Turf Management

for Golf Courses

A Publication of

The United States  *Golf Association*

by
James B. Beard
Professor of Turfgrass Science
Texas A&M University

With illustrations by
Steven M. Batten

 **Burgess Publishing Company**
Minneapolis, Minnesota

Editor: Gerhard Brahms
Production editor: Nelda Wright
Copy editors: Leslie Reindl, Nelda Wright
Production: Morris Lundin, Pat Barnes, Judy Vicars, Priscilla Heimann, Gloria Otremba
Design and layout: Priscilla Heimann, Mari Ansari
Additional illustrations: Nickolas Hyduke

Front cover photo: The seventeenth hole, Sunningdale Country Club, Scarsdale, N.Y. (Photo courtesy of A. M. Radko, USGA Green Section, Far Hills, N.J.)

Back cover photo: The tenth hole, Five Farms Course, Baltimore Country Club, Baltimore, Md. (Photo courtesy of M. J. Frank, Baltimore Country Club, Baltimore, Md.)

© 1982 by The United States Golf Association
Printed in the United States of America
Library of Congress Catalog Card Number 81-69092
ISBN 0-8087-2872-5

Burgess Publishing Company
7108 Ohms Lane
Minneapolis, Minnesota 55435

J I H G F E

All chemicals suggested for use should be applied in accordance with the directions on the manufacturer's label as registered under the Federal Insecticide, Fungicide, and Rodenticide Act. Mention of a trademark or proprietary product does not constitute a guaranty or warranty of the product by the author, the United States Golf Association, or the publisher and does not imply approval to the exclusion of other products that also may be suitable. The use of certain pesticides effective against turfgrass weeds, diseases, insects, small animals, and related pests may be restricted by some state, provincial, or federal agencies; thus, be sure to check the current status of the pesticide being considered for use.

This book is
dedicated to
my family
Harriet
Jim C.
John W.

Contents

Preface

This book has been written as a comprehensive reference and "how-to" book concerning the culture and management of golf turfs. It is oriented to golf course superintendents, golf club officials, course owners, green committee chairmen, golf course architects, novice golf course workers, and students of golf course turfgrass culture in adult short courses, night schools, technical schools, and undergraduate college courses. The book emphasizes the application of basic turfgrass principles to golf course turfgrass culture. These principles are not covered here in detail, since other authoritative textbooks are available, for example, this author's *Turfgrass: Science and Culture* (Prentice-Hall, Inc., Englewood Cliffs, N.J., 1973). Those wishing to study the principles on which the cultural practices discussed in this book are based are encouraged to pursue in-depth reading in this comprehensive text.

The subject has been organized into twelve chapters. Chapter 1 provides an overview of golf, its history, golf course measurement, course operations, and climatic regions. Golf course architect and site selection, architecture, construction, and rebuilding are discussed in chapter 2. The next four chapters cover the description, construction, turfgrass selection, establishment, and culture of putting greens, tees, fairways, and roughs. Material related to bunkers is presented in chapter 7. Golf course equipment needed and its selection, calibration, operation, and maintenance are considered in chapter 8, while chapter 9 discusses irrigation systems. Chapter 10 is devoted to turfgrass pests and environmental stresses, including their diagnosis, identification, and control. The management aspects of a golf course operation, including organizational structure, records, budgets, purchasing, contracts, personnel relations, and communications are covered in chapter 11. Finally, other aspects of golf course management and maintenance, such as tournament preparation; building and maintenance of shelters, cart paths, bridges, parking lots, security fences, ponds, and lakes; stream stabilization; and landscaping are discussed in the last chapter. The Appendices contain supporting reference tables and grass and seed illustrations. There is also a glossary.

Preparation of *Turf Management for Golf Courses* has been sponsored by the United States Golf Association (USGA). The goal was to provide a comprehensive, practical book that can be used by professional individuals in leadership and management positions on all types of golf courses, including private, municipal, and public fee facilities. It is hoped that the information presented will prove a useful guide and practical reference for the economical establishment and maintenance of golf course turfs, which in turn will provide optimum conditions for the game of golf.

This book is the third in a series sponsored by the USGA. It is not a revision but a completely new text. In 1917, the USGA sponsored publication of the first book on golf course turfgrass culture, *Turf for Golf Courses,* by Charles V. Piper and Russell A. Oakley. In 1950, *Turf Management* by H. Burton Musser was published under USGA auspices; it was revised in 1962.

The practices discussed herein represent the current state of the "art and science" of turfgrass culture. It is interesting to compare this third USGA book with the previous two and note the significant progress in technology that has occurred over the past sixty years. This is not to say that we now completely understand the science of turfgrass culture on golf courses. Considerably more research is needed. From these investigations will come even further refinements and improvements in cultural practices, turfgrasses, fertilizers, pesticides, and equipment.

I wish to express sincere appreciation to members of the USGA Editorial Board for their contributions during preparation of this book. The untiring efforts of Alexander M. Radko through the seven years of work deserve special acknowledgment. Most individuals on the Editorial Board provided not only editorial evaluations but also initial drafts ranging from short paragraphs to sections. The following USGA Green Section contributors formed the Editorial Board: Alexander M. Radko, William H. Bengeyfield, William G. Buchanan, James B. Moncrief, Carl H. Schwartzkopf, and Stanley J. Zontek. Other USGA Green Section contributors were William S. Brewer, Holman M. Griffin, and James T. Snow. Frank Hannigan wrote the Great Golf Holes narrative in chapter 2. Material was also provided by James R. Watson and Bruce C. Camenga.

Members of the USGA Review Board were also of great assistance in giving valuable critiques based on many years' experience in day-to-day golf course operations. I want to thank the following golf course superintendents for their participation on the Review Board: William D. Carson, Larry A. Eggleston, Palmer Maples, Jr., Sherwood A. Moore, Arthur A. Snyder, Robert M. Williams, and John A. Zoller. Inputs from members of the American Society of Golf Course Architects to the chapter on building a golf course are gratefully acknowledged, with special thanks to Cabell B. Robinson and Rees L. Jones.

The exceptional artistry of Steven M. Batten in preparation of most of the illustrations is appreciated and contributes substantially to the quality of this book. Photos not credited as to source were provided by the USGA Green Section or J. B. Beard. The numerous inputs from colleagues in turfgrass research at other state universities are gratefully acknowledged. Finally, the assistance of my wife, Harriet, in typing, frequent retyping, proofing, and assembling of the manuscript is gratefully acknowledged.

I also would like to thank the many professional golf course superintendents who, through their encouragement, cooperation, and thoughtful discussions, have been a significant force in furthering my knowledge and understanding of golf course turfgrass culture and management.

James B. Beard

Foreword

Golf is a unique game in many respects. Certainly, no other sport requires so many skills for the development, preparation, and maintenance of the surface on which it is played. Consider, for example, what a golf course requires as compared with a football field, a tennis court, a baseball diamond, or a bowling green. There is no sport, moreover, in which effective maintenance matters more than it does in golf. The accomplished architect takes the terrain God has provided and fashions it into eighteen challenging holes. The player takes the body and mind God has provided and makes them work together to fashion a golf swing. In the final analysis, however, all that God and the architect and God and the player are able to do matters very little if the golf course is not properly maintained. Conversely, proper maintenance can realize for the architect the fulfillment of a vision and for the player the reward for a skill.

Aesthetics are at the very heart of golf. The importance to play of what the player sees and how he or she feels about it is unique in this sport. But aesthetic values in the design of a golf course are meaningless unless the course is properly maintained. The artist may conceive a great painting, but the concept fails unless it is carried out on the canvas with the right combination of form and color. In golf, it is maintenance that gives the right texture and color to the forms conceived by the architect.

The United States Golf Association Green Section is in its sixty-second year of service to the game of golf. Its founders created it as a turfgrass research and advisory agency, but it has become, over the years, a national resource for turf management. The provision for turfgrass research and advice is at least as important as any other contribution the USGA makes to the game of golf. This book was planned by the Green Section with the same dedication and loving care that should be given to every golf course. Its purpose is to provide up-to-date information on golf course management to meet the needs of the modern golf course superintendent and golf club official.

In recognition of the importance of this book and to insure its quality and utility, Dr. James B. Beard, professor of turfgrass science in the Department of Soil and Crop Sciences at Texas A&M University, College Station, was chosen to write it. Dr. Beard is an internationally known turfgrass researcher and educator who has made major contributions through his research on turfgrass stress physiology. Among his honors are National Science Foundation Post Doctoral Fellow, Fellow in the American Society of Agronomy, Meritorious Service Award of the International Turfgrass Society, Honorary Award of the American Sod Producers Association, and the Oberly Award of the American Library Association. Dr. Beard has authored four other books: *Turfgrass: Science and Culture, Turfgrass Bibliography, Introduction to Turfgrass Science and Culture — Laboratory Exercises,* and *How to Have a Beautiful Lawn.*

The United States Golf Association dedicates *Turf Management for Golf Courses* to all those whose care and concern for the way a golf course plays and looks have made the playing of the game the consummate experience it can and should be.

William C. Campbell
President
United States Golf Association

Chapter 1

Golf and
the Golf Course

HISTORY

The Game

How did the game of golf, and eventually the profession of turfgrass management for golf, evolve? Unlike the origin of many modern sports (baseball, basketball, football, and so on) to which a precise date or at least an approximate year can be affixed, the exact origin of golf is shrouded in the darkness of centuries. Some suggest that the Romans brought the idea to early Europe and Britain during their northern conquests. Others say it started far earlier. Sir Walter Simpson in *The Art of Golf*[1] suggests:

> A Shepherd tending his sheep would often chance upon a round pebble, and, having his crook in his hand, he would strike it away; for it is inevitable that a man with a stick in his hand should aim a blow at any loose object lying in his path as that he should breathe.

An antique engraving found in Santiago, Chile, believed to have been completed between A.D. 1570 and 1600, shows a Chilean Indian swinging a crook at a round object on the ground, not unlike today's golfer. It is believed that prints of this sort were made to be returned to Europe to show the ways and habits of the natives.

Any number of ball-and-stick games may claim parentage to golf. The word ''golf'' is derived from the Dutch ''kolf,'' which is related to ''kolbe'' in German and ''holbe'' in Danish, meaning club. Perhaps the Romans did bring ''paganica,'' their ball-and-stick game, north with them to spread eventually over Europe. ''Cambuca'' was played in England, ''jeu de mail'' in France, ''het kolven'' in the Netherlands, and ''shinty'' in Scotland (still played today). There were many similar recreational forms. An old Dutch proverb reads, ''You must play the ball as it lies.''

Golf, as we know it today, was born and nurtured in Scotland over five-hundred years ago. St. Andrews was an ancient city even during medieval times. Evidence indicates it was once a prehistoric settlement, located on a cliff-protected peninsula with clear visibility for miles around. Certainly there was a monastery to which relics of St. Andrew were brought about A.D. 736. A cathedral was founded around 1160 that was to become the pride of the Catholic church in Scotland. St. Andrews became cloaked in medieval glory as the major ecclesiastical center, seaport, and trading post of its time. Early trade fairs attracted ships and commerce from all over the then known world. It was in this twelfth century that the marriage of golf (gowf) to the Land of the Scots took place.

---

[1]Simpson, W. G. 1887. *The Art of Golf*. David Douglas, Edinburgh, Scotland. 186 pp.

Figure 1-1. Sand-pit burrows made by sheep seeking shelter from cold winds. Sand bunkers evolved from such burrows.

Perhaps the best thesis as to the origin of the game we know today is that it evolved from the popular Dutch game het kolven. Some of the terms used in golf obviously came from this game. To reach St. Andrews from its harbor, Dutch and other traders traveled some distance across a sandy, grassy, seaside linksland. The ancient Swilcan Bridge can be seen today on what is now the eighteenth fairway of The Old Course, still hinting at the old pathway between town and harbor. The linksland was ideally suited for the Dutch traders' game. There were targets along the way in the form of rabbit scrapes, and the soft, naturally fine-textured turf seemed invented for het kolven.

The linksland along much of the Scottish coast was formed at the close of the Ice Age as the land rose above the sea. The resulting marshland and sand dunes formed an undulating terrain. The architect of this first golf course was nature. Gentle rains nurtured the grass and howling gales off the North Sea smoothed the gently rolling land. The traditional linksland had turf of very fine leaf texture which was sleek, smooth, and almost glassy when dry. It also had many natural hazards. Gorse, heather, reeds, pools, and pits of sand where sheep huddled for shelter from the wind were all characteristics of the linksland (Fig. 1-1). Gowf grew in popularity, became known along the coast, and eventually spread throughout the British Isles.

The Fifteenth and Sixteenth Centuries. The game persisted. Even with balls of roughly turned wood or of feathers bound in leather, the townsfolk of St. Andrews continued their romance with gowf. Some played the game to the extent that they began to neglect their practice of archery in the name of the King. Practiced archers were needed to counter the threat of invasion from England. In 1457, James II of Scotland decreed before his Thirteenth Parliament:

> . . . decreeted and ordained that wapinschawing is to be halden by the Lordis and Baronis spirituale and temporale, faure times in the zeir, and that the Fute-ball and golfe be utterly cryit downe and nocht usit.

The subject was raised again in 1471 and a third time in 1491, during the rule of James IV, when a decree was issued:

> Item, it is statute and ordained that no place of the Realme there be used Fute-ball, Golfe, or uther sik unproffitable sportes, but for common gude of the Realme & defense thereof.

Still, James IV developed into an avid golfer despite this decree.

There is no denying the medieval popularity of golf. Art references from 1500 to 1520 show three players with club and ball on a green with one of the players attempting to hole out. James V of Scotland and his daughter, Mary, Queen of Scots (1542-87), were known to have played golf at St. Andrews.

To the townsfolk, the narrow strip of turf bordered by masses of entanglements leading to the harbor became known as The Green. It was their property by heritage and birthright. Legal title was acquired in 1552 when the Town Charter reserved for the citizens of St. Andrews the right of using the links for "golfe, fute-ball, shuting and all games, as well as casting divots, gathering turfs," (to roof their houses) and for "pasturing of their livestock." The Charter legally confirmed the citizens' rights to play golf over the linksland.

The Seventeenth and Eighteenth Centuries. A magnificent advance came to the primitive game of golf in 1618—the feather ball was invented. A new "featherie" flew tremendous distances, even by today's standards. However, it soon lost shape and flight capabilities and it came apart rather easily when wet. It was also very expensive. The ball maker would almost completely sew a leather cover, invert it, and then, with a blunt, pointed iron shaft, force a standard measure of feathers (a hat full) through the small opening into the leather casing. The opening was closed and the ball painted with white oil for waterproofing and easy visibility. The feather ball was obviously difficult to manufacture. Even the best ball makers could turn out only one thousand to two thousand a year. But golf technology had begun, and the feather ball ruled the fairways for nearly 225 years!

So fanatical were the St. Andreans for golf that it has been said they could tell even from great distances who was playing the course just by watching the swing. Like fingerprints, no two swings were alike. Players would tee up with a handful of sand and try to drive the feather ball to the "fair green." Accuracy was of great importance with heather and gorse all around. Once on the fair green, the next target was the "play green," a relatively smooth area with a roughly prepared hole. The winner in early golf was determined by the number of holes won from the opponent, not by the total number of strokes taken in a round. It was not until 1759 that stroke play was developed.

The Nineteenth Century. The next major technological breakthrough in golf took place around 1845. A large, black marble idol of Vishnu arrived in St. Andrews from Singapore, consigned to a Dr. Patterson of St. Andrews University. The idol was cushioned and packed in a material known as gutta percha. From the discarded gutta percha, the two golfing sons of Dr. Patterson fashioned a round ball they thought might be used for golf instead of the very expensive featherie. It was a most unpopular idea at the time, especially among the feather ball makers. But the Patterson boys persisted, improving and eventually marketing the first gutta percha balls in 1846. Within a year or two, the gutta ball had taken over! It had greater durability and was far less expensive than the featherie, and with molded markings on its cover its flight pattern was every bit as good.

The Twentieth Century. Two giant steps lay just ahead for golf, one of them in America. The rubber core ball replaced the gutta percha by 1902, again improving the playability of the game and increasing its popularity. And a single event that occured in 1913 raised golf from its relative position of obscurity to a game played by the masses of North America. An unknown twenty-year-old caddie by the name of Francis Ouimet beat the greatest golfers of the day, English professionals Harry Vardon and Ted Ray, in the United States Open Championship at The Country Club, Brookline, Massachusetts! The popularity of golf soared within a few years' time. It was now a game for every American to learn. Subsequently, in 1930, amateur Robert Tyre Jones, Jr., achieved a grand slam. He won the United States Amateur and United States Open Championships plus the British Amateur and British Open Championships in the same year!

Golf Turf Care

Although the Old Course at St. Andrews belonged to the citizens of the city, it was open to all for play. In fact, golf was free at St. Andrews until 1913, when the first green fee was levied on visitors. With the Scots' obsession for the game and its spreading popularity, the Society of St. Andrews Golfers (later to become the Royal and Ancient Golf Club) sought special playing privileges on The Old Course in 1754. We would probably call these privileges ''starting times'' today. In return, the Society agreed to pay for the maintenance of The Old Course. This is a very interesting historical point. The Society was actually concerned with the care and maintenance of the golf course in 1754.

Long before there was golf on this side of the Atlantic Ocean, the Society of St. Andrews Golfers decided to rebuild some of the old greens. This was in 1832, the same year Andrew Jackson was reelected president of the United States. In this same era, Maine became a state (1820), the Erie Canal was completed (1825), and the Republic of Texas declared its independence from Mexico (1836). At St. Andrews the Society was busy rebuilding and enlarging the old greens, turning them into the famous ''double greens'' we know today.

Greenkeepers

By the end of the 1700's the first greenkeepers came into being. The term was ''greenkeeper,'' not ''greenskeeper,'' Historically, the term ''green'' referred to the whole golf course and not just to the putting greens. Not unlike today, the greenkeepers were charged with making things better for the golfer. In the records of the Aberdeen Golf Links in 1820, mention was made that the club agreed to pay Alexander Monroe four pounds a year for ''taking charge of the links and providing accommodations

Figure 1-2. Early view of the St. Andrews Golf Club of Yonkers, N.Y.

for the members' boxes.'' Monroe was also to pay particular attention to keeping the holes in good order. Two years later, Monroe's salary was reduced to three pounds a year!

And so care of the ''green'' had its beginning. The early golf professionals frequently became greenkeepers. Neither job was known for its security, even in those days. Old Tom Morris, four times winner of the British Open and still considered the grand old man of golf, became greenkeeper of St. Andrews in 1865 and remained so until 1904. He had two rules for his turf maintenance program:

> 'Mair saund Honeyman,' was his cry for his assistant, Honeyman, to apply ever more topdressing of sharp sand to the greens, tees, and fairways. Tom Morris said it was needed to 'maintain the character of the grass.'
>
> 'Nay Sunday play. The golfe course needs a rest even if the golfers don't.'

To this day there is ''nay Sunday play'' on The Old Course. The first patented hole cutter was developed by one Charles Anderson and presented to Old Tom Morris as a tribute in 1869.

Golf Courses in North America

Through the years golf cast its spell over the people of St. Andrews, their fellow islanders in Britain, and eventually on people around the world. Records indicate the game was introduced into Australia around 1820 and into India sometime in the early 1800's.

There is evidence of golf being played in North America during the 1700's. The earliest reference to the game appeared in a Charleston, South Carolina, newspaper in 1788. The article referred to the formation of a golf club there in 1786. There was also a golf club in Savannah, Georgia, around 1795; continuing references were made to it until the War of 1812. Apparently that war ended further active participation in the game of golf in North America, play that was not resumed until after the American Civil War.

The Royal Montreal Golf Club in Quebec, Canada, was organized in 1873 and is the oldest continuously operated golf course in North America. Four other Canadian clubs were also organized prior to 1880: the Royal Quebec Golf Club of Quebec (1874); the Toronto Golf Club and the Niagara-On-The-Lake Golf Club, both of Ontario (1876); and the Brantford Golf Club of Ontario (1879).

It was not until the late 1880's that the first permanent golf club came into being in the United States. St. Andrews Golf Club, Yonkers, New York, founded in 1888, is generally recognized as the oldest continuously operated club in the United States (Fig.1-2). Others have claimed organization at about the same time, for example, the Dorset Field Club, Vermont (1886); the Foxburg Country Club, Pennsylvania (1887); and the Middlesboro Golf Club, Kentucky (1889). However, only St. Andrews has complete documentation of the date it was formed. One of the earliest — if not the first — public golf courses, Van Cortlandt Park Golf Club in New York City, opened in 1889. It is still operating on the original site.

There is no doubt that golf was sinking its roots into this country. At least seventy-five clubs were in existence by 1895 (Fig.1-3). To administer the game, the United States Golf Association (USGA) was founded in 1894. There were five charter member clubs: St. Andrews Golf Club, New York; Newport Country Club, Rhode Island; Shinnecock Hills, New York; The Country Club, Massachusetts; and the Chicago Golf Club, Illinois. The Tuxedo Club of New York was not included through an oversight in communication.

Turfgrass Research

Prior to the twentieth century, the ''art'' of golf turf culture was developed through trial-and-error. Typically, unprocessed manures were used for fertilizer, bordeaux mixture for disease control, nicotine solution for insect control, and a knife for weed removal. The height of the grass was orginally controlled by the intense grazing of sheep, cattle, and rabbits. Hand scything was employed on some

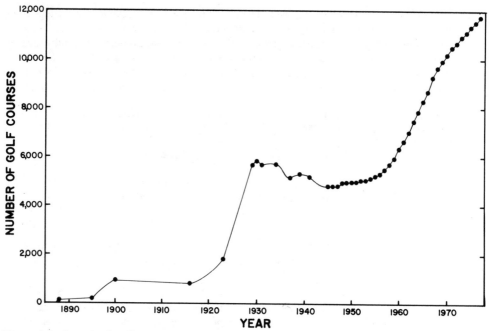

Figure 1-3. Growth of golf course facilities (nine-hole, eighteen-hole, and larger) in the United States from 1888 to 1977. (Adapted from data provided by the National Golf Foundation, North Palm Beach, Fla.)

turf areas. In 1830, Edwin Budding of Stroud, Gloucestershire, England, invented and patented a mechanical push mowing machine for turf (Fig. 1-4).

The first published report related to turfgrass research was initiated in 1880 by the noted botanist Dr. W. J. Beal of the Michigan Agricultural Experiment Station. Interest in the science of turfgrass culture was manifesting itself. The first formal turf garden was established by J. B. Olcott in 1890 at South Manchester, Connecticut, and existed until 1910. Starting in 1886, Dr. Olcott personally collected grasses from around the world. At one time he had nearly five-hundred strains under cultivation. This work was conducted under auspices of the Connecticut Agricultural Experiment Station. The Rhode Island Agricultural Experiment Station became active in turfgrass research in 1895 and expanded the program in 1905.

In 1904, Fred W. Taylor, an enthusiastic golfer and student of the game, initiated a series of turfgrass studies on his home grounds near Philadelphia. He purchased the finest turfs of Dr. Olcott and carried out extensive experiments with seeds, fertilization, and drainage. Taylor formulated the first recommendations for putting green construction and published many articles on turfgrass culture, including identification of brown patch as a disease of turfgrass in 1914.

Drs. C. V. Piper and R. A. Oakley established the Arlington Turf Garden at Arlington, Virginia, in 1916 under the auspices of the United States Department of Agriculture (USDA). The USGA Green Section joined the USDA in this major turfgrass research program in 1921. In fact, the USDA and the USGA had worked cooperatively in turfgrass research since before 1920, but the formal joint financial agreement was not drawn up until 1921.

A major concern during the 1920's was the extensive loss of turf to disease both summer and winter. Dr. John Monteith, Jr., a pathologist with the USDA, was hired in 1926 by the USGA Green Section to work on this problem. Dr. Monteith developed the first effective turfgrass fungicides. He directed

Figure 1-4. First mechanized reel mower. (Drawing courtesy of Ransomes, Sims, and Jefferies Ltd., Ipswich, England.)

extensive experimental work in turfgrass fertilization, types of soils, weed control, and grass selection. The development of pie-shaped test greens, insecticides, disease controls, and irrigation requirements began under Dr. Monteith and his Green Section staff.

Turf for Golf Courses Published

Recognizing the important relationship of good playing conditions to development of skill in and enjoyment of golf, the USGA supported the publication of a book in 1917 called *Turf for Golf Courses* by Drs. Charles V. Piper and Russell A. Oakley of the USDA. These men were not only agronomic scientists but golfers as well. Their book covered soils, fertilizers, composts, liming, grass species adaptation, establishment, culture, weed control, animal pests, and even machinery.

"Mowing machines," they wrote, "are the most essential elements on every golf course." Although the lawn mower had been invented in England by Edwin Budding in 1830, it was slow to be adopted. Sheep were still used on American golf courses in the early 1900's (Fig. 1-5). They were much less expensive and kept the grass not only mowed but nurtured as well. Piper and Oakley recommended horse-drawn equipment or gasoline mowing machines:

> On level or gently undulating courses, the motor machines are most efficient. The only serious objection is their weight, which on clayey soils results in too great compacting of the surface soil.

> When the soil on the fairways is clayey, horse-drawn machines are favored, because they are not so heavy as to cause undue compaction of the soil. The use of horses may involve some unevenness of the turf due to the footprints of the animals, but this can be largely obviated by mowing only when the soil is firm, or by using special shoes on the horses.

First Golf Turfgrass Advisory Service

The first turfgrass advisory agency in the world was organized in November, 1920, as the Green Section of the USGA. This evolved during the United States Open Championship held at the Inverness Club, Toledo, Ohio. Green chairman E. J. Marshall and greenkeeper W. J. Rockefeller were charged with getting the golf course into first-class condition. However, they found valid published information and substantiated concepts about golf course maintenance to be lacking. Only a few opinions were available and most were related to the selling of a special product.

During the search for reliable information, Marshall came into contact with many other green committees that needed the same types of information. It became evident that an agency for developing

Figure 1-5. Sheep grazing on a golf course to keep the grass short, circa 1917.

useful information on golf course maintenance practices was needed and could also serve as a focal point for cooperation among the growing number of golf clubs in the country, estimated at over two thousand. Marshall made many contacts throughout the summer and fall of 1920. In November, the Green Section of the USGA was formed. Dr. C. V. Piper of the USDA was elected chairman.

The new organization was to serve golf in three ways:

1. A monthly bulletin containing information on cultural practices, labor, budgets, seed analysis, diseases, weeds, and insects was to be sent to all members. *The Bulletin* was the first of its kind and became the classic turfgrass publication from 1921 through 1933.
2. A service bureau was to provide prompt information on subjects relating to the maintenance and upkeep of golf courses. The bureau was responsible for all Green Section publications.
3. An annual meeting was to be held and was to include a program consisting of papers on current problems and practices followed by an open discussion.

Thus, the USGA Green Section had its beginning. The benefits of this national organization became evident. District green sections were encouraged by the USGA, which had no desire for direct administrative control. It was to be a cooperative effort on the part of all those interested in contributing to golf.

Greenkeeper Association Formed

Interest in a national greenkeeper organization developed in the United States during the mid-1920's. John Morley of the Youngstown Country Club of Ohio was instrumental in forming a National Association of Greenkeepers of America in 1926. Morley recognized the need for an association to further the professional recognition and competence of greenkeepers through a continuing education program. John Morley served as the first president from 1926 until 1932. By 1927 there were some four hundred charter members and the National Association began publishing the *National Greenkeeper Magazine*.

The organization continued to grow and is today known as the Golf Course Superintendents Association of America (GCSAA). By 1975 the membership exceeded four thousand and had established permanent headquarters in Lawrence, Kansas. The Association sponsored its first golf course educational and equipment show in 1928 and has continued this event, which is now known as the International Turfgrass Conference and Show.

Current Status

Golf enjoyed an unprecedented growth in players and facilities following World War II. President Eisenhower did much to popularize the game, as did Arnold Palmer and extensive coverage of the game on television. Active and retirement communities were rarely developed without a golf course as the central attraction. Resort hotels around the world found that a golf course added to their popularity.

By the early 1950's, equipment manufacturers were marketing new, efficient, and greatly improved maintenance equipment. Chemical companies had developed new pesticide formulations for disease, insect, and weed control. New technical data became available, especially from the state agricultural experiment stations of the major land grant universities. There was now a need to interpret and bring this information directly to American golf courses.

Richard S. Tufts, chairman of the USGA Green Section Committee, announced formation of the Regional Turf Service of the USGA Green Section in February, 1953. Annual consultation visits to individual courses were made available at minimal cost. The purpose was to assist each club, through its superintendent and green committee, to keep abreast of the latest and best developments in turfgrass management. The Green Section agronomists were not to be super-superintendents. They were to provide the latest, unbiased information based on sound, proven turfgrass management operations and principles. The Green Section Turfgrass Advisory Service remains available today to all clubs concerned with providing the best golfing conditions. In addition, the Green Section provides substantial support for golf turfgrass research at selected state universities throughout the United States. Since inception of the Green Section in 1920, the USGA has invested more than $6 million in its activities.

By 1975, there were over twelve thousand golf courses in the United States and more than sixteen million golfers. The popularity of the sport spread to Japan and increased in Australia, New Zealand, South America, Spain, and Sweden. Astronaut Admiral Alan B. Shepard, Jr., hit the first golf ball on the moon!

The science of turfgrass culture has kept pace. Over fifteen state universities now offer major courses of study in turfgrass management and twenty-five state agricultural experiment stations have more than one faculty member assigned to conduct turfgrass research. Golf course maintenance of today little resembles that of even ten years ago. It has become big business. It is estimated that over $400 million is spent annually for the care and upkeep of golf courses in the United States. Turfgrass management, like golf, is a science, the study of a lifetime in which one may exhaust oneself but never the subject.

CONCEPT OF GOLF

Golf has been described in many ways but never better than as follows, by David R. Forgan.[2]

GOLF — It is a science — the study of a lifetime, in which you may exhaust yourself but never your subject.

It is a contest, a duel or a melee, calling for courage, skill, strategy and self-control.

It is a test of temper, a trial of honor, a revealer of character.

It affords a chance to play the man, and act the gentleman.

It means going into God's out-of-doors, getting close to nature, fresh air, exercise, a sweeping away of the mental cobwebs, genuine recreation of the tired tissues.

It is a cure for care — an antidote to worry.

It includes companionship with friends, social intercourse, opportunity for courtesy, kindliness and generosity to an opponent.

It promotes not only physical health but moral force.

---

[2]From a plaque at Golf House Museum, United States Golf Association, Far Hills, New Jersey.

Figure 1-6. Apparatus used by the United States Golf Association for testing the overall distance standard of golf balls.

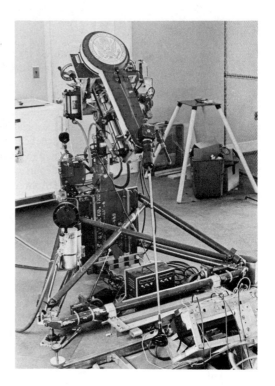

Others have described the game as fascinating, exasperating, aggravating, bewitching, and madness. Nevertheless, all those who have permitted themselves to become so entranced admit to its absorbing science. It is truly the sport of a lifetime!

The Game

Golf consists of playing a ball from a teeing ground into the hole by successive strokes, in accordance with the *Rules of Golf*. A variety of clubs (woods, irons, and putter) are used to propel a ball that weighs a minimum of 1.62 ounces (46 grams) and measures not less than 1.68 inches (4.27 centimeters) in diameter. These implements, that may not exceed fourteen in number, allow the player to hit the ball variable distances, depending on individual skill in relation to the requirements of the shot. The *Rules of Golf* states (1) that the golf club shall be composed of a shaft and a head, and (2) that all the various parts shall be fixed so that the club is one unit. The club is not adjustable, except for weight. The distance the ball travels depends on the club's angle of loft, the force and precision employed, and the player's ability to direct it accurately and have it stop within a reasonable distance of the target.

In 1976, the USGA incorporated into its *Rules of Golf* the concept called Overall Distance Standard (ODS) for golf balls. It was proclaimed by some golf observers as the most significant step ever taken by this organization with respect to golf equipment. In essence, the rule states that the average distance covered in carry and roll by a brand of golf ball, when tested on an apparatus approved by the USGA (Fig. 1-6) on the outdoor range at the USGA headquarters under the conditions set forth in the Overall Distance Standard for golf balls, shall not exceed 280 yards (256 meters) (with a tolerance of 8 percent which will be reduced to a minimum of 4 percent as test techniques are improved).

The game of golf requires finesse, force, precision, concentration, balance, and a delicate touch around greens. The equalizer is a handicap system derived from performance which allows golfers of varying ability to compete on an equitable basis. Most regulation eighteen-hole golf courses are made of four par-3 holes, four par-5 holes, and ten par-4 holes. Par for such a course thus is 72. However, there are courses that have a par of 69, 70, or 71. The range is 74 into the low 60's. Those in the 60's in no way detract from the pleasure of golf if they have been measured accurately and rated by competent authorities.

It is important for persons genuinely interested in golf turf management to develop an understanding and appreciation of the golf game. This is not to say that the golf course superintendent and crew must be low-handicap golfers. However, it is essential for them to understand the game, including the etiquette. Everyone employed on a golf course should be instructed as to the game's requirements. These include keeping noise to a minimum, not shouting or talking loudly at any time but especially when players are near, not moving when directly behind someone playing a shot, and being ever alert to the presence of golfers. Tasks that interfere most with play should be completed before daily play begins, whenever possible.

Conversely, it is important for the chairman of the Green Committee or the management to inform the club membership of workers' goals. For example, consideration on the golfer's part in allowing crew members to finish spraying a green before playing up or waving them off often helps workers do a better job. It also allows them to use their time more efficiently and effectively.

Golf Terminology

The *Rules of Golf* contains definitions and rules designed to insure that everyone plays golf by the same rules. The *Rules of Golf* is published annually as approved by the USGA and the Royal and Ancient Golf Club of St. Andrews, Scotland. Many definitions in the *Rules of Golf* are important from the agronomic as well as from the player's point of view.

> *Casual water* — Any temporary accumulation of water which is visible before or after the player takes his stance and which is not a hazard of itself or is not in a water hazard. Snow and ice are either casual water or loose impediments, at the option of the player.
>
> *Course* — The whole area within which play is permitted. It is the duty of the club officials to define its boundaries accurately.
>
> *Flagstick* — A movable straight indicator provided by the club officials, with or without bunting or other material attached, centered in the hole to show its position. It shall be circular in cross section.
>
> *Ground under repair* — Any portion of the course so marked by order of the club officials concerned or so declared by its authorized representative. It includes material piled for removal and a trench made by a greenkeeper, even if not so marked. Stakes and lines defining ground under repair are not in such ground.
>
> *Hazard* — Any bunker or water hazard. Bare patches, scrapes, roads, tracks, and paths are not hazards.
>
>> A *bunker* is an area of bare ground, often a depression, which is usually covered with sand. Grass-covered ground bordering or within a bunker is *not* a part of the hazard.
>>
>> A *water hazard* is any sea, lake, pond, river, ditch, surface drainage ditch, or other open water course (regardless of whether or not it contains water), and anything of a similar nature. All ground or water within the margin of a water hazard, whether or not it be covered with any growing substance, is part of the water hazard. The margin of a water hazard is deemed to extend vertically upwards.
>>
>> A *lateral water hazard* is a water hazard or that part of a water hazard so situated that it is not possible or is deemed by the club officials to be impractical to drop a ball behind the water hazard and keep the spot at which the ball last crossed the margin of the hazard between the player and the hole.

It is the duty of the club officials in charge of a course to define accurately the extent of the hazards and water hazards when there is any doubt. That part of a hazard to be played as a lateral water hazard should be distinctively marked. Stakes and lines defining the margins of hazards are not in the hazards.

Hole — Shall be 4.25 inches (10.8 centimeters) in diameter and at least 4 inches (10.2 centimeters) deep. If a lining is used, it shall be sunk at least 1 inch (2.54 centimeters) below the putting green surface unless the nature of the soil makes it impractical to do so; its outer diameter shall not exceed 4.25 inches (10.8 centimeters).

Loose impediment — Natural objects not fixed or growing and not adhering to the ball, and the like, dung, worms, and insects and casts or heaps made by them. Snow and ice are either casual water or loose impediments, at the option of the player. Sand and loose soil are loose impediments on the putting green but not elsewhere on the course.

Obstruction — Anything artificial, whether erected, placed, or left on the course, including the artificial surfaces and sides of roads and paths but excepting:

   Objects defining out of bounds, such as walls, fences, stakes, and railings.

   In water hazards, artificially surfaced banks or beds, including bridge supports when part of such a bank are obstructions.

   Any construction declared by the club officials to be an integral part of the course.

Out-of-bounds — Ground on which play is prohibited. When out-of-bounds is fixed by stakes or a fence, the out-of-bounds line is determined by the nearest inside points of the stakes or fence posts at ground level; the line is deemed to extend vertically upwards. When out-of-bounds is fixed by a line on the ground, the line itself is out-of-bounds. A ball is out-of-bounds when all of it lies out-of-bounds.

Putting green — All ground of the hole being played which is specially prepared for putting or otherwise defined as such by the club officials. A ball is deemed to be on the putting green when any part of it touches the putting green.

Rub of the green — Occurs when a ball in motion is stopped or deflected by any outside agency.

Teeing ground — The starting place for the hole to be played. It is a rectangular area two club-lengths in depth, the front and sides of which are defined by the outside limits of two tee-markers. A ball is outside the teeing ground when all of it lies outside the stipulated area. When playing the first stroke with any ball (including a provisional ball) from the teeing ground, the tee-markers are immovable obstructions.

Through the green — The whole area of the course except:

   a. Teeing ground and putting green of the hole being played,

   b. All hazards on the course.

COURSE MEASUREMENT AND RATING

Course measurement and course rating are inseparable and of great importance to golf. The two together offer par standardization so that golfers can judge with some certainty the test they face on any given course and can apply the USGA handicap system equitably anywhere.

The need for accurate yardage measurement of every hole on a golf course is not only self-evident but critical. Yardage is the predominant factor in the USGA handicap system and is the basis for all decisions the golfer makes while playing any hole. A golfer's most helpful single aid is a scorecard showing accurate yardage.

The golf course architect prescribes the yardage for each hole in the original design, giving consideration to the desires of the client and being guided by the standards for par as defined in the USGA's

Table 1-1. United States Golf Association Yardage Guidelines for Par Ratings

Par Rating	Yardage Maximum and Minimum	
	Men	Women (Front)
3	To 250 (228.5*)	To 210 (192)
4	251 to 470 (229 to 429.6)	211 to 400 (192.8 to 365.6)
5	471 (430.5) and over	401 to 575 (366.5 to 525.6)
6		576 (526.5) and over

*Meters.

Rules of Golf (Table 1-1). A further consideration in distance with respect to par standardization is the effect of altitude and the resulting air density on the distance a ball will travel. Controlled tests are needed to assess the degree of this effect. Such tests could result in future adjustments in distance with respect to par standardization in a specific region.

It is the responsibility of each club to arrange for its course rating through the golf association having jurisdiction within its section of the country. The USGA recommends that courses be rated by a single committee within each section to promote uniformity of rating. A club should not attempt to rate its own course because it is apt to interpret the rating principles differently.

The rating system used by the USGA places primary emphasis on course yardage, so course rating begins with accurate course measurement. If the course has already been measured, but some time ago, it should be measured before course rating is sought. Often changes are made after measurement that can affect handicaps. The USGA has set guidelines for measurement and rating in its publication *USGA Golf Handbook*.[3] It is the responsibility of a club or association of clubs to arrange for precise measurement of the golf course. The result is the yardage that appears on the scorecard.

Yardage Measurement

Permanent Yardage Markers. Precise measurement begins with the installation of permanent reference markers at a standard starting point, commonly the middle of each teeing area (Fig. 1-7). The preferred location is the side where golfers approach the tee from the preceding hole so that the marker can readily be observed. Markers are best made of concrete, steel, or a similar material that insures permanency. Each should bear a number indicating the true yardage from that precise point on the tee to the center of the putting green. The permanent yardage marker helps golfers determine the distance of the hole from the point where the tee markers are placed.

Method. Each hole should be measured horizontally (air line) with a steel tape, surveying instrument, or electronic distance meter from the permanent yardage marker to the center of the green along the designed line of play. Measurement must be made by a competent individual, preferably one with knowledge of civil engineering. Accurate measurement to the nearest yard is of great importance. Holes with a dogleg are measured on a straight line from the tee to the center of the fairway at the bend along the architect's intended line of play and then on a straight line to the center of the green. To locate the center of the green, measurement is made by tape from the front edge of the putting surface to the rear edge on the line of flight to the green. This distance is then divided by two to determine the approximate center.

Separate measurements and permanent yardage markers should be established on holes where more than one tee is commonly used. The color of each permanent yardage marker should be coordinated

[3]Available from Golf House, Far Hills, New Jersey, U.S.A., 07931.

Figure 1-7. Concrete permanent yardage marker embedded in tee for ease of mowing.

Figure 1-8. Two commonly used yardage measurement devices: measuring wheel *(left)*; electronic distance meter *(below)*.

with the associated set of tee markers. The USGA recommends the following standard colors and terms for tee markers:

Back tee: Blue or championship course

Middle tee: White course

Front or women's tee: Red course

The club scorecard and bulletin board should show the course ratings for each set of permanent yardage markers as previously described. If a single set of markers is used on any hole to designate two courses, it should show both colors, half and half. Nine-hole courses having separate tees or tee markers for each nine of an eighteen-hole round should have separate measurements and permanent yardage markers established for each nine holes. The yardage markers and respective tee markers should be identified with ''I'' or ''1'' for the first nine and ''II'' or ''2'' for the second nine.

Course measurement is best done over the physical layout, rather than from aerial photos. Distortion is possible due to camera angle or differences in height when the photos were taken. However, if aerial aids must be used, an aerial survey is preferable to an aerial photo. It is made to scale and is much more accurate.

Measurement Instruments. If golf courses were flat and devoid of hazards it would be a simple matter to measure them with a steel tape or measuring wheel. Since this is usually not the case, other measurement devices or combinations of devices are used, including steel tape, measuring wheel, transit, and electronic distance meter (Fig. 1-8).

Tees and other flat areas can be measured accurately with steel tape or measuring wheel. However, these devices cannot be used over large bodies of water, up and down steep terrain, or through other hazards, since the technique used is to measure in a straight line. That is, the course is measured as it is to be played: down the center of the fairway, bending on dogleg holes, again at the center of the fairway, and on to the center of the putting surface. Use of the transit requires that one man use the instrument and another the stadia rod; walkie-talkies are helpful in communications between the two.

Electronic distance meters are a recent innovation which employs laser beams. They are simple to operate, readily available on a daily rental basis, and accurate to 0.1 foot per 10,000 feet (1 centimeter per 1,000 meters). Thus, these units are preferred for golf course measurement.

Area Measurement

The area of each green, tee, and fairway is essential information needed by the golf course superintendent to determine the amounts of fertilizer, herbicide, fungicide, or insecticide needed for a particular use and to confirm that the material has been applied at the proper rate. The unit of measurement most commonly used on fairways is the acre (hectare in metric), while the area of greens and tees is usually expressed on a 1,000-square-foot basis (100 square meters, or 1 are, in metric).

If the number and size of greens, tees, or fairways to be treated are known, the amount of pesticide or fertilizer that must be added to a full spray tank when operated at a specified calibration pressure and ground speed can be calculated. For example, if nine greens totaling 54,000 square feet can be sprayed with one tankful of water and a particular pesticide is to be applied at a rate of 4 ounces per 1,000 square feet, one can readily calculate (54×4) that 216 ounces or 13.5 pounds pf pesticide must be added to the tank to apply the pesticide at the label rate. A similar procedure can be used to check whether a chemical has been applied at the desired rate.

Most golf course turfs have irregular shapes rather than distinct geometric configurations. For this reason, it is not possible to measure each green, tee, and fairway to within a few square feet. Fortunately, this degree of accuracy is not required for figuring fertilizer and pesticide applications. Nevertheless, it is important that measurement be as accurate as possible to insure that pesticides are efficiently, safely, and economically applied at the manufacturer's labeled rate. One method of measuring and calculating irregularly shaped turf areas, such as fairways, is summarized as follows:

Step 1.   Subdivide the area into the best possible fit of circle(s), rectangle(s), triangle(s), and trapezoid(s). A set of temporary stakes placed at the junctions will aid in sighting the lines and subsequently will facilitate accurate measurements.

Step 2.   Measure the linear dimensions of each geometric figure.

Step 3.   Make a drawing of the turf area, including the geometric figures used and linear measurements obtained.

Step 4.   Compute the area (usually in square feet) of each individual geometric figure (Fig. 1-9).

Step 5.   Calculate the total surface area by adding together the areas of each individual geometric figure (Fig. 1-10).

Step 6.   Check the calculations.

The following procedure may be used to determine the area of an irregularly shaped, basically circular putting green:

Step 1.   Select and mark an approximate center point on the green.

Step 2.   Divide the irregularly shaped area into 10° or 20° pie-shaped increments (Fig. 1-11). Use the 10° spacing when greater accuracy is desired or the green is more irregularly shaped.

Step 3.   Measure the distances from the center to the perimeter of the green: thirty-six measurements for 10° increments and eighteen measurements for 20° increments. This procedure can be accomplished most practically by anchoring the zero end of a measuring tape to a swivel staked at the estimated center of the green and traversing the perimeter of the green while holding the tape taut. Record the radius measurements at the appropriate intervals.

Step 4.   Determine the average radius by totaling the measured radii and dividing by the number of measurements.

Step 5.   Use the average radius with the forumla $A = \pi \ (radii^2)$, or 3.14 × (average radii × average radii) to calculate the area.

Step 6.   Check the calculations.

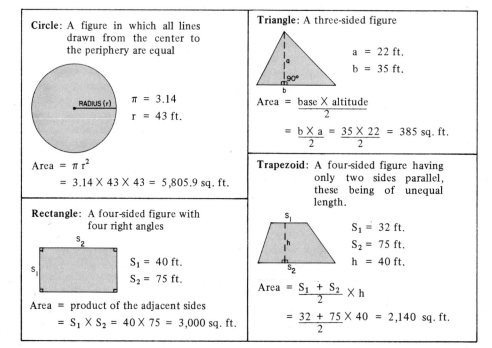

Circle: A figure in which all lines drawn from the center to the periphery are equal

RADIUS (r) $\pi = 3.14$
               $r = 43$ ft.

Area $= \pi r^2$

= 3.14 × 43 × 43 = 5,805.9 sq. ft.

Rectangle: A four-sided figure with four right angles

S_2
S_1 $S_1 = 40$ ft.
          $S_2 = 75$ ft.

Area = product of the adjacent sides

= $S_1 × S_2$ = 40 × 75 = 3,000 sq. ft.

Triangle: A three-sided figure

a $a = 22$ ft.
90° $b = 35$ ft.
b

Area $= \dfrac{\text{base} \times \text{altitude}}{2}$

$= \dfrac{b \times a}{2} = \dfrac{35 \times 22}{2} = 385$ sq. ft.

Trapezoid: A four-sided figure having only two sides parallel, these being of unequal length.

S_1
h $S_1 = 32$ ft.
S_2 $S_2 = 75$ ft.
       $h = 40$ ft.

Area $= \dfrac{S_1 + S_2}{2} \times h$

$= \dfrac{32 + 75}{2} \times 40 = 2,140$ sq. ft.

Figure 1-9. Formulae for calculating areas of primary goemetric configurations used in measuring the surface area of golf course turfs.

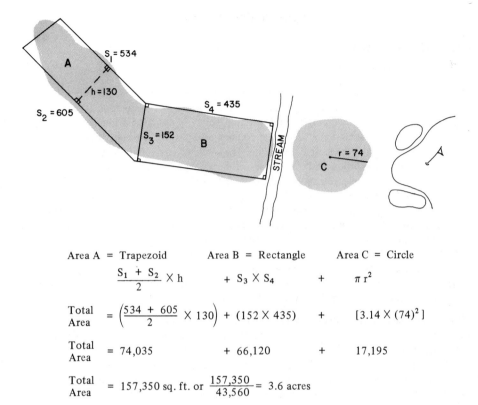

Area A = Trapezoid   Area B = Rectangle   Area C = Circle

$$\frac{S_1 + S_2}{2} \times h \qquad + S_3 \times S_4 \qquad + \qquad \pi r^2$$

Total Area $= \left(\frac{534 + 605}{2} \times 130\right) + (152 \times 435) \qquad + \qquad [3.14 \times (74)^2]$

Total Area $= 74{,}035 \qquad\qquad + 66{,}120 \qquad + \qquad 17{,}195$

Total Area $= 157{,}350$ sq. ft. or $\frac{157{,}350}{43{,}560} = 3.6$ acres

Figure 1-10. Sample calculation for area of a golf course fairway.

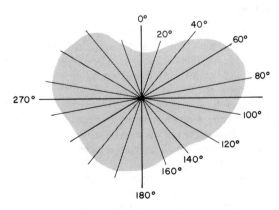

Figure 1-11. An irregularly shaped area divided into $20°$ pie-shaped increments.

COURSE OPERATION

Types of Golf Courses

The three major types of golf courses are:

1. *Daily fee golf course.* A course open to the public under conditions prescribed by the management. It is usually owned by an individual, partnership, or corporation and is operated as a business venture. Accordingly, the operating policy is designed to return a reasonable net profit to the owners. Some daily fee courses offer membership privileges in addition to encouraging use by the fee-paying public. The so-called pay-as-you-play country clubs are in this category. According to the National Golf Foundation, the largest increase in new facilities during the last twenty years was in the daily fee type courses. Many of these new courses are associated with resorts or land developments.
2. *Municipal golf course.* A course constructed and operated by a tax-supported agency such as a state, county, township, city, town, or park district. Its chief goal is to provide golfing facilities to its citizens at a reasonable cost.
3. *Private golf club.* A limited-use facility, usually nonprofit, designed to meet the specific needs and desires of a restricted membership. The membership may own a proprietary interest (equity-type club) or ownership may be vested in private enterprise that leases, rents, or in some manner makes the facility available to the members.

Closely enmeshed with the three major types of golf courses are the par-3 and executive golf courses. Sometimes these courses are built as separate facilities and, in some cases, in association with regulation facilities to accommodate the overflow. Most are municipal and daily fee operations. They are shorter than regular courses but offer much enjoyment. Though abbreviated in distance, these courses offer a good challenge against par, especially the longer ones. A par-3 course contains nine or eighteen par-3 holes, while executive courses include par-4 and sometimes par-5 holes.

Course Usage

The intensity of golf play on an annual basis for an eighteen-hole golf course can be categorized as (a) low—less than fifteen thousand rounds, (b) medium—fifteen thousand to thirty-five thousand rounds, (c) high—thirty-five thousand to fifty thousand rounds, and (d) very high—above fifty thousand rounds per year. The intensity of play is significant in that it influences both the annual maintenance budget and the specific types and level of turfgrass cultural practices employed.

Organizational Structure

Golf clubs are organized in several different structures, but all must operate with certain basic organizational arrangements. There must be direct and clear lines of authority and communication at all levels, and the people responsible for final decisions must be clearly designated.

In the case of private clubs, the membership elects a board of directors, who in turn elect officers— president, vice president, treasurer, and secretary. These elected officials are responsible for the entire operation of the facility. Although not always the case, it is highly desirable for committee chairmen to be members of the board of directors. Golf clubs normally have a house committee, golf committee, and green committee and may have other departments established within the overall club structure. Each department has separate functions but all are complementary and must be closely coordinated. This means open, continuing communication.

A triumvirate organizational structure is employed successfully in a majority of private golf clubs (Fig. 1-12). A house manager, golf professional, and golf course superintendent comprise the triumvirate. Each is in charge of a department and is responsible to the respective committee through its

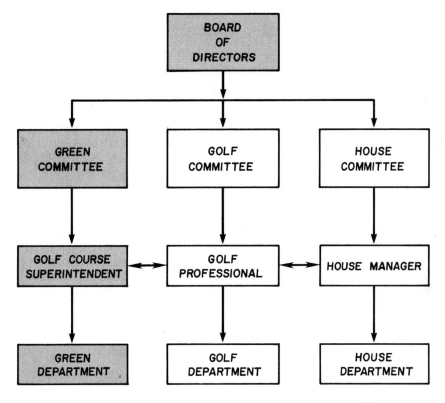

Figure 1-12. Typical triumvirate organizational structure for a golf club.

chairman. It is of utmost importance that these three individuals work in close harmony with each other and the board of directors.

Under certain circumstances, a general manager organizational structure is utilized (Fig. 1-13). The general manager is directly responsible to the board of directors, through its president, for all golf facility operations. This individual must also work closely with the various committees established by the board. In this structure, the golf course superintendent, golf professional, and house manager report to the general manager and sometimes to the chairman of the appropriate committee as well. In other circumstances, rather than a general manager position being budgeted in addition to the positions of the three major department heads, a dual position such as superintendent-general manager, pro-general manager, or house-general manager is established. The organizational arrangement that is most effective depends on the desires of the members or owners, size of the facility, and the professional expertise and competence of each unit manager.

In the case of a daily fee course or a golf club owned by an individual or company, the organizational structure is much the same except that all employees are ultimately responsible to the owner or an appointed representative. In almost every instance, the owner or contracted operator has the responsibility for final policy decisions even when committees have been set up for advisory purposes.

There are numerous other variations in the basic structure of golf course operation. Some clubs have found it advantageous to combine the golf committee and the green committee because of similarities in functions and the need for coordination. However, the structures described are the most common and have been the most successful.

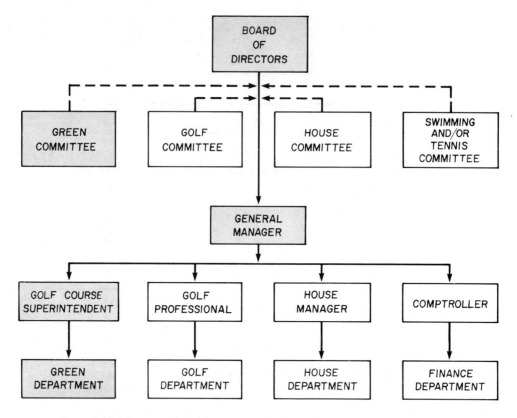

Figure 1-13. Representative general manager organizational structure for a golf club.

Specific responsibilities of each department head can be summarized as follows: The house manager is responsible for operation of the clubhouse, locker rooms, restaurant, and associated food services, including the halfway house. The golf professional is in charge of instruction, golf shop merchandising, caddies, carts, bag storage, golf club care, and practice range. The golf course superintendent is responsible for maintenance of the grounds and golf course complex, which may include landscaping, parking lots, tennis courts, skeet range, polo fields, and swimming pool. A comptroller, if employed, functions as a business manager for billings, statements, financial reports, records, purchasing, mail processing, master inventory, and general budgeting.

Communicating with Golfers Regarding Course Maintenance

Communication in one form or another is essential in every facet of golf course operation. Poor communication can cause disaster; good communication can smooth the way for progress. Whether referred to as public relations, keeping members informed, or maintaining credibility, communication among the golf course superintendent, other management departments, and the membership of the golf club must be good if the superintendent is to be an effective turfgrass manager.

By informing golfers about what is to be done on the golf course and why, the superintendent not only may avoid serious criticism but gain support. Proper communication generates pride in golfers, who feel knowledgeable and a part of what is happening. Knowledge also helps golfers schedule their

Figure 1-14. Notice regarding a future coring operation.

activities and avoid days when necessary but bothersome cultural practices are done. Golfers' normal pride in their golf course can be enhanced by keeping them informed as to what nonroutine maintenance or renovation will be done, when it will be initiated, why it is necessary, and when it will be completed, if known. Of all the cultural practices employed on the golf course, perhaps the most objectionable from a golfing standpoint is turf cultivation, which involves coring or slicing. Thus, it is very important that the dates for this operation be communicated to the golfers. Golfers are paying the bills and have a right to such information.

A number of methods can be used to communicate. Included are (a) posting news items on the club bulletin board, (b) writing periodic newsletters, (c) placing an item in the club newsletter or calendar of events, (d) placing signs at appropriate places like the first tee (Fig. 1-14), (e) placing notices in golfers' lockers, (f) speaking at meetings, and (g) talking with golfers at any time the occasion presents itself. These are very useful tools of communication which the golf course superintendent should utilize to the fullest.

Golf Etiquette from a Turf Standpoint

The golfer who drags spikes on putting greens, fails to rake disturbed sand in bunkers, does not repair ball marks, leans on the flagstick or putter on greens, takes several practice divots on every tee, never replaces a divot, and/or leaves a stream of litter behind is a detriment to the playing quality of a golf course, its appearance, and the ultimate cost of maintenance. Such a golfer either has not read or is not observing the first section in the *Rules of Golf*, the section on etiquette, which encompasses courtesy, priority, and care of the golf course. It states:

> Holes in Bunkers
>> Before leaving a bunker, a player should carefully fill up and smooth over all holes and footprints made by him.
>
> Restore Divots, Repair Ball Marks and Damage by Spikes
>> Through the green, a player should ensure that all turf cut or displaced by him is replaced at once and pressed down, and that any damage to the putting green made by the ball is carefully repaired. Damage to the putting green caused by golf shoe spikes should be repaired *on completion of the hole*.

Damage to Greens — Flagsticks, Bags, etc.
Players should ensure that, when putting down bags, or the flagstick, no damage is done to the putting green, and that neither they nor their caddies damage the hole by standing close to it, in handling the flagstick or in removing the ball from the hole. The flagstick should be properly replaced in the hole before the players leave the putting green. Players should not damage the putting green by leaning on their putters, particularly when removing the ball from the hole.

Golf Carts
Local Notices regulating the movement of golf carts should be strictly observed.

Damage Through Practice Swings
In taking practice swings, players should avoid causing damage to the course, particularly the tees, by removing divots.

In addition, there are other suggestions that aid in protecting turf and in providing the best possible playing conditions. For example:

1. Beginning golfers should not be allowed on the golf course unless in the company of an experienced player who can advise on turf care and golf etiquette. Beginners should also seek out the advice and guidance of a golf professional regarding proper golf turf etiquette. In particular, the beginner should be well informed on the proper techniques of replacing divots, repairing ball marks on greens, walking on putting greens so as not to scar turf, and entering and exiting bunkers.

2. All golfers should exercise good judgment while walking or riding by avoiding (a) worn, thin turf areas in order to allow recovery, (b) wet areas where traffic will increase rutting and soil compaction, (c) wilted turf areas under severe drought stress, and (d) roped-off areas and similar sites where ground is under repair.

3. The route of walking or traveling the golf course should be varied, especially around tees and greens. This will distribute traffic wear and soil compaction effects, thus minimizing damage to the turf. Taking the shortest route in key sites results in bare, compacted paths. The golfer should remember that one of the goals of play is physical exercise and enjoyment of the aesthetic setting of green grass and trees.

4. The ball should always be played as it lies, as this was the way the game was intended to be played from the beginning.

Observing good golf turf etiquette and being thoughtful of the course and other people while playing the game not only increases the golfer's pleasure but can yield financial savings in course maintenance. A lost spike from a shoe, which should have been tightened, can necessitate costly repairs to the delicate, complex mowers now used in golf course maintenance. Cleaning up litter and repairing turf damage caused by thoughtless golfers can run into many dollars during a full golfing season. Each golfer has a responsibility to the club, to the employees, and to fellow golfers to use the facilities properly. This responsibility is as much an attitude as anything else and is established by example from the leadership. Additional aids involve the posting of information on proper ball repair, divot replacement, and similar golf turf etiquette and making available a supply of ball-mark repair implements in the pro shop. Finally, pride of individual golfers in maintaining a quality golf course can be further enhanced by keeping the turf well groomed and free of litter and the sand in bunkers properly raked.

Operating Golf Carts on Turf Areas

Golf carts are a lucrative and sometimes helpful addition to the game. However, carts are damaging to golf course turf and their improper operation may result in injury to golfers. Golf carts may be electric or gasoline powered, three- or four-wheeled, and of various sizes and descriptions.

Golfers using a cart should be familiar with its operation before leaving the parking area. General rules of safety must be followed and common sense exercised to protect both the golfer and the turf. Local rules should be posted in a conspicuous place on the golf cart for ready reference. Unless these

Figure 1-15. Thinned, partially bare area caused by concentrated traffic.

rules are strictly enforced they are of little value. Successful approaches to enforcement include the use of rangers and policing by golf and/or green committee members with letters to violators. Some key guidelines designed to protect turfs during golf cart operation are as follows:

1. Follow the rules as prescribed by each golf club, including observing signs, directional markers, and barriers.
2. Whenever possible, vary the route of travel across the turf to distribute the detrimental effects of traffic and thus minimize soil compaction and turfgrass wear.
3. Vary the traffic pattern when thin, partially bare areas start to develop (Fig. 1-15). This may require the aid of roping or the use of appropriate signs.
4. Avoid operating carts in areas where they are not intended to be driven. For example, operation on steep slopes can cause serious side slippage, turf damage, and rutting as well as potential injury to passengers should the cart overturn.
5. It is never acceptable to bring hand or powered golf carts onto the greens, collars, or tees. Keep such vehicles as far away as practical and at least six to ten paces from the perimeter of the green or tee surface.
6. Guide carts away from water-saturated areas. Avoid cart traffic on turfgrass areas that are wilting or have frost covering the leaves. In the former situation, serious rutting and soil compaction can result, while in the latter, the turfgrass leaves can be killed.
7. Operate golf carts in a manner that will minimize damage to the turf. Avoid skidding or spinning the wheels by quick braking or rapid acceleration. Also avoid short, quick turns which can seriously bruise the turf and cause thinning.

A club with twenty or more carts should consider installing cart paths in high traffic areas. (A discussion of cart paths is included in chapter 12.)

Closing the Golf Course

Closing a golf course is probably one of the most difficult and emotional questions faced by the golf course staff. It adversely affects cash flow in all departments and may create dissension among the golfing clientele.

The two primary reasons for closing a golf course are adverse weather conditions and construction activities. Many factors influence the decision. Since most of these factors call for personal judgment, the decision is seldom left undisputed. This is especially true if the reasons are not clearly understood.

Even though judgment is involved, the decision should be based on all available facts, with the best long-term interests of the entire club membership being the primary governing factor.

The final decision is the responsibility of either the green committee chairman, who has direct responsibility to the membership for maintenance of the course, or the owner or designated authority, in the case of privately owned clubs. The decision is strongly influenced and usually solely dependent on the judgment of the golf course superintendent. A properly trained superintendent is capable of rendering expert professional advice on the subject. The golf course superintendent can recognize factors that have tremendous influence on the future well-being of a turf and its playability that are not recognized or understood by golfers. Thus, as a practical solution, the decision-making responsibility is frequently delegated to the golf course superintendent.

Adverse Weather Conditions. Weather can have adverse effects on both turf and underlying soil. Such effects are further aggravated by traffic over wet areas. Traffic has two main detrimental effects on golf course turf: soil compaction, the extent of which is determined by the pressure in pounds per square inch exerted on the soil, and turfgrass wear from abrasive action and pressure on grass shoots.

Bare feet are particularly destructive to greens in terms of soil compaction, as are high-heeled boots and shoes, because body weight is exerted on a relatively small surface area. For example, body weight is distributed on the heel and ball of a bare foot and on the heel and shoe sole of a foot wearing a street shoe or a golf shoe with recessed spikes. Body weight is distributed largely on the spike shoulders of regular golf shoes.

Hand-pulled golf carts exert more pounds of pressure per square inch than do most three- or four-wheeled powered golf carts. For this reason, hand-pulled carts should be under the same operating restrictions as are powered golf carts. However, the abrasive action of powered golf cart tires in turning, starting, and stopping makes these carts more likely to injure a turf than are pull carts.

The effect of traffic on soil compaction increases as soil water content increases. The soil becomes extremely pliable and soft and is then prone to serious rutting and compaction (Fig. 1-16). Serious problems arising from soil compaction include (a) exclusion of oxygen needed to maintain root growth, (b) loss of water absorption and retention capabilities in the soil, (c) increased water loss by surface runoff, (d) loss of resiliency (which affects the ability to hold a shot on a green), (e) destruction of surface smoothness (which can require weeks or even months to fully correct), (f) a weakened turf that is prone to disease, annual bluegrass invasion, insect injury, and such environmental stresses as cold and heat, and (g) need for a substantial number of man-hours for corrective procedures such as soil cultivation (e.g., coring and slicing), topdressing, spiking, and overseeding.

The degree of soil compaction caused by traffic under wet conditions varies depending on soil texture and drainage characteristics. Problems with compaction and rutting are great on fine-textured clay soils and in areas where drain lines and surface drainage have not been provided. In contrast, sandy soils drain quite rapidly and traffic can be reintroduced quickly after an intense rain. Thus, it is possible for one golf course to be closed due to wet conditions while another not far down the road is open, simply because of differences in soil texture and drainage characteristics between the two sites.

Turfgrass wear from traffic can also occur during the cold part of the year when there is frost on the ground, especially on greens. Mechanical pressure exerted on frozen leaves disrupts them physically and results in their death. Frost can be removed quickly by a light syringing if the air temperature is above freezing. In most cases, however, it is preferable simply to close the course until the normal rise in temperature has melted the frost.

Play on solidly frozen greens usually does not cause permanent damage if the grass is dormant. However, the greens may not stay frozen all day once play is allowed. Should surface thawing of the sod occur, the turfgrass roots can be sheared at the interface between the frozen soil and thawing sod. This is a second winter condition calling for closing of the course, but is one that is difficult for golfers to understand.

Finally, cart traffic should be confined to the rough and to cart paths during the spring transition of dormant bermudagrass fairways.

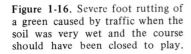

Figure 1-16. Severe foot rutting of a green caused by traffic when the soil was very wet and the course should have been closed to play.

Construction Activities. Play may have to be restricted or even stopped when construction or renovation is taking place on a course. Whenever members will be inconvenienced by construction activities, every effort should be made to inform them of the project well in advance and also to provide alternatives for the affected golf hole or holes. A more detailed discussion of rebuilding procedures is presented in chapter 2. Temporary tees and greens can serve as very satisfactory alternatives while construction is in process. If adequate time and effort are devoted to establishing these temporary surfaces, their quality can be quite acceptable, assuming they are properly maintained. Generally, construction projects should be planned well in advance so there is adequate time for establishment of alternate greens and tees before the actual construction work is initiated. In some cases of fairway renovation, one or more holes may have to be closed for a period of time. Whenever possible, such renovation should be scheduled at a time when golfing activity is minimal.

The Decision. The goal of good course maintenance is to have the course open and in optimum playing condition at all feasible times. Any decision that necessitates closing of the course should be made carefully, using sound reasoning. The potential damage, both immediate and long term, of allowing play must be weighed very carefully against monetary losses and golfer dissatisfaction if play is prohibited. Unfortunately, the decision is not easy to make. Frequently it involves a compromise, such as allowing foot traffic only or restricting carts to paths and/or the rough. The golf course superintendent's judgment based on sound agronomic knowledge is vital in the decison-making process, especially when closure is contemplated due to unfavorable weather conditions.

PHILOSOPHY OF GOLF COURSE MAINTENANCE

A well-maintained golf course allows the golfer to play the game with the least number of interfering and inconsistent factors. In the past, a substantial percentage of golf course superintendents knew little about the subtleties and strategies of the game itself. This was unfortunate, because the golf course is the single most important factor in determining how the game is played. This means that the golf course superintendent is a behind-the-scenes official of the game. It also means that the superintendent should pursue his or her responsibilities in a professional manner. Development of a sound working knowledge and understanding of the game of golf is crucial. The superintendent devises a philosophy of how the course should play, giving due consideration to the needs of the golfers. This philosophy is not just

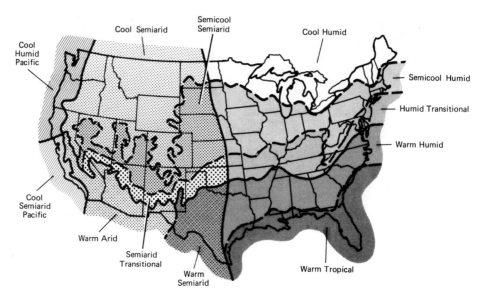

Figure 1-17. Major turfgrass climatic zones of the United States. The boundary lines are actually broad transitional areas. (From Beard, J. B., 1979. *How to Have a Beautiful Lawn.* Beard Books, College Station, Tex., p. 4.)

learned but evolves through a combination of education and experience over a period of time. Application of this philosophy involves coordinating all factors that allow a golf course to play to its full potential all the time.

The superintendent should strive to make the course the most equitable determinant in the sport. This must be done in every operation, be it routine daily practices, such as tee marker and cup placements, or major renovations that affect the physical nature of an entire hole. This does not imply that every inch of a well-maintained golf course must be perfectly groomed. Most renowned golf courses have areas of extreme contrast. Tees, greens, and fairways receive intense grooming, while roughs, bunkers, and other hazards are left naturally rugged.

A golf course is in truly ideal condition when it presents a challenge and yet always plays fair. The ultimate goal of the golf course superintendent is for the golf course to play at or near championship standards on a continuing basis, assuming the budget is adequate. Extraordinary measures should not be needed to elevate the course to championship form for any tournament or special event.

CLIMATIC REGIONS

References will be made to particular climatic zones or regions within the United States when discussing the use of turfgrass species and cultivars and cultural practices. Thus, the objectives of this section are to delineate these regions geographically and to describe some of the important climatic features of each zone.

Climate is a dynamic combination of environmental factors which influence the growth and development of turfgrasses. The four major components of climate influencing turfgrass growth are light, temperature, precipitation, and wind. Temperature extremes and precipitation patterns are the most significant determinants of zones of turfgrass species adaptation.

Each turfgrass species has a specific temperature range in which it can maintain growth. Growth ceases at the extremes of the range and the turf may die if stress continues. A turfgrass species is adapted to a particular climatic zone when it is able to persist on a long-term basis. The cool-season turfgrasses grow best at temperatures between 60 and 75 °F (16 and 24 °C). Root and shoot growth is severely restricted at soil temperatures above 80 °F (27 °C). In contrast, warm-season turfgrass species grow best at temperatures between 80 and 95 °F (27 and 35 °C). Shoot growth ceases, leaf chlorophyll is lost, and the turf becomes dormant with a brown to tan appearance at soil temperatures below 50 °F (10 °C).

Four major turfgrass climatic zones are shown in Figure 1-17. The boundaries are not absolute but rather indicate transition zones. There can also be considerable variation in climate within a region, particularly as influenced by altitude and rainfall distribution. Temperatures generally decrease in mountainous regions with increasing altitude.

Cool Humid Zone

This temperate zone represents one of the larger areas of turfgrass in North America. The zone has two distinct geographical regions. The larger portion is the northeastern and north central regions of the United States, extending from Maine westward into the eastern Dakotas. The western edge of this portion extends southward to the northeastern corner of Oklahoma; the southern transitional boundary is quite variable from northern Arkansas to southeastern Virginia, with the Appalachian Mountains extending the zone southward into Tennessee, Georgia, and the Carolinas. The smaller portion of the cool humid zone is represented by a narrow strip running north and south along the Pacific Coast and east to the Cascade Mountains.

The cool humid zone is characterized by mild to hot summers and cold winters (Table 1-2). Low-temperature kill of certain cool-season species can be a problem in the northern portions, while heat stress is a particularly severe problem in the southern portion. Temperatures are much milder along the cool humid Pacific coastline.

Total annual precipitation, which ranges from 25 to 45 inches (63.5 to 114.3 centimeters) in the northeastern and north central regions, is fairly evenly distributed throughout the year. A portion occurs in the form of snow, primarily in the months of December, January, and February. Precipitation is much higher in the northern Pacific cool humid zone, most of it occurring during the winter along with moderate temperatures. Relative humidity tends to be in the 50 to 80 percent range. Both precipitation and relative humidity are highest along the Atlantic coastline and lowest west of the Mississippi River. Evapotranspiration correlates directly with the seasonal temperature pattern. Water loss exceeds rainfall to the extent that supplemental irrigation is usually needed during June, July, and August if growth cessation and summer dormancy are to be prevented.

The eastern two-thirds of the cool humid region tends to have acidic soils, while in the western portion soil pH tends to be neutral to slightly alkaline. Saline and sodic soils are generally not a problem.

Cool Arid-Semiarid Zone

This climatic zone is one of the larger regions in the United States in terms of land area. It extends westward from the northern Great Plains, including portions of North and South Dakota, Nebraska, Kansas, and Oklahoma, to the Cascade and Sierra Mountain ranges in western Washington, Oregon, and California. The cool arid-semiarid zone encompasses two contrasting regions: to the east the vast Great Plains, where many of the native North American grasses originated; to the west the intermountain region of highly variable topography with extensive, elevated plateaus.

The climate is typically continental with hot summers and cold winters. Elevations within the zone vary from 1,000 to 14,000 feet (305 to 4,268 meters). Temperatures decrease with increasing altitudes

Table 1-2. Summary of Representative Weather Conditions for the Four Major Climatic Zones and Their Subzones

Climatic Zone	Subzone	Mean Monthly Temperature (°F)		Average Annual Temperature (°F)	Annual Precipitation (In.)	Average Monthly Relative Humidity at Noon (%)	
		January	July			January	July
Cool humid	Northern	0 - 25	65 - 70	35 - 45	25 - 35	70 - 80	55 - 65
Semicool humid and transitional	Southern	25 - 35	70 - 78	45 - 60	35 - 45	65 - 70	45 - 60
Cool humid Pacific	Northern	35 - 40	55 - 65	50 - 55	40 - 100	75 - 83	55 - 82
Cool semiarid Pacific	Southern	40 - 45	65 - 75	55 - 60	20 - 40	55 - 75	50 - 65
Cool semiarid	Northern	0 - 20	60 - 70	35 - 45	10 - 20	55 - 75	25 - 45
Semicool semiarid	Southern	20 - 30	65 - 75	45 - 60	10 - 35	40 - 60	20 - 45
Warm humid	Northern	35 - 50	78 - 82	60 - 65	40 - 50	60 - 75	50 - 60
Warm tropical	Southern	50 - 70	82 - 85	65 - 75	40 - 65	65 - 70	60 - 70
Warm semiarid and transitional	Eastern	42 - 62	82 - 88	62 - 73	15 - 40	40 - 70	35 - 65
Warm arid	Western	35 - 53	75 - 92	60 - 73	5 - 20	30 - 45	25 - 35

in the mountainous regions. Mean summer temperatures are in the 70 to 80 °F (21 to 27 °C) range in the plains of Kansas, Oklahoma, and Texas and in the 60 to 70 °F (16 to 21 °C) range in the intermountain region. Midwinter temperatures have a mean monthly average in the 20 to 35 °F (− 7 to 2 °C) range in Nebraska and Kansas and are as low as 0 to 10 °F (− 18 to − 12 °C) in the upper portion of the region. The intensity of sunlight is very high, especially in the mountainous region.

Rainfall tends to be low and variable, ranging from less than 10 inches (25.4 centimeters) in the intermountain plateaus to as high as 20 to 25 inches (50.8 to 63.5 centimeters) in the eastern subhumid region. Relative humidity is very low, which increases the evapotranspiration rate from turfs but also reduces disease problems. Rainfall distribution tends to be erratic, with the heaviest amounts occurring in the spring and early summer. Midsummer dormancy of turf may occur due to soil drought if supplemental irrigation is not provided. There is also a strong probability of winter desiccation injury in areas with minimal snow cover, especially if exposed to high winds. The soils tend to be alkaline; saline and sodic soil problems are encountered in certain locations.

Warm Humid Zone

This zone is represented primarily by the southeastern portion of the United States, which extends along the Atlantic coast east of the Appalachian Mountains, southward throughout Florida, and west to central Texas and Oklahoma. Elevations throughout most of the zone are relatively low, and there are numerous rivers and low-lying marshes.

The climate is characterized by subtropical areas along the coast, including the Gulf of Mexico and eastern Florida shorelines. The more northerly locations tend to have mild temperatures. The mean July temperatures throughout the region are near 80 °F (27 °C), with a humidity of 60 to 70 percent. The incoming warm tropical ocean current has a strong influence on the climate, resulting in rainfall ranging from 50 to 65 inches (127 to 165.1 centimeters) along the Atlantic seaboard and decreasing westward to 25 inches (63.5 centimeters) in eastern Texas and Oklahoma. Periodic droughts of two to three weeks duration may occur at irregular intervals, especially in the western portion of the region. The soils tend to be acidic, particularly in the more southeasterly area.

Warm Arid-Semiarid Zone

This zone encompasses a wide belt from Texas to California across the southwestern United States. The zone includes three subregions: (1) a transitional temperate area in the northern mountainous parts, (2) a subtropical area in southern California and southwestern Arizona, and (3) a tropical region along the Gulf Coast in south Texas. Midsummer temperature means are generally very hot, 80 to 95 °F (27 to 35 °C). January temperature means range from 42 to 62 °F (5.6 to 17 °C) in the eastern half of the zone and from 35 to 53 °F (2 to 12 °C) in the western half.

Precipitation ranges from less than 5 inches (12.7 centimeters) annually to about 20 inches (50 centimeters) along the eastern edge of the zone. Rainfall distribution usually includes relatively dry summers, particularly in the western two-thirds of the region. Irrigation is necessary to maintain green, actively growing turfs throughout much of this climatic zone because of the low rainfall and high evapotranspiration rate. Humidity is typically low except along the Texas Gulf Coast. Skies are clear for a large portion of the year, which accentuates the hot daytime temperatures and coolness of the nights. In the western portion of the zone, cool nights plus a low humidity of 25 to 45 percent, which enhances transpirational cooling, favor the growth of certain cool-season turfgrass species. Soils are primarily alkaline, with saline and sodic soils scattered throughout the region. Well water containing a high salt or sodium level is not uncommon in this zone.

Chapter 2
Building a Golf Course

The development of a good golf course is a major undertaking requiring a sizeable investment. Thus, it is important that the decision-making process and individual events follow an organized structure. A flow diagram with suggested guidelines for the development of a golf course is shown in Figure 2-1. Information concerning current construction costs for golf courses can be obtained from the National Golf Foundation (NGF) or the American Society of Golf Course Architects (ASGCA).

The developer of a golf course may be an individual or a group. Commonly the developer appoints a golf course advisory committee, usually after the construction decision has been made. This committee may or may not be involved in site selection. The overall role of the advisory committee is administration of the golf course development—to serve as a communications link between the decision maker(s) and the various consultants, professionals, and contractors necessary for the work.

One of the first responsibilities of the advisory committee is to interview possible architects and make subsequent recommendations to the decision maker(s). Selection of the architect is one of the most important decisions in the golf course development process. The architect is the one continuing link throughout the project. A good architect can build an acceptable golf course on a poor site, whereas an unknowledgeable architect often misuses a good site and produces a poor course fraught with long-term maintenance problems.

The golf architect, once selected, develops preliminary designs, after which a final design concept is selected by the decision maker(s) with advice from the advisory committee. The architect then prepares the working drawings. During both the preliminary design and working drawing stages, the architect usually will be required to assist the developer in obtaining any necessary zoning or general construction permits that relate to the presence of the course and/or its detail design.

It is important for successful construction that the architect prepare detailed specifications covering the construction standards and methods related to the work shown on the plans. Bids are then solicited from qualified contractors. Either a general contractor or several specialized contractors is or are selected, the decision being based on competitive bids or direct negotiation. At the same time, the position of construction supervisor/superintendent should be announced, applicants interviewed, and the best-qualified candidate hired. The length of time elapsing from selection of the architect to beginning of construction can be one half to one and a half years; an additional one and a half to two years typically elapses from the time golf course construction begins until the course is opened for play.

To reemphasize, good golf courses do not just happen! They are the result of careful planning, design, construction, and management.

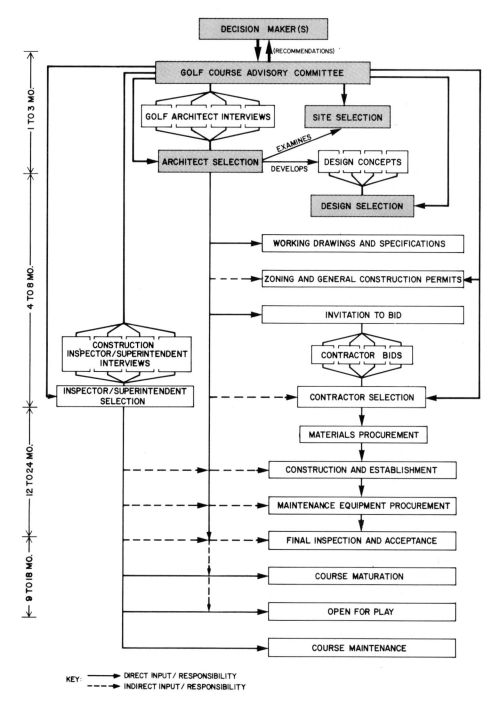

Figure 2-1. Suggested stepwise procedures and lines of communication in the development of a golf course.

ARCHITECT SELECTION

Designing a golf course requires the full attention of a competent golf architect. Selecting the architect thus is one of the most important acts in development of a golf course and should not be done in haste.

Procedures to follow in selecting an architect include an on-site interview with each candidate and personal inspections of courses previously designed by the candidates. Questions to ask during inspection include: Is the client pleased with the course? Do golfers enjoy playing the course? How much time did the architect spend on the site? How much time did the architect spend overseeing construction? Did the architect meet the budget agreed on? Were the specifications followed? Was the architect's work completed on schedule? Was the architect cooperative?

Finally, examination of a set of plans and specifications from a previous project by someone qualified to interpret them may prove helpful, but only in conjunction with a visit to the course itself. Plans and specs vary with the desires of the client, the projected budget, and the site, so the architect should be allowed to justify any criticisms of a particular project.

In evaluating proposals from various architects, the person(s) choosing the architect should ascertain that the quality of the work will be of an acceptable standard and will comply with the client's desires. It is important to determine that the architect has experience with the type of course design desired by the client. Unexpected problems may arise whose solutions will require time, close attention, and the practical experience of the architect. Thus, good rapport between the architect and the contractor, course superintendent, and golf course clients is of utmost importance.

The ASGCA will, on request, provide its membership list of golf course architects to interested clients. Unfortunately, some individuals arbitrarily declare themselves "architects" and are willing to undertake contracts of any magnitude. Thus, the candidate selected must have a demonstrated talent for golf course design, be knowledgeable about the game of golf, and understand the basic engineering necessary for the detail design, drawing, and construction phases. The architect must be willing to consult with competent agronomic advisors on matters of soil, drainage, irrigation, and turfgrass selection under the specific soil and climatic conditions. It is also the architect's responsibility to see that his or her plan of original design, together with more detailed plans and specifications, are in fact followed by the contractor and subcontractors.

The Architect's Contract

A written contract should specify the architect's responsibilities to the client during the design and construction phases of golf course development. To avoid possible misunderstandings, it is usually advisable to enumerate specific items for which the architect is not responsible.

Included in the contract will be the architect's fee structure and the payment schedule. The fee may be a lump sum or a percentage. If the latter, the base should be clearly stated. The fee often includes travel and living expenses for the architect during site visits if he or she does not live nearby. If not, these expenses should be shown or listed as being in addition to the basic fee. The costs for a golf course architect's work are less easily defined and generally more variable than those for the work of a building architect.

The contract should cover the following basic points:

Architectural Services

1. The type and number of preliminary concept drawings to be presented and the detail required (scale, yardages, black and white or color).
2. Type of cost estimates to be provided during the planning stage and the degree of cost breakdown.

3. Type and detail of working drawings and specifications to be provided for bidding purposes and subsequent use by the contractor.
4. Type of construction standards to be specified and the degree of detail required.
5. Responsibility for designing facilities directly related to the golf course layout and construction. Such items may include practice putting green, practice range, service roads, cart paths, lakes, dams, stream bank stabilization, course landscaping, water sources, and power supplies.
6. Responsibility for designing other structures such as shelters, restrooms, bridges, parking lots, pump-house, and maintenance area.
7. Responsibility and limits thereof in acting as the owner's representative in the administration of construction.
8. Type of architectural supervision or site inspections to be made during the actual construction, what such inspections entail, and, optionally, the number to be made. Also, arrangements and payment for extra visits requested.
9. The time when direct responsibility ceases. This may be when the course is planted or when it is opened for play.
10. Additional services or subsequent consultations.
11. Procedure to be followed if there is early termination of the contract.

Related Supporting Services

1. Who is to obtain and purchase the topographic maps, aerial photographs, soil surveys, and hydrologic surveys.
2. Who is to arrange and pay for the survey and staking of the golf course and the property limits.
3. Who is to be responsible for securing environmental impact studies, licenses, permits, and other official approvals.
4. Who is to be responsible for developing the bid document and selecting the contractor(s).
5. Who is to certify payments to contractors and the completion of work.
6. Who is to be responsible for hiring a construction inspector and/or the course superintendent. Who is to pay the salary(ies). To whom is the individual(s) responsible.
7. Who is authorized to approve ''change orders'' during construction.
8. Who is to be responsible for conducting physical and chemical tests of soil construction materials on greens, tees, and fairways to insure that the specifications have been met. Who is to pay for the tests.
9. Who is to provide a list of maintenance equipment and course furniture, and who is to be responsible for the purchase thereof.
10. Who is to be responsible for the design and installation of the irrigation system and pumping station.

Other points may be necessary in the contract owing to the particular nature or circumstances of the project, and numerous legal clauses are usually included as well. The advice of a legal counsel familiar with this type of service contract should be sought before a binding agreement is entered into.

Finally, ASGCA has formulated a standard design services contract, similar to that commonly used by the American Institute of Architects (AIA). This document simplifies the contract formalities for both architect and client.

SITE SELECTION

The individual or group involved in site selection for a golf course should seek professional counsel in this key decision. The guidance of a qualified golf course architect, and possibly of a soil scientist, should be obtained. For a small fee and/or expenses, most golf course architects will inspect and evaluate sites under consideration. Such an evaluation can be arranged with the clear understanding that it in no way commits the owner to retain the architect for the actual golf course design.

A number of factors enter into the site selection process. They can be grouped into economic and physiographic criteria.

Economic Criteria

Although it is not the intent here to discuss at length the golf course as part of a larger development project, it should be noted that a great majority of new golf courses are in fact an integral part of a larger real estate and/or resort project. With this in mind, two important factors should be considered in choosing the site: potential golfing demand and land cost.

Potential Golfing Demand. Market demand is of foremost importance in site selection, whether the golf course is to be part of a larger project or whether it is to be a public or private golf club on its own. Often a golf course is built in an outlying area where potential for population growth or resort development is great. However, patrons may be reluctant to travel to the course if a comparable facility is closer. Thus, the location of a golf course in terms of accessibility and convenience can play a major role in its success.

To help ascertain the demand for a new golf course in any area, the developer should contact the NGF for an assessment of potential demand and a golfer profile. Representatives of this organization are available to make on-site feasibility studies.

Land Cost. Costs, both for land and for construction of the golf course, must be considered in site selection. Prime industrial or residential sites near urban centers have become almost too expensive for the development of privately owned or operated courses. More distant sites on marginal land may be more economical to purchase but also may require a considerably greater construction expenditure.

Physiographic Criteria

Six major physiographic factors are important considerations when selecting a golf course site. They are (1) land area required, (2) topography, (3) soil suitability, (4) site drainage, (5) vegetation, and (6) availability of water and power. It is usually difficult to locate a site having an ideal combination of these characteristics, but significant savings can be realized in the construction of the golf course if these factors are carefully analyzed during the site selection process. These same factors also enter into whether the finished golf course is practical to maintain, has reasonable maintenance costs, and is enjoyable to play.

Finally, state and local ordinances require an environmental impact study, and therefore a thorough site analysis based on these six factors will help produce the positive conclusions necessary for obtaining construction permits.

Land Area Required. The actual area required for the course depends on topography; property configuration; course length desired; number and size of trees, ponds, lakes, and streams; amount of space planned between adjacent golf holes; and relationship of the golf course to surrounding real estate. A golf course length of 6,300 to 6,500 yards (5,758 to 5,941 meters) and a fairway width averaging 45 yards (41 meters) can be developed on a minimum of 120 acres (48.6 hectares). However, it is generally advisable to acquire from 160 to 200 acres (65 to 81 hectares) for an eighteen-hole golf course that will include a practice range, clubhouse, parking lot, and maintenance facility plus swimming and tennis facilities. This is especially important if the desire is to develop a golf course with unusual character and wide separation between holes. Although golf courses occasionally are built on less than the 120-acre minimum, this is to be avoided. An exception would be a nine-hole, executive, or par-3 course.

Topography. Golf course character is strongly influenced by the topography of the site. Topography, more than any other factor, dictates the flow and routing and the layout of individual holes. Flat

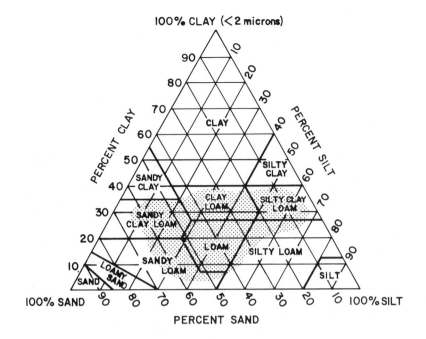

Figure 2-2. Soil textural triangle delineated in terms of turfgrass usage. Darkened area in lower center indicates preferred soil textural conditions for a golf course, assuming a depth of indicated textural materials to at least 18 inches (45.7 centimeters) without an abrupt textural change to subsoil materials. Local site conditions, such as soil drainage, clay mineralogy, and climate, may modify acceptable textural conditions.

sites afford an almost total and arbitrary use of the land, while more rugged topography will suggest designs that take advantage of natural features and avoid unnecessary earth moving and/or unappealing golf holes.

Golf courses are located on all types of terrain, ranging from the classic, flat seaside links to steep, hilly terrain. Most golfers prefer something in between, such as an aesthetically appealing site characterized by gently rolling hills, elevated plateaus that serve as natural green and tee sites, pleasing valleys with an occasional lake or meandering stream, and large trees which outline the fairways and provide backgrounds for the putting greens. Spectacular scenery, such as a background of ocean, sand dunes, or mountains, adds further interest to the site from an aesthetic standpoint.

Very hilly topography may necessitate considerable grading and soil movement to create acceptable fairway landing areas. Ideally, the final grade should provide maximum visibility from the tee to the landing area and from the landing area to the green to speed play, insure adequate safety, and provide the best possible playing qualities.

In contrast, relatively flat sites may present drainage problems that must be corrected. Such problems necessitate the excavation of ponds that can then also be utilized as water hazards and as a source for irrigation water. The excavated soil may be used to elevate the subgrade of fairways and possibly also to improve surface drainage. This technique can be used to develop elevated greens and tees as well as to create interesting contours and grassy mounds. It is essential that existing topsoil be stripped and stockpiled before the new subgrade is constructed. This topsoil can then be redistributed over the area after the final subgrade is established.

Large-scale soil excavation using earth-moving equipment should be held to a minimum. Extensive soil moving is expensive, may result in a loss of soil structure, and may destroy the natural character of the land. The soil moved may need a number of years to stabilize on fill sites. Thus, if the optimal design on a difficult site calls for extensive soil movement to achieve a playable golf course, it may be wise to consider a more suitable site.

Soil Suitability. It is possible to grow grass on most soil types provided surface drainage is good and the appropriate cultural practices are employed. However, there are limits in terms of practicability and economics. Unfavorable soil conditions translate to increased construction costs and difficulties as well as to higher expenditures for future maintenance programs. A relatively coarse soil texture is preferred (Fig. 2-2). A USDA Soil Conservation Service soil survey map can be consulted as to the soil characteristics of each prospective site, or a soil scientist can be employed to map each site and provide technical information concerning its suitability.

Loamy Soils. Sandy loam to loamy sand soils are preferred for golf course sites, since they usually present minimal construction problems and greatly reduce long-term turfgrass maintenance costs. The advantages of loamy soils include adequate subsurface water drainage with retention of significant amounts of water for turfgrass growth. The more rapidly the soil drains following intense rains, the sooner golfers can resume play. A significant reduction in green fees, golf cart rental, and other revenue may impair cash flow when a course is closed for several days due to water-saturated soil. An added benefit during construction is that sandy loam to loamy sand soils are easier to move, grade, and contour than heavier soils and thus savings are achieved in both time and money.

Sandy Soils. Sandy soils (more than 50 percent medium to coarse sand) have the advantages of (a) being less prone to compaction, (b) having rapid internal drainage, and (c) being favorable for turfgrass growth when compared with finer textured clay soils. Sandy soils provide uniform playing conditions throughout the year since seasonal variations in rainfall have minimum effects on them. An adequate irrigation system is necessary to maintain the desired moisture level during turfgrass establishment and subsequent maintenance of quality turf. Decaying grass roots contribute to the organic matter content of sandy soils over a period of years and thereby improve their water and nutrient retention capacities.

Gravelly Soils. It is generally preferable to avoid building a golf course on an alluvial gravel bed. Although gravelly soils are characterized by good internal water drainage, they require costly root zone modification to achieve adequate moisture and nutrient retention in the upper 6 inches (15 centimeters). Root zone preparation usually requires removal of large stones to a 3-inch (7.6-centimeter) soil depth by means of mechanical equipment, followed by placement of a fine-textured sand over the gravel to a 4- to 6-inch (10- to 15-centimeter) depth. This operation will increase costs substantially but is worthwhile in moderating long-term maintenance costs and cultural problems.

Gravelly sites are associated with alluvial floodplains. Thus, these areas should be checked carefully to assess their susceptibility to periodic flooding. Land prone to flooding may be relatively inexpensive to purchase, but problems associated with the debris cleanup, turf loss, and soil deposition resulting from flooding are expensive, especially where the turf must be reestablished. Also, the golf course is closed during flooding and the subsequent cleanup-recuperative period, which means a significant loss of income and dissatisfied golfers.

Clay Soils. Clay soils (more than 30 percent clay) are less desirable for golf course sites than are loam and sandy soils. Fine-textured clay soils are very prone to compaction when under intense traffic. Compaction severely restricts internal water drainage and eventually causes a decline in turfgrass quality. The ultimate result is inferior playing conditions and increased maintenance costs. Lack of internal drainage also causes the soil surface to become saturated during intensive rains. Traffic, especially golf carts, must be withheld from the area until sufficient water has evaporated from the surface to dry the soil. It is important to insure that the final grade on clay soils provides rapid removal of surface water. Failure to construct proper contours creates problems that are very difficult and expensive to correct.

Silty Soils. It is preferable to avoid soils high in silt (more than 50 percent silt). However, this may not be possible in certain regions of North America. River bottom soils frequently have a high silt and clay content. Their dark color and good physical appearance when dry can be misleading.

Rocky Soils. Shallow soils are found on rocky sites. The sites are either bedrock with a shallow soil mantle over the surface or surface and subsurface rocks interspersed with soil. Bedrock material can be highly variable. Golf course construction on such a site is very costly. Cuts and irrigation trenches may require blasting with explosives and the use of air hammers. Root zone soil mix will probably have to be hauled in to cover the exposed rock, a very expensive operation. Thus, it is important to check the depth of the root zone over an extensive rock formation in order to anticipate or avoid costly construction operations. However, high construction costs in covering bedrock may be preferred to the long-term maintenance problems and costs associated with golf course construction on poorly drained clay sites.

Sites where rock is mixed with soil are somewhat easier to work with than sites with soil over bedrock. Sufficient soil may be present to maintain adequate turfgrass growth. However, larger rocks will still have to be removed, possibly by blasting, and some supplemental soil hauled in to fill these areas (Fig. 2-3).

Swamps and Bogs. Problems can be encountered in wet, imperfectly drained or swampy areas where peat and muck have accumulated. Golf courses constructed on these sites usually will have increased construction costs. In addition, local or state law may require a permit for construction on so-called wetland and floodplain sites, and obtaining this permit may be quite difficult.

Whenever possible, construction of putting greens and tees on peat or muck deposits should be avoided. The gradual, uneven settling that occurs as the underlying peat is pushed outward may cause breakage of irrigation and drainage lines. The preferred approach is to remove the organic deposits if

Figure 2-3. Major rock problem on a proposed fairway area. Rocks must be removed or crushed at considerable expense.

they are shallow or to avoid placing greens and tees on them if they are extremely deep. The latter is possible if the deep deposits are small in size and are randomly distributed on undulating terrain.

Similarly, design and construction of fairways on organic soils should be avoided if at all possible. When they must be built on such soils, it may be necessary to recontour and reestablish a turf on the area every eight to ten years.

Similar problems are encountered with golf courses constructed on sanitary landfills. The subsidence rate varies unpredictably across the fill as the organic materials decompose. This may cause more breaks in irrigation and drainage lines and also necessitate periodic recontouring and reestablishment of turf to maintain an acceptable playing surface.

Saline and Sodic Soils. Potential golf course sites should be evaluated for saline and sodic (sodium) soils by means of a soil test. This is most important in semiarid and arid regions. In some cases, salinity problems can be corrected before construction is begun. Correction involves downward leaching of salts from the root zone. Salts cannot be removed in this way if the soil water percolation rate is restricted or if an adequate means for removal of the drainage water is not provided. Therefore, the ability to grow turfgrasses on saline soils depends on the existing salinity level, the soil percolation rate, and the salinity level of the irrigation water to be used.

Sodic soil problems can also be corrected if the soil can be leached and drained. In this case, gypsum or sulphur is incorporated into the soil to a 6- to 8-inch (15- to 20-centimeter) depth prior to leaching for the purpose of displacing sodium held on the clay particles. The sodium is then leached downward out of the root zone and into the drainage lines.

It is important that saline and sodic soil problems be corrected prior to turfgrass establishment.

Site Drainage. As a general rule, constructing a golf course in a low, poorly drained area will be much more expensive than constructing it on an elevated, well-drained site. Water-saturated soils and standing water on a golf course following intensive rain can delay play for prolonged periods, sometimes up to several days. In some regions this could mean a loss of twenty to forty golfing days per year with a substantial loss in revenue and many unhappy golfers. Also to be avoided are sites subject to periodic flooding, especially those at the lower end of an urban watershed (Fig. 2-4).

Visual signs of drainage problems include the presence of cattails, reeds, and sedges; peaty soil; and subsoil with a blue-gray or mottled coloration. These conditions indicate that prolonged water saturation has occurred at some time during the year.

Two types of drainage must be provided. Surface runoff is the most rapid and easiest method of removing excess water during intensive or prolonged rains. Surface drainage can be provided by having crowned fairways on flat areas and a minimum slope of 1 to 3 percent on rolling terrain. These modest slopes should direct the water into diversion ditches and eventually into grass waterways. The waterway cross section must be designed to handle the anticipated water volume at a moderate velocity to minimize erosion potential. Contours on the fairways and primary rough should be graded uniformly to avoid depressions where water may accumulate. Installation of dry wells and/or french drains will aid in removing excess surface water where surface depressions cannot be avoided.

The second dimension of good drainage is subsurface or internal soil water movement. This involves infiltration or entrance of water into the soil, its percolation or movement through the soil, and its eventual removal through subsurface drainage lines. A relatively coarse-textured, sandy or loamy sand root zone is particularly beneficial in this regard and should be provided on high-traffic areas such as tees and greens. Subsurface drainage can be further enhanced by a tile or plastic pipe drainage system on sites with tight, impermeable soil. Surface catch basins may have to be connected to the underlying drainage system on sites where large volumes of surface water cannot be handled through grass waterways.

Proper drainage is important in semiarid and arid regions for another reason. Salts can accumulate and result in a saline-sodic soil condition on sites with inadequate surface drainage and relatively impermeable soil.

Figure 2-4. Flooding on a golf course constructed in a lowland area.

Vegetation. Preservation of existing stands of mature trees and/or shrubs adds greatly to the development of an aesthetically pleasing and challenging golf course. A planting program can be initiated if trees are lacking, but many years are needed to produce a mature wooded appearance. The classic seaside golf courses of Scotland do not have many trees, and some American golf courses have been constructed in this motif, as trees are not a prerequisite for a challenging golf course. However, most American golfers and golf course architects prefer trees and shrubs in the secondary rough and particularly for separation between holes and as background for greens.

Some trees probably will have to be removed during construction. The clearing costs may be partially offset by selling the trees for lumber. Local governmental units in most regions require, by law, that environmental impact studies be made and approval be obtained before large-scale tree-clearing operations can be initiated. This adds to construction costs. Local laws restricting burning also result in expenses for the disposal of brush, small limbs, stumps, and other wood debris. Clearing costs notwithstanding, if the choice is between two sites having comparable topography, drainage, and soil conditions, the site with trees would be preferred.

Potential golf course sites which have been in agricultural production should be evaluated in terms of past herbicide usage. Herbicides with specific toxicity to grasses may have been used for years on some crop production land. The toxic residue can remain in the soil for many years where it may create problems in establishment of turfgrass.

Power and Water Availability. The availability of and distance to fuel and power adequate to operate the golf course facility should be determined. The irrigation pumping system may require a 480- to 220-volt (3-phase) power source. If the power source is a substantial distance away, the cost for connecting lines can become quite large. Nevertheless, this connection cost may be offset by the larger needs of a surrounding housing development.

The availability and quality of water are critical factors in selection of a golf course site. Water is a key cultural factor in the maintenance of quality greens and tees, with irrigation also needed to maintain quality fairway turfs on most golf courses in North America. Water source criteria include the minimum amount required per unit time, the total quantity of water available, the water quality, and the cost. The actual amount of water needed within a given period depends on such factors as the turfgrass species, evapotranspiration rate, physical properties of the soil, and amount and distribution of precipitation.

Water for irrigating golf courses may be obtained from a well, stream, river, lake, pond, drainage canal, municipality, utility company, or a combination thereof. An often overlooked source is effluent and similar waste water. This is an increasingly important water source, particularly in arid and semiarid climates. Golf courses are ideally suited to use waste water and thereby to play a key role in recycling and conservation of this most vital natural resource.

The preferred water source is one within the boundaries of the golf course property. This may become even more important in the future. A more detailed discussion of water sources can be found in chapter 9.

ARCHITECTURE

Golf course architecture in the United States has evolved from the varied moods and minds of many individuals. Scottish golf professionals influenced the architecture of early American golf courses. They had many years' experience in golf and thus their counsel was eagerly sought by individuals developing golf facilities in the United States. Subsequently, a few Americans became interested in golf course design and had sufficient family wealth to study abroad and self-educate themselves in golf course architecture. From this background evolved the professional golf course architect, who designs and oversees construction of a golf course on a fee basis. Today many golf course architects are trained in landscape architecture, civil engineering, and other technical aspects of the field.

Few individuals are truly talented in the art of golf course design. It requires a unique ability to view a vast expanse of undeveloped property, conceive an image of the completed golf course, make drawings, and then constantly rework the design until it is as near perfection as possible. The qualities enabling a person to accomplish this are a very special gift. In addition to having artistic ability, the truly capable golf course architect must have equal competence in the scientific aspects of soil science, drainage, irrigation, and turfgrass establishment/culture and in the concepts and strategic aspects of the game itself.

A golf course constructed from an architect's design is meant to be a relatively permanent inscription on the landscape and is the product of a major investment in time, money, and physical resources. The architect must develop the design under the restrictions imposed by terrain, landscape vegetation, budget, physical resources, and the desires of the golf club membership or owner. Essentially, the golf course architect defines the theories of the game of golf by the design developed for a particular site and client.

Philosophy of Design

A well-designed course is a challenge to all degrees of golfing skill without being burdensome or uninteresting. A good golf course architect takes advantage of the natural beauty of a site to create a course both aesthetically pleasing and enjoyable to play. Artificiality has no place in this concept of design. Playing a well-designed golf course should be a delightful, memorable experience.

Golf course design, or more specifically the design of individual golf holes, falls into three major categories: (1) strategic, (2) penal, and (3) heroic (Fig. 2-5). Penal-type golf holes were quite common during the early part of the century owing to the strong influence of British golf courses with their random placement of bunkers and other hazards. The classic penal architecture of fifty years ago is

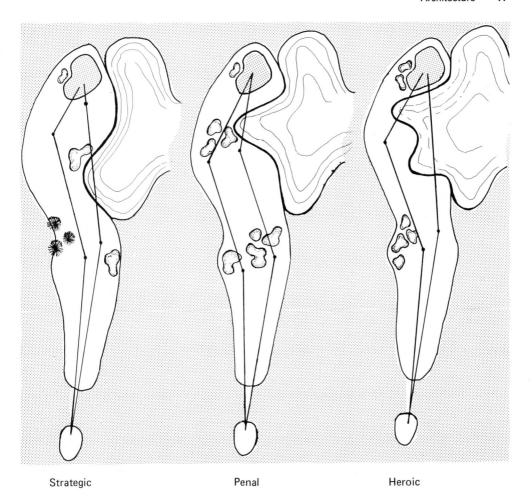

Strategic   Penal   Heroic

Figure 2-5. Comparative drawings illustrating the strategic, penal, and heroic philosophies of golf course design.

seldom seen on modern courses. Today the emphasis is on strategic design, but one frequently encounters a few holes on a course with heroic design. The combination of these two design principles usually results in a good test for all calibers of players, and the application of these principles to varying topographic conditions helps produce the uniqueness and individuality of character found on all good courses.

The degree to which design principles are applied varies according to the intended use of the golf facility. Public fee and municipal courses may exhibit only the elemental concepts of strategy, having few bunkers and other hazards, whereas courses designed specifically for hosting major championships usually have numerous bunkers and water hazards to accentuate the strategic, heroic, or penal nature of each hole and to create a high level of excitement during competition. The normal private club or resort course falls somewhere between these extremes.

Strategic Design. The most frequently utilized design philosophy on golf courses in the United States is the strategic. This design offers more than one way to play a hole and imposes on the individual responsibility for making the choice. Behind this design lies the principle that a good course should require thought as well as technical skill. A good course should also be a source of pleasure to all types of players, giving mediocre ones a chance while demanding the utmost to break par from experts.

No course is more representative of this school of design than the Augusta National Golf Club, Augusta, Georgia. The fairways are very wide, there is almost no rough, and there are very few fairway bunkers. Generally speaking, the player is not overly penalized for a bad shot. On the other hand, he or she must play for position on virtually every shot to score well.

On a strategically designed par-4 hole, it may be advantageous to approach the green or a specific pin placement area of the green from a certain angle or position on the fairway. The depth and orientation of the green and/or the relative position of the greenside bunkers guarding the entrance to the green may be more favorable from this point. On other holes, a certain part of the fairway may afford a better lie topographically or may offer better visibility to the flag. In either case, the golfer's drive must be positioned to take advantage of the more direct second shot opportunity that the architect has offered. The architect may introduce the element of risk by placing some form of hazard or tree near this ideal target zone, which necessitates precise execution of the drive. For the player who elects not to take the risk, the hole offers a large and relatively trouble-free target area from the tee. The second shot, however, will be more difficult, but even here an alternate, less challenging approach from just short of the green will usually be available. The only penalty, a self-imposed one, will be the third shot needed to reach the green, but there is still a chance of 1-putting for par.

In summary, when the ideal or direct route presents a hazard (bunker or water) beyond the player's shot-making ability, an alternate route should be offered which is less risky, less demanding, and less penalizing but also not characterless. It is the architect's creation of fair pitfalls, guarding against easy conquest of par, that makes a hole interesting. The challenging aspect of strategic design is that the player must plan and execute each shot properly.

Penal Design. Penal architecture as it flourished during the early part of this century resulted in courses that were both frustrating and humbling for many to play. Extensive use of deep, frightening bunkers; high rough; trees; and occasionally water left the golfer no choice in how to play the course. Basically there was only one route to follow for each hole. Following the line of play on any hole was an exacting, demanding assignment. Every shot had to be controlled and placed precisely to avoid the multiplicity of hazards. Accuracy was the paramount requirement, and any error was costly. It was extremely difficult to circumvent the dictates of the architect and still make par.

The increased popularity of golf, along with a greater emphasis on the pleasurable rather than the punishing aspects of the game, brought about the demise of the straight and narrow philosophy of penal design. Although the penal concept is still in use in a modified form, few courses today exhibit the formidable and intimidating design concepts of fifty years ago. Pine Valley Golf Club in Clementon, New Jersey, is one of these. Carved out of forest and sandy wasteland, it has been called the largest unraked bunker in the world. There is adequate turf for tees and fairways, but these are so designed that exacting shots are required to avoid severe trouble. Fairway bunkers are unraked, and this feature, together with the growth of natural vegetation within the bunkers, strikes fear into the hearts of even the most skilled golfers. The fairways are lined with dense trees and shrubbery, and natural vegetation is allowed to grow freely in the bunkers as well, making recovery shots extremely difficult. Anyone unable to cope with the island-hopping requirements of Pine Valley will find the course unforgiving. However, Pine Valley is one of the world's most formidable tests of golf for the player who can execute shots with accuracy and precision.

Absolute penal architecture in a golf course is a thing of the past. Today's concept of penal architecture is much softer, although the basic idea remains the same: A miss-hit shot is penalized. However, the severity of the penalty has been lessened. At the south course at Oakland Hills Country Club in Birmingham, Michigan, for example, bunkers are staggered along each side of the fairway in the landing areas to catch the errant drives of long and short hitters alike. However, the shape and depth of the bunkers, along with their well-raked condition, offer better players the choice of playing the recovery shot directly to the putting green. The penalty exacted, therefore, is slight. The famous Oakmont Country Club near Pittsburgh, Pennsylvania, has lost much of its original penal design. The originally awesome number of 350 bunkers has been cut in half. Those remaining — still twice the number on most courses — are no longer deeply furrowed. Both Oakmont and Oakland Hills have hosted major national tournaments. In the Open Championship, the United States Golf Association (USGA) usually requires that the fairways be narrowed and that the rough be allowed to grow to 4 inches (10 centimeters) or more. This practice further emphasizes the basic penal concept.

All modern courses may be loosely termed penal if they have hazards, woods, out-of-bounds, or rough. A fairway lined with bunkers and/or out-of-bounds stakes, a par-3 hole surrounded by bunkers with no real fairway, and a short par-4 with the approach shot over water may all be considered penal. Most architects judiciously employ a bit of the penal philosophy in their designs for added excitement and challenge.

Heroic Design. In the heroic concept of design, the architect challenges the golfer to the limit of his or her ability by requiring a truly monumental shot to reach the objective. Heroic design is generally more in evidence on par-5 holes where the architect is trying to preserve the original intent of the par-5 as a hole requiring three shots to reach the green. Nothing says that a player should not reach a par-5 green in two shots for the chance at a possible birdie or eagle. However, the architect will usually defend against this assault on par by requiring, through the use of hazards or other design factors, that these two shots be spectacular. The opportunities to cut across a bunkered dogleg or to carry a water hazard to shorten the distance to the green are typical of the temptations offered on a heroic hole. The reward for a well-played shot is clearly evident, but miscalculation may result in a severe penalty. The design may dictate that the greater the miss the greater the penalty.

While the concept of heroic design is usually associated with defending against a birdie or better on longer holes, it is equally viable as a defense against par on shorter holes. Reaching the par-3 sixteenth hole at Cypress Point, Pebble Beach, California, requires a prodigious tee shot on even a calm day. The second shot to the sixteenth green at Oakland Hills is no less demanding and thrilling. In both cases, there is a safer alternate route. In avoiding the risk, though, the golfer must invariably settle for a lesser achievement.

Heroic golf holes, regardless of length, add immeasurably to the character of a golf course and to the excitement players of all classes experience when playing them. Nearly all the great courses of the world possess a few such holes. Merion Golf Club near Philadelphia, Pennsylvania, presents one of the finest examples of the heroic design concept in its last five holes. These holes present one of the strongest finishes in golf, as each one demands either a tee shot or an approach of heroic proportions if the golfer is to achieve par or to have a chance for a birdie.

Integrated Designs. Elements of more than one design principle — especially the strategic-heroic combination — may be found in certain holes and may lead players of varying abilities to classify them differently.

Great Golf Holes

Most golfers either have played some of the great golf courses of the world or have seen them as a result of extensive television coverage of major golfing events. Great golf courses place a premium on accuracy and demand the use of every club in the bag.

What features make a golf hole an exhilarating experience when successfully played and induce fits of despair when the attack on par is unsuccessful? Perhaps the best way to answer this question is to examine some of the great golf holes in the United States: the seventeenth at Pinehurst Country Club, No. 2 Course (Fig. 2-6); the thirteenth at Augusta National Golf Club (Fig. 2-7); the sixteenth at Oakland Hills Country Club, South Course (Fig. 2-8); the eighteenth at Merion Golf Club, East Course (Fig. 2-9); the thirteenth at Pine Valley Golf Club (Fig. 2-10); the eighteenth at Pebble Beach Golf Links (Fig. 2-11); and the sixteenth at Cypress Point Club (Fig. 2-12).

Great Golf Holes
the seventeenth at Pinehurst Country Club, No. 2 Course

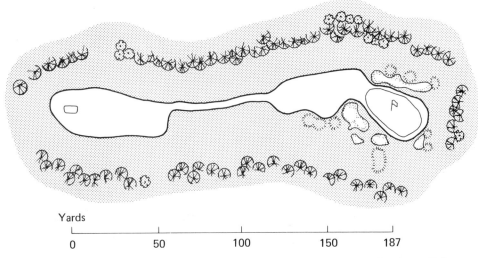

Yards

0	50	100	150	187

Figure 2-6. Seventeenth hole at Pinehurst Country Club, No. 2 Course, Pinehurst, N.C.

Pinehurst's No. 2 course was designed and exquisitely engineered by Donald Ross, one of the game's premier architects and certainly its most prolific. Ross, who learned the game as a child in the north of Scotland at Dornoch, was one of the band of immigrant Scottish pros who spread the word on the game in the United States when they came here early in the twentieth century. He is said to have built or modified nearly six hundred courses in this country.

Many consider Pinehurst No. 2 the ultimate expression of Ross's artistry because he lived in Pinehurst and, therefore, not only built the course but watched over its evolution.

The par-3 seventeenth hole plays from an elevated tee to a relatively flat green. It is guarded in the front and on both sides by bunkers and mounds.

The hole, like the best of Ross's works, is subtle, not flamboyant. He took great pains in contouring his greens, which he inevitably located on sites that seemed perfectly natural.

The first nine holes of the original course were installed with sand greens in 1900. The second nine were added in 1907. Ross thoroughly overhauled the old No. 2 Course in the 1930's, when improvements in grass strains enabled the sandhills of Pinehurst to hold grass greens.

Other memorable Donald Ross courses include Seminole in North Palm Beach, Florida; Inverness in Toledo, Ohio; Salem, near Boston, Massachusetts; and Oak Hill in Rochester, New York.

LEGEND

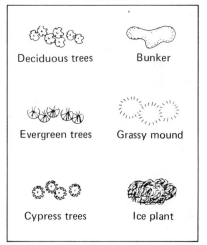

Great Golf Holes
the thirteenth at Augusta National Golf Club

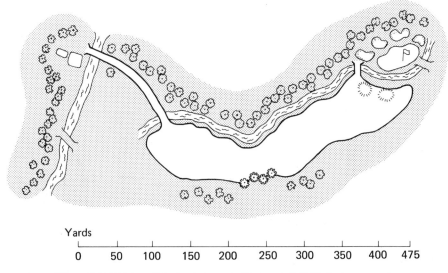

Figure 2-7. Thirteenth hole at Augusta National Golf Club, Augusta, Ga.

The thirteenth hole at the Augusta National Golf Club is a splendid example of a par-5 hole that can be reached in two, but with peril. The ideal location from the drive is down the left side of the fairway, which means flirtation with a creek that then becomes the vital element in the hole as it angles across the entrance to the green.

Like so much of the Augusta course, the thirteenth has been made beautiful by landscaping. The attractive features include splashes of sand in the woods behind the green and flourishes of azalea on the left side of the hole.

The Augusta National Golf Club course was the joint creation of Bobby Jones and architect Dr. Alister MacKenzie. Jones founded the club shortly after his retirement from competitive golf in 1930. It became the site of the annual Masters Tournament in 1934.

Jones, describing the thirteenth hole, wrote: "This is one of the finest holes for competitive play I have ever seen. The player is first tempted to dare the creek on his tee shot by playing in close to the corner, because if he attains this position he has not only shortened the hole but obtained a more level lie for his second shot.... Whatever position may be reached with the tee shot, the second shot as well entails a momentous decision whether or not to try for the green."

LEGEND

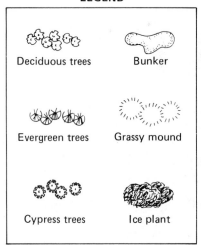

Great Golf Holes

the sixteenth at Oakland Hills Country Club, South Course

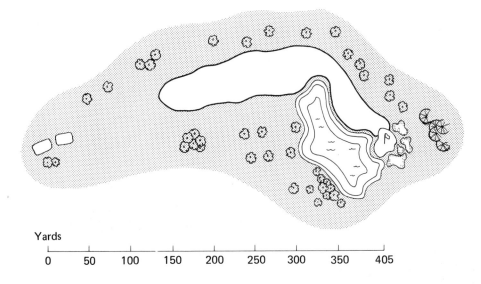

Figure 2-8. Sixteenth hole at Oakland Hills Country Club, South Course, Birmingham, Mich.

The par-4 sixteenth hole at Oakland Hills is renowned for its demanding second shot into a lovely setting—a peninsula green flanked by water and sand. A ridge runs through the center of the green to compound the challenge.

The sixteenth is basically the work of architect Donald Ross. It was revised by Robert Trent Jones prior to the 1951 U.S. Open Championship.

Oakland Hills has been the scene of four U.S. Open Championships, one of which was won by Ben Hogan in 1951 when the course was so severe that only two rounds under 70 were recorded.

The most dramatic stroke ever played on the sixteenth hole came during the final round of the 1972 PGA Championship, when Gary Player seemed about to drop out of contention when he drove far to the right behind trees. It seemed unlikely that he could both clear the trees and reach the green, but Player, using a 9-iron, carried his ball more than 150 yards to within 5 feet of the hole to set up a birdie he needed to win.

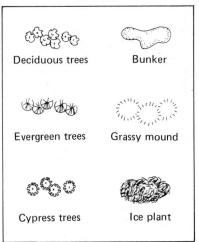

LEGEND

Deciduous trees   Bunker

Evergreen trees   Grassy mound

Cypress trees   Ice plant

Great Golf Holes

the eighteenth at Merion Golf Club, East Course

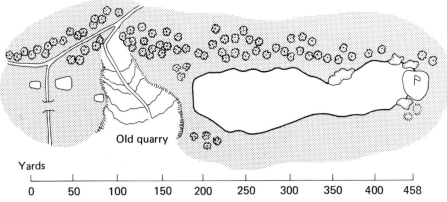

Figure 2-9. Eighteenth hole at Merion Golf Club, East Course, Ardmore, Pa.

The phrase "greatest finishing hole in golf" has become one of the game's sorry cliches, but the par-4 eighteenth hole at Merion deserves the utmost consideration of that accolade.

The drive from the back tee must carry 200 yards over an abandoned quarry and must be held up to the right lest the second shot be played from a hanging or sloping lie. The green is very large and properly so, since the second shot can be a full-blooded wood for even scratch golfers.

Merion has been the site of more USGA Championships and international matches than any other course, so the eighteenth hole is linked with great moments in the history of the game. One of the more poignant was in 1950 when Ben Hogan, needing a 4 to tie, ripped a 1-iron shot into the heart of this green to establish his par. He won the playoff and the U.S. Open the next day.

Merion and its eighteenth hole is the handi-work of Hugh Wilson, who was a member of the club and played on its original course. He was given the assignment of heading a committee that would lay out a new and improved Merion. Wilson traveled to Great Britain where he studied and sketched the storied links courses before laying out Merion. He was first assisted by William Flynn, who was in charge of the construction of the course and later became an eminent architect. The hole was modified, as was much of Merion, under the supervision of the legendary Joe Valentine, the Merion golf course superintendent, whose accomplishments include the discovery of what we now know as Merion Kentucky bluegrass, which he found in a patch near the course's seventeenth tee.

LEGEND

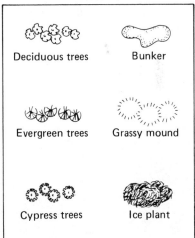

Great Golf Holes
the thirteenth at Pine Valley Golf Club

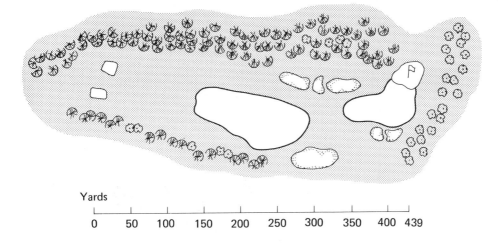

Figure 2-10. Thirteenth hole at Pine Valley Golf Club, Clementon, N.J.

Pine Valley was the sole architectural creation and vision of a Philadelphia hotel owner—George Crump—who slowly began to carve holes from forests in New Jersey's pineland in 1912. He made a sort of home on the barren site, living in a tent and then a bungalow.

Crump was assisted in the preparation of the course plan by the gifted English architect H. S. Colt, but the extraordinary and unique character of the course was divined by Crump.

Crump died in 1918 with four holes still to be finished. Work on the remaining holes was directed by Hugh Wilson, the architect of Merion, and his brother Alan.

The par-4 thirteenth was one of Crump's unfinished holes. Like the rest of the course, its basic design principle is the island target surrounded by shrubs, bushes, and sand.

The second shot makes the thirteenth at Pine Valley remarkable. It's a long shot from the crest of a hill over sandy wasteland to a huge green. If the drive isn't perfect, and it must be in order to get home in two, the hole can be safely converted to a three-shotter by steering the second shot down a slope to the right.

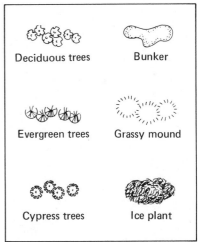

LEGEND

Deciduous trees	Bunker
Evergreen trees	Grassy mound
Cypress trees	Ice plant

Great Golf Holes
the eighteenth at Pebble Beach Golf Links

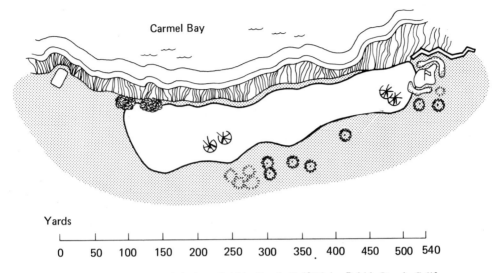

Carmel Bay

Yards

| | | | | | | | | | | | |
|0|50|100|150|200|250|300|350|400|450|500|540|

Figure 2-11. Eighteenth hole at Pebble Beach Golf Links, Pebble Beach, Calif.

The eighteenth at Pebble Beach is an exacting par-5 with a narrow fairway and Carmel Bay running along the entire left side. Trees and out-of-bounds border the right side. These features, along with shifting winds, make it one of the most carefully played finishing holes in the world. Most golfers attempt three well-placed shots to reach the green, hoping to 1-putt to beat par.

Students of golf course architecture generally hold that few architects have been able to build par-5 holes with enthralling second shots. The eighteenth at Pebble Beach is surely an exception, since the second has to avoid the Bay on the left, a boundary on the right, and a couple of isolated pines which seem to have no other purpose but to block a clear third shot to the green.

Pebble Beach was laid out shortly after World War I by Jack Neville, with Douglas Grant as a consultant. Neither was a professional golf course architect. Both were first-rate amateur golfers and former California state champions. Neville, in fact, represented the United States on the 1923 Walker Cup Team.

The course is operated by the Pebble Beach Corporation, which owns much of the land on California's Monterey Peninsula.

Pebble Beach was the site of the first national championship played west of.the Mississippi River in 1929, when Harrison Johnston won the U.S. Amateur Championship. Jack Nicklaus won the Amateur Championship in 1961 and the Open Championship in 1972 at Pebble Beach.

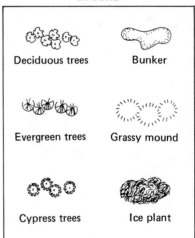

LEGEND

Deciduous trees   Bunker

Evergreen trees   Grassy mound

Cypress trees   Ice plant

Great Golf Holes
the sixteenth at Cypress Point Club

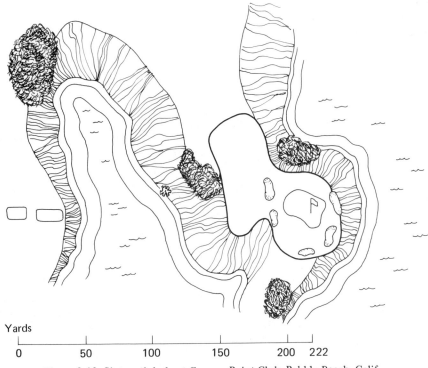

Figure 2-12. Sixteenth hole at Cypress Point Club, Pebble Beach, Calif.

The sixteenth hole at Cypress Point may be the most famous par-3 hole in golf. It is certainly the most photographed. The hole plays directly into the Pacific Ocean, a carry of 210 yards over a cove with the prevailing wind in the golfer's face.

For those who can't carry a ball 210 yards into the wind, an alternate route is available. An iron shot played away from the green, to the left, requires a carry of only about 150 yards and leaves a short iron or a pitch to the green.

The confluence of high land and sea on the Monterey Peninsula provides Cypress Point with as dramatic and glorious a setting as is to be found in American golf.

Cypress Point was laid out in the 1920's by Dr. Alister MacKenzie, a Scot whose first profession was medicine but who turned to golf course architecture after World War I. MacKenzie's rich body of work includes the Royal Melbourne course in Australia and the Augusta National Golf Club.

The course is one of three (with Pebble Beach and Spyglass Hill) used as sites for the Bing Crosby Pro-Amateur tournament each winter. It has never been the site of a national championship but was exposed to an international audience as host to the 1981 Walker Cup Match.

LEGEND

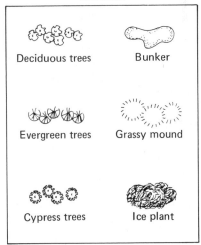

Deciduous trees	Bunker
Evergreen trees	Grassy mound
Cypress trees	Ice plant

Securing Permits and Licenses

The owner or appointed planning and/or engineering representative normally is responsible for securing all permits and licenses required to complete golf course construction, including the payment of any fees involved. Formal applications or requests and official permission may be required for (1) draining of tributaries or wetlands under the jurisdiction of the Corps of Engineers, (2) subsurface drainage developments controlled by state, county, or local authorities, (3) damming of rivers or streams where the normal volume of water flow may be interrupted to potential downstream users, (4) clearing of land with attendant steps to minimize topsoil loss by erosion, (5) use of the proposed water source for irrigation and/or drinking, and (6) use of electric, gas, or other power sources. An environmental impact statement covering all aspects of the golf course development may be needed.

Considerable time and expense can be involved in these steps, especially in making environmental impact studies, getting official approval for damming of streams, and getting permits for wetlands construction. In some cases, permits should be obtained prior to the detailed design phase, since some of the architect's options could be negated by restrictions imposed by the permit or license. Other situations allow these two phases to progress in concert.

Site Inspection

Once selected, the golf architect should make several inspections of the site. The initial visits normally consist of familiarization with the character of the terrain and the landscape, the general vistas from various parts of the site, and specific features that may be incorporated into the golf course design. With this general view in mind, the architect proceeds to make some preliminary layouts for the course. Additional visits to the site are then necessary to determine how well the various studies fit the land and how well they coincide with the general wishes and constraints of the client.

Site inspections are much more thorough and detailed at this point. Whereas initial visits gave the architect the general impression of the "forest," subsequent visits, with design ideals already in hand, enable him or her to inspect the "individual trees," adjusting aspects of the design to take advantage of specific features and characteristics of the site. It is obviously impossible to accomplish this in a single visit or by studying maps off the site.

It is important that the architect be provided with local soil maps from the U.S. Geologic Survey (USGS) or the Soil Conservation Service (SCS) at the time of the first site visit. These maps delineate the specific soil types and describe soil texture, infiltration rate, and associated properties vital to golf course construction and subsequent turfgrass culture. Good internal soil drainage is a critical feature in the maintenance of quality turfgrass areas. Thus, it is important to take advantage of any favorable soil drainage conditions existing on the site as well as to identify potential drainage problems that require corrective measures.

Design Guidelines

Topography dictates, to a certain extent, the flow or routing of golf holes. Routing that flows with the contour will produce a natural golf course with holes that are enjoyable to play. Fighting the contour, using it improperly, invariably necessitates excessive earthwork and results in a course that is unnatural and unpleasant to play. Seaside locations should suggest a links-land style course, while mountain and prairie sites adapt themselves better to styles that bring out their features.

Architectural styles based on modification of the unique features of a site through major earth-moving operations are costly, unnatural, and usually not advisable. Unnecessarily modifying the natural conditions of a site frequently results in difficult maintenance problems and even ecological disasters. Some leading authorities on golf course architecture feel that the more subtle details of a "natural golf course" are of much greater significance than the grand overall topography and design. That is, manipulation of the smaller, more subtle slopes, mounds, drainage ways, and contours around greens can be more significant in terms of the playing strategy on individual golf holes.

Proper use of topography when designing a golf course will minimize the extent of play oriented up steep hills. The course should flow with, not fight, the contour of the land. Sharp changes in elevation are best utilized by designing holes to be played downhill. If abrupt uphill changes are necessary, it is better to absorb the increase in elevation in the walk between a green and the next tee rather than along the length of the hole. Alternate, gentler routes may be required for older or weaker players.

An eighteen-hole golf course normally has two loops of nine holes each. Square or long-narrow property configurations are usually considered less conducive to an interesting layout of holes than other shapes. A rectangular parcel is preferred, with the longer dimension oriented north and south. An east-west lengthwise orientation frequently results in golfers playing into the setting sun on the finishing holes, which causes great sight difficulty and discomfort.

An early phase in planning a golf course involves determining the length of course required. The specific playing length of the course can range from 5,800 to more than 7,000 yards (5,301 to 6,398 meters) from the back "championship" tees. It is possible to offer playing lengths varying from 200 to more than 1,000 yards (183 to 914 meters) by designing alternate tees at various distances from the green. This approach has practical significance, since it offers a range of course lengths from the different tees — women's, men's regular, and championship. This allows golfers in all handicap ranges to compete fairly on the same golf course. For regular membership play, the women's course length is typically in the 5,800-yard range, while the men's course normally measures from 6,200 to 6,600 yards (5,667 to 6,032 meters). Most courses on which major tournaments are held measure from 6,600 to 7,000 yards. Yardage alone, however, does not determine how good the golf course is from a playing standpoint. A number of golf courses measuring 6,200 yards are excellent tests of golf.

A typical eighteen-hole golf course in the United States has four par-3 holes, four par-5 holes, and ten par-4 holes, making a total par for the course of 72. Each hole should have a distinct individuality while fitting into the overall style of design and playing quality. A varying sequence of 3-, 4-, and 5-par holes makes a far more interesting layout than back-to-back holes of similar yardage and par. This is especially true of the par-3 and par-5 holes. It is further advisable to avoid par-3 holes at the start of either nine. A relatively easy par-4 or par-5 makes a good starting hole, while a strong par-4 is generally considered a good finishing hole.

The increasing length of time it takes to play a round of golf today has placed great emphasis on design concepts that speed play. Thus, the sequence of par-3 holes within each nine-hole loop is important. A par-3 first hole or back-to-back par-3's tend to slow play, since one group of golfers usually waits on the tee until the preceding group has holed their putts and moved off the green. It is desirable to have a comparable number of par-3 holes on each nine. Finally, the distance between holes, or the walk from a green to the next tee, should be minimized and, for safety, players should be moving away from the line of approach to the green just played.

The route traversed between putting green and tee sites should be designed to minimize traffic in critical use areas. Sufficient entrance space onto tees is needed so that players can walk to the tee markers from numerous points. Similar concepts apply to routes between sand bunkers and the approach to a green. Severe turfgrass wear is likely if attention is not given to distributing traffic over multiple routes or over as large an area as feasible (Fig. 2-13).

Facilities Associated with the Golf Course. Adequate space and appropriate locations must be planned within an eighteen-hole golf course layout for a practice range, practice putting green(s), turfgrass nursery, and course maintenance facility. Failure to plan adequate practice areas is one of the most common errors in the design of new golf courses and this is one of the first improvements sought after such courses open for play. It is advantageous for practice areas to be a convenient distance from the golf shop, locker room, and first tee. Finally, golf course play must take into consideration the location and spatial requirements of the clubhouse, golf shop, golf-cart storage area, golf course maintenance facility, and parking lots plus the location of other sport facilities to be operated in conjunction with the course, such as swimming pool, paddle tennis courts, curling rink, lawn bowling greens, and riding stables. A plan delineating potential locations of service roads and golf cart paths is also needed. This is made following a comprehensive study of anticipated traffic flow patterns.

Putting Greens. Putting green size, contour, and shape, plus the location of associated hazards, vary in accordance with the length of the required approach shot. Normally, putting greens range in size from 5,000 to 7,500 square feet (465 to 697 square meters). Larger and smaller greens are designed to fit specific settings. While very large greens were in vogue a few years ago, the current trend is to intermediate-sized greens, owing in part to the high maintenance costs for large surfaces. The size of a green depends on the intended difficulty of the hole. Larger greens generally are used for holes that require long, difficult approach shots; for short holes requiring more controlled approach shots, the green is usually smaller and more difficult to hit. This places a premium on an accurate shot to the flagstick.

Contemporary greens typically are elevated above the fairway to provide adequate surface drainage, enhance depth perception, and necessitate a well-executed approach shot that must carry to the putting surface. An open entrance is not needed on the line of play where the intended line of play crosses a difficult hazard. A turfed opening onto the green off this line of play offers the high-handicap golfer a safer, but usually longer, route. Apart from drainage, the real design reason for elevation is to provide a specific target that the player must hit. The approach shot must carry to this target, which eliminates the chance that a poor shot, though improperly struck, might manage to roll onto the putting surface. This is the modern strategic or target golf concept, as opposed to the earlier pitch-and-run concept of the British and older U.S. courses.

The overall depth of a green depends on the length of the approach shot normally required. Long approach shots have low trajectories and the ball does not stop quickly when it hits the green. The high arc of a lofted approach on a shorter hole results in a shot that stops closer to where it lands. Holes requiring this shorter approach do not need the same depth of putting surface along the line of play. Many strategically designed greens combine these principles. A long hole may have the majority of its putting surface oriented to provide sufficient depth for the length of shot required while a small shallow area is located to one side and guarded by some form of hazard or mound. A golfer wishing to approach close to the flag placed in this part of the green will be required to make an extremely accurate shot. Alternatively, he or she can play to the larger safe area of the green with a resultant longer putt.

An interesting example of green shape and depth is the ''Redan'' hole, patterned after a famous par-3 hole by that name at North Berwick, Scotland. The axis of the green is on a diagonal to the line of play. The front of the green is nearly at tee level, but due to the fall of the adjacent land, the rear of the

Figure 2-13. Bare area resulting from intense traffic caused by a narrow exiting path from green to tee without reasonable alternate routes.

Figure 2-14. Typical Redan type of putting green design.

green forms an elevated plateau, the face of which is heavily bunkered. The putting surface gets narrower and falls away slightly to the side and rear. The farther a pin is placed along the diagonal, the more difficult is the shot. The player either can play to the more open front part of the green and hope to get a favorable roll toward the hole or face a long putt or may choose to carry the bunkers and aim directly at the pin in an attempt to set up a possible birdie. The risk of this approach is clear: if played short, the ball is in the bunker; if played long or off line, a challenging shot is required to save par (Fig. 2-14).

The general contour of a green should allow for pin placement over a majority of the surface area. A gently undulating putting surface is preferred, with significant changes in contour occurring only between clearly defined pin placement areas. Contours should be designed to allow rapid surface drainage and freedom from depressions. Terraces are utilized occasionally when the green is built into a slope or when the design of the hole calls for a particularly challenging pin position.

The total area of putting green surface to be constructed and maintained on a well-designed eighteen-hole golf course ranges from 2 to 3 acres (0.8 to 1.2 hectares). This does not include such associated parts of putting greens as the collar, grassy surrounds, and bunkers, which may add 10,000 to 20,000 square feet (9.3 to 18.6 ares) of area to be constructed and maintained around each green. Avoidance of steep slopes on the apron and green surrounds allows mowing with multigang units and greater freedom in traffic circulation, thus permitting economical maintenance. Sufficient width and gentle contours are needed on the apron and green surrounds for turning three-gang riding greens-mowers and similiar large-capacity maintenance equipment.

Tees. Golf courses designed prior to 1950 typically have small tees. The size was adequate for the low intensity of play typical of that period. However, their inadequacy in the face of increased play and the associated divots became apparent during the golf boom of the 1950's and '60's. As a consequence, tee enlargement has been one of the major rebuilding projects on many golf courses.

Rules of thumb for minimum usable tee sizes are (a) 100 square feet (9.3 square meters) per thousand rounds of golf annually for tees on par-4 and par-5 holes and (b) 200 square feet (18.6 square meters) per thousand rounds of golf annually for tees on par-3 holes designed for iron play. Optimum size is double these minimums. The tee size rule for par-3 holes designed to be played with a wood club is the same as that for par-4 and par-5 holes.

Turfs on tees that are shaded most of the day tend to be much weaker than turfgrasses growing in full sun. Therefore, it is advisable for shaded tees to be significantly larger than the recommended minimum. The first tee is generally subjected to more intense traffic stress than other tees owing to golfers gathering, warming up, and waiting prior to teeing off. For this reason, the first tee should also be larger than the recommended minimum. Where play is intense and the club allows starting on both the first and tenth tees, the tenth should also be considerably larger than the minimum. Typically, a well-designed eighteen-hole golf course has a total of 1.5 to 3 acres (0.6 to 1.2 hectares) of teeing area.

To provide flexibility in the playing length of a golf course it is desirable to utilize multiple tees, such as: (a) front or women's tee, (b) middle or men's tee, and (c) back or championship tee. Some clubs designate a shorter course for senior players by adding a set of tee markers forward of the markers for the middle or regulation men's course. In the case of a nine-hole course, it is possible to create two nine-hole loops with the same nine greens by designating two distinctly different sets of tees for each hole.

Rapid removal of surface water is as critical on tees as on greens, since the small area of the tee receives very concentrated traffic. The actual tee surface should be smooth with a very gentle slope of 1 or 2 percent. The pitch can be from front to rear, left to right, or right to left, depending on the surrounding terrain. A properly designed tee will actually look flat. On a large terraced tee it is important to avoid contours that cause water to accumulate at the rear of the lower terraces.

Varying the size and shape of tees is desirable since it adds interest to golf course design. Individual tees that are wider than they are long offer greater variety in play. The possibility of teeing off from a wide number of places on the tee may change the effect of fairway hazards, trees, and other natural features. This is especially true on multitiered par-3 holes where the resulting change in angle of the approach to a green can alter considerably the effect of adjacent bunkers on the varying pin positions.

Preferably, tees should be elevated to provide good drainage and visibility for the golfer, but this should be done carefully so that they blend naturally into the surrounding landscape. It is best to avoid small, isolated rectangular plateaus with steep side slopes. The area surrounding each tee should be gently sloped to blend into the existing landscape. Gentle contours allow more economical mowing of the tee surrounds by means of multigang units. The tee shape, whether rectangular or free form, should orient the golfer to the architect's intended direction of play for the hole. This can be accomplished by means of basic surface contours of the tee surrounds, by the turf boundaries delineating the mowed perimeter of the tee, or by associated landscape features, such as trees.

The location of tees depends primarily on topography and the quality of the shot a particular location offers. A number of other factors also are of concern. The tee relative to the previous green ideally is placed to avoid long walks and/or backtracking which may expose players to the risk of being hit by approach shots. Also, each tee should be protected against errant shots from adjacent tees and fairways. However, tees enclosed on three sides by trees and shrubs usually have a weak turf due to the excessive shade and lack of air movement (Fig. 2-15). Shaded turfs are disease prone, which creates added maintenance problems.

A final consideration is a rest area near the tee where golfers may relax and wait in comfort during periods of slow play. Sites under mature trees are particularly valuable in this regard.

Fairways. Whenever possible, fairways should be positioned to take advantage of the existing topography. This minimizes construction costs, maximizes use of the existing topsoil, insures good blending of the golf course into the natural terrain, and results in easily maintained golf holes. Specimen trees that can be used as part of the playing strategy on individual holes should be identified early in the design and staking stages and care taken to insure that they are protected during clearing operations.

Fairway width varies, depending on the degree of difficulty planned for the golf hole, from 35 to 60 yards (32 to 55 meters), the average being approximately 45 yards (41 meters). Typically, the fairway perimeters are contoured, the width being greatest in the landing areas. The total fairway area on an eighteen-hole golf course ranges from 30 to 60 acres (12 to 24 hectares), depending on widths and whether fairways are mowed from tee to green or from a distance of 50 to 75 yards (46 to 69 meters) in front of the regular tees.

Rough. Whether a primary mowed rough is included in the design and construction of a golf course depends on several factors. If the course is to be carved out of a heavily wooded site, the architect may decide to restrict the clearing of each hole to 150 to 180 feet (46 to 55 meters) and to establish the fairway from tree-line to tree-line. This approach is fairly common in forests of mature hardwood trees and in the pine woods of the southeast. In both cases there may be no mowed rough owing to the difficulty of establishing grass in the shade of trees, the only rough being the needle-covered or relatively bare forest floor. In coastal or other regions where vegetation is sparse and the holes are close together, the desire may be to grass the areas between the holes and to maintain the entire course as fairway. This philosophy is often popular in resort areas and for public courses where enjoyment and speed of play are paramount considerations and where ample water is available for irrigation. In arid regions there may be only enough water to irrigate the fairways, in which case the only rough will be the native landscape bordering the fairways.

The design of individual holes also influences the use of primary rough. On short par-3 holes, the intent may be to have primary rough cover the entire cleared area between the tee and the front apron of the green. On par-4 and par-5 holes, primary rough may be used for the first 50 to75 yards (46 to 69 meters) between the front of the tee and the beginning of the fairway, with only a swath of fairway grass the width of a gang mower connecting the tee to the fairway. This does not mean that the fairway itself will always have a primary rough on either side. On many courses with no primary rough adjacent to fairways, the outer edges of the fairways are allowed to grow several inches prior to the course hosting a major tournament. This "primary rough" is then restored to fairway at the end of the tournament, so it must be considered fairway for the purposes of construction.

Probably the most important determinant for the presence or lack of primary rough is the amount of land available for the course. Many courses today are so squeezed by surrounding property lines that there just is not sufficient area between the holes to allow for a mowed rough in addition to comfortably

Figure 2-15. Tee being constructed where it will be difficult to maintain due to a dense barrier of trees and shrubs on three sides.

wide fairways. It is common in these situations to remove all but the most important trees between the holes and to plant and maintain these areas as fairway. At best a narrow primary rough may be shared by two parallel holes.

Despite the pressures brought about by restricted land area and the desire to speed up play, the primary rough remains an integral part of the game. The inclusion of rough as part of the design is still important in most new courses, and careful consideration should be given to the construction and development of these areas.

The primary rough varies in width depending on the (a) tree proximity to fairways, (b) relationship to other golf holes, (c) presence of hazards, and (d) desires of the golfing clientele. Typically, the primary rough on each side of the fairway ranges from 10 to 15 yards (9 to 14 meters) in width. The outer perimeter should naturally blend into the surrounding landscape, while the inner perimeter should be sharply defined by the height of cut so that it is readily distinguished by players.

Well-placed trees and shrubs add to the beauty and aesthetics of the golf course landscape. Tree positioning in rough can also be important to the playing strategy of a golf hole. Existing trees should be evaluated when laying out the golf course. This is especially true in semiopen sites where specimen trees are common and in certain forested areas where old mature trees are present. A golf course design that, among other criteria, capitalizes on existing trees will be characterized by a mature appearance that minimizes the need for costly landscaping. Care should be taken in clearing golf holes to avoid monotonous straight lines of trees along the edges of the fairway or rough. An irregular undulating line of trees or random groupings produce a more interesting, natural setting.

The location of service roads in the secondary rough is another concern in rough design. It is desirable, where possible, to position roads in relation to the terrain, trees, and shrubs so that they are hidden from the view of players.

Hazards. A hazard is defined in the *Rules of Golf* as "any bunker or water hazard. Bare patches, scrapes, roads, tracks, and paths are not hazards." The most common form of hazard, an area of bare ground, often a depression, usually covered with sand, is called a *bunker*. Grass-covered ground bordering or within a bunker is not part of the hazard.

Wherever hazards exist, the associated contours should blend into the surrounding landscape. Contours that permit the drainage of surface water into bunkers must be avoided. It is preferable that the facings of bunkers and water hazards be visible to the golfer from the tee or from subsequent landing

Figure 2-16. Properly designed set of bunkers with the facings readily visible.

areas (Fig. 2-16). This visual dimension enhances depth perception and, more important, it makes the design strategy of the hole more evident, thereby enabling the golfer to plan how best to play the hole. Finally, bunkers are best designed to facilitate entrance and exit over a significant portion of the perimeter. Bunkers around greens should have a small vertical edge or lip on the greenside so that players cannot putt out of them.

Bunkers are best positioned so that they influence the strategy of play. Most bunker positioning is intended to direct the placement of shots rather than excessively penalize the golfer. Bunkers not critical to playing strategy are of minimal significance and can add substantially to the cost of maintenance.

Plans Prepared by the Architect

As the architect's concept of the golf course design evolves, it must be transformed into a general master plan for the course. Once the master plan has been accepted and/or modified as necessary, the golf architect will transform the overall design concept into working drawings that accurately portray the golf holes as envisioned. These working drawings must be accurate and easily read by construction personnel so that they can produce the original design concept. Accurate working drawings and specifications are also vital in determining realistic budget estimates and projected construction needs. The drawings prepared by the golf architect should include the following:

Golf Course Master Plan. The master plan delineates the property and shows the routing of individual golf holes, their yardages, and the functional relationships among them (Fig. 2-17). The tees, greens, fairway perimeters, and intended centerlines of play are shown, as are key hazards such as bunkers and water hazards. In addition to the golf course layout, the master plan should show schematically the proposed or potential location of associated facilities, such as the clubhouse, parking lot, practice range, practice green, shelters, service roads, and course maintenance facility. The boundary lines of the property must be shown. A frequently used scale for the master plan is 1 inch equal to 100 feet. The master plan is not a detailed working drawing.

Staking and Earthwork Plans. A staking plan depicts the location of all the points marked on the master plan. These points usually encompass the centers of putting greens and tees plus the fairway doglegs or turning points. An accurate staking plan consists of mathematically calculated coordinates from which a land surveyor can accurately locate the sites of individual features of each hole in the field. This insures that the yardages shown on the plan will be accurate in the field. The coordinates are calculated by the latitude and departure based on the yardages of each hole given to the nearest 0.5 foot (15.3 centimeters) and transferred to the staking plan. In this context, all boundaries and corners of the property must be correctly located, permanently marked, traversed, and closed by a professional surveyor. This avoids errors in the placement of the grids or the baseline. Use of a grid coordinate system allows a surveyor the convenience of selecting baselines in the field rather than following an arbitrary baseline coordinate system.

The architect usually checks the course once staking is completed. Frequently, slight adjustments in the location of greens, tees, or even entire fairway centerlines will prove advantageous from the point of view of both design and construction cost. These changes are then plotted on a revised staking plan.

The earthwork plan may be included as part of the staking plan or as a separate plan, if extensive excavation-fill work is required. It delineates those areas where excavation is required as well as sites where the soil will be placed, termed fill areas (Fig. 2-18). Typically, the subgrade for such features as greens and tees requires fill soil. The earthwork plan should be as exact as possible to facilitate reasonable estimates of excavation costs. Further, it should provide a systematic approach which balances excavations with nearby fill areas for maximum efficiency in haul routes.

Clearing Plan. A clearing plan is necessary in partially wooded or forested areas. This plan shows the area to be cleared on each hole as well as a typical detail of how clearing is to be done. Usually clearing is done in two phases. The first phase opens up perhaps 60 percent of the proposed width of the fairway, while the second phase, the area of which is frequently marked or flagged by the architect in

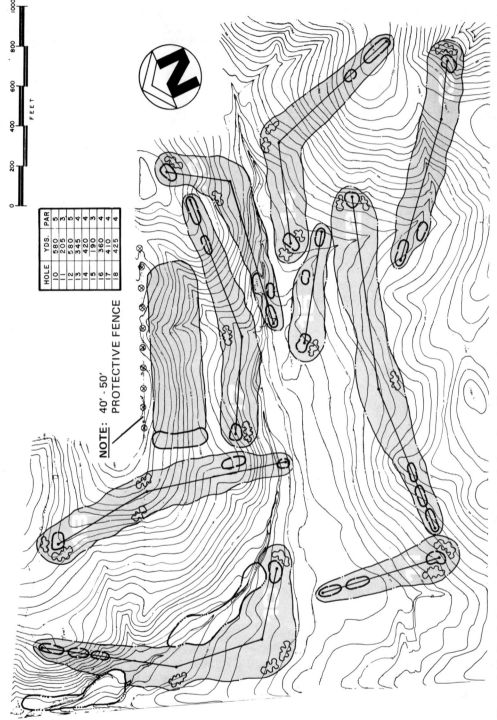

HOLE	YDS.	PAR
10	580	5
11	205	3
12	580	5
13	345	4
14	420	4
15	190	3
16	360	4
17	410	3
18	425	4

NOTE: 40' - 50'
PROTECTIVE FENCE

Figure 2-17. Typical master plan showing nine holes of a golf course layout. (Drawing courtesy of Rees Jones, American Society of Golf Course Architects.)

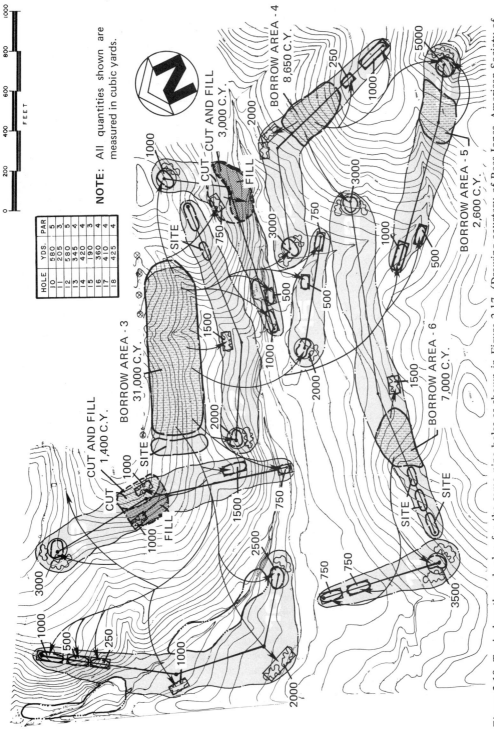

NOTE: All quantities shown are measured in cubic yards.

HOLE	YDS.	PAR
10	580	5
11	205	3
12	580	5
13	345	4
14	420	4
15	190	3
16	360	4
17	410	4
18	425	4

Figure 2-18. Typical earthwork plan for the same nine holes as shown in Figure 2-17. (Drawing courtesy of Rees Jones, American Society of Golf Course Architects.)

the field, completes the clearing of a particular hole or lake area. Marking before this second phase allows the architect to save important trees at the edge of a fairway by shifting the centerline or by altering slightly the proposed center of a particular green, tee, or bunker.

   Grading and Drainage Plans. The grading plan insures that needed surface and subsurface drainage facilities are incorporated to eliminate wet problem areas and that surface contours allow economical long-term maintenance. The specific cut and fill areas and their respective finish grades and slopes are shown for all tees, fairways, bunkers, and lakes. Finish grades for greens are shown on the putting green detail plans. Slopes around greens, tees, and bunkers and on fairways should be properly shaped and gentle enough so that excess water is diverted from these prime playing areas and slowed to a velocity that minimizes soil erosion, especially during the establishment period.

   The *drainage plan* must be coordinated with the grading plan but can be drawn separately, particularly if an extensive subsurface drainage system is required. This plan includes the locations of existing drainage outlets and their elevations plus the location, length, slope, and diameter of all proposed mains and connecting lateral drain lines (Fig. 2-19). The location and size of any catch basins needed for the removal of excess surface water are indicated, as are the location and slope of any needed french drains and/or dry wells. Although it is nearly impossible to foresee all of the drainage problems that ultimately will require solution, it is nonetheless important that the plan be prepared as accurately as possible to avoid large unanticipated increases in cost. An accurate detailed topographic map is essential in this regard. The grading and drainage plans involve an overall layout of the golf course and may include detailed drawings for each hole as required. The minimum scale for the grading and drainage plans is 1 inch per 200 feet.

   On completion of the drainage portion of construction, an *as-built drainage plan* should be drawn up based on accurate records kept on a daily basis during installation. The as-built plan is very important as a reference for future location of underground drains for cleaning, for adding to the existing system, and for repairing breakdowns. It is advisable for the contract with the architect to specify that an as-built drainage plan is to be provided.

   Details of Individual Putting Greens. Detailed plans must show the positions of all contours on the putting green surface as well as on the associated grassy surrounds and apron. They should be scaled to not less than 1 inch per 30 feet with contours shown at an interval not to exceed 0.5 foot (15.3 centimeters). These plans also show the locations of bunkers, drain line network and outlets, irrigation heads, and areas to be seeded or sodded. A typical cross-sectional profile of the subgrade, drain lines, and root zone modification details is also advisable along with the root zone specifications.

   Irrigation Plan. Most golf courses now being constructed include an irrigation system. A full chapter (9) is devoted to irrigation systems. The overall irrigation plan should encompass the entire golf course and possibly a series of detailed drawings for each hole. Included in the plan are the (a) placement and size of all irrigation pipe, (b) type, size, location, spacing, and distribution pattern of all sprinkler heads, (c) location and size of all quick-coupling valves, remote control valves, gate valves, control stations, and drain valves, (d) placement of master and satellite control stations, if automatic, and (e) pump-house site and site of associated support facilities. A suggested minimum scale is 1 inch equal to 50 feet. The irrigation plan should be closely referenced to the specifications.

   Once the irrigation system has been installed according to specifications, performance tests are conducted by the irrigation contractor to confirm that the design specifications have been met and to check for freedom from leaks.

   An *irrigation program control plan* may also be provided. This is usually prepared by a qualified architect or an irrigation specialist when system requirements and pipe sizes are determined to have a significant effect on the cost of the irrigation system. In the case of an automatic irrigation system, the program plan shows the order in which individual sprinkler heads or groups of heads are activated. Also shown is the relationship of the master and satellite controllers to individual heads or groupings.

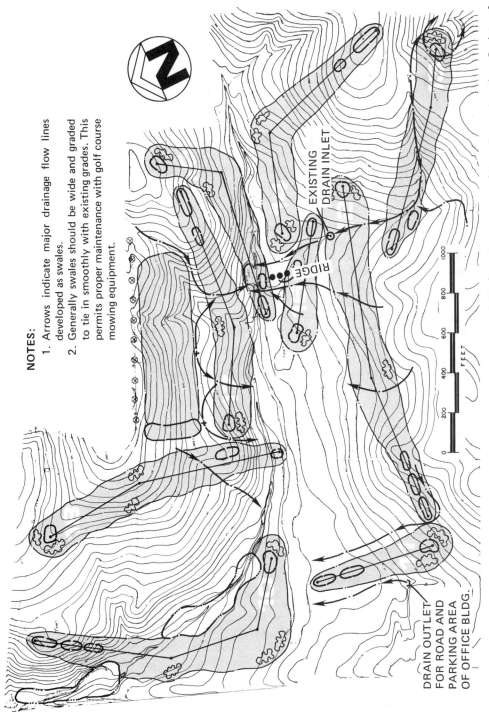

NOTES:

1. Arrows indicate major drainage flow lines developed as swales.

2. Generally swales should be wide and graded to tie in smoothly with existing grades. This permits proper maintenance with golf course mowing equipment.

EXISTING DRAIN INLET

RIDGE

DRAIN OUTLET FOR ROAD AND PARKING AREA OF OFFICE BLDG.

0   200   400   600   800   1000
FEET

Figure 2-19. Typical drainage plan for the same nine holes as shown in Figure 2-17. (Drawing courtesy of Rees Jones, American Society of Golf Course Architects.)

An *as-built irrigation plan* is required for future reference by course officials to properly service and maintain the system as well as to aid in locating main and lateral distribution pipes should repair or update of the system be needed at some future date. An as-built plan usually varies considerably from the original irrigation plan. Typically, numerous changes necessary to solve unanticipated problems are made during installation of the system. The contract with the architect or design engineer should specify that an as-built irrigation plan is to be provided.

Turfgrass Planting Plan. The specific turfgrass(es) or turfgrass mixture(s) utilized as well as the planting rate and method vary with the climatic region, soil condition, and cultural requirements for the putting greens, tees, fairways, and roughs. This justifies a planting plan (Fig. 2-20) that may involve a total plan for the golf course or detailed plans for specific areas. The specific locations and actual sizes of individual areas to be planted are shown. The written specifications for each area will cover the choice of seeds, seed mixtures, sod, sprigs, or stolons to be utilized along with the planting rate, method of planting, and preferred planting dates. The minimum scale for the planting plan is 1 inch equal to 100 feet. It is important that the planting plan be accurate in terms of the perimeters of fairways, tees, and putting greens. Different turfgrass species are planted in these areas and these turfgrasses delineate each hole.

Landscape Planting Plan. Trees are used in golf course design for one or more of the following purposes: depth perception, game strategy, windbreaks, noise and/or visual buffers, golfer safety, aesthetic value, and shade for golfer comfort. Therefore, a landscape planting plan is a key element of golf course design. The plan should show the locations of major existing trees and/or tree groupings in relation to individual golf holes, recommended locations where trees will enhance the golf course landscape, and a suggested list of major deciduous or coniferous trees to be used. A long-term tree planting plan developed in phases over a number of years may be desirable.

The inclusion of a detailed landscape planting plan may depend on whether the golf architect or a staff member is a qualified landscape architect. Even if not so qualified, the golf architect will usually provide a tree mass plan which satisfies the design intent. The superintendent, with the assistance of a local landscape architect or nurseryman, can then select trees that best fit the design.

CONSTRUCTION

The keys to successful golf course construction are detailed contracts and specifications to insure that the architect's design is executed as envisioned. These are discussed in this section, as are the first three major phases of golf course construction: surveying and staking, site clearing, and rough grading. Subsequent phases presented in other chapters include (a) installation of the irrigation system, (b) subsurface drainage system development, (c) construction of putting greens, tees, and bunkers, (d) final grading and preplant soil preparation, (e) planting, (f) postplanting care, and (g) landscaping. Successful execution of these major phases depends on the employment of a competent contractor and construction inspector/golf course superintendent.

Contracts and Specifications

The contract for construction of a golf course is a simple form of agreement. It includes descriptive articles on the (a) contract documents, (b) work involved, (c) time of commencement and/or completion of the work, (d) sum payable for the work, (e) form of progress payments, (f) purchase responsibility and payment schedule for materials, (g) final payment date, and (h) miscellaneous provisions. The form of a contract is fairly standard whether it covers the entire golf course construction or a particular phase thereof.

The contract documents referred to or listed in the contract include the general and special conditions for the work, the technical specifications describing the work, and all related plans and drawings.

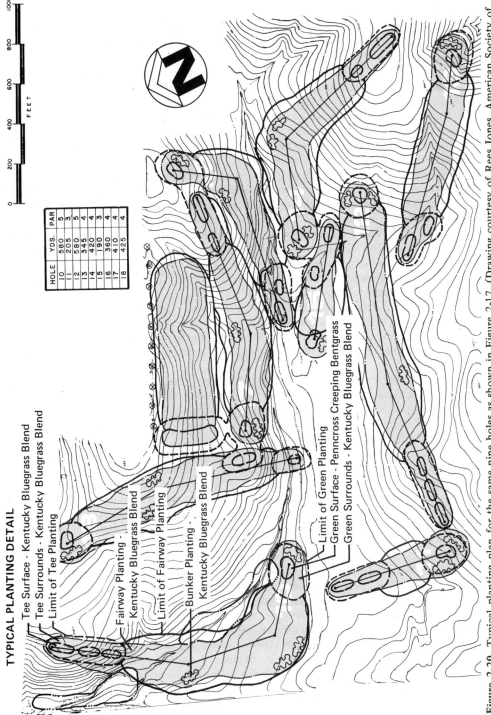

TYPICAL PLANTING DETAIL

Tee Surface - Kentucky Bluegrass Blend
Tee Surrounds - Kentucky Bluegrass Blend
Limit of Tee Planting

Fairway Planting - Kentucky Bluegrass Blend
Limit of Fairway Planting
Bunker Planting - Kentucky Bluegrass Blend

Limit of Green Planting
Green Surface - Penncross Creeping Bentgrass
Green Surrounds - Kentucky Bluegrass Blend

HOLE	YDS.	PAR
10	580	5
11	205	3
12	580	5
13	345	4
14	420	4
15	190	3
16	360	4
17	410	4
18	425	4

Figure 2-20. Typical planting plan for the same nine holes as shown in Figure 2-17. (Drawing courtesy of Rees Jones, American Society of Golf Course Architects.)

Technical specifications often differ considerably from one course to another owing to the variability of soils, drainage, topography, and vegetation and the unique features. The contract documents must be carefully tailored to the job. How well the architect does this determines the effectiveness of a contract and the ultimate quality of golf course construction.

The general conditions are contained in a somewhat lengthy set of articles defining in legal terms general aspects of the construction work. The document is standard in the construction industry. The special conditions modify the articles and definitions of the general conditions to suit the needs of a specific project. Of special interest are the articles on insurance and bonds. The general and/or special conditions normally specify the types and amounts of liability insurance the contractor must carry. Generally, the contractor must obtain a Certificate of Insurance to prove that he or she has met this requirement before being allowed to commence work.

The requirement for performance, payment, labor and material, and/or maintenance bonds is more variable and complex. Public projects may by law require any or all of these bonds as a form of guarantee. Large reputable construction companies can usually secure such bonds without difficulty. However, a substantial amount of golf course construction is done by small local contractors and subcontractors. Some of these are more experienced in specialized golf course work than many larger companies. Unfortunately, their small size may prevent them from being able to post the required bonds, which eliminates them from bidding on such contracts. For this reason, some bonding of selected contractors and subcontractors may be modified on privately financed projects. Care must thus be taken to select a reputable contractor.

The contract specifies the permits and licenses the contractor is responsible for securing. Usually included are licensing for business practices and certain construction permits, such as a burning permit for the clearing operation. Finally, the contract should specify that the contractor provide ''as-built'' plans, especially as they relate to installation of the subsurface drainage lines, irrigation system, and power lines.

The written technical specifications describe building procedures for the various phases of the construction work (Table 2-1). Included are sections on clearing; rough grading; major earth moving and lake excavations; surface and subsurface drainage; construction of the greens, tees, and bunkers; root zone modification of greens and tees; irrigation installation; final grading; preplant soil preparation; pH adjustment; fertilization; and planting.

Instructions concerning the removal and disposal of all obstructions and objectionable materials, including required depth of removal and disposal sites, are included as part of the above specifications or as separate sections. A separate section on blasting and rock removal may be included, as the amount of blasting that may be required is difficult to assess in advance. A separate unit price ''rock clause'' covers this contingency. Depending on the extent of the construction contract and/or the limit of the architect's design responsibilities, the specifications may also cover postplanting care, landscaping, stream bank stabilization, and construction of bridges, cart paths, service roads, and/or parking areas.

The contract usually calls for completion of construction in a stated number of working days and takes into account conditions related to rain, snow, wet soil, and climatic adversity. The contract sometimes states a date for the commencement of work and frequently a completion date. If the latter is included it should be carefully discussed among the owner, architect, and contractor before the contract is signed. Contracts with a completion date requirement often include a penalty clause, under which the contractor must pay a fixed daily amount for each calendar day beyond the designated completion date necessary to complete the work. The penalty clause is often accompanied by a bonus clause awarding the contractor a fixed daily sum for work completed ahead of schedule.

It is important that the contract documents clearly state the limits of the contractor's responsibility as a prerequisite for determining both the completion of work and the award of final payment. If the contract includes planting of the course, the technical specifications normally state that the contractor's responsibility terminates with the actual planting work. Most contractors do not have the personnel or machinery needed to maintain turf once it has been planted, and this becomes the responsibility of the owner.

Table 2-1. Activities to Include in a Golf Course Construction Contract

Surveying and staking
Staking of centerline
Bringing in of electric power and gas mains*
Development of water source*
Site clearing—trees and brush

Site clearing—bedrock and stone
Disposal of stone and debris
Rough grading—excavation and fill
Building of water-impoundment facilities (dam, emergency spillway, structural spillway)
Construction of surface drainage (catch basins, culverts, ditches, waterways, diversion ditches, dry wells)

Installation of subsurface drain lines (fairways and roughs)
Irrigation pumping-station construction
Installation of irrigation system (greens, tees, and fairways)
Final shaping of green and tee subgrades
Installation of subsurface drain lines (greens and tees)

Root zone soil modification (greens and tees)
Bunker construction
Topsoil redistribution (fairways)
Completion of final grading
Soil pH adjustments

Fertilization
Preplant soil preparation
Planting
Postplanting care
Cart-path construction*

Bridge construction*
Service-road construction*
Shelter, restroom, and water-fountain construction*
Landscaping*
Placing of sand in bunkers*

Final inspection
Contract completion acceptance

*May or may not be included in contract of prime contractor.

Some contractors may be willing to maintain planted areas until the turf is fully established (a difficult definition) or for a fixed period of time after the planting has been completed, e.g., thirty to ninety days. Such a maintenance clause is usually unnecessary and expensive. The contractor must carry the costs of the necessary machinery and personnel and the wait for final payment. The contractor may insist on an "acts of God" clause, escalating the postplanting maintenance cost still further. Meanwhile, the superintendent, assuming the position has been filled, is being paid not to be involved in what he or she knows best. Unless specific situations warrant, it is usually more satisfactory for the contractor's responsibility to terminate on planting, with a small final payment withheld pending the successful establishment or vegetative rooting of the areas planted.

The question of acceptable planting dates may be included in the general specifications. This will be redundant if the overall completion date stipulated is based on planting of the course during a favorable period. In either event, the contractor is responsible for the correction and repair of areas damaged by normal weather occurrences prior to planting.

Finally, the contract includes a payment schedule. Although some contracts stipulate an average or a weighted monthly payment to the contractor during the construction, most clearly define partial payments each month based on the percentage of work completed and materials purchased either for the total job or item by item. Whatever the form of progress payment chosen, it should be clearly stated in the contract.

Construction Inspector/Superintendent

The architect's supervision of construction is periodic in nature. The frequency and duration of visits depend on satisfactory progress, speed of the work under way, and possibly, the contractual commitment with the client. The conscientious architect is present often enough to mark out for the contractor in advance the work to be accomplished and to insure that work is being done in agreement with the plans, specifications, and general design intent. If both the architect and contractor have been carefully selected, periodic supervision should be sufficient to guarantee successful execution of the contract.

Many developers and/or their advisory committee feel, due to busy schedules or concern that the contractor may not always adhere to the construction standards specified, that the insurance of having their own qualified representative on site is worth the additional cost. The decision may be made to hire a construction inspector or owner's representative called a clerk of the works. The role of this person is to insure, in the interest of the client, that the terms of the contract are met. There is no involvement in supervision of the contractor's activities, as this responsibility rests with the architect. Rather, the construction inspector informs the architect and owner of any construction activities that do not meet the contract specifications so that appropriate corrections can be made. The salary of the inspector is paid directly by the owner or developer.

The primary qualifications for this position should be (a) integrity, (b) knowledge of construction engineering practices, especially those related to golf course development, and (c) an ability to interpret the drawings and specifications of the architect. The candidate should have formal training and experience as a golf course superintendent if he or she is to continue in charge of maintenance once the course is finished. Finding someone who possesses all of the above qualifications is usually difficult. Thus, a more realistic approach is to hire a construction inspector and subsequently, though overlapping somewhat in time, a qualified superintendent.

The value of a construction inspector is most evident during the early phases of construction, specifically during staking, clearing, rough grading, and site drainage. The diversity of operations occurring at any given time and the necessity of forming a communications bridge among owner, architect, and contractor demand that the individual be knowledgeable, observant, and articulate.

Selection of a construction inspector/superintendent should take place just before construction is scheduled to begin so that the person can become familiar with the working drawings and specifications prepared by the architect before work actually commences. Depending on background and local knowledge, the construction inspector/superintendent may participate in selection of the contractor and subcontractors.

Whether the construction inspector continues on as golf course superintendent depends primarily on the individual's training and experience. Whereas the presence of a construction inspector during the early phases of golf course construction is optional, the hiring of a qualified golf course superintendent should be considered essential well before the course is finished. It is very important that the individual who will be in charge of the course prior to its opening and for the first year or two thereafter becomes thoroughly familiar with the course during construction. His or her role, as a representative of the owner, is to assure, together with the architect, that the plans and specifications are being followed. By being present during golf course construction, the superintendent becomes familiar with the location of drainage lines and various components of the irrigation system. This information is extremely important for long-term maintenance of the course. The individual also helps to coordinate purchase of the necessary maintenance equipment and operational furniture for the course and can assist in the functional design and construction of the maintenance facility.

Although the ultimate responsibility for design decisions rests with the architect, a competent superintendent may have valuable ideas helpful in producing a great course with minimum long-term problems. The architect may assist the owner or advisory committee in the selection and hiring of a qualified superintendent. The architect and the superintendent must work together closely to achieve the mutually desired end result. It is advisable that the superintendent be employed in time to observe the irrigation installation; the finish grading and construction of the greens, tees, and fairway bunkers; and the preparation and planting of the entire course. This is especially important if a construction inspector is not employed.

Bid Procedure and Selecting a Contractor

A contractor is selected to accomplish the work described in the contract, which is based on the architect's completed plans, detailed working drawings, and specifications. Construction of a golf course may be done either by one general contractor responsible for all of the work required, or, as is often the case, by subcontractors specialized in such activities as clearing, grading, irrigation system installation, green and tee shaping, and other specific tasks. Federal, state, or other publicly financed projects may by law require an overall general contractor selected by competitive bid. Private clubs or privately financed development golf courses may opt for independent subcontractors. Choice in this case too usually depends on results of competitive bidding.

The bidding procedure for a general construction contract is covered by two basic documents, the invitation to bid and the instructions to bidders. If a project is to be bid on publicly, notices are published for a period of time in newspapers and/or invitations are sent out to potentially interested companies or individuals qualified in golf course construction. The invitation describes in general the work involved, its location, and for whom it will be done. It designates the place where bids are to be sent and the time and place of their opening. Details on obtaining the bidding documents are included, as is information on the form of contract. Finally, the invitation usually states the requirements for bonding, bid deposits, contractor qualifications, and other pertinent restrictions or limitations. Information on the invitation to bid should be complete enough to allow the prospective contractor to determine if he or she is interested in the job under the conditions stated and is in fact qualified to bid (Fig. 2-21).

Whereas the invitation to bid is a simple letter or advertisement, the instructions to bidders are an actual part of the bidding document. This document instructs the contractor on how to prepare and submit a bid and describes in greater detail than the invitation to bid the restrictions, limitations, and conditions relating to the bid, the bidder, and the job itself. Included may be information on bidder qualifications, any financial statements required, the type of bonds required, nondiscrimination clauses, the identification of subcontractors along with the right of approval, and the form of contract to be used. Information on the bidding procedure covers corrections, substitutions, and/or addenda to the bidding documents; bid forms; bid security; bid modification or withdrawal; the opening, rejection of bids, and the acceptance of a bid.

High general contractor qualifications, requirements for bonds, and other restrictions may limit the bidding on a project to large contractors. Such contractors may then rely on subcontractors to handle specialized items. Some owners may decide to fill the role of general contractor and award separate contracts for the various aspects of construction. The same bidding procedure and precautions should be followed in this case.

The owner may opt for more quality control by prequalifying the bidders on various aspects of the work. Procedures to follow when preselecting contractors from whom bids are desired include: (1) personal on-site visits to past projects to review contractor performance with the officials involved at the time of construction and to hold discussions with the course superintendent currently maintaining the course; (2) discussions with the architect regarding personal experience in working with the contractor under consideration; and possibly (3) discussions with the manufacturer's representative, especially in the case of an irrigation contractor. It is important to determine whether the contractor fulfilled the total obligation; followed the plans, specifications, and field direction of the architect; was cooperative; and completed the work on schedule.

INVITATION TO BID

Sealed proposals for a Nine Hole Addition to Newberry Golf Course, Bradford, Ohio, will be received at the office of the Mayor as ex-officio Director of Public Service at _____ , Bradford, Ohio 43805, until 2:00 P.M. local time on _____ , and at that time and place publicly opened and read aloud. All bids will be considered valid until sixty (60) days after the opening date, although not accepted or rejected.

The work for which proposals are invited consists of furnishing all the labor, equipment, and specified materials for the construction of a 9-hole golf facility addition and practice chipping green to Newberry Golf Course, complete and ready for play.

Copies of the Contract Bid Documents are available for inspection at the Engineering Division office, City of Bradford, _____ , Bradford, Ohio 43805, and the offices of _____ _____ , Golf Course Consultants, _____ , Piqua, Ohio 45356.

Contract Documents, Specifications, Plans, and Bid Forms may be obtained from the Engineering Division, City of Bradford, _____ , Bradford, Ohio 43805, only upon payment of $50.00 per set, which will not be refunded.

Each bid shall be accompanied by a Proposal Bond, in the form provided in the Contract Documents, with surety or sureties satisfactory to the City, or by certified check in the same amount on a solvent bank, within _____ county. Bond or check shall be in the amount of ten percent (10%) of the amount of the bid and shall be made payable to the City, conditional that if the bid is accepted, a contract will be entered into within 10 days after notice of acceptance.

Separate performance and payment bonds in the amount of one hundred percent (100%) of the amount of the contract, with a surety company satisfactory to the City, conditioned according to law, will be required for the faithful performance of the contract and for payment for labor and materials.

A maintenance bond of one hundred percent (100%) of the contract, with a surety company satisfactory to the City, conditioned according to law, will be required for a period of one year after date of final acceptance.

The work on this contract shall commence within two weeks after signing of the contract and shall be completed not later than _____ , exclusive of placing the sand in the bunkers, which shall be completed no later than _____ .

The work under this contract will be inspected by the Golf Course Consultant and his representative and by the designated agent of the City, for the purpose of concluding that the work performed is satisfactory or unsatisfactory.

The City reserves the right to reject any and all bids from any bidder which, in the opinion of the City, lacks adequate experience in golf course construction to assure proper performance under the terms of the proposed contract.

This project is Federally assisted. Contracts to be awarded under this invitation for bids will be subject to affirmative action for Equal Employment Opportunity.

A pre-bidding site review for all prospective bidders with the Golf Course Consultant and the City will be at 9:00 A.M. starting at Number 10 tee.

Figure 2-21. Typical notice to bidders. (Courtesy of Kidwell and Hurdzan, American Society of Golf Course Architects.)

Were any long-term maintenance problems the result of the contractor's workmanship? Other items may be of equal importance when prequalifying contractors. Does the prospective contractor have (a) sufficient capital to complete the work, (b) adequate machinery, or access thereto, to complete the work on schedule, and (c) adequate and experienced personnel, especially field foreman? And finally, are the contractor's equipment operators experienced in the artistic work involved in building a golf course?

Although it is possible to evaluate contractors once the bids have been received, it is often preferable to do so prior to soliciting bids. This may eliminate irresponsible or otherwise unqualified bidders and may be particularly advisable if the lowest price must be accepted. The owner should bear in mind that the lowest price does not necessarily mean the best job. Unless the contractors are equally qualified and experienced; bid prices are comparable; and in the case of irrigation the product quality, service standards, and design performance are equal, the owner should carefully consider all other related information about the bidding contractors prior to awarding the contract to the lowest competent bidder.

An additional aid in the bidding procedure, whether for a general contractor or for a particular phase of the construction, is to hold a prebid meeting on the construction site. Such a meeting should be held after the prospective bidders have obtained the plans and specifications and had enough time to examine them. The meeting provides an opportunity for the architect to answer questions that may have arisen. In addition, the prospective bidders have an opportunity to familiarize themselves more thoroughly with the project and the personnel involved so that responsible bids can be prepared.

A few golf course architects also act as contractors for all or certain parts of the golf course construction. This need not be a conflict of interest, provided the owner is aware of this point before selecting the architect. From the outset, the architect should indicate an interest in and perhaps reserve for a personal representative certain aspects of the construction, such as the artistic work in shaping the greens, tees, and fairway bunkers. If the architect has a financial interest, either directly or indirectly, with a contractor who will or may bid on the work, this must be indicated. In some situations, the contractor and the architect should not be the same person. This avoids potential problems, since the architect has the obligation to represent the client while the contractor is an independent operative.

Construction Planning

In any climatic region there are certain ideal months in terms of temperature and moisture conditions for the planting of turfgrass. Thus, it is very important for the architect to work closely with the owner in scheduling the construction completion date to coincide with this optimum planting period and thereby assure the best possible conditions for successful turfgrass establishment.

Inability to plant the golf course at the proper time owing to poor scheduling and/or construction delays can lead to numerous problems. For example, extensive failures in grass stands may require costly sodding or reseeding as well as loss of play and revenues for all or part of the first golfing season. Bare areas, especially on slopes subject to severe soil loss due to wind and water erosion, may require regrading to establish the original contours. The scheduled opening date may have to be postponed for periods up to six months, which could have a serious impact on the financial structure of the organization.

With these factors well in mind, the architect should prepare an overall construction flowchart for all phases of the golf course construction. Often this is accomplished by working backward in time from the ideal planting dates. Sufficient time should be allowed in the flowchart not only for the work involved under normal circumstances but also for delays caused by bad weather (rain days) and by other variables appropriate for climate and conditions in the region. The result will be a practical date for the commencement of work. The ideal dates for soliciting bids and awarding the contracts thus can be established.

The best method of portraying this time schedule is the use of a construction flow diagram based on the *critical path method*. It provides a logical system for integrating all construction activities into a

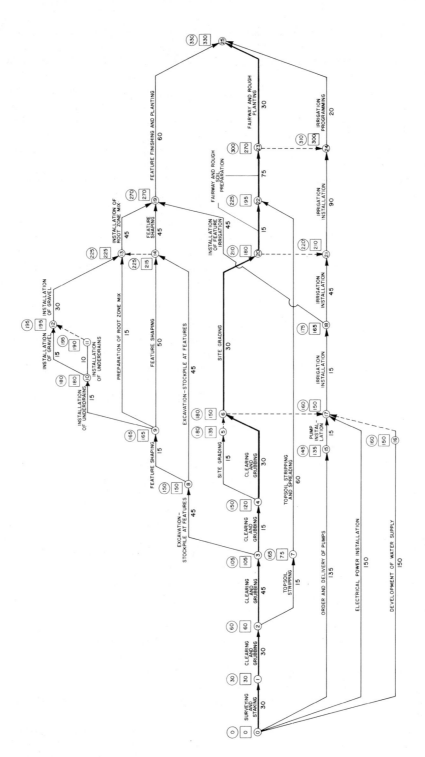

Figure 2-22. Representative critical path network for golf course construction. (Drawing courtesy of Rees Jones, American Society of Golf Course Architects.)

relatively simplified flow plan. The method involves a major critical path, designated by a wide solid line, and a series of shorter concurrent paths, designated by narrow solid lines which eventually tie into the main critical path (Fig. 2-22). These lines are connected by a series of circles which indicate that a specific construction task has either been initiated or completed. A number within the circle identifies each specific task or event with the numerical sequence reading from left to right. The various construction activities are plotted horizontally against a left-to-right time grid. The critical path designates the longest series of uninterrupted construction activities. The length of this path represents the overall duration of the golf course construction. The concurrent paths running parallel and above or below the critical path represent supporting construction activities which originate from and terminate back into the critical path at the proper times. A broken line, which indicates that no work is required, is inserted appropriately between specific work activity arrows. The slack activity arrows occur on concurrent critical paths.

The critical path construction plan may or may not be part of the contract documents. However, it is extremely useful for the architect to prepare such a plan prior to the contract being awarded, as it allows prospective bidders to evaluate any completion dates stipulated in the contract documents. It is one further step in clarifying the conditions of work.

Once the contract is executed, the critical path diagram will assist the contractor in organizing resources properly for the efficient and successful fulfillment of the contract obligations. Manpower allocation, materials acquisition, and equipment procurement can all be effected more efficiently with the aid of the construction flow plan. Coordination between the general contractor and the subcontractor(s) is facilitated as well. Finally, the critical path diagram will serve as a basis for progress communications among owner, architect, and contractor. A more simplified version of the construction flow plan that may be used in communications with the client is shown in Figure 2-23.

Resource Planning. Preconstruction planning should involve an assessment of the activities and resources that must be arranged prior to initiating actual construction. Resource planning involves three primary areas: manpower, materials, and equipment. The contractor should carefully examine the architect's plans and specifications to determine the exact activities to be performed and assess the resources required to accomplish these tasks.

The prime contractor must decide which activities will be accomplished within the organization and which activities are to be subcontracted. Similarly, for materials acquisition, it must be decided what materials, if any, are to be purchased by the prime contractor and which must be furnished by the subcontractors involved. Any of the surveying-staking, clearing, rough grading, irrigation system installation, drainage system development, and final planting phases may be accomplished under separate subcontracts. The prime contractor must usually specify the materials, equipment, construction permits, and inspections to be secured by a subcontractor. This process, or resource planning, aids the contractor in predetermining activities and resources that are essential for efficient implementation of each construction operation contributing to the overall project.

Contractors may draw up a resource flow plan which is basically similar to the construction flow plan previously discussed. The resource flow plan is closely interdeveloped with the construction flow plan. It should indicate what materials and equipment are to be available on specified workdays on the critical path. Due consideration must be given to the lead times required for ordering, manufacture, and delivery of specific items. The contractor may also prepare a *construction activity plan* as shown in Table 2-2. Essentially, this table lists (1) all distinct construction activities in the sequence to be performed, (2) the number of workdays required to complete each activity, (3) activities on the critical path and the specific number of days required for their performance within the path, and (4) the cumulative number of workdays accrued on the critical path of construction (Fig. 2-22).

The construction activity plan also may be used to designate the time when various material and equipment resources must be available on the construction site. These reference points aid the contractor in assessing specific lead time required to secure the needed materials. Preparation and mailing of

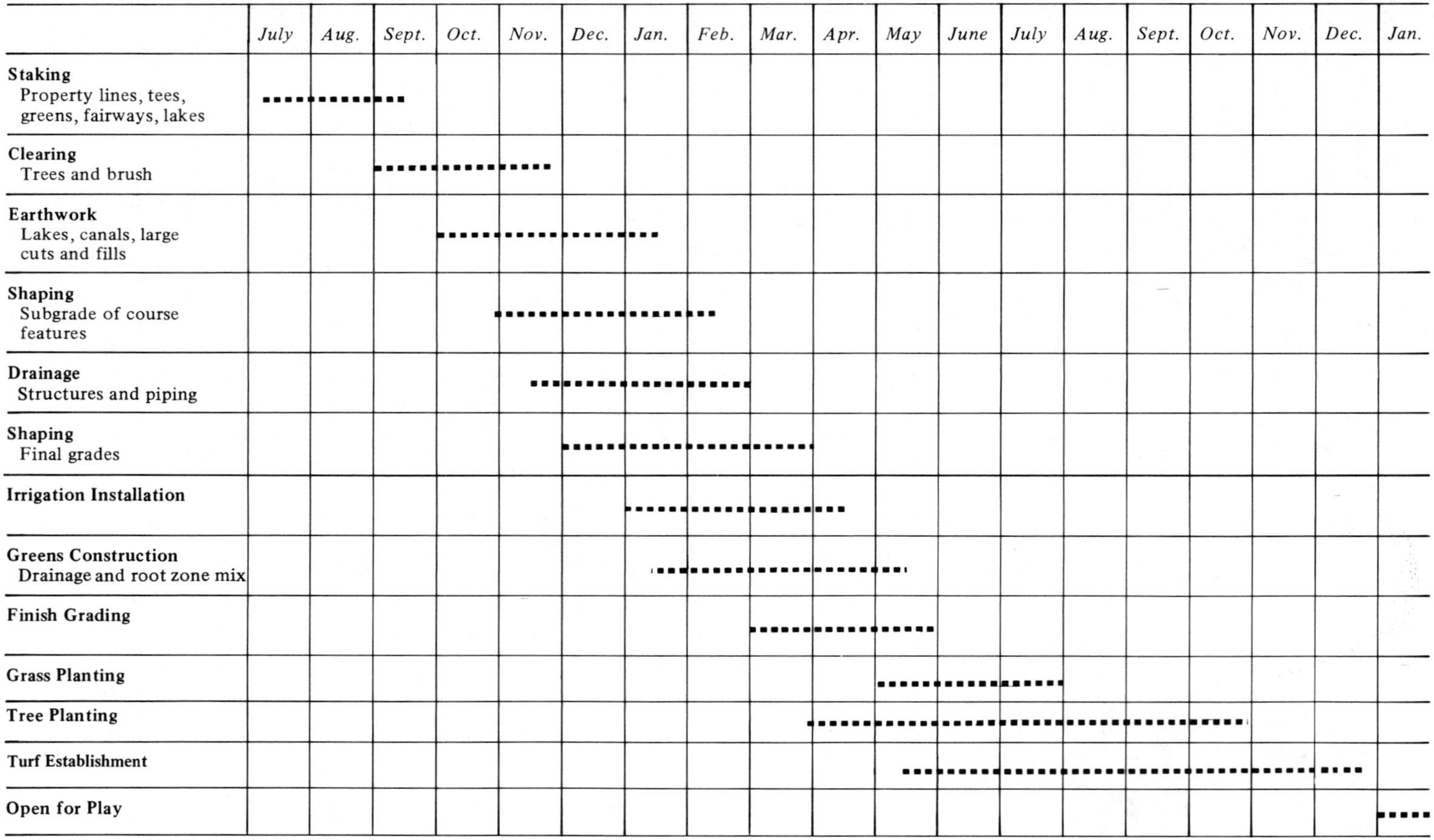

Figure 2-23. Simplified construction plan for a warm climatic region where construction activities can proceed year-round except for rain days. (Courtesy of T. Fazio, American Society of Golf Course Architects.)

	July	Aug.	Sept.	Oct.	Nov.	Dec.	Jan.	Feb.	Mar.	Apr.	May	June	July	Aug.	Sept.	Oct.	Nov.	Dec.	Jan.
Staking Property lines, tees, greens, fairways, lakes	■	■	■																
Clearing Trees and brush			■	■	■														
Earthwork Lakes, canals, large cuts and fills			■	■	■	■	■												
Shaping Subgrade of course features					■	■	■	■											
Drainage Structures and piping					■	■	■	■	■										
Shaping Final grades						■	■	■	■										
Irrigation Installation							■	■	■	■									
Greens Construction Drainage and root zone mix							■	■	■	■	■								
Finish Grading									■	■	■								
Grass Planting											■	■	■						
Tree Planting										■	■	■	■	■	■	■			
Turf Establishment											■	■	■	■	■	■	■	■	
Open for Play																			■

Table 2-2. Activity Plan for Construction of a Golf Course

Work Activity Number	Activity	Total Workdays	Critical Path* Workdays	
			No.	Cum.
0 - 1	Surveying and staking	30	30	30
0 - 15	Order and delivery of pumps	135		
0 - 16	Development of water supply	150		
0 - 17	Installation of electrical power system	150		
1 - 2	Clearing and grubbing	30	30	60
2 - 3	Clearing and grubbing	45	45	105
2 - 7	Topsoil stripping and stockpiling	15		
3 - 4	Clearing and grubbing	15		
3 - 8	Excavation—stockpiling at features	45	45	150
4 - 5	Site grading	15		
4 - 6	Clearing and grubbing	30		
6 - 20	Site grading	30		
7 - 22	Topsoil stripping and spreading	60		
8 - 9	Feature shaping	15	15	165
8 - 14	Excavation—stockpiling at features	45		
9 - 10	Installation of subsurface drainage system	15	15	180
9 - 13	Preparation of root zone soil mix	15		
9 - 14	Feature shaping	50		
10 - 11	Installation of subsurface drainage system	10		
10 - 12	Installation of gravel	15	15	195
12 - 13	Installation of gravel	30	30	225
13 - 19	Installation of root zone soil mix	45	45	270
14 - 19	Feature shaping	45		
15 - 17	Pump installation	15		
17 - 18	Installation of irrigation system	15		
18 - 19	Installation of feature irrigation system	45		
18 - 21	Installation of irrigation system	45		
19 - 25	Feature finishing and planting	60	60	330
20 - 22	Final fairway and rough soil preparation	15		
21 - 24	Installation of irrigation system	90		
22 - 23	Final fairway and rough soil preparation	75		
23 - 25	Fairway and rough planting	30		
24 - 25	Irrigation programming	20		

* Derived from critical path network shown in Figure 2-22.

requests for quotations, issuance of purchase orders, actual delivery time, and a reasonable contingency period all must be factored into this basic timetable. Much valuable time may be lost if materials or equipment vital to current activities on the critical path are not delivered on time. In the event of delays in material delivery, the activity plan provides a base from which contingency or alternate work schedules may be developed. A good contractor always plans for emergencies and is able to reschedule work to avoid delays in progress.

Surveying and Staking

The first actual step in the construction of a golf course is the staking of centerlines for each hole. By this time the architect is very familiar with the site and will have prepared a staking plan which indicates the alignment of each hole. Whereas some architects may stake the course themselves, this work is usually done in conjunction with a competent, registered surveyor employed by the owner.

Staking of the centerline for each hole begins at the rear of the championship tee, follows the center of the fairway (along the intended line of play), and terminates at the center of the green. Stakes are usually placed at intervals of 100 feet (30 meters) along the centerline, though greater intervals may be satisfactory in open areas. It is customary as well to stake the rear of any offset tees and to place a stake at each turning point or dogleg on par-4 and par-5 holes. Each stake should be 3 to 4 feet (0.9 to 1.2 meters) long and sturdy enough to remain in place throughout construction. Key stakes at tee, dogleg, and green locations should be coded and clearly labeled. Prior to but no later than concurrently with staking of the centerlines, the surveyor should clearly define the boundary of the entire golf course.

Once the centerlines have been staked in accordance with the plan, the architect, together with the owner and perhaps the contractor, examines the alignment of each hole. Minor adjustments are frequently necessary due to the dictates of good design principles and inaccuracies in the topographic maps. Any such changes agreed on between the architect and the owner are then plotted and the plans modified accordingly. Having the course boundary clearly marked prior to any centerline adjustments is essential.

Since many architects prepare their grading and earthwork plans using existing grades and elevations as datum points, it is necessary for the surveyor to establish a permanent bench mark on the site. All subsequent elevations used in surveying the greens, tees, bunkers, fairways, and lakes are referenced from this bench mark (Fig. 2-24). Additional reference hub stakes are often driven along the hole centerlines and these are used in the subsequent surveying and work measurements on individual holes. Such hub stakes should be semipermanent, as they will remain in place throughout construction.

Site Clearing

The potential natural beauty of a golf course can be irreparably damaged during clearing operations if the contractor does not heed carefully the plans and specifications and if the architect does not maintain close surveillance of the clearing by means of frequent on-site inspections. It is in the best

Figure 2-24. Surveying setup for checking elevations.

interests of everyone to preserve from damage or cutting those trees which will enhance the beauty of the golf course and/or will contribute strategically to its playing value.

At the start of clearing operations, the architect and the owner agree on an optimum general layout for the golf course. In arriving at this final plan, careful consideration is given to unique trees and/or vegetation areas of special interest. During stake-out of the course, the centerlines will be further refined as much as possible to accommodate topographic and vegetative details not apparent during the earlier stages of design. Equipment needed for clearing includes bulldozers, log rakes, root rakes, chain saws, and trucks. To insure that only those trees designated for removal are cut, the clearing operation should proceed in phases.

Phase I. Phase I clearing should encompass all trees along the staked centerline of each hole. Usually the contractor is given a set of dimensions in the plans and specifications indicating the width of the phase I clearing on each side of the centerline. Starting from the back of the tee, typical dimensions may be 20 feet (6 meters) on each side of the centerline for the first 300 feet (91 meters), the tee area, and 40 feet (12 meters) on each side from there to the center of the green. All vegetation within these dimensions is cut and piled in the center of the cleared area (Fig. 2-25). In most cases the contractor is responsible for marking the limits of the phase I clearing, although the architect may elect to do this in certain areas.

Phase II. After phase I clearing has been completed, and before commencement of phase II, the architect normally walks the holes. For the first time the planned holes are open from tee to green and the architect is better able to visualize how each will appear and to determine how each is likely to play when finished. As the 80-foot (24.4-meter) clearing represents slightly less than half of the ultimate fairway width, the architect can proceed to mark the limits of phase II clearing by marking equal distances on each side of the centerline or "weighting" the clearing more to one side than to the other, taking advantage of specific trees or topographic features.

The limits of phase II clearing should be marked personally by the architect so that he or she can fully express the envisioned aesthetic and strategic plan. The marking itself is usually done with brightly colored plastic ribbons tied securely around the trunks of trees forming the limits of the clearing. Tee and fairway areas are widened, and the areas for offset tees and for green surrounds marked. Finally, in phase II the architect marks for clearing any areas for proposed lakes or borrow pit excavation.

The design intent of phase II clearing is to widen each hole enough so that play characteristics are readily visualized. Additionally, the width should be great enough to facilitate the construction of greens, tees, and hazards. Aesthetically, clearing limits should be irregular or undulating lines of vegetation which preserve or enhance the setting and strategic value of a particular tree or group of trees.

Phase III. Most competent architects are sensitive to the beauty and importance of trees and the time necessary to grow a tree. As a result, phase II clearing on certain holes may be less than ideal for playing conditions. The consequence may be a limited amount of phase III clearing specifically marked by the architect in certain areas. This work is done almost concurrently with phase II. The architect usually tries to coordinate any such additional clearing with the contractor to avoid unnecessary delays. As a general rule, it is more advantageous in the long run for the architect to err on the conservative side in the marking of phase II limits than to remove too many trees.

Water Features. Lake and dam sites should be cleared of all vegetation below the water suface. This is especially important at sites proposed for earthen dams and within small lakes. In larger lakes the trees may be felled and tied down in groups with cables to insure that they will not float. These tree remains on lake bottoms serve as an ideal habitat and protection for fishes and associated aquatic life.

Clearing Roughs. The amount of work involved in clearing roughs varies from site to site. Trees that are to remain in the primary rough are marked for preservation by the architect during phase II-phase III operations. The wooded areas of the secondary rough usually commence at the limits of the phase II-phase III clearing. Some sites with mature forests may require little or no additional clearing work in the wooded areas between holes. Selective clearing may be required on sites with tangled undergrowth

Figure 2-25. Wooded site being cleared (*top*) and burned (*bottom*) for golf course development.

and immature second-growth woodland to facilitate finding of slightly miss-hit balls. Selective clearing of this sort normally is limited to a width of 20 to 30 feet (6 to 9 meters) on each side of the fairway. All ground-cover vegetation, brush, vines, deadwood, and smaller trees are removed to accommodate the use of large-capacity riding rotary or flail mowers. Although selective clearing of secondary rough areas is sometimes included in the general site-clearing operations, it may also be done during the growing-in period by maintenance personnel as part of course preparation for opening.

Stump and Root Removal. The final step in site clearing involves the removal of stumps, roots, and other objectionable organic material from cleared areas. The specifications usually define the limits of this grubbing operation in terms of the size of the stumps and roots to be removed and the soil depth to which the contractor must remove them. This work is essential to prevent irregular settling caused by the decay of stumps and roots. The overall intent is to leave the cleared areas free of organic debris which would interfere with subsequent construction operations, vegetative or seedbed preparation, turf establishment, and subsequent turfgrass cultural practices.

Stumps and roots are usually removed by means of bulldozers with toothed blades. Stumps may be pulled up if small or dug out with a bulldozer. A wood-chipping stump remover (Fig. 2-26) can be used to shave the stumps off below the soil surface if in the rough but not in the fairway. Stump holes are then smoothed over with a bulldozer to restore the cleared area to a smooth natural grade free of any unnatural water-holding depressions.

Because of the large amount of soil attached to roots and stumps, it is usually difficult to burn them completely even where burning is permitted. It is common, therefore, to bury this type of debris in small pits excavated in nonplay areas scattered throughout the site.

Although the cutting and removal or burning of trees appear to be the major aspect of clearing work, the removal of stumps and roots from the golf course play areas is no less an important part of the operation.

Disposition of Wood Debris. Owing to the increasing demand for firewood, it is now possible to arrange for harvesting of timber on a wooded site. This is desirable from a conservation point of view and it further avoids the costly and sometimes complicated removal of the cleared material. If sale of the timber is planned, the contract should indicate whether the income derived from such sale is the owner's or whether it simply offsets the contractor's cost of clearing the site. Also, it should be clear whether the responsibility and cost for removal of stumps and other debris is included in the harvesting contract.

In the past, when timber harvesting was not practical, burning was the most common means for disposal of trees, stumps, and other wood debris. Today, however, laws relating to open burning have become very strict in many areas. Thus, it is important for the developer to become completely familiar with local requirements before estimating costs and letting contracts. Some state or local laws permit burning as the land is cleared, but under specified conditions. Methods of burning which minimize atmospheric pollution are available. One technique is use of a pit constructed with a forced draft which insures rapid, complete combustion of wood. Whatever the method of burning, extreme care should be exercised by the contractor in selecting burning sites so that valuable trees and desirable native plants are adequately protected from damage by fire and heat drafts.

Figure 2-26. Powered stump removal chipper in operation. (Photo courtesy of Vermeer Manufacturing Company, Pella, Ia.)

The alternative approaches to disposal are to remove all debris from the site or to bury it on site. Removal of material for disposal in landfill areas may be very expensive and should be avoided whenever possible. The cost of excavating holes and burying the debris on site is also high when compared with the cost of burning. Additional land areas may be required for burial, as this must not be done within the golf course playing areas (greens, tees, fairways, and hazards) to avoid trenching problems for drainage and irrigation and the subsequent development of objectionable depressions due to subsidence.

Another less practiced option is to designate a specific area for the dumping of wood, which then is available to the public for collection and use as firewood. This practice, however, may be prohibited by local ordinances for purposes of insect control, and in the end what is left will still have to be disposed of by conventional methods.

Rough Grading

The rough grading phase encompasses all major excavation and fill work. It includes (1) placement of fill at such features as green, tee, and bunker sites, (2) rough shaping of the feature subgrades, (3) construction of dams, (4) excavation of lakes and ponds, (5) recontouring, filling, and grading of fairway and rough areas, (6) rock excavation, (7) construction or realignment of waterways, (8) construction of diversion ditches and other drainage ways to improve surface runoff, and (9) stripping, stockpiling, and respreading of topsoil over disturbed areas.

Where features such as greens, tees, and bunkers are to be constructed on level land, the architect specifies the amount of fill material required for each feature. Existing topsoil is stripped from each site requiring fill and stockpiled nearby for subsequent respreading. Fill material is then hauled in trucks or pans, or it may be pushed into place by bulldozers from adjacent borrow pit areas. When features are to be built on slopes or mounds or in other areas where sufficient material is available on site to carve out the feature, no additional fill material will be required.

The shaping of feature subgrades is done in one of two ways. Some architects indicate on the plans and feature details the finish subgrade contours along with spot elevations on mounds. These elevations are tied to a bench mark elevation on the site. Using these elevations, the contractor can rough grade and shape the subgrade. Some architects choose not to work with fixed grades, believing the resulting features to be too mechanical. In this case, a specialized subcontractor may be used to shape the features according to sketches and on-site supervision by the architect.

Construction of dams, ponds, lakes, or canals is often a major part of the rough grading work (see chapter 12). Water areas are often an integral part of the design strategy and frequently are used as a reservoir source for the irrigation system. Sites for earthen dams should be carefully selected and construction methods closely coordinated with the local Soil Conservation Service representative. Lake or pond size and location will depend on the overall design strategy as well as on the amount of fill required elsewhere on the site for the construction of dams and golf course features. Lakes also may be used to eliminate marshy or low bog areas and as a catchment for drainage systems, where needed. The amount of topsoil stripped from lake sites generally exceeds that required to cover the banks and berms and the excess can be used where existing topsoil is thin. Lake and pond excavation may be handled with large earthmovers or pans, loaders and trucks, and in very wet areas with draglines. The amount of material to be excavated is usually calculated to balance fill requirements.

On golf course sites with hilly terrain, a certain amount of reshaping is needed to provide contours suitable for play. Cutting down hills to prevent blind shots, covering or filling ditches that cross fairways, and cutting or filling to improve side slopes are typical fairway grading operations. Often this work is done with large bulldozers pushing and backblading (Fig. 2-27). Sometimes excess material is hauled to areas requiring fill by means of trucks or pans. It is important that existing topsoil be stripped and stockpiled prior to any fairway grading and that it be respread prior to finish grading.

Figure 2-27. Rough grading of a golf course.

Certain areas of a course may need fill to make them suitable for both play and general maintenance. Low, poorly drained areas can often be improved by adding a layer of stable fill material. If the existing topsoil is unsuitable or its removal is impractical, the fill material can be placed directly over it and the existing grade and this material then covered with topsoil brought in from elsewhere on the site. Old wells or cisterns should be filled with soil, not with bricks, stones, or wood debris that will settle and leave depressions. Allowance should be made for settlement of the soil before such well areas are covered with topsoil. Existing excavations or gravel pits may require fill if they are not to be left as a design feature. In some cases, such areas may be partially filled and smoothed over and topsoil added for ease of maintenance.

It is not uncommon to encounter rock during rough grading operations. Loose rocks and large stones should be removed when possible, as they may interfere with irrigation system installation. If the extent of the rocks or another factor makes their removal impractical, the area can be covered with a layer of topsoil. Thus, only the rocks uncovered during installation of the irrigation system need to be removed.

The existence of shallow topsoil over bedrock or of large rock outcroppings may cause other problems in construction and turf maintenance. Soil Conservation Service soil maps or other sources of information may enable the architect to make an initial identification of potential problem sites on the plans. In some cases, the architect may choose to utilize a unique outcropping as an integral part of the design. Otherwise, when the presence of rock of this nature is suspected, it may be advisable to conduct deep core samplings and drillings to identify problem areas so they can be anticipated in the contractor's bids. Although the information obtained is helpful in determining areas that may require blasting, the drilling operations are costly and time consuming and the information is not always complete. The normal practice, therefore, is to insert a "rock clause" in the specifications, which stipulates an extra amount to be paid. Rock excavation by blasting requires drilling and the use of explosives to break up the rock so it can be removed mechanically.

Stones and blasted rock should be removed to nonplay areas of the course. They may be buried in pits, piled in an out-of-the-way place not visible to players, used in stream bank stabilization, or hauled off site and sold to landscape contractors. Although not a very desirable solution, the extent of rock to be removed may necessitate that it be used for fill over culverts or in other low areas. This should only be done if sufficient soil material is mixed in with the rocks to prevent settling and if the area is then covered with a thick layer of subsoil followed by a layer of topsoil. Finally, the architect may elect to use large stones in certain nonplay areas for their landscape effect.

Rough grading and site drainage operations overlap somewhat during the construction process. Culvert pipes may have to be installed in a ditch or streambed crossing a fairway before the area is filled. Construction of diversion ditches to channel runoff to a particular area is another instance, as it may involve both grading work and installation of drainage structures. The architect may wish to preserve an existing waterway while at the same time changing its alignment to enhance the strategy of play. This work is often done during rough grading, as it may require the use of the bulldozers, backhoes, or front-end loaders commonly used in rough grading operations.

Finally, the plans may call for construction of surface swales in fairway or rough areas to improve existing runoff patterns, to solve new drainage problems that result from rough grading and fairway contouring, or to function as a water-harvesting strategy.

The rough grading phase of construction is normally finished when topsoil has been spread over all the work areas. General site drainage may be accomplished concurrently with the rough grading, so the spreading of topsoil in certain areas may have to await completion of this work. The green and tee surrounds are usually not covered with topsoil until after installation of the irrigation system and placement of the root zone mix.

Throughout the various stages of rough grading the architect should make frequent site visits to inspect progress. The number of visits will vary from site to site depending on the amount of rough

Figure 2-28. Protective rock wall around a tree in an area where substantial soil fill was required.

grading involved and the speed at which the contractor works. Certain aspects of the rough grading, such as molding and contouring of the feature subgrades, require closer supervision by the architect than does, for example, the excavation of a large lake. Close communication among the architect, the owner's construction inspector/superintendent, and the contractor is essential to assure that the job runs smoothly and according to the plans.

During inspection visits the architect should also observe if parts of the site outside the actual work areas are being protected or preserved. Open areas not requiring rough grading should be left undisturbed so that existing vegetation minimizes soil erosion prior to plant-bed preparation. The contract may specify construction of tree wells or protective retaining walls where fill around the base of trees might prove lethal (Fig. 2-28). Haul routes should be carefully located to avoid undesirable compaction in key areas and to protect the remaining vegetation. Servicing and repair of the heavy grading equipment should take place outside areas to be grassed, since oil and grease spills are detrimental to establishment and growth of turfgrass.

If the grading work is being done to specified elevations shown on the grading plan, the architect and/or the owner's construction inspector/superintendent usually requests resurveying of the site. Elevations of the final rough grades should be checked against the centerline grade stakes to assure correctness of the final subgrade. Spot elevation checks should be made elsewhere as necessary. Detailed contour grade checks are often made on the greens, tees, bunkers, drainage channels, and waterways.

Although the grades may check out accurately according to the plan, the owner should be prepared to accept and the contractor to implement modifications of the finish subgrades, as suggested by the architect. The imprecise nature of golf course architecture makes it very difficult to design and lay out a course perfectly in two dimensions on a plan. Consequently, a degree of artistic license must be granted the architect to modify grading during the course of the work. A final check of the rough grade should assure that all areas provide good conditions both for play and for establishment and maintenance of turfgrass. All areas should be left with slopes conducive to positive surface water runoff.

Subsequent phases in golf course construction, such as (1) subsurface drainage system development, (2) installation of the irrigation system, (3) construction of putting greens, tees, and bunkers, (4) final grading and preplant soil preparation, (5) planting, (6) postplanting care, and (7) landscaping are discussed in the following chapters.

REBUILDING

Many American golf courses constructed prior to 1935 have been or will be rebuilt to varying degrees. Reasons for rebuilding include:

1. *Desire to lengthen the golf course.* Modern golfers are stronger, play more, and use better equipment and improved golfing techniques that increase the hitting distance.

2. *Desire to improve the strategy of play on the course.* Course strategy may be enhanced by reshaping greens; lengthening holes; planting trees and ornamental shrubs strategically; and improving bunker placement, number, and shape. The desire to increase strategic difficulty occurs most often in clubs that wish to host major national tournaments and thus must have course designs that challenge the world's best golfers.

3. *Desire to provide flexibility to attract all classes of golfers.* This is usually done by adding tees, which can both lengthen and shorten the course depending on placement.

4. *Desire to speed or facilitate play.* Redesign can enhance the speed of play and increase revenues, which are especially important considerations in the case of public fee courses. Approaches may include elimination of unnecessary bunkers and rough, thinning of wooded areas to aid golfers in finding balls, elimination of blind shots, and rearrangement of par-3 holes if they fall in a bad sequence, e.g., holes one, two, ten, and eleven.

5. *Desire to correct unsafe playing conditions.* Examples include blind shots, adjacent holes located too close together, and tees facing the line of play of an adjacent hole. Redesign will help not only to achieve safer playing conditions but to provide a more enjoyable atmosphere.

6. *Desire to correct technical flaws in the original design or construction.* Design flaws may include penal-type hazards, such as poorly placed bunkers, that catch only high-handicap golfers and blind hazards or holes that make a course unfair for the average golfer. Typical construction flaws are greens constructed on clay soil that becomes severely compacted and prone to turf loss during stress periods, drainage of all surface water to the front of a green, and depressions on a green. Redesign that includes improvements in the root zone soil mix and in surface and subsurface drainage can be beneficial to both the playing condition of the course and the ease of turfgrass maintenance. Also, properly constructed greens that have good internal drainage are playable for a longer portion of the year than are poorly drained greens, which maximizes use of the facility.

7. *Need to minimize traffic effects from increasing numbers of golfers.* This usually is achieved by construction of greens and tees composed of sandy root zone mixes which minimize soil compaction. Enlargement and/or reshaping of greens and tees makes more area available for cup placement and tee marker movement, resulting in reduced traffic on any one area. Redirection of traffic reduces turfgrass wear around tees and greens (Fig. 2-29). Bunkers may need to be eliminated or reshaped. Also, walk-off areas from greens to tees may need to be widened in order to disperse traffic rather than encourage single-file movement.

8. *Need to redesign and reroute course after land has been lost to public domain or real estate development.* The acquisition of certain portions of golf courses by governmental agencies for road construction and similar public-interest activities is not uncommon. Redesign and rerouting may be required when this occurs.

9. *Need to increase the number of holes.* Such an expansion may be required to accommodate a growing membership or to generate added revenue through increased play.

Rebuilding Versus Moving

The extent of rebuilding may vary from a single green or hole to the entire golf course. In the latter situation, club officials should seriously evaluate the positive and negative aspects of rebuilding versus

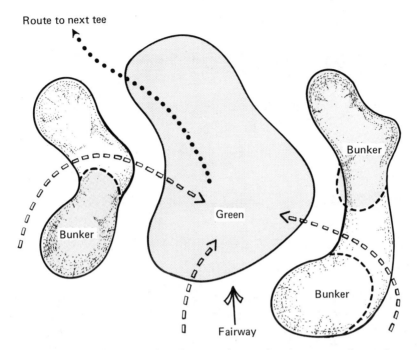

Figure 2-29. Proposed redesign of bunkers to reduce turfgrass wear around a putting green.

moving to a new location. It may be advisable to retain the services of a golf course architect to provide input about the design aspects involved in the decision. Factors to consider in evaluating the existing versus potential sites for a course are (1) land value versus acquisition costs, (2) taxation, (3) expansion trends in the city, (4) comparative access, (5) location of the membership relative to the course location, (6) comparative quality of rebuilt versus new course, (7) actual cost of rebuilding versus cost of constructing new course, (8) availability of adjacent property for future expansion, and (9) current condition and projected repair costs for other golf course facilities, such as the clubhouse, golf pro shop, parking lot, maintenance facilities, and utilities.

Comparative economics and long-term future success may dictate moving to a new site rather than rebuilding. In this case, construction on the new site can be accomplished while play and operations at the existing golf course continue without disruption. In rebuilding projects, potentially serious disruptions in play may result in numerous hidden costs, such as income reductions at the golf pro shop, restaurant, and other service facilities, and possible loss of members.

Redesign

There is no room for amateurism in golf course redesign. Redesign is a serious, challenging task that should be under the direction of a competent golf course architect. In many cases, redesign is more difficult than design of a new course. The architect must study and capture the course theme and character, and then must artistically blend the new with the old so that there is a single theme throughout the completed redesign. This goal must sometimes be compromised when only a partial redesign is involved.

The golf course architect should ask the appropriate club committee, the golf professional, and the golf course superintendent their views on needed improvements. Membership inputs are usually

Figure 2-30. New green being constructed while play continues on a temporary green in foreground.

conveyed through the club officials and/or the green committee. The club golf professional possesses an expertise which, when combined with detailed firsthand knowledge of the course, can lead to important suggestions for the architect. The golf course superintendent similarly can make suggestions concerning the agronomic and ornamental aspects of the course that will help insure long-term economical maintenance of a quality golf course. After assimilating these diverse inputs, the golf architect then prepares the redesign specifications. It is important that the architect draw up a plan for satisfactory staging of the redesign work.

Special Considerations in Redesign. During redesign, thought should be given to future renovation or expansion plans for the clubhouse, parking lot, swimming pool, tennis courts, pro shop, and/or golf course maintenance facility. Such future improvements frequently require additional land area. Thus, it is important that all related improvements be considered when the master plan for the redesign of a golf course is being prepared so that they can be carried out in future years with the least amount of disruption.

Existing facilities on the golf course are an important consideration when redesign is contemplated. The locations of existing water lines, power lines, easements, open drainage ditches, and sewer lines are of special concern. Costs for relocating such utilities can be very high, and consideration thus should be given to designs that avoid or minimize this expense.

The movement of heavy construction equipment across the golf course can cause loss of turf, severe soil compaction, rutting of wet soils, and damage to underground drainage lines and irrigation pipe. Accordingly, contingency funds need to be budgeted for correcting damage once the rebuilding project is completed.

Rebuilding Procedures

Some interference with play can be anticipated during rebuilding unless the golf course has considerable surplus land available. However, interference can be minimized by proper planning. One approach frequently used is rebuilding of only nine holes at a time, keeping the second nine open for play. If only one or two golf holes are being redesigned, positioning of the new green behind or to one side of the existing green enables construction to proceed while play continues on the old green (Fig. 2-30). However, such a convenience should not be the determining factor in placement of a new green. An alternate approach is construction of a temporary green well in advance of rebuilding in order to keep the hole open for play during the rebuilding phase on the original site. These techniques have an additional benefit in that there is less pressure to complete the project hurriedly and more time for the project to be completed correctly. It is important that time be allocated for the turf to mature before play is allowed to resume. Similar approaches can be used in rebuilding of tees.

Consideration should be given to use of existing materials in the rebuilding operation, where appropriate and economical. For example, stockpiling quality topsoil from existing turf areas before grading operations are initiated is very important. This topsoil can subsequently be redistributed over exposed subsoil sites to provide more favorable turfgrass growing conditions. Topsoil from old greens which contains a high silt or clay content should not be reused on newly constructed greens unless it is properly mixed on the basis of detailed laboratory tests. Quality sod from abandoned greens may be used on tees and slopes to control potentially serious soil erosion.

Salvaging buried irrigation pipe and drainage lines is usually not economical or practical. However, pop-up irrigation heads, swing joints, valves, couplers, switches, pumps, and controllers may be salvaged and reused if they are of adequate capacity and in good operating condition.

In sodding rebuilt greens, the use of sod grown expressly for this purpose is advisable. Sod from old greens should not be transplanted onto newly constructed greens if the (a) turfgrass composition is undesirable, (b) sod is excessively thatched, or (c) soil on the old green is different from that on the new green. Sod containing fine-textured clay from old greens can negate the beneficial effects of rapid water movement through the underlying sandy root zone if transplanted onto new greens. Similarly, sod high in annual bluegrass or composed of numerous grass strains should be avoided. If time is not a critical factor, seeding of new greens rather than sodding is better and less costly.

Finally, the golf course superintendent can extend the continuity of the golf architect's theme during reestablishment. The redesign can be complemented through subtle grooming of the golf course turf and through landscape improvements. For example, contour mowing of fairways, secondary roughs, and even more subtle aspects along the perimeters of tees and greens can add to the overall favorable impression of a rebuilding project. By emphasizing the natural contours of the landscape, the superintendent can integrate the golf course redesign into an aesthetically pleasing setting.

Implementing the Rebuilding Project. The procedures involved in the selection of an architect, development of plans, selection of a construction contractor, and establishment of a budget are basically the same in a rebuilding project as in construction of a new golf course.

BIBLIOGRAPHY

A limited number of references on golf course architecture are available. They are listed below. Many of these are older classics, are not widely available, or are outdated in some aspects. Copies are available in the O. J. Noer Turfgrass Libraries at Michigan State University, East Lansing, and Texas A&M University, College Station, and at the USGA library at Far Hills, New Jersey.

Anonymous. 1978. *Building Golf Holes for Good Turf Management*. United States Golf Association, Far Hills, N.J., 55 pp.

Anonymous. 1981. *Planning Information for Private and Daily Fee Golf Clubs*. National Golf Foundation, North Palm Beach, Fla., 500 pp.

Colt, H. W., and Alison, C. H. 1920. *Some Essays on Golf Course Architecture*. Charles Scribner's Sons, New York, 69 pp.

Cornish, G. S., and Robinson, W. G. 1971. *Golf Course Design . . . An Introduction*. National Golf Foundation, Chicago, 20 pp.

Finger, J. S. 1972. *The Business End of Building or Rebuilding a Golf Course*. Joseph S. Finger and Associates, Inc., Houston, 47 pp.

Gill, G. D. 1977. *Golf Course Design and Construction Standards*. Texas A&M University, College Station, Texas, 40 pp.

Hunter, R. 1926. *The Links*. Charles Scribner's Sons, New York, 163 pp.

Jones, R., and Rando, G. *Golf Course Developments*. Urban Land Institute, Washington, D.C., 105 pp.

Killian, K. K., and Nugent, R. P. 1981. *Planning and Building the Golf Course*. National Golf Foundation, North Palm Beach, Fla., 50 pp.

MacKenzie, A. 1920. *Golf Architecture: Economy in Course Construction and Greenkeeping*. Simpkin, Marshall, Hamilton, and Kent Co., Ltd., London, 135 pp.

Sutton, M. H. F. 1906. *Layout and Upkeep of Golf Courses and Putting Greens*. Simpkin, Marshall, Hamilton, and Kent Co., Ltd., London, 42 pp.

Sutton, M. H. F. 1912. *The Book of the Links: A Symposium on Golf*. W. H. Smith and Son, London, 212 pp.

Sutton, M. H. F. 1933 (Ed. 2 1950). *Golf Course—Design, Construction, and Upkeep*. Spottiswoode, Ballantyne and Co., Ltd., London, 152 pp.

Thomas, G. C. Jr. 1927. *Golf Architecture in America: Its Strategy and Construction*. Times-Mirror Press, Los Angeles, 342 pp.

Wethered, H. N., and Simpson, T. 1929. *The Architectural Side of Golf*. Longmans, Green, London, 206 pp.

Wethered, H. N., and Simpson, T. 1952. *Design for Golf*. The Sportsman's Book Club, Norwich, England, 203 pp.

In addition, some good articles on golf course architecture can be found in current periodicals. Older writings are cited in Beard, J. B.; Beard, H. J.; and Martin, D. P. 1977. *Turfgrass Bibliography: 1672 to 1972*. Michigan State University Press, East Lansing, Mich., 730 pp.

Chapter 3
The Putting Green

DESCRIPTION

A *putting green* is all ground of the golf hole being played which is especially prepared for putting. A ball is deemed to be on the putting green when any part of it touches the green. Two shots per hole, or 50 percent of seventy-two shots (par), on an eighteen-hole golf course are allotted to the putting greens, and a third shot per hole involves hitting an approach shot onto the green. In other words, the putting greens represent only about 2 percent of the golf course area but play a role in 75 percent of all golf strokes, assuming par rounds. Thus, proper design, construction, and maintenance of putting greens are very important. Good putting green design provides a fair but challenging test of skill and contributes to economical maintenance. A putting green should be large enough to provide variability in contours, offer a challenge to the golfer, and provide flexibility in cup placement and the associated rotation of traffic. It should not be so large that putting is overemphasized or unrealistic in terms of distance.

Putting greens in North America range from 1,200 to 27,400 square feet (111 to 2,548 square meters) in size, 5,000 to 7,500 square feet (465 to 697 square meters) being the most popular range. Generally, the longer par-3, -4, and -5 holes have large-sized putting greens whereas the short par-3, -4, and -5 holes have smaller greens with more tightly positioned bunkers, thus demanding more accuracy in approach shots. This philosophy tends to equalize the respective demands of individual holes. Good design dictates that each green on a golf course possess unique characteristics in size, shape, contour, and bunker location to provide variation in challenge and interest to the golfer. The placement of bunkers and the shaping of contours surrounding a green should insure that traffic is not concentrated in any one area and that maintenance operations can be accomplished economically.

Surface drainage from a putting green should be in two or more directions. Contouring a green so that all surface water drains to the front where traffic enters should be avoided. Gentle to moderate contours are preferred to avoid mower scalping on ridges and the development of localized dry spots caused by water running from mounds rather than entering the soil. The slope on a major portion of a putting green should normally not exceed 3 percent, although small portions may exceed this, for example, on difficult terrain or for special architectural effect. Contouring of the green should provide a minimum of three distinct areas for cup placement.

Two-Green System. The two-green system is employed to a limited extent in warm humid climates, and is used in Japan more often than in other areas. One green is composed of bermudagrass for summer use and the second green is composed of bentgrass for winter play. In this case, the bermudagrass green can be covered with straw or perforated black plastic for protection during the winter stress period, especially in the transition zone. The two-green system also provides freedom to perform needed maintenance practices without interrupting play. This can be particularly important on intensively used golf courses.

Figure 3-1. Newly prepared winter green in front of regular green.

Alternate Greens. Alternate greens are temporary in nature. They are smaller greens located on the fairway in front or to one side of the summer greens (Fig. 3-1). They are used during the winter, when play is minimal, in lieu of the regular greens. This protects the regular greens from damage by rutting and soil compaction during thaws and wet periods. Alternate greens are used primarily in the southern half of the cool humid region, including the transition zone, where winters are mild enough to permit intermittent year-round play.

Alternate greens are frequently controversial because they tend to provide less smooth putting than do regular greens. However, they serve a valuable function in protecting the regular greens against long-term damage caused by a relatively small percentage of the golfing clientele. A larger hole size occasionally is used on alternate greens where smoothness is a problem. To minimize objections to alternate greens, good planning and fall conversion efforts are needed to provide the best possible putting surface. Topdressing, fertilization, and possibly even overseeding can enhance surface quality. Reuse of the same alternate green location every year can result in improved surface smoothness.

Double Greens. Landmarks at the St. Andrews Golf Course in Scotland are the double greens. The sizes range up to 42,000 square feet (3,906 square meters), giving a potential putt of 150 feet (45.7 meters) or more. On these greens, one hole is located on the near portion of the green on the front nine and a second hole is placed on the far side on the back nine. There are a few double greens in the United States. They have been used rarely because of concern for golfer safety.

Associated Turf Areas. There are three turfed areas associated with the putting green that require distinct types of culture. The narrow turfed strip surrounding the putting green that is mowed at a height intermediate between the height of the fairway and that of the putting green is termed the *collar*. Adjoining the collar and in front of the putting green is an extension of the fairway known as the *apron*. The remainder of the turfed area to each side and in back of the green immediately outside the collar is maintained similarly to the primary rough and is called the *putting green surrounds*. These areas are illustrated in Figure 3-2. The characteristics and cultural requirements of the collar and apron are discussed in this chapter, while the surrounds is discussed in chapter 6. The putting green surrounds is considered part of the rough. Bunkers may be positioned within the apron and putting green surrounds.

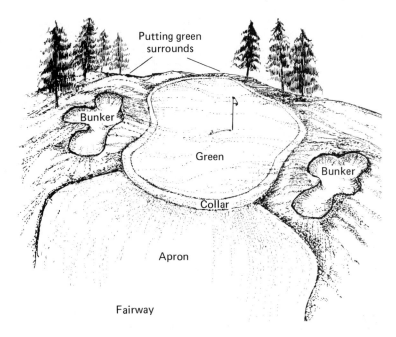

Putting green surrounds

Bunker

Green

Bunker

Collar

Apron

Fairway

Figure 3-2. Illustration of a putting green with the associated collar, apron, and grassy surrounds.

COMPONENTS OF PUTTING GREEN QUALITY

Components of turfgrass quality on a putting green include (a) uniformity, (b) smoothness, (c) firmness, (d) resiliency, (e) close mowing, and (f) absence of grain. *Ball roll* is the distance a golf ball moves after it strikes the green on termination of its air flight or as the result of a putting stroke. The speed or velocity of a green is determined primarily by the height of cut, mowing frequency, smoothness, firmness, and fertility level.

Typically, putting greens are closely mowed at 0.2 (3/16) to 0.25 (1/4) inch (5 to 6.4 millimeters) to achieve the uniformity and smoothness required for trueness of ball roll, speed of the green, and bounce for the approach shot. Close, frequent mowing results in very high shoot density and vertical leaf orientation (Fig. 3-3).

Firmness is important in minimizing footprinting and ball marks. A *ball mark* is a depression and/or tear in a putting green surface made by the impact of a golf ball. Greens should be free of grain, puffiness, and excessive mat or thatch. Some mat (thatch intermixed with soil) is desirable to provide the cushion needed for resiliency and wear tolerance. A depth of about 0.2 to 0.3 inch (5 to 7.6 millimeters) is preferred. A certain degree of resiliency is desirable from the standpoint of holding a properly played approach shot to a putting green. Thus, the green should not be excessively hard or soft.

Green Speed Measurement. A device called the Stimpmeter[1] has been developed for measuring the speed of greens. It is a 36-inch (0.9-meter) long, extruded aluminum bar with a V-shaped groove extending along its entire length. It has a precisely milled ball-release notch 30 inches (76 centimeters)

[1] Available from the United States Golf Association, Far Hills, New Jersey, U.S.A. 07931, at cost (plus mailing charges) to individual golf clubs.

Figure 3-3. Close-up of a
uniformly dense, firm
putting turf surface.

from the tapered end (the end that rests on the ground). The underside of the tapered end is milled away to reduce bounce as a rolling ball makes contact with the green. The V-shaped groove has an included angle of 145 degrees, thereby supporting a golf ball at two points 0.5 inch (1.3 centimeters) apart. A ball rolling down the groove has a slight overspin which is thoroughly consistent and has no deleterious effect on the ensuing measurements. The ball-release notch is so designed that a ball is released and starts to roll when the Stimpmeter is raised to an angle of approximately 20 degrees from the horizontal. This insures that the velocity of the ball is always the same when it reaches the tapered end. When the Stimpmeter is not in use it should be stored in a plastic tube or case. Even relatively slight damage to the release notch or to the groove may cause errors.

Items needed to measure green speed are a Stimpmeter, three small dimpled golf balls, three tees or small marker pegs, a data sheet, and a 10- to 12-foot (3- to 3.7-meter) measuring tape. The suggested procedure is as follows:

Step 1. Select a level area on the green approximately 10 by 10 feet (3 by 3 meters). (A simple means of checking for level is to lay the Stimpmeter flat on the green and place a ball in the V-shaped groove. Movement of the ball will indicate whether the area is reasonably level.)

Step 2. Insert a tee in the green, near the edge of the area selected, to serve as a starting point. Holding the Stimpmeter by the notched end, rest the tapered end on the turf beside the tee and aim it in the direction you intend to roll the ball. Put a ball in the notch and *slowly* raise the end until the ball is released and starts to roll down the groove. *Keeping the tapered end on the same spot*, repeat the same procedure with two more balls (Fig. 3-4).

Step 3. All three balls should come to rest not more than 8 inches (20 centimeters) apart. Should they be farther apart than that, the Stimpmeter motion of elevation may not have been smooth during the series, the area selected may not be as flat as it appears to the eye, there may be some obstruction on the Stimpmeter, or other unusual conditions may exist. In any event, a pattern larger than 8 inches is of dubious accuracy, and the three-roll series should be repeated.

Step 4. Assuming the balls stop within the prescribed 8-inch (20-centimeter) limit, insert a second tee in the green at their average stopping point. The distance between the two tees is the length of the first series of rolls.

Step 5. Repeat step 2, using the second tee as a starting point and the first tee as an aiming point. (In other words, roll a series of three balls along the same line, but in the opposite direction.)

Step 6. Repeat step 3, thereby establishing the length of the second series of rolls.

Step 7. Measure the distance for the first series and that for the second series and calculate their averages. *Note*: Should the difference in length between the first and second series be greater than 18 inches (45 centimeters), the accuracy of the resulting average is questionable. The area selected for the test may not have been sufficiently level — or sufficiently representative of the green — in which case it is advisable to select another area and repeat the test. Sometimes a green may be so severely undulating or sloping that a level area simply is not available. The data record should so indicate this fact.

Step 8. Record the measurements and subsequent calculations plus a description of the weather and green condition on that date.

Selecting a reasonably level test area is important. Measurements taken up or down a slope or over mounds result in misleading data. Conditions during a test are important. Initially, the greens should be tested under optimum conditions: a cleanly mowed, dry, smooth surface on a calm day. Once the basic speed has been established, speeds can be documented under unusual conditions: windy, wet, non-mowed, recently topdressed, different times of day, and before and after fertilizer applications. The data accumulated will lead to a better understanding of how different cultural practices affect the speed and consistency of each green on a golf course. Practice makes perfect. A relatively small amount of practice in using the Stimpmeter will increase the accuracy and consistency of the data obtained with it. Obviously, complete and accurate records, maintained over extended periods, are essential.

The Stimpmeter technique can be used by the golf course superintendent to monitor green speed on a continuing basis throughout the growing season. It can also be used to evaluate the effects of various cultural practices on green speed and to determine the degree to which these practices should be utilized to achieve the green speed desired by the membership. Preferences of the golfing membership may actually vary through the year, with faster greens preferred for championship play than for routine play.

The United States Golf Association (USGA) Green Section agronomists characterized green speed on some fifteen-hundred golf courses in thirty-six states during the 1976-77 playing season using the Stimpmeter technique. A reference chart has been developed from these observations that can serve as a basis for evaluating green speed (Table 3-1). Development of this chart should not be interpreted as an attempt to standardize green speeds on golf courses around the United States. The decision as to green speed should be made by the membership of individual clubs depending on local conditions, budget,

Figure 3-4. Stimpmeter being used to assess the speed of a green.

Table 3-1. Reference Chart of Green Speeds Calculated by Stimpmeter Technique

Relative Green Speed	Average Length of Roll *			
	Regular Play		Tournament Play	
	(in.)	(dm)	(in.)	(dm)
Fast	102	25.9	126	32.0
Medium fast	90	22.9	114	29.0
Medium	78	19.8	102	25.9
Medium slow	66	16.8	90	22.9
Slow	54	13.7	78	19.8

* Reduce length of roll by 6 inches (1.5 decimeters) for bermudagrass greens.

and standard of play expected. The Stimpmeter has been developed as a management aid for the golf course superintendent. It is against the *Rules of Golf* for a golfer to use any device of this type to evaluate green speed during active play.

CONSTRUCTION

The construction of putting greens is the most costly, time-consuming aspect of golf course construction because it usually involves installation of an extensive subsurface drainage system, special root zone modification, and very subtle surface contouring. It is also the most critical aspect, since improper construction due to cost cutting can result in higher long-term maintenance costs and problems in maintaining quality greens. The major steps in putting green construction are (a) surveying and staking, (b) construction of subgrade and surrounds, (c) installation of subsurface drainage system, (d) root zone modification, (e) installation of irrigation system, and (f) finish grading (Fig. 3-5). The staking, clearing, and rough grading have been discussed in more detail in chapter 2.

Surveying and Staking

The perimeter of each putting green is staked at intervals of 15 to 25 feet (4.6 to 7.6 meters) using a terminal reference stake from the earlier centerline staking plus the elevation established from the permanent bench mark reference stake. Additional grade stakes may be used to delineate major excavations or fill work needed for the putting green surrounds. The surface contours of a putting green are constructed based on the architect's detailed drawings. These drawings are used to stake the green by means of properly coded and clearly labeled hub elevation stakes. The important goal is for the finished green to have the shape and surface contours envisioned by the golf course architect.

Construction of Putting Green Subgrade and Surrounds

All tree stumps, roots, rocks, and similar debris must be removed from the putting green site. Most of the large debris should have been removed during earlier construction phases, as described in chapter 2. The primary activity at this point is a final grubbing and cleaning of the site before subgrade construction is initiated.

The first step in subgrade construction is stripping of any acceptable quality topsoil from the site. This topsoil can be stockpiled for future redistribution over exposed subsoils on the fairway and on the primary rough, if an adequate supply is available.

Depending on the particular site, the subgrade may be built onto the existing grade, cut into the subsoil, or built up to the desired elevation with fill material. When a putting green is to be constructed on a slope or mound, sufficient subgrade material may be available on the site so that the primary

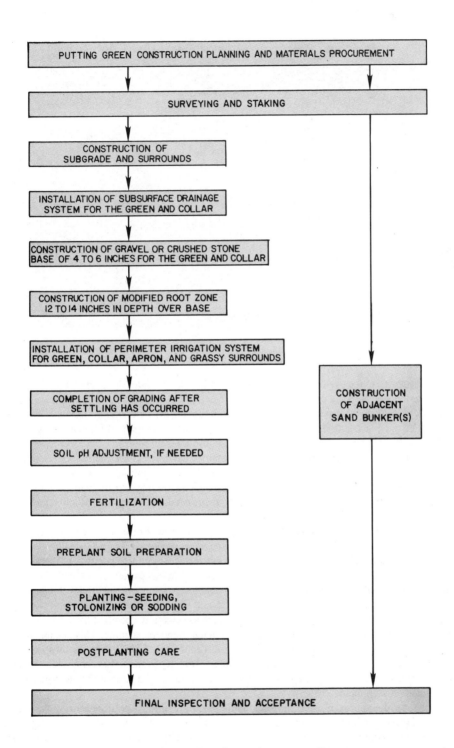

Figure 3-5. Flow diagram for the construction of a putting green, collar, apron, grassy surrounds, and associated bunkers.

Figure 3-6. Subgrade shaping of a putting green and its surrounds.

concern is reshaping to the desired design. More typically, some outside fill material will be needed to elevate at least some portions of the green for better definition and visibility and to insure adequate drainage. Depending on the distance to the putting green site, the fill material may be hauled in trucks or pans or pushed into place by bulldozers. The architect specifies the amount of fill material required for construction of the subgrade at each putting green and also the haul routes.

The subgrade should be constructed so that its final settled grade is 18 inches (45.7 centimeters) below the proposed finished grade. In some cases where fill is used, the subgrade must be firmed and even moistened to enhance settling. Failure to provide adequate time and mechanical provisions to insure full soil settling can result in objectionable depressions in the green which retard surface drainage.

The subgrade contours should conform to those proposed for the finished grade with a tolerance of ± 1 inch (2.5 centimeters). The actual shaping of subgrade contours (Fig. 3-6) involves an artistic dimension. There are two approaches to achieving the surface contours specified in the architect's detailed drawings. One involves placement of reference grade stakes tied to a known bench mark elevation, with the bulldozer operator being responsible for constructing subgrades that conform to these specified elevations. In this case, each green should be resurveyed on completion of subgrade shaping to confirm that the settled contour elevations are as originally specified by the architect. The second approach involves employment of a specialist in putting green shaping. This person, who may be an employee of the architect, has the artistic capability to shape subgrade contours by a study of the detailed drawings and on-site supervision by the architect. No fixed grade stakes are needed. Shaping is usually accomplished with an intermediate-sized bulldozer with an 8- to 10-foot (2.4- to 3-meter) wide, front-mounted, straight blade.

Regardless of the approach used, the subgrade of each green must be inspected by the architect before the next phase in putting green construction is initiated. At this time the architect may request corrections so the contours meet the original specifications or may make slight modifications in the original design to achieve the best possible contours for each golf hole.

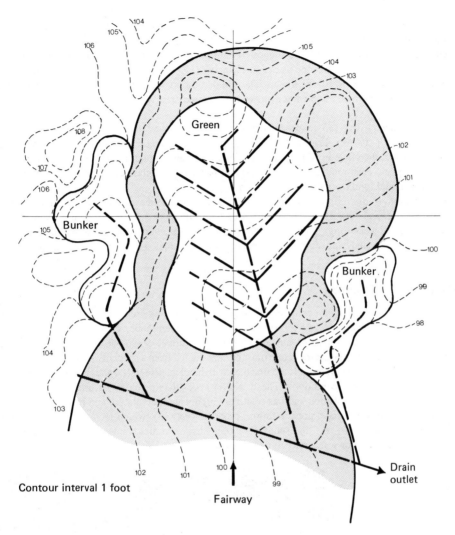

Figure 3-7. Detailed drainage-system plan for a putting green.

Installation of Subsurface Drainage System

Rapid removal of excess soil water is an essential attribute of putting greens. Thus, installation of a complete subsurface drainage system is vital. The first step in planning and construction is the location or development of an adequate-sized outlet for the drainage water. This is followed by a survey for grade. The system itself should be designed so that excess soil water will not have to move more than 10 feet (3 meters) to reach a drain line. Typically, the system consists of 15- to 20-foot (4.5- to 6-meter) lateral spacing of drain lines in either a herringbone or gridiron arrangement (Fig. 3-7). The drain lines are 3 to 4 inches (7.6 to 10 centimeters) in diameter and of clay tile, concrete tile, or flexible slit plastic. The continuous slit plastic drains have gained wide acceptance due to their ease of installation and comparatively low cost.

The first phase in installation involves siting, surveying and staking of drainage lines, and proper labeling for the desired depth of cut. The trench should be no deeper than is necessary to achieve the needed slope for proper drainage. The suggested minimum fall is 0.5 percent; the range is up to 3 or 4 percent. The trench width may range from 6 to 12 inches (15 to 30 centimeters). The wider the cut, the greater the cost for gravel to fill the trench. The soil dug during trenching may be distributed over the subgrade in a manner which establishes a crown between the drain lines or it may be removed from the site.

A 0.5- to 1-inch (1.3- to 2.5-centimeter) layer of gravel is placed in the bottom of the trench before the drain lines are put down. Prior to backfilling, all main and lateral lines should be checked with a level to insure that the grade or fall provides adequate drainage. Drain tiles, if used, should be butted together tightly and each joint covered with asphalt paper or fiberglass composition material, which prevents gravel and sand from entering the lines.

On completion of drain line installation, including appropriate tees and end caps, the trenches are backfilled with gravel of 0.25- to 0.4-inch (6- to 10-millimeter) diameter. It is important to avoid displacement of joint coverings during backfilling. This usually involves careful shoveling of gravel on the joint covers, tees, and connections before backfilling is completed with large mechanical equipment (Fig. 3-8).

Root Zone Modification

Golf courses occasionally are constructed on sites where putting greens can be formed by pushing the surrounding loamy sand-to-sand topsoil into the desired green shape. This is infrequent, however, if not rare. Most sites have soils dominated by clay, silt, stone, or similar objectionable materials, which dictate that a putting green root zone must be constructed from a specially prepared soil mix. The primary concerns in putting green soils are that they withstand intense traffic and drain well to provide a playable surface under wet conditions. These criteria necessitate a coarse-textured, sandy root zone which is less prone to compaction and has relatively high water percolation and infiltration rates. In addition, sandy root zones have good aeration, especially oxygen, which facilitates deep rooting. It should be recognized, however, that sandy root zones have the disadvantages of limited cation exchange capacity and poorer water retention characteristics.

Figure 3-8. Putting green with the trench, drain lines, and gravel being installed into the contoured subgrade. (Photo courtesy of Rees Jones, American Society of Golf Course Architects.)

Figure 3-9. Improperly constructed root zone mix with a serious soil-layering problem.

Root Zone Mix Selection. The selection of the most appropriate root zone mix is a critical decision that affects the long-term performance of a putting green in terms of surface quality, ease of turfgrass culture, and maintenance cost. Unfortunately, a majority of the golf courses built over the years have been constructed of improper soil materials (Fig. 3-9), which has necessitated costly rebuilding of the putting greens along with considerable disruption of play. Only a very naive person makes a final decision concerning the appropriate root zone mix to be used on the basis of appearance and feel of the dry mix. The sound approach involves a combination of (a) a physical soil test, (b) understanding the chemical and physical characteristics of the individual soil, sand, and organic components involved, and (c) practical field experience concerning the long-term performance of specific soil-sand-organic mixes.

The amount of soil, sand, and organic matter needed on a volume basis to prepare an acceptable quality root zone mix varies greatly depending on the physical and chemical characteristics of the individual components. These criteria cannot be assessed by a simple field examination. Rather, the best approach is to submit the individual components to a physical soil testing lab where specific quantitative measurements can be conducted to assess the best combination of soil, sand, and organic components that will achieve a root zone capable of functioning with acceptable rates of percolation, infiltration, and aeration.

Root Zone Laboratory Analysis. The starting point in root zone mix selection is acquisition of a detailed physical and chemical description of the components being considered for use as well as how these components perform when mixed in various combinations. This is accomplished by securing representative samples of the soil, sand, and organic components under consideration and submitting them to a reputable physical soil testing laboratory.

The laboratory will conduct a series of primary physical determinations which usually include the infiltration rate (hydraulic conductivity) and pore space distribution as well as particle size, moisture retention, aggregation, bulk density, and mineral derivation. The next phase in laboratory analysis is the selection and preparation of a series of trial soil mixes containing varying proportions of the soil, sand, and organic matter. Which trial mixes are selected is dictated by results of the previously conducted physical determinations on the individual components. The synthesized trial soil mixes are

Date: _____

Sample Number: _____
Sender or Club: _____
Address: _____
Phone: _____

PARTICLE SIZE ANALYSIS

SOIL MIX MATERIALS	GRAVEL >2mm (>9 mesh) %	TOTAL SAND (9-300) mesh %	SILT .002-05mm (<300 mesh) %	CLAY <.002mm %	SAND FRACTIONS					Organic Matter %
					VERY COARSE 1-2mm (9-16 mesh) %	COARSE 0.5-1mm (16-32 mesh) %	MEDIUM 0.25-.5mm (32-60 mesh) %	FINE 0.1-.25mm (60-140 mesh) %	VERY FINE 0.05-.1mm (140-300 mesh) %	
Sand	0.5	97.0	1.7	0.8	2.5	19.7	62.6	11.2	1.0	
Composted peat										30.5

PHYSICAL MEASUREMENTS

MIXES EXAMINED (% by Volume)

SAND	SOIL AMENDMENT	BULK DENSITY g/cm^3	% PORE SPACE		INFILTRATION RATE–INCHES OF H$_2$O/HOUR	PERCENT MOISTURE RETENTION AT PRESSURE INDICATED				pH OF MIX	LIME NEEDS lbs/1000 sq. ft.
			CAPILLARY	NON-CAPILLARY		40 cm of H$_2$O	1/3 atm.	2/3 atm.	1 atm.		
100	0	1.33	4.6	45.2	40.9	3.5	1.3	1.0	1.0	5.7	
90	10	1.36	10.8	38.2	14.8	8.0	4.0	3.2	2.8	6.7	
80	20	1.34	16.9	32.6	8.9	12.6	6.8	5.7	5.6	7.0	
70	30	1.31	23.2	27.3	0.7	17.7	10.2	9.1	7.5	7.1	

Lime values indicate rates of pure calcium carbonate (100% neutralizing value) uniformly incorporated to a six-inch soil depth. Adjust rate of application according to neutralizing value of material used and depth of soil to which it is applied.

Figure 3-10. Sample report issued by physical soil testing laboratory.

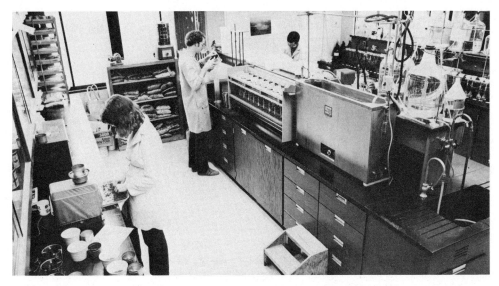

Figure 3-11. United States Golf Association Physical Soil Test Laboratory at Texas A&M University, College Station, Tex. (Photo courtesy of K. Brown, Texas A&M University, College Station, Tex.)

then compacted and evaluated for hydraulic conductivity and pore space distribution relative to an optimum standard. This is repeated until a ratio that approaches the optimum standard is found for each component. A recommendation as to the percentage of each soil, sand, and organic-matter component is then given. The recommendation applies only to that particular soil type, sand, and organic matter. The sand and organic-matter components may vary as greatly as the soil component.

Not only the root zone mix but also the gravel component used for underdrainage can be assessed by mechanical analysis. A recommendation as to the appropriate size distribution for the gravel can also be given to insure that the soil mix does not migrate into the underlying gravel layer and eventually block the drain lines.

A chemical assessment of the recommended soil mix should be requested along with the physical evaluation. This chemical characterization should include (a) pH, (b) levels of major essential elements including phosphorus, potassium, calcium, and magnesium, and (c) total soluble salt level. Specific requests can be made for the assessment of minor nutrient content, potential sodium problems, and boron level if potential problems are suspected.

After the laboratory analyses are completed, a report is sent to the individual who forwarded the material for testing (Fig. 3-10). It is preferable if the report includes an interpretation of the analytical measurements by a qualified soil scientist experienced in root zone modification of golf course putting greens.

Few soil testing laboratories in the United States possess the capability of physical soil analysis that meets golf course turf needs. The USGA Green Section supports such a laboratory, currently located in the Department of Soil and Crop Sciences at Texas A&M University, College Station, Texas (Fig. 3-11). Since this laboratory is subsidized, the fee schedule for physical analysis is modest. The cost ranges from $75 to $250 depending on the number of components and candidate soil mixes to be evaluated and the specific chemical analyses requested (Table 3-2). This is a minor expenditure compared with the overall cost of construction and the risk of failure from use of improper soil materials. Selection of a root zone mix on a relatively arbitrary basis without the aid of a reputable physical soil testing laboratory is likely to result in compacted, poorly drained problem greens which eventually must be rebuilt.

Table 3-2. Types of Soil Analyses
Conducted by the United States Golf Association Physical Soil Test Laboratory

Complete analysis, including total USGA testing procedure for sand, soil, and organic matter

Mechanical analysis (particle size) of individual sand or soil samples

Assay of organic amendment sample, including ashing

Chemical analysis for soil pH and for P, K, and total salt content

Analysis of a soil mix for particle size and ash

Infiltration rate of submitted root zone mix or a combined (laboratory-blended) mix

Moisture retention for 40 cm of water, $\frac{1}{3}$, $\frac{1}{2}$, and 1 atm

Analysis of a root zone mix for particle size, bulk density, pore-space distribution, infiltration rate, and 40-cm water retention

Sieve analysis of sand for bunkers

Sieve analysis of gravel for putting green underdrain

Obtaining Representative Materials for Laboratory Analysis. Laboratory analysis requires a minimum of 2 gallons (7.6 liters) of sand and 1 gallon (3.8 liters) each of soil, organic matter, and gravel to be used for the underdrain. If there is a choice of sands, soils, and organic materials, a sample of each should be sent with a note indicating a preference based on cost and accessibility. The laboratory will attempt to use the preferred materials in the recommended root zone mix.

Care must be exercised so that representative samples of all components are obtained. If the materials are stocked, several samples should be composited from the side or top portion of the stockpile. Materials near the edge or on a sloping surface may not be representative. It should be ascertained that a prospective vendor has a sufficient supply of uniform materials to be able to provide the same mix as the sample sent even if there is a delay of a few months. Sieved or processed sand is preferred to river or bank-run sand for this reason.

Soil sampling requires special consideration. Only the top 6 inches (15 centimeters) of soil should be used. An area from which topsoil can be stripped should be marked off and three or more samples from the area composited. Usually no more than 200 square feet (18.6 square meters) of root zone mix per green are needed, but it is good to have more available. Soils selected should be sands, sandy loams, or loams. The local Soil Conservation Service representative or a USGA Green Section regional representative can assist in soil selection, if necessary.

All materials should be packaged separately and securely. Strong plastic bags packed inside cardboard cartons or metal cans is the most satisfactory method. A paper bag containing moist soil or sand rarely arrives intact. When containers arrive broken and materials mixed, the laboratory must request more material. Such a delay can be inconvenient, aggravating, and time consuming.

Paper labels packaged with moist materials deteriorate very rapidly. Use of plastic labels inside and outside the packages is worthwhile. The more information provided, including a covering letter, the better.

Root Zone Amendments

Most modern putting greens are constructed by soil modification with use of one or more components from outside the course property. This entails both purchase and hauling of the appropriate materials to the course. Criteria to consider in the selection of root zone soil amendments include (a) effects on soil texture and related physical properties, (b) effects on soil chemical characteristics, (c) long-term strength and stability, (d) local availability, (e) amount required versus availability, (f) cost, including hauling, and (g) long-term availability.

Table 3-3. Characteristics of Soil Separates as
Established by the United States Department of Agriculture

Soil Separate	Particle Diameter (mm)	Number of Particles per Gram
Very coarse sand	2.00 - 1.00	90
Coarse sand	1.00 - 0.50	722
Medium sand	0.50 - 0.25	5,777
Fine sand	0.25 - 0.10	46,213
Very fine sand	0.10 - 0.05	722,074
Silt	0.05 - 0.002	5,776,674
Clay	< 0.002	90,260,853,860

The soil component of the root zone mix preferably is obtained within the property boundaries. The preferred component to be used in root zone modification is a loamy sand, sandy loam, or loam. Soils containing more than 5 percent silt or a substantial amount of clay should be avoided, if at all possible. It is frequently advisable to obtain the assistance of a qualified soil scientist in locating the best possible soil component to be used in root zone modification.

Sand Component. There is great variation in sands available in terms of particle size distribution, shape, hardness, color, and pH. Some sands are excellent for root zone modification, while others are excellent for making concrete. The sand component should represent a very high proportion of most root zone mixes used on intensively trafficked putting greens because it enhances aeration, infiltration, and percolation and is less prone to soil compaction than other components. Medium- to coarse-textured, washed sands with a particle diameter of 0.25 to 1 millimeter are preferred (Table 3-3). Even better moisture retention is achieved if at least 50 percent of the sand particles have a diameter in the 0.25- to 0.5-millimeter range. Seventy-five percent is considered ideal. Due to substantial variation in particle size distribution of sands as well as soils, it is best if the proportion of a specific sand component to be utilized in root zone modification be established by laboratory physical analysis.

Organic Component. The addition of well-decomposed organic material to the root zone mix improves nutrient and water retention, resiliency, and aeration. It enhances turfgrass establishment, especially from seed, on high-proportion sand root zone mixes due to the surface moisture it retains. Decomposed peat is the organic material most commonly used in root zone modification. However, there are all types of peats. They vary greatly in degree of decomposition, pH, and mineral content. A well-decomposed, fractionated peat with minimum mineral content is preferred. A ranking of types of peat from excellent to poor would be: peat humus, reed-sedge peat, hypnum moss peat, sphagnum moss peat.

Other organic matter amendments can also function well in root zone mixes if adequately decomposed and available locally in sufficient quantities. Among these are decomposed sawdust, shredded bark, lignified wood, and various animal/vegetable byproducts. These materials should be finely shredded to achieve the best possible mixing characteristics. Knowledge about previous experience with local sources of decomposed organic matter is usually helpful in selecting the best material.

Other Potential Amendments. Other potential amendments can function in much the same way as sand and may be considered for use in root zone mixes if readily available or less costly than sand. Calcined clay fired to the proper hardness has been used effectively. Blast furnace slag from the steel manufacturing industry has some good physical characteristics. The soil pH may have to be adjusted where slag is used in soil modification. Expanded shale can also be used effectively if properly graded from a physical standpoint. Washed ash and fly ash from the burning of coal fuels have proven effective in root zone modification, but these materials must be free of potential toxic chemicals or a high salt content. Colloidal phosphate has been used to modify high sand content soils in Florida to improve their water-holding and nutrient-retention capacities. Materials such as processed micas and expanded perlite have not been acceptable as soil amendments owing to their lack of mechanical strength under the intense traffic typically occurring on putting greens.

Soil Modification Procedure

On most golf courses constructed in North America, putting green soil modification is required to maintain a quality putting surface with minimal problems from turfgrass wear and soil compaction. Far too many putting greens are being constructed with a partially modified soil mix or objectionable soil layering which fails to meet minimum standards in terms of soil water movement, aeration, and compaction potential. This eventually leads to the unavoidable decision to rebuild the putting greens, using a reliable method of complete soil modification that provides a favorable environment for the culture of putting green turfs with a reasonable investment of time and materials.

Eight methods of soil modification are presented and discussed in *Turfgrass: Science and Culture* (by James B. Beard, 1973, Prentice-Hall, Inc., Englewood Cliffs, N.J.). Variations on these basic methods have been attempted with limited success. Three of the methods are oriented to putting green construction and thus will be discussed here. For the purposes of discussion, the collar is considered part of the total putting green from the standpoint of root zone soil monification. Regardless of the root zone modification method planned, an adequately designed and installed subsurface drain line system is essential.

USGA Green Section Method. Specifications for this method of putting green construction were first published in 1960 and were revised in 1973. This method is based on very extensive research and

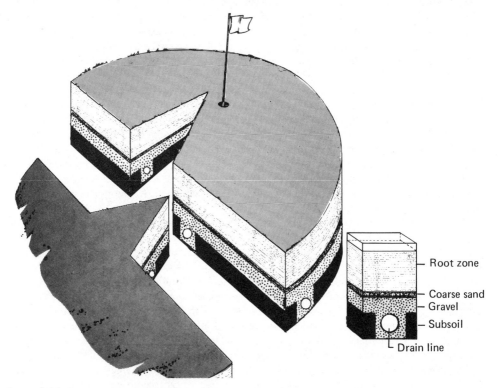

Root zone
Coarse sand
Gravel
Subsoil
Drain line

Figure 3-12. Cross section showing United States Golf Association Green Section method of putting green construction.

has been the most widely used method yet conceived. It combines a perched water table to provide a reserve supply of water in the root zone with a high sand content root zone which possesses good internal soil drainage and minimal proneness to soil compaction (Fig. 3-12). It was the first method to establish a procedure for physical soil analysis, including soil mix synthesis and testing based on sound physical principles, which permits specific recommendations concerning the proper proportion of each sand, soil, and organic-matter component to be mixed. The specifications for construction by the USGA Green Section method are as follows:

Subgrade. Contours of the subgrade should conform to those of the proposed finished grade with a tolerance of ± 1 inch (2.5 centimeters). The subgrade should be constructed at an elevation 18 inches (45.7 centimeters) below the planned finished grade. The subgrade should be firmed sufficiently to prevent future settling.

Drainage System. A herringbone or gridiron subsurface drainage system is utilized including 4-inch (10-centimeter) diameter drain lines spaced at 15- to 20-foot (4.6- to 6-meter) intervals with a minimum grade of 0.5 percent. Trenches for the drain lines should be cut into the subgrade as shallowly as possible and yet still provide the needed slope for drainage. Approximately 1 inch (2.5 centimeters) of gravel is placed in the bottom of the trenches. Drain lines are then laid in place. Additional gravel is placed over the drain lines in the trenches, care being taken to not displace the coverings over each joint.

Gravel Layer. Washed pea gravel of 0.25 to 0.4 inch (6.3 to 10 millimeters) in diameter (Fig. 3-13) should be obtained for filling the drain trenches as well as for covering the entire putting green and collar subgrade to a minimum settled thickness of 4 inches (10 centimeters). It is important that the proper sized pea gravel be obtained to insure functioning of the perched water table.

Coarse Sand Layer. A 1.5- to 2-inch (3.8- to 5-centimeter) deep layer of coarse sand is spread over the entire gravel base. The size of the sand particle must be within five to seven diameters that of the underlying gravel. Thus, if 0.25-inch (6.3-millimeter) pea gravel is used, the coarse sand layer particle should be not less than 1 millimeter in diameter. The purpose of the coarse sand layer above the pea gravel base is to prevent soil particles in the upper root zone mix from migrating downward into the pea gravel. This thin sand layer presents some difficulties in proper installation if the proper equipment, such as a mechanical sand rake, is not available. This dimension of USGA Green Section soil modification is important in the overall concept and is a modest investment compared with the duration of time that the green is expected to function.

Because of repeated difficulties in installation, many have asked if under certain conditions the coarse sand layer could be eliminated. Recent research indicates that the coarse sand layer can be eliminated if a physical soil test by an accredited soil testing laboratory indicates that the particle size

Figure 3-13. Desired size of washed pea gravel for use in the United States Golf Association Green Section method of construction.

Figure 3-14. Ringing phase in construction of a putting green. (Photo courtesy of R. Phipps, Shorehaven Golf Course, East Norwalk, Conn.)

relationship between the gravel and the root zone is exactly as specified in the USGA Green Section specifications for putting green construction. The correct root zone mix-to-gravel relationship is vital to proper water retention in the top mix and to insure that soil particles are prevented from migrating downward to impair drainage. Attempts have been made to substitute a nonbiodegradable woven or screenlike material for this layer. Problems have developed with some of these screens, since they tend to become clogged with the finer sand and soil particles to the extent that they become impermeable and cease to function as originally intended.

Ringing. A strip of polyethylene sheeting should be inserted as a vertical barrier between the outer soil and the sandy root zone mix to avoid lateral transfer of water into the adjacent dry soil (Fig. 3-14). This polyethylene ringing is positioned at the outer perimeter of the collar, which is 3 to 5 feet (0.9 to 1.5 meters) beyond the putting green perimeter.

Root Zone Mix. The root zone mix selected should be based on specific physical tests conducted in the USGA Physical Soil Test Laboratory. The report from these tests specifies the particular materials to be used and the percentage in which they are to be mixed. Because of the narrow acceptable limits in the physical properties, it is very important that the laboratory recommendations be followed in mixing the components of the root zone mix. The desired physical characteristics for a USGA root zone are as follows:

Sand Particle Size. The sand amendment should contain not more than 10 percent of particles larger than 1 millimeter (16 mesh) in diameter. The total root zone mix should contain a minimum of 25 percent particles in the 0.25-millimeter (60-mesh) to 0.5-millimeter (32-mesh) range, 15 percent below 0.25 millimeter (60 mesh) and 5 percent below 0.06 millimeter (160 mesh) (Table 3-4). Sand of the brick or mason class is preferred. Silica sands are recommended. Other sands are acceptable only in the rare cases when silica sand is unavailable.

Infiltration Rate. The ideal water infiltration rate for a compacted root zone mix should be in the range of 4 to 6 inches (10 to 15 centimeters) per hour. This is measured by compacting the root zone mix at a moisture content equal to field capacity and maintaining it under a constant head flow of water for twenty-four hours at a temperature of 68 °F (20.2 °C). The infiltration rate in the laboratory tests should not exceed 10 inches (25.4 centimeters) per hour and should be no less than 2 inches (5 centimeters) per hour for bermudagrass and 3 inches (7.6 centimeters) per hour for bentgrass.

Porosity. The root zone mix should have a total pore space (micropores and macropores) volume of between 40 and 55 percent. The ideal distribution would be 25 percent capillary and 25 percent

Table 3-4. Guidelines for Particle Size

Gravel	Very Coarse Sand	Coarse Sand	Medium Sand	Fine Sand	Very Fine Sand	Silt and Clay
≥2mm	1 - 2 mm	1.0 - 0.5 mm	0.50 - 0.25 mm	0.25 - 0.10 mm	0.10 - 0.05 mm	< 0.05 mm
Maximum 3%	Maximum 7%					Maximum 3% clay 5% silt

Maximum	Desired Range	Maximum
Not more than 10% of total	65% minimum 75% optimum	Not more than 25% of total, preferably 10% of total

noncapillary pore space. These characteristics are measured on a root zone mix that has been allowed to percolate water for twenty-four hours and then is drained at a tension of 15.7 inches (40 centimeters) of water.

Bulk Density. A root zone mix synthesized with a major sand component should ideally have a bulk density of 1.4 grams per cubic centimeter. The minimum acceptable bulk density for such mixes is 1.2 and the maximum is 1.6 grams per cubic centimeter.

Water Retention Capacity. The root zone mix should have a laboratory-established 40-centimeter water retention capacity of between 12 and 25 percent by weight on a 105- to 111 °C-oven dry-soil basis. Available water in the soil is estimated to be that water held at a tension of 40 centimeters of water (the distance from the putting green surface to the drain line) at 15 atmospheres. The ideal water retention capacity is approximately 18 percent, or 0.15 inch (3.8 millimeters) of water held per inch (2.54 centimeters) of soil.

The USGA Green Section method of putting green construction requires the following quantities of material per 1,000 square feet (92.9 square meters) of putting green surface: (a) washed pea gravel to 4-inch (10-centimeter) depth: 12.3 cubic yards (9.3 cubic meters); (b) coarse sand to 1.5-inch (3.8-centimeter) depth: 4.6 cubic yards (3.5 cubic meters); and (c) root zone mix to 12-inch (30.5-centimeter) depth: 37 cubic yards (28 cubic meters); plus approximately 100 linear feet (30 meters) of drain lines.

Soil pH. The ideal range is 5.5 to 5.7.

Organic Matter. The organic matter source selected should have no more than 15 percent ash content or mineral material, 10 percent being preferred.

Methods Involving a Permanently Elevated Water Table. The Purr-Wick system and similiar approaches utilize the principle of a permanently elevated water table in contrast to the perched water table concept previously discussed. This concept of putting green construction was first tested on an experimental basis in 1968 and has been used on a number of golf greens in the 1970's. The Purr-Wick system consists of a series of terraced compartments delineated by plastic sheeting on the bottom and sides plus drainage tubes that have adjustable outlets by means of which the water level can be controlled and/or the system fully drained, if desired (Fig. 3-15). This construction method has not worked well on steeply contoured greens.

Subgrade. The subgrade should be constructed at an elevation 16 to 20 inches (40 to 50 centimeters) below the proposed finished grade. The subgrade area of individual compartments will vary in width and length to obtain the desired contours of the final grade with minimum variation in sand depth. Appropriate internal vertical dividers should be installed for every 6-inch (15-centimeter) change in elevation. Each subgrade compartment should extend to the outer perimeter of the collar. There have been problems with water seepage from upper to lower terraces of contoured greens.

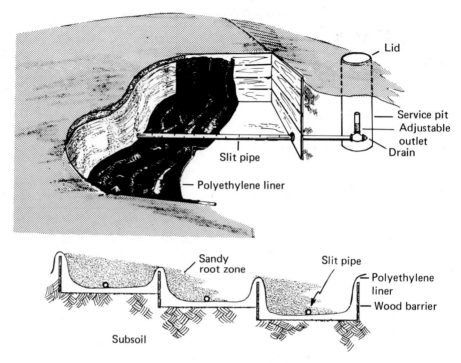

Figure 3-15. Purr-Wick system. Cross section of a single compartment plus the associated external drain control well (*top*). Side view of a typical series of compartments on a contoured green (*bottom*).

Impermeable Barrier. A heavy impermeable underlayer or barrier is placed across the subgrade. Four-mil polyethylene sheeting has been used successfully. Sufficient material should be procured to allow a 25 percent overlap of the edges and vertical compartment dividers. The edges between each sheeting should be overlapped 1 to 3 feet (0.3 to 0.9 meter) to obtain the desired seal. The vertical dividers for each compartment should extend to the proposed final surface elevation. Taping of the edges provides further assurance of a dependable seal. Where drain lines extend through the impermeable barrier, it is important that the proper seal for water retention be provided by means of flange collars, tape, or mastic. Special care must be taken in installation of the subgrade barrier, since holes punched in the polyethylene sheeting will result in leakage problems.

Drainage System. Two-inch (5-centimeter) drainage tubing possessing numerous narrow slits is then placed across the impermeable barrier at a spacing of 10 to 25 feet (3 to 7.6 meters). The drainage lines in this system are placed above the plastic barrier; thus, trenching and placement of drain lines into the subgrade are not done, as in the USGA Green Section soil modification system.

Water Control. Drain lines within the compartment are connected to a main which extends through the impermeable barrier wall of the compartment into a drain control well which is open to the surface for access to the controls. Outlet mains from several compartments may extend into the same drainage well. The water outflow main from each compartment includes a terminal tee with a removable plug to allow complete drainage during the winter and an upright nipple to control the desired water table depth above the subgrade barrier. The control well is connected to a subsurface drain line which removes all excess water immediately.

Root Zone Mix. Root zone specifications for the Purr-Wick system are not as well defined as those for the USGA Green Section method, discussed previously. Washed sand with a uniformly fine particle size is suggested. It is preferable to have less than 1 percent combined silt and clay with 100 percent of the particles below 0.5 millimeter in diameter. Following distribution of the sand root zone within the test compartments, the final subgrade is established and an additive, usually an organic material such as decomposed peat, is mixed uniformly into the upper 2 inches (5 centimeters). The organic material is added to provide resiliency and surface moisture retention during the establishment phase. All workers should be careful during these operations to avoid puncturing the impermeable subgrade barrier.

Methods Involving General Sand Modification. The previous two methods of complete soil modification involve maintaining a water reserve in the immediate root zone. The category discussed herein represents a composite grouping of many different viewpoints on soil modification. The objective is to remove excess water by amending with materials possessing relatively coarse particle size, no attempt being made to maintain a water reserve in the root zone. A majority of the approaches within this category now in use by various builders of putting greens were devised through trial-and-error rather than specific quantitative research. Many eventually fail. The end result is costly rebuilding to a more quantitatively controlled system based on sound physical principles. Some approaches to root zone modification within this category, however, are quite effective in a given region when a particular type of soil and sand is utilized.

Subgrade. The subgrade is constructed to conform with the proposed finished grade at an elevation of 10 to 20 inches (25 to 50 centimeters) below the final grade. Most approaches employ a subsurface drainage system involving a herringbone or gridiron arrangement with 4-inch (10-centimeter) diameter drain lines spaced on 15- to 20-foot (4.5- to 6-meter) intervals at a minimum grade of 0.5 percent. Some soil modification approaches do not employ a drain line system. Most of these are doomed to failure.

Drainage Layer. Many of the systems employ some kind of crushed aggregate or gravel which is placed over the drain lines and to a depth of 2 to 6 inches (5 to 15 centimeters) over the subgrade. This material may range from very large crushed stone down to the washed pea gravel specified in the USGA Green Section method. In some cases, this coarse aggregate layer is not included, which is generally a serious error. Almost any type of coarse aggregate is better than none, but for most situations washed pea gravel with a diameter of 0.25 to 0.40 inch (6.4 to 10 millimeters) is preferred.

Root Zone Mix. Above the coarse aggregate material is placed a sandy root zone, the material ranging from sand only to sand plus an organic material, such as decomposed peat, incorporated at a rate of 10 to 20 percent by volume to a mix of sand plus soil plus decomposed organic matter in varying percentages. While some of these mixes may perform successfully under a given set of situations, there is great likelihood of failure and eventual costly rebuilding for most of them. Also, although one approach may be successfully used in a given locality, the potential for its successful use over a wide range of soils, environmental conditions, and sand sources is limited.

Root Zone Installation Procedure

Quality control is the key to successful execution of any root zone modification method. All root zone mixing should be completed off-site. Every truckload of each component utilized in the soil mix, as well as the coarse sand layer and gravel, should be checked at delivery to insure that the specifications are met and that the materials are equivalent to the materials originally submitted for analysis to the USGA Physical Soil Test Laboratory.

Off-site mixing should include soil shredding, screening to remove any objectionable stones, and the addition of the appropriate proportions of each mix component into a rotary mixer. In some locations where the demand for root zone mix is great enough, a bulk soil mixing plant can be contracted to provide the desired root zone mix. After confirmation that the root zone mix meets the desired specifications, it is transported to the green construction site and dumped around the perimeter.

A small crawler tractor with blade is used to push the soil mix out onto the green (Fig. 3-16). Care should be taken that the tractor is always operated with its weight on the soil mix in a back-and-forth motion. This minimizes the chance of disturbing the lower profile, such as the coarse sand-pea gravel base or the impermeable barrier. The soil mix is carefully distributed from the collar perimeter toward the center of the green to the desired depth. Grade stakes placed at 10- to 15-foot (3- to 4.5-meter)

Figure 3-16. Small crawler tractor being used to move the root zone mix into place across the green. (Photo courtesy of Rees Jones, American Society of Golf Course Architects.)

intervals across the green in a grid pattern aid in establishing the desired final contours to the specified root zone depth. Completion of soil distribution across the green may be done manually by means of shovels, push boards, and/or drags.

Irrigation System Installation

An irrigation system is a standard component in golf course construction. The system should be installed and made operational before the putting green is planted. A detailed discussion of irrigation systems is presented in chapter 9 and thus is not included here. Only considerations unique to putting greens are discussed in this section.

Most modern putting green irrigation systems consist of an underground automatic pop-up system along with one or two quick-coupler hose-end outlets for use in syringing, spot watering, watering of localized dry spots, or supplying other emergency water needs. The preferred design for putting greens is a perimeter system with equilateral triangular spacing and head-to-head coverage to achieve the desired uniformity of coverage (Fig. 3-17). Because of the superiority of this design, the architect should consider it in the original shaping of each putting green. A system typically has a minimum of four to six heads per green with one or two pop-up heads under the command of a single control station. Single-head control is preferred, as it allows greater flexibility in providing only the amount of water needed for a given area of the green. Where two heads are utilized per control station, they should be grouped based on similarities in elevation and shade conditions or in relation to the prevailing wind direction. It is important for the system to provide a syringe cycle in which water can be applied lightly for cooling, prevention of wilt, frost removal, dew removal, or other specific conditions. The sprinkler head selected should deliver a relatively low precipitation rate.

To maintain the proper moisture level on a putting green, the surrounds may have to be irrigated, particularly where steep slopes are positioned in the direction of prevailing winds. Failure to provide adequate irrigation to such areas may result in drying of the green laterally from underneath. Where the putting green surrounds are constructed of soil possessing drastically different infiltration and percola-tion rates from those of the actual putting green surface, use of a separate set of irrigation heads with an adjustable application diameter may be desirable on the perimeter of the green. This provides flexibility in water application to the surrounds as needed and thus avoids either over or underwatering. If the

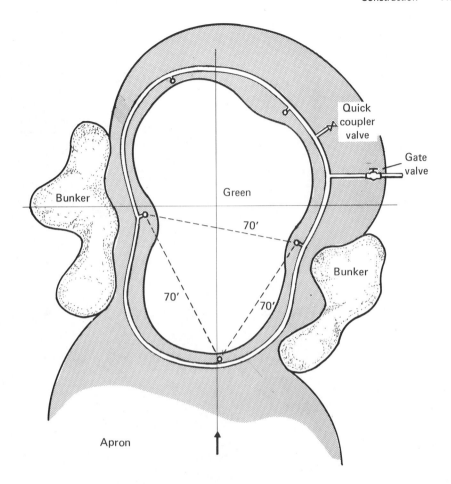

Figure 3-17. Detailed irrigation plan for a putting green having two zones and an equilateral triangular spacing of 70 feet (21.3 meters) with head-to-head coverage.

same heads are used to irrigate putting green surface and surrounds of distinctly different soil textures, the primary priority will be irrigation of the green.

One final consideration involves use of partial-circle heads positioned in such a way that minimal water is applied to bunkers. This reduces costs for bunker maintenance and provides better bunker playing conditions on a continuing basis.

Finish Grading

Once root zone mix distribution has been completed to the specified depth, the initial finish grading can be accomplished. A small crawler tractor equipped with a front-mounted blade can be used for initial rough grading. Grade stakes placed at 10- to 15-foot (3- to 4.5-meter) intervals in a grid system across the green are used to insure that the root zone mix is distributed to the correct depth and the green thus meets the contour specifications in the architect's detailed putting green drawing.

Figure 3-18. Final shaping of a putting green with a grader box (*top*) followed by firming of root zone with powered riding roller (*bottom*). (Top photo courtesy of M. Taylor, Bainbridge, Wash.)

The root zone mix must be firmed before finish grading can be completed. A significant amount of firming is achieved by operation of the grading tractor and other construction equipment across the surface (Fig. 3-18). In the past, firming of the putting green surface was achieved by ''footing,'' i.e., short, choppy foot movements made across the surface in an organized pattern by a large crew of workers. Footing was particularly effective on the clay soils used in green construction in early days. However, it is rarely used in modern putting green construction. Special efforts are needed to properly firm the sandy root zone mixes used today. Typically, a mechanically powered roller is operated across the surface repeatedly until the desired degree of firmness is achieved (Fig. 3-18). Irrigation can be used to enhance settling and firming of the surface during the late stages of grading.

Finish grading of the surface root zone involves mechanical raking, dragging, and sometimes even hand raking. Certain types of mechanical sand rakes are very effectively adapted for use in the final smoothing of putting green surfaces. Repeated raking of the surface in a looping pattern results in the most firm, uniform surface grade possible.

On completion of finish grading, the surface contours should be checked by means of a level or transit to confirm that the grades are within 1 inch (2.5 centimeters) of the elevations specified in the architect's original detailed drawings. Equipment used during finish grading may include various types of drags, a small crawler tractor with blade, a tractor with rear-mounted grader box, a mechanical sand rake, a power roller, and 3- to 4-foot (0.9- to 1.2-meter)-wide lightweight rakes.

TURFGRASS SELECTION

Turfgrass species and cultivars selected for putting greens must possess special characteristics including (a) a low, creeping growth habit and erect leaves, (b) tolerance to very close mowing of 0.2 inch (5 millimeters), (c) very high shoot density, (d) fine leaf texture, (e) uniformity, (f) freedom from excessive grain and thatch, and (g) good recuperative rate. Other features are also desirable, such as resistance to pest injury and tolerance to environmental, soil, and traffic stresses. A dark-green color does not affect putting quality but does enhance the aesthetics of the course.

Cool-Season Species

Bentgrass (*Agrostis* spp.) is the cool-season turfgrass used most commonly on greens in the cool and transitional climatic regions and in the cooler portions of the warm climatic region, especially the arid zone. Bentgrasses, especially Penncross, are being used increasingly on greens in the warm climatic region when (a) the atmospheric humidity is sufficiently low, (b) the proper sand root zone mix is utilized in green construction, and (c) a quality automatic irrigation system is installed. Elevations above 2,500 feet (762 meters) also enhance the culture of bentgrass greens in warm climatic regions.

Creeping bentgrass is the most commonly used *Agrostis* species in North America. The major creeping bentgrass cultivars in use are Cohansey, Penncross, Seaside, and Toronto (Table 3-5). Others are Arlington, C-52, Congressional, Emerald, Evansville, Nimisilia, Penneagle, Pennpar, and Washington. Penneagle is the most recently released and as yet is not totally proven, but is promising. Penncross, Emerald, Seaside, and Penneagle are established from seed, while the others are planted vegetatively by stolonizing. Penncross is the most widely used throughout North America, except for the hot, humid southeast. Those in moderate use include Toronto, in the northern cool climatic region; Cohansey, in the transitional and northern warm climatic regions; and Seaside, in maritime climates.

Colonial bentgrasses, such as Astoria, are occasionally utilized but are inferior to the creeping bentgrasses in tolerance to cold, close mowing, and wear as well as in disease resistance, recuperative rate, and competitiveness against annual bluegrass invasion. Velvet bentgrass, primarily Kingstown (Table 3-5), is used to a limited extent in the upper New England region on acidic soils, with frequent topdressing. Although not originally planted, the less desirable annual bluegrass (*Poa annua*) may invade and become a major portion of the putting green polystand if not controlled. Thus, it is sometimes a species to be considered when developing a cultural maintenance program.

Emergency Seeding. Use of a seed mixture of red or chewings fescue (*Festuca ruba*) at the high seeding rate of 20 to 25 pounds per thousand square feet (10 to 12 kilograms per are) in conjunction with use of the existing bentgrass cultivar at 0.5 to 1 pound per thousand square feet (0.25 to 0.5 kilogram per are) is effective in emergency seeding of damaged areas on seeded bentgrass greens when sod is not available or disruption of the surface cannot be tolerated. The fine-leafed fescues are effective temporary grasses because of their quick establishment rate, tolerance to close mowing, and minimal aggressiveness, which allow the creeping bentgrass eventually to become dominant. A seeded bermudagrass cultivar is not available for putting green use.

Table 3-5. Characteristics of Sixteen Cultivars Used on Putting Greens in North America

Cultivar	Establishment Method	Description	Adaptation	Pests	Other Comments
Creeping Bentgrasses					
Arlington (C-1)	Stolonize	Moderate olive-green color; fine texture; high shoot density; erect growth habit; tends to swirl; slow shoot growth rate; not aggressive; deep root system	Good tolerance to heat stress and wear; best adapted to droughty soils	Moderate resistance to dollar spot and *Helminthosporium* diseases; high susceptibility to brown patch	Slow establishment rate; medium intensity of culture required; good recuperative rate; frequently blended with Congressional
Cohansey (C-7)	Stolonize	Distinctive yellowish-green color; medium fine texture; medium high shoot density; erect shoots; medium aggressiveness	Good hardiness to heat and low-temperature stress; excellent tolerance to winter desiccation; good spring greenup rate	Moderate resistance to brown patch and *Helminthosporium* diseases; high susceptibility to dollar spot, copper spot, and *Typhula* blight	Good establishment rate; less prone to thatching; intermediate recuperative rate
Congressional (C-19)	Stolonize	Very dark-green color; very fine texture; very high shoot density; slow shoot growth rate	Good hardiness to heat and low-temperature stress; good low-temperature color retention and spring greenup rate	Good resistance to *Typhula* blight; moderate resistance to dollar spot; high susceptibility to brown patch	Less prone to thatching; intermediate recuperative rate; frequently blended with Arlington
C-52 (Old Orchard®)	Stolonize	Medium-green color; medium fine texture; medium high shoot density	Adapted to a wide range of soil types; intermediate heat tolerance; good spring greenup rate	Moderate resistance to dollar spot and brown patch; high susceptibility to copper spot	Medium intensity of culture required
Emerald (Smaragd)	Seed	Dark-green color; medium fine texture; high shoot density	Good low-temperature hardiness; poor wear tolerance	Good resistance to *Typhula* blight; high susceptibility to dollar spot	

Cultivar	Establishment Method	Description	Adaptation	Pests	Other Comments
Nimisilia	Stolonize	Moderate olive-green color; fine texture; high shoot density; rapid shoot growth rate	Good low-temperature color retention and spring greenup rate	Moderate susceptibility to dollar spot	Excellent establishment rate and recuperative potential
Penncross	Seed	Medium dark-green color; medium fine texture; high shoot density; vigorous shoot growth rate; less prone to segregation into mottled patches than other seeded types	Excellent wear tolerance; good hardiness to low temperature and heat stress; intermediate low-temperature color retention and spring greenup rate	Moderate resistance to dollar spot; susceptibility to stripe smut	Rapid establishment; good recuperative rate; prone to thatching at high nitrogen levels
Penneagle	Seed	Medium dark-green color; very high shoot density; moderately vigorous shoot growth rate; fairly upright shoot growth habit	Less prone to chlorosis than Penncross and Seaside	Good resistance to *Helminthosporium* leaf spot; moderate susceptibility to brown patch, *Fusarium* patch, and *Typhula* blight; high susceptibility to dollar spot	Medium nitrogen fertility requirement
Pennpar	Stolonize	Medium dark-green color; medium fine texture; high shoot density; intermediate shoot growth rate	Good wear tolerance	Good resistance to dollar spot, brown patch, and *Helminthosporium* diseases; susceptibility to *Typhula* blight	Good establishment rate and recuperative potential; medium high intensity of culture required

(Continued)

Table 3-5/Continued

Cultivar	Establishment Method	Description	Adaptation	Pests	Other Comments
Seaside	Seed	Medium light-green color; medium texture; medium shoot density; prone to segregation into mottled patches on putting greens	Excellent tolerance to winter desiccation and saline soils; intermediate low-temperature hardiness and wear tolerance; poor low-temperature color retention; good spring greenup rate	Moderate susceptibility to dollar spot; high susceptibility to brown patch, Fusarium patch, Helminthosporium leaf spot, and Typhula blight	Medium to low intensity of culture tolerated; good recuperative rate
Toronto (C-15)	Stolonize	Medium dark-green color; fine texture; high shoot density; vigorous shoot growth rate; shallow root system	Excellent low-temperature hardiness; good low-temperature color retention and spring greenup rate; fair wear tolerance; poor tolerance to winter desiccation	Moderate resistance to copper spot; high susceptibility to dollar spot, brown patch, red leaf spot, stripe smut, and bacterial wilt	High intensity of culture required; prone to thatching; poor recuperative rate
Washington (C-50)	Stolonize	Light-green color; medium fine texture; medium low shoot density; slow shoot growth rate	Good tolerance to heat stress; poor tolerance to winter desiccation; poor low-temperature color retention and spring greenup rate; turns purplish	Moderate resistance to brown patch; susceptibility to dollar spot, Fusarium patch, stripe smut, Typhula blight, and Helminthosporium diseases	Poor recuperative rate
Velvet Bentgrass					
Kingstown	Seed	Dark-green color; very fine texture; very fine shoot growth rate; soft leaf	Prefers acidic (pH 5-6), infertile soils; good shape adaptation and drought tolerance	Good resistance to dollar spot; susceptibility to copper spot; high susceptibility to brown patch	Slow establishment rate; poor recuperative potential; light, frequent topdressing needed; low nitrogen requirement

Bermudagrasses

Cultivar	Establishment Method	Description	Adaptation	Pests	Other Comments
Pee Dee	Stolonize	Dark-green color; medium fine texture; high shoot density; medium low growth habit	Poor low-temperature color retention, turns purple; good low-temperature hardiness		Minimal seedhead formation; high intensity of culture required; rapid establishment rate
Tifdwarf	Stolonize	Dark-green color; fine texture; high shoot density; slow growth rate	Poor low-temperature color retention, turns purple; late spring greenup; medium low-temperature hardiness; improved shade tolerance high susceptibility to smog injury	High susceptibility to sod webworm and spring dead spot; prone to invasion from off-type bermudagrasses and, in the fall, annual bluegrass	Minimal seedhead formation; medium high intensity of culture required; superior tolerance to close mowing; slow establishment rate
Tifgreen	Stolonize	Dark-green color; very fine texture; soft leaf blade; very high shoot density; low growth habit	Poor low-temperature color retention; good low-temperature hardiness and spring greenup rate; excellent drought and wear tolerance; prone to smog and 2, 4-D injury	Good resistance to *Helminthosporium* diseases and bermudagrass mite; susceptibility to armyworm, sod webworm, and scale insects	Minimal seedhead formation at high nitrogen levels; high intensity of culture required; good recuperative potential

NOTE: Comparisons (excellent, good, medium or intermediate, fair, poor, very poor) are made within each species only.

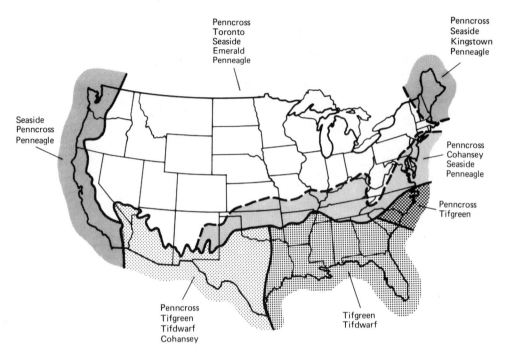

Figure 3-19. Geographic distribution of major bentgrass and bermudagrass cultivars used on putting greens in the United States.

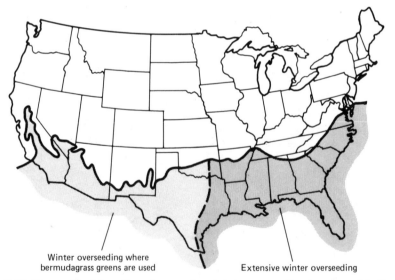

Figure 3-20. Geographic delineation of areas where winter overseeding is practiced in the United States.

Warm-Season Species

Bermudagrass (*Cynodon* spp.) is the warm-season turfgrass used most commonly on greens in the warm humid climatic regions, especially on compacted clay greens (Fig. 3-19). Bermudagrass putting greens have been viewed as inferior in quality to bentgrass greens. However, the development of improved grooming equipment and cultural techniques has narrowed the quality differential between the two species. Tifgreen has been the most widely used bermudagrass cultivar. Tifdwarf was utilized very extensively during the early 1970's in the southern half of the warm climatic region. However, an increasing problem with encroachment of off-type bermudagrasses into Tifdwarf has brought renewed interest in Tifgreen. Pee Dee is occasionally found on putting greens in the Carolinas.

The finer textured zoysiagrasses, such as *Zoysia matrella*, have been used, especially in Japan, on summer greens. The quality of zoysiagrass greens is inferior to that of bermudagrass greens because of the puffy nature of zoysiagrass.

Winter Overseeding of Bermudagrass Putting Greens

Winter overseeding of bermudagrass greens is practiced in the South where there is winter play (Fig. 3-20). The seed mixture selected should provide a minimum transition period while the bermudagrass is entering dormancy in the fall and during spring greenup. The overseeding mixture usually includes two to four species of the following cool-season turfgrasses: perennial ryegrass, red fescue, rough bluegrass, creeping bentgrass, Italian ryegrass, and certain low-growing Kentucky bluegrass cultivars (Table 3-6). The improved cultivars of perennial ryegrass, red or chewings fescue, and rough bluegrass are the species most widely used. Kentucky bluegrass has been used to a limited extent, primarily along the Gulf Coast and in Florida. The fine-leafed fescues make the strongest contribution under dry winter conditions. The mixture selected depends on climate, soil, and pest conditions.

Table 3-6. Eight Representative Winter
Overseeding Mixtures Utilized on Dormant Bermudagrass Putting Greens

Seed Mixture	Species Composition in Percentage by Weight				
	Perennial Ryegrass	Red and Chewings Fescues	Creeping Bentgrass	Rough Bluegrass (P. trivialis)	Kentucky Bluegrass
A	100*	. . . . .	. . . . .	. . . . .	. . . . .
B	65 - 85	15 - 35	. . . . .	. . . . .	. . . . .
C	55 - 75	10 - 25	3 - 5	. . . . .	. . . . .
D	35 - 55	20 - 35	3 - 5	5 - 15	. . . . .
E	30 - 50	. . . . .	5 - 10	20 - 35	15 - 30
F	80 - 90	. . . . .	. . . . .	10 - 20	. . . . .
G	. . . . .	30 - 50	5 - 10	30 - 50	. . . . .
H	. . . . .	45 - 65	5 - 10	15 - 30	15 - 30

*Blend.

ESTABLISHMENT

Golf course construction should be completed prior to the prime time for optimum turfgrass establishment. Since putting greens are irrigated, the main factor influencing optimum planting time is temperature. Cool-season turfgrasses germinate readily in the 60 to 85 °F (16 to 30 °C) range. In contrast, warm-season turfgrasses require temperatures of 70 to 95 °F (21 to 35 °C) for optimum seed germination with subsequent optimum growth temperatures in the 80 to 95 °F (27 to 35 °C) range. Thus, late spring-early summer is preferred for planting warm-season turfgrasses, while cool-season grasses are best planted in late summer-early fall. Exceptions are the northernmost areas, such as Canada and Alaska, and the higher elevations of the Rocky Mountains, which have a very short growing season. In these cases, late spring-early summer is the best planting time for cool-season turfgrasses. Proper timing of planting is critical to insure rapid, uniform turf establishment. Improper timing greatly increases the potential for development of numerous bare areas which subsequently erode and must be releveled and replanted.

Once the root zone mix has been placed on site according to the architect's specifications, representative soil samples from each putting green should be collected and submitted to a reputable soil testing laboratory for analysis. Results of testing provide the basis for decisions concerning pH adjustment and the quantities of phosphorus and potassium to be incorporated into the soil prior to planting. A special request may be made for the analysis of minor element content, salinity, sodium level, and/or boron content if a problem is anticipated. After these preparations are completed, the primary phases in putting green establishment are followed, as shown in Fig. 3-21. The same procedures are also followed for the collar.

Soil Reaction Adjustments

Major pH adjustments should be accomplished prior to planting. Materials should be incorporated into at least the upper 4 to 6 inches (10 to 15 centimeters) of the root zone. Calcium carbonate in the form of agricultural limestone is commonly used on acidic soils, a fine grade being preferred for rapid response. Dolomite limestone is utilized on acidic soils that also have a magnesium deficiency. Sulfur is usually incorporated into excessively alkaline soils. The amount of material incorporated is based on soil test recommendations. The amount should be the same for all putting greens, assuming the root zone mix is the same and has been properly mixed.

Major adjustments in soil reaction should be made well in advance of the planting date. The procedure involves incorporation into the root zone either after the root zone mix has been placed on the putting green site or at the time the root zone materials are being mixed. The latter approach insures more complete incorporation and pH adjustment throughout the entire depth of the root zone mix. A possible concern, however, is that a larger quantity of adjustment material is required.

Fertilization

Preplant incorporation of fertilizer into the putting green root zone is required in almost all situations. The specific rate of application and ratio of fertilizer incorporated should be based on soil test guidelines. Phosphorus (P) and potassium (K) are the two major plant nutrients whose application rates should be based on soil test results. Available fertilizer carriers are described in the appendix. There is no convenient, reliable test for soil nitrogen level. Nitrogen (N) is usually applied at a rate between 1.5 and 3 pounds of actual nitrogen per thousand square feet (0.73 to 1.5 kilograms per are). The higher rate is preferred, with 40 to 60 percent of the nitrogen being in a slow-release form. Selected minor elements may also be included in the complete (N-P-K) analysis fertilizer if deficiencies are indicated by soil tests or if previous experience indicates the need for a particular minor element. A minor nutrient deficiency is more likely on putting greens constructed of a root zone mix that is predominantly sand.

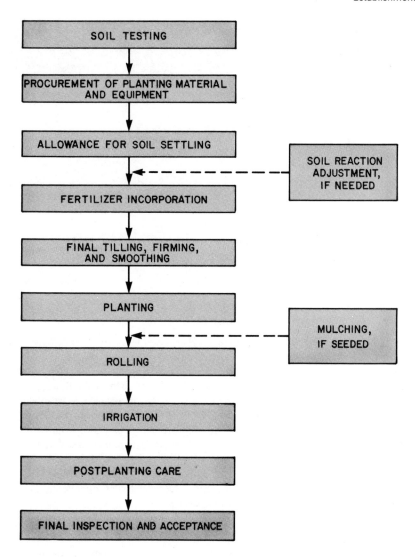

Figure 3-21. Flow diagram for planting putting greens and collars.

The fertilizer is usually applied just prior to planting by means of a gravity drop or centrifugal-type spreader. The fertilizer should be incorporated into the upper 3 to 4 inches (7.6 to 10 centimeters) of the soil root zone. Incorporation is accomplished with a low-velocity rotary tiller or with similar cultivation equipment that will mix the fertilizer to the desired depth in a uniform manner. In some instances, the fertilizer is incorporated throughout the soil root zone at the time the materials are being mixed.

Preplant Soil Preparation

Fumigation is usually advisable prior to final preplant soil preparation. The material most commonly used for fumigation is methyl bromide. Treatment requires about forty-eight hours, followed by

Figure 3-22. Final smoothing of a putting green surface prior to planting.

another forty-eight hours for aeration once the polyethylene cover is removed. Specific approaches to soil fumigation are covered in chapter 10.

Every effort should be made to insure that soil settling is as complete as is feasible before preplant soil preparation is initiated. Watering may be required at intervals to enhance settling. To achieve the desired degree of firming, especially on sandy root zones, the green may have to be rolled.

The surface root zone of the putting green should be lightly tilled just prior to planting to provide a moist, granular, clod-free plant bed. During final preplant soil preparation, a range of tools and techniques are used, including repeated hand raking and the dragging of large metal mats in a circular pattern (Fig. 3-22). Special care is needed to preserve the detailed contours of the green as designed by the architect. In addition, it is very important that the surface be as smooth as possible. Failure to take adequate time for smoothing operations can necessitate frequent heavy topdressing during the establishment phase and can even delay opening of the course.

Planting

The two primary methods of establishing putting greens on a new golf course are seeding and stolonizing. Either method can be used with bentgrasses, but bermudagrasses are planted solely by stolonizing. Suggested seeding and stolonizing rates for bentgrass and bermudagrass are shown in Table 3-7. There has been a general trend toward seeding of bentgrass greens, primarily because of the convenience and lower cost involved. It is imperative that certified bentgrass seed be specified in the purchase order. Sodding is usually restricted to situations where an individual green is being rebuilt and must be brought back into play as rapidly as possible. The sod used must have been grown on a root zone mix comparable to that utilized on the putting green.

Planting should not be initiated until the newly constructed root zone has settled into place. It is advisable for the final seedbed to be firmed by means of a powered roller. The most important concerns in execution of either seeding or vegetative planting are preservation of the surface contours and minimization of disruptions in surface smoothness.

Seeding. The traditional method of seeding involves application of seed by means of a gravity-drop spreader followed by shallow incorporation into the upper 0.25 inch (6.4 millimeters) (Fig. 3-23).

Table 3-7. Planting Rate Guidelines for Putting Greens

Turfgrass	Stolonizing Rate		Seeding Rate	
	bushels/1,000 sq. ft.	cu m/are (100 sq. m)	lb./1,000 sq. ft.	kg/are
Bentgrass	8 - 12*	0.26 - 0.4	0.5 - 1.0	0.25 - 0.5
Bermudagrass	12 - 16*	0.40 - 0.5	. . . .	. . . .

*Lower rates can be used if a longer establishment period is acceptable.

Figure 3-23. Seeding a putting green with a gravity drop spreader.

Immediately following seed incorporation, the soil should be firmed around the seed by means of a light roller. Every effort should be made by individuals walking across the surface to avoid making deep footprints in the soil surface. Complete, uniform seed coverage over the green is best insured by dividing the seed into two equal lots and applying each lot at one-half the rate in perpendicular directions.

An approach that avoids footprinting problems is the application of seed by means of a hydroseeder. Although hydroseeding does place the seed only on the surface, this usually creates no problems on putting greens, since irrigation water is available and can be applied as needed to maintain a moist surface during the establishment phase. Special care is needed to direct the hydroseeded material only onto the putting green and collar. It is preferable for the fertilizer to be incorporated into the soil prior to final surface smoothing rather than to be included in the hydroseeding tank mix. In contrast, a pulp fiber mulch is usually a desirable adjuvant when hydroseeding. It is critical for the surface to be kept constantly moist during the establishment phase and mulching helps to accomplish this.

Stolonizing. Vegetative stolonizing of greens with either creeping bentgrass or the improved bermudagrasses can also be accomplished by hydroplanting. As is the case with hydroseeding, hydroplanting offers the advantages of avoiding disruptions in surface smoothness and being a rapid method for planting of eighteen putting greens on a newly constructed golf course.

Figure 3-24. Steps in stolonizing a putting green: manually spreading stolons (*top*), and topdressing (*bottom*).

The traditional approach to stolonizing putting greens involves (a) manual distribution of stolons over the green, (b) pressing in of the stolons, (c) topdressing with material comparable to the original soil mix at a rate of 0.3 to 0.5 cubic yard (0.23 to 0.38 cubic meter) per thousand square feet, and (d) rolling with a light roller to provide good soil contact around the sprigs and to smooth the surface (Fig. 3-24). If considerable time is required for manual planting, the first planted portion of the green should be irrigated even while the remainder of the green is being planted. This approach insures the most rapid establishment. The placement of 4- by 8-foot (1.2- by 2.4-meter) plywood sheets across the green for workers to walk on minimizes footprinting during the planting activities.

Sodding. Sodding of an entire putting green usually is done only when an individual green is being rebuilt and must be brought back into play as rapidly as possible. A weed-free monostand of the desired cultivar should be selected for sod harvesting. It is imperative that the root zone of the sod be comparable to the root zone mix on the green to be sodded. Sodding of putting greens usually involves small 2-by-2-foot (.6-by-.6-meter) sod pieces laid flat (Fig. 3-25), in contrast to lawn sodding which involves rolled or folded 1- to 1.5-square yard (0.84- to 1.25-square meter) pieces. The sod should be harvested at a soil depth of less than 0.5 inch (1.3 centimeters).

The sod is carefully laid in place in a staggered or checkerboard pattern. Proper laying of sod on putting greens is an art requiring great patience and attention to detail to achieve a smooth surface in as short a time as possible. It is critical that the sod be handled gently to minimize stretching. Special care must be taken to insure that sod edges are butted tightly and neatly, without overlap. The use of 4-by-8-foot (1.2-by-2.4 meter) plywood boards around the area of sodding activity minimizes foot-printing problems.

Immediately following sodding, the area should be rolled and watered. In some cases this may mean initiation of watering on a portion of the green while the remainder is still being sodded. Light, spot topdressing may also be required immediately and at weekly intervals thereafter to achieve the desired smoothness. The topdressing material must be comparable to the underlying root zone.

Mulching

Mulching is advisable on almost all putting greens seeded to bentgrass. Mulching is one of the best insurance practices in achieving rapid, uniform turf establishment. It is especially important when seeding on droughty sand root zones. From 1.5 to 2 tons (1.4 to 1.8 metric tons) of weed-free straw per acre, preferably in combination with some type of asphalt binder, is an effective mulch. The straw usually can be applied by a mechanical mulch blower, which avoids additional footprinting on the putting greens. It may be appropriate to use a hand fork to selectively remove a portion of the straw mulch when the seedlings are approximately 0.5 inch (1.3 centimeters) high. This avoids excessive shading, which can impair further shoot growth. When hydroseeding, a pulp fiber mulch can be included in the tank mix. In this case, it is important to use a high application rate, preferably at the upper limit specified by the manufacturer.

Postplanting Care

Irrigation. Proper postplanting cultural practices are essential in achieving successful turfgrass establishment. The first priority is to irrigate immediately after planting, particularly in the case of stolonizing, to avoid the loss of plants by desiccation. Also, the quicker a seeding is irrigated, the faster seed germination will occur. The initial irrigation should be long enough to fully wet the root zone. Subsequent irrigations should be light and frequent to keep the surface moist. The goal is to maintain a moist surface during the first two to three weeks to insure successful establishment. This may mean irrigating one to two times daily if the area is properly mulched or as frequently as hourly on sand root zones without mulch and a high evaporative demand. Again it should be emphasized that irrigation is one of the most critical steps in achieving rapid, uniform turfgrass establishment.

Mowing. Postplanting mowing should be initiated when the young shoots are firmly rooted, which is at a height of 0.3 to 0.6 inch (7.6 to 15.2 millimeters). The preferred time for mowing is when the seedlings are dry, usually during midday. Clippings are not removed during these initial mowings. As a result, the severed elongated stolons fall to the soil surface and root, thus enhancing rapid establishment.

During the initial phases, mowing may be done three to four times weekly. This interval gradually shortens until daily mowing is required as the turf matures to the desired putting green quality. Catchers should be added to the mowers when a large enough quantity of clippings is being produced to create objectionable shading and an environment for disease activity.

A

Figure 3-25. Steps in sodding a newly constructed putting green. (Photos courtesy of E. Karcheski, Traverse City, Mich.)

A. Transport sod flat in as undisturbed a manner as possible.

B. Use a fork to lift, carry, and lay each piece of sod into place with minimum disruption of the sod.

C. Position each piece of sod manually to insure a tight, even fit on the edges.

B

C

Fertilizing. Postplanting fertilization requirements of putting greens vary greatly. The most extreme situation is on a very sandy root zone, where the first year's nitrogen requirement may be two to three times that of subsequent years. An initial fertilization at a rate of approximately 0.5 pound per thousand square feet (0.24 kilogram per are) should be made when the seedlings reach a 1-inch (2.5-centimeter) height. Subsequent fertilizations should be made at a rate of 0.2 to 0.6 pound of nitrogen per thousand square feet (0.1 to 0.3 kilogram per are) on a ten- to twenty-day interval, the more frequent rate being used on sandy root zones. Bermudagrass usually has a higher annual nitrogen requirement than does bentgrass. Each fertilization should be watered in immediately after application to avoid foliar burn. Individual fertilizations should alternate between use of a straight nitrogen carrier, possibly with a slow-release component, and use of a complete analysis fertilizer which may also include minor nutrients. This fertilization program should be continued until adequate turf establishment is achieved.

Weed Control. Owing to the very close mowing practiced on putting greens, a majority of weed problems are eliminated. The few broadleaf weeds, such as chickweed, clover, and henbit, that do persist can be controlled by careful use of mecoprop. Application of such phenoxy-type herbicides should be delayed at least six to eight weeks after seed germination. Annual weedy grasses, such as crabgrass, goosegrass, and certain sedges, can be controlled by repeat applications of an organic arsenical at seven- to fourteen-day intervals. However, the first application should not be initiated until at least six and preferably eight to ten weeks after seed germination. It is preferable to defer chemical weed control on bentgrass greens until the following spring.

Topdressing. Frequent topdressing during the establishment phase is critical in achieving a smooth putting green surface. The frequency required depends on the existing degree of surface smoothness. It is not uncommon for topdressing to be applied at weekly intervals during the first six to eight weeks of establishment. The initial topdressing rate may be as high as 0.3 cubic yard per thousand square feet, gradually being reduced to 0.1 cubic yard as the surface smoothness improves. The higher initial topdressing rate also functions as a covering for stolons, thereby enhancing rooting and tillering from the lateral stems. The material selected for topdressing must be the same as that used in construction of the underlying root zone. Topdressing is typically applied with a powered mechanical topdresser. Subsequently, the topdressing is worked in and smoothed over the surface by careful matting with a flexible steel drag mat.

Rolling. A postplanting cultural practice whose use varies greatly is rolling. The primary objective is to firm the soil, which aids in bringing moisture to the surface, especially on loose, droughty sand greens. Rolling also aids in firming the crowns and lateral stems into the soil. Rolling may be needed from one to four times, depending on the smoothness and firmness of the surface. It is usually accomplished with a powered mechanical roller. A limited degree of rolling is also achieved during the mowing process itself, particularly where a large cylinder greensmower is utilized.

Opening for Play. Traffic and play on newly planted putting greens should be withheld until a mature sod has been established. There is a distinct difference between a uniform, green cover of seedling grass and a mature dense sod formed through lateral stolon growth, tillering, and a deep root system. The last is necessary for the turf to survive the stresses imposed by traffic during play. Although seeding produces a green cover much quicker than does stolonizing, the time required to form a mature sod of acceptable putting green quality is usually not significantly different between the two. In the case of vegetative plantings, quicker establishment rates can be achieved simply by increasing the planting rate. Under optimum conditions, it is possible to establish a bermudagrass green in six weeks if a planting rate of 18 to 20 bushels (7.6 to 8.4 cubic meters) per thousand square feet is used. More typically, most seeded and stolonized greens require eight to ten weeks (bermudagrass) or ten to sixteen weeks (bentgrass). In contrast to its effect in vegetative plantings, increasing the seeding rate of bentgrass above the recommended range may delay successful establishment.

Finally, a sodded green can be opened for quality play within four weeks if growing conditions are optimum and sodding was done over a level, settled soil base.

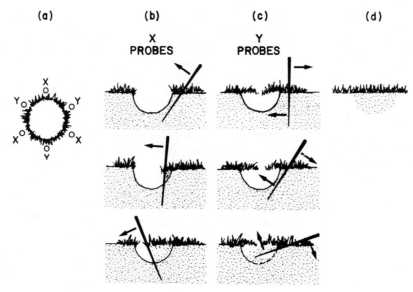

(a)   **(b)**   **(c)**   **(d)**

Figure 3-26. Procedure for repair of ball marks on putting green. (Concept by A. Radko, drawings by L. Record, United States Golf Association Green Section.)

(*a*)   *X*-marks indicate probe penetration to stretch turf over ball mark; *Y*-marks indicate probe penetration to loosen and raise soil.

(*b*)   Stretch turf by inserting sharp probe into soil at 45-degree angle 0.5 inch (1.27 centimeters) outside perimeter of ball mark and moving probe toward ball mark and down.

(*c*)   Loosen soil beneath ball mark by inserting probe vertically into soil 0.5 inch (1.27 centimeters) outside perimeter and pressing away from ball mark and down.

(*d*)   Firm turf with a putter, the palm of hand, or a shoe.

CULTURE

Mowing

The extremely close mowing required on greens is a costly cultural practice that also places severe physiological stress on the turf. Rooting depth, carbohydrate reserves, recuperative potential, and tolerance to environmental stresses are all adversely affected.

The green should be inspected for the presence of foreign objects prior to each mowing. Twigs, stones, acorns, metal and other hard objects must be picked up so that they don't become embedded in the green or stuck in the reel of the mower and nick the reel blade and/or bedknife. At the same time, the green can be checked for disease activity, insect damage, localized drying, wet spots, and leaf chlorosis. Any developing problems should be reported to the superintendent immediately.

Ball Mark Repair. Ball marks should be properly repaired prior to each mowing. Improperly repaired or neglected ball marks leave raised spots of turf in the green. These spots are scalped during mowing. The resulting unsightly bare marks remain for one to two weeks. Failure to repair deep ball marks can result in depressions and loss of surface smoothness.

The correct way to repair a ball mark is to stretch the turf back over the bruised area (without tearing it loose) and then to loosen the underlying soil so that the turf is able to root easily (Fig. 3-26). A pointed instrument is required to loosen the soil. The instrument must be sharp enough to penetrate the soil easily and strong enough to cut through soil laterally to a depth of 1 inch (2.5 centimeters) or less. A short, wooden-handled ice pick can be used. After the soil is loosened, the stretched turf must be firmed or pressed down to make contact with the soil; otherwise it may dry out or be scalped during mowing.

Figure 3-27. Twenty-one-inch walking greensmower (*top*) and three-gang riding greensmower (*bottom*) in operation on a putting green.

Mower Type. The use of eight- or nine-bladed reel-type mowers is necessary to maintain a uniform putting green surface of the desired quality. Two basic types of mowers are used: a walking greensmower with a 20- to 22-inch (50- to 56-centimeter) mowing width and a three-gang greensmower with a 58- to 62-inch (1.5- to 1.6-meter) mowing width (Fig. 3-27). The latter was developed to speed the mowing operation and substantially reduce labor costs. Its negative aspects are a potential increase in soil compaction, turfgrass wear, thatch, graininess, and hydraulic oil spills.

Mowing Frequency. Daily mowing is preferred to achieve the best playing conditions, especially during periods of active shoot growth. Less frequent mowing results in a green of somewhat reduced shoot density and coarser leaf texture. This causes unpredictable ball movements and a substantial reduction in the velocity of ball roll. Such a green is termed a slow green. Greens are preferably mowed in the early morning prior to initiation of play, since much leaf elongation is nocturnal. Omission of mowing one day in every seven results in improved overall turfgrass vigor on intensely played greens.

In some situations, greens are mowed twice daily, such as during the long midsummer days in the northern Canadian provinces and in Alaska. Leaf growth during a nineteen- to twenty-one-hour day necessitates twice-a-day mowing for maintenance of quality putting greens. *Double mowing,* or two mowings one immediately following the other, can be done prior to and during important tournaments to enhance the speed of rapidly growing greens turfs.

Mowing is sometimes omitted for at least one day after topdressing, cultivation, or fertilizing to allow time for extraneous materials on the surface to be worked into the turf by irrigation. An older greensmower is frequently retained for mowing greens after topdressing or cultivation in order to pick up surface debris. This also minimizes reel and bedknife damage to the regular mowing units from stones, coarse sand, and other abrasive materials.

Cutting Height. The preferred effective cutting height on greens is 0.19 ($\frac{3}{16}$) to 0.25 ($\frac{1}{4}$) inch (4.8 to 6.4 millimeters) but may vary from 0.12 ($\frac{1}{8}$) to 0.30 ($\frac{5}{16}$) inch (3 to 7.6 millimeters). The lower cutting height is preferred if proper shoot density can be maintained and the greens are not severely contoured.

Effective cutting height refers to the distance above the soil surface at which a turf is mowed. *Bench setting* is the height at which the bedknife is set above a hard, level surface. The effective cutting height may be significantly higher than the bench setting, sometimes by $\frac{1}{8}$ inch (3.2 millimeters). Also, some types of greensmowers may have different effective cutting heights even when adjusted to the same bench setting. A mower equipped with a new bedknife will cut higher than one with a worn bedknife when mowing at $\frac{3}{16}$ inch (4.8 millimeters) or less. Thus, three-gang riding mowers should be fitted with bedknives of approximately the same thickness or degree of wear. To achieve extremely close cutting heights for tournaments, a special thin bedknife can be purchased or the regular bedknives ground down to the desired thickness.

It is frequently advisable to temporarily raise the cutting height slightly ($\frac{1}{32}$ to $\frac{1}{16}$ inch) on bentgrass greens to minimize heat stress, scalping, and other problems associated with midsummer stress periods. Also, the cutting height should be raised $\frac{1}{16}$ to $\frac{1}{8}$ inch for a one- to two-week period before and after winter overseeding of bermudagrass greens.

Mowing Pattern. The operating direction normally is altered at each mowing in each of four directions to minimize the development of grain. This procedure can be described as round-the-clock in directions designated 12 to 6, 3 to 9, 4:30 to 10:30, and finally 1:30 to 7:30 o'clock. The cycle is repeated after the four directions are completed. This results in a distinctive checkerboard or striped pattern (Fig. 3-28). The mowing pattern made with a walking greensmower is much more striking than

Figure 3-28. A distinctive checkerboard striped pattern from proper mowing of a green with a walking greensmower.

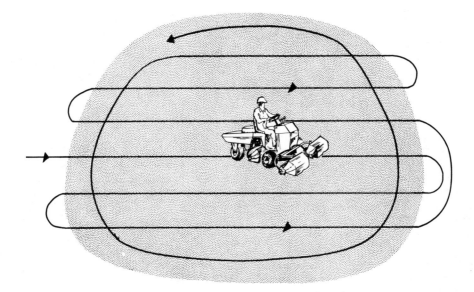

Figure 3-29. Preferred pattern of three-gang greensmower operation for a green.

that made with a three-gang riding greensmower. A consecutive ribbon pattern is suggested for each individual mowing (Fig. 3-29). It is attractive and minimizes compaction during turning on the surrounds.

Mower Operation. An experienced operator is careful to maintain a straight line of operation as well as minimum overlap. This is achieved through experience and concentration. It involves uniform pressure of both hands on the steering handles. The operator must avoid downward pressure when using a walking greensmower so as not to raise the cutting height. The operator of such a greensmower should adjust the speed of travel to avoid footprinting or making heel marks. (Heeled shoes or boots should never be worn while operating a walking greensmower.) Mowers should be carefully turned on the surrounds, never on the surface of a green or collar. Turns should be made in a wide arc rather than in a spinning action that can seriously bruise turf. The three-gang riding greensmower requires a much larger turning area than does the walking greensmower. A mower must not be stopped on a green with the cutting units operating, since serious bruising results.

Turfgrass wear and even thinning can be a problem around the perimeter of greens, especially those mowed with a three-gang greensmower. Periodically skipping the final outer-trim mowing can alleviate wear problems. Also, moving in or out one tire width (about 10 inches or 25 centimeters) each day reduces soil compaction from certain three-gang-mower wheel positions. Reducing the speed of three-gang riding greensmowers with rubber tires during the final outer trim mowing also aids in minimizing bruising of the turf.

Each mower should be checked frequently to prevent development of gas and oil leaks or grease accumulations that may drop on the turf and cause small dead spots. The operator must be constantly alert for hydraulic line leaks from three-gang riding units. In addition, the rollers must be kept clear of soil and clipping accumulations that can adversely influence mowing quality. When mowing of the green is finished, the flagstick should be placed back in the cup and the green checked for any problems or clipping accumulations. The latter is most likely to occur if mowing is done when the green is wet. Clipping accumulations can be dissipated with use of a whipping pole.

Clipping Removal. Clippings are caught in "baskets" attached to the mowing units and are then removed from the putting green. With certain walking greensmowers, these baskets must not be allowed to fill up, as their increasing weight causes a variance in mower performance, especially in cutting height. Grass clippings should be removed from the green surrounds every day after completion of the mowing operation. The operator who does the mowing usually empties the baskets of clippings into a carrier, such as a small truck or trailer, 55-gallon drum, tarp, or plastic bag, and removes them from the immediate area of the green after mowing. The clippings are used in composting or are scattered over a dump site. Clippings should not be piled or scattered in close proximity to the green, since they do not disperse well if wet and the resulting heavy clumps can smother a turf. If budget restrictions do not permit hauling of the clippings from a greens area, the operator should be trained to carry the clippings a substantial distance from the green into the secondary rough and to scatter them widely.

Turf Grain Control. Brush or comb attachments on greensmowers can be used as needed to correct or prevent a grain problem (Fig. 3-30). The Wiehle roller can also be used in some situations. A light vertical cutting at five- to ten-day intervals when the turf is growing vigorously is also effective in correcting a grainy condition on greens. This technique has been greatly facilitated by the development of vertical cutting attachments that can be interchanged with the mowing units on the three-gang greensmower. The comb or vertical cutter should be set to merely touch or slightly rough up the turf surface without gouging. Special care must be exercised not to gouge into slopes, terraces, or humps in greens. Frequent, light, cross-vertical cutting using a blade spacing of 0.25 inch (6.4 millimeters) can be used to alleviate an annual bluegrass seedhead problem on greens.

Scalping. Mower scalping usually indicates that puffiness and/or thatch problems exist or that the surface contours are excessively severe. Scalping caused by excessive thatch most commonly occurs during midsummer heat stress and after intense summer rains that cause swelling of the thatch and a resultant soft turf. If this condition is anticipated, the bench setting should be raised $\frac{1}{16}$ inch (1.6 millimeters) for several days or else mowing should be skipped for one or two days until the conditions favoring scalping dissipate. Scalping can also result from a drastic adjustment in the cutting height at any one mowing or a breakdown in the mechanical height-adjustment device or bearings on a mower (Fig. 3-31). Additionally, a mower will scalp if the bedknife blade is worn too thin.

Fertilization

The nutrient requirements of putting greens vary with the amount of water applied, soil nutrient holding capacity, climate, and turfgrass species/cultivar. Specific nutrient deficiency symptoms are

Figure 3-30. Attachments used on a greensmower for grain and mowing height control: (*left to right*), comb, brush, Delmonte rake, three-point roller, solid roller, Wiehle roller, and skids. (Photo courtesy of The Toro Company, Minneapolis, Minn.)

Figure 3-31. Serious mower scalping damage to a putting green collar.

described and illustrated in chapter 10, as is the chemical soil test procedure. No one fertilization program (type of carrier, application rate, and application time) or fertilizer covers all situations. The specific fertilizer program must be selected by the golf course superintendent based on an analysis of conditions on the golf course or even on individual greens. Criteria for selecting the most appropriate combination of fertilizer carriers, rates, and timings are discussed in this section. Characteristics of the common fertilizer carriers are presented in the appendix.

Time of Fertilization. A complete analysis (nitrogen-phosphorus-potassium) fertilizer is usually applied in the spring and in the late summer-early fall. The latter is generally preferred if only one complete analysis fertilizer application is made per year. Periodic supplemental nitrogen applications are made throughout the remainder of the growing season, as are applications of potassium and iron, based on need.

The interval between nitrogen applications depends on the carrier utilized, the application rate, the rate of nutrient leaching through the soil, and the turfgrass color/shoot growth rate desired. A reduced nitrogen fertility level should be maintained on bentgrass and annual bluegrass greens during periods of heat stress (midsummer) and of low-temperature hardening (midfall) in localities where low-temperature injury is a problem. Bermudagrass greens usually receive regular nitrogen fertilizations throughout the growing season except for the low-temperature hardening period just prior to winter dormancy and the spring root dieback period of two to three weeks just after shoot greenup.

Supplemental applications of iron and potassium may be required, especially during the summer on bentgrass and annual bluegrass greens. Iron chlorosis may also be a problem on bermudagrass greens, especially during spring greenup and root decline. Iron should be applied as needed to help maintain color and the chlorophyll synthesis capability, while potassium is applied prior to stress periods to improve the wear tolerance and hardiness to heat, cold, and drought.

Method of Application. A common method of greens fertilization is application of a dry carrier with a centrifugal spreader (Fig. 3-32) preferably in two directions at right angles to each other. The fertilizer, especially a water-soluble carrier, is usually applied to dry foliage and "watered in" immediately after application to avoid foliar burn.

Certain kinds of fertilizer particles may not fall through the turf to the soil due to very high leaf density on the greens. Fertilizer particles that remain on the leaf surface for a period of time have an increased probablity of causing foliar burn, especially if they are water soluble. Another potential problem is removal of particles during mowing if steps are not taken to insure fertilizer penetration into the turf by means of brushing and irrigation. Other preventive steps include (1) applying the fertilizer

Figure 3-32. Fertilization of a putting green using a centrifugal-type spreader.

just after mowing, (2) skipping of mowing the day after fertilizer application, (3) mowing without baskets, and/or (4) spiking the green prior to fertilizer application.

Water-soluble fertilizers can also be applied as a foliar feeding or a soil drench with use of a large-capacity sprayer or an irrigation-fertilization injection system. This procedure is termed fertigation. A small amount of fertilizer, especially iron, can also be included with pesticide spray applications, but in this case it is important to check the compatibility of the materials being mixed.

Nitrogen. Sufficient nitrogen must be applied to maintain turfgrass shoot density, adequate recuperative potential, moderate shoot growth rate, and, to a lesser extent, color. The nitrogen fertilization rate typically ranges from 3 to 6 pounds per thousand square feet (1.5 to 3 kilograms per are) per year on bentgrass and annual bluegrass greens and from 6 to 18 pounds per thousand square feet (3 to 8.8 kilograms per are) per year on bermudagrass greens. Bermudagrass requires a higher nitrogen level than do creeping bentgrass and annual bluegrass, while velvet bentgrass has a very low nitrogen requirement. Nitrogen rates as high as 8 pounds per thousand square feet may occasionally be required for Penncross creeping bentgrass growing on sand root zones. Minimal amounts or even no nitrogen should be applied to bentgrass and annual bluegrass greens during heat stress periods.

Nitrogen is generally applied at one- to three-week intervals during periods of normal shoot growth. The specific interval depends on the type of nitrogen carrier used, applications being more frequent with water-soluble carriers (ammonium sulfate, ammonium nitrate, and urea) and less frequent with slow-release carriers (natural organic, ureaformaldehyde, IBDU [isobutylidene diurea], methylurea, sulfur-coated, and other coated carriers). Water-soluble nitrogen carriers can be used in early spring on bentgrass-dominated greens to help increase its level in the turfgrass community.

Excessive nitrogen fertilization is frequently a greater problem on greens than is a nitrogen deficiency. The former leads to objectionable surface quality, thatch accumulation, increased disease problems, reduced tolerance to environmental stresses, decreased wear tolerance, a restricted root system, and lower recuperative potential caused by a lack of carbohydrate reserves. The best putting quality is achieved by low individual nitrogen application rates that avoid overstimulation of shoot growth. Nitrogen can always be added, but the immediate effects of excessive application cannot be counteracted.

A common rule of thumb for bentgrass greens during the summer months is to use the nitrogen fertilization rate at which one to two basketsful of grass clippings are removed per day on a green approximately 6,000 square feet (558 square meters) in area. Good results have been obtained on bentgrass and annual bluegrass greens using only 0.1 to 0.3 pound of nitrogen per thousand square feet (0.05 to 0.15 kilogram per are) per ten to fifteen growing days for a water-soluble carrier or 0.3 to 0.7

pound per thousand square feet (0.15 to 0.35 kilogram per are) per twenty to thirty growing days for a slow-release carrier. In the case of bermudagrass greens, 0.2 to 0.5 pound per thousand square feet (0.1 to 0.25 kilogram per are) per ten to fifteen growing days for water-soluble carriers or 0.5 to 1.2 pounds per thousand square feet (0.25 to 0.60 kilogram per are) per twenty to thirty growing days for slow-release carriers is effective. The upper portion of the nitrogen range commonly is used on coarse-textured (sand) root zones where leaching is a severe problem. Light, frequent nitrogen fertilizations are superior to monthly or occasional heavy applications.

Potassium. Potassium is prone to leaching through the soil, especially on sand root zones. It is quite important in maintaining heat, cold, drought, and wear tolerance as well as in enhancing root growth on greens. The potassium fertilization program is best determined by soil test results. As a general rule, the potassium requirement is approximately 50 to 75 percent that of nitrogen, although higher levels of potassium are sometimes desirable. Spring and late summer-early fall are the times when potassium applications are most commonly made. In some situations this schedule is adequate. Potassium can also be applied at twenty- to thirty-day intervals during heat, drought, and wear stress periods. Potassium chloride (58 to 62 percent K_2O) and potassium sulfate (48 to 53 percent K_2O) are the potassium carriers most commonly utilized. The latter is preferred because of a substantially lower foliar burn potential and the added contribution of sulfur.

Iron. Iron is the micronutrient most commonly deficient on greens, particularly where the pH, organic matter content, or phosphorus level is high. When iron chlorosis occurs, a foliar application of iron sulfate, chelated iron, or ferrous ammonium sulfate will correct the problem within one to two hours. Some complete analysis fertilizers contain iron. Chelated iron has some soil residual persistence. The iron carriers are commonly applied at a rate of 2 to 3 ounces per thousand square feet (60 to 90 grams per are) in a mixture with fungicide sprays at two- to four-week intervals. If severe iron deficiency exists, 3 to 6 ounces per thousand square feet (90 to 180 grams per are) of the iron carrier in 6 gallons (22.7 liters) of water may need to be applied when the leaves are dry. Higher rates can be used on bermudagrass than on bentgrass without foliar burn.

Phosphorus. Phosphorus is required in much smaller amounts on putting greens than are nitrogen and potassium. The phosphorus fertilization rate should be based on soil test results. This mineral usually is applied only one to two times per year, during spring and late summer-early fall, as one component of a complete fertilizer. It is sometimes questionable whether any phosphorus is required, particularly since visible growth responses are seldom observed.

High phosphate levels are quite common on older greens. It is important that excessively high phosphorus levels be avoided on high sand soils where a saturated phosphate level would result in downward leaching of phosphorus. Also, the phosphorus soil test can have misleadingly high readings on greens that have received arsenic applications for pest control, since the phosphorus and arsenic molecules are very similar both chemically and in size. Superphosphate (ordinary, 15 to 22 percent P_2O_5; treble, 37 to 53 percent P_2O_5) is the most commonly used phosphorus carrier if phosphorus is not applied in a complete fertilizer. Application of phosphorus fertilizers is preferable just after coring to achieve deep soil penetration of this relatively immobile nutrient.

Other Nutrients. Deficiencies of nitrogen, potassium, and iron are the most common nutrient deficiencies observed on putting greens. However, there are regional areas or localized soil types where deficiencies of other nutrients occasionally are observed. Of these, sulfur is probably the most common. It is required by grass in amounts comparable to those of potassium. In the past, adequate quantities of sulfur were applied in the commonly used complete analysis fertilizers in carriers such as ammonium sulfate (25 percent sulfur), superphosphate (11 percent sulfur), and potassium sulfate (17 percent sulfur) or was carried down in rainfall from atmospheric pollution in the form of sulfur dioxide. With the advent of high-analysis specialty fertilizers containing lower amounts of sulfur and the use of low-sulfur coal and petroleum fuels, sulfur deficiencies have developed in the Pacific Northwest, Florida, and Texas. A sulfur deficiency can be corrected by an application of elemental sulfur or of one of the three previously mentioned fertilizers which contain sulfur. Some complete fertilizers still contain sulfur, and it is listed as one of the components in the official analysis.

Calcium and magnesium are rarely deficient, although magnesium deficiencies do occur on the sandy soils of Florida. A deficiency of the former can be corrected by an application of agricultural limestone (32 percent calcium); of the latter by an application of dolomitic limestone (12 percent magnesium and 22 percent calcium). Other nutrients are occasionally deficient, for example, copper and manganese on bermudagrass growing on high pH, sandy greens in Florida and molybdenum and copper on high sand bentgrass greens in North Carolina. Micronutrient solutions are available that can be applied foliarly to correct these deficiencies. However, application of micronutrients on a regular basis is not advised unless an actual deficiency can be documented.

Soil Reaction Adjustments

The preferred pH range for optimum turfgrass growth and vigor is 6.0 to 7.0 for bermudagrass, 5.5 to 6.5 for bentgrass, and 6.2 to 7.2 for annual bluegrass. Adjustments are more likely to be needed on intensely irrigated, highly leached sand root zones or where irrigation water has a substantial alkaline effect. Major adjustments in soil reaction are best made prior to turfgrass establishment.

The materials used most commonly for raising the pH and for lowering it are agricultural limestone and sulfur, respectively. Dolomitic limestone can be used where magnesium deficiency exists. Continual decreases in pH can be caused by regular use of an acidifying fertilizer, such as ammonium sulfate. By the same token, acidifying fertilizers can be used effectively to lower the pH of alkaline soils. The reader is referred to *Turfgrass: Science and Culture* (by James B. Beard, 1973, Prentice-Hall, Inc., Englewood Cliffs, N.J.) for more detailed coverage.

Application is by means of a gravity drop or centrifugal-type spreader. The specific amount of material needed is dictated by soil test results. Agricultural limestone can be applied at rates up to 25 pounds per thousand square feet (12.2 kilograms per are) per application, while sulfur materials should not exceed 5 pounds per thousand square feet (2.4 kilograms per are) per application. The preferred time for applying pH adjustment materials is during the winter dormancy period. They should be watered in immediately if potential for foliar burn exists.

Irrigation

Irrigation is one of the most critical and difficult cultural practices in greens maintenance. Each green should be irrigated in accordance with its specific needs as affected by topography, exposure, soil texture, turfgrass species, intensity of traffic, rooting depth, and evapotranspiration rate. The sprinkler irrigation system used on putting greens is usually a permanent, underground, remote-controlled, perimeter rotary pop-up type (Fig. 3-33). The system should be designed to cover the collar and adjacent banks as well as the green to prevent lateral internal soil drought from the sides of exposed slopes and mounds.

Irrigation Frequency. Deep infrequent irrigation is preferred, insofar as is possible. However, the extremely close cutting height used on greens causes a substantial reduction in the depth and extent of the root system. The resulting limited water absorption capability necessitates an increased irrigation frequency. Light daily irrigation of greens may be necessary, particularly during midsummer on compacted fine-textured soils, very high sand content root zones combined with a shallow root system, or turfs composed primarily of annual bluegrass.

Irrigation Timing. Most deep intensive irrigation of greens is accomplished during the night. Soils with a very high water content are particularly prone to compaction, ball marks, heel marks, and disease. It is important to schedule deep irrigations well in advance of periods when intense traffic is anticipated so the excess water in the upper soil has an opportunity to drain downward. Similarly, programming intense greens irrigation early in the night allows more time for dissipation of excess surface water. A light irrigation at dawn is desirable in that it also functions in dew and exudate removal. This results in a less favorable environment for fungi activity and better playing conditions during the early morning hours.

Figure 3-33. Typical perimeter rotary pop-up sprinkler irrigation system in operation on a putting green.

Water Application Rate. Water application should be uniform over the green and collar to avoid wet or dry spots. The rate should be adjusted in relation to soil infiltration and percolation rates. Adjustment is made primarily through sprinkler head nozzle selection on greens where the irrigation system is already installed. The water use rate is normally in the range of 1 to 2 inches (2.5 to 5 centimeters) per week (0.14 to 0.30 inch per day), depending on local climatic conditions, turfgrass species/cultivar, cultural practices, soil type, water retention characteristics of the soil, infiltration rate, and available moisture. Greens with a high sand root zone are prone to hydrophobic soil problems, a condition best alleviated by application of an effective wetting agent.

Hand Watering. Hand watering of localized dry spots is sometimes necessary, particularly on high spots and along the edges of greens. A rose-type nozzle usually is used. The most effective correction for localized dry spots is use of intensive hand watering in conjunction with deep cultivation (hand forking or coring) and/or use of an effective wetting agent. Only a few of the available wetting agents are effective in correcting localized dry spots caused by a hydrophobic or water-repellent soil condition.

Syringing. Rooting of bentgrass and annual bluegrass frequently declines during midsummer heat stress periods at soil temperatures above 75 °F (24 °C). This impairs water absorption capability and results in an increased likelihood of midday wilting during periods of rapid transpiration caused by full sunlight, high temperatures, low relative humidity, and windy conditions. Death of the turf is likely if water is not applied immediately when visible wilt symptoms occur. Syringing should not be used routinely at midday but only as needed to correct wilting or alleviate midday heat stress. Syringing for the purpose of cooling is usually accomplished between 11 A.M. and 2 P.M., provided the atmospheric humidity is low enough to facilitate evaporation. Earlier times are preferred for maximum cooling effect. However, syringing to correct wilt must be done whenever water stress symptoms occur. Under severe conditions, syringing may be needed from two to four times a day within the 10 A.M. to 5 P.M. stress period. The amount of water required during syringing is only enough to wet the turf foliage and not the soil. Syringing can be done manually or with a remote-controlled rotary pop-up system having a syringe cycle control. The manual method is preferred for selective watering of localized dry spots, since water can be placed where it is needed without adjacent areas becoming overwatered.

Topdressing

Topdressing is the most effective practice available for biologically controlling thatch on greens. In addition, topdressing is used to correct irregularities in surface smoothness; provide a firm, tight, fine-textured turf; and control grain formation. It is somewhat expensive but well worth the investment in achieving a high-quality putting green surface. Proper topdressing requires long-term planning of up to one year in advance.

There are two basic approaches regarding the frequency of topdressing. One is to topdress only as needed to correct surface irregularities or a developing thatch problem. With this approach, cool-season turfgrasses usually are topdressed in the spring and/or fall, while bermudagrass greens may be top-dressed at six- to eight-week intervals during the summer period of rapid shoot growth and low traffic intensity. A second approach is to topdress frequently, such as biweekly or monthly, at light application rates. Topdressing of bentgrass and annual bluegrass greens during periods of heat stress can cause problems, especially when the application rate is high.

Light rates of topdressing are preferred for quality greens. The maximum rate for established creeping bentgrass and annual bluegrass greens is 0.3 cubic yard per thousand square feet with rates of 0.1 cubic yard per thousand square feet on greens topdressed monthly (Table 3-8). Established bermudagrass greens with a thatch problem are topdressed at a rate of 0.2 to 0.4 cubic yard per thousand square feet. Quality greens with minimal thatch may be topdressed at 0.05 to 0.10 cubic yard per thousand square feet. Tifgreen bermudagrass requires either a higher topdressing rate or more frequent topdressing than does Tifdwarf bermudagrass. Topdressing is normally applied with a powered mechanical topdresser and is then matted and/or brushed into the turf (Fig. 3-34).

Topdressing Soil Preparation. The topdressing material should be of a texture and consistency comparable to the existing underlying soil, assuming this root zone has good physical characteristics. Layering of soils of distinctly different textures should be avoided because movement of water and air through the soil is disrupted. The soil mix should be prepared well in advance of application. Selection of the sand, soil, and organic components is critical to insure that the soil mix is comparable to that used in construction of the green. The assistance of a soil physical testing laboratory to determine the proper mixing percentages can be of great value. On finer-textured problem soils, long-term use of a coarse-textured sandy soil mix may be beneficial.

Table 3-8. Depth of Soil Resulting from Different Rates of Topdressing

Topdressing Rate		Resulting Topdressing Depth	
cu. yd./1,000 sq. ft.	cu m/are (1,000 sq. ft.)	in.	mm
0.05	0.035	0.015	0.4
0.1	0.07	0.03	0.8
0.2	0.14	0.07	1.6
0.3	0.21	0.09	2.4
0.4	0.28	0.13	3.3
0.6	0.42	0.19	4.9
0.8	0.57	0.26	6.6
1.0	0.71	0.32	8.2

Figure 3-34. Equipment for mixing topdressing (*top*). A powered, mechanical topdresser being loaded (*center left*). Application of topdressing to a green (*center right*). Working in of the topdressing with a drag mat (*bottom*).

The dry soil mix should be passed through a shredder, screened to remove stones and other objects, and thoroughly mixed (Fig. 3-34). Subsequently, the soil mix may require fumigation, for instance with methyl bromide, to kill undesirable weed seeds, vegetative propagules, insects, nematodes, and disease-causing pathogens. The final step in topdressing preparation, which unfortunately is not commonly practiced, is composting for eight to ten months to regenerate the soil flora and fauna.

The composted topdressing soil mix should be stored in a well-ventilated soil shed. This insures that it is sufficiently dry at the time of application (uniform application with a mechanical topdresser requires dry soil). Sufficient topdressing should be on hand at any one time to topdress all greens and tees at a rate of 0.4 cubic yard per thousand square feet.

Thatch Control

Thatch accumulation is a common problem on greens, since the turfgrass species used are particularly prone to this problem. Thatching tends to be more severe with bermudagrass than with bentgrass. A limited mat accumulation is beneficial if it does not exceed 0.3 inch (7.6 millimeters). Mat involves thatch that has been intermixed with soil as a result of topdressing. A modest mat provides resiliency, improved wear tolerance, and less proneness to soil compaction. However, an excessive amount of thatch and/or mat accumulation can lead to increased disease and insect activity, potential hydrophobic restrictions in water penetration, increased puffiness, footprinting, slower putting, and proneness to mower scalping.

There are both preventive and corrective measures for thatch. From a preventive standpoint, avoidance of excessive nitrogen fertilization, which forces shoot growth, is an important consideration. Light, vertical cutting at a one- to two-week interval can also be effective. From a corrective standpoint, any practice that enhances the rate of biological degradation is beneficial. The most effective of these is topdressing.

Other cultural practices that contribute to thatch control include (a) light, frequent applications of lime under acidic conditions, (b) turf cultivation by coring, with the soil cores then broken up and worked back into the soil by matting, (c) light, frequent vertical cutting, (d) frequent, close mowing, and (e) light, frequent nitrogen applications. Light applications of hydrated lime at 2 to 3 pounds per thousand square feet (1 to 1.5 kilograms per are) two or three times annually aid in thatch decomposition. Frequent, light vertical cutting is particularly important in thatch control on bermudagrass greens. A typical schedule during periods of rapid shoot growth is once or twice weekly. A suggested setting for the vertical cutting blades is ⅟₃₂ to ⅛ inch (0.8 to 3.2 millimeters) below the current effective mowing height and at a 0.50- to 0.75-inch (1.3- to 1.9-centimeter) spacing. Under certain problem conditions, two passes in perpendicular directions are advisable.

Removal of Excessive Thatch. A serious thatch problem (more than 1 inch, or 2.5 centimeters) is quite difficult to correct. Deep vertical cutting or grooving can be practiced, but either approach results in severe disruption of play for an extended period of time. If extensive vertical cutting or grooving for thatch removal is required, it should be done when play is minimal and when subsequent environmental conditions favor rapid growth and recuperation. Also, the turf should be well rooted at the time, as otherwise portions of the sod may be lifted out. The vertical blades should be set deep enough to just barely touch the soil. The spacing between blades should be 1.5 inches (3.8 centimeters), in contrast to the 0.75-inch (1.9-centimeter) spacing used in preventive thatch and grain control (Fig. 3-35). An extensive, deep vertical cutting should be followed by topdressing.

An alternate approach is stripping of the entire sod plus thatch from the green using a mechanical sod cutter, followed by the appropriate soil preparation, leveling, and seeding or sodding. The nursery sod must be grown on a root zone mix comparable to the soil texture existing on the green. This approach is usually preferred for thatch 1.5 inches (3.8 centimeters) or more thick.

Figure 3-35. Powered walking vertical cutter being used for deep cutting of excess grass from a green (*top*) and the resulting appearance (*bottom*).

Soil Modification

Intense traffic on greens can result in a severe soil compaction problem. Soil modification is frequently practiced to achieve a soil texture having good internal water drainage and minimum compaction tendency. This usually means amending with sand or similar material and sacrificing a substantial amount of nutrient and water retention capacity. The resiliency factor should also be considered when selecting soil amendments for putting greens. Complete soil modification is generally preferred using one of the methods outlined early in this chapter.

Drainage

Rapid removal of excess water from the soil surface minimizes soil compaction and contributes to favorable playing conditions on greens. Also, shallow standing water in depressions can result in scald. Proper surface contours, soil modification to insure adequate percolation rates, and a subsurface drainage system can be utilized to achieve rapid removal of excess water. Details concerning drainage techniques on greens were covered in the construction section of this chapter.

Correcting Compaction

Soil compaction can be a severe problem resulting in restricted root growth, lack of water infiltration into the soil, and loss of resiliency. Symptoms of a compaction problem include (a) lack of rooting, (b) increased difficulty in pushing the hole cutter into the soil, (c) thinning of the turf, and/or (d) reduced rate of water infiltration into the soil as evidenced by puddling occurring earlier than usual in the irrigation cycle.

The best approach to compaction problems is prevention. Prevention involves construction with a sand root zone mix that has low compaction proneness and proper contouring for good surface drainage.

Compaction frequently becomes a problem on greens constructed with fine-textured soils. Corrective measures in this case involve turf cultivation. Turf cultivation results in improved turfgrass quality and vigor due to enhanced movement of water and air into the soil. However, it also disrupts the smoothness of the putting green surface and is controversial among golfers. Nevertheless, it is a necessary practice in certain situations. An important consideration is to inform all golfers about the scheduled date(s) of greens cultivation well in advance so that those who find this practice objectionable can arrange their golfing activities around this cultivation period.

Turf cultivation is utilized as required to (a) correct a compacted soil condition, (b) assist in controlling thatch, and/or (c) alleviate soil layering problems. Correcting compaction is the most significant aspect of turf cultivation in terms of effectiveness. Alternative approaches available for thatch control are discussed in an earlier section of this chapter.

Cultivation is generally practiced in the spring and/or fall, although it may be necessary monthly on certain fine-textured soils subjected to intense traffic. Late-spring cultivation may be needed to correct compaction that occurs due to winter-early spring play when the soil is quite wet. Spring or early summer cultivation is preferred to fall cultivation from the standpoint of minimizing annual bluegrass invasion, since seed germination is greatest in the fall. Late fall coring of dormant turfs should be avoided in regions where winter desiccation of greens is a potential problem.

Coring. Deep cultivation of greens to a depth of 3 to 4 inches (7.6 to 10 centimeters) can be accomplished by coring. The vertically operated, hollow tine-type unit is used for coring to minimize surface disruptions (Fig. 3-36). The diameter of coring tines used on greens ranges from 0.25 to 0.63 (¼ to ⅝) inch (6.4 to 16.0 millimeters), depending on the time of year and reason for coring. The larger tines usually are used on compacted problem greens and prior to topdressing. The 0.25- (¼-) inch (6.4-millimeter) tine is preferred for warm-weather coring to minimize surface disruption of the green during periods of intense use and to reduce water loss from the green.

Soil cores left on the surface after coring can be removed by using a catcher or sweeper or can be broken up by using a vertical cutter and worked back into the surface by matting. If the soil is undesirable, the cores are usually removed and the green topdressed with an improved soil mix at a rate of 0.2 cubic yard per thousand square feet. A light topdressing of 0.2 cubic yard per thousand square feet may be required ten to twenty days after coring to fully smooth surface depressions resulting from soil settling in the coring holes.

Slicing. Slicing is used much less frequently than coring for deep cultivation of greens. The depth of penetration is comparable to that of coring, 3 to 4 inches (7.6 to 10 centimeters). However, no soil is brought to the surface to serve as topdressing. Surface disruptions from slicing are less than those from

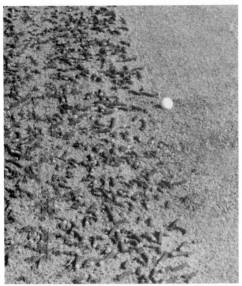

Figure 3-36. Greens cultivation: coring (*top*); soil cores lying on the surface (*center left*); breaking up the soil cores using a vertical cutter (*center right*), (photo courtesy of Jacobsen Division of Textron, Racine, Wis.); and matting the soil back into the surface (*bottom*).

Figure 3-37. Powered spiking of a putting green.

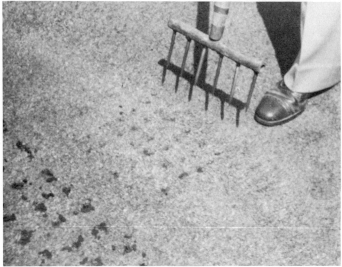

Figure 3-38. Manual forking of a dry spot on a putting green. (Photo courtesy of T. Mascaro, North Miami, Fla.)

coring. Nevertheless, a light topdressing is frequently required to achieve the desired surface smoothness. A rate of 0.1 to 0.2 cubic yard per thousand square feet is generally sufficient. The greens may have to be kept slightly more moist than normal until after the slicing openings have healed, especially if topdressing is not applied.

Spiking. Spiking (Fig. 3-37) can be practiced on greens for distinctly different reasons. One reason is a developing surface compaction problem in an area where intensity of play does not permit immediate coring or slicing. The effects of spiking are limited to a shallow surface soil zone of 0.5 to 1 inch (1.3 to 2.5 centimeters). It may partially alleviate surface crusting until coring or slicing can be accomplished. A second, more important benefit from spiking is the severing of rhizomes and stolons, which stimulates new shoot and root growth. When used primarily to sever lateral stems, spiking may be done as frequently as every seven to fourteen days. Finally, spiking can facilitate water penetration through a thatch, mat, and/or surface crust.

Forking. Localized dry spots are sometimes a problem. Hand forking (Fig. 3-38) to a depth of 6 to 8 inches (15 to 20 centimeters), followed by intensive spot watering, usually corrects the problem. Four- or five-tined forks are preferred. Application of an effective wetting agent and immediate drenching can follow hand forking if the dry spots are caused by a hydrophobic soil condition.

Shoot and Root Rejuvenation

There are times when stimulation of new root and shoot systems is desirable. A typical example is during slowed growth of bentgrass shoots and roots during a midsummer heat stress period. A prerequisite for new root and shoot generation is an adequate carbohydrate reserve. This is maintained primarily by avoiding excessive nitrogen fertilization and using cultural practices that insure a healthy turfgrass plant. Assuming that these preconditions are met, any practice that severs lateral stems will stimulate new shoot and root growth from nodes located nearest the point where the internode was severed. Thus, cultivation practices such as coring, slicing, spiking, and forking all stimulate new shoot and root growth. Among these, spiking is the most desirable because of a high perforation density and minimal surface disruption. In some cases, spiking is practiced in multiple directions and at intervals of one to two weeks.

Smoothing

Surface irregularities on putting greens result from ball marks; foot depressions during wet soil conditions; improper cup-changing techniques; insect and small-animal activity; vandalism; and cultivation, especially coring. Topdressing, discussed earlier in this chapter, is the common method for correcting these problems, along with hand repair work when needed.

Rolling. At one time in the early history of putting green culture, rolling was commonly practiced. However, the practice of rolling has fallen into disfavor because of the potential for compaction from the heavy rollers and because a limited degree of rolling is achieved with powered greensmowers.

Nevertheless, proper rolling can be used to advantage on putting greens under certain circumstances. Use of a water ballast roller to apply no more weight than is needed minimizes the potential for compaction. On properly constructed sand root zones, rolling can be done with minimum concern for compaction problems. Rolling may be used as a finishing technique to insure maximum surface smoothness for trueness of ball roll and to increase the speed of ball roll. Both effects can be important in a major tournament or championship.

Another circumstance in which rolling can be beneficial is in early spring prior to the first mowing when frost heaving has occurred. Rolling functions to push the sod, including grass crowns, back into proper contact with the soil as well as to level the surface to avoid scalping during the first mowing. Rolling may also be useful for leveling after sodding, to provide good contact between the sod interface and the underlying soil, and during seedling establishment.

Leaf and Debris Removal

Removal of fallen tree leaves, branches, and other debris is necessary during periods of active golf play. The practice is most needed in early spring following winter dormancy and in the autumn, especially if deciduous trees are nearby. Small amounts of leaves can be picked up during the regular mowing operation, since a grass catcher is used on the greensmower. Specific equipment can be used when larger accumulations occur. Examples of commonly used power equipment include vacuums, sweepers, and blowers (Fig. 3-39). Bags or similar collection devices are available in a range of sizes for most of these units.

Winter Overseeding

The use of cool-season turfgrasses in winter overseeding of bermudagrass greens is a common practice in the southern portion of North America. Specific characteristics of the cool-season turfgrass

Figure 3-39. Leaf blower being used to remove fallen leaves from a putting green.

species used for this purpose have been discussed in the turfgrass selection section of this chapter. It is important for the seed to be selected, purchased, and delivered well in advance of the projected date when overseeding is to be initiated. This allows flexibility in the seeding date depending on weather conditions. In the interim, all seed should be stored in a cool, dry location protected from rodent damage. A significant reduction in germination percentage can occur if seed is held under warm, humid conditions for an extended period of time.

Cultural Practices Before Overseeding. A properly maintained, healthy bermudagrass turf is in the best possible condition to survive the winter dormancy period and the spring transition in acceptable shape. In this regard, it is important to control excessive thatch accumulation by vertical cutting and/or topdressing, as needed, and to correct developing soil compaction problems by cultivation, usually coring. These cultural practices should be accomplished at least four to six weeks prior to overseeding so the bermudagrass has an opportunity to recover prior to entering winter dormancy. Fall fertilization should also be completed by this time.

Winter Overseeding Practices. The best timing for winter overseeding varies considerably from location to location and is based on experience gained over a number of years. The objective is for the overseeding to be done late enough in the fall so that bermudagrass growth has been slowed by low temperatures but early enough so that temperatures are favorable for germination of the overseeded cool-season turfgrasses. The former is important in minimizing excessive bermudagrass competition with the overseeded cool-season turfgrass seedlings. The goal is a uniform surface transition with no adverse effects on ball roll. The techniques used in winter overseeding have changed considerably over the past ten years, as have the turfgrass cultivars used. The basic steps in winter overseeding include:

1. Vertical cutting in several directions
2. Removal of loose debris
3. Application of a fungicide, if needed
4. Uniform seed application at the proper rate
5. Matting of the seed with a heavy rug
6. Topdressing lightly
7. Irrigation frequently as needed to maintain a moist seedbed during germination

Vertical cutting, usually with the appropriate reels in a three-gang riding greensmower, is done in several directions in a crossing pattern. The objective is to open the bermudagrass turf so the seed can fall into the turf canopy and near the soil surface where conditions are more favorable for seed germination and the chance of lateral seed movement by wind and water erosion is minimized. Vertical cutting is followed immediately by use of a separate unit, typically an older three-gang riding greens-mower with catchers, to remove the loose plant debris produced by the vertical cutting. If extensive vertical cutting is required, the greens were not properly maintained during the summer. Vertical cutting is usually scheduled approximately one week ahead of overseeding. Raising the cutting height ¼ to ⁵⁄₁₆ inch (6 to 8 millimeters) approximately one week prior to the scheduled seeding aids in reducing lateral movement of seed.

The final step prior to seeding is the application of a fungicide such as captan, for control of seedling diseases caused by organisms such as *Pythium* and *Rhizoctonia*. Some superintendents prefer to prevent seedling disease problems by purchasing seed that has been treated with the appropriate fungicide.

The actual seeding operation is best accomplished when wind activity is minimal. The normal plan is to overseed over a two-day period with the objective of completing nine holes each day, including matting and topdressing. This allows half of the golf course to remain in play throughout the over-seeding phase. Two or more properly calibrated centrifugal- or gravity-type seeders are utilized with half the seed applied in one direction and the second half in a direction perpendicular to the first to insure uniform coverage (Fig. 3-40). Typical seeding rates for putting greens (on a thousand square foot or are basis) are 30 to 40 pounds (15 to 19 kilograms) for perennial ryegrass, 35 to 50 pounds (17 to 25 kilograms) for Italian ryegrass, 24 to 30 pounds (12 to 15 kilograms) for fine-leafed fescues, 8 to 12 pounds (4 to 6 kilograms) for bluegrasses, and 3 to 5 pounds (1.7 to 2.5 kilograms) for bentgrasses. Seed mixtures containing two or more of these species are frequently used, with the seeding rate adjusted in proportion to the components comprising the mixture.

Immediately following seeding, the area should be matted to work the seed into the turf. The best technique is to pull a dense carpeting material over the turf. Sometimes a steel drag mat is tied on top if the carpeting is not sufficiently weighted. Movement of the mat in a zigzag pattern aids in working the seed into optimum contact with the soil. The seeding and matting operations should be limited to the putting green surface to avoid introducing seed onto the collar.

Topdressing has been a standard practice in the winter overseeding of greens for many years. The rate of soil application has decreased substantially and in some cases successful establishment is now being achieved without topdressing. The rate of topdressing normally ranges from 0.3 to 0.5 cubic yard per thousand square feet. It is important to utilize a soil mix comparable to the underlying root zone, unless the base is an impermeable soil high in clay. Following topdressing, the area should again be matted to work the topdressing material into the surface.

On completion of the seeding, matting, and topdressing operations, the greens should be irrigated immediately with a gentle shower of water to prevent lateral movement of seed off the greens. Many superintendents prefer to do this initial irrigation manually to insure proper surface wetting with minimal lateral seed movement. Note that fertilization is not practiced at the time of overseeding, since it stimulates excessive bermudagrass competition.

Cultural Practices After Overseeding. The seedbed must be kept moist during germination and initial seedling establishment. This is the most critical step in overseeding. One or more light midday applications of water are usually needed. Although an adequate moisture level is important, overwa-tering can encourage seedling diseases. The superintendent must be constantly alert for the develop-ment of seedling disease problems and prepared to make the appropriate fungicide application. Disease problems are most likely to occur during periods of high humidity and on compacted, poorly drained greens.

The cutting height during this initial establishment period is typically maintained at 0.3 inch (7.6 millimeters) and certainly no less than 0.25 inch (6.4 millimeters) until after the seedlings are fully

Figure 3-40. Winter overseeding of a bermudagrass green: seeding (*top*), topdressing (*center*), and matting (*bottom*). (Photos courtesy of Alan D. Hess, Texas A&M University, College Station, Tex.)

established. This can be as long as two weeks, or until the seedlings begin tillering. The first few mowings are accomplished without a grass catcher to avoid removal of seeds lying on the surface. Potential seedling injury is minimized if mowing is scheduled when the overseeded green is dry, such as just before midday watering. Also, it is important that the mower be especially sharp and properly adjusted during the initial mowings.

The initial fertilization following overseeding should be withheld until the seedlings are well established, usually sometime between the second and third week, depending on how quickly the bermudagrass enters dormancy. Subsequently, fertilization is continued at a two- to four-week interval at rates of 0.7 to 1 pound per thousand square feet (0.35 to 0.50 kilograms per are). All fertilizer should be watered in immediately after application.

One final question concerns the policy of allowing play during the establishment phase of overseeding. There is no doubt that traffic damages developing seedlings. The main issue is how severe the traffic stress will be. Overseeding is usually done on consecutive days on alternate nines. Some prefer to keep the course closed for two to three days following overseeding, especially when done on impermeable, high clay soils and where a very high topdressing rate is used. Others allow play to continue immediately after the overseeding procedure is completed. In this case, the course is never completely closed, since at least one nine is open on each of the two days when overseeding is being accomplished. Whether play can be allowed during this establishment period following overseeding depends on the anticipated intensity of play and the drainage characteristics of the greens involved. If play is allowed immediately after overseeding, it is critical that the cups be moved on a daily basis to distribute the stress of traffic as uniformly as possible.

Spring Transition. A successful winter overseeding program culminates with proper spring transition. This means a uniform putting surface maintained by gradual decline and loss of the winter overseeded grasses coordinated with spring greenup and shoot growth initiation of bermudagrass. Some of the improved turf-type perennial ryegrasses which perform so well during the fall overseeding establishment and winter playing season tend to persist too long into the spring and early summer. A result of this spring competition has been impairment in bermudagrass survival and in some cases a substantial stand loss. The approach most commonly used to minimize this spring transition problem is a series of light vertical cuttings while the ryegrasses are still actively growing. These vertical cuttings are best timed prior to initiation of spring greenup of bermudagrass so as not to aggravate problems with spring root decline of the bermudagrass.

Pests

Pest problems encompass weeds, diseases, insects, nematodes, and animals. A detailed discussion of problem recognition, causal diagnosis, cultural practices affecting severity of the problem, and chemical controls is found in chapter 10. The information in this section is a summary of potential pest problems unique to putting greens and of related cultural and chemical practices that have specific application.

Weeds. The extremely close mowing practiced on putting greens provides control for a wide range of large, erect-growing weedy species and restricts the potentially serious weeds to those shown in Table 3-9. Most persistent, prostrate-growing broadleaf weeds occurring on established greens can be controlled with use of selective herbicides. One caution in this regard is the high potential phytotoxicity of phenoxy-type herbicides. Mecoprop (2-MCPP) is the preferred herbicide for use on most broadleaf weeds for this reason. Dicamba may be used in combination with mecoprop where there is no annual bluegrass and no chance of damage to adjacent trees due to dicamba absorption by tree roots that extend under a green.

Goosegrass and nutsedge are serious problems on both bentgrass and bermudagrass greens. Acceptable selective controls have not been available in the past. However, several promising herbicides are in

Table 3-9. Weed Problems on
Established Bentgrass and Bermudagrass Putting Greens

Relative Weed Problem	Bentgrass Greens	Bermudagrass Greens
Severe; difficult to control with selective herbicides	Annual bluegrass Bermudagrass Goosegrass	Goosegrass Nutsedge
Widespread but can be controlled with selective herbicide(s)	Common chickweed Crabgrass Dandelion Mouse-ear chickweed Plantain White clover	Annual bluegrass Crabgrass
Occasional problem	Algae Black medic Moss Pearlwort Shepherdspurse Speedwell Spurge Velvetgrass Yarrow	Algae Common bermudagrass* Dichondra Kikuyugrass* Moss Sedges

*Difficult to control.

advanced stages of development. A few goosegrass plants scattered across a green are most easily removed manually by spudding.

Selective herbicides are available for controlling annual bluegrass in bermudagrass greens. However, a consistently effective herbicide for selective annual bluegrass control in bentgrass greens is lacking. Perennial strains of annual bluegrass are even more difficult to control with selective herbicides than are annual strains. Lead arsenate had been used effectively since the 1920's in many regions of North America, but its use now has been restricted by pesticide laws. A number of preemergence herbicides, such as benefin, DCPA, and bensulide, exhibit good control of annual bluegrass. However, most offer a high risk of injury to bentgrass. The preemergence herbicide that has proven the most selective is bensulide, but even this material can produce bentgrass injury with repeated use.

A potential herbicide for annual bluegrass control in bentgrass greens is endothall. Application techniques and timing are very critical in terms of the physiological condition of the grass and the temperature, and thus it is not easily used. The approach is one of gradual annual bluegrass reduction through repeated light applications rather than eradication in one single treatment.

Because of these potential problems, selective control of annual bluegrass should not be attempted on a given golf course without first evaluating the herbicide on a comparable nursery green. At least three years are needed to assess potential phytotoxicity to the bentgrass under the particular soil, climatic, and cultural conditions on the golf course and to allow the superintendent an opportunity to gain experience in proper use of the herbicide. Because of the wide-ranging problems associated with attempts to chemically control annual bluegrass, many superintendents choose to accept its presence on greens and to minimize its encroachment through manipulation of cultural practices to favor creeping bentgrass.

The basic concept in the use of a herbicide is that it be effective in annual bluegrass control and that a sufficient stand of bentgrass be present to rapidly fill in voids left by the dying annual bluegrass. Experience has shown that it is difficult to stimulate bentgrass coverage of substantial bare patches where the annual bluegrass has been eradicated with a preemergence herbicide. Thus, when annual

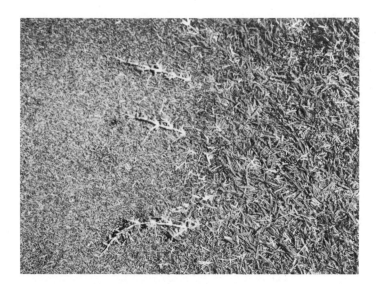

Figure 3-41. Objectionable bermudagrass encroachment onto a bentgrass green.

bluegrass represents the dominant component of a putting green polystand, the best option is reestablishment, in which the annual bluegrass is stripped off with a sod cutter and a bentgrass turf is established by seeding, sprigging, or sodding before an annual bluegrass control program is initiated. This is also an ideal time to correct any existing surface or subsurface drainage problems. The result will be a more favorable soil environment for growing bentgrass and one that discourages annual bluegrass encroachment. From one to three greens usually can be renovated per year with this approach.

A final point to stress is that most herbicides used on greens weaken the turf, which already has a short root system due to very close mowing. Thus, much caution is needed in selection and proper use of herbicides on greens. The preferred approach is application of a herbicide only as needed to control a developing weed problem, rather than use of a broad-spectrum preventive control program on a regular basis. Above all, a good cultural system is fundamental to successful, long-term weed control.

Encroachment Problem. The increasing use of creeping bentgrass in warm arid and even warm semihumid climates results in an added problem where warm-season species are used on fairways, aprons, and putting green surrounds—bermudagrass encroachment into bentgrass greens (Fig. 3-41). In southern California and Hawaii there is also the problem of kikuyugrass encroachment into both bentgrass and bermudagrass greens.

The concept in solving this problem is institution of preventive and corrective measures on the collar rather than on the putting green itself. In the case of bentgrass greens, the collars should be established and maintained as bentgrass monostands of at least 5 feet (1.5 meters) in width. The basic preventive program is for cultural practices to be oriented toward encouragement of the desirable species. One option that has achieved some success involves application of the appropriate growth regulator at a four- to eight-week interval. A second option involves sodding a 3- to 6-foot (0.9- to 1.8-meter)-wide Tifgreen bermudagrass or zoysiagrass border outside the collar as a barrier to encroachment. Both will gradually encroach into a bentgrass green, but at a much reduced rate compared with that of the vigorous creeping bermudagrasses or kikuyugrass. Insertion of vertical barriers from the soil surface downward generally has been unsuccessful in preventing encroachment.

Approaches to the removal of bermudagrass that has encroached into a bentgrass apron or green include manual removal and selective chemical control. Manual removal may need to be done as often as monthly during periods of rapid lateral shoot growth. Chemical control of bermudagrass has usually involved the use of siduron, which has variable effectiveness. Similar erratic results have occurred with

Table 3-10. Disease Problems on
Established Bentgrass and Bermudagrass Putting Greens

Relative Disease Problem	Bentgrass Greens	Bermudagrass Greens
Severe; difficult to control with fungicides		Spring dead spot
Widespread but can be controlled with appropriate fungicide(s)	Brown patch* Dollar spot* *Fusarium* patch* *Helminthosporium* diseases* *Pythium* blight* *Typhula* blight	Dollar spot *Helminthosporium* diseases
Occasional problem	Anthracnose Copper spot Downy mildew (yellow tufts) Fairy ring† *Fusarium* blight Red thread Slime mold Stripe smut Takeall patch Winter crown rot (LTB)	Brown patch Fairy ring† *Pythium* blight Slime mold

*Also on cool-season turfgrasses overseeded on dormant bermudagrass greens.
†Difficult to control.

organic arsenicals on kikuyugrass. A successful program, if instituted at five-year intervals, involves kill of the kikuyugrass with glyphosphate followed by reestablishment of the bermudagrass.

Diseases. The best preventive approach to minimizing the effects of turfgrass pathogens is maintenance of a healthy turf through proper cultural practices, including avoidance of excessive thatch accumulation. The major diseases occurring during the growing season are controlled either on a preventive basis or by corrective fungicide treatment as injury symptoms appear. In a preventive program, alternating between use of systemic and nonsystemic fungicides is better than using the same fungicide continuously. Sustained use of the same fungicide can lead to the development of resistant strains, as has occurred with dollar spot. There is a trend away from continuous applications of broad-spectrum fungicides toward selective preventive applications at the time of year when a potentially serious disease is most likely to occur. Scheduling is based on climatological information and experience. In addition, the fungicide selected is usually specific to the target disease of immediate concern.

Bentgrass putting greens are subject to damage from a wide range of turfgrass diseases (Table 3-10). Winter diseases, such as *Typhula* blight, *Fusarium* patch, and winter crown rot (LTB), are usually controlled on bentgrass greens by a preventive fungicide applied just prior to the first permanent snowfall. *Fusarium* patch also occurs in early fall. Dollar spot is more likely to occur during the cooler spring and fall periods. In contrast, brown patch and *Pythium* blight commonly occur during midsummer periods of hot humid weather, especially on poorly drained soils.

The range of disease-causing pathogens and the seriousness of disease attacks are usually not as great on bermudagrass as on bentgrass greens. Unfortunately, one of the few serious diseases is spring dead spot, for which no effective control is available. Tifdwarf is even more susceptible to spring dead spot than is Tifgreen. Spring dead spot is currently being called a disease although the specific causal organism has not been positively identified. It most commonly occurs in the northern portion of the warm climatic zone as well as in the transition region. The trend in disease control programs for bermudagrass greens is to apply fungicides on a corrective rather than a preventive basis.

The situation is somewhat different during the winter when cool-season turfgrasses are overseeded on bermudagrass greens. *Rhizoctonia* and *Pythium* seedling blights are particularly serious during the establishment period. Thus, preventive fungicide use is common during this period, particularly in humid regions and on poorly drained soils. An attack of dollar spot, *Pythium* blight, or *Fusarium* patch may also occur periodically during the winter. A preventive fungicide program may be used in the more humid regions for this reason. As with bentgrass greens, the fungicide program should alternate use of systemic and nonsystemic types.

Cultural techniques can be used to reduce the disease proneness of turfs. Included are maintenance of adequate potassium levels and avoidance of excessive nitrogen nutritional levels. Three diseases that are exceptions to the latter measure are dollar spot, rust, and red thread, which are most severe under low to deficient nitrogen fertility levels.

Another cultural aspect very important to disease incidence is water management. Most pathogens which cause turfgrass diseases respond to the presence of water. For example, free water on the leaf is usually needed for spore germination and invasion of the leaf. Excessive irrigation can lead to a water-saturated soil condition and enhanced pathogen activity. Daily, early morning removal of dew and leaf exudates, preferably by syringing or by poling, can be very significant in reducing disease problems. Cultural practices that avoid excessive thatch or mat accumulation can also be significant in minimizing disease incidence. Excessive thatch can absorb a portion of certain applied pesticides, necessitating the use of higher rates to achieve adequate control.

Insects. Insect problems tend to be greater on all greens in the warm humid climatic region than on bentgrass greens in cool climates (Table 3-11). The occurrence of insect problems increased noticeably on both bentgrass and bermudagrass greens during the mid-1970's. The increase is attributed to laws that eliminated use of the persistent insecticides, such as the chlorinated hydrocarbons. Thus, the trend has been away from broad-spectrum preventive applications to corrective treatment as an insect problem develops. The insecticide selected is usually specific for control of the problem of immediate concern. Mole crickets have been an increasing problem on bermudagrass greens in the southern region. Unfortunately, control of this pest is marginal with the available insecticides.

Nematodes. Nematodes, especially the spiral and stunt species, have been documented as a serious problem on bermudagrass greens on sandy soils in Florida. Striking response can be obtained by use of the appropriate nematicide.

Numerous putting green problems have also been attributed to nematodes attacking bentgrasses in the cool climatic region. However, actual documentation of detrimental activity by nematodes is frequently lacking. Usually the injury is from an environmental stress, disease, or improper cultural practice combined with parasitic activity. Correction of the nonnematode problem is usually sufficient to alleviate the problem on bentgrass greens.

Animals. A number of small animals can be very disruptive to putting greens because of their burrowing activities in search of food (Table 3-11). Two common approaches to minimizing the problem are control of the food source, which in turn discourages feeding activity, and trapping and removal of the animals from the area.

Both earthworms and ants create serious problems on greens in some regions due to the casts and soil mounds they leave on the surface. Earthworms make many beneficial contributions to soil, but must be controlled on greens due to the objectionable castings they produce.

Stress Damage

Putting greens are prone to a wide range of environmental stresses. Bentgrass generally is more subject to damage than is bermudagrass. Winter stresses include direct low-temperature kill, winter

Table 3-11. Insect and Animal Problems on
Established Bentgrass and Bermudagrass Putting Greens

Relative Problem	Bentgrass Greens	Bermudagrass Greens
Severe; difficult to control with insecticides		Mole cricket
Widespread but can be controlled with appropriate insecticide(s)	Black turfgrass ataenius Chinch bug Cutworm Sod webworm White grub	Armyworm Bermudagrass mite Cutworm Sod webworm White grub
Occasional problem	Armyworm Frit fly Japanese beetle Turfgrass weevil	Bermudagrass scale Ground pearl* Rhodesgrass mealybug
Animal problems usually involving disruption of the turf surface	Ants Coots Deer Earthworms Geese Ground squirrels Ground wasps Moles Pocket gophers Skunks Voles	Ants Armadillos Coots Earthworms Ground squirrels Moles Skunks

*Difficult to control.

desiccation, ice coverage, and frost heaving. Environmental stresses of concern during the summer growing season include shade, heat, wilt, flooding, scald, petroleum spills, and atmospheric pollutants. Putting greens are particularly prone to internal water stress because of the restricted root system caused by close mowing. Bentgrass greens are subject to winter injury problems in the northern portion of the cool humid region, as are bermudagrass greens in the transition zone. In addition, most bermudagrasses lack tolerance to shade stress conditions.

Soil stress problems include salinity, high sodium levels, soil deposition, and waterlogging. Localized dry spots can occur on the sand root zones frequently used in the construction of putting greens. The diagnosis, causes, and prevention of environmental and soil stresses are discussed in detail in chapter 10.

SUMMARIES OF CULTURAL SYSTEMS

Summaries of the cultural systems utilized in the maintenance of the three most common types of golf course putting greens are presented in this section. The two main turfgrasses used on greens are bentgrass and bermudagrass. A system is also presented for annual bluegrass putting greens, which are used in some regions of the country even though bentgrass is the preferred species. Exceptions, of course, exist to these general guidelines, and flexibility should be maintained in selection of the cultural system, depending on the environmental stress and pest problems most likely to occur in a given location. These systems are presented as a ready reference. For more details the reader is referred to the previous section of this chapter on putting green culture.

Cultural System for a Bentgrass Putting Green

Mowing Height   0.19 to 0.31 (3/16 to 5/16) in. (4.8 to 7.5 mm).
Mowing Frequency   Daily.
Mowing Pattern   Alter at each mowing in each of four directions.
Clippings   Remove.
Grain Control   Use comb or brush attachment on greensmower as needed to prevent grain formation. Light vertical cutting may be required once per week for several weeks where a serious grain problem has already developed.
Fertilization
   Nitrogen   Apply 0.5 to 0.7 lb. N/1,000 sq. ft. (0.25 to 0.35 kg/are)/growing month. Use 0.1 to 0.3 lb. N/1,000 sq. ft. (0.05 to 0.15 kg/are)/10 to 15 growing days for a water-soluble carrier or 0.3 to 0.7 lb. N/1,000 sq. ft. (0.15 to 0.35 kg/are)/20 to 30 growing days for a slow-release carrier. Avoid nitrogen fertilization during summer heat stress.
   Phosphorus   Apply at rate based on soil test. Spring or fall timing best. Usually part of complete analysis fertilizer.
   Potassium   Apply at rate based on soil test where fine-textured clay soils are involved. Coarse-textured soils require 3 to 5 lbs. K_2O/1,000 sq. ft. (1.5 to 2.5 kg/are)/yr., usually split into four to six applications over the growing season.
   Iron   Apply 1 to 2 oz. iron carrier/1,000 sq. ft. as needed to correct developing iron chlorosis symptoms. Most commonly a problem during summer months.
   Other Nutrients   Apply if specific nutrient deficiency diagnosed (an infrequent occurrence).
pH Correction   Maintain pH between 5.5 and 6.5. Apply limestone or sulfur materials as needed based on annual soil test.
Irrigation   Moisten to full depth of root zone with each irrigation; time prior to development of visual wilt symptoms. Midday syringing may be needed to prevent wilt, timing being based on footprint symptom development.
Topdressing   Apply two to six times per year as needed for smoothing and thatch control. Minimum of twice per year suggested, with spring and fall applications of 0.2 to 0.4 cu. yd./1,000 sq. ft. Use as follow-up to cultivation whenever possible at higher application rate. May be applied as often as every three to four weeks during periods of active shoot growth at rate of 0.1 cu. yd./1,000 sq. ft.
Cultivation   Utilize two to six times per year. Higher frequencies needed on intensively trafficked greens grown on fine-textured soil. Core or slice a minimum of twice yearly in late spring and early fall. Avoid cultivation during heat stress if possible.
Spiking   Practice as needed to correct developing surface compaction or impermeability problem. Can also use on weekly basis during midsummer stress to enhance shoot and root rejuvenation.
Weed Control   Control broadleafs in spring and fall as they appear. Use mecoprop (MCPP) and/or dicamba carefully at light rates. Avoid phenoxy herbicides, such as 2,4-D, because of potential phytotoxicity. Use selected preemergence and postemergence weedy-grass herbicides with great caution due to potential phytotoxicity to certain bentgrasses.
Disease Control   Practice on preventive basis or give corrective fungicide treatment as injury symptoms appear. Preventive program usually utilized for warm-weather diseases in humid climates; alternate several effective fungicides. Where winter diseases, such as snow mold, are a problem, preventive fungicide program usually needed.
Insect Control   Apply appropriate insecticide as needed to correct developing insect problem.
Drainage   Adequate drainage essential for culture of healthy bentgrass greens subject to intense traffic. Use of well-drained, coarse-textured root zone is particularly critical on greens in transitional and warm climatic regions which are at southern limits of bentgrass adaptation.

Cultural System for a Bermudagrass Putting Green

Mowing Height   0.19 to 0.31 ($\frac{3}{16}$ to $\frac{5}{16}$) in. (4.8 to 7.5 mm).

Mowing Frequency   Daily.

Mowing Pattern   Alter at each mowing in each of four directions.

Clippings   Remove.

Grain Control   Use vertical cutting as needed up to once per week for control of grain and variable growth. Adjust to produce very light combing effect. Combing or brushing may also be advisable.

Fertilization

   Nitrogen   Apply 0.5 to 1.2 lb. N/1,000 sq. ft. (0.25 to 0.60 kg/are)/growing month. Use 0.2 to 0.5 lb. N/1,000 sq. ft. (0.10 to 0.25 kg/are)/10 to 15 growing days for water-soluble carrier or 0.5 to 1.2 lbs. N/1,000 sq. ft. (0.25 to 0.60 kg/are)/20 to 30 growing days for slow-release carrier.

   Phosphorus   Apply at rate based on soil test. Spring or fall timing best. Usually part of complete analysis fertilizer.

   Potassium   Apply at rate based on soil test where fine-textured clay soils are involved. Coarse-textured soils require 4 to 8 lbs. K_2O/1,000 sq. ft. (2 to 4 kg/are)/yr., usually split into four to six applications over growing season.

   Iron   Apply 2 to 4 oz. iron carrier/1,000 sq. ft. as needed to correct developing iron chlorosis symptoms; common occurrence following spring greenup.

   Other Nutrients   Apply if specific nutrient deficiency diagnosed (an infrequent occurrence).

pH Correction   Maintain pH between 6.0 and 7.0. Apply limestone or sulfur materials as needed based on annual soil test.

Irrigation   Moisten to full depth of root zone with each irrigation; time prior to development of visual wilt symptoms.

Topdressing   Apply two to six times per year as needed for smoothing and thatch control. Minimum of twice per year suggested, with spring and late summer applications at 0.3 to 0.5 cu. yd./1,000 sq. ft. Use as follow-up to cultivation whenever possible with higher application rate. May be applied as often as every three to four weeks during periods of rapid shoot growth at rate of 0.1 cu. yd./1,000 sq. ft.

Cultivation   Utilize two to six times per year. Higher frequencies needed on intensely trafficked greens grown on fine-textured soil. Core or slice a minimum of twice yearly in spring and late summer. Avoid cultivation within thirty days of scheduled winter overseeding.

Spiking   Practice as needed up to weekly to prevent developing surface compaction or impermeability problem.

Weed Control   Control broadleafs and annual weedy grasses as they appear with either preemergence or postemergence herbicide. Be sure to apply late summer treatments sufficiently early to avoid phytotoxicity to winter overseeded cool-season grasses.

Disease Control   Use corrective or preventive disease control program, former generally being preferred, especially in arid and semiarid climates.

Insect Control   Apply appropriate insecticide as needed to correct developing insect problem.

Winter Overseeding   Usually used in southern half of warm humid climatic region. Accomplish adequate thatch control and soil compaction correction well in advance of scheduled winter overseeding. Follow overseeding procedures discussed in previous section.

Cultural System for an Annual Bluegrass Putting Green

Mowing Height   0.19 to 0.31 ($\frac{3}{16}$ to $\frac{5}{16}$) in. (4.8 to 7.5 mm).

Mowing Frequency   Daily.

Mowing Pattern   Alter at each mowing in each of four directions.

Clippings   Remove.

Grain Control   Use comb or brush attachment on greensmower as needed. Can also employ vertical cutting as needed up to once per week for control of grain and variable growth. Adjust to produce very light combing effect.

Seedhead Control   Use properly adjusted brush mounted on greensmower on daily basis during peak seedhead formation and three to four times per week during periods of light seedhead development. Similar effect can be achieved with light vertical cutting two to four times per week, especially if three-gang greensmower with vertical cutting units is available.

Fertilization

Nitrogen   Apply 0.3 to 0.7 lb. N/1,000 sq. ft. (0.15 to 0.35 kg/are)/growing month. Space at 10- to 20-day interval with rate between 0.25 and 0.5 lb. N/1,000 sq. ft. (0.13 to 0.25 kg/are)/application. Avoid nitrogen fertilization during summer heat stress.

Phosphorus   Apply at rate based on soil test and use program that maintains moderately high level of soil phosphorus. Applications best made in spring and fall, usually as part of complete analysis fertilizer.

Potassium   Apply at rate based on soil test where finer-textured clay soils involved. Coarse-textured soils require 3 to 5 lbs. K_2O/1,000 sq. ft. (1.5 to 2.5 kg/are)/yr., usually split into four to six applications over growing season.

Iron   Apply 1 to 2 oz. iron carrier/1,000 sq. ft./growing month, lower level being used in northeast. Three ounces in 3 gallons of water may be needed where chronic iron chlorosis occurs.

Other Nutrients   Apply if specific nutrient deficiency diagnosed (an infrequent occurrence).

pH Correction   Maintain pH between 6.2 and 7.2. Apply limestone or sulfur materials as needed based on annual soil test.

Irrigation   Maintain constantly moist soil root zone through daily, light, early-morning applications. Syringe as needed to prevent wilt, timing being based on footprint symptom development.

Topdressing   Apply two to four times per year as needed for smoothing and thatch control. Minimum of twice per year suggested, with spring application of 0.2 to 0.3 cu. yd./1,000 sq. ft. and fall application of 0.3 to 0.5 cu. yd./1,000 sq. ft. Use as follow-up to cultivation whenever possible, with higher application rate. May be applied as often as every three to four weeks during periods of active growth at rate of 0.1 cu. yd./1,000 sq. ft.

Cultivation   Utilize two to six times per year. Higher frequencies needed on intensely trafficked greens grown on fine-textured soil. Core or slice a minimum of twice yearly in very early spring, as soon as equipment can be taken onto green, and in early fall. Avoid cultivation during heat stress if possible.

Spiking   Practice weekly throughout summer, if needed, when soil temperature is above 70 °F (21 °C).

Weed Control   Control broadleafs as they appear. Use mecoprop (MCPP). Avoid phenoxy herbicides, such as 2,4-D and dicamba, because of potential phytotoxicity. Hand-weed goosegrass. Avoid organic arsenicals and preemergence weedy-grass herbicides because of potential phytotoxicity.

Disease Control   Use preventive fungicide program in which several effective fungicides are alternated. Dollar spot, brown patch, *Fusarium* patch, *Typhula* blight, and anthracnose are usually the most severe diseases.

Insect Control   Apply appropriate insecticide as needed to correct developing insect problem. *Ataenius spretulus* grub and turfgrass weevil of particular concern. Avoid emulsifiable concentrate formulations of insecticides.

Drainage   Adequate drainage is essential for culture of healthy annual bluegrass putting greens. If drainage poor, employ surface and subsurface drainage techniques for improvement.

CUP CHANGING

By definition the *hole* in a putting green is circular with a diameter of 4.25 inches (10.8 centimeters) and is at least 4 inches (10.2 centimeters) deep. A metal or plastic cup is commonly placed in the hole. The cup should be sunk approximately 8 inches (20.3 centimeters) deep, unless the nature of the soil makes this impractical, with its top at least 1 inch (2.54 centimeters) below the putting green surface. The outer diameter of the cup liner should not exceed 4.25 inches.

A flagstick is commonly placed in the cup. The *flagstick* is a movable straight indicator, with or without bunting or similar material attached, and circular in cross section, which is centered in the hole to show its position.

The ability to change the location of cups on putting greens is a vital tool available to the turf manager. It permits control over the concentration of traffic entering and leaving the green as well as on the putting surface. The frequency at which cup location is changed depends on the (a) intensity of play and resulting wear, including spike marks, (b) relative wear tolerance of the turfgrasses, (c) anticipated rate of recovery from wear, (d) compaction potential of the soil, and (e) need for changing the play strategies of the game. Changing of cup settings is normally done daily but may on occasion be done every second day or less often during periods of minimal use. However, the interval between cup changes should not be so long that inward turfgrass growth effectively decreases the diameter of the hole. Occasionally, cup location is changed twice a day during periods of limited shoot growth and very intense traffic, especially on public golf courses. Cup location should not be changed during a competitive round of a day's event.

Another approach, if the greens are large, is the use of two cups per green which allows players to alternate pin placement when each group completes putting. This two-cup technique can also be used to distribute traffic more widely on smaller greens during early spring and late fall when the recuperative rate of the turf is slowed.

Improper changing of cups, with the sod plug placed either too high or too low, must be avoided. Generally, one individual who pays sufficient attention to detail and is reliable is made responsible for this important daily task. Speed in performing the task should be secondary to a high level of quality, since an improperly changed cup can detract from an otherwise quality putting green.

Many different cup changing procedures have evolved through experience on individual golf courses. A detailed stepwise outline of a commonly used approach is presented and is illustrated in Figure 3-42.

1. After selecting a new location for the cup, and with the hole-cutting implement set to remove a plug to the desired depth, remove the plug from the green but let it remain in the implement. The cup cutter should be distinctly marked on the outside and used in such a way that cut and fill depths of the plug are comparable. Two cuts may be required in certain dense clay soils. Carefully place the first cut in a bucket and leave the second in the cup cutter.

2. Using the hooked cup puller and a slow, straight upward pull, carefully remove the cup from its old location. Place it in the new hole with its top 1 inch (2.54 centimeters) below the surface of the green, preferably with a cup setter.

3. With the hole-cutting implement placed in the abandoned hole, remove the plug from the implement.

4. Check the level of the plug with the adjacent surface of the green and make adjustments (if necessary) either by shaving the bottom of the plug or by adding root zone soil. Never resort to forcing the plug downward to achieve leveling.

5. Use thumbs to separate edges of the plug from the adjacent green area. This releases grass blades forced into the perimeter interface of the plug and surrounding soil.

6. Gently firm the perimeter.

7. Water the plug. Recheck to be sure the plug has retained its level position.

(a) New site is apart from old one.

(b) Cup is removed carefully.

(c) Topsoil is placed in hole.

(d) Soil in hole is tamped with a stick.

(e) Plug is shaved at bottom.

(f) Thickness of plug is checked against...

Figure 3-42. Procedure used in changing a cup on a putting green.

(g) . . . depth to tamped soil. Further adjustments by shaving plug or adding topsoil insure even surface.

(h) Plug is broken by pressing up with fingers; plug is then rotated and broken again.

(i) Plug is placed into hole and surface is firmed with thumbs.

(j) Edges are separated to release grass blades forced into slit around the perimeter.

(k) Perimeter is firmed as plug is watered.

(l) Job completed. Plug outline has disappeared.

Figure 3-42/*continued*

Cup Placement

The primary principle in cup placement is fairness. A location should not be selected that will not fully reward the properly struck shot played from the right fairway position. A number of factors should be weighed, including (1) change in slope, (2) turf surface quality, (3) visual appearance, (3) distance to edge of green, (5) holding quality of the green, (6) length of the shot to the green, (7) probable prevailing wind conditions for the day, (8) design of the hole, and (9) type of play. Ideally, there should be no changes in slope for a radius of 3 feet (0.9 meter) around the hole. This does not mean that the area must be flat; rather, there should be no change in the angle of slope over the area and the slope should not be so steep that a rolling ball can gather speed. There have been instances where holes have been set on slopes so severe that as the green dried out during the day it would not hold a ball.

The area around the hole should be as free as possible of ball marks, other blemishes, and changes in grass texture. It is around the hole where the ultimate action takes place. Thus, the particular spot should be selected with careful thought. The location should "look" right. Care should be taken to avoid placements which, from the player's point of view, present a distorted picture. Golf is a visual game, and the overall vision is of the location of the hole. To better assess the player's viewpoint, the person placing the cup can bring along a putter to roll the ball at the selected spot before the hole is cut to assure that it will, in fact, play properly.

The USGA suggests at least 5 paces (approximately 15 feet or 4.6 meters) between the hole and the edge of the green. The distance should be greater if the approach shot must carry over a hazard near the edge of the putting green. The cup should be positioned so that traffic entering and leaving the green will be at least 15 feet (4.6 meters) away from the old position. It is preferable to position the cup in the front portion of the green during wet soil conditions, when compaction potential is high, and during winter when play is minimal. This serves to protect the rest of the green against damage by compaction and rutting. If rain is forecast, an elevated site should be selected rather than a low, depressed area that is subject to water saturation and maybe even standing water.

A systematic method of cup placement is used on many golf courses, particularly when the workers involved lack experience in this key activity that is so important to golf play. For example, both the greens and tees have designated front, middle, and back portions. A more uniform yardage is maintained with use of the combinations front green—back tee, back green—front tee, and middle green—middle tee. In addition, cup placement should be rotated left and right. The net result over an eighteen-hole golf course at any time is six front, six middle, and six back placements on the greens along with nine right and nine left placements. This systematic method tends to minimize player complaints that the course is playing "long" or "short."

Tournament Cup Placement. Preplanning should be done by analyzing the course and generally determining the four major areas on each green providing hole locations. In addition to the design of the hole, other factors such as weather, wind direction, firmness of the turf, and how the particular hole will play that day should be considered.

A balanced course should be set for each day's play, avoiding too many left side-right side or front-rear sequential settings. A common error, particularly during tournaments, is to set up the course to play more difficult each day by using all the easiest pin placements on the first day and proceeding progressively to all of the most difficult settings on the last. This tends to distort the course, at least on the first and last days.

In a four-day USGA Championship, each of the four areas preplanned for each green are evaluated. The most difficult is rated 1, the easiest 4, and those intermediate 2 and 3. Each day's setting process involves planning to avoid an "18" course (i.e., eighteen number 1 settings) on the one hand or a "72" course (i.e., eighteen number 4 settings) on the other. The optimum for each day would be a 45. An effort should be made to get as close to that number each day as conditions allow. For a ten-day period prior to a tournament it is desirable for the cups to be placed in portions of each putting green that will not be used during the event. Also, the practice round settings must be planned so that the four key setting areas are preserved for tournament play.

Figure 3-43. Cutting height differential on well-maintained collar of a putting green.

Flagsticks. The flagsticks used should be 8 feet (2.4 meters) in height with a diameter no greater than 0.75 inch (1.9 centimeters) from a point 3 inches (7.6 centimeters) above the hole to the bottom of the hole. Flagsticks are usually painted a solid white or cream color. The color selected for the flags on top of the flagsticks should be such that the flags are easily seen. A yellow flag against the typically green background of a golf course provides excellent visibility. Flagsticks should be collected each day after play and put out again the next morning. Periodic loss of flags and/or flagsticks can be anticipated due to vandalism. Such losses should be reported to the superintendent or foreman immediately so replacement can be made with minimum disruption of play. At least two sets of flagsticks, cups, and flags should be maintained as replacements.

COLLAR

Description

The *collar* is the turfgrass area surrounding the putting green that is mowed at a cutting height intermediate between that of the fairway and the green. This height usually allows a golfer the option of using a putter when a ball lands on the collar (Fig. 3-43). Collar width is determined by the capabilities of the available equipment, size of the putting green, contours of the green, and membership desires. The width ranges from one to three widths of the walking greensmower but normally averages 3 feet (0.9 meter) to 5 feet (1.5 meters) if cut with a three-gang riding greensmower. The collar can pose special maintenance problems. Thus, the construction procedure and soil texture used should be the same as those on the green so that fertilization, irrigation, cultivation, topdressing, and pesticide requirements are comparable. This simplifies the cultural system needed on greens and collars.

Turfgrasses Used

The collar is preferably planted to the same species and cultivar used on the green. This commonly involves a creeping bentgrass in cool climates and one of the improved bermudagrasses (Tifgreen or Tifdwarf) in warm climates. Such an approach simplifies the cultural program. However, several of the improved Kentucky bluegrasses, preferably blended, have been used on the collars of bentgrass greens.

Culture

The cutting height of the collar is higher than that of the green to provide a distinct definition of the boundary. It normally ranges from 0.4 to 0.7 (⅜ to ¾) inch (1 to 1.8 centimeters). The frequency of mowing is usually three times per week, but can be as often as six times per week at the lower cutting height on high-budget courses. Clippings are normally removed. The collar and adjacent surroundings should extend out from the green a sufficient distance so that there is an adequate turning radius for the greensmower. This is particularly important with the three-gang riding greensmower.

The collar should receive the same fertilization, cultivation, topdressing, and pesticide programs as those employed on the green. In some portions of the collar where thinning occurs due to intense wear, use of a higher nitrogen fertility level than on the green may be desirable to enhance the recuperative rate. However, this practice should not be followed on the collar where wear is not a problem because severe thatch and puffiness problems could result. In fact, a lower nitrogen level than that used on the green may be preferred on higher cut, infrequently trafficked collars to avoid thatching.

The irrigation system should be designed to apply water uniformly not only to the immediate green area but also to the collar and adjacent grassy mounds. This prevents the development of soil drought on elevated greens due to internal drying from the sides. Supplemental hand watering of exposed, elevated portions of the collar may be required, similiar to the procedure followed on the green. Thatch and puffiness can become a problem on collars, since bentgrass and bermudagrass are usually the species involved. This problem is generally most severe on portions of the collar that receive minimal traffic. An annual or semiannual vertical cutting is usually required on bentgrass collars, while bermudagrass collars may require more frequent vertical cutting of up to once per month during the prime growing period. The suggested reel setting is $\frac{3}{16}$ inch (.48 centimeter) below the current height of cut with a blade spacing of 0.75 to 1 inch (1.9 to 2.5 centimeters).

Traffic Problems

Compaction is a common problem on portions of collars. The front approach and areas immediately adjacent to bunkers receive the most intense traffic. Additional turfgrass wear and soil compaction result from the turning of maintenance equipment. Thus, periodic core cultivation of the entire collar is required to minimize compaction. Cultivation may be needed more frequently than on the putting green, with monthly intervals sometimes being necessary on intensively trafficked collars having a fine-textured underlying soil. A preventive approach to the traffic problem involves the use of ropes, painted lines sprayed on the turf, and/or signs to divert traffic around the green or away from seriously compacted, thin turf areas. Such an approach provides a rest and recuperative period. The effects of intense traffic are most commonly observed on narrow collars where the bunker is positioned too close to the green and on the side nearest to the next tee. Good architectural design avoids this problem by judicious placement of bunkers.

Sand Deposition

Sand deposition from nearby bunkers as a result of explosion shots and wind erosion can cause a gradual rise in the elevation of the collar. This problem can be corrected by cutting and lifting the sod, removing a portion of the underlying sand, tilling the remaining soil, and transplanting the original or new sod onto the collar. This procedure may be required every five to ten years. At times, sand deposition may extend out onto the green. In this situation, the problem should be corrected on both green and collar at the same time.

Tree Root Problem

Tree roots can be a problem if trees are located near the putting green. Such a green requires unusually intense irrigation on the affected area and is prone to wilting. Surface tree root problems under greens can be partially alleviated by trenching around the outer edge of the collar. Trenching to a 2- to 3-foot (0.6- to 0.9-meter) depth severs a major portion of the surface roots. A significant improvement in turfgrass growth and quality on the green usually results. A strip of sod should be lifted prior to trenching. This practice permits easier trenching, finishing, and cleanup. Subsequently, the soil should be returned and firmed and the sod transplanted back into place.

Figure 3-44. A trencher being used in the surrounds to cut tree roots (*top*). Severed tree roots that had extended under the green and had been competing excessively for nutrients and water (*bottom left*). Turf can recover quite rapidly if root pruning is properly executed (*bottom right*).

A three-point hitch, deep-soil chisel attachment mounted on a tractor has been used in severing tree roots where soil conditions permit and subsurface drain lines are not present. This method leaves the surface relatively undisturbed and is usually not detectable after one to two weeks of soil settling and turfgrass regrowth. Placing an artificial root barrier in the trench has usually proved ineffective for any significant length of time. Periodic root pruning by trenching at three- to four-year intervals has proven to be the most acceptable practice (Fig. 3-44). Precautions should be taken to avoid severing drain lines, irrigation pipes, hydraulic lines, and electrical wiring.

APRON

Description

The turf that is an extension of the fairway in closest proximity to and in front of the putting green or adjoining the collar is termed the *apron*. It normally extends outward from near the center line of the hole to an acceptable distance from key hazards such as bunkers or to grassy mounds that are mowed at a higher cutting height. The apron extends sufficiently out into the fairway so that the turning zone for the fairway gang mower can be varied. This procedure reduces the turfgrass wear and soil compaction that result if the turning is concentrated in a narrow zone at the end of the fairway.

Turfgrasses Used

The turfgrass species and cultivar used on the apron are normally the same as those on the adjacent fairway. Creeping bentgrass or a blend of the improved Kentucky bluegrass cultivars is commonly utilized in the cool climatic region, while the bermudagrasses and, to a lesser extent, the zoysiagrasses are used in warm climates. Annual bluegrass frequently invades the apron, especially if the turf is subjected to constant intense wear and is growing on a compacted, fine-textured soil. Every effort should be made to keep the annual bluegrass population in the apron to a minimum.

Culture

The cultural practices employed on the apron are comparable to those used on the adjacent fairway. The cutting height on aprons can range from 0.5 to 1 inch (1.3 to 2.5 centimeters). Frequently the apron is mowed at the same cutting height as the fairway. Mowing frequency ranges from two to three times per week. Typically, a three-gang riding mower is used. Quite frequently the same mower is used for both the apron and tee areas. Clippings are usually returned, although some higher budget courses prefer to remove clippings if the apron is mowed quite low. It is important for contours on the apron and associated approach areas of the green to be designed so that multigang mowing units can be utilized where economy in mowing costs is needed. The actual size and mowing pattern of the apron in terms of its extension into the fairway shift back and forth throughout the growing season in relation to the fairway zone where the multigang mowing units are turned. This is done to distribute traffic and the resultant potential soil compaction and turfgrass wear over as large an area as possible.

The apron normally receives the same cultural program as the fairway in terms of fertilization, irrigation, cultivation, and pesticide usage. Application of a somewhat higher nitrogen rate on apron areas that receive severe wear enhances the recuperative rate. It is very important that excessive irrigation of the apron be avoided. A soggy turf is an unfair area for play, since the ball will ''die'' as it strikes it. Also, a high percentage of the traffic entering the green passes over the apron, and a high soil moisture level can lead to increased soil compaction. If soil compaction is a continuing problem on the apron, cultivation, usually either coring or slicing, may need to be scheduled at shorter intervals than on the adjacent fairway. In some cases, golf carts are not allowed on apron areas (Fig. 3-45). The differential cutting height used on the apron can function as a natural boundary that delineates the apron. This, combined with appropriate signs, aids in keeping golf carts off aprons.

PRACTICE GREEN

The practice green presents a special challenge to the golf course superintendent. It probably receives more intense traffic than any other putting green on the course. It is one of the first turfgrass areas that the golfer views and plays. Thus, the appearance and playability of the practice green can set an impression concerning playing conditions that may carry through the remainder of the golf course. Finally, the practice putting green should offer a putting surface quality comparable to that on the regular eighteen holes of the golf course.

The practice putting green is generally located in the vicinity of the golf shop and first tee. It should be large enough to allow space for nine to eighteen cups plus alternate cup placement locations. The actual size depends on the membership's desire, the intensity of use, and the amount of space available. The practice green is commonly, but unfortunately, developed as one of the last steps after the golf course design and clubhouse location are decided. Preferably, the size of the practice putting green should be established early in the planning stages and adequate space allocated for this area in the design plan. A single, large practice green usually is preferred. Practice putting greens that are too small for the intensity of practice putting at a particular club are extremely difficult to maintain. They become quite thin, worn, and not representative of playing conditions on the golf course. Although not in common use, two practice greens offer some advantages in certain situations. One green can be closed as needed

Figure 3-45. Directional sign used to keep golf carts off apron in front of a putting green.

for special cultural practices, repair, or just a recuperative rest period if the green becomes excessively thin.

Design of the practice putting green should offer a relatively level surface but one that has sufficient slope, preferably up to 3 percent, to facilitate rapid drainage of surface water. The turfgrass cultivar selected for the practice green should be the same as that used on the eighteen regulation greens. The construction procedure, root zone soil mix, subsurface drainage, establishment, and cultural practices utilized should also be comparable to those on the eighteen regulation greens. Compaction problems can be severe, since the intensity of play on the practice green is frequently greater than on any other green on the golf course. This emphasizes the importance of proper watering and use of a root zone soil mix that minimizes potential problems.

Finally, the frequency of cup changing and cup placement procedures can be critical in maintaining a quality turfgrass surface on practice putting greens. The frequency of cup changing should be based on the intensity of practice putting and resulting turfgrass wear. An even higher frequency than used on the actual course may be needed if the golfing membership is very active in practice putting.

PUTTING GREEN TURF NURSERY

A nursery of putting green turf should be maintained on the golf course. The size should be comparable to the average size of the greens on the golf course but not less than 5,000 square feet (465 square meters) for an eighteen-hole course. Excessively large nurseries are costly to maintain. Much larger nursery greens may be maintained during periods of renovation or rebuilding when sodding of greens is planned.

The nursery is usually roughly rectangular or square, depending on the space available, with rounded corners for ease of mowing. It should have a minimum slope of 2 percent to provide surface drainage. Locating the nursery near the maintenance building increases its accessibility and encourages more frequent observation by the golf course superintendent. The putting green nursery serves two main purposes. First, it is a readily available source of sod for repair of unforeseen damage on greens (Fig. 3-46). Second, the nursery can be used for testing new pesticides, fertilizers, cultural practices, and cultivars before using them on the regular greens. Detailed records should be kept concerning the chemicals or cultivars used in experimental tests as well as their location and the timing, rate, and method of application.

When establishing a nursery, the area should be fallowed for a time or fumigated to insure that no off-type bentgrasses or bermudagrasses are present. The soil mix and subsurface drainage system used on the nursery area should be comparable to those on the regular greens. The nursery should also be composed of the same cultivar as is found on the regular greens and receive the same cultural practices. Seedheads should never be permitted to form in or around the nursery to avoid the introduction of off-type plants. This is accomplished through daily mowing at the normal putting green height used on

Figure 3-46. Sod cutter being used to cut sod from a putting green nursery (*left*) for repair of a green damaged by a hydraulic oil spill (*right*).

the golf course. The absence of traffic on the nursery may require some adjustments in the cultural practices used compared with those used on regulation greens should a thatch problem develop. Appropriate steps include a low nitrogen rate, increased topdressing, and/or more frequent vertical cutting.

STOLON NURSERY

Bentgrass

A stolon nursery is established when (a) large quantities of vegetative material will be required for stolonizing new greens constructed during rebuilding or expansion and (b) the cultivar selected for the greens cannot be propagated with genetic uniformity from seed. The stoloniferous species most commonly propagated in stolon nurseries is creeping bentgrass.

The stolon nursery should be located in close proximity to the maintenance shop where adequate irrigation facilities are available. The size is dictated by the total area of green to be stolonized. After a full growing season, 1 bushel (0.42 cubic meter) of stolons can be produced from 4.5 feet (1.4 meters) of row. Thus, 1,000 linear feet (305 meters) of sprigged row will produce 222 bushels (93 cubic meters) of stolons. The stolonizing rate is 8 to 10 bushels (3.4 to 4.2 cubic meters) per thousand square feet. Accordingly, stolonizing a 7,000-square-foot (650-square-meter) green requires 315 linear feet (96 meters) of sprigs.

The site should be well drained and composed of a moist, fertile soil. Soil preparation is comparable to that discussed in the previous sections on green construction and establishment. The planting bed is tilled, leveled, and firmed. Any needed soil pH corrections indicated by the soil test are made. The indicated amounts of phosphorus and potassium are incorporated to a 4- to 6-inch (10- to 15-centimeter) depth. Soil fumigation usually is required to eradicate off-type strains and difficult-to-control weeds. Metam or methyl bromide may be used.

The stolons are planted in rows spaced 4 to 5 feet (1.2 to 1.5 meters) apart (Fig. 3-47). The sprigs are planted end to end in furrows at a depth of 1 to 2 inches (2.5 to 5 centimeters). The soil is pressed firmly around the sprigs. The preferred planting times are spring for bermudagrass and late summer for bentgrass.

Following planting, the stolon nursery should be kept moist and weed free. Monthly fertilization at a rate of 1 pound of nitrogen per thousand square feet (0.5 kilogram per are) is suggested during the

Figure 3-47. Properly established and maintained creeping-bentgrass stolon nursery. (Photo courtesy of B. Warren, Warren Turf Nursery, Inc., Palos Hills, Ill.)

establishment period. A final critical point is removal by hand of all bentgrass seedheads immediately on formation. This time-consuming manual procedure prevents contamination from off-type strains and other serious problem weeds.

Bermudagrass

The common procedure for obtaining vegetative planting material involves the use of a vertical cutter operated across a nursery turf. The chopped vegetative material is brought to the surface, collected by sweeping, and then immediately planted. The procedure is most commonly used on the improved bermudagrasses. It is vital that the nursery turf utilized be completely free of any off-type strains. A cutting height of 0.4 to 0.8 inch (1 to 2 centimeters) is preferred in terms of obtaining high yields of vegetative planting material. The vertical cutter used should have every other blade removed. The resulting wide spacing produces a good yield and at the same time does not disrupt the turfgrass surface so much that it cannot be brought back into an acceptable cover within a short period of time. Generally, application of a fertilizer immediately after collecting the stolons encourages rapid recovery and minimizes invasion of weeds or off-type strains. The vegetative plant material produced by this procedure is of ideal length for easy distribution and uniform coverage of a green during stolonizing.

SAND GREEN

Although rare, sand greens still exist in certain arid western plains states such as Colorado, Kansas, Nebraska, North Dakota, and South Dakota. They tend to be quite small in comparison with grass greens, usually ranging from 2,000 to 3,000 square feet (186 to 279 square meters). This smaller size is used because the ball does not bounce as it does on a grass green but rather dies where it strikes and because play would be seriously slowed by the extensive sand smoothing that would be needed prior or putting on large sand greens. Sand greens are economical to maintain as they require little care compared with grass putting greens. Thus, they have a place on extremely low-budget golf courses, particularly where turf loss due to heat and drought is severe.

Construction

The first step in building a sand green is construction of a 4- to 6-inch (10- to 15-centimeter) thick, compacted clay soil base. This subbase should be contoured with a minimum grade of 0.5 to 1 percent to facilitate drainage of surface water from the green. Washing of sand and floating of lighter fuel oil off the green onto fairways can be a problem during intense rains. Therefore, it is important to consider building a raised lip around the perimeter during the subgrade construction. Swales, diversion ditches, or waterways can be constructed to divert water around the green where the topography is quite sloping and thus to prevent flowing surface water from entering the green. Installation of two to three small catch basins or french drains at the lower front edge of a sand green aids in rapid removal of surface water and prevents the oily water from running out onto the apron where turfgrass injury could result.

After a firm subgrade is completed, a heavy fuel oil is distributed over the clay base and allowed to soak in for a few days. A final leveling can then be accomplished. Where water drainage into the cup is a problem, the cup and surrounding 2 feet (0.6 meter) of soil can be raised approximately 0.5 to 1 inch (1.3 to 2.5 centimeters) above the adjacent subbase to minimize it. An additional aid is installation of a french drain 2 to 3 feet (0.6 to 0.9 meter) below the cup, filling it with stone, and connecting it to the cup by a small sand channel to facilitate rapid drainage.

Sand Preparation. The sand to be distributed over the subbase usually is prepared off-site. A medium to fine, sharp sand (0.1 to 0.5 millimeter) is preferred, as it holds pitch shots well and putts better than finer textured sands. A variety of particle sizes within this range is preferred because the sand "sets up" better and is firmer. Very fine sands (less than 0.1 millimeter) of uniform particle size tend to have slow putting characteristics and increased ball tracking. The sand used must be free of sand sized larger then 1 millimeter, pebbles, and gravel. An angular, sharp sand is firmer to walk and putt on than are round sands.

The surface sand is mixed with oil, which functions as a bonding agent. It is important to select a rather heavy oil for mixing with the sand. The heavier oils are preferred because they are less prone to wash onto the fairway where serious grass kill can occur. Oil drained from crankcases is good but is prone to wash from the sand unless burned beforehand in a furnace or in a large sheet-iron pan. The sand is placed on a hard surface and the heavy oil poured over it and mixed continually until the sand has absorbed all the oil possible. This involves approximately one-half barrel of oil per cubic yard of sand. The sand should be spread over the subbase to a depth of 1 to 2 inches (2.5 to 5 centimeters), depending on the specific particle size distribution of the sand utilized.

After the sand is placed on the subbase, it is desirable to place at least one and preferably two strips of sod around the perimeter to provide good definition and stabilization of this apron area.

Sand-Asphalt Green. A second method of sand green construction involves building of the clay subbase, as just described, over which an asphalt base is poured. A 1-inch (2.5-centimeter) layer of fairly coarse sand, previously treated with crude mineral oil, is then applied. It is important that the sand be screened beforehand to remove all small pebbles.

Maintenance

One of the main reasons for using sand greens is the very low maintenance cost, particularly in areas where water is not available for irrigating grass greens. The primary maintenance practice on sand greens is dragging with a mat or heavy piece of carpeting, usually on a daily basis. This smoothing operation involves pulling the drag mat or carpet in a circular motion starting at the cup and working outward. In another method, which is used primarily on greens having a sand covering over an asphalt base, the surface sand is lightly swept with a coarse fiber broom in a circular motion. In addition, a small, T-shaped instrument with a long handle may be provided at each sand green which the player is permitted to use to smooth the line of putt between the ball and the cup (Fig. 3-48). Other courses provide a small drag mat which each player uses to smooth over footprints and ball marks for the following players.

Sand greens with a clay subbase may need to be loosened with a spiked drag at a depth of 0.5 to 1 inch (1.3 to 2.5 centimeters) at regular intervals. The interval depends on how rapidly the sand becomes compacted. This operation is followed immediately by dragging with a mat to achieve the desired surface smoothing. After intense rains the sand may need to be redistributed over the green using a wooden rub-board. This washing problem varies depending on the slope of the green and intensity of precipitation. An occasional follow-up application of oil to the sand surface may be required at annual

Figure 3-48. Sand green with a clay subbase, on which golfer is smoothing his putt. (Photo courtesy of R. Keen, Kansas State University, Manhattan, Kans.)

intervals or even less often, depending on the type of sand and degree of washing that occurs. Periodic edging of the perimeter to prevent surface encroachment of strong creeping, perennial grasses may also be required as the problem develops.

The maintenance requirements for sand greens should be minimal if the greens are properly constructed. Much time and money can be spent on improperly constructed sand greens which are prone to surface water overflow and erosion. Included is labor to repair eroded areas and to sweep up the washed sand, clean it by screening, and redistribute it over the green. The sand may even have to be retreated with oil as well. Additional labor may also be required to reestablish areas in adjacent fairways that have been killed by oil being washed onto them.

CHAPTER 4
The Tee

DESCRIPTION

The *Rules of Golf* does not give a precise definition for a tee. The specific term used is *teeing ground,* which is the starting place for the golf hole being played. It is described as "a rectangular area two club-lengths in depth, the front and sides of which are defined by the outside limits of two tee markers." A ball is outside the teeing ground when all of it lies outside the stipulated area.

The teeing ground as described was adequate for the intensity of seasonal golf play during the early days of golf. Thus, tees on old golf courses were typically quite small, square to slightly rectangular in design, and usually elevated with steeply sloped sides.

For the purpose of this text, the *tee* is defined as the area of the hole being played which is specially prepared for hitting the first shot of each hole. It encompasses the teeing ground, which is delineated by two tee markers. The tee is typically cut at a height intermediate between those of the putting green and the fairway.

There has been a major shift to a large tee size since 1950 because of increased play and improved maintenance equipment. The size of tees should be large enough to accommodate frequent movement of the tee markers as needed to maintain a turf cover despite intense play. Providing adequate-sized tees avoids unnecessary turf wear and enhances the rate of turfgrass recovery. A rule of thumb for tee size is discussed in the architecture section of chapter 2.

The trend in design of tee shape is for the tee to blend into the existing terrain and to be easy and economical to maintain. Tees may be of any shape, the most common configurations being rectangular, square, semicircular, circular, S-shaped, U-shaped, and L-shaped. Multilevel, terraced, and abruptly elevated tees restrict the usable teeing area and increase maintenance costs substantially. For a more detailed discussion, see the architecture section of chapter 2.

COMPONENTS OF TEE QUALITY

The components of quality for good playability of golf tees include (a) smoothness, (b) firmness, (c) density, (d) uniformity, (e) resiliency, and (f) close cut. Smoothness is particularly critical on golf tees so that golfers can achieve a level, firm, and balanced stance. Turfs having proper density possess adequate leaf area to produce the carbohydrate reserves needed to achieve rapid turf recovery following divot removal and the deep root system and strong sod formation needed to survive intense traffic and severe turfgrass wear stresses. The smoothness, density, and close cut components of quality contribute to overall tee uniformity which provides a well-groomed, favorable impression and quality playing

Figure 4-1. Properly maintained tee allows players the option of teeing the ball high or low, according to preference.

conditions. Resiliency is needed in the surface soil zone to allow wooden or plastic tees to be inserted readily into the soil. Resiliency is best achieved with relatively coarse-textured root zones. On clay soils not recently irrigated it may be almost impossible to insert a tee.

The tee is characterized by a mowing height intermediate between the green and the fairway heights. The height of the grass should be such that a ball stands clear of the leaf tips when positioned on a wooden tee (Fig. 4-1). The height should also allow each golfer a preference in the height at which a ball is teed.

CONSTRUCTION

The techniques employed in tee construction are similar to those described for putting greens in chapter 3. Thus, only the key activities are reviewed here, along with any significant variances.

The major steps in tee construction are (a) surveying and staking, (b) shaping of subgrade, (c) installation of a subsurface drainage system, if needed, (d) installation of an irrigation system, (e) construction of a modified root zone, and (f) finish grading (Fig. 4-2). The earlier construction phases, such as centerline staking, clearing, and rough grading of individual holes, have been discussed in detail in the construction section of chapter 2.

Surveying and Staking

With use of the earlier established centerline stakes as references, the shapes of individual tees are outlined according to the architect's staking plan. Hub stakes with grade designations are used as a reference to check the construction elevations and slopes.

Subgrade Shaping

Major excavations involving extensive cuts or fills are accomplished first according to the grading plan specifications. Sufficient time must be allowed for soil settling if deep fills are involved. For example, allowing settling over the winter months is quite effective. Subsequently, final subgrade shaping is carefully done to achieve the specified subgrade elevations. The final subgrade contours should conform to the finished grade within a tolerance of ± 1 inch (2.5 centimeters) and at an elevation 6 to 12 inches (15 to 30 centimeters) below the proposed finished grade. If adequate time is not available for needed settling, mechanical firming procedures should be used to accelerate it.

Subsurface Drainage System Installation

Good internal soil drainage is essential on tees to minimize soil compaction and provide favorable turfgrass growing conditions. Subsurface drain lines probably are required if the soil utilized in

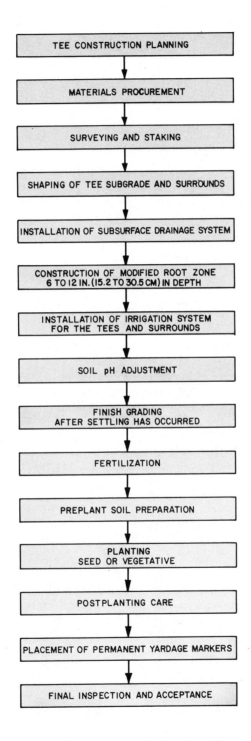

Figure 4-2. Flow diagram for construction of a golf course tee.

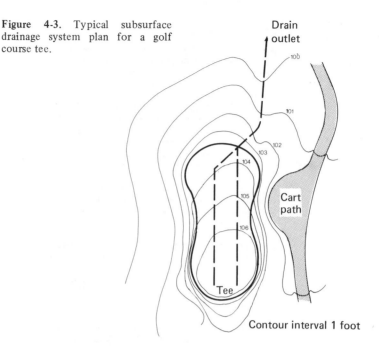

Figure 4-3. Typical subsurface drainage system plan for a golf course tee.

Drain outlet

100

101

102

103

104

105

106

Cart path

Tee

Contour interval 1 foot

establishing the subgrade is relatively impermeable. The drainage system for tees is similar to that for putting greens discussed previously. It consists of a 4-inch (10-centimeter) main line connected to an outlet of adequate size or, if there is no other option, to a large dry well/gravel drain bed in the adjacent rough. The lateral drain lines are typically 4 inches in diameter and arranged in a parallel herringbone or gridiron configuration with a spacing between of 15 to 20 feet (4.6 to 6.1 meters) (Fig. 4-3). Drain lines may be of clay, concrete, or flexible perforated plastic. The last is the most popular due to low cost and ease of installation.

The first step in installation is staking of the drainage system, including grade stakes. Trenches are then dug at a shallow depth into the subgrade using a mechanical trencher. The minimum slope of drain lines should be 1 percent. A 0.5- to 1-inch (1.27- to 2.54-centimeter) layer of pea gravel (0.5 to 0.7 inch in diameter) should be placed in the bottom of the trench if the subgrade soil is somewhat loose or unstable. The drain lines are then installed and the trenches backfilled with pea gravel, usually to the top of the subgrade unless the drain lines have been dug unusually deep. A sand root zone mix is placed in the trench above the gravel to insure rapid removal of excess water.

Root Zone Modification

Due to their limited size, tees are subjected to very intense traffic. Thus, potentially serious problems with soil compaction and poor turfgrass growth can occur if the proper root zone soil mix is not utilized. Characteristics desired in a soil mix for tees are minimum proneness to compaction, good soil water infiltration and percolation rates, and a resilient surface which allows ready insertion of a golf tee. The preferred root zone mix is basically the same as that described for golf greens and will not be discussed in detail here. The depth of a modified root zone above the subsoil grade of tees is typically in the 6- to 12-inch (15- to 30-centimeter) range.

Most tees are normally elevated, which enhances drainage. However, if the tee is not elevated, placement of a gravel layer between the subsoil and modified root zone is beneficial, as is the ringing of tees with soil prior to the distribution of the modified soil mix, as previously described for putting greens. The soil used to ring a tee and cover the tee surrounds should be a good quality topsoil which has been previously stockpiled or a relatively coarse-textured soil mix which will provide adequate internal soil water drainage.

Irrigation System Installation

Modern construction of most golf tees includes installation of an irrigation system. The system should be installed and made operational prior to planting. If installed early enough, the irrigation system can be used to enhance soil settling during very dry periods.

The irrigation system should be designed to meet the needs of the particular tee shape. On larger free-form tees, it is helpful for tee shapes to be designed so that equilateral triangular spacing can be achieved by means of perimeter sprinkler-head placement. The irrigation heads for each tee should be on a separate controller. In addition, a quick coupler valve is installed at each tee for manual access to water as needed.

Finish Grading

Finish grading of tees is usually accomplished just prior to planting. The grading operation should not be attempted until the underlying soil is completely settled and firm. The final surface grade must be adequate to insure surface drainage and yet level enough to assure a player a reasonably level stance. A slope of 1 to 2 percent is generally adequate and so slight that it can be oriented in most any direction. The direction of slopes is usually dictated by the surrounding terrain. On a multilevel tee, it is important for the slope to be either toward the right or left so that water does not collect between the terraces. It is also advisable for the slope to drain away from the side where golfers approach, thus avoiding wet spots in the trafficked areas. It is essential that adequate time, manpower, and equipment be devoted to achieving a uniform, smooth final grade that is settled and free of depressions.

TURFGRASS SELECTION

Key characteristics desired in turfgrass species and cultivars utilized on golf course tees include (a) rapid recuperative rate, (b) adaptation to a cutting height of 0.3 to 0.8 inch (7.6 to 20.0 millimeters), (c) tight, dense turf, and (d) tolerance to soil compaction and turfgrass wear. The turfgrass selected should have a low spreading or creeping growth habit so that it can tolerate close mowing heights and achieve rapid healing of divot marks. In addition, the traffic concentration on tees necessitates that the grass selected have good wear tolerance and recuperative potential. The grass should be rather tight and dense with minimum puffiness to insure the golfer a firm, stable stance. Species and cultivars characterized by good tolerance to environmental stresses such as heat, cold, drought, and shade and that are less susceptible to major disease and insect problems should be selected whenever possible, assuming the previously listed criteria are also met.

Cool-Season Species

Creeping bentgrass (*Agrostis palustris*) and Kentucky bluegrass (*Poa pratensis*) are the cool-season turfgrasses most commonly used on tees in the cool climatic region (Fig. 4-4). Penncross is the most commonly used creeping bentgrass cultivar; Seaside, Penneagle, and Emerald are used to a lesser extent. Creeping bentgrass performs best at a high intensity of culture, including irrigation, and relatively close, frequent mowing of 0.5 to 0.7 inch (1.3 to 1.8 centimeters). Improved cultivars of Kentucky bluegrass are used on tees mowed at a higher height and subject to medium to low intensity of

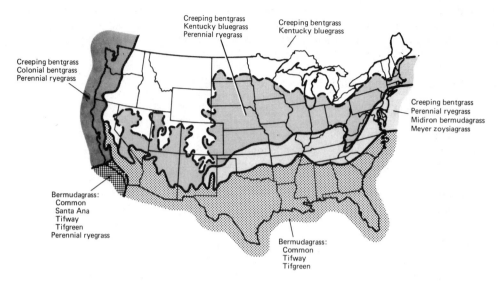

Figure 4-4. Geographic distribution of turfgrass species commonly used on golf course tees in the United States.

culture. These cultivars are listed in Table 5-2, page 206. Some colonial bentgrass is also used, primarily in the maritime areas of the Pacific Northwest. Although not originally seeded, annual bluegrass may become the dominant component of golf course tees, particularly in shaded sites and in the northern half of the cool climatic region. Some improved turf-type perennial ryegrass cultivars are being overseeded onto tees in the southern half of the cool climatic region and in the transitional zone, where continual intense traffic causes thinning.

Warm-Season Species

Bermudagrass (*Cynodon* spp.) is the most widely used warm-season turfgrass species on tees in the warm climatic region extending from Florida to California. Tifway and Tifgreen have performed quite well. Common seeded bermudagrass is utilized widely on low-budget, minimal-maintenance golf courses. Santa Ana has been effective in southern California owing to its superior smog tolerance, while Tifgreen is used to a limited degree in the Southeast on high-budget, intensely maintained courses.

The two most commonly used turfgrasses in the transitional zone are Midiron bermudagrass and Meyer zoysiagrass (*Zoysia japonica*). Midiron possesses better low-temperature hardiness than any other available bermudagrass cultivar. Meyer zoysiagrass also has good low-temperature hardiness for a warm-season turfgrass but its rate of recovery from divoting is somewhat restricted. This means that its performance is better under medium to low intensities of use. Also, zoysiagrass is preferred to bermudagrass on shaded tees.

Winter Overseeding of Bermudagrass Tees

Winter overseeding of bermudagrass tees is practiced in the South where significant winter play occurs. However, the practice of winter overseeding on tees is not as extensive as on greens. Perennial ryegrass is usually one of the species utilized. Most overseeding mixtures contain from two to four species selected from such cool-season turfgrasses as perennial ryegrass, rough bluegrass, creeping bentgrass, red fescue, Italian ryegrass, and certain low-growing Kentucky bluegrass cultivars.

Figure 4-5. Tee being planted by the hydroseeding method.

ESTABLISHMENT

The criteria and chronological steps involved in establishment of golf course tees are basically the same as those for putting greens, discussed previously. The reader is referred to the section on turfgrass establishment of greens in chapter 3. The hydroseeding method of planting tees is illustrated in Figure 4-5.

CULTURE

Many of the principles and specific practices utilized in the culture of golf course tees are the same as those discussed for putting greens in chapter 3. Thus, the material covered in this section relates primarily to aspects of tee culture that are distinctly different from those on putting greens. For specific details on tee culture not covered in this section, the reader is referred to the earlier discussion on culture of putting greens.

Mowing

The cutting height on tees should be low enough so that when a ball is teed up at the desired height, leaf growth does not obstruct clean contact between the club face and ball. A relatively low cutting height also insures golfers a firm, stable stance. These considerations dictate a height that is usually intermediate between those on putting greens and fairways of from 0.3 to 1.0 inch (7.6 to 25 millimeters). Kentucky bluegrass and Common bermudagrass perform best when mowed frequently at a height in the upper portion of the range, while the bentgrasses, zoysiagrasses, improved bermudagrasses, and annual bluegrass respond best at cutting heights of 0.5 inch (1.3 centimeters) or less.

The mowing frequency on tees is usually two to four times per week. More frequent mowing is preferred, and usually required, where high nitrogen fertility levels and/or high cutting heights are used. Clippings may or may not be removed, although removal is preferred. High intensities of culture, including very close mowing, necessitate the removal of clippings.

Tees are usually mowed with a three-gang, six- to eight-bladed reel mower. A three-gang riding greensmower may be used on intensively maintained tees where a close cutting height is utilized (Fig. 4-6). Before a mower is driven on a tee the area should be inspected for foreign objects. Any metal (shoe spikes) or wooden (golf tees) objects which could damage the reel blades or bedknife must be picked up. In addition, all divots should be replaced or the marks filled. The mowing pattern is usually in two perpendicular directions, with the mower also being alternated in opposite directions within each of the perendicular mowings to minimize grain development. Mower operating procedures are basically the same as those described for putting greens in chapter 3.

Fertilization

The philosophy of tee fertilization is slightly different from that of greens. Extensive damage caused by divoting dictates a more rapid shoot growth rate to enhance turf recovery. Sufficient nitrogen must be applied to maintain adequate turfgrass color, shoot density, and recuperative rate in terms of lateral shoot growth and tillering. The nitrogen fertilization rate ranges from 3 to 6 pounds per thousand square feet (1.5 to 3.0 kilograms/are) per year on bentgrass, Kentucky bluegrass, zoysiagrass, and annual bluegrass tees and from 5 to 10 pounds per thousand square feet (2.5 to 5.0 kilograms/are) per year on bermudagrass tees. The frequency of nitrogen fertilization is typically at intervals of fifteen to thirty growing days.

The nitrogen fertilization rate utilized on individual tees within a golf course may vary even though root zone mix and irrigation practices are comparable. Tees that receive extensive divoting, such as the par-3's and the first tee, may require up to twice the amount of nitrogen applied to larger tees, which receive minimal traffic stress and divoting. A higher nitrogen fertilization rate is needed in the former situation to enhance the recuperative rate from traffic stress and divot marks and is particularly important if the tee is small. In the case of a large, minimal use tee, a high nitrogen level may result in increased thatch formation, which will necessitate use of corrective measures.

Principles concerning the seasonal timing of nitrogen applications, selection of the appropriate carrier(s), and method of application are essentially the same as those discussed in the putting green culture section of the previous chapter.

Figure 4-6. Three-gang riding mower with catchers being used to cut an intensively maintained tee.

Good results have been obtained on bentgrass, Kentucky bluegrass, zoysiagrass, and annual blue-grass tees using 0.25 to 0.75 pound of nitrogen per thousand square feet (0.13 to 0.38 kilogram/are) every fifteen to thirty growing days. In the case of bermudagrass tees, a higher rate of 0.5 to 1.2 pounds per thousand square feet (0.25 to 0.60 kilogram/are) every fifteen to thirty growing days has been effective. The upper portion of the range is commonly used (a) on coarse-textured sand root zones where leaching is a problem, (b) where clippings are removed, (c) where intense divoting and traffic stress occur, and (d) on sites with full sun exposure.

The phosphorus, potassium, iron, and sulfur nutritional programs for tees are basically the same as those previously discussed for putting greens. Descriptions of the commonly used carriers can be found in the appendix. Potassium is particularly important in promoting turfgrass wear tolerance. Soil tests are used as the primary guideline in both phosphorus and potassium fertilization, as previously discussed. Analyses should be conducted for each tee at one- to three-year intervals, depending on the soil texture, irrigation intensity, and site conditions.

Soil Reaction Adjustment

The preferred pH range, application rate, time of application, carrier, and method of application are essentially the same as those discussed for putting greens. The need for pH adjustment should be based on regular soil test analyses.

Irrigation

Proper irrigation of tees is just as exacting as proper irrigation of putting greens. Tees should be maintained at a somewhat drier moisture range than are putting greens to provide a firm stance for golfers. Fortunately, the higher cutting height on tees and resulting deeper rooting does permit main-tenance of a drier surface zone through deeper, less frequent irrigations than are commonly used on putting greens. In addition, the higher cutting height and deeper rooting reduce the need for frequent syringing, as is utilized on bentgrass greens in midsummer. Other than these aspects, the basic principles and practices of irrigation of golf course tees are comparable to those discussed in the putting green culture section of the previous chapter.

Topdressing

Properly maintained tees need to be topdressed periodically. Unfortunately, this important practice tends to be neglected on many golf courses. It is particularly important on par-3 holes where extensive divoting occurs. Topdressing of divot marks enhances the recuperative rate and also smooths the area, which provides a level stance. The rate of topdressing application is usually higher than that typically used on putting greens, ranging from 0.25 to 0.50 cubic yard per thousand square feet. Topdressing is usually needed at least once per year and as frequently as four times per year on selected tees. Other than these small modifications, the procedures utilized in topdressing selection, preparation, and application are basically the same as those described in the putting green culture section of the previous chapter.

Thatch Control

The need for thatch control on tees varies greatly. Tees on par-3 holes that are intensively divoted or tees that are excessively small for the amount of play they receive rarely develop a thatch problem. On the other hand, large tees with a modest intensity of use and a high nitrogen nutritional level may require regular thatch control measures, such as vertical cutting (Fig. 4-7). In addition, the topdressing utilized for smoothing divot-marked areas proves beneficial in thatch control. Other procedures for thatch control on tees are essentially the same as those discussed for putting green culture in the previous chapter.

Figure 4-7. Medium-severe dethatching of a tee with a powered vertical cutting machine.

Cultivation

Soil compaction is a more common problem on tees than on putting greens. This is because fewer root zones have been properly modified on tees than on putting greens. Construction of tees too small for the intensity of play further accentuates the soil compaction problem. Thus, the frequency of soil cultivation of tees ranges from never on large tees with properly modified root zones to every three to six weeks on small, intensively trafficked tees. Most tees that lack properly modified root zones require cultivation at the minimum of every spring and fall. Coring and slicing are the two main cultivation approaches employed. If coring is practiced, the turfed cores are usually broken up, the soil matted back into the turf unless it is an extremely objectionable clay, and the grass debris removed. Spiking, forking, grooving, and shattering are forms of cultivation rarely utilized on tees.

Other than these specific points concerning correction of soil compaction on tees, the basic principles relating to problem diagnosis, timing of cultivation, and types of cultivation are basically the same as those discussed in the putting green culture section of the previous chapter.

Winter Overseeding

Winter overseeding in the southern portion of North America is less widely practiced on bermudagrass tees than on putting greens. It is most commonly employed on high-budget and winter resort golf courses. The preoverseeding cultural practices utilized are comparable to those for putting greens, with particular attention needed concerning elimination of any existing thatch problem. The ryegrasses are the most popular species utilized in overseeding of golf course tees. Seeding rates tend to be 20 to 40 percent less than those for putting greens. The actual overseeding procedures are comparable to those used on putting greens with the exception that topdressing is rarely used for seed coverage. The postplanting cultural practices are usually comparable to those normally used on bermudagrass tees during the summer. Particular attention needs to be given to frequent movement of the tee markers during the seedling establishment period to minimize injury and thinning.

Pest and Stress Problems

The weed, disease, insect, nematode, animal, environmental, and soil stress problems of tees are basically comparable to those discussed for putting greens in chapter 3. Detailed coverage of problem

Figure 4-8. Divot repair by topdressing with a seed-soil mix.

recognition, causal diagnosis, cultural practices affecting severity of the problem, and chemical controls can be found in the chapter on pests and stresses (chapter 10). A few additional comments related only to golf course tees are warranted.

Continual divoting of tees increases weed problems. First, the divot marks provide ideal openings for invasion of weeds, especially annual bluegrass, crabgrass, and goosegrass, which have light requirements for seed germination. In addition, extensive deep divot marks on par-3 tees may disrupt a protective surface layer of preemergence herbicide, which also increases the potential for weed development. Because of these potential problems, it is important that proper cultural practices, including nitrogen nutrition, be utilized to enhance divot mark recovery and that overseeding or plugging practices be employed as needed to facilitate recovery.

The disease, insect, animal, and nematode problems of tees are comparable to those previously discussed for putting greens. The higher nitrogen nutritional level utilized on tees increases proneness to invasion by certain pathogens, such as brown patch and *Pythium* blight. On the other hand, irrigation practices that leave a drier surface discourage disease development. Nevertheless, serious injury may occur periodically and necessitate use of the appropriate chemical control measures to prevent extensive turfgrass loss.

Potential for stress damage on tees is not quite as great as on closely mowed putting greens but is still a substantial concern. Utilization of the appropriate preventive cultural practices contributes significantly to reducing the potential for injury from environmental and soil stresses.

Divot Mark Repair

A program of divot mark repair is needed on most golf courses, with primary emphasis placed on the par-3 holes, the first tee, and the practice tee. The foundation of any divot mark repair program is a cultural system that enhances the rate of tillering and lateral stem development. Proper irrigation and nutritional levels are important. Many par-3 holes are subject to sufficiently intense divoting so that a formal program of divot mark repair should be followed. The two primary approaches involve filling the divots with a soil-seed mix (Fig. 4-8) or, less commonly, by plugging. The frequency with which either of these approaches is used may vary from daily to biweekly, depending on the intensity of divoting. The seed-soil mix typically consists of nine parts root zone mix to one part seed mix. The latter consists of the existing species monostand or polystand plus a turf-type perennial ryegrass or fine-leafed fescue to enhance the rate of germination and seedling establishment. In some cases the problem of divoting is so intense that periodic resodding is required. This is especially true on the practice tee. Thus, maintenance of a tee nursery is important where sodding or plugging is anticipated.

Figure 4-9. Bare, compacted tee caused by failure to construct tee of adequate size and root zone texture.

Rebuilding

The intensity of divoting, soil compaction, shade, and traffic stress is so severe on certain golf courses that it is impossible to sustain adequately turfed tees on the par-3 holes. Such bare, compacted tees are usually excessively small relative to the amount of traffic and/or have a fine-textured, clayey soil which is very prone to soil compaction problems (Fig. 4-9). The only long-term solution is rebuilding. In rebuilding, it is important that corrective measures be taken to minimize the chance that the problem will recur. These include design of a sufficiently large teeing surface, use of a modified root zone possessing minimum proneness to compaction, and use of a subsurface drainage system to remove excess water. Finally, it is important that the surface of the tee be reconstructed with a slight slope to insure rapid removal of excess water. The specific principles and procedures utilized in rebuilding a tee are basically the same as those covered in the section on tee construction.

Tee Surrounds

Tee surrounds refers to the turfed area immediately adjacent to the more closely mowed tee surface. The turfgrass species and cultural practices used on tee surrounds are comparable to those used on the primary rough, including the cutting height used, mowing frequency, disposal of clippings, fertilization, irrigation practices, and weed control. The mowing frequency interval may need to be somewhat shorter than in the primary rough because the tee surrounds tend to receive the same intense irrigation as the tee area. Additional attention may be needed on those portions of the surrounds where most golfers enter and exit from the tee, including a higher nutritional level to enhance turf recovery and more frequent cultivation by coring or slicing. Slopes on the tee surrounds should be contoured with sufficient moderation so that mowing can be accomplished with multigang units. This is particularly important on golf courses where budget restrictions make it advantageous to mow the tee surrounds with the same five- to seven-gang mowers utilized on the primary rough and putting green surrounds. The tee irrigation system should be designed to cover the associated surrounds so that all slopes are adequately watered to prevent drying from the sides.

A problem frequently encountered on the tee surrounds is associated with trees. The tee may have been constructed adjacent to or within a tree stand. The objective is to offer comfort on hot days to golfers who are waiting to tee off. While a tree stand is a desirable feature, it can pose serious problems to turfgrass culture if the trees are too close to the tee. A tee enclosed on three sides by trees and shrubs is subjected to an environment unfavorable for turfgrass survival. The grass is generally weak and spindly, possesses a very low wear tolerance, and is prone to disease. This problem occurs on densely shaded tees regardless of the root zone mix and specific cultural program employed. Approaches to partially solving it include selection of shade-tolerant turfgrass species and cultivars, raising of the mowing height, use of a low nitrogen fertility level, utilization of moderate irrigation practices, and control of potentially serious disease problems as they occur. In addition, the environment for turfgrass growth can be improved through such actions as (a) selective tree and shrub removal, particularly in the direction of the prevailing wind and the rising sun, (b) selective thinning of tree limbs, particularly the lowermost parts, (c) immediate removal of fallen leaves in the autumn, and (d) trenching of the surrounds to sever tree roots which compete for nutrients and water.

SUMMARIES OF CULTURAL SYSTEMS

Summaries of the cultural systems utilized in the maintenance of five types of golf course tees are presented in this section. The two main turfgrasses used on tees are bentgrass and bermudagrass. Systems are also presented for Kentucky bluegrass, zoysiagrass, and annual bluegrass. Exceptions of course exist to these general guidelines, and flexibility should be maintained in selection of the cultural system, depending on the environmental stress and pest problems most likely to occur in a given location. These systems are presented as a ready reference. For more details the reader is referred to the previous section of this chapter on tee culture.

Cultural System for a Bentgrass Tee

Mowing Height   0.3 to 0.6 in. (7.6 to 15 mm).
Mowing Frequency   Two to four times per week.
Mowing Pattern   Opposite mowing in each of two perpendicular directions.
Clippings   Return or remove (latter is preferred).
Fertilization
> **Nitrogen**   Apply 0.25 to 0.75 lb. N/1,000 sq. ft. (0.13 to 0.38 kg/are)/15 to 30 growing days.
> **Phosphorus**   Application rate based on soil test. Spring and fall timings usually best, preferably just after coring, usually as part of complete analysis fertilizer.
> **Potassium**   Application rate based on soil test where fine-textured clay soils are involved. Coarse-textured soils and clippings removed require 4 to 5 lbs. K_2O/1,000 sq. ft. (2 to 2.5 kg/are)/yr., usually split into four to six applications over the growing season.
> **Iron**   Apply only when visual deficiency symptoms appear. Deficiency occurs occasionally, particularly during the midsummer months.
> **Other Nutrients**   Apply if specific visual deficiency is diagnosed (a rare occurrence).
pH Correction   Maintain pH between 5.5 and 6.0. Apply limestone or sulphur materials as needed based on soil test.
Irrigation   Each irrigation should moisten to full depth of root zone and should be timed prior to development of visual wilt symptoms. Midday syringing usually not needed unless very close, frequent mowing practiced.
Topdressing   Apply one to four times per year as needed for smoothing. Spring and fall applications suggested at rate of 0.25 to 0.50 cu. yd./1,000 sq. ft.
Thatch Control   Practice vertical cutting if thatch problem develops. Usually only occurs on large nonintensively divoted tees. Vertical cutting best accomplished during first half of growing season.
Cultivation   Core or slice as needed to correct developing soil compaction problem. Frequency may be as high as every two to three weeks on small tees with fine-textured clay soil.

Weed Control   Apply herbicides only as needed to correct developing weed problem. Early fall application of mecoprop (MCPP) and/or dicamba is suggested. Avoid phenoxy herbicides, such as 2,4-D, because of potential phytotoxicity. Use selected preemergence and post-emergence grass herbicides with great caution due to potential phytotoxicity to certain bentgrasses.

Disease Control   Practice on preventive basis or give corrective fungicide treatment when injury symptoms appear. Preventive program usually utilized for warm-weather diseases in humid climates, use of several effective fungicides being alternated. Where winter diseases, such as snow mold, are a problem, a preventive fungicide program is usually needed.

Insect Control   Apply appropriate insecticide as needed when potentially serious insect injury symptoms first appear.

Drainage   Adequate drainage is essential for culture of healthy bentgrass tees subjected to intense traffic.

Divot Mark Repair   Place soil-seed mixture in divot marks on daily to weekly basis (or hand plug).

Cultural System for a Bermudagrass Tee

Mowing Height   0.3 to 0.6 in. (7.6 to 15 mm).
Mowing Frequency   Two or three times per week.
Mowing Pattern   Opposite mowing in each of two perpendicular directions.
Clippings   Return or remove.
Fertilization
   Nitrogen   Apply 0.5 to 1.2 lb. N/1,000 sq. ft. (0.25 to 0.6 kg/are)/15 to 30 growing days.
   Phosphorus   Application rate based on soil test. Spring and fall timings usually best, preferably just after coring, usually as part of complete analysis fertilizer.
   Potassium   Application rate based on soil test where fine-textured clay soils are involved. Coarse-textured soils and clippings removed require 4 to 8 lbs. K_2O/1,000 sq. ft. (2 to 4 kg/are)/yr., usually split into four to six applications over growing season.
   Iron   Apply only when visual deficiency symptoms appear. Deficiency occurs occasionally, particularly on alkaline soils and following spring greenup.
   Other Nutrients   Apply if specific visual deficiency is diagnosed (a rare occurrence).
pH Correction   Maintain pH between 6.0 and 7.0. Apply limestone or sulphur materials as needed based on soil test.
Irrigation   Each irrigation should moisten to full depth of root zone and should be timed prior to development of visual wilt symptoms.
Topdressing   Apply one to four times per year as needed for smoothing. Spring and fall applications suggested at rate of 0.25 to 0.50 cu. yd./1,000 sq. ft.
Thatch Control   Practice vertical cutting if thatch problem develops. Tends to be more of problem with bermudagrass than bentgrass, especially at higher nitrogen levels. Vertical cutting best accomplished during first half of growing season.
Cultivation   Core or slice as needed to correct developing soil compaction problem. Frequency may be as high as every three to four weeks on small tees with fine-textured clay soil.
Weed Control   Control broadleafs or annual weedy grasses as they appear with a preemergence or postemergence herbicide. Best accomplished during first half of growing season. Control of winter annual weeds may be required after bermudagrass enters winter dormancy, assuming overseeding not practiced.
Disease Control   Use corrective or preventive disease control program, with former generally preferred, especially in arid and semiarid climates.

Insect Control   Apply appropriate insecticides as needed when potentially serious insect injury symptoms first appear. Major insect problems include bermudagrass mites, sod webworms, armyworms, and grubs.

Winter Overseeding   May or may not be used in southern half of warm humid climatic region. Use procedures for overseeding described in chapter 3 for bermudagrass putting greens.

Cultural System for a Kentucky Bluegrass Tee

Mowing Height   0.6 to 1.0 in. (15 to 25 mm).

Mowing Frequency   Three to five times per week.

Mowing Pattern   Opposite mowing in each of two perpendicular directions.

Clippings   Return or remove.

Fertilization

   Nitrogen   Apply 0.25 to 0.75 lb. N/1,000 sq. ft. (0.13 to 0.38 kg/are)/15 to 30 growing days.

   Phosphorus   Application rate based on soil test. Spring and fall timings usually best, preferably just after coring, usually as part of complete analysis fertilizer.

   Potassium   Application rate based on soil test where fine-textured clay soils involved. Coarse-textured soils and clippings removed require 4 to 5 lbs. K_2O/1,000 sq. ft. (2 to 2.5 kg/are)/yr., usually split into four to six applications over growing season.

   Iron   Apply only when visual deficiency symptoms appear. Occurs occasionally, particularly during midsummer months.

   Other Nutrients   Apply if specific nutrient deficiency is diagnosed (a rare occurrence).

pH Correction   Maintain pH between 6.0 and 7.0. Apply limestone or sulfur materials as needed based on soil test.

Irrigation   Each irrigation should moisten to full depth of root zone and should be timed prior to development of visual wilt symptoms.

Topdressing   Apply one to four times per year as needed for smoothing. Spring and fall applications usually suggested at rate of 0.25 to 0.50 cu. yd./1,000 sq. ft.

Thatch Control   Usually not needed.

Cultivation   Core or slice as needed to correct developing soil compaction problem. Frequency may be as high as every three to four weeks on small tees with fine-textured clay soil. Best accomplished during the first half of growing season.

Weed Control   Control broadleafs or annual weedy grasses as they appear with either preemergence or postemergence herbicide. Best accomplished in early fall.

Disease Control   Best accomplished by selecting appropriate disease-resistant cultivars, especially *Helminthosporium*-resistant. Fungicides infrequently used.

Insect Control   Apply appropriate insecticide as needed when potentially serious insect injury symptoms first appear. White grubs, sod webworms, billbugs, and cutworms are most common problems.

Divot Mark Repair   Place soil-seed mixture in divot marks on daily to weekly basis (or hand plug).

Cultural System for a Zoysiagrass Tee

Mowing Height   0.3 to 0.5 in. (7.6 to 13 mm).

Mowing Frequency   Two to three times per week.

Mowing Pattern   Opposite mowing in each of two perpendicular directions.

Clippings   Return or remove.

Fertilization

   Nitrogen   Apply 0.25 to 0.75 lb. N/1,000 sq. ft. (0.13 to 0.38 kg/are)/15 to 30 growing days.

   Phosphorus   Apply at rate based on soil test. Spring and fall timings usually best, preferably just after coring, usually as part of complete analysis fertilizer.

Potassium   Apply at rate based on soil test with fine-textured clay soils. Coarse-textured soils and clippings removed require 3 to 6 lbs. $K_2O/1,000$ sq. ft. (1.5 to 3.0 kg/are)/yr., usually split into three to five applications over growing season.

Iron   Apply only when visual deficiency symptoms appear. Deficiency occurs occasionally during the midsummer months.

Other Nutrients   Apply if specific visual deficiency is diagnosed (a rare occurrence).

pH Correction   Maintain pH between 6.0 and 7.0. Apply limestone or sulphur materials based on soil test.

Irrigation   Moisten to full depth of root zone with each irrigation; time prior to development of visual wilt symptoms.

Topdressing   Apply one to four times per year as needed for smoothing. Adjust spring and fall applications at rate of 0.25 to 0.50 cu. yd./1,000 sq. ft.

Thatch Control   Practice vertical cutting as thatch problem develops (highly likely with zoysiagrass). Best accomplished during first three-quarters of growing season.

Cultivation   Core/slice as needed to correct developing soil compaction problem. Frequency may be as high as every three to four weeks on small tees with fine-textured clay soil. Best accomplished during first half of growing season.

Weed Control   Control broadleafs or annual weedy grasses as they appear with preemergence or postemergence herbicide. Best accomplished during first half of growing season. Control of winter annual weeds may be required after zoysiagrass enters winter dormancy.

Disease Control   Use corrective disease control program when specific problem develops which threatens serious turf loss. Fungicides infrequently used.

Insect Control   Apply appropriate insecticide as needed when potentially serious insect injury symptoms first appear. Hunting billbugs, grubs, cutworms, and sod webworms are most common problems.

Cultural System for an Annual Bluegrass Tee

Mowing Height   0.4 to 0.7 in. (10 to 18 mm).

Mowing Frequency   Two to three times per week.

Mowing Pattern   Opposite mowing in each of two perpendicular directions.

Clippings   Usually return.

Fertilization

Nitrogen   Apply 0.25 to 0.75 lb. N/1,000 sq. ft. (0.13 to 0.38 kg/are)/growing month.

Phosphorus   Apply at rate based on soil test. Spring and fall timings usually best, preferably just after coring, usually as part of complete analysis fertilizer.

Potassium   Apply at rate based on soil test where fine-textured clay soils involved. Coarse-textured soils probably require 3 to 5 lbs. $K_2O/1,000$ sq. ft. (1.5 to 2.5 kg/are)/yr., usually split into four to six applications over growing season.

Iron   Apply as visual deficiency symptoms appear, at rate of 1 to 3 oz. ferrous sulfate/1,000 sq. ft./growing month. Typically applied monthly during summer.

Other Nutrients   Apply if specific visual deficiency diagnosed (a rare occurrence).

pH Correction   Maintain pH between 6.2 and 7.2. Apply limestone or sulphur materials as needed based on soil test.

Irrigation   Maintain moist but not wet soil through light frequent irrigations, usually as daily early morning applications. Syringing may be needed occasionally to prevent wilt.

Topdressing   Apply one to four times per year as needed for smoothing. Spring and fall applications suggested at rate of 0.25 to 0.50 cu. yd./1,000 sq. ft.

Thatch Control   Vertical cutting usually not needed for control of thatch problem.

Cultivation   Utilize two to four times per year, higher frequencies being needed on intensely trafficked tees with fine-textured soil. Core or slice a minimum of twice yearly, in very early spring as soon as equipment can be taken onto tee and in early fall. Avoid cultivation during heat stress, if possible.

Spiking   Practice on weekly to biweekly basis throughout summer when soil temperature above 70 °F (21 °C).

Weed Control   Control broadleafs as they appear. Use of mecoprop (MCPP) suggested. Avoid phenoxy herbicides, such as dicamba and 2,4-D, because of potential phytotoxicity during heat stress. Hand-weed goosegrass. Avoid organic arsenicals and preemergence weedy-grass herbicides because of potential phytotoxicity.

Disease Control   Use preventive fungicide program in which several effective fungicides are alternated. Dollar spot, brown patch, *Fusarium* patch, *Pythium* blight, and anthracnose usually most severe diseases, depending on climatic region. Where winter diseases, such as snow mold, are problem, preventive fungicide program usually needed.

Insect Control   Apply appropriate insecticide as needed when potentially serious insect injury symptoms first appear. Turfgrass weevil and black turfgrass ataenius grub of particular concern.

TEE MARKERS AND ACCESSORY EQUIPMENT

Tees became necessary on golf courses as a result of the evolution of the game and the advent of refined turf areas called putting greens. In the early days of the game, the teeing ground was the area one club-length from the hole just completed. Today, the teeing ground is a rectangular area two club-lengths in depth, the front and sides of which are defined by the outside limits of two tee markers. The teeing ground is located on a turfed tee, which is a separate entity from the putting green, and serves as the starting point for the hole to be played.

The advent of the teeing ground has led to a number of important revelations in the game of golf. One of the most important is the course yardage rating for handicapping purposes. A course must be accurately measured from the center of each tee along the centerline of the fairway, as the architect intended the hole to be played, to the center of the green. Once the distance for each hole has been established in this manner, a yardage rating is assigned to the course. Permanent yardage markers should be installed midway on one side of each tee to designate the exact location from which the measurements were taken. Many golf courses elect to install three such permanent yardage markers on each hole, one for the championship or blue course, one for the regular or white course, and one for the women's or red course.

Tee markers are an essential feature of each tee. They are utilized to designate the area from which play begins on each hole for a given day. Moving the tee markers in a planned pattern provides some variation in how individual holes are played from day to day and allows the turf manager to manipulate the distribution of traffic and divoting across the teeing area so as to avoid excessive damage to a given area as well as to allow time for damaged areas to recover.

Tee markers can range from simple inexpensive markers to very extravagant figurines on engraved plaques (Fig. 4-10). The individual courses within a golf facility are generally designated by different-colored tee markers. The accepted color scheme is blue markers for the championship course, white markers for the regular course, and red markers for the women's course. At some courses gold markers are used for the seniors' course, which may be designated the short course.

The frequency with which tee markers are moved is dictated to a certain extent by the intensity of play and associated damage to the turf. The greatest degree of divoting is usually on par-3 holes and on the first tee. In addition, relatively frequent rotation of tee markers on a golf course enhances golfers' enjoyment of a course because of the variations in tee shots offered from day to day.

Figure 4-10. Representative types of tee markers used on golf course tees.

An attempt should be made to keep the overall distance of the course as consistent as possible through a planned program of tee marker placement as well as cup placement on the putting greens. A typical program of tee marker rotation on an eighteen-hole golf course involves placement of six tee markers behind the permanent tee markers, six at approximately the same length as the permanent tee markers, and six to the front. Cup placement on greens is similarly coordinated to insure balance in the golf course, so that total yardage essentially remains comparable to that based on the permanent tee markers.

A number of accessories are utilized in association with golf course tees. Signs are generally positioned at each tee indicating the hole number, yardage, par, and handicap stroke in effect on the hole. In addition, some golf courses now display a sign on the tee which shows the design of the hole about to be played. Another accessory is a ball washer, one of which is placed at least at every other hole around the golf course. Each ball washer is accompanied by a stand with a towel attached for wiping the ball clean. In addition, a trash receptacle is positioned in the immediate area, usually with a bench of some type. Benches may vary from hewn logs to standard manufactured metal units to wood structures. All must be of a sturdy, outdoor type of construction. Finally, shoe spike cleaners may be attached to the stand or positioned close to the ball washing unit so that golfers may clean debris from the spikes of their shoes prior to starting on the next hole.

PRACTICE TEE

A common shortcoming in golf course design is a practice tee woefully deficient in size or even nonexistent. A usable practice teeing area can range from 15,000 to 30,000 square feet (1,394 to 2,788 square meters), depending on anticipated intensity of use. A minimum of 20,000 square feet (1,860 square meters) is suggested. Practice tees are generally in an elongated rectangular or gentle crescent-shaped design with the longest width perpendicular to the direction in which balls are hit. The practice tee is preferably elevated above the driving range.

The practice tee is one component of a practice range, which is discussed in detail in chapter 5. Site preparation for the practice tee, drainage, root zone modification, irrigation system, turfgrass selection, and turfgrass maintenance are basically the same as those discussed for regulation tees. However, two aspects vary due to the intensity of use of a practice tee: techniques of tee marker movement and reestablishment practices.

Large, readily visible tee markers should be utilized to delineate the designated hitting area on a practice tee for any particular day. Markers must be moved systematically at an appropriate interval such that sufficient turf remains to facilitate rapid recovery and repair of divot marks. Tee markers may need to be moved more than once per day during very intense use. On many courses, a topdressing-seed mix is applied whenever the tee markers are moved.

Small practice tees, which receive very intense divoting, may require overseeding following each period of intense use to reestablish a desirable cover. In this case, the markers should be rotated around the practice tee in a program coordinated with the tee renovation schedule of the golf course superintendent. For example, a practice tee could be divided into quarters, sixths, or eighths. With this plan, groundsmen can be initiating renovation on one sector of a tee, including irrigation, fertilization, and topdressing, while other portions of the tee are in play. Typically, rotation is from front to back.

The reestablishment procedure usually involves initial topdressing to achieve a level surface followed by spiking in two to four directions. Next comes application of the seed, then a second spiking in two directions, and possibly a final topdressing to achieve the desired degree of soil cover. It is important that adequate nutritional levels exist prior to planting. If the intensity of divoting is quite high, leveling of the tee by topdressing at fairly high rates (0.2 to 0.4 cubic yard per thousand square feet) is usually necessary. It is a practice on some golf courses to topdress the divot marks each time the tee markers are moved. The topdressing may contain seed, and the soil mix selected should be the same as the underlying root zone mix, assuming it is of acceptable quality. To insure quick, successful reestablishment, the surface zone must be kept continually moist for the first two to three weeks. It is advantageous if the irrigation system on the practice tee is designed with groups of heads under one station in an arrangement such that new reseedings on a portion of the tee can be lightly irrigated two to three times daily during the first three weeks of establishment, while the remainder of the tee is irrigated at a normal frequency.

The turfgrass seed mixture usually is the same as the original mixture used. However, if the intensity of divoting is severe and the practice tee is very small, it may be necessary to alter the seed mixture to achieve a more rapid cover. A quick establishing, wear-tolerant, turf-type perennial ryegrass cultivar can be utilized at up to 70 percent of a seed mixture by weight.

TEE NURSERY

Establishment of a tee nursery is not a common practice, unfortunately. Rather, the typical procedure is either to cut some quality turf from an out-of-the-way primary rough area or to purchase it from a sod farm. This approach can result in the introduction of an undesirable soil or of a cultivar that does not blend with the existing turf on tees.

Sod from the tee nursery may be required for (a) periodic resodding of densely shaded tees, (b) resodding of turfs damaged by petroleum, fertilizer, or pesticide spills or breaks in irrigation lines, (c) plugging of severe divot marks, and (d) periodic resodding of badly worn tees. The tee nursery can also be utilized as an experimental site for evaluating new pesticides, fertilizers, cultural practices, and cultivars which the superintendent is considering for use on the regular tees.

The best approach for golf courses utilizing grass species or cultivars on tees that differ from the grasses used on greens and fairways is the establishment and maintenance of a tee nursery. Characteristics desired include (a) a soil texture comparable to that on the regular tees, (b) the same turfgrass monostand or polystand as is grown on the regular tees, and (c) an intensity of culture similiar to that on the regulation tees. In line with this concept, a tee nursery of adequate size should be constructed at the same time as the regulation tees, using the same internal drainage system and root zone mix. It is advisable for the root zone mix to be somewhat deeper in the nursery, since periodic removal of shallow soil layers will occur. An irrigation system of adequate design should be installed. The tee nursery is best located where it is readily accessible for regular turfgrass maintenance but well away from the playing area. It is generally located near the maintenance building in the vicinity of the green nursery and fairway nursery. Sometimes the tee and fairway nurseries are combined if space is limited and/or the same grasses are used on the tees and fairways. The suggested size for a tee nursery on an eighteen-hole golf course is in the 10,000 to 25,000 square feet (929 to 2,323 square meters) range.

The tee nursery site should be fallowed for a period of time and fumigated to insure that no undesirable off-type weedy grasses are present prior to planting. Soil preparation and planting procedures are the same as those previously described for the regular tees. Special attention must be given to achieving a smooth surface, which facilitates future sod cutting. The same monostand or polystand should be planted on the tee nursery as on the regular tees. Comparable postplanting cultural practices are also employed.

Long-term maintenance of the tee nursery should be basically the same as that on regulation tees. One exception is that a somewhat lower nitrogen level should be used once the sod is established. There is no need to force grass growth on a tee nursery, as there is on regulation tees. Use of a high nitrogen level only increases thatch accumulation. In this regard, it may be necessary to periodically dethatch by vertical cutting and/or topdressing to control excessive thatch accumulation.

The tee nursery will need to be reestablished periodically as the sod supply is exhausted. Special emphasis should be given to irrigation and fertilization during reestablishment. The objective is to grow grass, and a distinctly different cultural regime is needed from that employed on established regulation tees.

Chapter 5
The Fairway

DESCRIPTION

There is no precise definition in the *Rules of Golf* for the term ''fairway.'' The term ''through the green'' encompasses the fairway and rough and is defined as the whole area of the golf course except for (a) the teeing ground and putting green of the hole being played and (b) all hazards on the course. In this text, a *fairway* is the turfed area between the tee and the putting green which is mowed at a lower cutting height than the surrounding rough. Fairway turfs are mowed relatively close to provide a tight, uniform turf and thus to reward the golfer who has accurately placed a shot onto the fairway. The *landing area* is that portion of a fairway where the golfer should drive the ball to have the most desirable position from which to play the next shot. Golfing terminology refers to certain fairways as *dogleg* holes. That is to say, there is a bend to the left or right in the area of the drive zone.

The total land area devoted to fairway turf on an eighteen-hole golf course varies depending on the playing length and the fairway width. Additional factors are whether the fairway extends from tee to green and whether there is an initial primary rough with the fairway starting at a distance of 50 to 75 yards (46 to 68.5 meters) in front of the regular tee. Fairway widths vary from 35 to 60 yards (32 to 55 meters), the norm being 50 yards (46 meters). The perimeters of the fairway, which delineate the beginning of the primary rough or in some cases the intermediate rough, should be aesthetically contoured. The width is typically greater in the landing area and narrower in other portions of the fairway. An eighteen-hole golf course typically has a total fairway area of 30 to 60 acres (12 to 24 hectares), the average being approximately 50 acres (20 hectares).

Associated with the fairway may be a water hazard such as a sea, lake, pond, river, ditch, surface drainage ditch, or other open water course which extends into the fairway or may even pass across the fairway. Bunkers may also be constructed within the fairway. Occasionally positioned in fairways are grassy hollows, grassy mounds, and/or a large tree or trees which are considered an integral part of the playing strategy for the hole involved. Not all golf holes on a course must have fairways. Some par-3 holes may be designed with a large apron area but no fairway.

COMPONENTS OF FAIRWAY QUALITY

Quality components for good playability of fairways include (a) density, (b) uniformity, (c) smoothness, (d) firmness, and (e) resiliency. The characteristics desired in fairways are not a great deal different from those desired for putting greens. Rather, the difference is in the degree of uniformity, smoothness, and firmness. A primary concern is proper shot control, which translates to a firm fairway surface to hit against.

Figure 5-1. Golf ball properly positioned on a dense fairway turf (*left*) and positioned too low in a fairway turf of inadequate density (*right*).

A high shoot density is needed to hold a ball in the proper position (Fig. 5-1). Thin, open turfs are particularly undesirable because a ball nestles too deeply into the turf. The tendency is to correct this problem by mowing too close to produce the desired shoot density. Other characteristics of a quality fairway are firmness, smoothness, and uniformity so that both ball positioning and hitting stance are uniform for all players throughout the fairway. Firmness also allows the ball a short roll after it hits the turf. Resiliency facilitates a modest ball bounce and ease of walking.

Particularly undesirable fairway conditions include turfs that have developed excessive thatch and rapid shoot growth that results in puffiness and/or sponginess. One indicator of fairway playing condition is divot size. A small divot is a sign of better condition than is a larger divot, assuming the same basic type stroke and turfgrass species are involved. A soft, lush, overwatered turf is typically associated with larger divots.

Fairway turfs are mowed relatively close to achieve the required density, firmness, and uniformity. In fact, close mowing is critical in achieving proper ball positioning on the turf and control in hitting the shots. The preferred effective mowing height is below 0.8 inch (2 centimeters). The cutting height typically ranges from 0.5 to 1.2 inches (1.3 to 3.0 centimeters), depending on the turfgrass species involved. Cutting heights above 1 inch (2.5 centimeters) should be avoided if possible. Selection of cultivars adapted to close cutting is the best approach to achieving the desired ball positioning. The turf is best maintained at a moderate shoot growth rate so that it possesses good recuperative potential in terms of carbohydrate reserves. This insures a fairly rapid rate of recovery from divot injury and wear.

CONSTRUCTION

Fairway development involves the largest land area of any golf course construction phase. The cost and time required can vary greatly depending on the extent of tree, stone, and rock clearing needed and whether extensive excavation or fill work is specified. The major steps in fairway construction are (a) surveying and staking, (b) site clearing, (c) rough grading, (d) installation of subsurface drainage lines, if needed, (e) installation of an irrigation system, if desired, (f) stone removal, if needed, and (g) finish grading (Fig. 5-2). The staking, clearing, and rough grading aspects are discussed in more detail in the construction section of chapter 2.

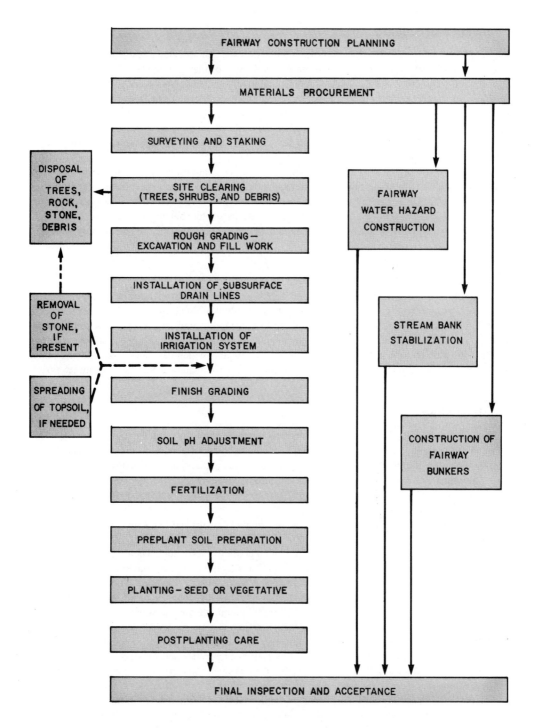

Figure 5-2. Flow diagram for construction of a golf course fairway.

Surveying and Staking

The first step in fairway construction is the staking out, examination, and adjustment as necessary of the centerline of each hole. The perimeter of each hole may or may not be staked at the same time, depending on whether the site is densely wooded or relatively open. On wooded sites, the perimeters of the holes usually are marked during the second phase of clearing operations, previously described in chapter 2. Typical clearing widths for holes in wooded areas range from a very narrow 35 yards (32 meters) to a spacious 70 to 80 yards (64 to 73 meters), the average being 50 to 60 yards (46 to 55 meters). The percentage of this cleared width that is planted as fairway as opposed to primary rough varies considerably (see chapter 6).

It is helpful if the centerline stakes are permanent, but efficient bulldozer clearing operations may make this impossible. If centerline stakes are destroyed, they should be reestablished after clearing operations have been completed. Permanent centerline stakes can be established from the outset on open holes. It is also feasible on open holes not only to stake the perimeters but also to establish location and grade stakes for major fill or excavation work including waterways, drainage ditches, fairway bunkers, water hazards, ponds, and canals.

Site Clearing

Essentially all trees, shrubs, large roots, and stumps must be cleared from the open or playing area of each hole. The preservation of specimen trees and the method of doing the work in phases has been covered in detail in chapter 2. Deep holes resulting from the removal of large roots and stumps should be filled with soil and firmed as thoroughly as possible to minimize future settling. This procedure is critical if the fairways are to be free of bumps and depressions which can cause drainage and other maintenance problems. The guideline for most soils is approximately 2 inches (5 centimeters) of settling per 12 inches (30 centimeters) of fill.

Rough Grading

Centerline stakes should be checked or reestablished on completion of the clearing phase. The perimeter of each hole, including any proposed primary rough, may not require staking if the remaining trees adequately define the hole. Location and grade stakes as necessary are placed on each hole to mark areas requiring major excavation or fill work. This also includes tees, fairway bunkers, and green sites which call for fill material. Lakes and water hazards, along with proposed drainage ditches and waterways, are usually staked as well. Finally, any specimen trees, rock outcroppings, or other special features preserved during initial clearing operations should be rechecked to insure that they are clearly marked and suitably protected.

The above work is done in preparation for the rough grading of each hole. The first step in the rough grading operation is the stripping and stockpiling of available quality topsoil from any part of the fairway-rough area indicated on the plans as requiring major fill or excavation work. Stockpiling of topsoil at green, tee, and fairway bunker sites needing subsoil fill is done concurrently; construction of these features is discussed in detail elsewhere. After the appropriate quantities of soil have been moved in accordance with the architect's plans, all work areas must be graded. Adequate time must be scheduled to achieve the smooth, gentle surface contours needed for easy, safe operation of maintenance vehicles and golf carts as well as a pleasing natural appearance and satisfactory playing conditions. Sharp dips and rises, potholes, furrows, and depressions should be avoided and/or eliminated.

Site clearing operations usually pertain only to the removal of vegetation. Another aspect in rough grading is the removal of large stones, rocks, and other debris. The importance of properly filling and firming any holes resulting from this work has been discussed in chapter 2. Lastly, the finish subgrade contours should insure the rapid removal of excess surface water from the fairway area so that the course can be opened for play as soon as possible after intense rains.

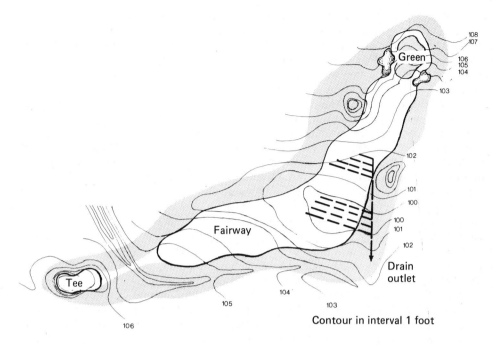

Figure 5-3. Subsurface drainage plan for a poorly drained fairway.

Once the basic fairway subgrade has been established, the contractor can proceed with subgrade shaping of grass waterways and fairway bunkers. Work on proposed water hazards and lakes usually proceeds concurrently with any recontouring of the fairway subgrade.

Installation of Subsurface Drain Lines

One aspect of golf course design and construction that is frequently overlooked is the need for adequate subsurface drainage on sites where excessively wet soil conditions are anticipated. If major drainage problems are not properly corrected at the time of construction, the needed drain lines will have to be installed at some future date, usually at a greater cost and with objectionable disruptions in play. The extent of drainage problems is usually greater where extensive fairway excavations are planned. A local Soil Conservation Service specialist can assist in the design and layout of more elaborate subsurface drainage systems.

Drainage systems normally consist of one or more mainline drains with a series of regularly spaced laterals extending outward across the fairway. Lateral drain lines are typically 4 inches (10 centimeters) in diameter and the mains usually are 6 to 8 inches (15 to 20 centimeters) or more in diameter. Types of drain lines available include perforated plastic, clay, and concrete. Perforated plastic is the most widely used owing to ease of installation and low cost.

Fairway subsurface drainage systems may range from a series of individual drain lines running through the low areas of undulating fairways to a comprehensive system of a herringbone or gridiron type (Fig. 5-3). The former is more commonly utilized. Drain lines are placed at a depth of 20 to 40 inches (0.5 to 1.0 meter) with a lateral spacing of 30 to 60 feet (9 to 18 meters). Drain lines should be placed closer to the surface and have smaller lateral spacings in areas with reduced water percolation rates. Placing a layer of pea gravel over the drain line prior to backfilling is advisable. The remainder of the trench should be backfilled with a porous sandy soil to the existing surface grade. Coarse sand is an ideal backfill material for drains located in depressions and valleys where large volumes of water must be accommodated by downward percolation to the subsurface drains.

Construction of dry wells or french drains should be considered in the case of isolated depressions or where the drainage problem is modest. Isolated depressions frequently collect surface water. Dry wells can be dug by backhoe or tree auger to eliminate a surface accumulation of water. The resultant hole is filled with coarse gravel and topped off with a thin layer of medium-coarse sand. Excess surface water quickly enters the dry well, where it can slowly percolate into the subsurface soil. Grass can be established directly on the sandy surface root zone.

French drain construction involves the excavation of a narrow (2 to 6 inches [5 to 15 centimeters]) trench of from 6 to 30 inches (15 to 76 centimeters) in depth. Such a trench can be quickly dug with the small riding or walk-behind power trenching machines available today. The open trench is backfilled nearly to the surface with 0.25- to 0.8-inch (0.6- to 2.0-centimeter) diameter pea gravel or stone, which can be covered with a shallow surface layer of sandy soil. The result is a subsurface gravel-filled channel for draining excess surface water. French drains may be used as laterals in a herringbone pattern if the problem area is small. Sometimes connection of the french drain into a dry well or a subsurface drain line is possible.

Installation of a catch basin may be advisable in situations where high volumes of water are concentrated. Such surface drains are best located in nonplaying areas, if at all possible. The associated drain lines should have a capacity adequate for the anticipated volume of water entering the catch basin.

Although it would be ideal for all drainage installations to be included in the original construction of a golf course, this is not always possible nor practical. Major drainage problems can and should be identified early in the planning stages. Other problems may become obvious only after clearing or rough grading operations. There are, however, always some questionable areas which may or may not prove to be a problem. Some settling problems invariably occur despite the precautions taken and may result in the development of wet areas after the course is in play. To cover all these contingencies may require a costly, comprehensive drainage installation in excess of what is actually necessary. Furthermore, smaller drain lines and french drains may silt up due to the erosion that occurs before a turf is established.

Therefore, an approach used on some sites is to install only those drainage lines that are obviously necessary and to leave certain doubtful areas for later. Any areas with evident drainage problems after one or two years of play can be corrected. Thus, it is important that the sizes and locations of drain lines be clearly marked on the as-built plans and that a clear understanding exists among owner, architect, and contractor as to who is responsible for correcting future drainage problems which were not evident during the initial construction and/or not covered by the terms of the original contract.

Irrigation System Installation

Most modern golf courses are constructed with the capability of irrigating fairways. It is critical that the irrigation system be installed and made fully operative prior to planting to insure a favorable soil moisture level during turfgrass establishment. A detailed discussion of irrigation systems is presented in chapter 9 and thus only a few comments will be made here.

A typical design for a two-row fairway irrigation system having an equilateral triangular spacing of 65 feet (20 meters) with head-to-head coverage is shown in Figure 5-4. The design and installation of a system having as uniform a water distribution capability as is practical is imperative. Two common problems, often present on the same hole, must be taken into account in the design of the system: major variations in topography and in soil types with their associated differences in drainage characteristics. It is important to have the flexibility of applying water in different amounts and frequencies to each of these uniquely different areas. That is, sprinkler heads located on different soil types or elevations should be controlled by different stations on the controller. An optimum of one to three and a maximum of six heads per control station is advised for flexibility in fairway irrigation. This is a critical aspect in fairway irrigation design and it should not be overlooked or its importance minimized on the pretense of cost savings.

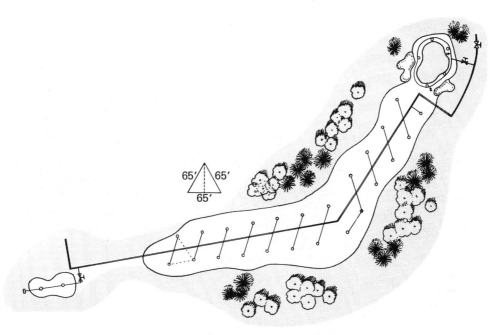

Figure 5-4. Detailed plan for a two-row fairway irrigation system that has head-to-head coverage of 65 feet (20 meters) and equilateral triangular spacing between sprinkler heads.

Finish Grading

The first phase in finish grading involves redistribution of topsoil over areas where topsoil has been removed during deep excavations or fills and also over undisturbed sites where topsoil is lacking. The topsoil should be distributed to a minimum settled depth of 4 inches (10 centimeters), with 6 inches (15 centimeters) being preferred, if available. Where the topsoil supply is limited, preference should be given to the fairways over the roughs.

Special attention must be given to stone removal in fairways. Failure to remove surface stones results in increased wear and frequent breakage of equipment used in coring and slicing. Adequate stone removal is important for playing conditions as well. The constant feel of golf spikes striking rocks just beneath the surface is annoying to players, as is the possible injury and damage resulting from a club head striking a buried stone. It is usually necessary to go over the fairways several times to achieve adequate removal of surface stones. Mechanical stone pickers can be used to remove the larger rocks and to bring rocks to the surface (Fig. 5-5). Mechanical tiller rakes can also be used to collect and windrow surface rocks for removal. Few mechanical devices do a thorough job, however. Eventually some hand pickup work is required to achieve the desired degree of stone removal, that is, the removal of surface stones of golf ball size and larger to a soil depth of 2 to 3 inches (5 to 7.6 centimeters). Stone cleanup during construction means less problems encountered during the first five years after fairway establishment.

Finish surface grading of fairways should be much smoother than of roughs. Smoothness is required so that high-quality fairways may be mowed as close as 0.5 inch (1.3 centimeters). Equally important is the provision for a fairway lie that offers the potential for an exacting shot. In contrast, the rough is designed as a penalty area and thus the degree of smoothness is not as critical. When finally completed, the fairway should possess a smooth, firm, granular plantbed which facilitates rapid turfgrass establishment.

Equipment utilized in finish grading may include landlevelers, graders, tiller rakes, disks, drags, and cultipackers of various designs (Fig. 5-6).

Figure 5-5. Mechanical stone picker operating on a fairway. (Photo courtesy of Rees Jones, American Society of Golf Course Architects.)

Figure 5-6. Grader being used in final shaping of a fairway. (Photo courtesy of R. P. Nugent, American Society of Golf Course Architects.)

TURFGRASS SELECTION

The key characteristics desired in turfgrass species and cultivars utilized on golf course fairways include (a) high shoot density, (b) adaptation to a cutting height of 0.5 to 0.8 inch (1.3 to 2.0 centimeters), (c) minimum thatching tendency, (d) rapid recuperative rate, (e) tolerance to compacted soil conditions and intense wear, and (f) at least moderate resistance to the major disease and insect pests. The monostand or polystand selected should also possess a rapid establishment rate, especially when used on sloping fairways having a high erosion probability.

The best shot control from fairways requires a firm surface to hit against. A high shoot density and adaptation to relatively close mowing are particularly important characteristics on fairways to facilitate skillful shots. Species and cultivars having good tolerance to environmental stresses, such as heat, cold, flooding, shade, and drought, should also be selected whenever possible, provided the previously listed criteria are also possessed by the particular turfgrass species or cultivars under consideration. The turfgrass species used for golf course fairways vary across the United States (Fig. 5-7). Characteristics of these species are given in appendix A.

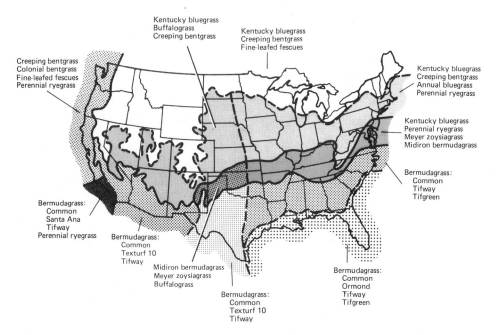

Kentucky bluegrass
Buffalograss
Creeping bentgrass

Kentucky bluegrass
Creeping bentgrass
Fine-leafed fescues

Creeping bentgrass
Colonial bentgrass
Fine-leafed fescues
Perennial ryegrass

Kentucky bluegrass
Creeping bentgrass
Annual bluegrass
Perennial ryegrass

Kentucky bluegrass
Perennial ryegrass
Meyer zoysiagrass
Midiron bermudagrass

Bermudagrass:
Common
Tifway
Tifgreen

Bermudagrass:
Common
Santa Ana
Tifway
Perennial ryegrass

Bermudagrass:
Common
Texturf 10
Tifway

Midiron bermudagrass
Meyer zoysiagrass
Buffalograss

Bermudagrass:
Common
Ormond
Tifway
Tifgreen

Bermudagrass:
Common
Texturf 10
Tifway

Figure 5-7. Geographic distribution of turfgrass species used on golf course fairways in the United States.

Cool Climates

Bentgrass. A high cultural intensity on fairways involves use of cutting heights of less than 0.8 inch (2 centimeters), mowing at a one- to two-day interval, heavy irrigation, moderate fertilization, and the use of fungicides for disease control, usually on a preventive basis. Creeping bentgrass is the primary turfgrass species utilized on intensively maintained fairways in cool climates (Table 5-1). It has the characteristics required for intensively maintained fairways. The primary bentgrass cultivar used in North America has been Penncross. Seaside is also widely used, especially along the east and west coasts. Both are established from seed, require the use of fungicides as disease problems arise, and tend to be thatch prone. Other seeded creeping bentgrass cultivars, such as Emerald and Penneagle, have not yet been used to any extent. Colonial bentgrass is occasionally included with a creeping bentgrass as a polystand on fairways.

Annual Bluegrass. Within a few years after establishment, closely mowed, intensively irrigated bentgrass fairways will have some encroachment of annual bluegrass. Annual bluegrass may become a significant or even dominant component of the fairway polystand within five years, particularly if the fairway is closely mowed and excessively irrigated. In fact, in many portions of the cool humid climatic region, the fairways on many older golf courses are basically composed of annual bluegrass, primarily the perennial types.

Kentucky Bluegrass. Monostands and blends of low-growing Kentucky bluegrass cultivars are utilized on fairways across a wide range of cultural intensities from medium-high to low levels. Prior to 1970, few Kentucky bluegrass cultivars were adapted to the close mowing heights required on golf course fairways. More recently, a number of improved cultivars have been released which can be utilized in blends for best overall performance (Table 5-2). Even with these improved cultivars, Kentucky bluegrass fairways must generally be mowed at higher cutting heights than are bentgrass, bermudagrass, and annual bluegrass fairways. The nitrogen requirement, thatching tendency, and irrigation need are generally less than for bentgrass. Most cultivars are established from seed, with the

**Table 5-1. Turfgrass Species Used on
Golf Course Fairways Under Various Climatic and Cultural Regimes**

Cultural Intensity	Extent of Use	Cool Climate	Warm Climate	Arid Transition Climate
Medium- to low- intensity maintenance	Wide	Kentucky bluegrass Annual bluegrass*	Common bermudagrass	Common bermudagrass
	Limited	Colonial bentgrass Red fescue Chewings fescue Perennial ryegrass	Zoysiagrass	Buffalograss Zoysiagrass
High- intensity maintenance	Moderate	Annual bluegrass† Creeping bentgrass†	Improved bermudagrass‡	Improved bermudagrass‡

*If irrigated.
†May require fungicide use.
‡May be winter overseeded with cool-season turfgrasses.

establishment rate being superior to that of bentgrass. Recuperation from underground rhizomes is very good. The Kentucky bluegrasses utilized on fairways generally have fewer disease problems than are encountered with bentgrass and annual bluegrass.

Kentucky Bluegrass Polystands. Kentucky bluegrass is typically utilized in combination with the fine-leafed fescues in the northern portion of the cool humid region and in polystands with the improved turf-type perennial ryegrasses in the southern portion of the cool humid region, especially the transition zone. These polystands generally require a higher cutting height than does either the bentgrass or annual bluegrass previously discussed. A major invasion of annual bluegrass can be anticipated if Kentucky bluegrass is mowed too closely or if it is maintained at an excessively high irrigation level. Both the fine-leafed fescues and perennial ryegrasses have a quicker establishment rate than does Kentucky bluegrass. The fine-leafed fescues lack the heat and disease tolerance needed to survive in the more southerly portions of the cool humid region. Most perennial ryegrass cultivars are prone to low-temperature injury and snow mold diseases in the more northerly portions of the cool humid region. Many of the improved turf-type perennial ryegrasses have good wear tolerance but are lacking in recuperative potential.

Fine-leafed Fescues. Use of the fine-leafed fescues should be considered on unirrigated fairways in the northern half of the cool humid region. Even though the turf may be brown during periods of summer drought stress, the high density of the fine-leafed fescues provides an excellent lie for golf balls. Both chewings and red fescues perform best under droughty, sandy soil conditions and with minimal nitrogen fertilization levels. On finer textured soils having a somewhat higher fertility level and no irrigation, the fairway species composition is more likely to be a polystand of fine-leafed fescue and Kentucky bluegrass.

Warm Climates

Bermudagrass. Bermudagrass probably possesses the best overall turf characteristics for fairway use and culture. Unfortunately its adaptation is limited to the warm climatic regions. The improved, vegetatively established bermudagrasses are used on the more intensively maintained and trafficked fairways (Table 5-1). Tifway is the most widely used improved cultivar throughout the warm climatic region. Other cultivars utilized include Ormond, primarily in Florida; Santa Ana, primarily in southern California; and occasionally Tifgreen. U-3 has been widely used in the past in the more northerly transitional areas. More recently, Midiron has been receiving considerable attention for use in the same northerly transition zone due to better low-temperature hardiness. The improved bermudagrass cul-

Table 5-2. Available Cultivars of Major Turfgrasses Used on Fairways

Bentgrasses	Kentucky Bluegrasses	Fine-leafed Fescues	Perennial Ryegrasses	Bermudagrasses
		Improved Cultivars		
Emerald	A-20	Agram	Barry	Midiron
Penneagle	Adelphi	Atlanta	Belle	Ormond
Penncross	America	Banner	Birdie	Santa Ana
Seaside	Aquila	Biljart	Blazer	Texturf 10
	Banff	Checker	Caravelle	Tifway
	Baron	Dawson	Citation	Tifway II
	BenSun	Ensylva	Dasher	Vamont
	Birka	Fortress	Delray	
	Bonnieblue	Highlight	Derby	
	Bristol	Jamestown	Diplomat	
	Cheri	Koket	Elka	
	Columbia	Ruby	Eton	
	Eclipse	Shadow	Fiesta	
	Enmundi	Wintergreen	Goalie	
	Enoble		Jackpot	
	Fylking		Loretta	
	Georgetown		Manhattan	
	Geronimo		Manhattan II	
	Glade		NK-200	
	Majestic		Omega	
	Merion		Palmer	
	Merit		Pennant	
	Midnight		Pennfine	
	Mystic		Prelude	
	Nugget		Premier	
	Parade		Regal	
	Plush		Yorktown	
	Ram I		Yorktown II	
	Rugby			
	Scenic			
	Shasta			
	Sydsport			
	Touchdown			
	Vantage			
	Victa			
		Less Improved Cultivars		
Astoria	Delta	Cascade	Game	Common seeded
Highland	Kenblue		Linn	Sunturf
	Newport			Tufcote
	Park			U-3

tivars have excellent wear, heat, and drought tolerance plus a rapid recuperative rate. Their most common problems are a potential for thatching, poor shade adaptation, and susceptibility to a number of insect pests.

Common bermudagrass, a seeded cultivar, is widely used on fairways maintained at medium to low intensities of culture. It requires periodic insecticide applications when potentially serious insect attacks occur. Common tends to form a more open turf with less wear tolerance and thatching tendency than the improved bermudagrasses previously discussed.

Zoysiagrass. Another warm-season turfgrass used on fairways with a medium to low intensity culture, primarily in the cooler transitional zone, is zoysiagrass. The main cultivar utilized is Meyer

(*Zoysia japonica*). Zoysiagrass is more low-temperature hardy and thus better adapted to the transitional zone than are the bermudagrasses and it also has excellent wear, drought, and shade tolerance. Zoysiagrass is typically established vegetatively, usually by plugging. It is extremely slow to establish, has a slow recuperative rate, and is prone to thatching. Seed is seldom used because of poor germination and lack of seedling vigor, although recent research may change this.

Winter Overseeding. Fairways maintained at a medium to high intensity of culture in the warm climatic zone may be winter overseeded with cool-season turfgrasses for winter play. One of the primary concerns is seed cost because of the large area to be overseeded, especially at the high seeding rates required. Thus, common perennial ryegrass and Italian ryegrass are most widely utilized, usually at low seeding rates of 10 to 15 pounds per thousand square feet (4.9 to 7.3 kilograms per are). On high-budget courses, one or more of the improved turf-type perennial ryegrasses and fine-leafed fescues, previously discussed in chapter 3, may be seeded at a rate of 20 pounds per thousand square feet (9.8 kilograms per are).

Arid-Semiarid Transitional Climates

The turfgrass species utilized in the transition zone are usually similar to those used in the warm climates just discussed. A native grass used on nonirrigated fairways is buffalograss. It is very tolerant to close mowing and drought but forms a rather open, low-density turf. Buffalograss can be established from seed but not without difficulties and high seed cost. Improved turf-type cultivars include Comanche and Texoka.

ESTABLISHMENT

The golf course construction phase should be completed prior to the prime time for optimum turfgrass establishment. Late spring-early summer is preferred for planting warm-season turfgrasses, while cool-season turfgrass species are best planted in late summer-early fall. An exception is in cold northern areas, such as Canada and Alaska, that have a short growing season where late spring-early summer is the best planting time for cool-season turfgrasses. Time of establishment is less critical from a moisture standpoint for fairways than for roughs, because the former are usually irrigated. Thus, the most important factor controlling the timing of fairway establishment is an optimum temperature range.

Representative soil samples should be collected and submitted to a reputable soil testing laboratory for analysis once the final fairway contours have been established. A separate soil sample should be obtained from each fairway and from different portions of individual fairways where variations in soil type exist. Results of these soil tests will provide guidelines for any needed pH adjustments and will indicate the amounts of phosphorus and potassium to be incorporated into the soil prior to planting. Specific requests may be made for analyses of minor elements, salinity, sodium level, and/or boron content if a problem is suspected. With these preparatory aspects accomplished, the primary steps in establishment are (a) soil reaction adjustment, (b) fertilization, (c) preplant soil preparation, (d) planting, (e) mulching, and (f) postplanting care.

Soil Reaction Adjustment

Major pH adjustments are best accomplished prior to planting so that immobile materials such as agricultural limestone and sulfur can be incorporated into the upper 4 to 6 inches (10 to 15 centimeters) of the root zone. Calcium carbonate in the form of agricultural limestone is usually utilized on acid soils. The finer grades are preferred, as the soil pH response is faster. Dolomitic limestone is utilized on soils with magnesium deficiency. Sulfur is commonly incorporated into excessively alkaline soils. The application rate should be based on soil test recommendations and may vary from fairway to fairway

Figure 5-8. Soil tillage by disking. (Photo courtesy of A. Bruneau, Department of Horticulture, University of Nebraska, Lincoln, Neb.)

across the golf course. It is desirable that these adjustments in soil reaction be made well in advance of the planting date.

Fertilization

While adjustments in soil reaction may or may not be required, preplant incorporation of fertilizer is almost always needed. The specific ratio and amount of fertilizer applied should be based on soil test results. Phosphorus (P) and potassium (K) are the two major nutrients whose rates are guided by soil tests. Specific fertilizer carriers are described in appendix C. There is no convenient, reliable test for soil nitrogen level. Nitrogen is usually applied at a rate of 40 to 100 pounds of actual nitrogen per acre (45 to 112 kilograms per hectare). The higher rate is desirable if the budget permits. If the higher rate is used, one-half of the nitrogen can be in the form of a slow-release carrier. The fertilizer should be incorporated into the upper 3 or 4 inches of the soil. Selected minor elements may also be included with the complete (N-P-K) analysis fertilizer in those few situations where a deficiency is indicated based on soil tests or where previous experience indicates the need for a particular minor element. The fertilizer is usually applied just prior to planting. Most fertilizers are applied with either a gravity drop or centrifugal-type spreader. A bulk truck method of fertilizer application is frequently utilized.

Preplant Soil Preparation

Final plantbed preparation of fairways is best accomplished just prior to planting. The objective is to prepare a soil surface that is smooth, firm, moist, and granular. If the soil has been firmed by rains since soil pH adjustment and fertilization were done, a final shallow tillage should be accomplished which results in a granular condition with soil particles in the 1- to 5-millimeter range (Fig. 5-8). Subsequently, an appropriate drag and/or landleveler should be utilized to achieve a smooth, firm plantbed surface. It is particularly important that adequate time be allocated for proper smoothing of fairways.

Planting

Planting methods utilized on fairways are more varied than those used on roughs. Seeding and vegetative planting rates for turfgrasses commonly planted on fairways are presented in appendix B. Most cool-season turfgrasses, such as bentgrass, Kentucky bluegrass, and fine-leafed fescue, are usually seeded. Common bermudagrass is also seeded in warmer climates. A cultipacker seeder is the best method for seeding fairways (Fig. 5-9). The resultant firming of soil around the seed at a shallow depth of 0.1 to 0.4 inch (2.5 to 10.0 millimeters) is very important in promoting rapid seed germination. This planting procedure also aids in achieving the final smoothness needed on fairways.

Figure 5-9. Fairway being seeded by means of a culti-packer seeder. (Photo courtesy of Brillion Iron Works, Brillion, Wis.)

Improved bermudagrasses such as Tifway are typically planted by sprigging, although stolonizing is occasionally used. Mechanical spriggers are usually employed for planting fairways (Fig. 5-10). The procedure involves insertion of sprigs into 1- to 2-inch (2.5- to 5.0-centimeter)-deep furrows followed by firming of the soil around the sprigs. Fairway sprigging consists of a 10- to 18-inch (25- to 45-centimeter) row spacing with the sprigs placed 3 to 6 inches (7.6 to 10.0 centimeters) apart in each row. The narrower the spacing between rows and between sprigs within rows, the more rapid the establishment rate.

Mechanical planters are also available where a fairway is to be planted by plugging. The suggested planting rate is 2- to 4-inch (5- to 10-centimeter) plugs set on 12- to 16-inch (30- to 40-centimeter) centers. Zoysiagrass is usually planted by plugging or strip sodding (Fig. 5-11). Sodding is not utilized in the initial establishment of fairways due to excessive cost.

Mulching

Mulching of new seedings is always a good practice. It provides soil erosion control and favorable moisture conditions for successful turf establishment. However, mulching is not as critical on fairways where erosion is unlikely as on roughs, since an irrigation system is usually available to provide adequate moisture. Fairway slopes having a high soil erosion probability should be mulched. Application of a straw mulch at 2 tons per acre (4,480 kilograms per hectare), preferably in combination with some type of binder such as asphalt, is the most common mulching technique. Sodding or either jute net or excelsior mat can be used in grass waterways and in low areas where a high-velocity water flow is anticipated. Mulching is normally not utilized on vegetative plantings done by sprigging or plugging.

Postplanting Care

Postplanting cultural practices are vital in achieving successful turf establishment. For example, it is critical for newly set sprigs to be irrigated immediately after planting to avoid loss by desiccation. The timing is not as critical with plugs, but still is best accomplished as soon as possible after planting. Similarly, the quicker new seedings are irrigated, the faster seed germination occurs.

Subsequently, new plantings should be irrigated once daily at midday or even more frequently as needed to maintain a moist surface soil. The irrigation frequency can be reduced in the case of seedings which have been mulched. Frequent surface irrigation should be continued for a two- to three-week period until establishment is achieved. The amount of water applied per irrigation on a daily basis is not great, since the objective is to rewet the surface zone. Proper irrigation is one of the most critical steps in achieving rapid, successful turfgrass establishment.

Figure 5-10. Mechanical sprigger planting bermudagrass into a fairway. (Photo courtesy of Southern Turf Nurseries, Inc., Tifton, Ga.)

Figure 5-11. Fairway area strip sodded with zoysiagrass.

The timing of other postplanting cultural practices, such as mowing and fertilization, is also important. Mowing is initiated when the grass seedlings reach a height of 2 inches (5 centimeters). The most effective mowing is achieved during midday, when the seedlings are dry. Clippings are returned to the soil. The initial cutting height is generally in the 1- to 1.5-inch (2.5- to 3.8-centimeter) range, depending on the particular turfgrass species involved. This cutting height is continued for a six- to ten-week period, at which time it is gradually lowered in steps to the ultimate fairway height desired. Frequency of mowing should be such that no more than 30 percent of the leaf area is removed at any one time.

The application of approximately 20 pounds of actual nitrogen per acre (22 kilograms per hectare) when the seedlings reach 1 to 1.5 inches (2.5 to 3.8 centimeters) in height is quite beneficial. In the case of vegetative plantings, fertilization at two- to three-week intervals at a rate of 20 to 40 pounds per acre

(22 to 45 kilograms per hectare) promotes rapid establishment. Each fertilization should be watered in immediately after application to avoid foliar burn. Phosphorus and potassium applications are usually not needed unless adequate quantities were not incorporated into the soil prior to planting.

Herbicide applications for weed control should be withheld as long as possible. Broadleaf weed control with phenoxy-type herbicides is best delayed for at least four weeks following seed germination. An even longer delay of six or more weeks is desirable for the organic arsenicals, such as MSMA or DSMA, that are used in weedy annual grass control. Earlier herbicide applications can result in substantial damage to turfgrass seedlings, especially the root system. A decision must be made whether the advantages of a longer delay in use of a herbicide will be overshadowed by the loss in grass stand caused by increasing competitiveness of the weeds.

Turfgrass seedlings are particularly prone to injury from traffic. Thus, operation of vehicles over the new seeding should not be allowed for the first six to eight weeks except as required for postplanting maintenance operations.

CULTURE

Mowing

The position of a golf ball relative to the upper turfgrass surface and the soil surface is critical to the golfer in achieving proper control when hitting a shot from the fairway. Ball position is controlled by the stiffness and number of turfgrass leaves beneath the ball. Leaf number is determined primarily by the cutting height and fertility and irrigation levels, while leaf stiffness is influenced by the irrigation and potassium levels. Unfortunately, golf course supervisory personnel who fail to manage fairway turfgrasses properly will be pressured by the playing membership to lower the cutting height to the extent that the ball essentially is supported by the soil surface rather than by a stand of closely mowed, stiff turfgrass leaves. This excessively close cutting height severely weakens the turf, which increases its susceptibility to environmental stresses, weed invasion, diseases, and turfgrass pests as well as reduces its rate of recuperation from injury.

Mower Type. Five- to ten-bladed reel mowers are used to maintain proper fairway surface quality. As the fairway cutting height is lowered, a higher frequency of clip is required to achieve a uniform,

Figure 5-12. Pull-type, ground-driven, nine-gang mowing unit in operation. (Photo courtesy of Jacobsen Divison of Textron, Racine, Wis.)

smooth cut. Reel mowers are usually operated in five, seven, or nine gangs which are either pulled or tractor mounted (Fig. 5-12). The latter is equipped with independent hydraulic lift controls for each mower. The five-, seven-, and nine-gang units normally give an effective mowing width of 11, 15, and 18.5 feet (3.4, 4.6, and 5.6 meters), respectively. More recently, hydraulically driven reel mowers have been introduced. These produce an excellent quality cut under closely mowed fairway conditions and provide improved mowing capabilities under wet soil conditions and especially on steep slopes.

Mowing Frequency. The frequency at which a fairway turf must be mowed is influenced primarily by the turfgrass shoot growth rate. Irrigated turfs are generally mowed on a regular basis, with a two- to three-and-one-half-day interval between mowings (Table 5-3). In contrast, unirrigated turfs, which are subject to periodic drought stress, may be mowed at a frequency ranging from two to three times per week during peak growth periods of optimum temperature and moisture to as-needed during hot, droughty periods. More frequent mowing is required during periods when the temperature and moisture are most favorable for the particular turfgrass species involved; for turfgrass species and cultivars having a rapid vertical shoot growth rate; and for cultural systems involving high nutritional levels, especially nitrogen. The ultimate in fairway quality is achieved by mowing daily. This approach is usually practiced during tournaments or key club events. Daily mowing may also be practiced where good lies are desired on Kentucky bluegrass fairways maintained at a cutting height of over an inch (2.5 centimeters). Such an intense mowing frequency is quite costly in terms of manpower and equipment.

Fairway mowing should be done in early morning, ahead of intense play, and when the surface is not wet, if at all possible. This minimizes soil compaction problems, prevents the accumulation and clumping of clipping piles across the fairway, and produces better overall mowing quality.

Cutting Height. The cutting height selected will vary depending on the desires of the golfing clientele, the turfgrass species, and the available operating budget. Thus, the cutting height may range from a low of 0.5 inch (1.3 centimeters) for annual bluegrass, bentgrass, bermudagrass, and zoysiagrass to a high of 1.2 inches (3 centimeters) for the fine-leafed fescues and Kentucky bluegrasses maintained under low-budget restrictions (Table 5-3). Generally, the closer cutting height is preferred, assuming it is within the cutting height tolerance limits of the turfgrass species involved. Since the best shot control is achieved from a very closely mowed turf, the best quality fairways generally have

Table 5-3. Mowing Practices Utilized on Golf Course Fairways

Turfgrass Species	Cutting Height* (in.)	(cm)	Interval of Days Between Mowing†
Annual bluegrass, intensively irrigated	0.5 - 0.8	1.3 - 2.0	2 - 3.5
Bentgrass, irrigated	0.5 - 0.9	1.3 - 2.3	2 - 3.5
Bermudagrass: Irrigated	0.5 - 0.8	1.3 - 2.0	2 - 3.5
Not irrigated	0.7 - 1.0	1.8 - 2.5	7 - 14
Buffalograss	0.7 - 1.0	1.8 - 2.5	7 - 21
Fine-leafed fescues, very limited irrigation	0.7 - 1.0	1.8 - 2.5	7 - 21
Kentucky bluegrass: Irrigated	0.7 - 1.0	1.8 - 2.5	2 - 3.5
Not irrigated	1.0 - 1.2	2.5 - 3.0	7 - 14
Kikuyugrass, irrigated	0.5 - 0.7	1.3 - 2.8	2
Zoysiagrass, irrigated	0.5 - 1.0	1.3 - 2.5	2 - 3.5

*Effective cutting height.

†Frequency interval shortens as nitrogen or irrigation levels are increased. Two-day interval would be from Monday to Wednesday.

Figure 5-13. Suggested mowing patterns for a fairway: longitudinal (*left*), cross pattern (*right*).

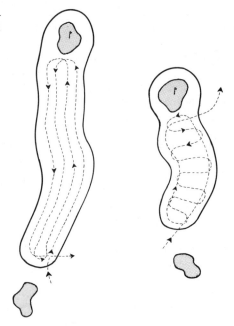

creeping bentgrass or an improved bermudagrass mowed at a 0.5-inch cutting height at a two-day interval. More upright growing species, such as Kentucky bluegrass, usually must be mowed at a somewhat higher cutting height to achieve the desired turf density and minimize annual bluegrass invasion. Thus, the decision concerning cutting height for the more upright growing species usually involves a compromise between the agronomic needs for adequate turf performance and the needs of golfers to achieve proper shot control from the fairway.

During periods of intense midsummer heat stress, it may be advisable to raise the cutting height temporarily by ⅛ to ¼ inch (3 to 6 millimeters) on fairways composed of cool-season species. The turf growth rate slows drastically at this time and the greater leaf area serves to prevent thinning caused by midsummer stresses. The temporary increase in height is particularly beneficial on bentgrass and annual bluegrass fairways mowed at 0.5 to 0.6 inch (1.3 to 1.5 centimeters).

In the case of warm-season species, such as bermudagrass, it is helpful to cease mowing sufficiently early in the fall so that the dormant turf enters the winter with an increased layer of shoots above the normal cutting height. This practice provides an increased dormant biomass which enhances wear tolerance during winter play and increases the insulation effect, which in turn reduces low-temperature kill and winter desiccation.

Mowing Pattern. Alternating the mowing direction on fairways encourages upright growth of the turfgrass shoots for better ball lie. Mowings on fairways mowed only longitudinally should be alternated in opposite directions. Preferably a fairway should be cross mowed at least once a month. The decision as to whether cross mowing is practiced is dictated by the operating budget, availability of hydraulic lift mowers, and mower turning capabilities in the primary rough. With periodic cross mowing, the direction should be altered each time, as with longitudinal mowing (Fig. 5-13). This alternation of mowing pattern enhances upright shoot growth, reduces compaction from tractor tracks, and provides a more attractive visual pattern. The natural beauty of the setting is further enhanced if the fairway perimeters are varied in an artistically contoured arrangement that blends with the terrain rather than being a series of uninteresting straight lines. A contoured perimeter also dictates more precise placement of shots on the fairway.

Figure 5-14. Rippling of turf on a fairway caused by operating a mower at excessively fast speed.

Mower Operation. A good operator will maintain uniformly spaced mowing swaths with minimum overlap. The ground speed of the tractor is critical in achieving quality mowing of fairways. Too often the operator runs the mower at an excessive speed. This can cause bouncing of the mower units, which produces a rippling effect on the turf (Fig. 5-14) and excessive wear on the mower. The operating speed should not exceed that specified in the manufacturer's operating manual. The actual speed that can be maintained depends on the type of mower, grass species, soil moisture, and smoothness of the fairway. Generally, a mower ground speed of 4 to 5 miles per hour (6.4 to 8.0 kilometers per hour) is recommended. The reel drive on hydraulically driven mowers should be disengaged whenever the tractor is stopped.

The mower operator should be constantly checking ahead along the mowing line for any metal or stone objects that could damage the bedknife or reel as well as for any pop-up sprinkler heads stuck in the up position. The mower should be stopped and any foreign object removed and returned to the maintenance facility for disposal. In addition, the operator must be constantly alert for mechanical breakdowns in the mower unit, which can cause scalping or a poor quality cut, and for hydraulic line leaks if the mower has either a hydraulic lift or a reel drive capability.

Mower turns should be made at a reduced speed and in a sufficiently wide arc so that roller bruising and tearing of the turf does not occur. The arrangement of individual mowing passes either longitudinally or across the fairway should be planned to achieve this wide turning arc. In the case of cross mowing of fairways, this may involve skipping every other mower pass and then mowing these skipped areas on a return series of loops back down the fairway. The adjustment of each mower unit should be checked by a qualified individual at two- to four-hour intervals. Any mechanical difficulties or malfunctions, no matter how minor they appear, should be reported immediately to the mechanic for correction.

A concern on fairways mowed primarily in a longitudinal direction is that the tractor wheels have a tendency to operate constantly in the same paths, which leads to compaction and thinning of the turf. This typically occurs because the operator starts mowing each fairway by making a perimeter pass first. To reduce this problem, it is advisable that the mower width of the initial perimeter mowing be altered by shifting the draw bar position sideways in the case of pull-type units or by lifting one or more hydraulic reel units before the initial perimeter pass. In this way, the tractor wheel pattern is constantly shifted and distributed over a large area of the fairway turf.

Other Considerations. As a general rule, clippings are returned on fairways. Thus, the proper mowing frequency must be maintained so that clippings are not objectionable from either an appearance or playing standpoint. There are instances, particularly on poorly drained fairway turfs growing on clay soil, when continuous rain makes mowing impossible for an extended period of time. Subsequent mowing then produces an excessive amount of clippings which may need to be removed by means of a blower, vacuum, or sweeper-type leaf removal unit. Where shoot growth is quite vigorous and long, raising of the cutting height may be necessary at the time of the initial mowing, with the cutting height being slowly lowered to the normal level over a period of successive mowings. This approach should be used where serious scalping is anticipated due to the excessive growth.

The development of grain on fairways is not as critical a problem as on putting greens. However, there are certain types of grasses and conditions where grain can be a problem if the turf is mowed constantly in the same direction. Usually this problem can be prevented by varying the mowing direction, possibly including cross mowing.

Scalping is a much less frequent occurrence on fairways than on greens. It usually occurs due to a mechanical breakdown or an inability to mow the area owing to excessively wet conditions over an extended period of time. The operator must be constantly alert for the former situation, while in the latter scalping can be prevented by raising the cutting height and bringing it back down to the regular height in successive mowings.

Aprons. By the nature of golf course design, the fairway area nearest the green tends to be quite narrow, particularly if large bunkers or grassy mounds are placed on one or both sides of the approach to the green. This narrow neck results in concentration of mower turning activities immediately in front of the green. Serious thinning will occur if this practice continues over an extended period of time. Should such a problem appear to be developing, a shift in the turning area of the heavy fairway mower to a wider portion of the fairway more distant from the green is advisable. The narrow zone and apron immediately in front of the green can be mowed with a lighter three-gang riding unit (Fig. 5-15). The result is a surprisingly rapid improvement in turf density. This has been so effective in many situations that it is now a common practice on a number of golf courses for the apron and any narrow area extending farther out in the fairway to be mowed on a regular basis with a three-gang riding unit. The interface between the fairway and the apron mowed with a three-gang riding mower can be shifted back and forth as needed to avoid damage and thinning in the zone where fairway mower turning is concentrated. The cutting height may be the same as for the remainder of the fairway or a height intermediate to that of the collar. Where an extremely high-quality turf is desired on these sites, clippings are regularly removed.

Figure 5-15. Apron being mowed by a three-gang riding unit with catchers. (Photo courtesy of Jacobsen Division of Textron, Racine, Wis.)

Fertilization

The nutrient requirements for fairways vary with the soil type, soil nutrient-holding capacity (CEC), amount of water applied, climate, turfgrass species/cultivar, and amount of play. Specific nutrient deficiency symptoms are described and illustrated in chapter 10, as is the chemical soil test procedure. No one fertilizer program (type of carrier, application rate, and time of application) or fertilizer can suit all situations. The type of program must be the decision of the golf course superintendent based on the specific conditions on the particular golf course or even on portions of an individual fairway. To aid in this decision, the criteria for selection of the most appropriate combination of fertilizer carrier, application rate, and timing are stressed in this section. Characteristics of the common fertilizer carriers are presented in appendix C.

Time of Fertilization. A complete analysis (nitrogen-phosphorus-potassium) fertilizer is usually applied in spring and late summer-early fall. The latter time is generally preferred if only one application is made per year. Periodic supplemental nitrogen applications are made throughout the remainder of the growing season, iron and potassium also being applied as needed.

The interval between nitrogen applications depends on the carrier utilized, the application rate, the rate of nutrient leaching through the soil, and the turfgrass color and shoot growth rate desired. Warm-season grasses, such as bermudagrass and zoysiagrass, usually receive regular nitrogen fertilizations throughout the growing season, except for the low-temperature hardening period just prior to winter dormancy and the spring root decline period of two to three weeks just after greenup. A reduced nitrogen fertility level is maintained on cool-season grasses during periods of heat stress (midsummer) and low-temperature hardening (midfall) in areas where low-temperature kill is a problem. The cool-season species usually receive from two to four nitrogen applications per year, except for the fine-leafed fescues which are more typically fertilized one to two times. The modern trend is to more frequent, light applications of fertilizer.

Supplemental applications of iron and potassium may be required, typically during midsummer on annual bluegrass fairways and to lesser extent on bentgrass. Spring iron chlorosis frequently occurs on bermudagrass fairways and necessitates corrective treatment. Finally, some iron chlorosis can be anticipated during the summer on bermudagrass and Kentucky bluegrass fairways growing on strongly alkaline soils. Iron is applied to maintain color and chlorophyll synthesis capability, while potassium is applied prior to stress periods to enhance both wear tolerance and hardiness to heat, cold, and drought.

Method of Application. Fairway fertilization may be done in either dry or liquid form. Dry fertilizers typically are applied by a centrifugal-type spreader (Fig. 5-16) or by means of a bulk applicator truck. The former has been the more commonly used approach, while the latter has been used increasingly in the past decade. It may be advisable to water in dry fertilizer applications by means of the irrigation system if (a) the turf has a very high density, (b) the water solubility of the fertilizer is high, and/or (c) there is a high potential for foliar burn, such as during periods of heat stress. Dry applications are advisable when the soil is fairly dry, to minimize soil compaction. This is especially true when a bulk applicator truck is used.

Interest is increasing in the application of liquid fertilizers through the irrigation system as a soil drench, termed fertigation. Effective use of this technique is dependent on a well-designed and installed irrigation system that can apply the liquid uniformly over the entire fairway area. There is also the possibility of including a small amount of fertilizer, such as iron, with pesticide spray applications for foliar feedings. In this case, it is important to ascertain that there is sufficient compatibility among the materials being mixed. In some areas, foliar nitrogen applications at light rates of 0.15 to 0.20 pound per thousand square feet (73 to 98 grams per are) are sprayed on cool-season turfgrass fairways during summer stress periods, usually in combination with iron.

Nitrogen. Sufficient nitrogen (N) must be applied to fairways to maintain proper turfgrass density, adequate recuperative potential, a moderate shoot growth rate, and, to a lesser extent, color. The actual amount of nitrogen applied can vary significantly depending on the particular turfgrass species utilized.

Figure 5-16. Large centrifugal-type spreader being used to apply a dry form of fertilizer to a fairway.

Among the cool-season grasses, the bentgrasses and Kentucky bluegrasses usually require 80 to 160 pounds of nitrogen per acre (90 to 180 kilograms per hectare) per year. In contrast, the fine-leafed fescues require only 40 to 120 pounds (45 to 134 kilograms). Annual bluegrass is intermediate, with a requirement of 60 to 120 pounds of nitrogen per acre (67 to 134 kilograms per hectare) per year. Small amounts or no nitrogen should be applied to the cool-season turfgrasses during heat stress periods. Among the warm-season grasses, bermudagrass requires 10 to 40 pounds of nitrogen per acre (11 to 45 kilograms per hectare) per growing month, depending on the particular cultivar, while zoysiagrass requires 10 to 20 pounds (11 to 22 kilograms). The upper range of nitrogen levels is commonly used on coarse-textured soils, where leaching is a greater problem.

The frequency of nitrogen application may vary from three to six weeks with warm-season grasses to four to ten weeks with cool-season species. The specific application interval depends on the type of nitrogen carrier utilized, being more frequent with water-soluble carriers (ammonium sulfate, ammonium nitrate, and urea) and less frequent with slow-release carriers (natural organic, ureaformaldehyde, methylurea, sulfur-coated, IBDU, and other coated materials). Typically, the nitrogen rate is adjusted to maintain rather moderate shoot growth rates to minimize mowing requirements. However, use of higher fertilization rates on landing areas where divot marking is severe may be desirable to encourage recovery. The same selective fertilization approach can be used on turf areas where golf cart traffic is intense. On the other hand, it is sometimes wise to maintain a minimal fertility level during the spring when frequent, intense rains are anticipated. This approach limits shoot growth during rainy periods and reduces need for mowing when the soil is excessively wet.

Phosphorus and Potassium. Soil tests should be utilized as a basic guide for potassium and phosphorus applications to insure that adequate soil levels are maintained. The phosphorus fertilization rate is based solely on soil test results. Phosphorus is usually applied only one to two times per year, spring and/or late summer-early fall, as one component of a complete fertilizer.

Potassium applications may be made at supplemental rates above the base level indicated by the soil test results. This approach is used to enhance heat, cold, drought, and wear tolerance on fairways. As a general rule, the potassium requirement is approximately 50 to 75 percent that of nitrogen, although even higher levels of potassium are sometimes used. Spring and late summer-early fall are the times when potassium applications are most commonly made. In many situations, this application frequently is adequate for fairways. Potassium can also be applied during summer heat, drought, and wear stress periods. Potassium chloride (58 to 62 percent K_2O) and potassium sulfate (48 to 53 percent K_2O) are the most common potassium carriers utilized. The latter is preferred because of the substantially lower foliar burn potential and the added contribution of sulfur.

Iron and Other Micronutrients. Iron is the micronutrient most commonly deficient on fairways. This is especially true of annual bluegrass, bentgrass, bermudagrass, and Kentucky bluegrass fairways on alkaline soils as well as of annual bluegrass during the midsummer period and of bermudagrass during spring root decline. Correction of an iron deficiency can be accomplished by including iron sulfate, chelated iron, or ferrous ammonium sulfate with pesticide spray applications or by use of complete analysis fertilizers, which contain iron. Under conditions of severe iron chlorosis, applications may be needed at three- to four-week intervals as long as the problem persists. The rate of application is generally in the range of 1 to 4 ounces per thousand square feet (30 to 122 grams per are).

Nitrogen, potassium, and iron are the nutrients most commonly deficient on fairways. Deficiency problems with other nutrients occur only occasionally and typically within a region or on an isolated soil type. Sulfur (S) deficiency is the fourth most frequently observed. Sulfur is required by the grass plant in amounts comparable to those of potassium. Sulfur deficiencies have been reported in the Pacific Northwest, Florida, and east Texas. The problem can be corrected by application of elemental sulfur, ammonium sulfate (25 percent S), potassium sulfate (17 percent S), or superphosphate (11 percent S). Some complete fertilizers contain a sufficient amount of sulfur for it to be listed as one of the components in the official analysis.

Calcium (Ca) and magnesium (Mg) are rarely deficient, although magnesium deficiencies do occur occasionally on the sandy soils of Florida. Should either deficiency occur, it can be corrected by an application of dolomitic limestone (12 percent Mg and 22 percent Ca). Other micronutrients occasionally deficient include copper and manganese on bermudagrass growing on high pH, sandy soils in Florida and molybdenum on high sand soils in North Carolina. Micronutrients are available that can be applied foliarly to correct these deficiencies. However, application of micronutrients on a regular basis is not advised unless an actual deficiency can be documented.

Soil Reaction Adjustments

Major adjustments in soil reaction are best made prior to turf establishment. The preferred pH range for optimum turfgrass growth and vigor is 5.5 to 6.5 for the bentgrasses and fine-leafed fescues; 6.0 to 7.0 for bermudagrass, Kentucky bluegrass, and zoysiagrass; and 6.2 to 7.2 for annual bluegrass. Adjustments in pH are most likely to be needed (a) on intensely irrigated, highly leached, coarse-textured soils, (b) where the parent soil material is high in acid, and (c) where the irrigation water possesses a substantial alkaline effect. Sulfur is used for lowering the pH, while agricultural limestone is the material most commonly used for raising the pH. Dolomitic limestone may be used where a magnesium deficiency exists. Continued use of an acidifying fertilizer such as ammonium sulfate is effective in lowering the pH of alkaline soils.

The specific amount of material to be applied is dictated by soil test results. Agricultural limestone can be applied at rates up to 25 pounds per thousand square feet (12 kilograms per are), while the rate of application of a 90-percent sulfur material should not exceed 5 pounds per thousand square feet (2.4 kilograms per are) in most situations. The preferred time for applying pH adjustment materials is early spring, late fall, or periods of winter dormancy and/or after coring. They should be watered in immediately if foliar burn potential is high. The equipment used in application may be a centrifugal-type spreader or a bulk applicator truck (Fig. 5-17).

Irrigation

Determining the specific irrigation practices to be employed on fairways is one of the most difficult day-to-day decisions made by the golf course superintendent. Each fairway or portion of a fairway should be irrigated individually in accordance with the topography, exposure, soil texture, turfgrass species, intensity of traffic, rooting depth, and evapotranspiration rate. Most modern golf course

Figure 5-17. Bulk applicator truck applying limestone to a fairway.

Figure 5-18. Double-row rotary pop-up irrigation system with equilateral triangular spacing between sprinkler heads.

operations have a permanent, underground, remote-control, double-row, rotary pop-up system with equilateral triangular spacing (Fig. 5-18). The heads should be grouped in a zonal arrangement of one to four heads as dictated by major variations in topography and soil type.

The higher cutting height on fairways results in higher evapotranspiration as compared with that on greens. Fortunately, the higher cutting height also results in increased rooting depth. This enhances the capability of a turf to absorb moisture from a deeper soil depth and thus delays drought stress. Of the six turfgrass species utilized on fairways, bentgrass and annual bluegrass usually require irrigation, while the fine-leafed fescues are irrigated on a very limited basis if at all. Bermudagrass, Kentucky bluegrass, and zoysiagrass may or may not be irrigated, although a more functional fairway turf is achieved by irrigation during periods of drought stress.

The basic concept in fairway irrigation is moistening of the full depth of the root zone just prior to appearance of footprinting and symptoms of visual wilt. The irrigation interval may range from seven to fourteen days for deep-rooted turfs during periods of optimum growing temperatures and moderate evapotranspiration rates to as short as every day on closely mowed, shallow-rooted turfs under conditions of supraoptimal temperatures, high evapotranspiration rates, and/or a severely compacted soil.

The preferred time for fairway turf irrigation in most regions is the predawn-early morning period. (One exception is in the arid Southwest, where nocturnal irrigation is practiced.) This timing has the added benefit of dew-exudate removal, which reduces the disease potential. However, many golf courses have irrigation systems which, due to the nature of the design and/or water source, must be operated throughout the night to accomplish complete fairway irrigation.

Midday syringing with water for cooling or immediate correction of an internal water stress is occasionally practiced where the need is critical. These situations typically involve closely mowed bentgrass or annual bluegrass fairway turfs during periods of severe heat stress. A more limited arrangement is syringing only selected exposed sites where stresses are known to occur more frequently. The practice of fairway syringing presents a problem in terms of play disruption. This problem can be minimized with an irrigation system designed with satellite zonal controls which can be activated by an on-site operator who views the area in question to insure that no golfers are in the vicinity.

The rate of water application among and within fairways varies significantly depending primarily on topography and specific soil texture. The correct rate is achieved through proper sprinkler-head nozzle selection in relation to the rates of soil percolation and infiltration. Proper selection minimizes water loss through surface runoff and areas of excess water accumulation. Unfortunately, there is a greater problem with overirrigation than with underirrigation. The resulting soggy soils and even standing water in low areas lead to problems with turfgrass scald, soil compaction, rutting from golf carts, and generally objectionable playing conditions. Overwatering also encourages the invasion of certain weeds, such as annual bluegrass. Actually, annual bluegrass fairway turfs perform best when irrigated at one- to three-day intervals, since this grass is well adapted to wet soil conditions. Allowing bentgrass and Kentucky bluegrass turfs to be partially water stressed occasionally discourages annual bluegrass invasion. Similarly, restricted irrigation with occasional periods of water stress minimizes Kentucky bluegrass and annual bluegrass invasion into fine-leafed fescue fairways.

The water use rate ranges up to 2 inches (5 centimeters) per week (0.3 inch [7.6 millimeters] per day). Maximum water utilization on fairways is accomplished through cultural practices that provide the deepest, most extensive root system possible under the relatively close cutting heights. Fairway turfs that are subject to periodic hydrophobic soil problems, especially on sandy sites, may require application of an effective wetting agent to insure the desired rate of water penetration into the soil.

Topdressing

Topdressing is usually not practiced on fairway turfs. This is not to say that situations do not exist where topdressing could not be used effectively for both thatch control and smoothing. However, the immense volumes of soil needed, the high labor demand, and the slowness of the operation translate into an extremely high cost relative to what can be accomplished. Fortunately, there are alternatives to thatch control involving biological approaches as well as the use of vertical cutting. In the case of smoothing, occasional topdressing is done in selected portions of fairways where very severe problems exist. In addition, coring brings soil cores to the surface where the soil can function as topdressing after being matted into the surface.

Thatch Control

Thatch becomes a problem on fairways when it accumulates to a depth where there is increased potential for mower scalping, disease development, and localized dry spot formation. The potential for a thatch problem on fairways varies with the turfgrass species and intensity of culture. Certain bermudagrass cultivars are particularly prone to thatching, as is zoysiagrass. Among the cool-season grasses, creeping bentgrass presents the most serious potential thatch problem. Irrigated fairways maintained at high nitrogen fertility levels and on which pesticides are used are the most prone to thatch formation.

On a majority of the golf courses in North America, the thatch problem is avoided through preventive cultural practices, i.e., use of the appropriate turfgrass cultivar, moderate nitrogen fertilization sufficient to meet the needs of recuperation from traffic stress, and use of pesticides only as needed to correct a developing pest problem that may threaten extensive damage to the fairway turf. Of equal importance is the enhancement of the environment for decomposing organisms such as earthworms and fungi through (a) maintenance of the pH in the range of 6.0 to 7.0, (b) soil cultivation to enhance oxygen levels, and (c) irrigation as needed to maintain a moist but not excessively wet soil condition.

Corrective measures for thatch control, usually vertical cutting, must be employed if the accumulation exceeds a depth of 0.6 inch (15 millimeters). One option involves the use of a vertical cutting machine followed by a separate sweeper to pick up and remove the thatch debris. Equipment is also available with the capability to perform vertical cutting and sweeping in a single operation (Fig. 5-19).

Vertical cutting for thatch removal is best accomplished during periods of active turfgrass shoot growth so that recovery occurs as rapidly as possible. Follow-up fertilization immediately after vertical cutting enhances the recovery rate if the basic nutritional level is low. Vertical cutting is best avoided at times of the year when weed invasion is most likely to occur, especially annual bluegrass invasion. In most situations, vertical cutting is best accomplished during the first half of the growing season. The specific height and spacing at which the vertical cutting unit is set will depend on the growth habit of the particular turfgrass species, the thatch depth, and the extent of rooting.

The best approach is avoidance of thatch accumulation through preventive biological measures. In those infrequent situations where excessive accumulation does occur, it should be corrected immediately through vertical cutting. Adjustments should then be made in the cultural program to reduce the rate of thatch accumulation. Coring of fairways followed by matting of the fractioned cores into the soil also aids thatch decomposition. A thick thatch accumulation should not be allowed to develop, since it is extremely difficult to correct or remove without severe disruption of the turf and associated playing conditions.

Drainage

Surface and subsurface drainage systems are vital for efficient, economical maintenance of fairways as well as for optimizing playing conditions. Soggy areas and standing water in depressions lead to increased soil compaction, disease potential, scald, rutting, and generally unfavorable playing conditions. Every effort should be made during initial construction to provide the surface contours and subsurface drain line systems needed to facilitate removal of excess surface water. Nevertheless, additional drainage facilities are usually necessary as problems become apparent following turf establishment. Anticipation of all drainage problems is impossible during the golf course design and construction phases. Postestablishment drainage installations may involve supplemental drain lines, catch basins, french drains, and dry wells. The details of such drainage techniques are discussed in the construction section of this chapter. Root zone modification to correct a drainage problem is generally not practiced on fairways.

Another dimension in water management involves early morning dew/exudate removal. This water on the surface of fairway turfs results in objectionable playing conditions in early morning. It can be removed by dragging a hose or chain across the full length of the fairway. The hose or chain is pulled by two utility vehicles, one driven down each side of the fairway. This practice has the added benefit of reducing disease problems.

Correcting Compaction

Soil compaction can become a severe problem on golf course fairways located on fine-textured clayey soils. Extensive use of golf carts accentuates the problem. Soil compaction results in (a) a restricted root system due to lack of aeration, (b) decreased soil water percolation and infiltration rates, which increase water loss by runoff, and (c) a decline in turfgrass health, vigor, and density, which decreases the quality of the playing surface. Symptoms of a developing soil compaction problem include (a) decreased root growth, (b) reduced rate of water infiltration into the soil as evidenced by runoff occurring earlier in the irrigation cycle, and (c) actual thinning of the turf. Once a soil compaction problem has been diagnosed, it must be corrected through turf cultivation, usually by either coring or slicing.

Figure 5-19. Two methods of vertical cutting for fairways: vertical cutting (*top left*) followed by a blower (*top right*) and a combined vertical cutting-sweeping unit (*bottom*).

Coring usually involves semiopen spoons or hollow tines mounted on a circular reel which remove soil cores by rolling action of the reel over the surface. The typical 6- to 9-foot (1.8- to 2.7-meter)-wide coring tool contains a series of reels positioned on a center shaft, which is mounted either as a three-point tractor hitch or as a pull-type unit (Fig. 5-20). The spoon-type tine is designed to move in a wide arc under the turf, which results in a significant amount of soil loosening in addition to removal of a soil core. The typical spoon size used on fairway turfs ranges from 0.5 to 1.0 inch (1.3 to 2.5 centimeters). The spacing of tine penetrations is a function of the number and spacing of spoons on the circular reel and the number of passes over the turf area. The soil cores removed during cultivation are broken up and returned by use of a drag mat operation. It is important that matting be accomplished immediately after coring so that there is sufficient moisture remaining in the cores to facilitate ready breakup. The remaining tufts of turf-thatch can then be blown onto the rough by a high-speed leaf blower mounted on a three-point hitch of a tractor.

Slicing is a form of cultivation that produces deep vertical cuts in the soil. Unlike in coring, no soil is removed. Slicing is accomplished by means of discs or V-shaped knives mounted on heavy circular reels. Slicing units are typically 5 to 6 feet (1.5 to 1.8 meters) wide and designed to be pulled across the turf surface (Fig. 5-20). It is preferable that each reel of knives be independently suspended and sufficiently weighted so that it will operate freely over the varying contours of the fairway.

Figure 5-20. Two types of fairway turf cultivation units: a coring unit (*top*) and a three-gang slicer (*bottom*). (Top photo courtesy of T. Mascaro, North Miami, Fla.)

Soil cultivation by coring or slicing should be practiced as needed to correct a soil compaction problem. In the case of both coring and slicing, a 3- to 4-inch (7.6- to 10.0-centimeter)-depth of penetration should be achieved. It is always best to schedule coring and slicing operations during periods when the soil is moist to insure a maximum depth of penetration. The preferred time for soil cultivation is when conditions are favorable for turfgrass growth so recovery of the disturbed areas is rapid. Late spring is generally preferred for cool-season grasses, while either spring or summer cultivation can be practiced as needed on warm-season turfgrasses. Unless a severe soil compaction problem exists, it is preferable to avoid soil cultivation in the fall when invasion of weeds is more likely. This is especially true of annual bluegrass. In this vein, either coring or slicing throughout the spring, summer, and fall is suggested on annual bluegrass fairways to encourage new seedling growth. In some cases, turf cultivation may only be needed on selected portions of a fairway where golf cart traffic is concentrated.

Steps that can be used to reduce potential for soil compaction include installation of adequate surface and subsurface drainage systems to insure adequate drainage of excess surface water. This is important, since wet soils are particularly prone to soil compaction. Avoidance of excessive irrigation is also important for the same reason. Deep irrigations should be scheduled well in advance of anticipated intense golf play. Also, measures should be taken to encourage the distribution of golf cart traffic across as wide a portion of the fairway as is possible. Techniques include educational communiques to the golfing clientele, proper design of cart path exit and entrance areas, and use of route signs and ropes where necessary.

Finally, it is important that the scheduled date of fairway cultivation be posted well in advance so that concerned golfers can arrange their golf activities around this period.

Divot Mark Repair

A divot mark repair program is budgeted as part of regular maintenance on some higher quality golf courses. Primary emphasis is placed on landing areas, where divoting is most intense. The procedure is basically the same as that discussed in chapter 4, and the reader is referred to this chapter for further coverage.

Winter Overseeding

Winter overseeding of bermudagrass fairways is practiced to a limited extent in the southern portion of the warm climatic region, but much less frequently than on putting greens. It is most commonly utilized on winter resort and high-budget courses. Preplant preparation of the turf on fairways, in contrast to that on putting greens, is minimal. In many cases, the seed is distributed over the fairway by means of a centrifugal spreader without any preplant soil cultivation or vertical cutting. A preplant fungicide application for the control of seedling diseases is usually used only in areas where the probability of seedling disease development is high.

The two species most commonly utilized for overseeding fairways are perennial ryegrass and Italian ryegrass. Annual ryegrass should not be used in the more northerly areas, where the potential for low-temperature kill is high. The seeding rates are 25 to 40 percent of that used on putting greens due to economic considerations. Postplanting practices may include matting in of the seed, especially where the fairway turf is quite dense. Topdressing is rarely practiced. Following planting it is important that adequate surface soil moisture levels be maintained during the establishment period. Also, an application of the appropriate fungicide may be necessary during periods favorable for severe disease attacks.

Use of a Colorant

An alternative to overseeding is use of a colorant to provide green color (Fig. 5-21). This approach lacks the dimension of recuperation from divot marks and wear which is achieved by winter overseeding. It is used primarily during major winter golf championships and tournaments to provide short-term green color. The pigment-type colorants are generally preferred, since they are more persistent. The turf should be completely dormant at the time of application. Pretreatment preparation includes mowing, clipping removal, and debris removal if any significant quantity of material is present on the surface. The actual application should be made when air temperatures are above 40 °F (5 °C) and there is no free water present on the leaves. Achievement of a uniform green color is dependent on a good, experienced operator and a sprayer adjusted to deliver a uniform spray.

Pests

A detailed discussion of pest problem recognition, causal diagnosis, cultural practices affecting severity of the pest problem, and chemical control is found in chapter 10 on pests and stresses. In this section are presented only a summary of potential pest problems unique to fairways and the related cultural and chemical practices that have specific application.

Weeds. A much more diverse range of weeds can occur on fairways than on putting greens (Table 5-4). Nevertheless, most major weeds found on putting greens are also a significant problem on fairways. Caution is always in order in the selection and use of herbicides on fairway turfs. The

Figure 5-21. Turfgrass colorant applied to a dormant bermudagrass fairway turf. (Photo courtesy of W. R. Kneebone, University of Arizona, Tucson, Ariz.)

Table 5-4. Weed Problems on Established Fairways

Relative Weed Problem	Cool-Season Turfgrasses	Warm-Season Turfgrasses
Severe; difficult to control with selective herbicide(s)	Annual bluegrass Goosegrass Nutsedge Tall fescue	Dallisgrass Kikuyugrass Nutsedge
Widespread but can be controlled with selective herbicide(s)	Common chickweed Crabgrass Dandelion Henbit Knotweed Mouse-ear chickweed Plantain Spotted spurge White clover	Annual bluegrass Crabgrass Goosegrass Henbit Knotweed Spotted spurge Spurweed White clover
Occasional problem	Algae Barnyardgrass Black medic Curly dock English daisy Foxtail Ground ivy Healall Knotgrass Mallow Moss Nimblewill Pearlwort Purslane Shepherdspurse Speedwell Spurge Thistle Velvetgrass Wild carrot Wild onion Yarrow	Algae Bahiagrass Barnyardgrass Dichondra Filaree Johnsongrass Knotgrass Moss Quackgrass Rescuegrass Sandbur Sedges Smutgrass Speedwell

preferred approach is application of a herbicide only as needed to control a developing weed problem, rather than use of a broad-spectrum preventive control program on a regular basis. In support of this philosophy, planning and execution of a sound cultural system are fundamental to successful long-term weed control on fairways. The development of a weed problem, especially one with weedy annual grasses, is most likely in landing areas where divot marks are extensive.

The control of broadleaf weeds in bentgrass and annual bluegrass fairways is most effectively achieved by a fall application of herbicide. Mecoprop is preferred in terms of selectivity, while the use of 2,4-D should be avoided on both species. Control of broadleaf weed problems in warm-season turfgrasses should be accomplished during the first half of the growing season. In addition, control of winter annual weeds may be required after the bermudagrass enters dormancy, assuming winter overseeding has not been practiced. Preemergence herbicides for the control of most weedy grasses are applied in the spring in the case of both warm- and cool-season turfgrass species. The approaches to annual bluegrass control in bentgrass and Kentucky bluegrass fairways are basically the same as those previously discussed for putting greens. The reader is referred to chapter 3 for further information concerning this problem.

Diseases. The first requisite in disease control on fairways is the development of a cultural program that insures a healthy turf with minimal thatch accumulation. Avoidance of overwatering can be especially beneficial in maintaining conditions that are unfavorable for development of disease-causing pathogens.

In the case of bermudagrass, fine-leafed fescue, Kentucky bluegrass, and zoysiagrass fairway turfs, the use of fungicides is infrequent, if done at all. Spring dead spot can be a problem on bermudagrass fairways, but approaches to controlling this problem are as yet unclear. Fungicides are usually not used on fine-leafed fescue fairways. The main problems on Kentucky bluegrass fairways are the *Helmintho-sporium* diseases, which can be avoided by use of a blend of resistant cultivars. Rust is an occasional problem on zoysiagrass in certain regions.

Severe disease problems which necessitate the use of a seasonal fungicide program are more likely to occur on intensely maintained fairway turfs composed of bentgrass and annual bluegrass than on others. Both species are susceptible to a wide range of diseases, including dollar spot, brown patch, *Pythium* blight, *Fusarium* patch, and *Typhula* blight (Table 5-5). Anthracnose has been a problem on annual bluegrass in certain regions. Thus, a preventive fungicide program may be needed on these intensively maintained fairways. The preferred approach is alternation between systemic and nonsystemic types of fungicides.

A more limited fungicide program might encompass a late-fall preventive snow-mold fungicide application in the more northern cool climatic regions, followed by two to three systemic fungicide applications during periods when the potential for dollar-spot development is high.

Insects. Insects tend to be more of a problem on warm-season fairway turfs in the warm humid climatic regions than is the case on cool-season grasses in the cool climates (Table 5-6). This is especially true of bermudagrass. The preferred approach is application of the appropriate insecticide as needed when potentially serious injury symptoms first appear. The insecticide selected is usually specific for control of the particular insect problem diagnosed.

Nematodes. The nematode situation on fairway turfs is basically the same as that on putting greens. The reader is referred to chapter 10 for information on nematodes.

Animal Problems. The animal problems on fairway turfs are basically the same as those on putting greens. The reader is referred to chapter 10 for information on animal problems.

Stress Damage

Fairways are subject to a broad array of environmental and soil stresses. Environmental stresses of concern include such winter problems as low-temperature kill, desiccation, ice coverage, and frost heaving and such summer problems as shade, heat, wilt, flooding, scald, petroleum spills, and atmospheric pollutants. Soil stress problems, which occur with varying degrees of severity, include

Table 5-5. Common Disease Problems on Fairways by Turfgrass Species

Disease	Annual Bluegrass	Bentgrass	Bermudagrass	Fine-leafed Fescues	Kentucky Bluegrass	Perennial Ryegrass	Zoysiagrass
Anthracnose	X	X					
Brown patch	X	X	X			X	
Copper spot		X					
Dollar spot	X	X	X	X	X	X	
Downy mildew (yellow tufts)	X	X	X	X	X		
Fairy ring	X	X	X	X	X	X	X
Fusarium blight					X		
Fusarium patch	X	X			X	X	
Helminthosporium diseases	X	X	X	X	X	X	
Nematodes			X				
Powdery mildew			X	X	X		
Pythium blight	X	X	X	X	X	X	
Red thread	X	X		X	X	X	
Rust					X	X	X
Slime mold	X	X	X	X	X	X	X
Smut	X	X			X		
Spring dead spot			X				
Takeall patch		X					
Typhula blight	X	X		X	X	X	
Winter crown rot	X	X		X	X		

salinity, high sodium levels, soil deposition, and waterlogging. The diagnoses, causes, and prevention of environmental and soil stresses are discussed in detail in chapter 10 on pests and stresses. After the cause of the stress damage has been corrected or has disappeared, the turf can be reestablished by sodding, plugging, or renovation-seeding (Fig. 5-22).

Leaf and Debris Removal

On putting greens, much of the debris is removed in the course of daily mowing, since clippings are collected and removed. This aspect of debris removal does not exist on fairways, since clippings are returned. Timely removal of fallen tree leaves, branches, and other debris is always important but is of special concern during the spring and fall. Fallen tree leaves may hide golf balls and thus lead to disgruntled golfers. Every effort should be made to remove fallen leaves as rapidly as possible. Early spring removal of tree limbs and debris accumulated during the winter dormancy period is equally important.

Leaf removal can be accomplished by one of three methods: (a) use of a leaf shredder, which fractionates and returns the leaf material to the soil in a recycling approach, (b) use of a combination rake and vacuum, which removes the leaves and places them in a collection hopper so that they can be hauled to an appropriate dumping area, and (c) use of a leaf blower, which produces an air blast to push the leaves off the fairway into the rough where one of the two previously mentioned methods can be

Table 5-6. Common Insect Problems on Fairways by Turfgrass Species

Insect	Annual Bluegrass	Bentgrass	Bermudagrass	Fine-leafed Fescues	Kentucky Bluegrass	Perennial Ryegrass	Zoysiagrass
Ants	X	X	X	X	X	X	X
Armyworm	X	X	X	X	X	X	X
Bermudagrass mite			X				
Bermudagrass scale			X				
Billbug					X		X
Black turfgrass ataenius	X	X				X	
Chinch bug	X	X		X	X	X	
Cutworm	X	X	X	X	X	X	X
Frit fly	X	X			X		
Ground pearl			X				
Japanese beetle	X	X	X	X	X	X	X
Mole cricket			X				
Sod webworm	X	X	X	X	X	X	X
Turfgrass weevil	X						
White grub	X	X	X	X	X	X	X

Figure 5-22. Mechanical renovation-seeder being used to plant into a stress-damaged sod.

Figure 5-23. Large leaf blower being used to remove fallen tree leaves from a turf.

utilized for actual removal (Fig. 5-23). The specific method used depends on the actual quantity and frequency with which the leaves and litter accumulate. The third method is the most common, since it can be done the most rapidly and frequently at the lowest cost. Branch and loose debris removal is much less of a problem during the remainder of the summer growing season. Usually the few scattered branches and litter that are present can be picked up by mower operators or other crew members as they pass through the area.

SUMMARIES OF CULTURAL SYSTEMS

Summaries of the cultural systems typically utilized in the maintenance of six major turfgrasses grown on golf course fairways are presented in this section. Exceptions of course exist to these general guidelines, and flexibility must be maintained in selection of the cultural program, depending on the environmental stresses and pest problems most likely to occur in a given location. These programs are presented as a ready reference. For more details the reader is referred to the previous section on fairway culture.

The programs outlined for creeping bentgrass, bermudagrass, fine-leafed fescue, Kentucky bluegrass, and zoysiagrass have been developed based on specific research and subsequent field evaluation and modification. Some readers may be surprised that a cultural program is also proposed for annual bluegrass (*Poa annua* L.) fairways. However, the actual situation must be approached realistically. Most closely mowed, intensively irrigated fairways in the northern and cool humid regions that are more than five years old contain a major component of annual bluegrass in the polystand. There are also many golf course superintendents in the cool humid region who essentially are maintaining annual bluegrass fairways. Thus, a cultural program for annual bluegrass is included. It should be recognized that the program is based on experience and field observation and is not adequately supported by specific research. Thus, some aspects may be modified and improved as more complete understanding is developed through research.

Cultural System for an Annual Bluegrass Fairway

Mowing Height   0.5 to 0.8 in. (1.3 to 2.0 cm).
Mowing Frequency   Two to three times per week.
Mowing Pattern   Mow longitudinally; occasional cross mowing beneficial.

Clippings   Return.
Fertilization
> **Nitrogen**   Apply 60 to 120 lbs. N/acre (67 to 134 kg/ha)/growing season split in two to four applications. Apply no more than 30 lbs. N/acre (33.5 kg/ha)/application.
> **Phosphorus**   Apply at rate based on soil test, usually once per year.
> **Potassium**   Apply at rate based on soil test, usually at 50 to 70 percent of the nitrogen rate.
> **Iron**   Apply as visual deficiency symptoms appear, typically monthly during the summer, at 1 to 4 oz. of iron carrier/1,000 sq. ft. (30 to 122 gm/are). Deficiency most commonly occurs on wet, alkaline soils.
> **Other Nutrients**   Apply if specific nutrient deficiency diagnosed (rare occurrence).

pH Correction   Maintain pH between 6.2 and 7.2. Apply limestone or sulfur materials based on soil test.
Irrigation   Maintain moist but not wet soil through light, frequent irrigations at one- to three-day intervals.
Thatch Control   Vertical cutting seldom needed. Topdressing not normally practiced.
Cultivation   Core/slice in spring, summer, and fall to encourage new seedling growth as well as to correct soil compaction.
Weed Control   Apply herbicide only as needed to control a weed problem; use minimal rates. Mecoprop (MCPP) preferred for broadleaf weed control. Usually applied in fall.
Disease Control   Preventive fungicide program may be needed for dollar spot control where it is serious problem. May need to consider late-fall preventive snow-mold fungicide program in northern cool climatic region. Where it occurs, anthracnose can be serious problem necessitating preventive fungicide program and increased nitrogen fertility level.
Insect Control   Apply appropriate insecticide as needed when potentially serious insect injury symptoms first appear; turfgrass weevil and black turfgrass ataenius grub of particular concern.

Cultural System for a Bentgrass Fairway

Mowing Height   0.5 to 0.9 in. (1.3 to 2.3 cm).
Mowing Frequency   Two to three times per week.
Mowing Pattern   Mow longitudinally; occasional cross mowing beneficial.
Clippings   Return.
Fertilization
> **Nitrogen**   Apply 80 to 160 lbs. N/acre (90 to 180 kg/ha)/growing season split in two to four applications.
> **Phosphorus**   Apply at rate based on soil test, usually once per year.
> **Potassium**   Apply at rate based on soil test, usually at 50 to 70 percent of nitrogen rate.
> **Iron**   Apply only when visual deficiency symptoms appear, an occasional occurrence during midsummer months.
> **Other Nutrients**   Apply if specific nutrient deficiency diagnosed (rare occurrence).

pH Correction   Maintain pH between 5.5 and 6.5. Apply limestone or sulfur materials based on soil test.
Irrigation   Bentgrass fairways usually irrigated. Each irrigation should be timed prior to development of visual wilt symptoms. Allow bentgrass to be partially water stressed occasionally to discourage annual bluegrass invasion.
Thatch Control   Practice vertical cutting if thatch problem develops. Intensive maintenance, particularly high nitrogen and irrigation levels, plus lack of an active earthworm population can result in excessive thatch accumulation requiring annual vertical cutting. Best accomplished during first half of growing season. Topdressing not normally practiced.

Cultivation   Core/slice when needed to correct developing soil compaction problem. Special attention needed on sites subject to intense cart traffic.

Weed Control   Apply herbicide only as needed to control developing weed problem, usually on postemergence basis. Avoid use of 2,4-D. Mecoprop (MCPP) preferred in fall application.

Disease Control   Bentgrasses quite prone to wide range of diseases including dollar spot, brown patch, *Pythium* blight, *Fusarium* patch, and *Typhula* blight. Preventive fungicide program frequently used, preferably with alternation between systemic and nonsystemic types.

Insect Control   Apply appropriate insecticide as needed when potentially serious insect injury symptoms first appear.

Cultural System for a Bermudagrass Fairway

Mowing Height   0.5 to 1.0 in. (1.3 to 2.5 cm) (unirrigated common bermudagrass mowed at higher height).

Mowing Frequency   Two to three times per week, if irrigated; weekly to biweekly, if not irrigated.

Mowing Pattern   Mow longitudinally; cross mowing especially desirable if irrigated.

Clippings   Return.

Fertilization

    Nitrogen   Apply 10 to 40 lbs. N/acre (11 to 45 kg/ha)/growing month; use lower rate if not irrigated.

    Phosphorus   Apply at rate based on soil test, usually once per year.

    Potassium   Apply at rate based on soil test, usually at 50 to 70 percent of nitrogen rate.

    Iron   Apply only when visual deficiency symptoms appear. Deficiencies most likely on alkaline soils and following spring greenup.

    Other Nutrients   Apply if specific nutrient deficiency diagnosed (rare occurrence).

pH Correction   Maintain pH between 6.0 and 7.0. Apply limestone or sulfur materials based on soil test.

Irrigation   May or may not be irrigated. If irrigated, moisten to full depth of root zone prior to appearance of visual wilt symptoms (footprinting stage).

Thatch Control   Vertical cutting may be needed if thatch problem develops. Best accomplished during first half of growing season. Thatch most likely to develop with improved bermudagrasses, especially at higher nitrogen and irrigation levels. Topdressing not normally practiced.

Cultivation   Core/slice as needed to correct developing soil compaction problem. Special attention needed on sites subject to intense cart traffic. Best accomplished during first half of summer.

Weed Control   Apply herbicide only as needed to control developing weed problem. Best accomplished during first half of growing season. Control of winter annual weeds may be required after bermudagrass enters winter dormancy, assuming overseeding not practiced.

Disease Control   Fungicides used infrequently. Spring dead spot can be problem; thatch control and maintenance of moist soil conditions reduce severity. Nematode problems are infrequent occurrence, except in certain limited areas.

Insect Control   Insect problems are much greater threat on bermudagrass than on cool-season grasses. Apply appropriate insecticide as needed when potentially serious insect injury symptoms first appear. Major problems include bermudagrass mites, sod webworms, armyworms, and grubs.

Winter Dormancy Practices   Winter overseeding may be practiced on high-budget courses. Low seeding rates and Italian ryegrass used to control costs. Other options include application of green colorant. In southernmost regions where discoloration is infrequent and caused primarily by chilling injury, application of gibberellic acid used to counteract color loss.

Cultural System for a Fine-Leafed Fescue Fairway

Mowing Height   0.7 to 1 in. (1.8 to 2.5 cm).
Mowing Frequency   Once per week if irrigated; every ten to twenty-one days if not irrigated.
Mowing Pattern   Mow longitudinally, although can be cross mowed.
Clippings   Return.
Fertilization
> **Nitrogen**   Apply 40 to 120 lbs. N/acre (45 to 134 kg/ha) in one to three applications per growing season.
> **Phosphorus**   Apply at rate based on soil test, usually once per year.
> **Potassium**   Apply at rate based on soil test; usually at 50 percent of nitrogen rate.
> **Iron**   Apply only when visual deficiency symptoms appear (rare occurrence).
> **Other Nutrients**   Apply if specific nutrient deficiency diagnosed (very rare occurrence).

pH Correction   Maintain pH between 5.5 and 6.5. Apply limestone or sulfur materials based on soil test.
Irrigation   Irrigate on very limited basis or not at all; otherwise annual bluegrass and Kentucky bluegrass invasion will occur.
Thatch Control   Usually not required.
Cultivation   Core/slice as needed to correct developing soil compaction problem. Special attention needed on sites subject to intense cart traffic.
Weed Control   Apply herbicide only as needed to control developing weed problem, usually on postemergence basis. Rates selected generally lower than those for Kentucky bluegrass.
Disease Control   Fungicides rarely used.
Insect Control   Apply appropriate insecticide as needed when potentially serious insect injury symptoms first appear. Insect problems less common in more northerly locations.

Cultural System for a Kentucky Bluegrass Fairway

Mowing Height   0.7 to 1.2 in. (1.8 to 3.0 cm).
Mowing Frequency   Two to three times per week if irrigated; every one to two weeks if not irrigated.
Mowing Pattern   Mow longitudinally; occasional cross mowing beneficial.
Clippings   Return.
Fertilization
> **Nitrogen**   Apply 80 to 160 lbs. N/acre (90 to 180 kg/ha)/growing season split in two to four applications.
> **Phosphorus**   Apply at rate based on soil test, usually once per year.
> **Potassium**   Apply at rate based on soil test, usually at 50 to 70 percent of nitrogen rate.
> **Iron**   Apply when visual deficiency symptoms appear; most likely to occur on alkaline soils.
> **Other Nutrients**   Apply if specific nutrient deficiency diagnosed (very rare occurrence).

pH Correction   Maintain pH between 6.0 and 7.0. Apply limestone or sulfur materials based on soil test.
Irrigation   May or may not be irrigated. If irrigated, moisten to full depth of root zone just prior to appearance of visual wilt symptoms (footprinting stage). Avoid overwatering, which encourages annual bluegrass invasion.
Thatch Control   Vertical cutting not usually needed if not irrigated or if excessive nitrogen fertilization avoided. Topdressing not practiced.
Cultivation   Core/slice as needed to correct developing soil compaction problem. Special attention needed on sites subject to intense cart traffic.
Weed Control   Apply herbicide only as needed to control developing weed problem. Broadleaf weeds best controlled in early fall.

Disease Control   Best accomplished by selecting appropriate disease-resistant cultivars, especially *Helminthosporium* resistance. Fungicides used infrequently.

Insect Control   Apply appropriate insecticide as needed when potentially serious insect injury symptoms first appear. White grubs and sod webworms common problems.

Cultural System for a Zoysiagrass Fairway

Mowing Height   0.5 to 1.0 in. (1.3 to 2.5 cm); closer mowing preferred.

Mowing Frequency   Two to three times per week, depending on irrigation and fertility level.

Mowing Pattern   Mow longitudinally; occasional cross mowing beneficial.

Clippings   Return.

Fertilization

    Nitrogen   Apply 10 to 20 lbs. N/acre (11 to 22 kg/ha)/growing month.

    Phosphorus   Apply at rate based on soil test, usually once per year.

    Potassium   Apply at rate based on soil test, usually at 50 to 70 percent of nitrogen rate.

    Iron   Apply only when visual deficiency symptoms appear (very rare occurrence).

    Other Nutrients   Apply if specific nutrient deficiency diagnosed (very rare occurrence).

pH Correction   Maintain pH between 6.0 and 7.0. Apply limestone or sulfur materials based on soil test.

Irrigation   May or may not be irrigated. If irrigated, moisten to full depth of root zone just prior to appearance of visual wilt symptoms (footprinting stage).

Thatch Control   Utilize vertical cutting as needed to control developing thatch problem. Zoysiagrass quite prone to thatch development, especially under high nitrogen and irrigation levels. Topdressing not practiced.

Cultivation   Core/slice as needed to correct developing soil compaction problem. Special attention needed on sites subject to intense cart traffic.

Weed Control   Apply herbicide only as needed to control developing weed problem. Best accomplished during first half of growing season. Control of winter annual weeds may be required while zoysiagrass in dormant stage.

Disease Control   Fungicides utilized infrequently. Rust can be severe problem in certain regions.

Insect Control   Apply appropriate insecticide as needed when potentially serious insect injury symptoms first appear. Hunting billbugs, grubs, cutworms, and sod webworms common problems.

PRACTICE RANGE

All too often a practice range is not included in the original golf course master plan. As a result, the location eventually selected may not be particularly desirable either from an accessibility standpoint or in terms of favorable conditions for turfgrass culture. Whenever possible, it is desirable to have the practice range within reasonable distance of the golf shop. The location selected should insure that errant golf balls do not threaten golfers playing nearby holes. The overall practice range size will depend on the number of golfers at the club and intensity of use anticipated. The typical length is 300 to 350 yards (274 to 320 meters), which includes the actual teeing area. The width varies from 100 to 200 yards (91 to 183 meters). This size requires a total area of 7 to 14 acres (2.8 to 5.7 hectares).

The surface of the practice range should be relatively level with a slight grade of 1 to 3 percent to insure rapid removal of excess surface water and to facilitate retrieval of golf balls. Drain tile or plastic drain lines should be installed if soil conditions warrant. Construction and establishment procedures for a practice range are basically the same as those for the regular fairways, including the turfgrass monostand or polystand selected. An irrigation system is sometimes installed if such a system is also planned for the regular fairways. Finally, the cultural practices employed on the practice range should be the same as those utilized on the regular fairways to insure comparable turf conditions and to facilitate ball retrieval. Details concerning the tee portion of the practice range are covered in the previous chapter on tees.

Also included on some practice ranges will be one or more small target greens of from 1,000 to 3,000 square feet (93 to 279 square meters) in size. These greens are usually not maintained at an intensity comparable to that used on the regular greens on the course. Golfers at some clubs may desire the inclusion of large sand bunkers on the practice green. The green is then used for practicing both sand blast shots from the bunkers and chipping from the surrounds. In this case, culture of the practice green, collar, apron, and grassy surrounds is usually comparable to that on the regulation greens.

FAIRWAY NURSERY

A nursery of fairway turf is not commonly found on golf courses. Typically, when sod is needed to replace damaged turf in the fairway, it is either cut from some better quality turf stands in the primary rough or purchased from a sod farm. These approaches may involve the introduction of an undesirable soil or of a cultivar that does not match the turf currently being grown on the fairways.

Sod from a fairway nursery may be required at unanticipated intervals for use in resodding turf worn severely at the entrances and exits of golf cart paths; turf severely damaged by a break in an irrigation line and during subsequent repair; or turf damaged by petroleum, fertilizer, or pesticide spills. The fairway nursery can also be used as a sod source for the grounds around the clubhouse, pro shop, course entrance, parking lot, swimming pool, tennis courts, bowling greens, and shelters. As with the green nursery, the fairway nursery can be used as an experimental site for evaluating new pesticides, fertilizers, cultural practices, and cultivars which the superintendent is considering for use on the regular fairways. Thus, the preferred approach, especially on golf courses having quality fairways, is the maintenance of a fairway nursery containing the same turfgrass monostand or polystand as is grown on the fairways and maintained at a comparable intensity of culture.

The site selected for the fairway nursery should have a soil comparable to that found on most of the fairways, whenever possible. Other site criteria include adequate surface and subsurface drainage plus an acceptable water supply for irrigation. The latter is particularly important during the establishment phase. The nursery preferably is located where it is accessible for routine maintenance. The site is typically in the more distant secondary rough, usually near the maintenance facility in the vicinity of the green nursery. A rectangularly shaped nursery is generally preferred to facilitate mowing. The suggested size for a fairway nursery on an eighteen-hole course is in the 0.3- to 0.5-acre (0.12- to 0.20-hectare) range.

Prior to establishment of a fairway nursery the area must be fallowed for a period of time and/or fumigated to insure that no undesirable, off-type weedy grasses are present. Soil preparation and planting procedures should be the same as those described for regular fairways. It is particularly important to insure that the surface is smooth to facilitate mechanical sod harvesting. The same monostand or polystand must be used in the fairway nursery as on the regular fairways. Postplanting care is also comparable. Increased fertilization and irrigation at this time aids rapid, complete establishment. Subsequent long-term maintenance of the fairway nursery should be the same as is employed on the regular fairways.

GROUND-UNDER-REPAIR

Damage to turf areas termed ''through the green'' occasionally occurs from rutting by equipment and golf carts, foot traffic on soft ground, damage by vandals, excesses in weather, accidents, or errors in judgment. The injured turf area is marked off as *ground-under-repair* if deemed by the Rules

Figure 5-24. Pressurized aerosol applicator being used to paint a line that delineates ground-under-repair.

Committee as being unfair to play. Sometimes even improved areas, such as newly sodded spots, are classified as ground-under-repair because the sod has not rooted sufficiently to provide a fair lie.

Ground-under-repair is usually delineated with a white paint line that encircles the area. The commonly used applicator consists of a pressurized aerosol can placed on a trigger-type applicator (Fig. 5-24). The latter directs pressure on the nozzle, which in turn releases a spray of paint. The pressurized can is positioned to aim down at the turf. Paint line width is determined by the height the can is held above the turf. This is an easy way to mark ground-under-repair. It is far more desirable than use of ropes and stakes, which must be moved for mowing, spraying, fertilizing, and similar cultural practices. The paint line usually lasts two to three weeks. It poses no problem to maintenance or to turfgrass growth. Lastly, the scorecard should bear a notation that any area in play marked off by white lines is to be considered ground-under-repair.

Chapter 6
The Rough

DESCRIPTION

The turfed area surrounding each golf hole (putting green, tee, and fairway) is commonly referred to as the *rough*. Like the fairway, the rough is not specifically defined in the *Rules of Golf*. Rather, it is included in what is termed "through the green," which encompasses the entire golf course except for teeing grounds, putting greens, and hazards. Since golf is a game that rewards accuracy and penalizes poorly placed shots, the higher cut turf in the rough should impose some penalty on golfers whose shots stray from the fairway. Such a penalty implies that the ball can be advanced but not the full distance to the target. The actual degree of penalty depends on the cutting height and density of the turf. The latter is determined primarily by the particular turfgrass species, fertilization level, irrigation pattern, and weed population.

The rough surrounds each golf hole and thus provides the background in which the game is played. The extent of rough on an eighteen-hole golf course varies greatly depending on the total acreage available and the design. Golf courses encompassing 100 to 150 acres (40 to 60 hectares) typically have a rough area of 40 to 90 acres (16 to 36 hectares).

The higher cut turf immediately adjacent and on each side of the fairway is termed the *primary rough*. Except on classical seaside and desert golf courses, it is common to have a scattering of trees randomly planted in the primary rough adjacent to the fairway. The taller turf with dense groves or woodlands more distant from the fairway is termed the *secondary rough*. Many golf courses now being constructed are planned with a minimum amount of secondary rough, especially those associated with real estate developments or public play. Golf cart paths extend through the primary rough and even the secondary rough of most courses. Service roads for maintenance vehicles should be located in distant parts of the secondary rough whenever possible.

The intensity of maintenance on rough areas is quite low compared with that on putting greens, tees, and fairways. However, this does not imply that the rough is not properly maintained in relation to golf play. In other words, a low intensity of culture does not mean neglect. Since no maintenance standard exists for roughs, there is variation in cutting height and fertility level depending on the turfgrass cultivar(s), intensity of play, speed of play desired, and degree of difficulty sought by the officials in charge of the golf course.

DESIRABLE CHARACTERISTICS

Characteristics desirable for roughs include (a) conditions insuring some degree of penalty, (b) ease in finding golf balls, if desired, (c) soil erosion control, and (d) minimal maintenance requirements.

Figure 6-1. Three common types of rough: semiopen with tall-growing grass (*top*), bare soil with tufted grass (*center*), and fertilized and irrigated dense, fluffy turf mowed at intermediate height of 3 inches (7.6 centimeters) (*bottom*).

The turf-soil condition of a rough must impose a penalty on shots being hit from the area. This can be achieved in several different ways (Fig. 6-1). Traditionally, it has been provided by tall, moderately dense grass stands. The use of bunch-type, tufted grasses can offer the same penalty situation, particularly in locations where summers tend to be droughty and/or on sites with sandy, droughty soils. Individual grass tufts typically become elevated 1 to 2 inches (2.5 to 5 centimeters) above the surrounding bare soil. Thus, the golf ball tends to rest on the bare soil between individual tufts. The ball can be readily seen but its position makes negotiation of a successful shot difficult. A third approach to obtaining a penalty shot condition is use of sod-forming turfgrass species combined with adequate fertility levels and irrigation, in some cases. The result is a turf of sufficient density to produce a fluffy lie from which it is difficult to hit a firm, controlled shot.

The second characteristic relates to time needed to find golf balls where speed of play is a major concern. It is generally controlled by the cutting height in relation to the turfgrass species involved, either tufted or sod-forming. A shorter cutting height increases the ease with which errant balls can be found.

In regard to the third characteristic, the rough is typically a minimal maintenance area in terms of mowing, fertilization, and irrigation. Establishment of a turfgrass species that provides good soil erosion control is important. Golf balls straying into eroded areas offer unplayable lies and unwarranted penalties. Erosion-free roughs can be readily mowed and comfortably traversed by golfers and their carts without fear of personal injury or damage to the carts. Maintenance equipment is also less prone to breakage.

Finally, the turfgrass species and cultivar selected should require a cultural intensity lower than that for greens, tees, and fairways. Considerable economy can thus be achieved in the operating budget while the golf course still offers playing conditions that challenge and please the golfer.

CONSTRUCTION

Many of the site construction activities for roughs are similar to those previously discussed for fairways. The major steps in rough construction are (a) surveying and staking, (b) site clearing, (c) rough grading, (d) installation of subsurface drain lines, (e) irrigation system installation, if desired, and (f) finish grading (Fig. 6-2). Some of the aspects of surveying and staking, site clearing, and rough grading are discussed in the construction section of chapter 2.

Surveying, Staking, and Site Clearing

The proposed primary rough area is normally delineated on the architect's plans. Once the centerline of each hole has been staked and adjusted, it is helpful for the perimeter of the primary rough to be staked as well. This facilitates clearing operations by defining the actual work limits of each hole.

Normally the phase II-phase III (see construction section of chapter 2) clearing limits coincide approximately with the outer limits of the mowed primary rough. The border between the fairway edge and the beginning of the primary rough is usually shown on the plans but is seldom staked prior to planting operations. Major excavations, waterways, ponds, diversion ditches, and other features in the rough requiring grading work can be surveyed and staked when the site has been adequately cleared.

With a golf course built on ideal or adequate acreage, as previously discussed, a hole may have a mowed primary rough on each side of the fairway from 10 to as much as 25 yards (9 to 23 meters) wide. Allowing for an average fairway width (beginning 200 yards [183 meters] from the back tee and through to the green) of 30 to 50 yards (27 to 46 meters), the phase II-phase III clearing on a hole may vary from 60 to 90 yards (55 to 82 meters) in width. As a rule of thumb, most golf holes are cleared, or selectively cleared, to a width of 60 to 70 yards (55 to 64 meters) for construction of the fairway and the primary rough. An additional 5 to 10 yards (4.6 to 9.1 meters) of grubbing, brush removal, and selective tree thinning produces an unmowed secondary rough on both sides of a hole.

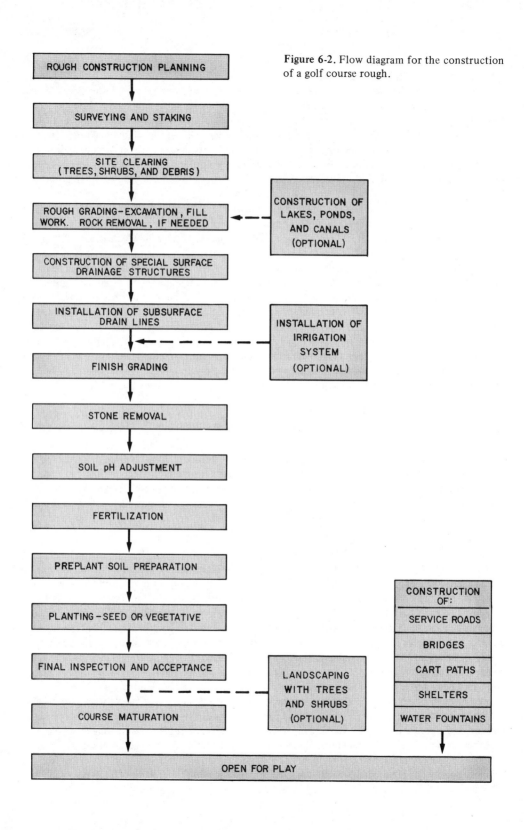

Figure 6-2. Flow diagram for the construction of a golf course rough.

The width of the primary rough varies considerably depending on the par and length of a hole, the intended fairway width, the land available, and whether a hole shares its rough with an adjacent hole. Where holes border the limits of a property, and particularly along roadsides, a minimum width of 20 yards (18.2 meters) is recommended for the primary and/or secondary rough. Where possible, trees should be left standing in such border areas for added safety and protection.

Rough Grading

Rough grading is initiated on completion of clearing and is coordinated as part of the overall site grading. The first step is stockpiling of topsoil from areas where deep cuts and fill are required. The subgrade established during rough grading should provide gently flowing surface contours which allow easy, safe operation of golf carts and of mowers and other maintenance equipment over the primary rough. Finish contours should provide rapid surface drainage, including removal of excess water from adjacent fairways, tees, and greens. Depressions where standing water can accumulate and cause turf kill should be avoided if they cannot be adequately drained.

Consultation with the local Soil Conservation Service representative is advisable in the preparation of construction specifications for ponds, diversion ditches, grass waterways, and terraces. Diversion ditches may need to be installed on long, steep slopes where the probability of erosion is high. Grass waterways should be shaped with a 2 to 3 percent gradient and sufficient cross-sectional size to handle the anticipated maximum volume of water at nonerosive velocities. Placement of fill around the bases of specimen trees that are to remain should be avoided during rough grading work. Also, use of the primary rough for the burial of rocks, stumps, and other debris must be avoided to eliminate possible settling and other future problems. Finally, fairway bunkers and grassy mounds in the rough area can be roughed out and shaped at this time. For details see chapter 7.

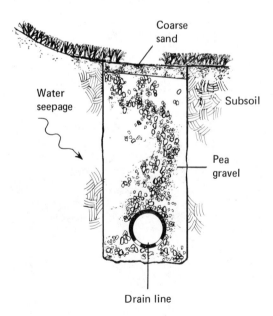

Figure 6-3. Cross-sectional drawing of a lateral drain line at the base of a slope designed to intercept water draining from hillside seepage veins and springs.

Installation of Subsurface Drain Lines

Next, the subsurface drain lines, catch basins, french drains, and dry wells are installed where appropriate, including those needed for drainage of nearby bunkers and unavoidable depression areas in fairways. Adequate drain outlets must be provided, and the drains should be of sufficient size to accommodate the anticipated volume of drainage water. It may also be necessary for interceptor drain lines to be installed at the base of slopes located just above the fairway to keep water from seeping down from intermittent springs or lateral seepage veins (Fig. 6-3). If these precautions are not taken, the resulting problems may include an inability to mow at regular intervals, increased rutting, actual loss of turf from scalping, soil compaction, and inferior playing conditions.

Installation of Irrigation System

An irrigation system is usually not used on roughs in the humid and semiarid climatic regions. However, use of such systems became more common during the late 1960's and early 1970's, and they are now considered important in arid climatic regions. The installation and operation of an independent irrigation system for the roughs greatly increases costs. Irrigation of the rough, if included, is usually part of the entire irrigation system. Modern irrigation programmers allow considerable flexibility in the use of this part of the system, so an independent system for roughs is not practical. In any case, if the entire fairway area is thoroughly covered, the primary rough on either side will be at least partially covered as well.

Finish Grading

First, any available topsoil should be redistributed over deep excavations and where topsoil has been removed. A minimum settled topsoil depth of 4 inches (10 centimeters), and preferably 6 inches (15 centimeters), is suggested. This is excellent insurance, because quality topsoil can provide otherwise

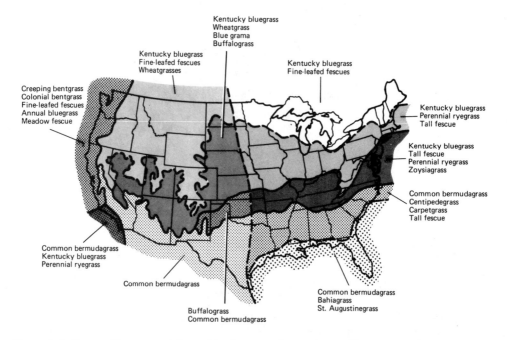

Figure 6-4. Geographic representation of turfgrass species used on golf course roughs in the United States.

lacking fertility on minimal-maintenance roughs. Also, postestablishment fertilizer requirements of turfgrasses grown on topsoil are less than those of turfs grown on less fertile soils.

A smooth, granular, firm plant bed is then prepared, although smoothness is not so critical as for the fairways. Equipment that can be utilized includes landlevelers, tiller rakes, disks, drags, wooden floats, and/or cultipackers of various designs.

Planting and Landscaping

Whenever possible, the planting of roughs should be scheduled for a period when temperature and moisture conditions are favorable for rapid turfgrass establishment. This is especially true if the rough will not be covered by the irrigation system. Specific procedures are discussed in the next two sections.

Once the rough has been established, any additional landscape plantings envisioned by the golf course architect can be made. A landscape plan is generally provided by the architect as part of the total service, unless the site is totally wooded. In some cases, a site may have a number of small trees suitable for transplanting, which will be lost during the clearing operation. Usually, their loss is more than compensated for by workmen not having to work around them during either the clearing or the rough preparation phases of construction.

It is important that spacing between individual shrubs and trees be of sufficient distance so that mowing units can be operated readily between them in the primary rough. The multigang mower units require a minimum distance of 15 to 22 feet (4.6 to 6.7 meters). The specifics of landscaping golf course roughs are covered in chapter 12.

TURFGRASS SELECTION

Turfgrass species and cultivars used on roughs must possess certain unique characteristics, including (a) a semierect growth habit, (b) adaptation to a 1.5- to 4-inch (3.8- to 10-centimeter) cutting height, (c) a relatively low fertility requirement, particularly nitrogen, (d) good resistance to drought stress, and (e) the ability to stabilize soils against wind and water erosion. In addition, a rapid establishment rate is desirable on unirrigated roughs and on sloping sites that have a high erosion probability.

The use of turfgrass species possessing a relatively slow vertical shoot growth rate is desirable in reducing the mowing frequency of roughs. Species and cultivars that are less prone to serious disease and insect injury should also be selected whenever available, provided they possess the previously listed criteria. Turfgrass species used for golf course roughs vary across the United States (Fig. 6-4).

Cool Climates

Polystand turfgrass communities are utilized on most roughs in the cool humid and cool arid climatic regions. Combinations of Kentucky bluegrass and red or chewings fescue are the most common mixtures used (Table 6-1). The cultivars of these three species selected for unirrigated roughs should have a low nitrogen requirement and good drought resistance. Cultivars for irrigated primary roughs are usually selected from among those listed in chapter 5 on fairways. Improved turf-type perennial ryegrass cultivars may be included in regions where low-temperature kill is not a problem and on rolling terrain where the slopes create a high erosion potential which necessitates rapid turf establishment.

The semistable polystand community formed will vary depending on soil, climatic, and cultural conditions. Kentucky bluegrass tends to dominate on roughs having moist, fertile soil conditions with a pH near neutral. In contrast, red, chewings, and sheep fescues become dominant on droughty, infertile, coarse-textured, sandy soils having a pH below 6.0. Sheep fescue may naturally invade roughs in the more northerly portions of the cool humid region. Kentucky bluegrasses provide a more dense sod, whereas the fine-leaved fescues, particularly sheep fescue, tend to form clumps, leaving spaces of bare soil between individual tufts. The use of creeping bentgrasses on roughs is usually avoided owing to its relatively high maintenance requirement compared with that of the other available turfgrass species and

Table 6-1. Turfgrass Species Used on
Golf Course Roughs Under Various Climatic and Cultural Regimes

Cultural Intensity	Extent of Use	Cool Climate	Warm Climate	Arid Transition Climate
Low-intensity maintenance	Wide	Kentucky bluegrass Red fescue Chewings fescue	Common (seeded) bermudagrass	Buffalograss Common (seeded) bermudagrass
	Limited	Hard fescue Perennial ryegrass Sheep fescue Tall fescue* Colonial bentgrass Meadow fescue	Zoysiagrass* Bahiagrass St. Augustinegrass Centipedegrass Carpetgrass	Wheatgrass Lovegrass Blue grama
High-intensity maintenance (irrigation plus higher fertilization)	Limited	Improved Kentucky bluegrass Creeping bentgrass	Improved bermudagrasses	Improved bermudagrasses

*Used primarily in the transition zone.

to problems with fluffiness, thatch, and disease at the higher cutting heights. Highland colonial bentgrass is used in certain locations, primarily in polystands. The cool-season turfgrass cultivars selected for use on medium- to low-budget courses should have relatively low maintenance requirements in terms of fertility and irrigation.

Warm Climates

Monostands are more commonly used on roughs in the warm climates than in the cooler regions. Seeded Common bermudagrass is the most widely used turfgrass on roughs throughout the warm climatic region (Table 6-1). In addition to meeting the previously listed criteria, Common bermudagrass also has excellent wear, heat, drought, and salt tolerance. Centipedegrass has been utilized in the southeastern United States on soils having a pH of 5.5 or lower. However, it does not make a good rough because the ball is held on top of the turf. Carpetgrass will become dominant on poorly drained sites having a low pH when planted in combination with centipedegrass. Bahiagrass and St. Augustinegrass are used occasionally in the subtropical region of the Gulf Coast and in Florida. As with cool-season turfgrasses, the cultivars selected for use on medium- to low-budget courses in the warm climatic zone should require a low intensity of culture, especially the fertility level and irrigation intensity.

Transition Zone

Arid Portion. The Great Plains region is an arid transition zone extending well into both the cool and warm climatic regions. Common seeded bermudagrass and buffalograss are very effective species for use on unirrigated roughs in the more southerly portion, while the wheatgrasses, Kentucky bluegrass, and fine-leafed fescues are used in the more northerly regions (Table 6-1). Weeping lovegrass and the grama grasses can occasionally be found in the intermediate transition zone. All are satisfactory for use on unirrigated roughs within their arid-semiarid region of adaptation.

Humid Portion. Tall fescue, perennial ryegrass, and zoysiagrass are occasionally used in the humid transition zone between the warm and cool climates. The preferred zoysiagrass for roughs is Meyer *(Zoysia japonica),* owing to the coarser leaf texture and more open density. Two limitations of zoysiagrass are very slow establishment and poor recuperative rate. Tall fescue, perennial ryegrass, and zoysiagrass possess good wear tolerance and require a medium to low intensity of culture. The former two possess a superior establishment rate but are lacking in recuperative potential because of a bunch-type growth habit. Tall fescue is a relatively coarse-textured species which creates a striking, almost objectionable contrast with the fine-textured turfgrass species more commonly used on golf courses. If not seeded at a sufficiently high rate, tall fescue tends to become clumpy due to its bunch-type growth habit. This causes added difficulty in negotiating recovery shots. The improved turf-type perennial ryegrasses are fairly compatible in polystands with Kentucky bluegrass in terms of leaf texture and relative competitiveness. They also possess good mowing quality and low-temperature hardiness. Turfgrass breeding programs are now producing similar improvements in the tall fescues.

ESTABLISHMENT

The turfgrass establishment procedures utilized on golf course roughs are quite similar to those previously discussed for fairways. The first concern is to obtain a description of the soil chemical properties that must be manipulated to insure effective establishment and subsequent long-term maintenance. Soil tests should be conducted on representative samples from each of the soil types in the rough. The specific locations from which soil samples should be collected can be determined from the soils map utilized in planning the golf course. Information provided by soil tests includes adjustments needed in major nutrients to support adequate turfgrass growth. The phosphorus and potassium levels are of particular importance, and information also is provided for calcium and magnesium. Minor element analyses can also be obtained from most soil test labs on specific request. Determination of the soil reaction (pH) is another key aspect in assessing the soil chemical properties and cation exchange capacity. If a potential problem is suspected, analyses of the soil salinity, sodium, and/or boron levels can be requested.

The other concern in planning the establishment phase is the projected planting date. The preferred time for planting cool-season species is late summer-early fall, while warm-season turfgrasses are best planted in late spring-early summer. Whenever possible it is best to time completion of fairway and rough construction so that plantings can be made at these optimum times, as dictated by the particular turfgrass species utilized. Failure to plant at the proper time can result in a poor stand and may require time-consuming, costly reseeding. Displacement and loss of topsoil by erosion can also be a serious threat.

Assuming these two preliminary aspects of establishment have been accomplished, the key steps in rough establishment can be initiated.

Soil Reaction Adjustment

If the soil test results indicate a need for pH correction, either liming with agricultural or dolomitic limestone to raise the pH or adding a sulphur-containing material to lower the pH should be done at this time. It is particularly important to accomplish major pH corrections at this time since these materials are most effective when incorporated into the upper 4 to 6 inches (10 to 15 centimeters) of the soil root zone well in advance of planting.

Fertilization

The next step involves incorporation of the appropriate fertilizer into the seedbed. The ratio and amount of fertilizer applied should be based on the phosphorus and potassium needs indicated by the soil tests. Substantial corrections in the phosphorus level are best done prior to establishment, since this nutrient does not move readily through the soil profile. In addition to phosphorus and potassium, between 40 and 80 pounds of actual nitrogen per acre (45 to 90 kilograms per hectare) should be applied. This is the third component of a complete analysis fertilizer. The higher level is preferred if the budget permits. One half of the nitrogen can be in the form of a slow-release carrier if the higher rate is selected. The fertilizer should be incorporated into the upper 3 to 4 inches (7.6 to 10 centimeters) of the soil root zone.

Although the long-term maintenance fertilization program on most roughs is quite low, it is important that adequate nutritional levels be provided during turfgrass establishment. Many soil types are deficient in one or more major nutrients. Thus, obtaining a preplant soil test and applying the specified amounts of nutrients are essential steps. Attempts to save a relatively modest amount of money by reductions in the fertilization program during the critical establishment phase may result in only partial turfgrass establishment and the need for costly reseeding and repairs. There is also an increased likelihood of severe soil erosion, particularly on slopes, which will necessitate expensive reshaping and replanting of the eroded areas.

Preplant Soil Preparation

Final plantbed preparation of roughs should be the same as described for fairways to insure rapid, complete establishment. Just because the roughs will not be maintained at as high an intensity as the fairways does not mean that any less effort can be tolerated in final soil preparation for planting. The objective is to prepare a soil that is moist, granular, firm, and clod free. A granular soil surface is one with 1- to 5-millimeter particles, not one that is fine and dusty. Final tillage encompasses both a firming and a leveling dimension, which are accomplished just prior to the scheduled planting.

Planting

Most turfgrass species utilized on roughs are established from seed. Exceptions are the vegetatively propagated bermudagrasses, zoysiagrass, and St. Augustinegrass. Firming the soil around the seed at a shallow depth of 0.1 to 0.4 inch (2.5 to 10 millimeters) is extremely important in promoting rapid seed germination. Thus, seeding preferably is done with a cultipacker seeder. Another method is distribution of the seed onto the soil surface, which previously had been cultipacked, and then cross cultipack. Hydroseeding should be considered on very steep slopes and on rocky terrain. This method is subject to seed loss by wind displacement. Vegetative planting procedures are the same as those discussed in chapter 5. Planting rates for the turfgrasses commonly used on primary roughs are given in Appendix B.

Mulching

Application of straw mulch through a mulch blower at 2 tons per acre (4,480 kilograms per hectare) is one of the best approaches to successful rough establishment (Fig. 6-5). Application of an asphalt or similar-type binder to the straw is advisable. Mulching of sloping sites with a high soil erosion probability is especially critical. Jute net and excelsior mat mulching or sodding are quite effective in waterway erosion control where high-velocity water flow is probable during rainstorms. Mulching is not used on vegetative plantings.

Postplanting Care

Successful rough establishment is dependent on use of the proper postplanting cultural practices. If feasible, it is advisable to provide irrigation for new seedings, particularly during extended drought periods. Irrigation of roughs is particularly important for vegetative plantings done by methods such as sprigging. The best approach is irrigation immediately to a 4- to 6-inch (10- to 15-centimeter) soil depth followed by daily light midday irrigations to maintain a moist soil surface. Irrigation as needed to maintain a moist environment should be continued for two to three weeks or until the turfgrass is established. The irrigation frequency generally is less if the seeding has been mulched. The amount of water applied per irrigation after the initial deep watering is not great, since the objective is simply to rewet the surface zone. On sites that cannot be irrigated, it is advisable to plant at a time of the year when adequate soil moisture levels are most likely to occur due to normal rainfall.

Figure 6-5. Mechanical mulch blower with asphalt applicator being used to apply straw mulch onto a slope that has just been seeded.

Initiation of other postplanting cultural practices at the correct time is also important. Mowing should be started when the grass seedlings reach a height of 3 to 5 inches (7.6 to 12.7 centimeters), depending on the particular species involved. The cutting height is generally in the 2- to 3-inch (5- to 7.6-centimeter) range. The mowing frequency should follow the rule of thumb of removing no more than 40 percent of the leaf area at any one mowing.

Nitrogen fertilization at 20 pounds per acre (22.5 kilograms per hectare) is beneficial when the turfgrass seedlings reach a 1.5- to 2-inch (3.8- to 5-centimeter) height. The postplanting fertilization program for roughs should be the same as that for fairways, even though subsequent maintenance fertilization levels will be distinctly different. The fertilizer should be watered in immediately after application to avoid foliar burn. Phosphorus and potassium applications are not required unless the amounts incorporated into the soil prior to planting were inadequate.

The use of herbicides should be delayed as long as possible. Phenoxy-type herbicides utilized for broadleaf weed control should not be applied for at least four weeks following seed germination. An even longer delay of six weeks or more is desirable for such organic arsenicals as MSMA or DSMA that are used in annual weedy grass control. By following these guidelines, potential phytotoxicity to the grass seedlings will be minimized. The decision as to when a herbicide should be applied depends on the merits of delaying the herbicide application relative to the loss in turfgrass stand that could result from increasing competitiveness of weeds.

As with fairways, grass seedlings in roughs are quite prone to injury from traffic. For this reason, it is important that traffic be withheld from the roughs for at least six to eight weeks after planting.

CULTURE

Mowing

Traditionally, roughs were maintained in an unmowed condition. Unmowed roughs composed of dense, tall-growing grasses impose a maximum penalty and create great difficulty in finding golf balls hit into them. This slows play, which is very objectionable on courses receiving a high intensity of use.

Primary Rough. To accommodate an increased intensity of use, particularly on public golf courses, the trend has been to maintain a relatively close cutting height in the primary rough (Fig. 6-6). This aids golfers to find golf balls, thus speeding play. A penalty is imposed in this situation by maintenance of a cutting height slightly higher than that of the fairway combined with fertilization and/or irrigation

Figure 6-6. Hydraulic lift, nine-gang mower being used to mow a short-cut primary rough. (Photo courtesy of The Toro Company, Minneapolis, Minn.)

which produces a dense, fluffy grass stand. The most difficult roughs of this type generally are composed of either an improved bermudagrass or a dense, well-fertilized Kentucky bluegrass.

The mowing height and frequency selected for primary roughs depend on the objectives of the course management and golfing membership in terms of degree of course difficulty and rapidity of play desired. The most common cutting height is in the range of 1.5 to 3 inches (3.8 to 7.6 centimeters). A dense bermudagrass rough should be mowed closer than roughs of noncreeping species to achieve a comparable degree of penalty. A cutting height of 4 inches (10 centimeters) or higher is utilized for the United States Golf Association Open Championship to achieve a more severe penalty.

A typical mowing frequency interval is one to two weeks, depending on shoot growth rate. That is, the frequency should be adjusted so that no more than 40 percent of the leaf area is removed at any one mowing. The frequency may be at intervals longer than two weeks during droughty periods when shoot growth is greatly reduced. However, the primary rough is best maintained by mowing on a regular basis. Clippings are almost always returned.

Turfgrasses such as bermudagrass and Kentucky bluegrass, which have vigorous lateral stem growth, are generally mowed slightly closer with a reel-type gang mower. In contrast, bunch-type species are commonly mowed at a higher cutting height with tractor-mounted rotary or vertical mowers. The reel mowers are usually either pull-type or tractor-mounted hydraulic five- or seven-gang mowers with independent lift controls and drive for each reel. The reel mowers operated at higher (2 to 3 inches [5 to 7.6 centimeters]) cutting heights are generally four- to five-blade units. The speed of operation, especially of mowers having an adjustable reel speed independent of ground speed, is dictated by the smoothness of the rough to minimize bouncing and the resulting rippling effect. Mowing on roughs is generally in a random, single direction, compared with the cross mowing utilized at intervals on fairways. Mowing of the rough perimeter adjacent to the fairway should be contoured to add interest. Preferably, the outline is artistically contoured to blend with the terrain rather than being mowed in a series of straight lines.

Intermediate Rough Zone. A further refinement on some golf courses is maintenance of an *intermediate rough zone* of one- or two-gang-mower widths parallel to the fairway (Fig. 6-7). This zone is mowed at a height intermediate between those of the fairway and the primary rough every five to ten days at a 1- to 2-inch (2.5- to 5-centimeter) cutting height and a width of 6 to 9 feet (1.8 to 2.7 meters). This cutting height provides a lesser degree of penalty to shots straying only slightly off the fairway compared with those hit deeply into the rough. It also avoids excessively fluffy lies where prostrate growing species, such as creeping bentgrass, encroach into the rough. Irrigation water and fertilizer applied to fairways usually reach into the primary rough, causing increased turf density and a more severe penalty for a shot straying slightly off line than for an errant shot hit farther into the rough. This is another reason why closer, more frequent mowing of an intermediate zone in the primary rough is desirable.

Trimming. Trimming is very costly but necessary for a well-groomed golf course. The presence of trees increases the cost of mowing the primary rough. Therefore, selection of equipment that has the flexibility of a short turning radius and the ability to mow relatively close to trees without causing damage is important. Additionally, grass around the trees must be trimmed periodically with rotary mowers, cord trimmers, or chemical trimming materials. Chemical trimming materials that have been used with varying degrees of success include fuel oil, paraquat, and glyphosate. The chemical selected should be of a type that is quickly biodegraded or tied up by the soil to minimize toxicity to trees. Chemical trimming is used more commonly on warm-season turfgrasses than on cool-season species. Application to green bark should be avoided, and even then there is concern for potential phytotoxicity to certain tree species. Information on tree species selectivity is very limited. Special care must be taken during application so that only a small-diameter ring of grass is killed, since rings of dead grass wider than 15 inches (38 centimeters) have an objectionable appearance. An additional objection is that broadleaf and annual weedy grasses have a tendency to invade these dead areas.

Secondary Rough. On some golf courses a distant secondary rough is allowed to grow in an unmowed condition, particularly in locations where golf shots seldom stray. The inner perimeter generally is mowed with subtle flowing contours that blend with the surrounding terrain and landscape, thus enhancing the aesthetic environment surrounding golf holes. Wild flowers can be planted and encouraged in this unmowed secondary rough.

Fertilization

Optimum fertilizer applications should be used during the establishment of roughs, as discussed earlier. This relatively high fertility level should be continued through the first growing season or until

Figure 6-7. Turf area of a primary rough with a low-cut intermediate zone in the foreground.

a mature sod completely covers the rough. At this point, fertilization can be decreased to a lower level, as dictated by the type of rough turf desired and the funds available for rough fertilization and mowing.

The fertility level utilized depends on the turfgrass species, soil conditions, and climate. Roughs on relatively fertile soils that are not prone to nutrient loss by leaching may rarely require fertilization, particularly if the turfgrass species utilized has a low fertility requirement. In contrast, roughs on sandy soils with rather intense nutrient leaching from rainfall and a turfgrass species of somewhat higher fertility level may require fertilization twice per year.

The fertility level selected may also be dictated by the desired penalty conditions of the rough. The level may be increased to maintain a dense, fluffy turf on a closely mowed rough, where the goal is for golfers to locate stray shots quickly.

In contrast, bunch-type grasses form roughs with interspersed bare soil. These grasses are infrequently mowed and at a high height, have a low fertility requirement, and are rarely fertilized. Bahiagrass, buffalograss, centipedegrass, chewings fescue, hard fescue, red fescue, and sheep fescue are rough grasses that have a very low nitrogen fertility requirement. An application of 40 pounds of actual nitrogen per acre (45 kilograms per hectare) per year is very adequate. These species seldom need fertilizing when grown on soils with a good nutrient retention level.

A typical fertilization program on high-quality rough turfs is one application per year of a complete analysis fertilizer, assuming the soil tests indicate a need for phosphorus and potassium. This single application is usually applied in the fall in the case of cool-season species and in the spring in the case of warm-season turfgrasses. The fertilizer may be applied to the rough in dry form by means of a centrifugal-type spreader, a truck bulk applicator, or a drop spreader (Fig. 6-8).

Selective, differential fertilization can be used in some situations. For example, a high fertility level may need to be maintained where foot and golf cart traffic is intense, as this program enhances turf recovery.

Weed Control

Broadleaf weed control is practiced on most mowed roughs because these weeds serve as a seed source for reinfestation of adjacent fairways. A combination of 2,4-D plus 2-MCPP or 2,4-D plus 2-MCPP plus dicamba is frequently utilized. Dicamba should not be included if trees are present because of potential phytotoxicity problems. Fall broadleaf herbicide applications are preferred on cool-season species and spring applications on warm-season turfgrasses. More difficult to control broadleafs, such as veronica, may require specific treatment with selected herbicides (see chapter 10).

Figure 6-8. Drop spreader being used to apply fertilizer to a rough.

Annual weedy grasses are usually not an objectionable problem on unirrigated roughs and the use of herbicides for their control may not be required. Preemergence or postemergence herbicides are occasionally used on irrigated primary roughs if annual weedy grasses such as crabgrass become a problem. Winter annual weeds, both grasses and broadleafs, may also need to be controlled in dormant warm-season turfgrasses.

Other Cultural Practices

Irrigation is seldom practiced on roughs except in semiarid and arid climates. If it is used, the irrigation practices should follow those previously discussed for fairways (see chapter 5).

Insecticides may be used on a curative basis to correct severe insect attacks which could spread into adjacent fairway turfs. Some preventive control of white grubs, armyworms, mole crickets, and Japanese beetles is practiced where these are a major problem. Fungicides are rarely utilized on roughs except occasionally on irrigated primary roughs.

Cultivation, such as coring and slicing, is practiced less often on roughs than on fairways. The main areas of emphasis are selected locations where the soil becomes compacted from intense traffic or on steep slopes where water penetration is lacking. Cultivation practices should be comparable in such situations to those discussed for fairways. Thatch is rarely a significant problem necessitating control measures. Thus, vertical cutting and/or topdressing are not practiced in roughs.

Adjustments in soil reaction are sometimes made, principally on acid soils in northeastern and northwestern North America. Lime is applied at one- to three-year intervals at rates dictated by soil test results.

A distinct definition in height between the fairway and primary rough is desirable, particularly on golf courses being prepared for championship play. This can be a problem with low-growing turfgrass species such as bermudagrass and creeping bentgrass. A 3- to 4-inch (7.6- to 10-centimeter)-high rough can be obtained from bermudagrass in four weeks by the proper application of gibberellic acid. The effect of this plant hormone is to stimulate stem elongation. It is sprayed at a rate of 5 grams of active ingredient per acre (2 grams per hectare) at two-week intervals. Application should be initiated in late spring after turfgrass shoot growth is initiated. A more complete response can be obtained under cooler conditions by coordinated applications of water-soluble nitrogen fertilizer and gibberellic acid.

Leaf Removal

Leaf removal is a must on golf courses having deciduous trees. A majority of leaf drop occurs in the rough during a four- to six-week period in the autumn. It is important that leaves be removed or mulched at frequent intervals to prevent accumulation of a leaf mantle which increases the difficulty of finding errant golf balls and excludes light needed to maintain turfgrass growth.

A number of methods can be utilized in leaf removal. One method involves use of a machine that picks up, shreds, and blows the fragmented leaf material back onto the turf in a recycling approach. This operation can be quite noisy and dusty. It has the advantages of contributing to the surface soil organic matter content and solving the leaf disposal problem. Dry leaves can also be pulverized with a tractor-mounted rotary mower. A low-cost method of partially mulching small quantities of leaves if they are very dry involves dragging with a double-layer, chain-link fence.

A second method of leaf removal involves use of a combination rake and vacuum that lifts the leaves off the turf and deposits them into a hopper (Fig. 6-9). The rakelike pickup device consists of a reel on which flexible rubber tines or nylon bristles are mounted. Hoppers are available with a hydraulic self-dumping capability.

A third method consists of use of a leaf blower that produces an air blast to push the leaves into large piles or rows where they can then be picked up by vacuum tubing or a sweeper and drawn into a collection hopper. This third method is the most commonly used, especially when the leaves are relatively dry. It is also faster than sweeping when large areas are involved.

Figure 6-9. Leaf-litter removal unit in operation. Pickup involves use of a flexible vacuum tube and rakes.

Finally, a combination of the three methods can be used. For example, the leaves may be blown off the fairway and mulched in the roughs. Unfortunately, most of these leaf removal methods are quite noisy and thus leaves should be removed when play is minimal.

Litter Removal

One characteristic of a well-groomed golf course is the absence of litter, tree branches, and trash, particularly in the roughs. A preventive approach to litter disposal is appropriate placement of adequate sized litter cans and baskets around the golf course. Commonly used sites for litter baskets are on or near each tee and in shelters. Litter containers should be emptied at a sufficient interval, usually daily, so that they never overflow. Also, golfers should be encouraged to use good golf etiquette and take pride in their golf course by not littering.

Litter removal from turf areas can be achieved mechanically with a litter pickup unit. Many types of designs are available. Most feature some combination of a vacuum, a flexible rake on a reel, an air blower, and/or a nylon bristle sweeper on a reel. The effective operating size of such units is a width of 4 to 6 feet (1.2 to 1.8 meters) and a hopper size of 100 to 200 cubic feet (2.8 to 5.7 cubic meters). Unfortunately, most units tend to be cumbersome and have a very slow operating speed. Some vacuum-rake-sweeper units also feature hydraulically operated lifts which dump the accumulated litter and leaves from the hopper.

Litter is minimal during periods of light play and can usually be picked up manually during or between regular golf course maintenance activities. The significance of even small amounts of litter should not be overlooked. Litter can mean the difference between an impression of a well-groomed golf course or that of a sloppily maintained golf course. Each greens staff member should be alert to litter and keep it picked up at all times.

Communication Cables

Television and associated communication cables are usually installed permanently on golf courses that host major tournaments yearly. Whenever possible, establishment of specified cable lanes that avoid disruption of the existing irrigation system and associated electrical or hydraulic control lines is desirable. The cable lanes should be in "out-of-play" areas.

Typical TV lines now being installed consist of six cables each about the size of a large pencil. Their installation on golf courses is rather simple compared with installation of the bulky, large-diameter cables used in the past. Machines with a vertical sod knife attachment pull the cable into the soil to a depth sufficient to protect them from ground-level traffic. The cables are attached permanently within connector boxes, to which a TV camera hookup can be attached each time the tournament is held. The connector boxes are usually placed in concrete and have vandal-proof lids. Permanent blueprints should show the locations and depths of all cables to prevent their possible severing during construction and renovation activities on the golf course.

When not installed permanently, the cables can be placed at a shallow depth using the same machine with a sod-edging attachment. The cables can be readily pulled out on completion of the tournament with minimal damage to the sod. Whenever possible, permanent TV cables should be installed in conduit. However, this is an expensive procedure which most TV companies are reluctant to follow, since their contracts are usually of a short two- to three-year duration.

Companies tend to run cables by the shortest routes, disregarding potential damage to existing irrigation control lines and turf areas that come into play. The golf course superintendent should be given responsibility for specifying the sites of all TV cables and also of areas for TV towers, vans, and related equipment as well as routes of travel to these locations. These sites should be well away from possible playing areas.

SUMMARY OF A CULTURAL SYSTEM

A summary of a cultural system for golf course roughs is presented in this section. There will be some variance depending on the particular turfgrass species involved. Exceptions, of course, exist to these general guidelines, and flexibility must be maintained in selection of the cultural system, depending on the environmental stress and pest problems most likely to occur in a given location. This system is presented as a ready reference. For more details the reader is referred to the previous section on rough culture.

Cultural System for Roughs

Mowing Height   1.5 to 4 inches (3.8 to 10 centimeters) in primary rough; 1.5 to 2 inches (3.8 to 5 centimeters) for irrigated primary roughs of bermudagrass; secondary rough may not be mowed.

Mowing Frequency   Seven- to fourteen-day interval; five- to ten-day interval on irrigated primary roughs.

Clippings   Return.

Fertilization   Minimum levels once fully established.

Nitrogen   Apply up to 80 lbs. N/acre (90 kg/ha)/yr.; 40 lbs. N/acre (45 kg/ha)/yr. is typical. Use higher rate in irrigated intermediate primary roughs.

Phosphorus   Apply up to 40 lbs. P_2O_5/acre (45 kg/ha)/yr. Usually not needed if phosphorus is brought into proper range prior to establishment.

Potassium   Apply up to 40 lbs. K_2O/acre (45 kg/ha)/yr.

pH Correction   May not be required if done during establishment, although liming may be needed every two to three years in certain regions where soil pH drops below 5.5.

Irrigation   Not usually done, except in semiarid and arid climates.

Thatch Control   Not usually needed.

Cultivation   Not utilized except in selected problem areas of intense traffic. Coring and slicing are most common types of turf cultivation. Usually done once per year in early fall on cool-season turfs and in spring or early summer on warm-season turfs.

Weed Control   Apply phenoxy-type herbicide mixture at one- to three-year intervals as broadleaf weed problem develops. Annual weedy grasses may occasionally need chemical control, especially in irrigated primary roughs; use preemergence or postemergence herbicide.

Disease Control   Not normally done.

Insect Control   Not done unless severe infestation occurs or where white grubs, armyworms, mole crickets, and Japanese beetles are major problems.

Tree Leaf Removal   Necessary in autumn if trees are deciduous.

Out-of-Bounds Markers   Inspect periodically to check for proper placement and alignment.

150-YARD MARKER

The use of 150-yard markers is an increasing trend on North American golf courses. The markers delineate the fairway position that is 150 yards (137 meters) from the center of the putting green. It is the option of each club whether to use 150-yard markers. Some golf clubs reject the use of yardage markers because they view the capability to assess distances accurately and select the proper club as an important part of the game which should be retained.

The 150-yard mark can be delineated by means of trees, shrubs, painted stakes, removable painted stakes set in buried concrete, blocks buried in the fairway or rough, or special marking devices placed on trees (Fig. 6-10). The markers typically are placed in the primary rough on each side of the fairway. The preferred placement is in a conspicuous site close to the tree line where there is minimal obstruction of play. Some courses employ plastic yardage markers set in concrete embedded in the center of the fairway. In some cases, the irrigation head nearest to the 150-yard mark is painted a specific color and the actual distance to the green for each hole designated on the scorecard or on another card available to players before starting their rounds. An approach used by some golf clubs is for the scorecard to include a layout map of the holes showing distinguishing landmarks (tree, shrub, bunker, and so on) and the yardage to the center of the green from each landmark.

OUT-OF-BOUNDS MARKER

A characteristic associated with quality golf courses is proper marking of the out-of-bounds so that the game of golf will be played as intended by the rules. It is the duty of the Rules Committee at each club to clearly define the course boundaries and the area where play is permitted. Except for extenuating circumstances involving the safety of people or property, the committee should strive to limit out-of-bounds markers to the outside perimeter of the golf course property. Boundaries should be continued as far as there is the remotest possibility of a ball going out.

Out-of-bounds is normally defined by large stakes or fence posts. Most clubs use 1 × 2- or 2 × 2-inch stakes long enough to allow their protrusion approximately 3 feet (0.9 meter) above the ground (Fig. 6-11). Stakes should be painted so that they are easily seen as well as to preserve them. White is now used almost universally. Marker stakes should be large and strong enough to be driven into the ground. Consideration might also be given to using removable stakes inserted into holes in permanent concrete bases. The concrete base positioned in the soil insures permanent positioning, while the removable stake facilitates mowing and ease of painting or replacement. An adequate supply of

Figure 6-10. Three types of 150-yard markers: small, trimmed decorative shrub near fairway (*top left*), permanent marker embedded in center of fairway (*top right*), and easily movable and replaceable, inexpensive wooden yardage marker (*bottom*).

replacement stakes should be kept on hand. All out-of-bounds stakes should be repainted at least annually.

The marker spacing selected should allow the golfer or official to conveniently and comfortably sight between two out-of-bounds markers, without intervention from bushes or trees, to determine whether a ball is in- or out-of-bounds. The spacing usually ranges from 12 to 25 yards (11 to 23 meters), the former being more commonly used. The wider spacing is used where the stakes are well away from playing areas. Out-of-bounds markers are considered fixed and permanent with respect to the *Rules of Golf*. They should be periodically checked, since the stakes are sometimes removed by vandals or other unthinking individuals. The proper positioning of each out-of-bounds marker must be checked before every tournament and at two- to four-week intervals, depending on the frequency of displacement. An important detail is to inform players about how the boundaries are defined. This is normally done on the back of the scorecard. The exact boundary line is defined by the inside lines, at ground level, of fence posts and large stakes. Thus, fences and stakes themselves are out-of-bounds. If white lines are used, the lines themselves are out-of-bounds.

Figure 6-11. Series of out-of-bounds markers of proper size and spacing to facilitate sighting.

PUTTING GREEN SURROUNDS

Putting green surrounds refers to the turfed area immediately adjacent to and outside the collar but not including the apron. The surrounds encompass a varied topography of relatively steep slopes and distinct grassy mounds interspersed with sand bunkers.

The turfgrass species and cultural practices used on the surrounds are similar to those used on the primary rough. Where budget restrictions are a concern, it is important that mound contours and bunker placement be designed so that a majority of the green surrounds can be cut with multigang mowing units, preferably of five- to seven-gang widths. Some walking mower work may be required in selected areas that cannot be reached by multigang units, for example, isolated strips of turf between the bunker and green and narrow peninsulas of turf extending into bunkers. Extremely steep slopes that cannot be mowed safely with multigang units will also need walking mower work. Mowing frequency may need to be at shorter intervals than in the primary rough because the surrounds typically receive more intense irrigation. Clippings are normally returned.

The putting green irrigation system should be designed to cover the associated surrounds so that all slopes are adequately watered. This approach prevents drying of the green interior from beneath. In some cases, installation of a separate set of irrigation heads controlled independently from the putting green irrigation system is advisable. This approach is needed where the infiltration and soil percolation rates of the putting green and its surrounds are distinctly different.

Cultivation of sloping surrounds that receive intense traffic greatly facilitates water infiltration and reduces water loss by surface runoff. Fertilization and pesticide programs are comparable to the programs discussed earlier for the primary rough.

GRASSY HOLLOWS AND MOUNDS

Some golf course architects utilize grassy hollows and mounds in their basic golf course design. These are not considered hazards under the *Rules of Golf*. Grassy hollows are sometimes referred to incorrectly as grass bunkers. However, use of the term ''bunker'' should be avoided, since a bunker is by definition a hazard. Grassy hollows and mounds are usually located in the primary rough near the fairway or even projecting into the fairway. They function in the playing strategy of golf holes and add interesting variations to the golf course landscape. The turfgrass species and cultural practices utilized for these features are usually the same as those used on the rough, including a cutting height of 2 to 4 inches (5 to 10 centimeters).

Grassy Hollows

Grassy hollows are constructed with shapes similar to those of sand bunkers, except that the edges are contoured to facilitate mowing. They are frequently used on sites having severe drainage problems which make it impractical to maintain sand bunkers in satisfactory playing condition. Grassy hollows are sometimes developed on sites originally constructed as sand bunkers, most commonly bunkers in nonstrategic positions. Use of grassy hollows is usually an economy measure, since sand bunker maintenance is one of the more expensive components of a golf course maintenance budget.

Grassy Mounds

Grassy mounds are sometimes referred to as "chocolate drops." They offer variations in construction that add interest to the golf hole. If strategically positioned, they can cause a ball to take erratic bounces when striking the mound or slope (Fig. 6-12). An important consideration in the use of grassy mounds in golf course design is that steep slopes and facings usually restrict mowing operations to the use of small walking units. This means higher maintenance costs unless these areas are to be mowed very infrequently at a cutting height similar to that of the secondary rough or are to be left unmowed.

UNMOWED NATURAL AREAS

Secondary roughs are distant from the fairway and thus are frequently maintained in an unmowed condition, particularly in "out of play" locations where stray golf balls seldom intrude. Techniques for establishing secondary rough turf are similar to those for the primary rough. It is important that optimum fertility levels be provided and the soil pH adjusted into the desired range. Cultural practices such as fertilization, mowing, and even weed control are discontinued once an adequate turfgrass cover has been established. The grass is allowed to grow in its natural state. The attractiveness of these

Figure 6-12. Grassy mounds located in the rough on the edge of a fairway. They have been effectively shaped to add interest to the golf course landscape.

Figure 6-13. Secondary rough being maintained as an unmowed, natural area.

unmowed natural areas is enhanced if the demarcation between the primary and secondary rough is mowed in a contoured pattern rather than in a straight line. Natural areas need to be given much thought and effort, since there is a fine line between a pleasing natural setting and a sloppy, unkempt area that appears to have been forgotten.

The grass stand can reach heights of 24 to 48 inches (0.6 to 1.2 meters) during seedhead formation, depending on the particular turfgrass species involved (Fig. 6-13). Varied colors appear during seedhead ripening of various species, ranging from reddish to purplish to tan to brown. The interspersal of wild flowers with the grass in the unmowed secondary rough can provide striking variations in color of significant ornamental and aesthetic value to the golf course. They also serve as a cover and food source for a diverse range of wildlife species that add further interest to the golf course.

Chapter 7
The Bunker

DESCRIPTION

The most accepted explanation for the origin of bunkers is that they resulted from a combination of circumstances associated with the seaside links of Scotland where golf as we know it today evolved. Strong, chilling winds blowing off the North Sea caused grazing sheep to burrow into the rolling sandy terrain to seek protection. The combination of continual burrowing by sheep and wind erosion caused small depressions to become enlarged to what are now known as bunkers.

A *bunker* is defined in *Rules of Golf* as a hazard consisting of ''an area of bare ground, often a depression, which is usually covered with sand. Grass-covered ground bordering or within a bunker is not part of the hazard.'' Similarly, the grassy hollows discussed in the chapter on roughs are not hazards. ''Grass bunker'' is a misnomer for a grassy hollow and is not a true hazard. Many golfers refer to bunkers as sand traps. This usage has become commonly accepted, even though the word ''trap'' does not exist in the official *Rules of Golf*.

Bunkers are an integral part of golf strategy, aesthetics, and golf course maintenance. They also function to (a) provide depth perception, (b) protect tight green-tee areas by preventing balls from bouncing onto a tee and into players, (c) catch wayward shots which otherwise might result in an unplayable lie, a lost ball, or an out-of-bounds penalty, and (d) direct traffic patterns of players and golf carts. The components of a bunker are shown in Figure 7-1. The two basic types of bunkers are termed greenside and fairway bunkers.

DESIGN

There are no prescribed limits for the size and shape of bunkers. Specific dimensions are a result of the artistry and imagination of the golf course architect. The primary function of a bunker is the exaction of a penalty for a badly hit shot. The one guideline, therefore, in bunker design and construction is that the bunker be of sufficient depth or conformation to prevent the golfer from playing out of the bunker as easily as from a fairway or greenside lie.

Bunkers range in size from what are called pot bunkers to sandy areas of more than an acre. Pot bunkers are quite difficult to play from because they typically are small and very deep. In contrast, some golf courses have sand areas covering several acres of fairway/rough (Fig. 7-2). Apart from their strategic and penal importance to a hole, bunkers can greatly enhance the golfing landscape owing to the striking contrast in color between the sand and the healthy turf. This is true whether they are large or small. Often architects vary the size of bunkers as well as their shapes and number to provide overall variety and visual interest.

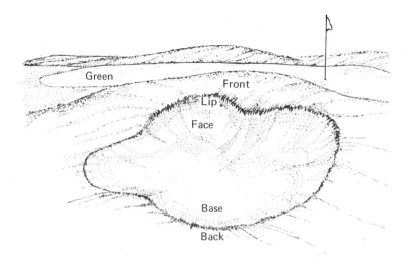

Figure 7-1. Graphic representation of the features that are found in most bunkers.

Figure 7-2. One-acre bunker parallel to a fairway at Saucon Valley Country Club, Bethlehem, Pa.

The tendency among architects today is away from small pot bunkers toward larger free-form bunkers. This change is the result of two factors. The development of powered mechanical sand rakes in the 1960's favored the use of large bunkers because mechanization made them easier and less costly to maintain. This increased efficiency also helped reverse the trend toward elimination of marginal or out-of-play bunkers which were nonetheless desirable from an aesthetic standpoint. Bunkers on modern courses should be large enough so that they can be maintained primarily with a mechanical sand rake and little or no hand raking, especially if a modest operating budget is anticipated. A second force behind larger bunkers, also a financial one, is that the bulldozers commonly used for constructing bunkers can more easily shape a large bunker than a small one.

The size, shape, and number of bunkers can vary greatly depending on the architect's design concept, the budget available for bunker maintenance, and the physical characteristics of a site, such as the land available, topography, and amount of natural vegetation. The design concept will depend in part on the category and amount of play envisioned. Speed of play may be a prime concern on intensely used public courses, as may be operating costs. Bunkering here will probably be limited to key areas of the course in order to avoid slow play. A private golf course of limited membership, or a course designed to host tournaments, may be dotted throughout with bunkers to emphasize its strategic design and to enhance its visual appeal. Budgetary considerations are usually secondary in this case.

The topography of a site is a major determinant in bunker usage and conformation. Flat land, whether covered with vegetation or not, lacks the three-dimensional appeal of a hilly site. Large, bold bunkers can be used to alleviate this monotony and, at the same time, to create strategic shot values, which would be missing without bunkers. In constrast, rugged terrain is not only more interesting but also demands greater shot-making skills owing to changes in elevation and in the lie of the ball. On such terrain bunkering may be both undesirable and unnecessary. Furthermore, large bunkers constructed on hilly land will of necessity have steeper slopes and will be subject to erosion damage. Thus, golf courses in south Florida typically have numerous large bunkers, whereas courses on the more rugged terrain of the northeast are normally characterized by bunkers of a smaller size.

Bunkers are usually larger and bolder on open sites than they are on heavily wooded sites where the fairways are narrow. Large mounded bunkers are sometimes used on treeless holes for visual definition as well as for hazards. When such sites have limited acreage, the bunkers also serve as a form of physical separation between adjacent holes. The total area of the golf course is equally important in this regard. The famous No. 2 course at Pinehurst Country Club, Pinehurst, North Carolina, is wooded, but sufficient acreage permitted exceptionally wide fairway clearing to accommodate wide roughs on either side of the fairways together with numerous, rather large bunkers. Modern courses that are less fortunately endowed with acreage usually have fairways extending from tree line to tree line. As a result, the fairway bunkers are smaller and usually oriented parallel to the hole. In the case of densely wooded sites, the architect tends to rely on the trees themselves rather than on numerous bunkers to provide much of the strategy for a hole.

Bunker sizes usually range from 1,500 to 4,000 square feet (140 to 372 square meters) with a few fairway bunkers being more than 25,000 square feet (2,323 square meters) and others being so small that they have scarcely enough room for a golfer to stand. The number of bunkers per eighteen-hole golf course has declined during the last two decades owing to high maintenance costs. Most of today's eighteen-hole golf courses are constructed with forty to eighty bunkers. Additional bunkers are sometimes added or some are removed or realigned as playing requirements dictate.

Bunker Face

The *face* refers to the slope or incline of the bunker that normally is visible to a golfer when playing the hole. It is generally that part of the fairway or greenside bunker nearest the putting surface. However, bunkers located behind the green usually have the main face on the slope away from the green. Also, fairway bunkers and lateral greenside bunkers may, depending on the supporting mounds, have the face positioned away from, but parallel to, the fairway or green.

The original function of the face was to make the recovery shot out of a bunker even more difficult. Invention of the sand wedge, however, makes such recovery shots relatively easy, especially around the green where distance is not a factor. A pronounced face between the golfer and the green can still be a formidable obstacle on fairway bunkers, since the player is sometimes forced to abandon hope of reaching the green and to use a lofted club simply to get back on the fairway.

With today's emphasis on strategic design in golf courses, the primary function of a bunker face is to alert the golfer to the existence of the hazard so the shot can be planned accordingly. This is a very important distinction between the modern strategic approach to golf course design, where all hazards are clearly visible, and the older penal style, in which many bunkers were pits hidden from the view of an unsuspecting player.

The height of the face on the green side of fairway bunkers varies with the terrain and the shot requirement envisioned by the architect. Greenside bunkers are normally constructed with higher, steeper faces than those of fairway bunkers. The steeper the slope of the face, the less likely the sand will remain in place. Slopes of 35 degrees or less are better from a maintenance standpoint, while steeper faces are more visually striking and usually present a more difficult challenge. Bunkers with steep faces are costlier to maintain because they are subject to erosion during every rain. Finally, sand on the face should not be so soft or deep that the golf ball can become buried or lost.

On some of the historic courses in Scotland, the Royal Troon Golf Club at Troon being a notable example, the practice of *revetting* is often used in the construction of bunker faces (Fig. 7-3). Strips of sod layered one on top of the other form a near-vertical face possessing excellent stability. There is no lip as such in these bunkers, and the sand is not flashed up on this sod wall. This practice was useful in the sandy linksland soil to stabilize the face against wind erosion. The binding root systems of the native fescue grasses have kept these faces intact for hundreds of years. The labor and amount of sod required are excessive by today's standards, and the severity of the face forces many golfers to play their recovery shot laterally or sometimes back in the direction of the tee. For these reasons, sod revetting of bunker faces is rarely practiced in America.

It was not uncommon on early Scottish courses to have wooden steps as part of the bunker face. This practice is no longer advisable, as such artificial structures not only add to maintenance costs but also pose a potential danger, since the ball may ricochet and injure the player.

Bunker Lip

The upper part of the bunker face should be, but is not always, defined by a vertical lip. The *lip* is in fact the vertical edge of the turf that forms over the bunker sand. A lip, if present, is normally 3 to 4 inches (7.6 to 10 centimeters) high; that is, the grassy lip and turf surrounding the bunker should be this height above the level of sand in the bunker (Fig. 7-4). The grassy lip of the bunker serves three purposes: (1) to prevent players from putting out of greenside bunkers, (2) to prevent shots that land in the bunker from rolling out, and (3) to define clearly the edge of the bunker for trimming operations.

Bunker lips should be present on the putting green side of all greenside bunkers. The edge away from the green need not have a clearly defined lip. Fairway bunkers are frequently without lips, as the sand normally is raked to meet the edge of the bunker.

The bunker lip is usually the result of excavation or building up of the bunker area. The face nearest the green is then undercut 6 to 8 inches (15 to 20 centimeters); after 3 to 4 inches (7.6 to 10 centimeters) of sand is spread on the face, a 3- to 4-inch vertical edge results. Bunker mounds that are sodded create an abutment of sod several inches above the final sand level.

The nature of the lip calls for a clearly marked edge. Normal lateral stem growth from the lip outward into the bunker produces a shaggy, unkempt appearance. As a result, bunker lips should be reedged and trimmed periodically as needed, an expensive and time-consuming operation. For this reason, lips are often eliminated on fairway bunkers. In this case, only an annual edging and trimming of the grass that has encroached into the bunker is necessary.

Location

Placement of bunkers is an integral part of the design of a hole and thus is the responsibility of the architect. Placement depends on how the architect envisions the play of the hole and what degree of difficulty is to be imposed on the various shots required to reach the green. Bunker placement on fairways should be strategic in nature in that it should cause the player to think about the proper placement of the tee shot to avoid trouble and set up the next shot. Occasionally the architect may add a nonstrategic bunker if a topographic feature provides a natural setting. However, in an era of increasing

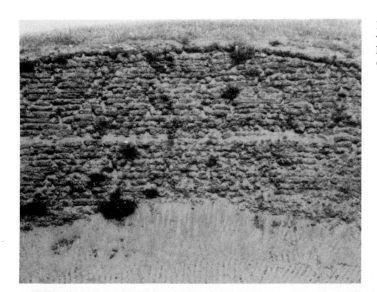

Figure 7-3. A bunker revetment constructed by layering sod pieces to the desired height.

Figure 7-4. Good grassy lip on a bunker.

maintenance costs, use of such nonessential bunkers should be avoided unless they greatly enhance the aesthetics of the hole. Normally the location of fairway bunkers is determined by distance from the championship teeₛ. The design of loₙg tees brings the bunker(s) into play for all classes of golfers from their respective forwarᵈ tees. On par-5 holes, bunkers associated with the second landing area generally are located to affect the better player and are not intended to pose problems for the average golfer.

Bunker location may also depend on drainage characteristics of the site, if additional fill material is not available for their construction. Bunkers require excellent surface and subsurface drainage. There is nothing worse for either the player or the course superintendent than a bunker full of water. In flat areas or in other areas where soil infiltration is poor, the floor of the bunker should be elevated above the surrounding grade to assure adequate drainage. Where surface drainage is good and adequate subsurface drainage can be provided, or on sandy soils with good soil infiltration, bunkers can be constructed below the surface of the terrain. Potential surface water runoff from slopes or from a green or apron should also be considered when locating and constructing bunkers so that water does not flow into the bunkers and is not impounded on or beside the green.

From a maintenance point of view, greenside bunkers should be situated no closer than 10 to 12 feet (3 to 3.7 meters) from the putting surface. This separation allows the area to be mowed by larger machines and provides sufficient area for the three-gang greensmowers to be turned off the green surface, thus minimizing damage to the putting green itself. This distance also minimizes the amount of bunker sand blasted onto the putting surface. Some architects believe that the design of major golf courses scheduled to host important tournaments necessitates placing bunkers very close to the green surface to defend certain pin positions. Such design practices, while demanding greater golfing accuracy, can result in higher labor requirements and maintenance costs. The quality of bunker sand is of considerable importance in this case.

Bunker configuration around a green can significantly affect the distribution of traffic between the green and the next tee. This in turn affects turfgrass wear and soil compaction around the green. The architect must weigh optimum design and aesthetic intent against the necessities of practical maintenance. Where intense play will be a major factor, a large greenside bunker should be avoided if it will lie in the natural exit from the green to the next tee. Traffic would thus be concentrated in one narrow area or, equally bad, players might have to exit from the green in the direction of oncoming players. A better solution would be to create two or more separate bunkers with a wide turfed area between them. When entrance to and exit from the green are made easier, speed of play is increased. Traffic will be more evenly distributed if the turfed areas are sufficiently wide, and in turn the problems of wear, compaction, and thinning of the turf will be greatly reduced.

Sand Depth

The sand depth of greenside bunkers should be at least 4 inches (10 centimeters) at the base and about 2 inches (5 centimeters) on the face. A shallow depth on the face aids in maintenance, since a golf ball striking a 2-inch face normally will not bury but will roll down onto the flatter base. As a result, sand raking and repair of the face are minimized because the golfer does not need to climb it to play a shot. Additional benefits are enhanced speed of play and less cost for sand replacement. From a quantitative standpoint, a 2-inch uncompacted sand depth is equivalent to 6.2 cubic yards per thousand square feet (4.4 cubic meters per are), while the 4-inch uncompacted depth is equivalent to approximately 12.4 cubic yards per thousand square feet (8.8 cubic meters per are). Anticipated settling to the final depth would be less than 10 percent. The sand depth of fairway bunkers is typically more shallow than that of greenside bunkers. The shallower depth provides a firmer lie for distant shots.

SAND SELECTION

Size

Selection of the correct sand particle-size distribution is an important decision, since it affects playing quality from bunkers as well as bunker maintenance. Thus, the decision should be based on a physical sand textural analysis, such as is conducted at the United States Golf Association (USGA) Physical Soil Test Laboratory at Texas A&M University, College Station. With sand of the proper texture, a variety of lies are provided, depending on the angle of entry and force of the ball at impact. The preferred sand size distribution, as specified by the Green Section of the USGA, is shown in Table 7-1. Sand in the recommended range for bunkers must go through a 16-mesh screen and be retained on a 60-mesh screen. Ideally, a major portion of it, and 75 percent at minimum, should be in the 0.25- to 0.5-millimeter range (medium-grain sand). Sands in the prescribed range provide the best all-around conditions in terms of (1) ball lie, (2) firmness of footing, (3) minimum surface crusting, (4) internal water drainage, and (5) ease of bunker maintenance.

Table 7-1. Size Specifications for Sand Particles Used in Bunkers

	ASTM* Mesh	U.S. Series (NBS†)	Particle Diameter (mm)	Sieve Opening (in.)		
	4	4	4.76	0.187		
	5	....	4.00	0.157		
	6	6	3.36	0.132		
	7	....	2.83	0.111		
	8	8	2.38	0.0937		
	9	10	2.00	0.0787		
	10	12	1.68	0.0661		
	12	14	1.41	0.0555		
	14	16	1.19	0.0469		
	16	18	1.00	0.0394		
	20	20	.84	0.0331		
Range	24	....	.71	0.0278	Coarse	
for	28	30	.59	0.0234		
bunker	32	35	.50	0.0197		
use	35	40	.42	0.0176	Medium	Ideally, minimum of 75% medium sand
	42	45	.35	0.0139		
Sharp, angular	48	50	.30	0.0117		
sand only	60	60	.25	0.0098		
	65	70	.21	0.0083		Round or angular sand acceptable
	80	80	.18	0.0070		
	100	100	.15	0.0059	Fine	
	115	120	.13	0.0049		
	150	140	.11	0.0041		
	170	170	.09	0.0035		
	200	200	.07	0.0029		
	250	230	.06	0.0025		
	270	270	.05	0.0021		
	325	325	.04	0.0017		

(Middle boxed section, ASTM 16 through 60, marked: Range for putting green root zone mixes)

*American Standard Testing Materials.
†National Bureau of Standards.

Ideally, sand that provides the proper ball lie in greenside bunkers should be of such nature that the ball penetrates to approximately half its diameter, the so-called "fried egg" lie (Fig. 7-5). Sand that sets up too firmly normally provides little or no penalty, while sand that is too soft frequently causes the ball to become embedded. Sand of one size or of a very narrow size range is undesirable because it remains too loose. Thus, sand of various sizes, but within the prescribed range, is preferred, since it sets up better and is firmer. Also, sands of the proper particle size range pose minimal maintenance problems when exploded onto the putting surface. They readily fall through the turf and thus present no problem to golfers, who meticulously lift every grain of sand in the line of putt, or to mowing operations. Particles in excess of 1 millimeter should be screened out, since they can damage greens-mowers and can also slow play owing to players taking time to pick up visible sand particles in the putting line.

Bunker sands in the range prescribed by the USGA Green Section are within the range of sand particle sizes specified for putting green root zone mixes (Table 7-1). Thus, bunker sand accumulating on the green from explosion shots creates minimal problems in terms of root zone growing conditions.

Wind Displacement. The one major exception to this discussion is in areas where high velocity winds are a recurring problem. Golf course personnel may be forced to use sands with a diameter larger than 1 millimeter in climatic regions where wind velocity is severe enough to blow finer sands out of

Figure 7-5. Close-up of poor ball position (*left*) and good ball position (*right*) in a bunker.

bunkers. Experience gained through trial-and-error will dictate just how large a sand size is required to achieve stability against wind deposition in a given climatic region. In addition, the wind displacement problem can be partially alleviated if the architect designs deep bunkers and/or bunkers well protected by surrounding mounds. The use of several small bunkers rather than a single large one is also advisable on windy sites.

Shape

Sharp, angular sands are preferred for bunker use since they "set up" better than round sands and are firmer surfaces from which to play. Smooth or round sands have a tendency to shift underfoot and are "heavy" to blast through, since they give the same feeling in playing a ball as does a water hazard. The likelihood is also great that the ball will become buried if the smooth, round sands are of uniform particle size.

Color

Light-colored sands, such as white, tan, or light gray sands, are preferred to darker ones. Light colors contrast more sharply with the surrounding green turf, thus providing a more visually aesthetic setting. Sand size and shape should be given a higher priority than color, however. For example, if the only sands available are a white sand that does not meet size and shape specifications and a dark sand that is within the specifications, the latter should be selected. In some cases, a sand may be so white that it causes golfers difficulty in seeing and hitting the ball. Very white sand can also possess objectionable glare characteristics.

Composition

Sands can vary in composition. Hard, silicate-type sands are preferred to soft, calcareous sands such as coral sands. The more stable composition is a much better choice. The softer sands break down under constant weathering and thus tend to stick together, which necessitates daily raking to prevent objectionable crusting.

Purity

The sand selected should be free from foreign materials. These include clay and silt, which tend to solidify the sand and cause crusting, and viable seeds or vegetative propagules, which can introduce serious weed problems into bunkers. It is advisable that each truckload of sand delivered be inspected to insure that the sand is of acceptable purity before it is dumped.

CONSTRUCTION

The first criterion in good bunker construction is proper drainage, including both surface and internal water drainage. The ultimate goal in surface drainage is to move the water away so that it does not enter the bunker and cause erosion of sand, especially on the face (Fig. 7-6). Replacing eroded sand in bunkers is one of the most costly labor operations on a golf course. Not only does it involve the time-consuming and costly task of replacing the sand, but there is the added problem of the sand becoming discolored and contaminated with eroded silt, clay, and organic debris. Thus, the major theme through all phases of bunker construction is proper surface and internal drainage (Fig. 7-7). Drainage system installation, lip construction, and finish grading should be done just prior to sand filling for the same reasons.

Surveying and Staking

The first step in construction is surveying and staking of each bunker location in accordance with the architect's staking plan. Fairway bunker locations will be clearly marked on the plan. Greenside bunkers are an integral part of an entire green complex, so the area normally is staked as a complete unit. The positioning and elevations are usually referenced to centerline hubstakes or to a specific bench mark. Bunkers are usually staked after clearing and grubbing has been completed and before rough grading and general earthwork are done. Most bunkers—fairway or greenside—require fill and so must be staked to show where fill stockpiles should be deposited.

Rough Shaping

A small bulldozer is usually used for rough shaping of bunkers. In cases of small bunkers built on steep slopes or the presence of large rocks that make use of a bulldozer difficult, a backhoe is sometimes used to excavate the bunker. As the modern design approach is to have bunkers clearly visible, placing of fill material at the location of each proposed bunker is often necessary. This material is used for the construction of bunker mounds and faces. The use of fill material, especially on flat terrain, also aids in assuring adequate bunker drainage. Fill material may not be needed to create visibility where bunkers are to be carved out of an existing slope or into the side of a green.

In either case, existing topsoil should be stripped from the entire work area (this will already have been done in the case of greenside bunkers) and stockpiled for redistribution once the bunker is built.

Figure 7-6. Failure to direct surface water away from face of improperly constructed bunker has resulted in erosion of the face and soil deposition in the base. Erosion can be controlled by proper contouring of bunker surrounds and installing a subsurface drainage system in bunker.

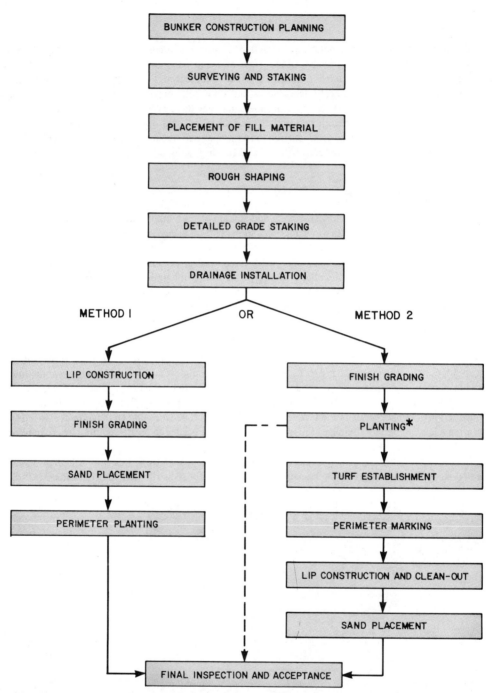

*Inspection and acceptance in Method 2 may take place after planting is completed if it is clearly understood that the contractor's responsibility terminates with this operation and that the lip construction, clean-out, and sand placement will be done by the course green staff.

Figure 7-7. Flow diagram for the construction of a bunker.

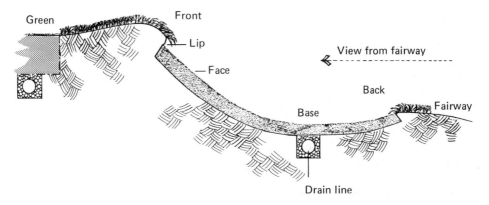

Figure 7-8. Vertical cross section showing the shaping suggested for bunkers to achieve drainage and visibility.

Many bunkers are built so that the *back,* or side nearest the tee, is flush with existing ground level, while the *front,* or side nearest the green, is elevated to create a visible face (Fig. 7-8). The height of this face depends on the need for visibility as well as on the degree of penalty intended. In general, faces of fairway bunkers are not pronounced and permit the player to advance the ball a considerable distance, perhaps even as far as the green, with exceptional execution. Faces of greenside bunkers are frequently high, as distance to the green is not a deterring factor. In free-form, amoebalike bunkers it is quite common for low-mounded peninsulas or ''fingers'' of turf to protrude into the bunker and for additional faces to be constructed on these fingers for visibility. On long fairway bunkers, bold-turfed mounds may flank the side of the bunker away from the fairway to create three-dimensional relief. Sand is then ''flashed'' on the faces of these mounds to enhance visual appeal.

The slope of the bunker floor, or *base,* should blend smoothly and concavely from the face(s) of the bunker toward the front or the sides. Large free-form bunkers may have more than one slope direction, depending on the configuration and shaping. The surface level of sand at the back or sides of the bunker (wherever the drainage exit occurs) is normally flush with the adjacent terrain. This facilitates surface drainage and eliminates the presence of a vertical lip which might interfere with a golfer's swing. The latter situation could force a golfer to play out of the bunker laterally rather than offering a chance to advance the ball toward the hole.

Detailed Grade Staking

Assuming the architect's plans have sufficient information on elevations and dimensions, grade stakes can be placed around the perimeter mounds and face(s) of the bunker to help establish the desired shape during the construction process. Some architects show on plan only the location and schematic form of the bunkers; the heights of the mound(s) and face(s) are less important as fixed dimensions. These architects rely on on-site supervision to create the final forms and desired visual and playing effects. In either case, it is important that an instrument check be made to confirm that a minimum base slope of 2 to 3 percent is achieved. The slope of the face is usually much greater to provide the desired visual effect. A 30- to 35-percent slope is generally considered maximum for this purpose, although bunkers built into natural hillsides often exceed this grade at the price of higher maintenance costs.

Drainage Installation

Special design features are needed where the overall topography slopes into a bunker. Failure to intercept and direct excess surface water around a bunker will create sand erosion problems after rains, early contamination from clay and silt, and a continuing need for costly replacement of the displaced sand. Interception of surface water can be accomplished by use of a swale, waterway, or small diversion ditch positioned above the bunker. These surface interceptor channels can be constructed with a small bulldozer at the time of rough shaping of the bunker. A subsurface interceptor drain line positioned parallel to the center of this drainage way may also be needed on imperfectly drained soils.

The interior of each bunker should have a 2- to 3-percent slope along the base, directed into a drain line to insure adequate internal drainage. Large bunkers with complex slope patterns require more than one drain line and provision of additional branch lines in a herringbone pattern often is advisable. Normally, 4-inch (10-centimeter) diameter, perforated plastic pipe or tubing is used for these drain lines. Nonbiodegradable plastic or glass fiber fabrics are available that can be wrapped (or come prewrapped) around the plastic drain lines to help prevent soil and bunker sand from entering and plugging the pipe.

Rain water commonly collects in the low point during bunker construction. It is very important that an outlet be provided for this water. Prior to installation of the drain lines, a swale often can be opened to the surrounding terrain. Once the drain line(s) has been installed, however, an adequate outlet must be provided. This may involve connection into a nearby drain line or into a swale or dry well, preferably located in the rough. Drain lines from greenside bunkers are normally connected into the putting green drainage system. Normal erosion runoff occuring prior to establishment of turf around the bunker and placement of sand in the bunker may cause the drain line(s) to silt up periodically. Therefore, it is frequently necessary for the contractor (if specified in the contract) or the golf course green staff to unblock and clean out the bunker drain line outlets just before the course is opened for play. Because of these clogging problems, some architects prefer to install drainage outlets for fairway bunkers after the turf is established.

Lip Construction

The lip, or vertical edge between the sand surface and surrounding turf, of all greenside bunkers, when finished, should be 3 or more inches (7.6 centimeters) high along the putting surface perimeter to prevent players from putting out of the bunker. There are basically three ways the lip may be created during construction.

If the perimeter of the bunker can be clearly staked from information given on the plan or under supervision of the architect, the base of the bunker can be undercut 6 to 8 inches (15 to 20 centimeters) at the edge of the perimeter where the lip is to be located. The depth of this undercut will vary depending on the slope of the face at the lip. Steep faces may have only a thin 2-inch (5-centimeter) layer of sand at the base of the lip, whereas relatively shallow faces should have 4 inches. Whatever the slope-sand depth combination, the undercut should be sufficient to leave a lip averaging 4 inches (10 centimeters) above the finished sand level. Elsewhere in the bunker, where no lip is intended, the undercut need only be about 4 inches to accommodate placement of the sand. For bunkers excavated in this manner, the integrity of the lip contour and depth must be protected during construction. This is best done by placing and staking pliable plastic, exterior plywood, or metal sheets (0.25-inch or less in thickness) along the face of the lip to keep it from breaking down due to erosion or general construction activity (Fig. 7-9).

A second method of lip construction, one more commonly used today, involves waiting until the sand is to be placed in the bunker. With this method, the mounds, faces, and fingers of the bunker are shaped by the bulldozer and then finish graded. The base of the bunker, whether a flat plane or concave, is similarly shaped and blended in smoothly with the mounds and fingers. Just prior to the placement and spreading of sand, the architect marks with paint or similar material the actual limits of the bunker. A backhoe or manual digging is then used to undercut the entire perimeter of the bunker, 6 to 8 inches (15 to 20 centimeters) along the proposed lip and 4 inches (10 centimeters) elsewhere, to accommodate the proper depth of sand. The depth of the undercut tapers to zero (the existing base grade) about 2 to 5 feet (0.6 to 1.5 meters) from the perimeter. The excavated material is then hauled away. Where bunkers

Figure 7-9. Use of plywood sheeting to preserve lip shape of bunker during turf establishment and subsequent sand filling.

are large and fairly concave and the soil is of good quality, excess soil can be "wasted" or spread evenly over the base of the bunker. Undercutting and cleanup are done after turf has been established on the bunker surrounds. This approach to bunker construction has the advantages that it (a) is fast, (b) relies on machines rather than manual labor, (c) makes finish grading/planting quick and efficient, and (d) enables the final outline of the bunker to be determined or altered under more favorable conditions of the presence of a turf.

Although sodding of the slopes and mounds of bunkers is a less common practice on new courses, this method of planting a bunker and creating the lip is preferred for remodeling projects where bunker changes are minimal and there is a pressing need to finish the project quickly. The procedure for shaping the bunker is the same as in the second method described above. However, instead of undercutting the bunker perimeter just prior to placing the sand, sod is laid around the perimeter to create the desired difference in elevation. Where a lip is intended, several inches of additional fill provides the proper lip height. This lip fill tapers back smoothly from the perimeter to tie in with the existing grade. Around the remaining perimeter, 1 to 2 inches (2.5 to 5 centimeters) of fill may be required to raise the sod sufficiently to accommodate the 4-inch (10-centimeter) depth of sand.

Finish Grading

The finish grading of bunkers requires a certain amount of manual labor, though the use of small machinery is desirable where possible. Bunkers with preconstructed lips require greater hand work. Shovels, rakes, wheelbarrows, a small front-end loader, and perhaps a tiller rake are required. In the case of large bunkers without preconstructed lips, finish grading is usually accomplished mechanically with use of a low-profile agricultural tractor. Useful accessories include a box scraper, a scotch chain or other drag, and even a modified side-delivery hay rake. Mechanical sand rakes with drag floats are also useful for fine grading. Apart from speed and efficiency, the use of mechanized implements results in smooth, flowing lines as well as surrounding slopes that are appealing and easy to maintain once a turf is established.

If definite grades, elevations, and perimeters are shown on the architect's plans, these dimensions should be carefully checked before the bunker is filled with sand. The original grade stakes can be used as reference points. A simple level and measuring tape are usually sufficient for this work. As stated previously, some architects consider the actual form and visual appeal of bunkers more important than fixed elevations and dimensions. In this case, the architect will approve on site the finish grading and general appearance of each bunker. Such an approach dictates timely site visits by the architect.

In preparation of a bunker for sand placement, all stones must be removed from the floor and especially from the face(s). This is necessary to avoid serious damage to mechanical edgers and golf clubs and possibly even injury to players. Care should also be taken to smooth the base of the bunker. Protruding humps covered by only a thin layer of sand can be struck by rakes or by the player's club, thus bringing soil contaminants to the surface of the sand and obstructing proper execution of a shot.

During the entire finish grading operation, care should be exercised to not damage the drain lines and trenches previously installed. All drain lines and outlets should be cleaned and inspected for proper functioning just prior to the placement of sand.

Sand Placement and Perimeter Stabilization

These two finish operations are discussed together because the methods vary with the types of bunker construction, as described earlier. Although the sand should already have been examined at origin for cleanliness and freedom from weeds, it is wise for each truckload to be inspected on arrival. In bunkers with preconstructed lips, the sand is placed in the bunker prior to planting of the perimeter. In bunkers shaped without a lip, the perimeter and part of the bunker are planted and only after the grass is well established is the lip formed and the sand put in place.

In the case of bunkers with preformed lips, the sand may be hauled and dumped into the bunkers in one of two ways. In new construction, the sand may be hauled directly to each bunker with the same large-capacity trucks which deliver it to the site. It is dumped right into the bunker (Fig. 7-10). This saves additional hauling time and cost. On established courses, and in the second method of finishing bunkers to be described, it is more common for the delivery trucks to dump the sand in one or more storage areas. The sand is then loaded onto tractor-drawn trailers by the golf course crew and hauled to each bunker as construction and clean-out are completed. For larger bunkers, the sand should be dumped in several preselected points along the edge of the bunker where the natural slope minimizes any danger of the truck tipping over while dumping and where destruction of the established bunker edge will be minimized.

A recently introduced method of sand placement involves the use of a gunite machine positioned in the rough. This unit is capable of accepting bulk sand and forcing it under high pressure through a hose for several hundred feet. The sand is delivered into the bunker with sufficient force so that it is

Figure 7-10. Sand dumped in bunkers for spreading. (Photo courtesy of R. A. Strait, Boca West Club, Boca Raton, Fla.)

favorably compacted and at the same time efficiently spread with minimal disruption to the perimeter, lip, and face of the bunker.

Just before the sand is hauled to and dumped into the bunker, the lip and perimeter edge should be checked and repaired as required. This involves removal of any stakes and of the plastic, metal, or plywood sheeting previously installed to shore up the edge. Any deterioration along the perimeter edge should be corrected, a task usually accomplished manually.

Distribution of sand in large bunkers can be done by a small bulldozer, although a small tractor with a rear-mounted blade is more commonly used. Mechanical sand rakes are now available with a small front-mounted, dozer-type blade which is very useful for spreading sand in smaller bunkers. Spreading sand out to the perimeters and up on the face(s) is usually done by hand using shovels and rakes. A uniform sand depth of 4 inches (10 centimeters) throughout the bunker is ideal except on the steep faces, where the thickness can taper down to 2 inches (5 centimeters) to provide firm footing and to reduce the possibility that a ball will embed itself in the face. The entire bunker can then be smoothed and raked by hand or with a mechanical sand rake.

Method One. Immediately thereafter, the bunker is finished by sodding the perimeter plus any adjacent mounds or slopes particularly prone to erosion and soil washing into the bunker. Although the entire bunker complex may be sodded, economic considerations usually dictate that the remaining areas be sprigged or seeded.

For bunkers built on steep slopes or with bold mounds and "fingers," the design intent may be for turf to extend down these slopes nearly to the base. Sodding is the most practical way of avoiding erosion in such areas. Stabilization is best achieved by using 6- to 8-inch (15- to 20-centimeter) wooden pegs to anchor the sod to the slope. The tops of pegs should be driven beneath the mower cutting height to avoid interference with mowing operations. Protruding pegs can be removed later when sod is well rooted or, if of soft wood, simply be allowed to decompose in place.

This first method involving sand placement and sodding of the bunker perimeter has the advantage on an existing course that the bunker can be finished and "in play" rather quickly with minimal disturbance to ongoing course usage and to overall appearance of the course. However, it is costly and labor intensive and requires a considerable amount of sod. It also has several important drawbacks when used in new construction. Sod, especially in quantities sufficient for sixty to eighty bunkers, may not be available if the bunkers are to be finished concurrently with the entire course, as is generally the case. The time, labor, and materials involved may be excessive and very costly. Finally, the readiness (sand in place) of the bunkers six to eight months prior to the opening of the course poses additional, unnecessary maintenance problems. During that period the bunkers will be subject to erosion, a certain degree of unavoidable contamination, and the encroachment of weeds and most probably will require at least one trimming operation.

Method Two. A second method of finishing bunkers involves turf establishment on the bunker surrounds first, followed by placement of the sand after the turf is well established and just before the course is opened for play. After fine grading of the slopes, mounds, fingers, and faces that comprise a bunker, topsoil is spread and smoothed over these areas. The soil is then prepared and fertilized in readiness for planting. Sodding is rare in this method of bunker construction due to cost, time, and labor requirements. Seeding of the entire bunker complex is more common, with the base preferably seeded to a bunch-type species. In the case of fairway bunkers, this work is done concurrently with establishment of the fairways and rough. Greenside bunkers are planted at the same time as the putting surface and surrounds. As no perimeter edge or lip yet exists, the faces and fingers are planted along with the surrounding mounds. The limit of planting may be the base of the bunker. The additional seed required to plant the entire bunker, including the base, is minimal and usually worth the cost in terms of erosion control.

The bunker is watered and mowed along with the fairways during the four- to eight-month establishment period. A month or so prior to course opening, the architect marks the proposed outer limit of the sand in each bunker. Cans of pressurized spray paint are ideal for this purpose. After outlining each bunker, the architect can stand back to examine how the faces will appear and make any adjustments necessary to improve the visual effect. This check is more effective against a background of turf than against a mound of soil. If there is concern that the painting will be lost during mowing operations before all bunkers are cleaned and filled with sand, the outlines quickly can be made permanent by hoeing or by spraying each outline with a nonselective herbicide by means of a backpack sprayer.

The next step is removal of the grass from within the bunker as outlined. This is most effectively done with a small tractor-mounted backhoe from inside the bunker. The lip or edge can be constructed and the turf loaded on a trailer in one operation. If all or part of the bunker base has been planted, the grass on the base can be cleaned out in the same way. In the case of bunkers constructed with deep, concave bases, it is sometimes felt that the turf must be removed from only the 2 or 3 feet (0.6 to 0.9 meter) along the perimeter and that a herbicide or fuel oil can be used to kill the remaining turf prior to placing the sand. This practice should be avoided. It is potentially dangerous and can be harmful to surrounding turf areas. Also, any sod mat thus left can interfere with proper drainage.

It is common practice to cut sod from the base of bunkers prior to marking and clean-out operations so that it can be used in repairing erosion damage elsewhere on the course. Bunkers can thus serve as provisional turf nurseries. A certain amount of erosion damage and/or poor turf establishment often occurs on bunker faces. Frequently, the architect can eliminate the need for repairing these areas by adjusting the marking so that a good portion of them is inside the bunker.

Depending on the skill of the backhoe operator, the bunker may have to be smoothed out by hand with shovels and rakes. Drain lines should be inspected and cleaned out as necessary. The bunker is then ready for sand placement. Since the turf is already established throughout the course, sand placement is usually done by tractor and trailer as described earlier to avoid damage from large trucks. If the turf is sufficiently established in the fall for the bunkers to be cleaned out during the winter when the ground is frozen, it is possible for sand to be hauled directly to the bunkers in medium-sized trucks with relatively little damage to the fairways.

The most important advantages of this second method of finishing bunkers are that (a) the bunkers can be fine graded and planted more quickly and with less costly hand labor, (b) the bunkers are less apt to become contaminated and require less maintenance prior to course opening, and (c) the bunker outline can be defined with greater flexibility and exactness. Use of the bunker bases as possible sod nurseries can also be helpful. The principal drawbacks are the extensive clean-out required and the difficulty of establishing complete turf coverage of the fingers and tops of mounds from seed.

Bunker Liner

On occasion, perforated polyethylene sheets have been placed over the base of bunkers prior to sand filling to control weed growth. This practice proves effective in some situations when bunkers are raked manually. However, weed problems can be minimized by the use of a powered sand rake on a regular basis. Such a rake can tear into a plastic liner if the sand depth has become too shallow. Torn edges are then dragged to the surface, where their presence is objectionable. Therefore, if a liner is used it is important that it be of heavy strength and that an adequate depth of sand be maintained in the bunker.

Another type of bunker liner involves a matrix pattern which restricts upward movement of stones from the subsoil while at the same time allowing adequate drainage. The liner may be some type of plastic, rubber, or synthetic net. The preferred installation procedure is to cover the net liner with a layer of screened soil before placing the sand in the bunker. Again, it is important that the net be covered with sand to a sufficient depth so that contact with it does not occur during raking activities and normal play.

MAINTENANCE

Because of the size, shape, and number of bunkers, the cost of maintaining them in a well-groomed, playable condition is high. Bunkers also require periodic renovation, including the addition of sand, restructuring of edges, and sometimes rebuilding of faces. Although bunkers represent a very small portion of the total golf course playing area, they are a unique, integral part of golf course design and playing strategy. Thus, proper maintenance is very important.

Raking

The primary maintenance practice associated with bunkers is sand raking to maintain the proper playing condition. Also, a well-groomed bunker encourages golfers to repair disruptions in the sand surface after playing from it.

Prior to development of mechanical sand rakes in the 1960's, bunkers were maintained by hand raking. Thus, bunker maintenance was one of the most laborious, time-consuming, and costly operations on a golf course. When labor costs increased during the 1950's and 1960's, there was a trend toward reducing the number of bunkers. In some cases, the reduction was as much as 50 to 60 percent. However, this trend was reversed with the development and successful introduction of mechanically powered sand rakes (Fig. 7-11). These units require a relatively small amount of manpower and provide good sand playing conditions in those bunkers where they can be operated efficiently.

Figure 7-11. Three types of mechanical sand rakes in operation.

Raking Frequency. Sand in bunkers should be raked frequently enough to maintain a semisoft, dry condition of the desired smoothness. The specific frequency of raking depends on the irrigation and rainfall frequency and the intensity of play. Water from irrigation or rainfall causes sand to become compacted, and thus bunkers should be raked after every measurable precipitation or irrigation. This may even dictate a daily raking schedule at times. Similarly, the more intense the play on a course, the greater the need for raking bunkers, even though most golfers are relatively considerate in smoothing their footprints. Thus, bunker raking may be required daily on weekends and on holidays during intense play, while during the week and the off-season raking may be required only at two- to three-day intervals or as dictated by intensity of play and water compaction from irrigation or rainfall. Tournaments and major golfing events require prime playing conditions. This includes proper sand conditions in all bunkers, which means raking on a daily basis.

Hand Raking Procedure. Surface characteristics of a sand bunker depend on the preference of the golfing clientele, varying from a relatively smooth surface to one with distinct grooves. Deep furrows are not desirable. Very shallow or no furrows are preferred for USGA championships. The actual surface effect achieved depends on the raking procedure and type of rake utilized.

Hand raking involves a forward and back movement of the rake as the worker moves laterally to the left or right. Care should be exercised so that ridges of sand are not left at the termination of either the forward or back stroke. The bunker can be raked from one side to the other or from end to end or even in a circular pattern. Manual raking should be done carefully, since rapid movements tend to leave vertical "waves" in the sand surface.

Special care is needed in raking the perimeter of bunkers. Sand must be worked toward the edge of the bunker in proportion to the amount moved toward the center. In the case of the bunker face, the proper procedure involves working along the edge of the bunker, either pulling sand up the face (if the groundsman is above), or pushing it up (if the groundsman is in the bunker). Raking down the face causes a downward movement of sand which eventually results in a thin face and excess sand in the base of the bunker. In contrast, the raking procedure on the opposite or back side of a bunker should insure that the sand surface is nearly level with the nearby turf-soil interface in order to avoid difficult lies (Fig. 7-12).

The type of rake selected depends on the particular effect desired (Fig. 7-13). Short, heavy-toothed rakes (2 inches [5 centimeters]) have the advantages of requiring less manual power and facilitating faster raking than long-toothed rakes. They are commonly used for dry, loose sand and are less effective in loosening wet, hard sand and in weed removal. Long-toothed rakes (3 to 4 inches [7.6 to 10

Figure 7-12. Back edge of a bunker with properly prepared edge (sand raked level with the adjacent soil) (*left*) and a deeper, more difficult edge (*right*).

Figure 7-13. Short, heavy-toothed rake (*left*) and long-toothed rake (*right*) used for manual raking of bunkers.

centimeters]) are not used as much because of the greater difficulty in manual raking and the cost involved. Their deeper penetration into the sand provides more sand loosening plus better weed control.

Mechanical Raking Procedure. Raking of bunkers using the mechanically powered sand rake involves driving into the bunker, lowering the rake, and traveling slowly over the sand surface in a circular or overlapping figure-eight pattern. The operator should try to enter and exit at a different location each time to avoid creating a worn path. One outside finishing pass should be planned, which also functions as an exit pass for the mechanical rake. Lifting of the rake before the machine exits from a bunker is important to avoid depositing excessive sand on the turfed edge outside the bunker. Subsequently, the operator should smooth out any sand mound left inside the bunker. Some bunkers are designed with steep faces or narrow, deep bays which cannot be negotiated by mechanically powered sand rakes. Supplemental hand raking by the machine operator is required in these situations. A manual sand rake should be carried on the machine at all times for this purpose.

Face Maintenance. Sand on faces tends to work downward into the base of the bunker because of continual erosive washing from rains and irrigation, wind displacement, raking, and activities of golfers. Thus, a crew must be assigned periodically to shovel sand from the base of bunkers back up on the face followed by a finish raking. This must also be done immediately after each intense rain.

Edging

Encroachment of grass into bunkers from the margins is a continuing problem, since sand is a favorable medium for the growth of grass and weeds. If not checked, grass sod typically grows inward, reducing the size of the bunker and/or altering its shape. The edges of bunkers must be reestablished periodically as originally designed by the course architect. Bench marks should be established as references for use when reestablishing the original perimeter. Edging is usually required at least once a year. It may be necessary on a more frequent interval if grass encroachment is rapid.

Special attention must be given to reestablishing the original edge of a bunker when removing encroaching vegetation. The original bunker design is usually apparent to the discerning worker. Several different types of equipment can be used in edging bunkers, ranging from straight-bladed hand spades to mechanically powered edgers (Fig. 7-14). The latter is more commonly used because of the lower cost and well-defined edge produced.

The next step is complete removal of the severed vegetative material. Addition of some new sand may or may not be necessary, depending on how much sand adheres to the sod pieces that have been removed.

Figure 7-14. Mechanically powered edger being used to reestablish the original edge of a bunker.

There are some preventive approaches to reduce the rate of grass encroachment into sand bunkers. One option that has achieved some degree of success involves an application of the appropriate growth regulator at a four- to eight-week interval. Another is the sodding of a zoysiagrass border 2 to 3 feet (0.6 to 0.9 meter) in width around the perimeter of the bunker as a barrier to slow bermudagrass encroachment. The zoysiagrass does gradually grow into the sand bunker but at a rate much reduced compared with that of the vigorous bermudagrasses common to the warm climatic region.

Weed Control

Bunkers must be kept free of weeds at all times. Vigorous lateral creeping grasses are a particularly difficult problem. Cultivation of the sand by frequent deep raking is one of the most effective weed control programs for bunkers. Mechanically powered sand rakes are usually the most effective tool for achieving weed control because of their deep cultivation capability. Weeds are a greater problem in bunkers where the sand is contaminated with a significant amount of soil. Golf courses that do not have mechanical sand rakes or cannot use them because of the bunker design usually employ a combination of hand raking and selected physical removal of weeds by hoeing and possibly even the application of an appropriate herbicide.

Particular attention must be given to selection of the proper herbicide. Safety to the nontarget grass species is the major concern. Characteristics desired include (1) minimum phytotoxicity to the desirable species surrounding bunkers, (2) ready biodegradability with a minimal residual period, and (3) low water solubility which minimizes movement in surface water. The herbicide should not be prone to washing out of the bunker where it can cause injury to the adjacent turf. Minimum phytotoxicity is necessary because sand with adhering herbicide can be tracked or thrown out of the bunker during explosion shots. The herbicide should be applied only to the sand area within the bunker to avoid destroying the forward grassy lip and bunker outline.

Types of herbicides that have been used include (1) phenoxy herbicides for the control of broadleaf weeds on a spot application basis, (2) nonselective herbicides with a short residual period, such as glyphosate and paraquat, which also present minimal problems from surface runoff or foot tracking of sand, and (3) a preemergent herbicide which is occasionally incorporated into the sand before germination of the target weed species. This is effective in killing weeds as they emerge but has little effect on established weeds.

Figure 7-15. Sand blasted onto a collar from bunker shots.

Stone Removal

The presence of stones in bunkers can cause problems from both a playability and maintenance standpoint. When thrown onto the green during explosion shots they can damage the greensmower. Stones in bunker sand must be removed either by cleaning the sand or by completely replacing the existing sand with one of proper texture. Both are very time-consuming, difficult tasks but are necessary if this condition exists.

If the sand is badly contaminated with small stones and pea gravel, total removal of the sand to a depth of 4 to 6 inches (10 to 15 centimeters) usually is advisable. New sand of the particle-size distribution range specified earlier in this chapter is then added. Consideration should also be given to installing a nonbiodegradable plastic net or similar synthetic liner below the sand where stones rise from the subsoil. The net or liner must be placed at a sufficient depth below the sand surface so that normal bunker raking will not cause contact with the liner.

An alternative is cleaning of the existing sand if the number of stones and gravel is limited or if funds are not available for total sand replacement. Two primary procedures are followed when cleaning sand in bunkers. One involves the use of a 0.25-inch (6.3-millimeter) mesh, slanted screen. The sand is either hand-fed or mechanically conveyed onto the screen, which may or may not be set up with a mechanical shaker. The former is preferred. The sand is moved to one side of the bunker, the screen positioned in the center, and the sand processed through the screen and placed in the opposite side of the bunker until all sand has been processed. Subsequently the clean sand is redistributed over the bunker. Some new sand may have to be added after this process is completed to achieve the desired depth.

The second procedure for cleaning sand involves the use of one of the numerous fine-toothed rakes that are available. Hand raking is much faster than screening but allows the sand to be cleaned only to a relatively shallow depth. Thus, the sand must usually be reraked on a periodic basis as stones work their way to the surface. This method is most effective when a very fine-toothed rake is used on sand that is completely dry. A mechanical stone picker specifically designed for the removal of objectionable stones from bunkers may become available someday.

Sand Blasting and Accumulation

Golf shots from bunkers usually result in the blasting or throwing of sand onto the green and adjacent collar (Fig. 7-15). A gradual rise in elevation of this area occurs over time. Some sand deposition may also occur by wind erosion. Eventually this continual rise in elevation necessitates that the sod be stripped from the raised area, excess underlying sand be removed to bring the surface grade down to the original level, and sod be transplanted onto the site. The rate of sand buildup varies greatly. It may be as

Figure 7-16. Wind displacement of sand from a bunker.

frequent as every five years around bunkers where sand blast shots commonly occur, whereas it may not occur at all in bunkers where sand blasting rarely occurs. Bunkers located near greens are likely to require elevation adjustment as described, while fairway bunkers rarely need it.

Wind Problems

The loss of sand from bunkers caused by wind erosion can be a problem, particularly in the semiarid plains, coastal areas, and intermountain regions (Fig. 7-16). In addition to loss from the bunker, there is also the problem of sand deposition onto adjacent turf areas. Fine-textured sands of a relatively loose nature are particularly prone to wind erosion. A number of steps can be taken to minimize wind effects in areas where wind erosion from bunkers is a continuing problem. They include (1) use of a coarser textured sand that is less prone to blowing, (2) placement of windbreaks, such as snow fences, across or around bunkers during the dormant winter period of minimal play, and/or (3) redesign of the bunkers to reduce high sand faces that are particularly prone to wind erosion. Deep ''pot'' bunkers are particularly effective in minimizing sand displacement problems in areas of high-velocity winds.

Sand Replacement

Continual loss of sand caused by sand blast shots, wind displacement, and removal during edging necessitates periodic sand replacement. The addition of new sand is required at intervals of one to five years depending primarily on the seriousness of the wind displacement problem and the frequency with which golfers play out of an individual bunker. Fresh sand should be added whenever the depth has decreased below the minimum of 4 inches (10 centimeters) throughout the base and 2 inches (5 centimeters) on the face. The sand selected should be comparable in particle-size distribution, shape, and color to that previously utilized in the bunker, assuming it has proven satisfactory.

Sand replacement is best scheduled for a time of year when minimal play is anticipated. Fresh sand of 1 inch (2.5 centimeters) or less in depth should be added at least one month before a scheduled major tournament. Special precautions must be taken to avoid disruption of the bunker perimeter and lip during the sand filling process. In many cases, the truck drivers delivering sand are instructed to dump in a storage area. Then the crew loads and hauls the appropriate amounts of sand to each bunker. The sand should be unloaded at carefully preselected points where disruption of the bunker edge will be minimal. Soaking the sand through irrigation will aid in settling and firming if a significant rainstorm does not occur.

ORNAMENTAL GRASSES

A few golf courses in the United States have constructed islands in bunkers on which large clumps of bunch-type grasses, heather, or scotch broom are grown. The grass species selected usually is not mowed and should not possess rhizomes or stolons. It also should produce ornamental seedheads. Grass clumps in bunkers have been more commonly used in Scotland and England than in the United States. They add a uniqueness to the golf course and aesthetic interest to bunkers and can significantly affect playing strategy (Fig. 7-17).

DEFINING WATER HAZARDS

A majority of this chapter has been devoted to only one form of hazard, the bunker. By nature of its construction and maintenance, the bunker has well-defined boundaries. However, this is not necessarily the case with water hazards. Thus, it is important that such hazards be properly marked so that the game of golf can be played as intended by the rules. It is the duty of the rules committee at each club to clearly define the water hazards.

Water hazards are defined in one of two ways: (1) by small stakes or (2) by lines painted on the turfed ground. Stakes usually consist of 1- by 2-inch (2.5- by 5-centimeter) stakes sufficiently long to allow them to protrude approximately 12 inches (30 centimeters) above the ground. Stakes painted yellow indicate a regular water hazard, while red stakes indicate a lateral water hazard. An adequate supply of replacement stakes should be kept on hand, and all stakes should be repainted at least annually. The distance between stakes is governed by the nature of the hazard, sharp bends dictating closer spacing. It is important to keep all parts of the hazard inside the stakes. All hazard boundary stakes should be checked, at two- to four-week intervals, depending on their proneness to movement by unthinking individuals or vandals and on a daily basis during tournaments. The exact boundary line is defined by the inside line, at ground level, of the stakes. Thus, the stakes themselves are within the hazard.

For tournament play, lines may be painted on the turf in place of stakes. The lines should be continuous and follow the same line that stakes would follow. Either yellow or red paint is used depending on whether the hazard is a regular water hazard or a lateral water hazard, respectively.

Figure 7-17. Fairway sand bunker containing unmowed clumps of ornamental bunch grass.

Chapter 8
Equipment

There was a time when the golf course green staff used hand tools almost exclusively. That age of cheap manpower has been replaced by the age of mechanization. Efficient, properly maintained equipment designed to perform specific functions is an important component in modern golf course maintenance. However, it should be recognized that equipment alone will not produce a properly groomed golf course in prime playing condition. Also required are concerned, intelligent, hard-working individuals capable of effectively using the sophisticated maintenance equipment.

GOLF COURSE EQUIPMENT

A summary of equipment and supplies required for the optimum operation of an eighteen-hole golf course follows. Figure 8-1 illustrates a portion of it. There will, of course, be variations from the suggested optimum depending on the (a) region of the country, (b) total acreage of the golf course and associated turf facilities to be maintained, (c) extent to which the various turfgrass areas are irrigated, (d) number and size of the hazards maintained within the golf course proper, (e) local topographical features, (f) intensity of maintenance desired by the golfing clientele and allowed by the budget available, and (g) amount of play. The list for a nine-hole golf course would be somewhat less than that presented here, but would not be reduced by one-half. Golf courses larger than eighteen holes require correspondingly larger amounts of equipment in about the same ratio.

Mowing Equipment

Greens

2 to 3 Riding 3-gang greensmowers (with brush, spiker, and vertical cutting attachments), *or*
1 to 2 Riding 3-gang greensmower(s) (with brush, spiker, and vertical cutting attachments) and 2 to 4 walking single-unit greensmowers, *or*
5 to 7 Walking single-unit greensmowers

Collars, Aprons, and Tees

2 Riding 3-gang reel mowers/greensmowers, *or*
1 Riding 3-gang reel mower/greensmower and 2 walking single-unit reel mowers, *or*
2 to 3 Walking single-unit reel mowers

Green and Tee Surrounds

1 to 2 3-gang heavy-duty reel mower(s), *or*
1 to 2 Heavy-duty riding rotary mower(s)

Figure 8-1. Portion of the equipment needed to maintain turf for a modern-day golf course.

Fairways

1 to 2 Hydraulically driven reel and lift 7- to 9-gang fairway mower(s), *or*

1 Hydraulic lift 7- to 9-gang fairway mower and 1 tractor-pulled 7- to 9-gang fairway mowing unit, *or*

2 Tractor-pulled 7- to 9-gang fairway mowing units

Rough

1 to 2 Tractor-pulled 5- to 7-gang mower(s)

Heavy-Duty Mowing

1 PTO (power takeoff) tractor-mounted, 6- to 7-foot rotary mower (leaf mulcher attachment where needed), *or*

1 Flail mower, 6-foot (leaf mulcher attachment where needed), *or*

1 Sickle-bar 5-foot mower attachment for tractor

Trimming

2 to 6 Powered 20- to 24-inch, walking rotary mowers (heavy-duty commercial type preferred)

1 to 2 Heavy-duty 70- to 82-inch, triple-bladed riding rotary mower(s) (cutting unit in front of the drive preferred)

1 to 4 Portable spinning nylon-cord trimmer(s)

Edging

1 to 2 Power edger(s)

Tractors and Trucks

2 to 3 Golf course tractors, 1 to 2 equipped with PTO

1 Utility tractor with front-end loader and backhoe attachments

1 Pickup truck, ½ to 1½ ton (4-wheel drive with snowplow where required)

1 Light-duty pickup truck (stretch 7-foot bed preferred)
2 to 5 Utility turf vehicles (for light work and transportation)
1 Utility tractor with PTO (optional)
1 Jeep-type 4-wheel-drive vehicle with snowplow attachment where required (optional)
1 Dump truck (either stake side or metal box) (optional)

Sprayers and Spreaders

1 to 2 Sprayer(s), 200 to 300 gallons with 100 to 200 feet of high-quality hose; multipurpose guns (for turf and tree usage); small spray boom; and large spray boom for fairway and rough spraying
1 Sprayer, 50 to 150 gallon, sled-mounted on a utility vehicle or 3-point hitch, tractor-mounted type with hose, gun, and boom
2 to 3 Portable 3-gallon sprayers
1 Drop spreader, 6- to 10-foot width
2 to 4 Walking centrifugal spreaders
1 Large-capacity, tractor-mounted or trailer-pulled, centrifugal spreader
1 Mist sprayer (optional)
1 Insecticide fogging unit (optional)

General Maintenance Equipment

1 to 2 Single-unit powered vertical cutter(s) (if there are no 3-gang units)
1 Tractor-pulled or PTO-powered vertical cutter/leaf litter sweeper
1 to 2 Powered coring machine(s)
1 to 2 Powered walking spiker(s)
1 Tractor-pulled fairway cultivation machine with spoon and slicing attachments
1 Powered soil shredder
1 Powered soil screen
1 Powered topdressing machine (walking or utility truck-mounted)
1 Powered drag mat (or equivalent utility vehicle-drawn type)
1 Powered sod cutter (automatic cutoff attachment preferred)
1 Tractor pulled or PTO-mounted leaf blower
2 to 4 Powered, high-velocity, walking blowers
1 Small, powered, walking water-ballast roller
1 Rotary tiller (powered walking or tractor-mounted)
1 to 2 Tractor-drawn trailer(s) (one with hydraulic dump)
1 Tractor-mounted grader blade and/or tiller rake
1 to 2 Chain saw(s)
1 Powered brush saw (with attachments)
1 to 2 Portable pump(s) and hose
1 to 2 Powered leaf sweeper(s) (where applicable) or one large-capacity all-purpose sweeper or vacuum
Assortment of hose, nozzles, and portable sprinklers
1 to 2 Snowplow(s) for trucks with appropriate accessories, chains, lights, and power tilt blade (optional)
1 to 3 Mechanical powered sand rake(s) (optional)
1 1- to 3-Gang fairway water ballast roller (optional)
1 Walking powered slicer-seeder (optional)
1 Tractor-mounted fairway slicer-seeder (optional)

1 to 2 Trenching machine(s) (1 small and 1 large) (optional)
1 Box scraper with teeth (tractor-mounted unit) (optional)
1 Powered hedge trimmer (optional)
1 Powered tree trimmer (optional)

Accessories

2 to 3 Hole cutters
36 to 40 Hole cups (extra set for repainting)
2 Cup extractors
2 Cup setters
40 Flagsticks and flags (or more as per expected yearly loss rate)
9 to 18 Practice green cups and markers
3 Sets of tee markers (red, white, and blue preferred with extras of each color as per expected yearly loss rate)
18 Golf ball washers, stands, and trash containers
20 to 25 Tee benches (or more as per expected yearly loss rate)
18 Shoe spike cleaning brushes
10 to 20 Bag stands (driving range)
50 to 100 Magnesium sand rakes (number dictated by size and number of bunkers)
Assortment of rule signs

General Tools

2 to 4 Divot repairers
1 to 2 2-inch plugger(s)
1 to 2 4-inch plugger(s)
1 8-inch plugger
1 to 2 Soil-sampling probe(s)
6 to 12 Bamboo or fiberglass whipping poles
2 Large rubber-tired wheelbarrows
1 8-foot stepladder
1 20- to 30-foot extension ladder
1 Distance-measuring wheel
1 Engineer's level and rod
3 to 4 Mole traps

Hand Tools

Shovels, spades, scoops, stone forks, spading forks, post-hole digger, sod lifters, turf edgers, cultivators, metal and wooden rakes, leaf rakes, picks, mattocks, cultivating hoes, pole pruners, pruning saws, lopping shears, pruning shears, hedge trimmers, grass shears, axes, brush hooks, hand sickles, crowbars, sledgehammers, wedges, tamps, and brooms

Tools for Service Area

Portable steam cleaner or electric high-pressure water cleaner
Air compressor with hose, spray paint gun attachment, filters, regulators, tire gauge, and air blowing gun
Alemite high-pressure pump assembly
Portable generator

Mower reel grinder, bedknife grinder, portable lapping machine, bench grinder, 5-ton chain hoist or 5-ton mobile hydraulic floor crane and/or 5-ton mobile hydraulic jack, 3-ton hydraulic jack, axle stands or steel ramps, portable drum on stand or recirculating solvent cleaning table, spark plug cleaner and tester, battery charger, electric and acetylene welding units, ¼- and ½-inch heavy-duty electric drills, drill stand with press, electric or air impact wrench with attachment kit, 6¼- to 8-inch circular saw, high-speed drill set, tap and die set, small vise, large vise, accurate small- and large-capacity weighing scales, trouble light with extension cord, and work benches

Complete sets of tools

Plumbing—wrenches, threaders, cutters, reamers, taps, soldering tools, blow torches, copper-tube flaring kit

Wood-working—hammers, saws, chisels, screwdrivers, levels, planes, bits, rulers, squares

Machinery—magnetic screwdrivers, hacksaws, pliers, calipers, chisels, bolt cutters, punches, files, wrenches

Wrenches—socket, open end, box (both short and long sockets preferred)

Concrete and masonry—trowels, markers, mixers

Engine repair—valve lifters, valve compressors, ring compressors, battery tools, pullers

Miscellaneous shop accessories such as oil cans, grease guns, safety-approved gasoline cans, paint brushes, and funnels. Other useful shop tools including a tire changer for golf cart, utility truck, and 3-gang mower low-pressure turf tires and a larger-capacity tire changer for trucks and tractor tires

Three- to four-drawer storage units for nuts, bolts, screws, nails, washers, and other parts appropriately marked or index numbered. Appropriate bins for pipe fittings, dresser couplings, and sundry plastic parts to repair PVC, cast iron, transite, and galvanized irrigation lines; irrigation heads, nozzles, valves, controller units, solenoids, and associated irrigation system components; and pump bearing packings, bearings, clay valves, and fuses. File cabinet for parts books, catalogues, manuals, and service records

Communication Facilities

Personnel communicators are being used increasingly to more quickly and efficiently react to changing golf course situations that arise during the day. Two-way radios, citizen band radios, walkie-talkies, and paging "beepers" are potentially useful tools that are becoming part of the modern golf course operation. Also, a blackboard, bulletin board, slide projector, and 35-mm camera

SELECTION

Selection of the appropriate type, design, size, and model of equipment for a particular use is the responsibility of the golf course superintendent. This is because the superintendent supervises those individual(s) who must operate the unit and is ultimately responsible for its proper adjustment, preventive maintenance, and repair. Useful guidelines to consider in equipment selection include the following:

1. *Acceptability in performing a specified function.* Can the unit adequately perform the job specified? Selection of a compromise machine that will be underutilized, mechanically overtaxed, or only partially effective in its assigned function is best avoided. Actual on-site demonstration of the various models and/or types of machines being considered is a key step in determining whether a unit will perform the specified function under potentially difficult conditions that may be unique to a particular golf course. It is important that the unit be designed for turf usage, such as having low-pressure tires to reduce soil compaction (Fig. 8-2).

Figure 8-2. Golf course maintenance tractor with special low-compaction turf tires.

2. *Availability of parts and service*. A machine cannot perform its function when needed if it is inoperable for extended periods due to unavailability of repair parts or lack of a professional repair service. Extended periods of down time are unacceptable for certain key golf course maintenance machines such as greensmowers, fairway mowers, and sprayers. Thus, it is important that equipment suppliers be assessed as to whether they maintain adequate stocks of repair parts, deliver them rapidly, and also have an adequate repair facility staffed with sufficient qualified mechanics. In some situations, purchase of a higher priced unit may be appropriate because a local distributor provides more acceptable parts delivery and equipment servicing than a competitor with a lower priced unit.

3. *Quality*. Some aspects of equipment quality are readily apparent to the golf course superintendent knowledgeable in equipment construction. However, some aspects of durability and functional usability are best determined through actual use in the field. Thus, communication among golf course superintendents at local meetings, seminars, field days, and conferences is important in terms of obtaining information on the quality and performance characteristics of equipment. Quality features of concern include sturdiness of construction for the particular operations involved, design features that insure ease of servicing and repair, as simple a design as possible, adequate safety features, and coordination of the appropriate power unit for the particular operation(s).

4. *Cost*. Cost is a consideration after performance, quality, and serviceability. The initial purchase price is not the only dimension in cost analysis. The evaluation of cost should also include consideration of the anticipated operational life and projected preventive maintenance–repair costs. Purchase of a machine that can do several operations and still not have to be run at maximum power all the time pays in the long run. Finally, the comparative advantages of purchase versus lease of major turfgrass equipment should be investigated.

OPERATION

How equipment is operated affects its ability to function in a particular job, its operating longevity, the interval between servicing, and the repair frequency. An operating manual provided with each piece of equipment includes information on operating procedures such as ranges in speed, turning limits, climbing ability, and starting and stopping. This manual should always be read before a piece of equipment is operated for the first time. Information on operating procedures not included in the manual should be obtained from the local distributor. Operating a particular piece of equipment outside the prescribed limits can be dangerous to the operator and may even cause damage to the turf. In addition, the effective operating life can be significantly shortened and/or maintenance and repair costs greatly increased. Also, the manufacturer's warranty may be voided, causing additional aggravating service problems. A different piece of equipment should be selected if conditions are such that a particular unit must be operated beyond or under its limits.

General guidelines for equipment operation include the following:

1. *Don't ever rev an engine.* This places extreme stress on the connecting rods, bearings, cooling, and lubrication systems. It usually results in accelerated deterioration and eventual failure of one of the engine's moving parts.

2. *Don't turn the machine too sharply.* Failure to observe this guideline may result in damage to the turf as well as potential injury to the operator should the unit overturn. In addition, sharp turns are abusive to the machine owing to increased tire wear and added stress on the suspension system.

3. *Don't operate a machine in areas or for functions for which it is not intended.* It is important to avoid operation on terrain where the unit may overturn or turf scalping can result. Similarly, equipment should not be used in functions for which it is not specifically designed.

4. *Don't underinflate or overinflate tires.* Proper inflation extends the operating life of tires and provides favorable ride and traction characteristics.

5. *Don't allow equipment abuse.* Racing, improper shifting, or quick starts and stops of maintenance equipment cause needless parts failure due to overstress. In addition, it can cause needless bruising and tearing of the turf.

6. *Do start the engine as outlined in the operating manual.* The Occupational Safety and Health Act (OSHA) requirements precisely dictate safe starting steps for equipment. Following proper starting instructions minimizes battery drain and best insures successful starting.

7. *Do service equipment according to the time schedule specified in the operating manual.* Preventive maintenance insures proper machine operation and a long operating life. Particular attention should be paid to servicing the air filter and to specified lubrication needs.

8. *Do instruct employees to report any malfunctions or operating irregularities to the superintendent, foreman, and/or mechanic as soon as possible.* Failure to correct operating malfunctions immediately often leads to expensive repair problems later. Be sure to use the machine only for the purpose for which it was designed so that the particular operation is completed safely and with a reasonable work load on the operator.

9. *Do make sure all OSHA-approved finger and foot shields are in place to avoid needless injuries.* Following such precautions may protect against the loss of a finger, toe, foot, or other serious injuries.

10. *Never eliminate or bypass safety switches.* Inform all operators where all safety switches are located and how to operate them.

SERVICE

The service schedule for each piece of equipment can determine how well it performs and how long it will operate satisfactorily. The best insurance for optimum equipment performance is a program of preventive maintenance so that objectionable field breakdowns are kept to a minimum. A preventive maintenance schedule is given in the service manual that should accompany every new piece of equipment. There are preventive maintenance schedules for engines, ignition systems, cooling systems, transmissions, differentials, belts, hydraulic systems, carburetors, filters, and general lubrication of all moving parts. A preventive maintenance service wall chart posted in the service shop will serve as a ready reference and reminder. Chart schedules indicate the last time the machine was serviced, what was done, and the date for the next servicing. A complete set of service records on each piece of equipment is a valuable asset in a modern mechanized golf course operation.

Small Engine Servicing

An eighteen-hole golf course typically has from ten to twenty types of maintenance equipment, powered by two- and four-cycle engines. Such machines are utilized for many rugged operations that place considerable stress on the engine. Thus, proper servicing is very important to maintain the power units in good working condition.

The two primary types of engines are the two cycle and four cycle. The primary differences between these two power units are the method of lubrication and the power strokes. Servicing criteria for keeping these engines working efficiently on a long-term basis are summarized as follows:

Two-cycle engine. Oil lubrication to piston and rod is supplied by a gas-oil mixture.

1. Use the proper ratio of gas-to-oil specified by the manufacturer. Also check to be sure the proper type of oil (detergent versus nondetergent) is used.
2. Keep exhaust ports clean. Deposits of debris can form rapidly, reducing engine power and efficiency.
3. Clean grass clippings and other debris from engine-cooling fins and housing. Failure to do this regularly with air-cooled engines will result in overheating, which causes a loss in efficiency, shorter life expectancy, and potential for vapor locks.
4. Change or clean air filters periodically in accordance with the intensity of usage. The appropriate interval is specified in the operating manual.
5. Clean spark plugs and check to be sure the gap meets the manufacturer's specifications. Also confirm that the proper type of spark plug in the specified heat range is used.
6. Check that recoil-type starters are tight and operative.
7. If the engine exhausts into the mower housing, be sure the exhaust openings are kept clear.
8. If the engine is equipped with points and condenser, be sure they are properly set and operative.

Four-cycle engine. Oil lubrication to piston and rod is supplied by a crankcase reservoir.

1. Make sure the carburetor is adjusted to the correct air/fuel mixture. The engine either will not start or will run very poorly if the carburetor is not properly adjusted.
2. Use the type of oil specified by the manufacturer and change it at the specified interval.
3. Change air and oil filters at the intervals indicated in the operating manual.
4. Check that recoil starters are tight and operative.
5. Clean grass clippings and other debris from engine-cooling fins and housing. Failure to do this regularly with air-cooled engines will result in overheating, which causes a loss in efficiency, shorter life expectancy, and potential for vapor locks.
6. Clean spark plugs and check to be sure the gap meets the manufacturer's specifications. Also confirm that the proper type of spark plug in the specified heat range is used.
7. If the engine exhausts into the mower housing, be sure the exhaust openings are kept clean.
8. If the engine is equipped with points and condenser, be sure they are properly set and operative.
9. Since four-cycle engines usually have a splash-type lubrication, avoid long-term operation on steep slopes. Otherwise the resulting inadequate oiling of the engine's internal parts causes increased wear and reduced operating life. For this reason, two-cycle engines are generally preferred for continuous mowing of steep slopes.

Either type of engine will give long-term, efficient performance if properly maintained according to the operating-manual instructions and if operated under reasonable conditions. The latter includes selecting the appropriate piece of equipment for the particular job so that the equipment is not over-stressed. Also, small engines should not be operated continually at full throttle. High RPM usage increases stress and wear on an engine and also accentuates vibration problems. Finally, it is important that regular checks be made for proper adjustment of belts, chains, and pulleys. Excessively loose or tight adjustments increase wear on the motor powering the machine.

Mower Servicing

The mower is one of the most important pieces of equipment on a golf course. Thus, proper mower servicing and preventive maintenance are critical to the playing quality of a golf course turf. Because of the important role of mowers, their preventive maintenance is discussed here in some detail.

Bedknife Grinding. The basic purpose of a bedknife is to function as one of the two cutting edges which sever grass leaves. The cutting height is determined by the height of the bedknife cutting edge above the soil surface. Typically, the bedknife is securely bolted to a backing plate mounted on the mower; once bolted it must be trued up owing to manufacturing irregularities in the steel.

The bedknife is "chucked" into the bedknife grinder and leveled and the grinding procedure is then initiated (Fig. 8-3). Most mower manufacturers specify a grinding angle on the upper flat surface of the bedknife, which is inclined approximately 15 degrees from the horizontal with the trailing edge lower than the leading edge. Once a smooth surface with the prescribed angle is achieved across the entire raised surface of the bedknife, the front edge is ready for truing by a final grind across the bedknife surface to offset irregularities in alignment due to variations in the mounting surfaces of the bed bar (Fig. 8-3). The bedknife assembly is ready for use when these steps are completed. The frequency of bedknife grinding during the season depends on the amount of use and whether the bedknife becomes rippled through misadjustment or knicked from hitting stones, irrigation heads, or other hard objects.

Reel Grinding. Grinding of the reel is the second important phase in the preparation of sharp cutting edges on reel mowers. The reel assembly from the mower is secured into the grinding machine (Fig. 8-4). A movable, adjustable grinding stone is then passed over each blade of the reel to evenly grind, sharpen, and true all blades on the reel. If the reel grinding steps are properly accomplished, all blades on the reel will be the same so that they cut the grass leaves against the bedknife in exactly the same manner.

Bedknife and reel grinding procedures vary depending on the particular mower and grinder apparatus model and manufacturer. Thus, the appropriate operating manuals must be studied in detail before initiating them.

Figure 8-3. Bedknife properly positioned in a bedknife grinder (*left*) and diagrammatic representation of bedknife grinding angles (*bottom*). (Drawing by S. M. Batten, Texas A&M University, College Station, Tex. Reprinted from Beard, J. B., et al. 1979. *Introduction to Turfgrass Science and Culture: Laboratory Exercises.* Burgess Publishing Co., Minneapolis, Minn., p. 74, with permission.)

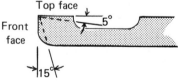

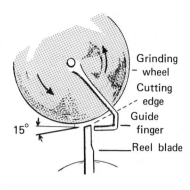

Figure 8-4. Reel assembly from a mower properly positioned in the grinding machine (*left*) and diagrammatic representation of the reel blade, grinding wheel, and guide finger (*right*). (Drawing by S. M. Batten, Texas A&M University, College Station, Tex. Reprinted from Beard, J. B., et al. 1979. *Introduction to Turfgrass Science and Culture: Laboratory Exercises.* Burgess Publishing Co., Minneapolis, Minn., p. 75, with permission.)

Reel Mower Lapping. The fine sharpening of reel mowers can be accomplished with an electrically powered lapping machine and emery-based lapping compound. It is best not to attempt to remove knicks or irregularities in either the bedknife or reel by lapping. Such problems are best corrected by grinding. Rather, the objective of lapping is to put an extremely fine, sharp edge on the actual cutting surfaces of the reel mower. Lapping is sometimes referred to as back-lapping, since it involves turning the reel backward during the sharpening operation.

The first step in lapping involves removal of the correct end plate on the reel mower according to the manufacturer's instructions. The lapping machine socket is then fitted into the reel shaft (Fig. 8-5). Activation of the lapping motor causes the reel to turn in a reverse rotation. A semiliquid lapping compound is then brushed onto the rotating reel blades. This emery compound serves as an abrasive base for fine sharpening as it is pinched between the rotating reel blades and the stationary bedknife. As the lapping noise becomes fainter it indicates that additional lapping compound needs to be brushed onto the reels or that the reel mower needs to be tightened slightly should the lapping process need to be continued.

The cutting quality of the mower should be checked periodically by disconnecting the lapping machine and test cutting a few pieces of paper between the reel blades and bedknife at various locations along the bedknife as well as with the various blades on the reel. When it is ascertained that the mower has been sharpened properly, the end plate is bolted on again and the lapping compound is completely washed off the mower. Water-soluble oils mixed with dry grinding compound wash off more easily than do motor oil mixes.

Reel Mower Adjustment. The scissorlike cutting action on grass leaves by a reel mower does not actually involve contact between the metal of the reel and the metal of the bedknife. If there were metal contact the bedknife would quickly wear out, necessitating costly, time-consuming replacement. A properly adjusted reel mower requires less energy to pull or drive, which saves on fuel costs. Proper, frequent adjustment of reel mowers is vital for high-quality mowing of turfs. It is a skill achieved through experience based on sound knowledge of the mower adjustment mechanism and the specific procedures recommended by the mower manufacturer.

The cutting quality of a reel mowing unit can be assessed with the aid of newspaper cut into 1- to 1.5-inch (2.5- to 3.8-centimeter)-wide strips. These strips are then inserted between the reel blade and the bedknife, with positioning perpendicular to the latter. Tilting of the reel unit backward, if this is

Figure 8-5. Lapping machine in operating position on the shaft of a reel mower.

possible, aids in accessibility. Rotation of the reel is then initiated, care being taken to not catch fingers or knuckles. Cleanly cut paper indicates a sharp reel, a rough or ragged cut indicates a dull reel, and no cut indicates the mower is out of adjustment. A sharp, well-adjusted reel unit should cut newspaper along the entire length of the bedknife with any blade on the reel. If this does not occur, the reel mower should be either lapped, if the problem is not too serious, or reground. Where misadjustment is a problem, the adjusting bolts or screws can be either loosened, if the reel does not spin freely, or tightened, if the paper is not cut.

Both visual and audible indicators can be used in assessing whether a reel mower is properly adjusted. Shredded tips on grass leaves indicate the reel mower is out of adjustment or dull. This is not easily assessed on turfs containing ryegrass. A good audible indicator is the occurrence of a singing or high-pitched squealing of the reels as they spin. In this case, the misadjustment relates to the reel being set too tightly. A visual indicator of reel problems is a ripple or wavy surface characteristic on the reel or bedknife cutting edge.

Rotary Blade Sharpening. Rotary mowers are frequently operated in areas where the blades come in contact with rocks, stumps, metal, and similar hard objects that cause the blade to become knicked and dull. Thus, an important part of rotary mower servicing is to keep the blade sharp so that grass blades are cut rather than shredded from the impact of the rotary blade. Some variation on the following procedure is typically used in the sharpening of rotary mower blades.

1. Disconnect the spark plug wire.
2. Carefully remove the blade from the engine shaft. Sometimes it is a left-hand thread. Use of an impact wrench is the safest method.
3. Grind the cutting portion of the rotary blade to the desired edge, being sure to use the appropriate eye guards and grinding wheel shields. A well-defined edge on the outer cutting portion of the blade is needed, but the edge need not be razor sharp.
4. Check the blade to determine if it is balanced (Fig. 8-6). This may involve the use of a commercially available magnetic balancing unit or of a less sophisticated procedure, such as the insertion of a screwdriver shaft through the center hole. Balanced blades should rest in a position perpendicular to the vertically positioned fulcrum on which the blade center point rests. Should one side prove heavier by dropping, that side should be ground sufficiently to bring the blade into balance. A properly balanced blade minimizes vibrations in the motor and mower housing and thus enhances the operating life of the mower.
5. Reattach the blade tightly to the engine shaft.
6. Connect the spark plug wire.

Figure 8-6. Newly sharpened rotary blade being checked for proper balance on a magnetic balancing unit. (Photo courtesy of The Toro Company, Minneapolis, Minn.)

Rotary Mower Maintenance. The underside of the rotary mower housing should be kept as clean as possible. A buildup of clipping debris results in loss of efficiency; increased weight, which makes the mower heavier to push; engine stalling if the grass accumulation is too great, especially when mowing wet grass; and reduced effectiveness in leaf-clipping fractionation, especially in the case of mulching mowers. The spark plug must be disconnected before the housing is cleaned. A scraping tool may be required if the accumulation is dense and dry. The housing should be washed after scraping. An application of silicone to the clean housing will discourage clipping accumulation.

Winterizing Equipment

Preventive maintenance does not involve only in-season work. It also includes winterizing and storage of all equipment during the off-season in those sections of the country having winter nonuse periods. Proper winterizing is particularly important if unheated storage areas are used. A brief set of guidelines follows concerning the procedures involved in winterizing for storage. More specific information can be obtained from the appropriate service manual.

Engines. Drain gasoline tanks. Introduce a small amount of oil into the head of the engine through the spark plug hole to minimize rust and corrosion. Drain the engine oil and add clean oil of the proper winter viscosity if the machine is to be used during the winter.

Ignition systems. Make sure the battery is fully charged at the time the equipment is stored. Protect battery terminals against corrosion by applying grease or a similar coating. Remove battery and store in a warm area if the equipment is to be stored in an unheated area in which the electrolyte solution would be subject to freezing. Waterproofing of the ignition systems is advisable. Spray condensation-prone areas before and after use to avoid condensation. Disconnection of the ignition system may or may not be necessary.

Cooling systems. Proper antifreeze protection is imperative for water-cooled engines in those regions of the country prone to winter freezing. Use a hydrometer to check for the proper level of protection. Add new antifreeze at least every two years, with annual replacement preferred in some cases.

Transmissions. Check for proper oil level and insulation against moisture. Also, be sure to check the operating manual for recommended oil change intervals for the transmission, differential, and other gear cases, since these tend to be overlooked.

Hydraulic systems. Inspect for proper sealing and oil levels. Condensation of water in hydraulic systems must be avoided. Protect exposed hydraulic piston shafts against pitting by applying the appropriate coating.

Carburetors. Drain all gasoline to avoid "gumming." This is especially important if leaded gasoline is used. If draining is not possible, add "dry gas" or gasoline antifreeze to the tank to reduce gum deposits and water formation.

Metal surfaces. Equipment being stored for the winter should have a full coat of paint over all metal surfaces to avoid rust and corrosion. A small scratch to bare metal can soon cause a rust blister that must be scraped and repainted.

Rubber surfaces. Treat rubber surfaces with a protective material, such as a silicone-base spray, to slow the deterioration process. This is especially effective on rubber tires of golf course equipment.

Mowing units. Protect newly sharpened reels and bedknives from rust and pitting by applying a liberal layer of oil or grease to exposed metal cutting surfaces.

Sprayers. Keep spray tanks open, well ventilated, and dry. The tank is best stored with the bottom drain plug removed. Be sure the pump is free of water to avoid freezing problems. Disconnect hoses, drain them completely, and store inside.

Spreaders. Clean, paint, grease, and/or oil, and dry spreaders.

Topdressers. Clean of all residual soil, oil/grease, and dry topdressers.

Water ballast rollers. Drain rollers and allow to dry out.

Dump bodies and trailers. Store in an elevated position to avoid accumulations of water, ice, or litter that can cause deterioration of metal or wood surfaces.

Snow plows and chains. Stock repair links for chains and spare shear pins for plow blades. Position the units for easy hookup.

Equipment Storage

Proper storage facilities for turfgrass maintenance equipment are important to achieve full operational longevity with minimum service and repair costs. An adequate storage facility insures that equipment is protected from weather adversities. Typically, the storage facility consists of an enclosed area with a raised concrete floor for dry storage to minimize corrosion. The area should be large enough so that operators have easy access to the equipment with minimum chance of bumping and possibly damaging equipment stored nearby. Equipment storage facilities are discussed further in this chapter in the section on the maintenance building.

CARE

Equipment requires day-to-day care by the operator as well as a sound preventive maintenance program. Properly cared for equipment runs better and has a higher trade-in value. Well-cared-for equipment is usually a reflection of the operating personnel. An observant, conscientious operator can enhance the effective operational life of golf course equipment. Respect for and proper care of equipment must be instilled into workers during their initial training period and continually reinforced throughout their working tenure. Such pride in and respect for equipment is sometimes hard to achieve but when accomplished is a valuable asset in insuring proper equipment performance. Some guidelines for proper equipment care follow.

Mowers. It is important to thoroughly wash mowers when the operating day is completed. Most maintenance facilities include a washing apron for this activity (Fig. 8-7). Care should be taken not to get water on a hot engine, and water under high pressure should not be used around bearings or seals. Excess water should be removed, either by blowing off with compressed air or by wiping dry.

Figure 8-7. Typical washing apron.

After the machine is cleaned, it should be (a) filled with gasoline for the next use, (b) greased and oiled (care being taken to remove any excess), (c) inspected and any needed adjustments accomplished, and (d) moved to a protected storage area or turned over to a mechanic if preventive maintenance is scheduled or repair needed.

The observant operator of a mower becomes aware of the operating motions and sounds and thus usually notes when malfunctions occur. Early recognition of malfunctions can save on repair costs and downtime at a later stage. The operator who observes any malfunction such as loss of oil or grease, any unusual sounds, or irregularities in the operation of the machine should report these to the mechanic or golf course superintendent as soon as possible.

Sprayers. Sprayers are utilized to apply a wide range of pesticides at the correct rates without contamination. Thus, it is extremely important to carefully wash and clean the tank after every use. Not only the tank but the pump, hose, nozzles, screens, filters, and exterior of the sprayer should also be cleaned. A minimum of two washings is usually required for all components of the sprayer. The addition of a detergent cleaner may be advisable in the initial washing. Directions for such an addition, if required, are included on the label of the pesticide container. Sprayer cleaning should be accomplished in a prescribed area where there is minimal potential for the pesticides to be washed off in surface water or to enter subsurface drainage systems.

After the sprayer has been thoroughly washed, the shaft bearings should be greased, packings checked for leaks, and the gasoline motor serviced and cleaned. If a power takeoff unit is involved, the shaft should be cleaned and greased. It is particularly important to check the packings for leaks, since immediate repairs are required to avoid leakage of potentially toxic chemicals onto the turf.

Spreaders and Seeders. On completion of a given operation, it is important to remove all excess seed, fertilizer, granular pesticides, or similar materials from spreaders and seeders to avoid inadvertent mixing. Unused materials in the hopper should be either spread on an adjacent area or returned to the container, if possible. Compressed air is quite effective in cleaning out many of these materials but should be used only on nontoxic materials. Quick, thorough drying after washing is very important in minimizing rust. Rust can seriously damage the spreader openings, which are critical in uniform material application at the proper rate. After washing, it is advisable to apply a thin layer of oil to protect the exposed metal surfaces from rusting.

Cultivation and Vertical Cutting Equipment. Coring, slicing, spiking, grooving, shattering, and vertical cutting machines require constant servicing because of their many moving parts that are subjected to severe stress during operation. Oil cups, grease fittings, drive belts, and similar moving parts should be constantly checked during operation. All soil, clippings, chaff, and dust should be removed from the unit when a particular task is completed. This is particularly true of the cooling louvers on air-cooled engines. Removal of the metal shroud may be necessary to achieve thorough cleaning. After cleaning is accomplished, the machine should be oiled, greased, and checked for wear on shafts, bearings, tines, and blades. If any parts are loose or worn, the mechanic should make the appropriate replacements immediately.

Trucks, Tractors, and Utility Vehicles. The care of tractors, trucks, and utility vehicles is essentially the same as that for automobiles, with one exception. The former are scheduled for service based on operating hours rather than miles traveled. Thus, these vehicles must be equipped with an hour gauge to insure the proper preventive maintenance and service schedules. Daily maintenance of these vehicles should include a thorough cleaning and removal of debris from truck beds. Mud, dust, grass, and sand can be removed by washing.

Soil-Handling Equipment. Topdressers, soil screens, and soil shredders are involved in dusty, highly abrasive processing of soils and thus require careful maintenance. Grit finds its way into all parts of this equipment, so that careful, periodic cleaning and servicing are necessary to avoid excessive wear of moving parts. The engine air cleaner should be checked regularly during operation for dust accumulation. Also, all grease and oil fittings should be checked frequently and relubricated when necessary. On completion of a given operation, the equipment should be thoroughly cleaned and washed to remove all trapped soil and stones. Particular attention should be given to cleaning screens.

Small Hand Tools. Good-quality tools will last many years if a regular maintenance program is followed. The standard procedure after each use is to wipe metal garden tools with a coating of oil to reduce rust problems. Periodic waxing of wood and metal handles is an excellent preservative practice. Wooden handles should also be inspected periodically and if rough or splintery should be rubbed down to the desired smoothness with a light-grade sandpaper.

Other Turf Equipment. Sod cutters, sweepers, blowers, and other associated turf maintenance equipment require care similar to that discussed for soil-handling equipment. Most of these operations subject equipment to dusty, debilitating conditions. Frequent lubrication of fittings is important to minimize the chance of grit entering moving parts. Frequent servicing of engines is required, including regular checks of engine air cleaners. On completion of an operation, all parts should be thoroughly cleaned, greased, and appropriate engine care followed. Sod blades should be checked and sharpened, if needed.

REPAIR

Equipment breakdowns occur occasionally even though good preventive maintenance programs are followed. It is imperative that broken equipment be returned to operation as soon as possible, especially if no backup unit is available. An efficient machine is a time- and labor-saver only when operating. A good mechanic, a well-stocked parts inventory, an up-to-date parts and service manual, and a rapid system for acquiring other needed parts from distributors are all important in equipment repair. Coordinated application of these components is critical for quick repair of inoperative equipment.

Diagnosis of equipment breakdowns is the responsibility of the mechanic. It can be facilitated by the equipment operator. The individual operating the equipment at the time of malfunction must be

Figure 8-8. A well-stocked and organized parts room within a golf course maintenance building. (Photo courtesy of D. Miller, Saucon Valley Country Club, Bethlehem, Pa.)

prepared to describe exactly what occurred. This may include an abnormal sound and its location, a pull to one side or the other, and/or sticking of a specific mechanical part before breaking. All such leads can be helpful to the mechanic in identifying the problem and in its subsequent repair. Ultimately, diagnostic information is sought from the service manual for the particular unit involved.

Parts Availability. Appropriate parts must be secured once the problem has been diagnosed. Ordering parts by their numbers is imperative in obtaining the correct replacement. The appropriate number can be found either on the part itself or in the parts section of the service manual. An additional aid in ordering parts is having the correct model and serial number of the machine.

A good parts inventory is invaluable in insuring continued machine operation with minimum downtime from breakdowns (Fig. 8-8). A record-keeping procedure for cataloguing and reordering parts is important in highly mechanized golf course operations.

Certain parts need replacement on a regular basis throughout the season. Thus, experience with golf course equipment greatly aids in intelligent stocking of an adequate repair parts inventory. It is important that a good quantity of those parts prone to severe wear or frequent breakdown be stocked. In contrast, certain more reliable parts need not be stocked under normal conditions, unless the distributor is relatively inaccessible or a great distance away and/or the particular machine parts are difficult to acquire owing to age or model discontinuation. One other source of parts should also be mentioned, cannibalizing junk machines. This is an especially good source for older equipment whose parts are difficult to acquire. While retaining old nonfunctioning machines can be carried to objectionable extremes, an adequate junk part inventory can prove advantageous.

CALIBRATION

When using chemicals, the goal is uniform application at the proper rate. This is particularly important in the case of pesticides and is emphasized by Environmental Protection Agency regulations. Thus, accurate calibration of sprayers, spreaders, and seeders is essential in the golf course operation. Calibration should be done at least annually for each unit as well as at any time when there is a change in applicator components or operating procedure. Detailed records of the calibration, including calculations, should be kept.

Sprayer Calibration

The basic concept in sprayer calibration is to determine how many gallons of spray are applied to a given surface area with a particular sprayer under certain operating procedures and turf conditions. There are a number of variations in the procedure. The most commonly used approach is presented here.

Once calibration has been accomplished, the application rate should be checked regularly during the growing season in terms of the amount of spray being applied to a particular turf. Knowledge of the area covered by one tankful of spray is useful for this. This check allows the person doing the spraying to confirm that the calibration rate remains stable each time a spray operation is accomplished.

Finally, recalibration should be done whenever (a) a new part is added or replaced on the sprayer (such as a pump or nozzles), (b) the operating pressure is changed, (c) the ground speed is changed, (d) the ground surface or turf conditions are changed, and (e) a new season begins.

Both sprayer calibration and routine spraying activities are more reliably executed if the responsibility is assigned to one individual designated the sprayman. This individual, as well as the golf course superintendent, should have successfully completed the state pesticide applicators certification exam and should be properly certified under guidelines of the Environmental Protection Agency.

Calibration Procedure. The sprayer should be thoroughly checked to be sure it is in good working condition. The next step is selection of the appropriate operating conditions. This includes a check of the manufacturer's operating instructions. Other considerations are previous experience and the type of material being sprayed. Operating criteria include the pressure, nozzle type, nozzle spacing, nozzle height, boom width, and ground speed. Use of a tractor having a speedometer or tachometer is advisable for accurate ground speed monitoring. Otherwise, the gear used should be recorded and the throttle setting marked and recorded. An example of representative sprayer operating conditions for use with fungicides, insecticides, and soluble fertilizers is: 60 pounds per square inch (4.2 kilograms per square centimeter) pressure, 4 miles per hour (6.4 kilometers per hour) ground speed, 8004 flat fan nozzles, and a nozzle spacing and height adjustment that provide even coverage. Where herbicides are applied, a lower operating pressure of 30 to 40 pounds per square inch (2.1 to 3.2 kilograms per square centimeter) typically is utilized.

The steps for calibrating a sprayer are as follows:

Step 1. Measure off a calibration test area of at least 200 feet in length over a level, representative turf area. Multiples of an acre facilitate calculations. For example, a ⅛-acre area requires a distance of 340.3, 302.5, 272.25, and 247.5 linear feet for 16-, 18-, 20-, and 22-foot boom widths, respectively. In general, the larger a test area the more accurate the calibration.

Step 2. Place sprayer on a level surface and fill the tank with water. Note the spray level in the tank or fill the tank full if there is no gauge.

Step 3. Activate the power unit to the pump and adjust the operating pressure to the specified psi.

Step 4. Approach the predetermined starting point on the test course at the specified ground speed and turn on the spray boom at the starting mark.

Step 5. Maintain the specified speed, pressure, and nozzle output over the full distance of the test course. Turn off the spray boom at the end point.

Step 6. Turn sprayer around and repeat steps 4 and 5 from one to three times.

Step 7. Return sprayer to the original position where the tank was filled and determine the amount of water needed to refill the tank to the original level. An alternate approach is to collect the spray output from all nozzles on the boom and measure the total quantity delivered.

Step 8. Calculate the rate of spray application, usually expressed on a per-acre basis. For example:

(A) Area sprayed (acres) $= \dfrac{\text{Spray width} \times \text{length of area (feet)} \times \text{number of passes}}{43{,}560 \text{ (square feet)}}$

(B) Application rate (gallons/acre) $= \dfrac{\text{Amount of spray applied (gallons)}}{\text{Area sprayed (acres)}}$

(C) Area sprayed per tank (acres/tank) $= \dfrac{\text{Volume of tank (gallons)}}{\text{Rate of application (gallons/acre)}}$

Step 9.   Confirm that the proper spray calibration rate has been achieved by applying a known quantity of spray solution to a known area on the golf course. This has the additional advantage of allowing a final assessment of spray coverage uniformity. It also establishes that the ground speed selected is not too fast for proper maneuvering on the more uneven terrain of the golf course. Recalibration is in order if this is a problem.

Step 10.   Proceed with recalibration, if needed. Should small adjustments in the gallons of spray applied per acre be needed, make alterations in either the operating pressure or ground speed. Switching to a different set of nozzles is the preferred approach where large adjustments are required. After selecting a new set of operating criteria for the sprayer, repeat the calibration steps just outlined.

Spreader Calibration

Two main types of spreaders are employed for the application of dry materials: the centrifugal and the gravity, or drop. The primary principle involved in calibrating either type is determination of the quantity of a specific material applied per unit area under a given set of operating conditions. The actual application rate varies depending on the (a) size and weight of the material being applied, (b) ground speed, (c) surface roughness, and (d) size of the feeder-gate opening.

Each spreader should be calibrated for the specific material being applied. Dry materials may vary from a material of a uniform granular size to vermiculite or corncob carriers to relatively dusty materials possessing a wide range of particle sizes.

Control of the operating ground speed should be given special attention, particularly in the case of small, manually pushed spreaders. An easily repeatable pace should be selected. Usually this is a fast walk; it should be practiced before calibration and then used each time the spreader is operated. For the most consistent results, one person should be assigned responsibility for applying dry materials when manually pushed spreaders are used. Also, the spreader should be recalibrated whenever a different person is to make the application. Finally, the surface selected for spreader calibration should be comparable in roughness to the area where the material is to be applied.

Spreader parts wear with use, which can affect the rate of application. For this reason, spreaders should be recalibrated periodically to avoid misapplication of materials. Also, it is important that the spreader be thoroughly cleaned and dried after each use. This prevents accumulation of pesticide or fertilizer residues, which can block and corrode the essential spreader parts that affect the application rate. A light application of lubricant following cleaning prevents rusting problems.

The steps for calibrating a spreader are as follows:

Step 1.   Determine the amount of a specific material to be applied per unit area (usually 1,000 square feet).

Step 2.   Select a setting for the spreader and make the appropriate mechanical adjustments.

Step 3.   Mark the spreader hopper at a given level and fill to that mark.

Step 4.   Apply the material to a specific measured area. Be sure the turf area selected is of a roughness comparable to that on which the material is to be applied and that a consistent, repeatable ground speed is maintained based on the surface conditions and material being applied.

Step 5.   Weigh the amount of material required to refill the spreader hopper to the preapplication mark. In the case of small spreaders, it is sometimes easier to weigh the amount originally put into the hopper and then the amount left after application to the measured area. The difference between the two weights is the amount applied to the area.

Step 6.   Calculate the application rate.

$$\text{Application rate} = \frac{\text{Amount applied (pounds)}}{\text{Area covered (square feet)} \times 1,000}$$
(pounds/1,000 square feet)

Step 7.   Should the application rate calculated not correspond to the desired rate, adjust the spreader setting and repeat the previous steps. Continue this procedure until the appropriate rate is achieved.

Step 8.   Be sure to keep a written record of all calibration work for future reference and to recheck the calculations.

Step 9.   A variation on this technique frequently used when calibrating drop spreaders is as follows: Attach a metal or plastic trough beneath the drop spreader to catch all material as it falls. Operate the spreader across a known distance at the selected setting and operating speed. Weigh the collected material and calculate the application rate as follows:

$$\text{Application rate} = \frac{\text{Amount applied (pounds)}}{\text{Distance (feet)} \times \text{spreader width (feet)} \times 1,000}$$
(pounds/1,000 square feet)

Note: There are numerous variations on the basic technique for particular situations.

THE MECHANIC

One of the most important employees on a golf course is the mechanic. A conscientious, competent mechanic qualified in the maintenance and repair of golf course equipment insures the smooth operation of a modern mechanized golf course. Finding and keeping a good golf course mechanic is not easy. Having a separate mechanic for each eighteen-hole unit in the case of a thirty-six-hole golf course is desirable. The efficiency of the golf course superintendent is greatly reduced if the superintendent must also fulfill the responsibilities of a mechanic. The many hours spent by a superintendent in maintenance and repair of equipment are hours lost to supervision and programming of golf course maintenance.

Job Description

A detailed job description should be written for the mechanic's position. It is the responsibility of the golf course mechanic to keep all equipment performing as intended with minimum downtime and operating costs. Specific activities include bedknife and reel grinding; mower lapping; mower adjusting; engine repairing; hydraulic system servicing; replacing of broken parts; record keeping; stocking of parts, gasoline, and oil; insuring that a preventive maintenance program is followed; and checking that workers follow the proper operating procedures on all equipment, including daily cleaning and lubrication.

The work load and important responsibilities justify a full-time mechanic on most eighteen-hole golf courses. This is especially true where the individual is also responsible for golf cart maintenance. In addition, a mechanic can answer phones and forward messages to the superintendent, since the individual is in the maintenance building most of the day. When mechanical activities do not demand the full time of a mechanic, free hours can be spent on other specialized responsibilities such as spraying, fertilizing, cultivation, and topdressing. However, proper priorities should be maintained so that the mechanic's first responsibility is keeping of all equipment in proper operating condition.

Qualifications

A mechanic should have extensive training and experience in small-engine repair and maintenance rather than just large vehicle work. A good mechanic is capable of troubleshooting, diagnosis, repair, and proper adjustment of equipment rather than simply being a parts changer. In other words, the approach of changing one part after another until the faulty one is finally found is not desirable because it is time consuming and very expensive. A qualified golf course mechanic need not be classroom educated or certified, although vocational-technical schools are now training persons who have good potential for this type of work.

Continuing Education

The ultimate development of a good golf course mechanic is achieved only through experience on the job. Interested, energetic mechanics should be encouraged to attend equipment repair, service, and adjustment clinics sponsored by local equipment distributors. Also, several of the larger equipment manufacturers hold worthwhile extended workshop-seminars on equipment servicing and adjustment.

MAINTENANCE FACILITY

The maintenance facility is the hub of the golf course operation. It is where the golf course personnel begin and end their working day; where equipment is housed, maintained, and repaired; where seed, pesticides, fertilizers, and other chemicals are securely stored; and where the irrigation master control center may be located. Thus, the golf course maintenance facility is much more than just a place to store equipment. In the truest sense, it is the nerve center of the golf course and should be designed, constructed, and organized to fulfill these important functions. The discussion in this section relates primarily to an eighteen-hole golf course.

Site Selection

The site selected for the maintenance facility should be as close to the center of the golf course as possible. This minimizes the distance that must be traveled to the turf areas to be maintained and thus provides better overall efficiency in both travel costs and employee travel time. The site must be free from flooding and generally well drained. The area chosen should be relatively flat so that large equipment can be maneuvered easily and safely. Positioning of the maintenance facility relative to adjacent golf holes should be such that there is no potential hazard from golf balls striking workers or equipment at the facility and that noise from the facility poses minimal distraction to nearby golfers (Fig. 8-9).

Other considerations in evaluating potential sites are the accessibility and cost for hooking up such utilities as gas, electricity, and water plus an acceptable area or outlet for sewage disposal. The location of the entrance road for the maintenance facility must be considered in the original design of the golf course. The access road should be in the distant secondary rough, out of view of golfers playing adjacent holes. The main entrance road must be constructed with a reasonable grade and load capacity to handle large, heavy trucks as well as normal employee vehicle traffic. Paving, either asphalt or cement, is desirable. Bumpy, rocky roads are hard on workers and on finely adjusted mowing equipment which frequently traverse the access road as one of the routes to turfgrass areas.

Components of a Maintenance Facility

Components of the central maintenance facility include an exterior work apron, a washing apron, an area for petroleum storage, a soil-topdressing area, a parking lot, and the maintenance building itself

Figure 8-9. Two properly sited golf course maintenance facilities that are well screened from the playing area by landscape plantings.

(Table 8-1). There may also be separate buildings for fertilizer, pesticide, and golf cart storage. The minimum area for an adequate maintenance facility on an eighteen-hole golf course is 1 acre (0.4 hectare), with 2 acres (0.8 hectares) preferred.

It is advisable that a perimeter of tree and shrub plantings be established around the maintenance facility to protect workers against errant balls as well as to provide a visual and sound buffer which isolates the facility from the surrounding golf course landscape (Fig. 8-9). In addition, appropriately sited tree and shrub plantings within the central maintenance facility provide a favorable working environment. In some locations, the central maintenance facility should be fenced to provide security against theft and vandalism. In this regard, it may also be desirable for the buildings, work apron, and parking lot of the maintenance facility to be lighted.

Exterior Work Apron. Hard surface aprons are usually located at the primary entrances to the maintenance building. They should be large enough to accommodate all anticipated activities. Typi-

Table 8-1. Space Allocations for a Golf Course Maintenance Facility

Facility and Type of Use	Suggested Space Allocation* (Sq. Ft.)
Maintenance Building	
Total Floor Space	7,000 to 12,000
Operations office(s)	200 to 300
Employee area:	
Meeting and lunchroom	200 to 300
Locker rooms	100 to 300
Showers and restrooms (men and women)	150 to 300
Service shop	1,000 to 2,500
Tool room	200 to 400
Parts room	200 to 300
Steam cleaning and paint room	300 to 600
Equipment area	4,000 to 7,000
Pesticide room(s)	200 to 300
Fertilizer storage	500 to 1,000
Seed room (optional)	100 to 400
Maintenance Area	
Total Area	40,000 to 80,000
Work apron	1,500 to 2,000
Washing area	400 to 900
Soil and topdressing apron	1,500 to 2,500
Soil storage shed	1,000 to 3,000
Petroleum storage (gasoline and diesel fuel)	1,000 to 2,000 (gals.)
Parking area	For 12 to 14 vehicles

*Suggested functional range, not minimum to maximum.

cally they are constructed of either reinforced concrete or asphalt to insure proper operating efficiency for work activities and ease of cleaning and to allow easy maintenance of an orderly appearance in line with the remainder of the golf course. Reinforced concrete of specifications proper to carry the anticipated weight loads of vehicles is required. The minimum area for the main entrance into the equipment and service areas of the maintenance building should be 1,500 square feet (140 square meters). A structure frequently associated with the work apron is a raised platform ramp or loading dock. This ramp or dock greatly facilitates safe loading and unloading of bulky or heavy equipment and materials from fixed-bed trucks.

Equipment Washing Area. All equipment that has been operated on the golf course should be cleaned, whether it is being brought in for one night or for months. Typically this involves washing with water. Cleaning is greatly facilitated by a properly designed washing apron. The design must include a water line of adequate size terminating in a hose bib arrangement at a convenient location. The apron surface should slope gently toward a surface drain of adequate capacity. The upper portion of the drain should contain a debris trap to collect clippings as they are washed from the equipment. The minimum dimensions for a washing apron on a golf course are 20 by 20 feet (6 by 6 meters), with 30 by 30 feet (9 by 9 meters) preferred.

Petroleum Storage. Construction of a petroleum storage facility must be in accordance with regulations of OSHA. Specifications concerning storage and venting of petroleum fuels may also fall under local governmental laws and ordinances. The fuel storage area should be located away from the maintenance building to prevent the spread of fire or explosions into the maintenance building itself. Large, underground storage tanks should be placed in low hazard locations to minimize danger of explosions, fires, and spillage runoff. Siting of the fuel storage area should also allow easy access from

Figure 8-10. Gas pump station positioned a safe distance from the maintenance building and enclosed by a security fence.

the maintenance building, whenever possible. Typically, the gas pump is located in the area of the storage tank (Fig. 8-10). Special precautions are needed to insure that the fuel storage tank is properly vented. Gasoline and/or diesel fuel storage tanks typically range from 1,000 to 2,000 gallons (3,785 to 7,570 liters) for an eighteen-hole golf course. Larger sized tanks may be advisable where the supply source is occasionally unreliable or limited.

Another consideration is construction of a fireproof oil, lubricant, and grease storage structure separate from the maintenance building. The structure should not only be fireproof but should be locked, ventilated, without windows, and constructed of materials that protect against vandalism. Typically, the building has reinforced concrete floors and concrete block walls. The storage structure should be 100 to 200 square feet (9.3 to 18.6 square meters) in area.

Soil-Topdressing Area. Topdressing is one of the more important maintenance practices on many golf courses. Thus, it is important that adequate amounts of topdressing material be stored under dry conditions to insure its ready availability, especially where topdressing is practiced at frequent intervals. An exception is where premixed topdressing is purchased from a dealer. It is generally advisable for the soil-topdressing area to be separate from the maintenance building. The mixing apron area should be of sufficient size to accommodate operation of a tractor with front-end loader, a soil shredder, and a soil screen and should also have a soil-handling area (Fig. 8-11). The suggested size for the mixing apron is 1,500 to 2,500 square feet (140 to 232 square meters). In some cases, a portion of the apron is set aside for long-term storage of soil mixes that are to be composted outside. It is preferable for the apron to be constructed of reinforced concrete with appropriate specifications to accommodate the anticipated weight loads.

In humid climates construction of a simple topdressing shed is advisable. This insures ready availability of dry topdressing (mechanical topdressers require dry topdressing soil to achieve uniform application). The structure can be relatively large and completely enclosed or can be a more modest structure with three sides enclosed and a fourth side open and facing away from prevailing winds. A relatively high roof (16 feet [5 meters]) facilitates operation of a front-end loader within the storage shed. The interior of the soil shed may be divided into several large bays (Fig. 8-12). This arrangement permits the separation of several distinctly different materials, including the actual topdressing mix, sand for mixing, bunker sand, and construction sand. It is not necessary that sand be stored within the topdressing shed but it should be stored on a raised concrete or asphalt apron. The size of the topdressing shed may range from 1,000 to 3,000 square feet (93 to 280 square meters).

Figure 8-11. Hard-surface apron used for mixing topdressing and also for parking.

Figure 8-12. Low-cost topdressing storage shed with interior divided into bays.

A fertilizer storage area can be constructed in conjunction with the topdressing shed. Potentially corrosive fertilizers generally should not be stored in the vicinity of equipment. Thus, a good approach is a combination of fertilizer and topdressing storage areas in one facility. A minimum of 500 square feet (46.5 square meters) should be allocated for fertilizer storage.

Parking Lot. A designated area should be set aside for employees and visitors to park their cars. All too often this need is overlooked in the original design. The site selected should not interfere with normal day-to-day activities at the maintenance facility but should be within a convenient distance and preferably shaded. Adequate space should be allocated for twelve to twenty-four vehicles, depending on the anticipated size of the green staff. More specific information on the size and arrangement of parking lots is in chapter 12.

Golf Cart Storage. A cart storage area is sometimes constructed at the maintenance facility, if this facility is reasonably close to the first tee. The number of golf carts in use determines the size of the storage building. In recent years, the trend has been toward increasing numbers of golf carts on individual courses. Thus, the building size should be based on projected future needs as well as on current requirements. It is better that the storage building be too large and grown into rather than adequate but grown out of in a few seasons.

Maintenance Building

Golf course maintenance buildings are as unique as the golf course design itself. Seldom are two alike. The building may range from a renovated barn from the original farm site to a modern facility expressly designed for its role. Because of the great variability in need from one golf course to the next in various climatic regions, no one design for a maintenance building can be recommended as superior. However, most golf course maintenance buildings have a number of similar key functions that require a certain amount of space for efficient, safe operation. Specific use areas include an operations office, employee area, service shop, tool room, parts room, steam cleaning and paint room, equipment area, pesticide room, and fertilizer area (Table 8-1). A representative floor plan is shown in Figure 8-13.

In selecting a design, it is important that provisions be made for future expansion of the maintenance building and surrounding facility. The design specifications should adhere to local building codes. An L-shaped or modified U-shaped arrangement is an efficient, compact design which facilitates future expansion of the structure. Major doors should not face in the direction of prevailing winds. The total floor space of the maintenance building usually ranges from 7,000 to 12,000 square feet (650 to 1,115 square meters) for an eighteen-hole golf operation. Construction of a mezzanine above the heated employee area adds substantial storage space at minimal cost.

The building should be constructed of relatively fire-resistant building materials, since it will house much valuable equipment. Use of fire-resistant concrete blocks and steel is advisable. The materials and construction design selected must meet specifications needed to withstand local weather adversities, including heat, high winds, heavy snows, and torrential rains. Typically, the foundation and floor are reinforced concrete of a specified load capacity, with bolts and cables embedded at required intervals for the attachment of walls and rigid roofs. The construction materials selected should be durable and have minimal long-term maintenance cost.

Doors and windows should be structurally sound and secured against potential theft and vandalism. The number of windows should be limited for security reasons. Another advisable security measure is the installation of exterior floodlights. An electric alarm system may also be needed in locations prone to theft and vandalism damage and/or relatively isolated. Such security precautions more than pay for themselves if they prevent just one extensive theft or vandalism attack. A separate security fence is sometimes needed around the maintenance building.

Operations Office. The complex, diverse responsibilities of a modern golf course superintendent necessitate a well-equipped operations office of adequate size. Furnishings include a desk, table, bookcases, file cabinets, and chairs. Typically, an overall map or aerial photo of the golf course is on the wall, along with overlays illustrating (a) the ''as built'' location of irrigation lines, gate valves, sprinkler heads, and subsurface control wires, (b) subsurface drain lines, french drains, and dry wells, (c) the proposed location of future tree plantings, sand bunkers, and course modification of tee, green, and fairway sites, (d) property survey, and (e) underground electric and gas power lines. Specific facilities included in the operations office usually include the master irrigation control system and communication equipment such as telephone, walkie-talkies, two-way radios, and/or a citizens band base station. Other key support equipment includes a typewriter, adding machine, weather radio, environmental monitoring equipment, microscope, slide projector, and camera. These items are

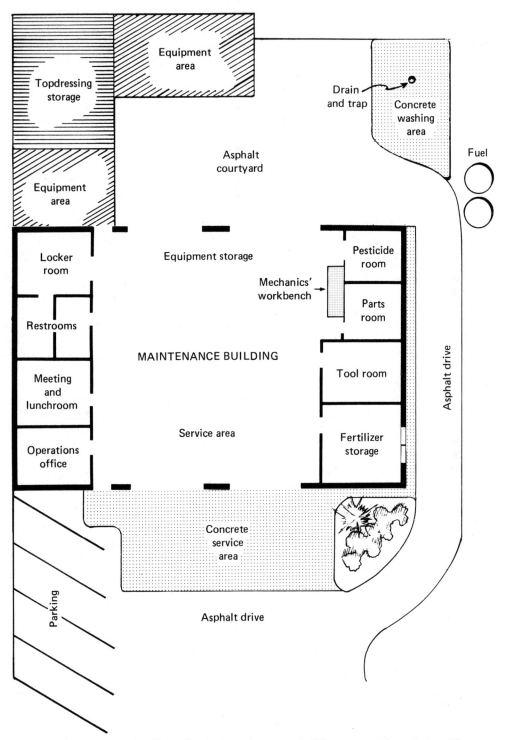

Figure 8-13. Representative floor plan for a maintenance building on an eighteen-hole golf course.

needed in the day-to-day diagnosis of problems, in decision making concerning turfgrass maintenance practices, and for employee in-service training programs. To protect this valuable equipment, it is important that the operations office be properly secured from theft and vandalism by the appropriate locks on windows and doors.

The operations office may range in size from 200 to 300 square feet (18 to 28 square meters), depending on the extent of activities anticipated and whether space is needed for an assistant superintendent. The area should be properly lighted, heated, and also air conditioned in warmer climates. Two or three operations offices may be needed if several assistant superintendents and multiple eighteen-hole courses are involved.

Employee Area. The employee locker room, lunchroom, shower, and lavatory facilities are included within this area. Specifications for these facilities are now controlled by federal and state health and safety laws. In some cases, the size of these areas is determined according to such statutes by the number of employees. Separate facilities for male and female employees are also becoming standard. General guidelines for the size of the employee areas include: shower and restroom facilities (with hot and cold water) of 150 to 300 square feet (14 to 28 square meters); locker room of 100 to 300 square feet (9.3 to 28 square meters), containing one locker for each employee; and a meeting/lunch room of 200 to 300 square feet (18 to 28 square meters). Occasionally, one or two of these rooms can be combined into one larger facility, such as a joint employee lunchroom and locker room. The area should be heated and, in certain more southerly locations, air conditioned as well.

In some cases, living quarters are provided in the maintenance building for college students studying to be golf course superintendents who are working during the summer. Such facilities have a dual function in that they provide the student with modest, low-cost housing, which is particularly important in high-cost urban areas, and at the same time offer readily available manpower in the case of emergencies as well as a valuable security service. In some situations, housing is provided in a trailer located adjacent to the maintenance building.

Service Shop. This area serves as the primary focal point for servicing and repair of golf course equipment (Fig. 8-14) and is under the immediate supervision of the mechanic. Most of the larger service equipment listed in the first part of this chapter are housed in the service shop. Since human activities of a very detailed nature occur in this area, it is important that the service shop be well lighted and properly heated and/or cooled, depending on the particular climate. An explosion-proof floor drain system is also needed.

One item which should be considered for inclusion in the service shop is a hydraulic automotive-type lift. This is a time-saving accessory for many types of equipment repair, particularly the larger sized self-propelled equipment used on golf courses.

The service shop may range in size from 1,000 to 2,500 square feet (93 to 232 square meters), depending on the inventory of equipment to be maintained. An even larger area is needed if golf carts are also maintained in the shop. Sometimes a separate grinding room of 250 to 300 square feet (23 to 28 square meters) is provided.

Tool Room. Tools that cannot be kept safely in an open service shop are best stored in a tool room that can be locked. Such items as expensive wrench sets, plumbing tools, electric drills, surveying equipment, and specialized engine repair kits are usually kept within the security of a tool room. Tools should be well organized, since not being able to find a needed tool is the same as not possessing it. The tool room can range from 200 to 400 square feet (18 to 37 square meters) in area, depending on the completeness of the tool stock maintained for use by the mechanic. The room should be located adjacent to and with easy access to the service shop.

Parts Room. Also located adjacent to the service shop should be a parts room. Such items as air and oil filters, spark plugs, engine gaskets, carburetor parts, bedknives, sprinkler head parts, control valves, pipe fittings, gate valves, coring tines, slicing blades, and vertical mowing blades are stored in the parts room. Each category of items should be kept in a designated bin or on a properly labeled shelf to insure easy access when needed. The parts room typically ranges from 200 to 300 square feet (18 to 28 square

Figure 8-14. Well-organized and maintained service shop within the maintenance building.

meters) in area. In some situations, the tool and parts rooms are combined into one larger room located just off the service shop.

Steam Cleaning and Paint Room. In certain golf course operations where activities dictate, a separate room is needed for steam cleaning and painting. The room must be well ventilated for painting activities and must have an adequate floor drain trap system for steam cleaning plus be heated and properly lighted. Steam cleaning and painting operations can be adequately accommodated in an area of 300 to 600 square feet (28 to 56 square meters). This room is particularly prone to safety inspections and thus must meet the safety specifications of OSHA, plus any local codes.

Equipment Area. This relatively large area houses the extensive inventory of costly maintenance equipment necessary for operation of a modern golf course. The complexity of turfgrass equipment needed to offset increasingly costly manual labor also necessitates that the equipment be stored under a roof and, if at all possible, in a heated environment. Equipment protected from the weather has quicker engine starting, less rusting, less dirt accumulation, and minimal soft-trim deterioration compared with equipment stored out of doors.

An eighteen-hole golf course requires from 4,000 to 7,000 square feet (372 to 650 square meters) of dry, preferably heated, post-free storage space. Enough space must be provided for maneuverability when equipment is brought into or taken from the area. Access should be by at least two overhead doors 10 to 12 feet (3 to 3.7 meters) wide and strategically placed for optimum accessibility.

Pesticide Room. Existing laws require that pesticides be stored in an area which (1) can be locked to prevent access by unauthorized individuals and (2) is properly ventilated to avoid a buildup of potentially noxious or toxic vapors. Electrical switches controlling the mechanically powered ventilation/exhaust fan(s) should be located outside the room and adjacent to the entrance doorway. A deluge-type shower with quick valve should be located near the door. The room should be designed and constructed so that a warm, dry atmosphere can be maintained. Thus, the room is usually heated, insulated, and without windows. Shelving of appropriate spacing should be constructed within the pesticide room to provide orderly storage so that the desired pesticide can be found readily. An inventory log of pesticide use and restocking should also be kept in the room.

The size of the pesticide room may range from 200 to 300 square feet (18 to 28 square meters). The room must be located at some distance from zones of concentrated human activities, especially the employee eating, restroom, and shower areas.

Fertilizer Area. A dry area is needed for fertilizer storage regardless of the particular product involved. Heating is usually not required except for liquid fertilizers. The area should be designed to insure ease in handling of bulky fertilizers during both delivery and removal for application on the golf course. High, wide doors and an adjacent exterior open area are needed for easy access by trailers or trucks being backed into the storage area. Fertilizer handling is greatly facilitated by a forklift, which can move pallet loads of fertilizer.

The size of the fertilizer area varies greatly depending on the particular objectives and types of fertilizer to be used. Fertilizer supplies can frequently be purchased during the off-season at considerable savings, provided adequate storage area is available. In addition, delivery and unloading during the off-season avoids problems with manpower restrictions, compared with deliveries made during the growing season when the labor force is needed for ongoing maintenance activities. The space required also varies with the type of fertilizer to be used, since the amount of fertilizer stored can vary from several hundred 50-pound (22.7-kilogram) bags to tons.

The fertilizer area can range from 500 to 1,000 square feet (47 to 93 square meters). It is important that it be located in a portion of the maintenance building where corrosive salt-type fertilizers can be distinctly separated from maintenance equipment. Because of potential corrosion problems, the fertilizer storage area is sometimes constructed as a portion of the soil-topdressing shed (Fig. 8-15). Another alternative involves bulk fertilizer handling, where the material is stored in a special outdoor hopper or silo positioned for ready accessibility by spreader trucks.

Seed Room. A seed storage area is sometimes required in portions of the country where large quantities of seed are utilized annually in winter overseeding of warm-season turfgrasses. From 5,000 to 8,000 pounds (2,268 to 3,628 kilograms) of seed may need to be stored in a dry area. The seed room should be constructed to minimize the intrusion of mice and other rodents. The space required can range from 100 to 400 square feet (9 to 37 square meters). When not being used to store seed the room can be used for other purposes.

In many parts of the country large quantities of seed are not kept on hand and thus a seed storage room is of no importance. In this case, the seed can be stored in the tool or parts room, provided the area is dry, partially heated, free of rodents, and of adequate size. Seed germination is best maintained for extended periods under dry conditions and at temperatures in the 50- to 60-degree Fahrenheit (10- to 16-degree Centigrade) range.

Figure 8-15. A dual fertilizer and topdressing soil-mix storage shed constructed separately from the maintenance building.

SAFETY

OSHA, by its current definition, encompasses golf course maintenance facilities and employees. This law is designed to protect employees through better and safer working conditions, equipment, and tools. The following is a selected list of the major regulations to be met at the time of this writing, along with some suggestions regarding compliance with this law. However, each golf course superintendent is responsible for full compliance with current OSHA regulations and, therefore, must regularly check the full text of the OSHA law.

Notices and Records
1. OSHA Safety and Health Protection Poster prominently displayed in the working area.
2. Log of occupational injuries maintained as part of both the permanent employee and golf course records (OSHA Form No. 100).
3. Record of occupational injuries and illnesses kept up to date (OSHA Form No. 101).
4. Summary of occupational injuries and illnesses posted (OSHA Form No. 102).
5. Emergency instructions posted, including names and phone numbers.
6. Employee safety meetings scheduled at regular intervals. An employee can be designated as the safety representative.

First Aid
1. First-aid supplies approved by a physician, properly stocked, and readily available with medicines that are kept current.
2. Each area where workers may be exposed to corrosive, injurious chemicals has a shower immediately adjacent for flushing eyes and body.

Maintenance Building

1. Passageways, storerooms, service rooms, and work areas clean and clear.
2. All floors clean and dry.
3. Exits not obstructed, locked, or fastened from inside.
4. Exits of reasonable width.
5. Exits visible, clearly marked, and illuminated where necessary.
6. Work areas with at least two exits.
7. Signs pointing to exits are posted if exits are not visible from work areas.
8. Exit signs of proper size.
9. Exits in poorly lighted areas illuminated by means of a light bulb or illuminated sign, with bulbs kept in stock as replacements in case of failure.
10. Nonexit doors clearly marked.
11. Vertical openings protected to prevent spread of fire or smoke.
12. Permanent passageways and aisles appropriately marked.
13. Permanent openings of all types have railings constructed around the open space.
14. All permanent stairs have handrails.
15. Load limits marked where storage is on the second floor, balcony, or other overhead area.
16. Adequate lighting of work areas for the jobs being performed.

Equipment and Materials Within Maintenance Building

1. Approved containers available for flammable materials.
2. Oil-absorbent materials available for use on spills.
3. Oil rag disposal can that meets approved specifications.
4. Trash containers for metal, wire, glass, etc.
5. Cylinders, tanks, and air receivers checked for: dents, cuts, gouges, corrosion, pitting, hairline cracks, or nicks in cylinders; safe storage in dry, clear area; and drainpipe or valve at low point.
6. Welding equipment inspected for hazards.
7. Welding tanks secured upright and in good condition.
8. Oxygen and acetylene tanks stored separately.
9. Acetylene equipment clean, free of oil, and in working order.
10. Portable power tools have three-wire cords and three-tong plugs for grounding.
11. Employees using portable power tools must wear safety glasses or shields where necessary.
12. Power tools, grinders, lathes, and turning machines inspected for the following: equipment properly grounded; goggles hung at all machines where necessary; machines under repair marked with "Do Not Operate" signs; and guards on all belts, pulleys, and areas hazardous to operator's body.
13. Wooden ladders stored out of the elements and inspected for structural soundness.
14. Wooden ladders have wire support under rungs.
15. Metal ladders equipped with nonslip metal on rungs.
16. All materials stored in a safe manner.

Dust and Inhalation Precautions

1. Proper respirators provided in spray paint areas or other inhalation hazard areas plus exhaust fans of adequate volume installed where necessary.
2. Employees instructed as to use of the proper respirators.
3. Respirators checked regularly and disinfected after every use.
4. Collectors or exhaust equipment provided for operations resulting in dust or hazardous particles.
5. All fans with blades located less than 7 feet (2.1 meters) above the floor have guards with openings no more than 0.5-inch (1.3-centimeter) wide.

6.   Proper ventilation and protective clothing provided in areas utilized for battery filling and charging (golf carts).

Fire Protection

1.   Fire extinguishers for necessary classes of fires properly mounted and visible.
2.   Unused or abandoned electric receptacles are plate covered.
3.   Approved electrical extension cords checked for frays or other damage which exposes the wires.
4.   No open electrical junction boxes or fuse boxes.
5.   Electrical panel door checked for damage.
6.   Watch kept for loose wires, worn insulation, or oil-soaked insulation.
7.   Spark-proof plugs and approved lighting in areas used for spray painting and storage of volatile materials that are flammable or explosive.

It is not the purpose of this section to list all official regulations relating to golf course safety but rather to point out some regulations which emphasize the extensiveness of the safety regulations and the need for compliance with current safety laws. Compliance with OSHA regulations is the responsibility of the golf course superintendent. Many golf course maintenance facilities should have little problem complying. An open, clean, safe maintenance facility promotes good worker attitudes and job performance. Safety suggestions and OSHA regulations are updated from time to time. Thus, it is important that periodic checks be made with a local representative for possible redefinitions in the state and federal laws that affect golf course operations. Periodic inspections by an OSHA official for compliance with the current laws can be expected.

First Aid Procedures

Every superintendent needs a well-planned procedure to follow when a medical emergency occurs on the golf course. The telephone number of the nearest emergency care facility should be posted near every telephone. It is important for the superintendent and key employees to know the location and most rapid route to the emergency room of the nearest hospital, in case an ambulance is not available. The superintendent and assistant superintendent should have completed a first-aid training course and all permanent employees should be encouraged to do the same. Free instruction is offered by the Red Cross in many areas. It is also important for the superintendent and the assistants to seek training in CPR — cardiopulmonary resuscitation. CPR is a method used by one or two persons to restart breathing and heartbeat in an injured person. In support of the first-aid program, a full-complement first-aid kit must be kept in the maintenance building and more modest first-aid kits at selected locations around the golf course. These kits should be checked periodically to be sure they have been properly restocked.

Mower Safety

Workers operating mowers on the golf course should wear either toe guards or steel-toed shoes. This is especially important for mowing of sloping areas with a walking mower. Other types of protective devices, such as goggles, are needed in situations where the operator's eyes may be exposed to debris thrown up by a mower, edger, trimmer, or vertical cutter.

Special precautions should be followed when mowing steep slopes, since mowers can readily overturn, especially under wet conditions. The operator may loose footing and fall or the mower may overturn resulting in a dangerous runaway mower, in the case of a self-propelled unit, and/or a dangerously spinning blade, especially in the case of a rotary mower. Ropes are sometimes attached to the machine and/or operator and held by an individual at the top of the slope to minimize the chance of overturning or slippage. This latter precaution is particularly important on steep slopes.

The rotary mower has more potential for accidents than any other type of equipment used on the golf course. Thus, it is imperative that proper safety practices be followed by workers using it. It is important for new employees to be properly instructed on the safe operation of rotary mowers.

SAFE OPERATING PRACTICES FOR NONRIDING MOWERS AND OTHER EQUIPMENT

Preparation

1. Read the operating and service manuals carefully. Become thoroughly familiar with the controls and proper use of the unit.
2. Memorize how to stop both equipment and motor quickly.
3. Never allow children to operate a power mower.

Before Starting

1. Inspect for proper lubrication and engine oil level.
2. Check the fuel level before starting engine (does not apply to electric mowers). Do not fill a gasoline tank indoors, when the engine is running, or while the engine is hot. Use an approved gasoline container. Wipe off any spilled gasoline before starting engine.
3. Thoroughly inspect the area where a mower is to be used and remove all stones, wires, sticks, bones, and other foreign objects.
4. Always wear substantial footwear. Do not operate the equipment when barefooted or when wearing open sandals.
5. Always disengage the self-propelled mechanism or drive clutch on units so equipped before starting the engine or motor.
6. Never operate the equipment without proper guards, plates, or other protective safety devices in place.
7. Keep wash-out ports and mower-housing service openings closed when mowing.
8. Keep the operations area clear of persons, particularly small children. This is very critical in the case of rotary mowers.

During Operation

1. Do not alter the engine governor setting or over rev the engine (does not apply to electric mowers).
2. Do not put hands or feet near or under rotating parts. Keep clear of the mower discharge opening at all times. Never operate a mower without discharge deflector.
3. Stop the mower blade(s) before crossing gravel drives, walks, or roads.
4. When the mower strikes a foreign object: stop the engine or motor, disconnect the spark plug wire, thoroughly inspect for damage, and repair any damage before restarting and operating.
5. If equipment should start vibrating abnormally, stop the engine or motor immediately and check for the cause. Abnormal vibration is usually a warning of trouble.
6. Stop the engine or motor before leaving the equipment, making repairs or inspections, or cleaning a mower housing.
7. Make certain the blade(s) and all moving parts have stopped before inspecting, cleaning, or repairing the mower. Disconnect the spark plug wire and keep the wire away from the plug to prevent accidental engine starting. Always disconnect line-operated electric mowers.
8. Shut the engine or motor off and wait until the blade(s) come to a complete stop before removing the grass catcher or unclogging the chute.
9. Do not run an engine indoors unless properly ventilated.
10. Never attempt a mower wheel-height adjustment while the engine is running.
11. Operate equipment in daylight or in good artificial light.
12. Whenever possible avoid operating equipment on wet grass. Always be sure of your footing, keep a firm hold on the handle, and walk, never run.
13. Mow across the face of slopes, never up and down. Exercise extreme caution when changing directions on slopes. Do not attempt to mow excessively steep slopes.

Maintenance and Storage

1. Thoroughly wash and clean after use.
2. To reduce the fire hazard, keep the engine free of debris, leaves, and excess grease (does not apply to electric mowers).
3. Check for and replace any excessively worn parts. Check the grass catcher bag frequently for wear or deterioration. Replace with a new bag as needed for safety protection.
4. Keep all nuts, bolts, and screws tight to insure that the equipment is in safe working condition. Pay special attention to the blade and engine mounting bolts.
5. Lubricate before storing.
6. Never store equipment with gasoline in the tank inside a building where fumes may reach an open flame or spark. Allow the engine to cool before storing in an enclosure.

SAFE OPERATING PRACTICES FOR RIDING MOWERS AND OTHER EQUIPMENT

Preparation

1. Read the operating and service manuals carefully. Become thoroughly familiar with the controls and proper use of the unit.
2. Memorize how to stop both equipment and motor quickly.
3. Never allow children to operate the vehicle. Do not allow adults to operate the vehicle without proper instruction.
4. Do not carry passengers on a vehicle unless it is specifically designed and constructed for this function.

Before Starting

1. Inspect for proper lubrication and engine oil level.
2. Check the fuel level before starting engine (does not apply to electric mowers). Do not fill a gasoline tank indoors, when the engine is running, or while the engine is hot. Use an approved gasoline container. Wipe off any spilled gasoline before starting engine.
3. Thoroughly inspect the area where a mower is to be used and remove all stones, wire, sticks, bones, and other foreign objects.
4. Always wear substantial footwear. Do not operate the equipment when barefooted or when wearing open sandals.
5. Always disengage all attachment clutches and shift into neutral before attempting to start the engine.
6. Never operate the equipment without proper guards, plates, or other protective safety devices in place.
7. Keep wash-out ports and mower-housing service openings closed when mowing.

During Operation

1. Do not alter the engine governor setting or over rev the engine (does not apply to electric mowers).
2. Do not put hands or feet near or under rotating parts. Keep clear of the mower discharge opening at all times. Never operate a mower without discharge deflector.
3. Watch out for traffic when crossing or operating near roadways. Stop the mower blade(s) before crossing gravel drives, walks, or roads.
4. Stop and inspect the vehicle and attachments for damage immediately after striking a foreign object. Any damage should be repaired before the unit is restarted and operated.
5. If equipment should start vibrating abnormally, stop the engine or motor immediately and check for the cause. Abnormal vibration is usually a warning of trouble.

6. Disengage power to attachment(s) and stop the engine before leaving the operator's position and before making any repairs or adjustments.
7. Disengage power to attachment(s) when transporting or not in use.
8. Shut the engine off and wait until the blade(s) come to a complete stop before removing the grass catcher or unclogging the chute.
9. Never make a cutting-height adjustment while engine is running if you must dismount to do so.
10. Take all possible precautions when leaving the vehicle unattended, such as disengaging the power-take-off mower attachment(s), shifting into neutral, setting the parking brake, stopping the engine, and removing the key.
11. Operate equipment in daylight or in good artificial light.
12. Whenever possible avoid operating equipment on wet grass.
13. Reduce speed on slopes and when making sharp turns to prevent tipping or loss of control. Exercise caution when changing directions on slopes. Do not stop or start suddenly when going uphill or downhill. Mow up and down the face of steep slopes, never across the face.
14. Stay alert for holes in the terrain and other hidden hazards so they can be avoided.
15. When using any attachment(s), never direct discharge material toward bystanders or allow anyone near the unit when in operation.
16. Use care when pulling loads or using heavy equipment. For example, use only approved drawbar hitch points, limit loads to those that can be safely controlled, do not turn sharply, use care when backing, and use counterweight(s) or wheel weights as suggested in the operating manual for a particular activity.

Maintenance and Storage

1. Thoroughly wash and clean after use.
2. To reduce the fire hazard, keep the engine free of debris, leaves, and excess grease.
3. Check for and replace any severely worn parts. Check the grass catcher bag frequently for wear or deterioration. Replace with a new bag as needed for safety protection.
4. Keep all nuts, bolts, and screws tight to insure that the equipment is in safe working condition. Pay special attention to the blade and engine mounting bolts.
5. Do not operate an engine in a garage unless it can be properly ventilated.
6. Lubricate before storage.
7. Never store equipment with gasoline in the tank inside a building where fumes may reach an open flame or spark. Allow the engine to cool before storing in an enclosure.

Chapter 9
The Irrigation System

A PERSPECTIVE

Water comprises 80 to 85 percent of the weight of a grass plant. Adequate water supplies are needed to maintain quality golf courses in most locations throughout North America. Essentially all grass greens are irrigated, as are a majority of tees. Fairway irrigation has been increasing since 1950, and some roughs are also irrigated. This trend may reverse in the future as water supplies become more limited and costly.

When to irrigate is one of the most difficult decisions in all of golf course turfgrass culture. The decision must be made daily for various turfs and locations on the golf course. Golf course irrigation problems are unique because the variables are numerous and many are beyond any reasonable degree of control.

Unfortunately, irrigation practices are widely abused, misused, and misunderstood. Many golfers tend to rate the golf course superintendent's abilities by how green the turf is maintained. Too frequently a lush, green golf course is expected at all times; however, such a turf is not necessarily healthy and wear tolerant. Proper irrigation practices are essential for good playing conditions and are of greater concern than whether irrigation produces a lush, green cover.

Overhead irrigation, as it is known today, had its beginnings in 1910. The first Skinner Irrigation Line system, complete with patented hydraulic oscillators, was used in agriculture at that time. The Nelson Lark Sprinkler, patented in 1920, was the first to have a roller base and long-arm rotary nozzles. The slip joint was introduced in 1925. Quick couplers, impact heads, and part-circle sprinklers were developed in the early 1930's. The first pop-up rotary turf sprinkler appeared in 1935. The first fully automatic golf course irrigation systems were installed in California in the early 1950's. Irrigation is critical for turfgrass culture in the semiarid areas of the western United States. It was natural for much of the turfgrass irrigation industry to originate there.

A golf course irrigation system is a complex, costly capital investment. It must be properly designed, engineered, installed, and operated to achieve maximum return on the investment in terms of a quality turf that is uniformly irrigated at the desired water application rate and timing. The decision-making processes involved in development of a golf course irrigation system are summarized in Figure 9-1. Each process is discussed in detail in this chapter. This chapter, however, is not intended as a comprehensive text on the design and installation of golf course irrigation systems. Rather, the objective is to discuss the procedural steps involved in development of an irrigation system and the range of alternatives available in design, types of systems, and system components, plus their advantages and disadvantages. The information presented should provide guidelines for those in decision-

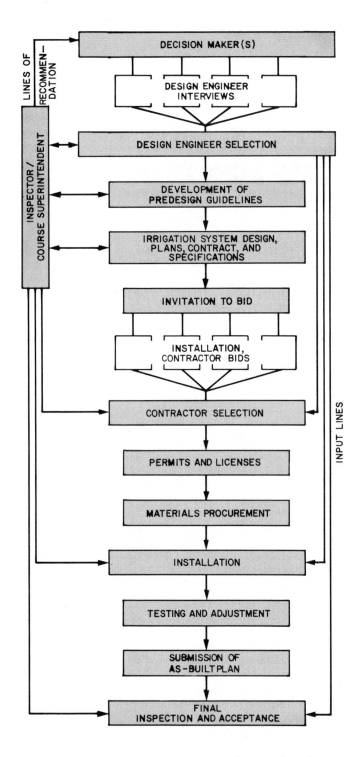

Figure 9-1. Flow diagram for development of a golf course irrigation system.

making positions to confirm that they are proceeding in an organized, stepwise manner with minimum chance of encountering unanticipated problems and costly construction or design errors which may have to be corrected.

TYPES OF IRRIGATION SYSTEMS

There are three main types of turfgrass irrigation systems in use on golf courses in North America: (a) automatic, (b) semiautomatic, and (c) manual quick coupler. All are basic forms of overhead irrigation. The automatic irrigation system is by far the most popular type being installed on today's golf course. The comparative advantages and disadvantages of each type of system for golf course use are discussed in this section.

Automatic Irrigation System

An automatic irrigation system is comprised of fixed pop-up sprinkler heads automatically activated by control valves at times preset on a controller (Fig. 9-2). The valves are operated by an electric or hydraulic signal received from a complex controller into which the golf course superintendent has preset an irrigation program. That is, the specific day, time of day, and operating duration can be established for any one or more of the control valves, each of which controls one or more sprinklers. The automatic irrigation system may or may not be integrated with an automatic sensing unit.

The term "automatic irrigation system" is somewhat of a misnomer. Although this type of system is automatic in terms of operating the heads at the time water is applied, experience has proven that it requires constant scheduling and maintenance. Nevertheless, it is by far the most popular and effective type of golf course irrigation system installed today. When properly designed, engineered, installed, and operated, it has the capability of irrigating a golf course in a most acceptable and efficient manner.

Automatic irrigation has the initial appeal of greatly reducing labor costs for the actual irrigation activity. To a degree this supposition is met. However, an automatic irrigation system still requires one man, usually on a full-time basis, for maintenance and repair. The golf course superintendent must also devote time to daily irrigation decisions and the setting of time schedules for the control units. The cost for repairs, parts, and replacement equipment can also be substantial after five to ten years.

What are the advantages of automatic irrigation? First and foremost, this system places the essential control of golf course turf irrigation directly with the most competent individual on the staff — the golf course superintendent. Second, there is precise timing of each sprinkler head in operation. When a green requires ten minutes of water, it receives ten minutes, not fifteen or twenty. Therefore, an automatic system that is properly designed, engineered, installed, and operated brings greater control and dependability to irrigation practices. With a manual system, one person is capable of handling only so many quick coupler heads at a time. That individual is usually stretched beyond the limit. The entire irrigation schedule is thrown off balance should there be a breakdown or delay of any kind. Water efficiency is greatly increased with an automatic system, since only the prescribed amount of water is applied at each irrigation. This means a savings, since more area can be satisfactorily irrigated with the same amount of water and sometimes even less.

Another advantage is that an automatic system does not require a night irrigator. In the case of manual and semiautomatic systems, one or two night irrigators must be carefully and properly trained as to the responsibilities of the position. This can be a long, arduous task. Not everyone is interested in a demanding nighttime occupation which sometimes must be conducted under cold, wet, and dangerous conditions. In addition, relatively few individuals have the knack and desire to carry out the precise scheduling assignments required for proper irrigation on a nightly basis. It is the fortunate golf course superintendent who trains and retains only one or two competent night irrigators per year.

Cost Considerations. An automatic irrigation system is the most expensive type to purchase and install. Thus, there is a tendency to cut costs, which leads to compromises in design of the system and

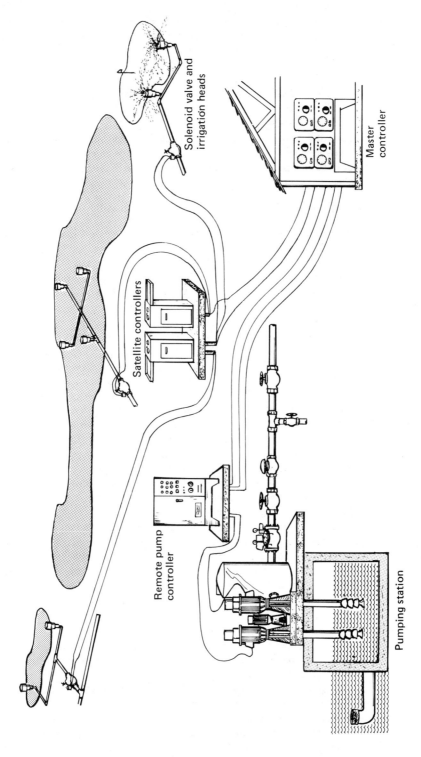

Solenoid valve and
irrigation heads

Satellite controllers

Master
controller

Remote pump
controller

Pumping station

Figure 9-2. Key components of a golf course automatic irrigation system.

later to difficulties in irrigation coverage and flexibility. Cost cutting in automatic irrigation systems is easily accomplished. For example, the spacing between sprinkler heads may be increased, reducing the number of heads required; a large number of heads may be placed under the control of each individual valve, thus reducing the number of valves required; and many valves can be placed under the control of each station, thus reducing the number of costly controllers required. The alternatives are endless and tempting. Although great savings in installation costs of an automatic irrigation system can be realized by employing one or more of these cost-cutting alternatives, the final system will not necessarily be capable of irrigating the golf course satisfactorily (Fig. 9-3). In contrast, there are instances of overdesign and overengineering of automatic irrigation systems. Such a system may offer a high degree of options and sophistications but the practicality of its use is questionable in relation to the cost involved. Overdesign is rare, while cost cutting occurs frequently.

Semiautomatic Irrigation System

A semiautomatic irrigation system involves valves that respond directly to a manually operated remote control switch. Such a system usually is installed on golf courses where long-range plans call for conversion to a fully automatic system when additional monies are available. The semiautomatic system has the advantages of low initial cost with potential for future upgrading. It is very important that the system be properly designed and installed so conversion to an automatic system can be achieved with minimum difficulty and expense. There are three variations of a semiautomatic system:

1. Only the pop-up sprinkler heads and control valves are permanently installed. Irrigation operations are conducted manually.
2. Quick coupler sprinkler heads are manually engaged into selected quick coupler valves in those locations where irrigation is required. The heads are then activated through valves and automatic controllers.
3. A portion of the golf course, such as the greens, is designed with a fully automatic system in terms of pop-up heads, valves, and automatic controllers, while other turf areas, such as fairways and tees, have a semiautomatic system which can be converted to a fully automatic arrangement later.

Figure 9-3. Spotty areas of green and brown dormant fairway turf owing to improper water distribution caused by poor design of the automatic irrigation system.

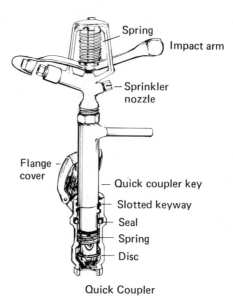

Figure 9-4. Diagram of a quick coupler valve and an impact-type sprinkler head with a manual coupler key in the base.

Quick Coupler

Manual Quick Coupler System

A quick coupler system requires the manual insertion and removal of each sprinkler head into quick coupling valves positioned at appropriate intervals throughout the golf course (Fig. 9-4). The quick coupling valves are connected to water distribution lines that may be under constant water pressure. The valve is opened as the manual coupler key is inserted into the valve and turned. The quick coupler sprinkler irrigation head is activated immediately and operates continuously until the head is manually disengaged from the quick coupling valve. The most common quick coupler head utilized is an impact type in which the nozzle assembly is driven by a spring-loaded arm that moves in and out of the water stream. The quick coupler system is also adaptable to hand-set hose sprinklers or to traveling sprinklers which are connected to the quick coupler outlets.

The initial cost of a quick coupler system is the lowest of the three irrigation systems discussed. The cost may be 35 to 50 percent that of a fully automatic system. This is because there is no need for electronic equipment and only as many sprinkler heads are purchased as can be operated at one time. The main disadvantages of a quick coupler system are the lack of reliable labor and the ever-increasing costs of labor to operate the system. From one to three night irrigators are usually employed on an eighteen-hole golf course for operation of a quick coupler system. Other disadvantages are the difficulties in employing people to work at night, the time required to train them, their typically low reliability, the potential for human error, and the greater amount of water used in comparison with a automatic system.

Even fully automatic irrigation systems require some quick coupling valves and keys, typically one valve at each green and tee and at intervals of 200 to 300 feet (61 to 91.4 meters) along fairways, in order to provide a manually activated source of water for emergencies and other uses. Some designs include quick couplers at every head on single-row fairway sytems as a complete manual backup.

Other Types of Irrigation

Flood irrigation was sometimes practiced on flat golf courses in earlier days. It involved a series of soil berms approximately 3 to 4 inches (7.6 to 10 centimeters) high constructed to hold water within a given area. These individual sections would then be flooded by a fire hose or by open ditch irrigation. Flood irrigation is relatively inexpensive in terms of initial cost but is inefficient in water utilization and inconvenient from the standpoint of turf use. Thus, it is rarely used on golf courses today.

There has been periodic interest in various types of subirrigation for a number of years. Subirrigation has been employed on a limited basis on some relatively level greens and tees. A typical subirrigation system involves a series of subsoil terraces defined by an impermeable plastic base layer. Water level within each terrace is controlled to a specific depth in the root zone. Advantages of the subsurface irrigation technique include minimum water loss through atmospheric evaporation and reduced disease and soil compaction problems. Construction of a subirrigation system presents difficulties where extensive contouring of the surface is involved. In addition, there are questions concerning the long-term performance and maintenance of such a system where saline or anaerobic conditions prevail. Thus, further research is needed concerning this irrigation technique.

SYSTEM COMPONENTS

The principal components of an irrigation system are a sequential chain: (1) water source, (2) pump station, (3) water distribution lines with associated gate and drain valves, (4) control valves, control lines, and their associated controller, if an automatic system, and (5) sprinkler heads. A fully automatic irrigation system utilizes all of these components, while other types of systems may use selected portions. Auxiliary components that may be used include systems for automatic moisture sensing and for chemical injection. Each major component within an automatic irrigation system is discussed in this section, with the exception of the water source, which is covered later in this chapter.

Pump Station

The function of a pump or pumping station is to draw water from a source, such as a well, lake, pond, or stream, raise the pressure, and subsequently release the water into the irrigation system at the pressure and rate required by the irrigation system design specifications. In addition, a pump is sometimes installed in a pressurized line to increase the pressure to the level needed for operation of the irrigation system. This is referred to as a booster pump and is usually of a centrifugal or vertical turbine type. Most golf course pumping stations are mounted on a permanent concrete base, but may or may not be constructed with a protective pump house. Use of a pump house is dictated by the need for protection from weather conditions, vandalism, and animal activity problems in the area. The pumping station may range from a single main pump with booster to an elaborate multiple pump arrangement with the appropriate controls and valves. The particular type of system depends on the design needs of the irrigation system plus the location and type of water source.

Pump Types. Most pumps used in turfgrass irrigation are of the impeller type with pressurizing achieved by centrifugal action. Energy is imparted to the water in the form of velocity by means of a rotating impeller, which is positioned within a pump housing. In this design, the water enters the impeller at the center, is forced to rotate outward in a circular motion, and is discharged through openings at the outer rim of the impeller. The force of the water as it is discharged from the outlet of the pump housing is translated to pressure relative to the prevailing conditions. The discharge head, or pressure generated by the impeller, is a function of the velocity of the impeller at the rim, which in turn is dependent on the diameter and speed of the impeller. The pump discharge rate is determined by the width, diameter, and rotating speed of the impeller. Centrifugal pumps characteristically possess a high efficiency over a wide range of operating conditions. Nevertheless, each pump design has a certain head and discharge at which it operates most efficiently. Most centrifugal pumps used for turfgrass irrigation are either of the volute or tubine type. The major difference between the two is the device that receives the water from the rotating impeller.

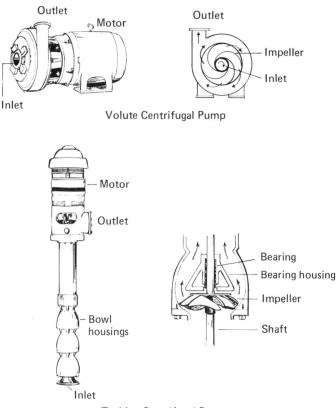

Figure 9-5. Basic design features of a volute centrifugal pump (*top*) and a turbine centrifugal pump (*bottom*).

Volute Pump. The volute centrifugal pump design involves a spiral case or volute that surrounds the impeller rim to receive and conduct water away from the rotating impeller. From the point of discharge at the impeller rim the volute increases in size in the direction of water rotation until the water is released into the discharge pipe (Fig. 9-5). The progressive enlargement of the volute functions in converting velocity energy to pressure energy. The volute centrifugal pump is a single-stage operation involving one bowl housing. It performs efficiently over a wider range of speeds than does the turbine pump. Both the motor and pump are mounted aboveground in some form of closed or flexible coupling, often on the same base frame. Both units are mounted with a suction line extending into the water source. The volute centrifugal pump is generally most effective when the water source is less than 20 feet (6 meters) below the pump. It is also used in a booster pump arrangement.

Turbine Pump. The discharge outlet design of a turbine pump consists of diverging passages or diffusers formed by veins to direct the water and to change the velocity energy to pressure energy. The pump consists of a multistage bowl assembly in which a series of rotating impellers impart increasing centrifugal forces on the water until the desired water pressure is achieved (Fig. 9-5). Owing to this design the turbine pump must operate over a more limited range of speeds than does the volute centrifugal pump. The most common turbine pump employed for water sources at a depth of more than 20 feet (6 meters) is the vertical type. The deep-well vertical turbine pump consists of (a) a motor installed aboveground, (b) a drive shaft positioned within a discharge column or pipe assembly which

1. Pressure gauge
2. Manual gate valve
3. Check valve
4. Strainer
5. Pressure tank
6. Pump
7. Union
8. Pressure relief valve
9. Pump electrical junction box
10. Pressure switch
11. Manual-off-automatic switch
12. Sight glass
13. Gate valve
14. Pump discharge to
    sprinkler system
15. Water level minimum 2 ft
    above pump inlet

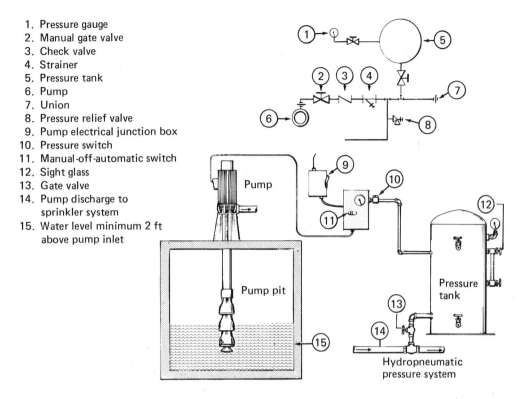

Figure 9-6. Profile of a vertical turbine pump installation.

extends from the base of the motor, and (c) a centrifugal turbine pump suspended from the base of the discharge column-drive shaft assembly (Fig. 9-6). The shaft transmits power from the drive motor to the pump and may be either oil or water lubricated. The pump itself extends into the water in the form of a flooded sump; thus there are no problems with the pump losing prime. Performance characteristics of this type of pump are determined primarily by the design of the bowl assembly and the speed of the impeller shaft. The advantages of a vertical turbine pump include good efficiency and elimination of suction pipe, foot valve, and priming system. This pumping system does have the added cost of construction of a pump pit.

Pump Selection. A qualified pump engineer should select the type of pump to be used based on the site conditions and the requirements of the irrigation system as furnished by an irrigation design engineer. Site conditions include the topography and the highest and lowest known water levels. In addition, potential sources of power for the motor should be outlined.

The pump engineer and the irrigation design engineer will confer once the preliminary design phase for the irrigation system has been completed. The pump engineer should be provided with information concerning (a) the maximum discharge rate or flow anticipated for the design layout plus any significant variations in discharge rate where the pressure requirement remains relatively constant, (b) the maximum head or pressure required for the system at the pump discharge outlet, and (c) the maximum vertical height of water lift required. A pump is then selected which has a performance rating suitable for the operating conditions proposed by the irrigation system designer.

With the preliminary pump specifications in hand, the irrigation design engineer proceeds with final design of the system. The pump engineer and irrigation design engineer then meet again to confirm that the final design specifications of the irrigation system will be met by the proposed pumping station.

Pump selection should be based on the maximum anticipated, or "worst case," discharge rate and head specifications calculated by the irrigation design engineer. Performance curves of the pump should be carefully evaluated. In addition, all combinations of operating conditions should be reviewed to insure that the pumping system will provide the desired flexibility under these varying conditions. Economy of pump operation should also be assessed prior to final selection. The pump engineer can calculate the fixed and operating costs for both the pump and power units proposed. Comparisons among several proposed pump systems may reveal significant savings in pumping costs without any deficiencies in meeting the irrigation system design specifications in terms of discharge rate and head.

Pump System. In addition to the basic pump, motor, and power source, the pumping station may include such components as a jockey pump, check valve, gate valve, pressure-reducing valve, automatic vent valve, bypass control valve, pressure gauge, pressure switch, drain valve, shutoff valve, pump control valve, pressure tank, strainer, and the associated electrical system (Fig. 9-7). The actual pump system design may be of varying degrees of complexity depending on which of these components are incorporated into the design. It is important that the pumps and associated power units be properly matched over a full range of speeds and pumping conditions.

Proper installation of the pump system requires a qualified electrician experienced with pumps, as well as appropriate plumbing personnel. Because knowledgeable installation personnel are not available in many parts of the country, purchase of a preassembled pump system may be advantageous. With such a station, all components are designed and built at the factory to the specifications of the particular golf course irrigation system. On-site installation can be accomplished with minimal professional expertise.

Most large golf course irrigation systems require a multiple pump system. It involves a set of either centrifugal pumps with individual suction pipes or vertical turbine pumps, each drawing from a single pit with the discharge pipes connected into the main irrigation system. Multiple pumps connected in series give a constant discharge rate but a cumulative pressure, while multiple pumps connected in

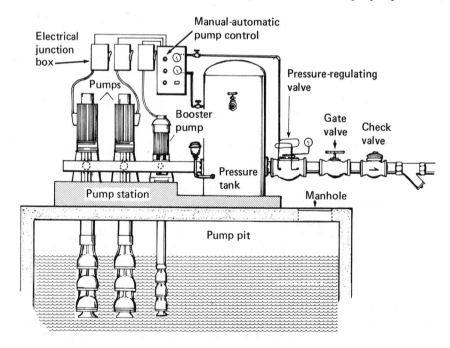

Figure 9-7. Diagram of the components of an automatic pumping system.

Figure 9-8. Typical multiple pump system with jockey pump and pressure tank.

parallel maintain a constant pressure while the discharge gallonage is cumulative. A typical eighteen-hole golf course multiple pumping system has two to three main pumps plus a jockey pump (Fig. 9-8). In a representative three-pump system, each pump is selected with a capacity to provide one-half the maximum discharge requirement for the irrigation system. This provides a very important backup capability in case one of the pumps fails. Activation of one or more of the pumps is accomplished automatically by pressure switches designed to maintain the programmed pressure. The jockey pump functions in (a) maintaining pressure in the system at all times to minimize water hammer caused by water being pumped into empty lines, (b) meeting small discharge requirements needed in filling water and spray tanks, deep watering of trees and shrubs, and irrigation of selected small zonal areas of turf, thus avoiding start-up of the main pumps, and (c) supplementing the pressure and flow requirements of one or more main pumps when the demand is not large enough to require activation of an additional main pump.

The pump operation should be automatically controlled by means of the appropriate pump matched with the proper-sized pressure tank and the necessary control devices. Maintenance of an automatically pressurized system on a constant basis insures ready water availability for small supplemental requirements and minimizes water hammer. A pressure tank is particularly important in dampening water hammer caused by the closing of automatic valves and activation of pumps. Typically, the pressure tank is filled approximately 50 to 60 percent with water and the remainder with compressed air. The compressed air stored in the pressure tank functions in absorbing water energy generated by the pumping system. Pressure switches are adjusted with a high and a low pressure requirement to maintain system pressure within the desired operating range. Associated with the pressure tank is a pressure switch and air valve. It is very critical that the pressure tank not be undersized. A smaller pressure tank can be used if a variable speed pump is incorporated into the pumping station.

Water Distribution System

Pipe. Most water distribution lines for turfgrass irrigation systems are installed permanently underground. The piping system involves relatively large main lines at the pump discharge point with the piping gradually sized downward through the more distant lateral lines to the most distant sprinkler head. Materials used in the manufacture of irrigation pipe include plastic, asbestos-cement, and metal. Each type of pipe possesses certain advantages and disadvantages in terms of strength, capacity, dimensions, longevity, and cost. Based on these, a type of pipe is selected that meets the needs of the particular irrigation system being installed.

Two terms associated with pipe are pressure rating and schedule. *Pressure rating* is the estimated maximum pressure that water in a pipe can exert continuously with a high degree of certainty that the pipe will not fail. This pressure rating encompasses both the maximum static pressure and pressure surges caused by water hammer action. Thus, the pressure rating and the working pressure of a pipe are related. *Schedule* designates a standard series of wall thicknesses for all sizes in which a specified type of pipe is manufactured. Thus, with a 40, 80, and 120 schedule series, the wall thickness increases with the schedule number. A larger pipe diameter is associated with a smaller pressure rating for the same pipe material.

In the selection of a particular piping material, it is important that the manufacturer's recommendations be followed concerning the specific kinds of fittings (couplings, reducers, ends, tees, crosses, and inserts) that can be used in association with that pipe.

Plastic Pipe. Plastic pipe has the advantages of being relatively low in cost and completely inert. Thus, such debilitating actions as rust and electrolytic corrosion are avoided. The relatively light weight of plastic piping facilitates easy installation, the life expectancy is excellent, and the flow capacity for specified pipe size is greater than that of other piping materials owing to the very smooth interior finish. Plastic pipe can be characterized in terms of the *standard dimension ratio* (SDR), which is a ratio of pipe diameter to wall thickness. The lower the SDR the higher the internal pressure the pipe can withstand. Pipes manufactured of one material and having the same SDR rating have the same pressure rating regardless of pipe diameter, with only the wall thickness varying. Plastic pipe is marked at intervals of not more than 5 feet (1.5 meters) along its length with the following specifications: nominal pipe size, type of material, standard dimension ratio, pressure rating in pounds per square inch of water at 74.3 °F (23 °C), and whether potable water can be transported in it.

Although numerous kinds of plastics have been utilized in the manufacture of pipe, only two are currently of any significance in the turf irrigation systems. Used primarily is polyvinyl chloride (PVC), while polyethylene (PE) is also used to a limited extent. Other types of plastic pipe used in the past include acrylonitrile-butadiene-styrene (ABS) and polybutylene (PB).

PVC pipe is semirigid and permits itself to be bowed somewhat during installation. In comparison with the other types of plastic pipe, PVC possesses (a) greater strength, (b) the most durability, (c) more resistance to a wider range of chemicals, (d) greater carrying capacity, and (e) a simpler way of attaching fittings. PVC pipe is typically available in 20-foot (6-meter) lengths; pressure ratings of 160, 200, and 315; and schedules of 40, 80, and 120. Most lateral piping of 4 inches (10 centimeters) or less in diameter now used on golf courses is PVC. There is also a trend toward the use of PVC even on main lines as large as 30 inches (76 centimeters). Fittings used on smaller diameter PVC pipe are of the exterior type and are chemically fused to the pipe by what is termed a solvent weld (Fig. 9-9). It is critical that the procedures followed in the solvent welding of fittings to PVC pipe are in accordance with the manufacturer's specifications, since this is typically the weakest point in the pipe line.

The high rate of expansion and contraction of PVC pipe presents a problem when there is a long run of pipe sized 3 inches (7.6 centimeters) and larger. Thus, there is a likelihood that the pipe may be pulled apart at its weakest point, a fitting. To avoid this problem, PVC fittings of the socket and bell type are available (Fig. 9-9). One end of each pipe section is designed with an ''0'' gasket to prevent leaks. The normal end of another section can be inserted into this fitting to form a movable joint which can expand and contract within itself, yet avoid pulling apart.

PE pipe generally has been less expensive than PVC and is easier to work. However, its use has declined because its lower strength results in a low pressure rating. In addition, its resistance to solvent welding techniques has necessitated use of insert-type fittings, which impede water flow (Fig. 9-9).

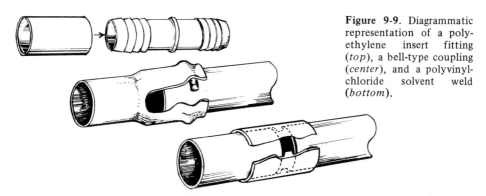

Figure 9-9. Diagrammatic representation of a polyethylene insert fitting (*top*), a bell-type coupling (*center*), and a polyvinylchloride solvent weld (*bottom*).

Thus, molded plastic, cast brass, and forged steel insert–clamp-type fittings are utilized with PE piping. If clamps and/or bolts are used they should be of stainless steel to prevent rusting. PE pipe is made in varying densities, which affect the relative flexibility of the piping. The more flexible pipe is available in long coils, which facilitates laying and calls for fewer couplings.

Asbestos-Cement Pipe. Asbestos-cement (AC) pipe is manufactured from an asbestos, cement, and silica combination. Since it has no metallic component it is free from electrolysis and galvanic corrosion problems. AC pipe is characterized by high strength, freedom from rust and corrosion, and relatively light weight compared with metal pipe of similar size. One problem is its somewhat brittle nature, which dictates very careful handling, installation, and backfilling procedures. It is available in 13-foot (4-meter) lengths and sizes ranging from 3 to 36 inches (7.6 to 91.4 centimeters) in inside diameter, with classes of 100, 150, and 200 pounds per square inch (7, 10.5, and 14 kilograms per square centimeter) working pressure. Pipe lengths other than standard length can be produced on request or the AC pipe can be cut and machined in the field. Fittings and couplings composed of asbestos-cement material are available for use with AC pipe. The coupler fittings contain a rubber ring fitted into a groove insert at each end. A specialized puller device is utilized for inserting the tapered machine end of the pipe onto the rubber ring fitting. The techniques used in the installation of AC pipe should follow closely the manufacturer's recommendations. Installation is best accomplished by properly trained, experienced personnel.

Metal Pipe. The three types of metal pipe worthy of mention are cast iron, galvanized steel, and copper. Cast iron pipe was widely used at one time, especially for large-diameter main lines. However, it has been almost completely replaced by AC pipe. Cast iron pipe is available in sizes from 3 to 60 inches (7.6 to 152.4 centimeters) in diameter with a standard length of 16 feet (4.9 meters). It should be installed strictly according to the manufacturer's directions. Also, it is quite brittle and thus should be firmly supported along the full length of the trench bottom. The main problems with cast iron have been serious rusting and corrosion on the inside of the pipe, which affects its functional carrying capacity. Disturbances in the pipe may cause the rust to be dislodged and carried outward to the sprinkler heads, where serious clogging problems can result.

Galvanized steel pipe has been used occasionally in the past, primarily for main distribution lines. However, it has substantial problems with both corrosion and chemical deposits on the inside surface. The result is serious impairment of flow capacity, which worsens through the years until operation of the sprinkler system is threatened. Also, rust and scale flaking may clog the sprinkler heads. An additional problem with galvanized pipe is its proneness to electrolytic corrosion, which occurs when two pipes of dissimilar metals are attached. For this reason, either dielectric plastic or plastic fittings should be used between two different types of metals.

Finally, copper water tubing has very limited use on golf courses. It is most commonly used as a riser for shrub heads. It is resistant to inside rusting and at the same time the external surface readily tarnishes to the extent that it blends well with shrubbery. Copper tubing is subject to dezincification in certain soil and water conditions.

Risers. A riser functions in connecting a sprinkler head or quick coupler valve to an underground lateral pipe. There are various types of riser arrangements, ranging from short lengths of pipe extending directly upward into the base of a sprinkler head to more complex single and double swing-joint assemblies. The latter are more commonly used in golf course installations, since they function in protecting both the underground pipe and the sprinkler head from damage when the wheels of vehicles and equipment pass directly over the sprinkler head. The swing-joint assembly is a combination of elbows which flex under pressure from above and thereby absorb the surface shock from wheels passing over the attached sprinkler head (Fig. 9-10). The swing-joint assembly also allows postinstallation adjustments in sprinkler head height as turfgrass growth and soil settling alter the surface grade surrounding each sprinkler head.

Gauges. Allied with the pump system and water distribution lines are an assortment of gauges whose function is to insure that water pressure and flow characteristics are maintained at certain levels in relation to the original design of the irrigation system. Pressure gauges are needed to monitor the pressure at various points throughout the system. One or more pressure gauges are permanently installed in the pumping system, including the pressure tank and point of water discharge from the pump into the main line. Portable gauges are also available to check the pressure of individual heads or other points along the lateral water-distribution lines. Consideration should be given to installation of a seven-day electric pressure recorder at the pumping station to monitor pressures in the system during periods, such as night cycles, when the superintendent is not present. Allied with certain pumping stations is a vacuum gauge positioned on the suction inlet of the pump to indicate the level at which the pump is functioning.

Control Valves

Valves are used to release water into either the distribution lines or into a sprinkler head, to retain water in a certain portion of the water distribution system or pumping station, to maintain a specified pressure, and to drain lines. A valve may be manually controlled, actuated by remote control, or automatic. Various types of valves are discussed here in terms of their functional relationships to water distribution lines, sprinkler heads, and the pumping station.

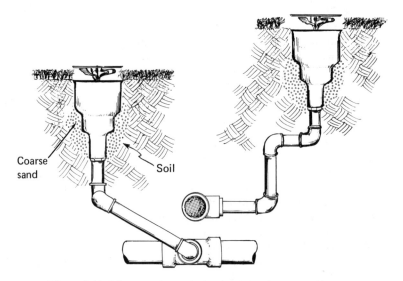

Coarse sand

Soil

Figure 9-10. Diagram of a typical swing-joint riser assembly.

A manually controlled irrigation system usually involves either globe or angle-type valves turned by hand to release water to the nearby sprinklers. In contrast, modern automatic irrigation systems commonly employ remote control valves whereby actuation of the irrigation heads is controlled from a centralized and/or field satellite controller. Although most remote control valves are designed for underground burial, their placement in a valve box allows easy access for servicing and, if necessary, for manual operation.

Opening and closing of remote control valves may be done either hydraulically or by an electrically operated solenoid valve. The control valve itself is operated by hydraulic pressure, with the exception of the thermal motor valve, which uses electric power to raise or lower a valve disc. Most remote control valves are of the globe design. Valve operation is based on a pressure differential between the top and bottom of a diaphragm or piston. Control of water movement through specially designed ports and chambers within the valve allows water pressure to be applied in such a manner as to open or close the valve assembly, which may be of either a diaphragm or piston type. The diaphragm-type valve is more commonly used, owing to minimal wear problems compared with the piston valve, which possesses washers and rings that require periodic servicing and replacement.

The manner in which the automatic valve is actuated is termed either normally open or normally closed (this is the position that the valve assumes if the hydraulic or electric control lines are cut or broken). Should an electric or a hydraulic line be severed or broken for any reason in a normally closed system, the valve will close itself automatically. Electric valves are normally closed, while hydraulic valves may be of either type.

The water used to operate remote valves through hydraulic control tubing must be clean. In regions of the country where freezing is a possibility, all water must be blown out of the hydraulic control tubing with an air compressor.

Larger pop-up sprinkler heads are now being manufactured with what is termed a valve-in-head design. The valve may be an electric or a hydraulic type and is incorporated in the base of the sprinkler head housing. This positioning offers certain advantages owing to its allowing independent control of each sprinkler head. The valve-in-head unit can also be used in the economical conversion of existing quick-coupler irrigation systems to an automatic irrigation system.

Other types of valves utilized in association with the water distribution lines include the gate, drain, clay, pressure-relief, and vacuum-relief valves. The gate valve is typically a manually operated type which functions in shutting off the flow in a line. It is advisable for a gate valve to be positioned at the start of each major lateral line. Thus, if a break occurs, the problem line can be isolated, shut down, and drained without affecting the entire irrigation system.

Drain valves may be manually operated and opened occasionally, as needed, to drain a line. There are also automatic drain valves which are adjusted to open when subjected to very low pressures. They permit the line to drain whenever the pressure drops near zero in the distribution lines. Automatic drain valves are used on pipelines that are not constantly pressurized, while manual drain valves are used on lines that are normally under constant pressure.

The third form of drain valve involves a manually operated, flushing type which is positioned on the outer end of a line for the purpose of flushing out dirt and debris which may be present in the distribution lines. The pressure-relief valve is usually a spring-loaded type adjusted to open at pressures above the normal operation level for the purpose of relieving excessive pressure surges. There is also a vacuum-relief valve, which is positioned on main lines that drain downhill for the purpose of preventing a vacuum stress that could collapse the pipe.

Quick coupling valves are positioned at the upper terminus of risers, usually of the swing-joint type. The line connected to the quick-coupling valve is normally under constant water pressure. Thus, a spring assembly holds the valve closed. A coupler is used to activate the valve by means of a screw or notched assembly which forces the spring-loaded valve seat down and thus opens the valve for water to flow through the coupler (Fig. 9-11). Mounted on the coupler may be either an above-ground rotary sprinkler or a swivel ell assembly to which a hose connection can be attached. The quick coupling valve normally has a hinged cover positioned so the top is flush with the turf.

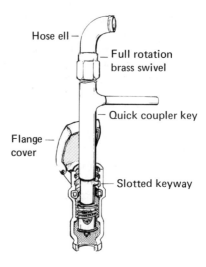

Figure 9-11. Diagram of a quick coupler assembly with a swivel ell hose connection.

Hose ell —

— Full rotation brass swivel

— Quick coupler key

Flange — cover

— Slotted keyway

Three types of valves may be associated with the pumping station. A foot valve is positioned at the base of the suction intake pipe to maintain water in the pump and suction pipe when the pump is not in operation. As a result, the foot valve serves to keep the pump in a primed condition. There may also be a manually operated discharge valve, which is generally kept closed for priming. A check valve is positioned on the discharge side of the pump where it maintains water in the pipeline above the pump when the pump is not in operation.

Finally, there are accessories such as pressure regulators. A unit located at the pump station regulates pressure at that point but has no control over losses or gains of pressure in the downstream water distribution lines. Pressure regulators located at the base of each sprinkler head maintain a constant operating pressure through the sprinkler head regardless of whether there are water pressure losses, caused by friction loss or uphill pipe runs, or pressure gains, due to downhill runs.

Controllers

A vital component in an automatic irrigation system is the controller that actuates the remote valves. The basic features include (a) a twenty-four-hour electric clock to keep controller time and pulse a rotary selector, (b) a day-of-the-week programming dial, (c) a control station indicator and timing device, and (d) a pump circuit. Controllers are available with varying numbers of stations. Each station usually has a timing capability of zero to sixty minutes and controls one or more remote valves. The golf course superintendent presets each station timing to the specific duration of irrigation desired for the turf area controlled by that station. A signal goes out from the controller by means of electric wire or hydraulic tubing to activate a remote valve and in turn initiate operation of one or more sprinkler heads. More specifically, the rotary switch channels 24-volt electric power to the valves, in the case of an electric control system, or a rotary selector valve may either apply or release hydraulic pressure to the remote valves, in the case of a hydraulic control system.

Most modern automatic irrigation systems designed for golf courses utilize some variation of this control system, usually involving a central programmer combined with a series of satellite field controllers. The main function of the central programmer is to initiate cycles for the satellite controllers. On command, the satellite controllers assume the actual programming and operation of that portion of the irrigation system under their control. Each field controller is positioned at a strategic location overlooking the sprinkler irrigation heads under its direct control. The satellite controller can be operated or overridden by the connecting central programmer. The satellite controller can also be operated manually at its field station, which gives added flexibility to activate a specific portion of the irrigation system.

The central programmer can be designed with accessories which permit monitoring of key components in the irrigation system. Included may be (a) gauges indicating pressure levels in various portions of the system, (b) operating indicators for the various pumps associated with the pumping station, (c) automatic cutoffs when a predetermined high- or low-pressure condition occurs, (d) an automatic signal system to indicate which portion of the system is in operation at a given time, and (e) an automatic rain cutoff control. The automatic control system has the advantage of placing the golf course superintendent in direct control of the irrigation practices employed throughout the golf course. The net result, if the system is properly operated, is increased efficiency of water utilization, more uniform irrigation of various turfgrass areas, and avoidance of overwatering with its associated soil compaction and disease problems.

A recent innovation in automatic controllers is an electronic solid-state computer system which permits more complex programming based on automatic monitoring of certain meteorological data. A further refinement in the central programmer is a precipitation-sensing device which countermands the controller program and thus shuts off the irrigation system when a specified amount of precipitation occurs.

Sprinkler Heads

The sprinkler head is at the end of a long chain of automatic irrigation system components including the water source, pump station, water distribution lines, remote control valves, and automatic controller. Types of sprinkler heads include fixed sprays, pop-up sprays, strip sprays, bubblers, stream sprays, and rotary sprinklers. The rotary sprinkler head is the type most commonly used on golf course turfs. It produces a slowly rotating, fine-velocity stream of water which is distributed relatively uniformly over a large circular to semicircular area of 50 to over 200 feet (15 to 60 meters) in diameter. The midrange in performance of rotary pop-up sprinkler heads is 70 to 170 feet (21.3 to 51.8 meters) in diameter. Many types of drive mechanisms are utilized in rotary sprinklers, including gear, cam, impact, ball, friction, and reaction drive. In one way or another they all depend on flowing water to create the drive force in a head. Sprinkler nozzles are available in various sizes, shapes, and descriptions to meet the needs of different pressure, gallonage, wind, and soil infiltration conditions.

Most rotary sprinkler heads utilized on golf courses are of the pop-up type. That is, the head is completely concealed below ground except for a cover plate level with the turf (Fig. 9-12). On activation of a remote valve, pressure on the pop-up assembly causes the sprinkler head to be elevated. A spring assembly is sometimes used to insure that the sprinkler head and cover plate retract into the sprinkler housing when the remote control valve is closed. A wide range of rotary sprinkler heads are available to choose from. Factors to be considered in selection of sprinkler heads include the (a) condition of areas to be irrigated, (b) available water volume in the water distribution lines, (c) anticipated operating pressure at the sprinkler head, (d) distribution pattern of the head, and (e) reliability and serviceability.

The rate and pattern of water distribution from a sprinkler head is the primary concern in golf turf irrigation. The normal distribution curve is highest near the head and gradually declines toward the extremities (Fig. 9-13). Thus, proper spacing and overlap of fixed automatic sprinkler heads are critical in achieving uniform water application. Improper operating pressure can adversely affect the water distribution pattern of a sprinkler. An additional complicating factor is that the water distribution curve becomes unreliable when wind velocities exceed 10 knots (11.5 miles or 18.5 kilometers) per hour.

Chemical Injection

It is feasible to apply fertilizers and other chemicals to golf course turfs through the irrigation system. This approach, termed fertigation, has received considerable interest recently in certain parts of

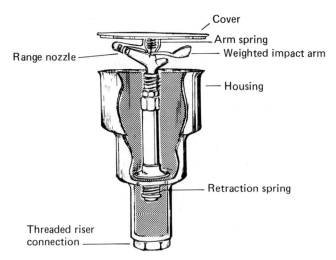

Figure 9-12. Diagram of a rotary pop-up sprinkler head.

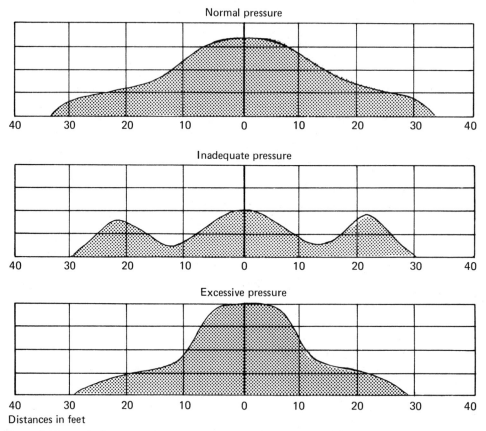

Distances in feet

Figure 9-13. Typical water distribution patterns from rotary sprinkler heads operating normally (*top*), with inadequate pressure (*center*), and with excessive pressure (*bottom*).

the United States. The preferred approach to chemical injection involves the use of a proportioner pump, which has the capability to adjust to variances in flow rates. Further, the relatively small orifices in valves and nozzles of the typical turfgrass sprinkler irrigation system dictate the use of chemicals in liquid form. The key to successful use of fertigation is an irrigation system properly designed and installed to insure uniform application of water over the entire turf area. Unfortunately, all too many systems fail to meet this important criterion. Chemical action on pipe, valve, riser, and sprinkler materials must be considered carefully when fertigation is used.

SYSTEM DESIGN

A properly designed and engineered irrigation system is essential in meeting the ultimate objectives of uniform application of water at rates desired for the varying conditions found on a golf course. The complexities of an automatic irrigation system necessitate incorporation of sound design and engineering principles. This is especially true since the system must function under a wide range of climatic, soil, and turfgrass cultural variables.

Selecting a Design Engineer

The first step in development of a golf course irrigation system is selection of a qualified design engineer. Applicants for the project position should be interviewed by a selection committee. In addition, the committee should visit with officials at golf courses where each qualified applicant has designed an irrigation system. The golf course superintendent should be interviewed regarding the design engineer's competence, cooperativeness, and type of plans and specifications prepared. It is also advisable that some of the original designs, plans, specifications, and final as-built plans developed for earlier projects be inspected.

The design engineer selected preferably should be an independent professional who has nothing to sell except engineering and design services. Willingness to work very closely with both the golf course superintendent and the irrigation installation contractor are also important. It is the design engineer's responsibility to provide detailed plans, bid documents, cost estimates, material lists, component specifications, and installation specifications for development of the golf course irrigation system. On installation of the system, the engineer must prepare an accurate as-built plan of the system based on daily records kept by the contractor. The goal is to integrate all aspects of the irrigation system design into a final functioning facility that is both efficient and reliable.

Contract. A contract should be prepared that specifies the engineer's responsibilities to the client during the design and construction phases of golf course irrigation system development. Included are statements regarding the (a) fee structure and payment schedule for the engineer, (b) specific types of plans, specifications, bid documents, and installation contracts to be prepared, as well as the degree of detail desired, (c) comprehensiveness of the irrigation system design, such as who is responsible for planning and development of the water source, pumping station, and any associated ponds or reservoirs that must be constructed, and (d) who has responsibility for staking the location of sprinkler heads. Also, the contract may call for the design engineer to inspect the system periodically during the installation phase. Actually, the design engineer's contract can be just as comprehensive as that previously discussed for the golf course architect in chapter 2.

Design Decisions

The first step in design development is for the decision-making committee or individual and the golf course superintendent to thoroughly study and decide on the irrigation performance expectations and the system capabilities. A statement of objectives and needs is then written. The type of system desired should determine the cost, rather than cost determining the type of system installed. Once the predesign

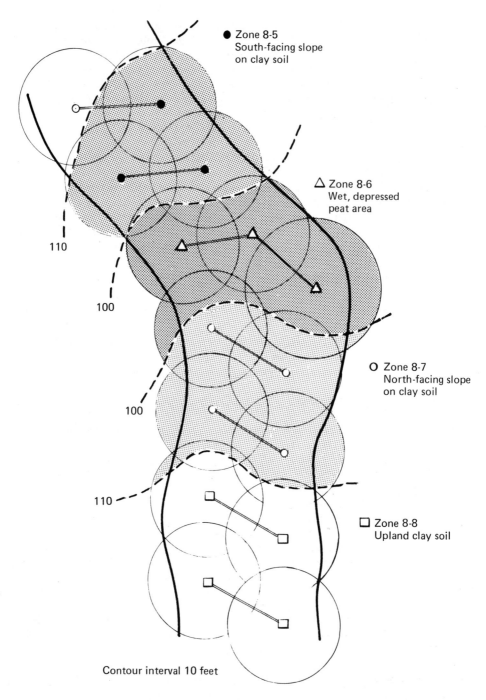

Zone 8-5
South-facing slope
on clay soil

△ Zone 8-6
Wet, depressed
peat area

○ Zone 8-7
North-facing slope
on clay soil

□ Zone 8-8
Upland clay soil

110

100

100

110

Contour interval 10 feet

Figure 9-14. Proposed sprinkler-head zoning arrangement on a fairway as influenced by topography and soil texture.

guidelines have been prepared by the decision maker(s), the design engineer evaluates and proposes a basic system design concept. In assessing and approving the design concept proposed by the engineer, it is important to evaluate it on an optimum operating basis rather than on the maximum performance basis which is sometimes presented. Counsel of the golf course superintendent should be sought at this point, especially for practical turf maintenance aspects. When approval is given, it is the engineer's responsibility to develop the irrigation system design, plans, contracts, specifications, and bid documents.

Design Development

Much thought and time must be given to developing a sound system design concept before preparation of detailed engineering specifications. The first step in the design procedure is selection of the method to be used to operate the sprinkler heads. This decision influences not only the type of sprinklers selected but also the types of valves, piping, fittings, and control lines. There are times when even competent design engineers will disagree over which method is best in a given golf course situation as well as which design techniques and data interpretation should be employed to effect the method.

Criteria to be taken into account in the design of a golf course irrigation system include the (a) maximum turfgrass water use rate for the particular situation, (b) amount of water available from the source per unit of time, (c) number of hours available per day for irrigation, (d) anticipated amount and frequency with which irrigation is to be employed, (e) water infiltration characteristics of the soil projected under intense traffic, (f) topography of the area, and (g) direction and intensity of prevailing winds. The design usually is based on the supplemental water requirement over a long term during the driest months to avoid over- or under-design. The design engineer must have a basic understanding of turfgrass cultural principles and practices to design an effective operating system from the practical turfgrass maintenance standpoint. It is extremely important in the design phase to insure that the operating pressure specified for the sprinkler heads selected can be maintained throughout the entire system under maximum operating conditions.

The design steps include preparation of a plot plan of the golf course to be irrigated, development of a sprinkler head layout, determination of flow requirements and associated pipe sizing, zoning of the sprinkler head system, development of a trenching plan, and selection of materials to achieve the design objectives along with detailed specifications concerning the individual sprinkler components needed. Each group of heads, termed a *zone,* is controlled independently by a separate controller station. Thus, the water supply delivered to a particular zone limits the maximum number of sprinkler heads that can be operated within the zone. When determining a zone, consideration must be given to differences in grass species, soil conditions, drainage, intensity of culture, slope, shade versus sun exposure, wind, and the presence of trees (Fig. 9-14).

The design engineer must walk every hole on a golf course and make specific notes of features that might affect the irrigation system's effectiveness. Unfortunately, too many golf course irrigation systems have been designed at the drawing board with little or no field investigation. This typically results in increased construction costs which could have been avoided through studious on-site inspections.

It is critical that an accurate irrigation plan be prepared (Fig. 9-15). Key permanent and semipermanent features, including buildings, major tree groupings, rock outcroppings, fence lines, and roads, should be accurately positioned on the plan. Attention to detailed accuracy at this time will avoid errors in head layout and subsequent cost estimates.

Once the design, plans, and specifications are completed, it is also the responsibility of the design engineer to prepare the appropriate bid documents, issue an invitation to bid, and distribute the appropriate design plans, specifications, and construction contracts to the irrigation installation contractors qualified to bid on the project.

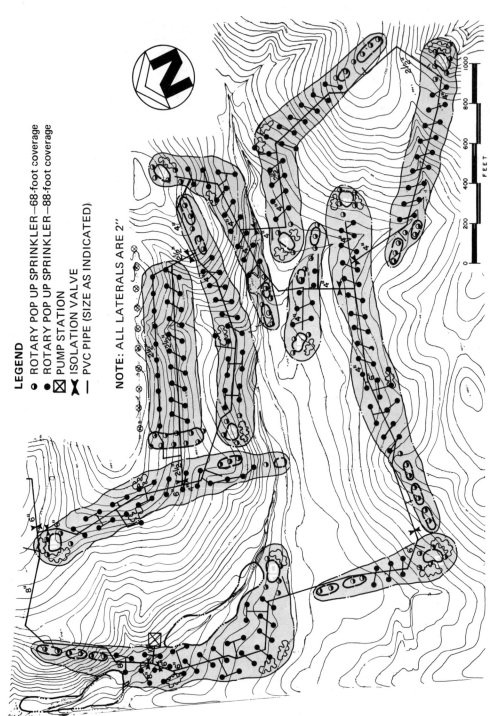

LEGEND

◑ ROTARY POP UP SPRINKLER—68-foot coverage
● ROTARY POP UP SPRINKLER—88-foot coverage
⊠ PUMP STATION
⋈ ISOLATION VALVE
— PVC PIPE (SIZE AS INDICATED)

NOTE: ALL LATERALS ARE 2″

Figure 9-15. Representative design plan for a nine-hole golf course irrigation system. (Drawing courtesy of Rees Jones, American Society of Golf Course Architects.)

Design Guidelines

Specific books are available on golf course irrigation system design and there is no intent here to cover the detailed steps involved. However, some of the more obvious but frequently overlooked guidelines in the design of an automatic irrigation system should be mentioned.

1. Main lines should be looped (i.e., interconnected) where possible to assist in balancing pressures throughout the system. Some engineers may suggest this is not necessary because of their "design characteristics." Nevertheless, looping is a valuable feature of any design layout, even if additional costs are involved. The greater amount of pipe used usually is offset by use of smaller pipe.

2. A multirow system is preferred to insure uniform fairway coverage. Most single-row systems are physically unable to furnish an overall pattern of equal precipitation rates, especially in arid-semiarid regions subject to frequent, high-velocity winds. An exception would be in high-rainfall areas where the goal is to insure turf survival between rains.

3. Overlap (i.e., the radius of coverage for a sprinkler head in relation to the distance between heads, expressed in percentages) is critically important in relation to sprinkler head spacing. Experience has proven that 100 percent overlap (i.e., each sprinkler throwing to the base of those adjacent to it) affords the best overall coverage. An overlap of 70 to 80 percent stretches the coverage and, in turfgrass irrigation, has not proven adequate under most circumstances.

4. The most practical spacing for automatic pop-up sprinkler heads (greens, tees, fairways, or roughs) has been found to be no more than 65 to 70 feet (20 to 21.3 meters) in an equilateral triangular pattern. Larger sprinkler heads at greater spacings may reduce the total cost of the system but frequently apply too much water too rapidly for most soil types. A gentle rain is far more effective than a heavy downpour.

5. The equilateral triangular spacing of 65 to 70 feet is especially important for putting green irrigation. It provides relatively uniform coverage because of the triangulation. Very large greens may preclude use of this design, although its use may be possible if the putting green perimeter is reshaped. Simply spacing heads every 65 feet around the perimeter of a green will not provide uniform coverage. There must be triangulation.

6. Equilateral triangular shaping is preferred over square or rectangular patterns (Fig. 9-16). The point is demonstrated by placing coins in similar configurations. Triangulation produces the smallest void. Square or rectangular patterns of spacing cause a more unequal precipitation rate and less uniform coverage. The ultimate goal in any golf turf irrigation system is uniform coverage.

7. It is totally inappropriate to have putting green, tee, and fairway sprinklers controlled by the same station or remote control valve. These areas have different irrigation requirements. Therefore, the sprinklers must be separated and under different, individual controller stations.

8. It is not good design to place full-throw sprinkler heads and part-circle sprinkler heads on the same control valve or controller station. There may be instances where a precipitation rate balance can be achieved through different nozzle sizes or head combinations, but complications hardly warrant the effort. Full-throw and part-circle sprinklers are generally incompatible from a precipitation rate/operating time viewpoint.

9. A single control station should generally have no more than two pop-up heads under its command, with single-head control preferred. For example, if six heads are needed for coverage of a particular green, at least three stations should be provided for them at the controller. This produces a greater degree of irrigation control on a green and is far superior to the practice of having all six heads operating at the same time. The separation of heads may be based on elevation similarities, upwind or downwind characteristics, shade, and so on.

   A similar design requirement is recommended for tees, i.e., no more than two sprinkler heads under the control of any one station. For fairways and roughs, a maximum of six

Equilateral head spacing   Square head spacing

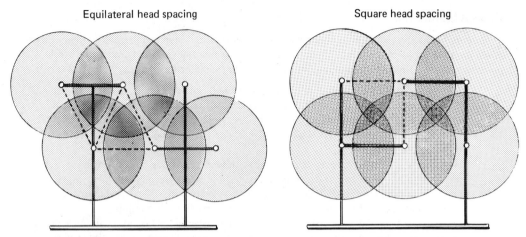

Figure 9-16. Graphic illustration of the comparative coverage achieved with equilateral versus square sprinkler head spacing.

sprinkler heads per station is used on multirow systems. In contrast, single-row systems may need individual head control on some sites. This degree of control may add to the initial cost of installation but also enhances the versatility and effectiveness of the system and lowers the operating cost.

10. Sprinkler heads under the control of the same station should be located at or near similar elevations. This permits proper irrigation scheduling for high ground as well as low. Uniform irrigation becomes impossible if heads under the same control station are at widely differing elevations. Similiar considerations might be given to those areas in intense shade (compared with full sun), with a particular slope or exposure (north versus south exposure), or where cultural practices vary.

11. Each pop-up sprinkler head should have a check or backflow valve. This prevents the irrigation line from back draining to the lowest sprinkler head after each irrigation cycle. Some automatic heads include a built-in valve for this purpose. Without some type of backflow stoppage, very wet areas develop at the base of the lowest sprinkler head on each line, water is wasted, and air enters the system to increase water hammer and surge damage. Installation of dry wells or drain lines offers a less satisfactory solution to the problem.

12. In every automatic irrigation system, quick coupling valves should be installed on live lines at every green and tee, plus at 200- to 300-foot (60- to 91.4-meter) intervals along the fairway, as a minimum. They are relatively inexpensive and will prove extremely useful during the life of a system. Practices such as spot watering, syringing, filling spray tanks, watering young trees, backup support, and emergency use are but a few justifications for their installation.

13. *Windage,* or sprinkler head offset to compensate for wind effects, seems to have been over-stressed in early irrigation design. Unless the wind is constant and continually from the same direction, offset sprinkler heads can be as much of a problem as the variable wind itself. Closer spacing between heads seems the best solution where wind is an important factor.

14. The location of satellite controllers should provide an unobstructed view of the sprinkler heads directly involved (Fig. 9-17). This affords an easy visual check of system operations.

15. Gate valves should be installed throughout the main lines of a system in a manner that permits easy main-line and lateral isolation. Gate valves are low-friction-loss valves used to control the flow of water. They should never be used as a throttle valve to restrict water flow in the line, since excess wear of the brass will void their use as shutoff valves when needed. Maintenance and repair are necessary from time to time during the life of any automatic system. The

Figure 9-17. Satellite controller positioned so that it is possible to visually assess whether all sprinkler heads under its control are operating properly.

placement of gate valves in strategic locations permits isolated shutdown without inactivation and draining of the entire irrigation system.

16. Every course has certain isolated areas where automatic irrigation coverage is difficult. A tee isolated in a wooded area illustrates the point. Under these conditions, optimum irrigation coverage can be achieved by the use of small pop-up heads closely spaced in an equilateral triangular pattern. This type of design provides better coverage than a single row of pop-up sprinkler heads. It also avoids overly wet and overly dry areas on the tee.

17. Most modern automatic controllers have the capability of repeating or recycling the irrigation program. This means that instead of one twenty-minute set, it is possible to program two ten-minute sets. This is an option on soils with a poor infiltration rate and should be included in all automatic systems.

18. In regions where winter weather necessitates system drainage, the designer must provide irrigation-line drainage capabilities. Manual drain valves should be placed at a level lower than any portion of the pipe to be drained. Use of a portable air compressor to blow the lines out in late fall provides added insurance.

WATER USE RATE

An assessment of how much water is needed for irrigation of a golf course is used in designing the system and in obtaining an adequate water source. The assessment includes both the maximum daily water requirement and the total seasonal need. Potential evapotranspiration rates and resultant water use requirements vary substantially across North America (Table 9-1). In some locations, irrigation is used only to supplement natural rainfall, while in other areas, irrigation is the sole source of water during the growing season. In establishing the maximum daily water use rate and seasonal water requirement for a golf course turf in a given area, reference information should be obtained from both the Weather Bureau and the appropriate state agricultural extension service.

A frequently used term related to irrigation practices is the *evapotranspiration rate*. It is a measure of the total amount of water lost by evaporation from the soil plus the water lost from plants through transpiration. The daily water use rate varies substantially from region to region (Table 9-2), and to a

Table 9-1. Average Monthly Rainfall and Potential Evapotranspiration for Thirty-Five Locations in North America

Location	Inches of Water per Month											
	Jan.	Feb.	Mar.	Apr.	May	June	July	Aug.	Sept.	Oct.	Nov.	Dec.
Alabama, Birmingham	4.9	4.8	4.2	1.2	-1.8	-3.2	-2.7	-2.9	-1.9	-0.1	2.6	4.4
Arizona, Phoenix	0	-0.4	-1.8	-3.8	-6.3	-8.2	-9.1	-7.4	-5.9	-3.5	-1.3	-0.2
British Columbia, Vancouver	8.3	5.3	4.0	1.5	-0.2	-1.6	-3.5	-2.4	0.9	4.1	7.5	8.3
California, Los Angeles	2.3	2.4	0.5	-1.5	-3.8	-4.9	-6.1	-5.6	-4.3	-2.5	-0.6	2.0
California, San Francisco	3.3	2.7	0.9	-1.2	-3.1	-4.3	-5.0	-4.5	-3.7	-1.9	0.2	3.0
Colorado, Denver	0.5	0.6	1.0	0.7	0.3	-1.8	-2.7	-2.3	-1.3	-0.3	0.6	0.5
Florida, Ft. Lauderdale	0.1	-0.3	-1.0	-1.3	-1.1	0.2	-1.2	-0.7	3.1	3.1	-0.5	-0.2
Florida, Jacksonville	1.2	1.6	1.0	-1.1	-3.0	-1.4	-0.3	-0.7	0.5	0.1	-0.4	1.0
Georgia, Atlanta	4.4	4.2	3.8	1.4	-1.6	-3.0	-2.2	-2.7	-1.7	0	2.0	4.2
Illinois, Chicago	1.9	1.6	1.9	1.3	-0.2	-1.8	-3.6	-2.7	-1.0	0.6	1.5	1.9
Iowa, Des Moines	1.2	1.1	1.5	0.6	0.1	-1.0	-3.5	-2.4	-0.7	-0.1	1.3	1.1
Kansas, Kansas City	1.0	0.7	1.0	0.3	-0.1	-1.3	-4.1	-2.8	-0.9	-0.3	0.6	0.9
Louisiana, New Orleans	3.1	3.0	2.3	0.4	-1.7	-2.2	-0.4	-0.9	0.6	-1.1	1.6	3.5
Maryland, Baltimore	3.0	2.4	2.8	1.1	-0.2	-2.2	-2.7	-1.6	-0.4	1.0	2.3	2.8
Massachusetts, Boston	4.0	3.4	3.5	2.2	-0.1	-1.8	-3.3	-1.6	0.1	1.3	3.2	3.4
Michigan, Detroit	1.9	1.9	1.7	1.2	-0.3	-2.2	-3.8	-2.8	-1.1	0.7	1.6	1.9
Minnesota, Minneapolis	0.9	0.9	1.8	0.6	0.1	-0.9	-3.2	-1.7	-0.3	0.1	1.3	0.9
Missouri, St. Louis	1.8	1.5	1.8	1.0	-0.5	-1.9	-4.0	-3.3	-1.3	0.5	1.5	1.6
Montana, Helena	0.6	0.6	0.8	-0.3	-0.8	-0.9	-4.3	-3.6	-1.5	-0.4	0.4	0.6
Nevada, Las Vegas	0	-0.3	-1.5	-3.2	-5.4	-7.4	-8.8	-7.6	-5.4	-2.9	-1.0	-0.2
New Mexico, Albuquerque	0	-0.2	-1.0	-2.3	-4.0	-5.7	-5.7	-4.8	-3.2	-1.7	-0.6	0
New York, New York	3.4	2.8	3.5	1.7	-0.2	-2.3	-3.1	-1.3	-0.2	1.1	3.0	3.3
North Carolina, Raleigh	3.1	2.9	2.5	0.4	-1.5	-3.1	-2.0	-1.7	-0.9	0.2	1.7	2.9
Ohio, Columbus	2.9	2.1	2.4	1.4	-0.4	-1.8	-3.0	-2.9	-1.3	0	1.7	2.2
Oklahoma, Tulsa	1.4	1.4	1.1	0.9	0.5	-2.1	-5.0	-4.6	-1.1	0.5	1.0	1.2
Ontario, Toronto	2.7	2.4	2.6	1.3	0	-1.7	-2.5	-2.0	-0.3	0.8	2.3	2.6
Oregon, Portland	7.3	5.5	4.6	1.1	-0.6	-2.0	-4.7	-3.9	-1.5	2.9	6.4	8.1
Pennsylvania, Philadelphia	3.0	2.4	2.9	1.2	-0.4	-2.1	-2.7	-1.5	-0.6	0.9	2.6	2.8
Quebec, Montreal	3.8	3.0	3.5	1.5	0	-1.3	-1.7	-1.3	0.6	2.0	3.5	3.6
Tennessee, Nashville	5.5	4.4	3.8	1.1	-1.2	-3.1	-3.4	-3.5	-1.7	-0.2	2.8	4.0
Texas, Dallas	1.4	1.3	-0.1	-0.2	-1.2	-4.6	-6.6	-6.4	-3.1	-0.8	0.6	1.4
Texas, El Paso	-0.1	-0.7	-1.8	-3.2	-4.6	-6.1	-5.8	-5.5	-3.6	-2.2	-1.2	-0.4
Texas, Houston	2.2	2.1	-0.2	-1.1	-2.4	-4.3	-4.0	-3.3	-1.7	-0.6	1.2	2.5
Utah, Salt Lake City	1.6	1.2	0.8	0.4	-2.0	-4.0	-6.3	-5.2	-3.0	-0.5	0.8	1.3
Washington, Seattle	5.2	3.9	2.8	0.4	0.5	-2.4	-4.1	-3.4	-1.1	2.3	4.8	5.8

SOURCE: *Rainfall Evapotranspiration Data*, The Toro Company, Minneapolis, Minn., 1966, 63 pp.

Table 9-2. Daily Water Use Rates Associated with Major Climatic Regions in North America

Climatic Region	Daily Water Use Rate	
	In./Day	In./Week
Coastal climates having considerable fog	0.10 - 0.15	0.7 - 1.0
Northern temperate region having moderate summer temperatures and humidities	0.12 - 0.15	0.9 - 1.0
Midtransitional region having high summer temperatures	0.15 - 0.27	1.0 - 1.9
Interior continental climate of the plains and interior valleys having hot, dry summers	0.25 - 0.35	1.8 - 2.5
Dry desert areas	0.30 - 0.45	2.1 - 3.1

certain degree from location to location within an individual golf course. Environmental factors controlling the evapotranspiration rate include the solar radiation level, surface temperature, atmospheric humidity, and wind velocity. Evapotranspiration rates are highest on sunny days characterized by high temperatures, low relative humidities, and a moderate wind velocity.

The actual water use rate depends on the soil water-retention capacity, rooting depth, and particular turfgrass species being grown. Highest water use rates typically occur during the summer, with comparatively low rates occurring during the spring and fall as well as during the winter in warm climates.

These water use rate data can be related to irrigation as follows. Using the midtransitional region water use rate of 0.15 to 0.27 inch per day (Table 9-2) and the fact that 1 acre-inch of water equals 27,154 gallons, a daily water requirement of 4,000 to 7,300 gallons of water per acre per day can be calculated.

Once estimates of the daily and seasonal water use patterns have been established, the average contribution expected from natural rainfall is determined. These data can be obtained from the long-term precipitation records of the Weather Bureau. The supplemental irrigation requirement can then be determined. Across the United States, the annual supplemental irrigation requirement may range from a maximum of 45 inches (114 centimeters) in arid regions with a twelve-month growing season to 6 inches (15 centimeters) in the northern cool humid regions having a six-month growing season.

WATER SOURCE

The first priority in development of an irrigation system is to secure an adequate water source in terms of both quantity and quality. Restrictions in the amount of water available per unit of time can alter key aspects of the system design. The presence of particulate matter may necessitate the incorporation of strainers, filters, sand separators, or holding tanks. Finally, the presence of sodium or soluble salts in a water source signals substantial long-term turfgrass maintenance and soil management problems. There are advantages to most water sources. The comparative benefits must be established for the particular golf course sites being considered. Thus, the following provides a basis of reference when considering alternative water sources.

Wells

Underground water sources usually prove excellent for turfgrass irrigation purposes. A common source of water for golf course irrigation is from one or more wells. Wells 20 to 50 feet (6 to 15 meters) in depth may supply ample quantities of water in some locations, while in others wells must be drilled 1,500 to 2,500 feet (457 to 762 meters) deep at substantial cost to obtain an adequate sustained capacity. The water yield (gallons per minute) and drawdown level of the well must be determined. Wells having a flow rate in the 500- to 1,000-gallons per minute range are generally considered adequate for an eighteen-hole automatic irrigation system, which typically requires 2,000 gallons per minute. In certain parts of the country, such as Colorado, it must be ascertained whether water drilling rights are held by the property under consideration and also what is the relative priority of water rights assigned to the site. In the future, this may become even more important throughout the arid and semiarid regions.

Wells usually have the advantages of being in close proximity to where the water is used and having less variability in yield than most surface sources. Well water is usually more uniform in temperature and soluble mineral content. On the other hand, wells are more expensive to develop than are surface water sources. Also, groundwater levels are dropping in many areas of the country owing to ever-increasing demands of agriculture, industry, and urban housing development. Finally, water quality problems occasionally are encountered in wells in certain locations. The most common concerns are high soluble salt and sodium levels. Salt intrusion into groundwater supplies is becoming a problem in certain coastal areas, such as Florida.

Well water can be pumped directly into the irrigation system or into a pond or reservoir and then into the irrigation system. With the former, some type of pressure regulator or relief valve arrangement must be incorporated into the system design. The latter is used when the water delivery rate of the well does not meet the water application rate demand of the irrigation system. Use of a reservoir also has the advantages of increasing pump efficiency and decreasing pumping costs. The latter is achieved by use of a smaller jockey pump when there is less demand on the system, such as during spot watering. However, when the demand increases and the line pressure falls below a preset level in the pressure control valve, the larger pump is activated automatically and the maximum design flow becomes available. If an irrigation pond or reservoir is used as an intermediate pumping source, it is preferable to locate it where it can also serve as an aesthetic attribute and/or water hazard which comes into play on one or more golf holes (Fig. 9-18).

Lakes, Ponds, and Reservoirs

Surface water from a large natural or man-made lake, pond, or reservoir, if of sufficient size, is an excellent water source for golf course irrigation purposes. The water may originate from springs and/or surface runoff from the surrounding drainage basin. The minimum size for a lake water source where there is no pumping from wells is 10 acre-feet in cool climates and 20 to 30 acre-feet in warm

Figure 9-18. Pond serving the dual purpose of a reservoir for irrigation water and an aesthetic hazard that influences the playing strategy of the golf hole.

climates for a fully irrigated eighteen-hole golf course (1 acre-foot equals 325,850 gallons or 1,233,342 liters). In relatively high rainfall areas, the minimum size of a pond with a good recovery rate could be as small as 5 acre-feet. It is preferable for the lake to be located entirely within the boundaries of the golf course property.

One of the main problems encountered in water from lakes, particularly with an automatic irrigation system, is particulate matter, such as algae, aquatic weeds, sand, organic debris, fish, frogs, and snails. The problem is usually greater in small reservoirs and lakes than in larger bodies of water. Aquatic herbicides are available that can be used to control water weeds and algae but are not harmful to wildlife. The problem is that these herbicides must be retained in the lake for several days to achieve adequate control. For this reason, many architects develop a two-lake system, both lakes being available as a water source for golf course irrigation. Each lake should be of sufficient size to meet irrigation needs for at least three to four days. Through this arrangement it is possible to isolate one reservoir for chemical aquatic weed control while the other serves as the water source for golf course irrigation. The severity of problems that can develop in the form of clogged nozzles, valves, and intake pipes as a result of a high concentration of debris and particulate material in the lake or reservoir should not be underestimated.

Perennial Flowing Streams and Rivers

Surface water from perennial flowing rivers and streams is acceptable if the rate and permanence of flow are reliable. The pattern of stream flow during wet or dry years must be determined. State hydrological engineers and the U.S. Geological Survey are potential sources for this type of information. The ebb flow should exceed the maximum potential demand for golf course irrigation by at least 50 percent. The flood stage should also be determined. In some cases, a permit may be required for use of water from streams and rivers. This is quite common if part of the water eventually enters a municipal water reservoir. To secure a permit, proof must be shown that ample flow will continue for downstream users.

A potential problem with this water source is water quality. Industrial plants located upstream may dump waste water that is potentially toxic to turfs into the stream. Recent actions by the Environmental Protection Agency are minimizing this type of problem. Another problem is the organic debris or solids frequently carried in flowing streams and rivers. Appropriate precautions to remove this objectionable particulate matter must be made to insure that the materials do not enter the irrigation system. Fouling, plugging, and abrasive wearing of the irrigation system components are minimized by construction of the proper type of water intake (Fig. 9-19).

Water from the river can be pumped directly into the irrigation system, if the flow rate is adequate, or into a pond on the golf course and then into the irrigation system, as in the method previously described for wells. Pumping directly from a flowing stream into the irrigation line generally is impractical because of difficulties encountered with stream velocity, changing water level, and varying amounts of debris, silt, and sand. Thus, best results are obtained by the construction of a pond or holding basin located at least 50 feet (15 meters) from the river. A channel is then constructed to connect the river to the pond. Typically, the pond depth should be from 6 to 8 feet (1.8 to 2.4 meters) below the mean low water level of the river. The pond must be of sufficient size to hold a six-day supply of irrigation water. Construction of this type of pond provides a water source relatively free of debris and sand compared with water pumped directly from the river.

Canals

Drainage canals serve as a source of water in parts of North America, such as Florida. Typically these water lanes are under public control, which increases the potential for restrictions to be placed on the quantity of water that can be used, particularly during periods of drought. Problems with debris and particulate material are similiar to those previously discussed for rivers.

Figure 9-19. Gravel filter intake unit that prevents particulate material from entering the irrigation system.

Water Utilities

Public or private water companies function as the source of water for many golf courses. A public source is less desirable than others because of the high potential for restricted water supplies during prolonged drought owing to the low priority assigned to golf courses. This could lead to disaster. Another disadvantage is that public water sources are becoming more and more expensive. Although the initial hookup cost is relatively modest in comparison with the cost of drilling a well or constructing a reservoir, the long-term expense of purchasing water can be quite high. An advantage of obtaining water from an outside agency is that it is delivered under pressure, and if the source is dependable, can be connected to the irrigation line at a considerable cost savings. Another advantage is the better quality and greater freedom from debris compared with perennial flowing streams and lakes.

Purchasing water from public utilities may be difficult to avoid in some areas of the country. For partial protection against potential water restrictions, construction of an intermediate reservoir into which the water is pumped, similar to that described for wells, may be advisable. Whether the water is pumped directly into the irrigation lines or through an intermediate storage reservoir, it is imperative that some type of antisiphon device be installed to prevent back flow of potentially contaminated water into a domestic water supply.

Effluent Water

A water source now being used for irrigating golf courses and which will be of increasing interest in the future is effluent water. Turfs can accept effluent water containing moderate levels of heavy metals and other elements which cannot be used in crop production because of potential problems in entering the human food chain or restricting crop yield. Thus, turfgrass irrigation offers one of the best approaches to disposing of certain types of effluent water. In addition, many golf courses are usually within reasonable delivery distance of treatment plants.

Sewage treatment plants have three levels of possible treatment. The primary level is concerned with removal of solids. The secondary level removes many dissolved impurities, while the tertiary level removes even more impurities. Each level is more expensive. In contrast, soils function as very good water filters and offer an economical means of advanced water treatment. Soils have a great capacity to handle organic wastes. Some sodic soils have actually been reclaimed through the use of sewage effluents having good inorganic qualities.

The reliability of an effluent water supply is a positive factor. In addition, the cost is fairly attractive compared with that of most alternatives, especially in arid regions. In some areas, effluent water is available at no cost or at only the pumping charge involved. In other areas, effluent water is being sold for from 25 to 35 percent of the price of domestic water. The cost of effluent water will probably rise in the future but still will remain economically attractive compared with that of other sources.

Chemical analyses of typical effluent water sources from fifteen California cities have shown that nitrogen, chiefly in the form of ammonia, is present in an amount of 60 to 100 pounds (27 to 45 kilograms) per acre-foot of water, while potassium is in the 220- to 240-pound (100- to 109-kilogram) range and phosphates between 60 and 100 pounds. Thus, each effluent water source may serve as a bonus source of beneficial nutrients for turfgrass growth and should be monitored for plant nutrient content.

Some chemicals present in effluent water can be injurious to turfgrass growth, and for this reason the water used for turfgrass irrigation should be monitored on a routine basis as required by Environmental Protection Agency regulations. (Usually tertiary-treated effluent is used for irrigation due to possible wind drift of spray.) The main chemical problems arise in the form of industrial wastes present in the effluent. These wastes include brines, heavy metals, and stable organic chemicals. The preferred approach in handling such wastes is for them to be separated from domestic sewage through zoning restrictions or a dual sewer system.

Another source of salts in effluent water is certain types of domestic water softeners. One cycle through an effluent treatment process removes approximately 300 parts per million total dissolved salts.

Five trace elements are of particular concern in effluent water quality and require close, frequent monitoring. Current guidelines suggest that effluent water used regularly for turf irrigation purposes should not contain more than 0.005 part per million cadmium, 0.2 part per million copper, 0.5 part per million nickel, 5 parts per million zinc, and 0.5 to 1 part per million boron. In addition, effluent water should be constantly monitored for possible contamination by mercury.

WATER RIGHTS

Simply stated, a so-called water right is the right to the use of water accorded by law. A review of water laws across North America reveals a crazy-quilt pattern of water rights. Each state has its own system of water laws. In some cases, conflicting laws are operative within the same state. Basically, the rights to surface water and to underground streams are subject to the law of water courses. These rights are governed by two conflicting doctrines — riparian and appropriation.

The *riparian doctrine* recognizes that the owner of land contiguous to a stream has certain rights to its flow. However, upstream location gives the riparian no preference for irrigation purposes. The right to use water for irrigation is coequal with the rights of all other riparian owners on the stream.

The *prior appropriation doctrine* accords a person who first takes water from a stream and makes use of it the right to continue diversion of the water. He or she has preference to all who come later.

Because of the great variability of laws governing development, retention, and use of surface waters and ground waters, further discussion of water rights is not warranted. The best advice for those planning a water source for an irrigation system is to seek the advice of competent local legal counsel.

WATER QUALITY

There are two major aspects of water quality from the standpoint of turfgrass irrigation. One involves the presence of particulate material, which affects the operating characteristics of the irrigation system itself. The second involves the presence of dissolved salts or chemicals, which are potentially detrimental to turfgrass growth either directly or indirectly through adverse effects on physical soil characteristics. Whenever possible, it is advisable that a clean water source for turfgrass irrigation be obtained to minimize the maintenance costs of the sprinkler system and to avoid adverse grass and/or soil effects which increase the difficulty of long-term turfgrass culture.

Figure 9-20. Manual strainer (*left*) and mechanical strainer (*right*) used to clean a raw water supply containing much debris. (Photo on right courtesy of David O. Miller, Saucon Valley Country Club, Bethlehem, Pa.)

Particulate Materials

Foreign debris present in the water supply results in inferior performance of the irrigation system and increased frequency of malfunctions. It necessitates frequent cleaning and flushing of the system plus servicing and cleaning of strainers and/or sand separators. The two main types of problem particulate debris are organic materials and sand.

Organic Materials. Organic materials usually are associated with a pond, lake, or river water source. Included are leaves, stems, sticks, algae, and relatively undecomposed peats, such as peat moss. These materials can cause clogging of orifices and sticking of valves, malfunctions that require costly flushing and cleaning.

Strainers. Where problems with organic materials in the water source are anticipated, installation of a strainer near the pumping station is advisable. Such a strainer usually is positioned aboveground to facilitate cleaning (Fig. 9-20). An important factor in strainer selection is the screen opening size, or mesh. It should be sufficiently small to remove the anticipated objectionable particulate material from the water source. The screen will generate a known pressure loss, which should be considered in the original design of the irrigation system. The frequency of strainer cleaning varies depending on the amount of irrigation water pumped and the amount of organic material present in the water source. The rate of strainer clogging can be monitored by means of pressure gauges installed on both sides of the strainer. Automatic self-cleaning strainers are also available. They should be considered for golf course irrigation systems which will be operated unattended for long periods and where organic debris in the water supply will be a continuing problem.

Sand. Water from wells and reservoirs with sandy bottoms can cause numerous problems, including sticking valves, eroded orifices, fouled orifices, sticking sprinklers, and accelerated wear of valves, impellers, and sprinkler heads. Thus it is imperative that facilities be installed for sand removal where a sand problem is anticipated. Sand separators are available designed specifically for the removal of such sand. The most common method of removing sand from water is by pumping the water into a covered holding tank or water reservoir. This approach is advantageous where pressure loss through strainers and sand separators is critical.

Holding Tank. A holding tank is basically a reservoir used to store water pumped from the original water source until it is pumped into the actual irrigation system. Use of a holding tank is particularly desirable when the water source contains objectionable quantities of organic material or sand. In case of a very dirty water source, the tank can be divided into sections, each separated by a removable screen. The screens vary in mesh size, the largest mesh being located at the end where the water enters and the mesh being reduced in size across the tank in increments of approximately ⅜-, ¼-, ⅛-, and ⅟₁₆-inch mesh. A screen system of this type must be cleaned at appropriate intervals. The size of the holding tank should be at least ten times the anticipated maximum flow rate for the system. Thus, an 800-gallon (3,028-liter)-per-minute maximum flow requirement would dictate an 8,000-gallon (30,280-liter) holding tank or reservoir.

Introduced Particulate Contaminates. Particulate matter can be introduced into the irrigation system as a result of carelessness during the original installation or during subsequent repair of the pipe lines. In addition, it can be introduced into public utility water as a result of rust particles breaking loose from inside cast-iron and steel pipe. The latter situation can only be corrected through installation of strainers at the golf course. The best prevention for particulate matter problems when an irrigation system is installed is proper flushing of the water distribution lines before the irrigation heads are connected and the system put into operation. Thus, good-quality workmanship is essential during this phase of installation. Similarly, it is important during repair of distribution lines to avoid the introduction of any particulate material. If some debris has been allowed to enter the system during repair, it is important that it be flushed out before the irrigation system is returned to its normal operational level.

Dissolved Salts and Chemicals

Essentially all irrigation water contains some dissolved salts and chemicals. Many of the soluble salts are beneficial to turfgrass growth, but some can be phytotoxic. The rate at which salts accumulate to undesirable levels in the soil depends on the concentration of soluble salts in the irrigation water and the physical/chemical characteristics of the soil in question. The major salt problems of concern in regard to water quality are the (a) total concentration of soluble salts, (b) relative proportion of sodium and bicarbonate to calcium and magnesium, and (c) amount of boron in the water.

Salinity. Most water of acceptable quality for turfgrass irrigation contains from 100 to 1,000 parts per million soluble salts. Soluble salt levels above 2,000 parts per million are very undesirable and can be directly injurious to turfgrass shoots. It is suggested that water used for turfgrass irrigation have a maximum soluble salt concentration of 800 to 1,000 parts per million unless the soil has exceptional permeability and good subsoil drainage characteristics. These two criteria permit the turf manager to leach excessive soluble salt concentrations from the root zone by periodic, intense irrigations.

The total concentration of soluble salts in irrigation water and soil is expressed in terms of *electrical conductivity* (EC). This type of water quality information can be obtained from analyses made at either state or reputable commercial laboratories. An EC of water of 0.75 mhos per centimeter is the approximate upper limit for growing turfgrasses without potential for problems which necessitate costly specialized adjustments in the cultural program. In contrast, a soil having an EC analysis (EC $\times$ 10^3) below 4 is considered quite satisfactory for growing most turfgrasses. Soil with an EC reading over 15 will support only a very sparse population of turfgrass plants.

Irrigation waters have been divided into four classes with respect to electrical conductivity. The classification is based on average conditions of soil, drainage, climate, and salt tolerance.

Class 1 (C1)—Low-salinity water (EC of 0.1 to 0.25 mhos/cm). Safe to use on practically all grasses and soils with little chance of saline problems developing. Some leaching is desirable to keep soluble salts moving downward through the soil profile. Leaching may be insufficient in soils of extremely low permeability under ordinary practices; these soils should be checked occasionally.

Class 2 (C2)—Medium-salinity water (EC of 0.251 to 0.75 mhos/cm). Can be used to irrigate relatively permeable soils and grasses with medium salt tolerance. Special practices for salinity control not required unless insufficient leaching occurs.

Class 3 (C3)—High-salinity water (EC of 0.751 to 2.25 mhos/cm). Should not be used on soils with inadequate subsurface drainage. Use of salt-tolerant grasses should be considered and soil-water management practices maintained in cases where this water is used. Adequate subsurface drainage should be installed if saline spots occur which cannot be eliminated by normal leaching procedures.

Class 4 (C4)—Very high-salinity water (EC above 2.251 mhos/cm). Should not be used for irrigation under ordinary circumstances. Occasional use is possible under special conditions of permeable soil, adequate subsurface drainage, and application of excessive irrigation water to assure adequate leaching of salts. Only grasses with a very high salt tolerance should be considered.

Chlorides and Sulphates. Chlorides and sulphates in irrigation water contribute to its total soluble salt concentration. Excessive concentrations of chlorides and sulphates can cause turfgrass tip burn and even total kill of the shoots. Concentrations of 250 to 400 parts per million are considered undesirable for irrigation of some salt-sensitive grasses. Fortunately, chloride and sulphate salts are quite soluble and thus can be leached from well-drained soils if there is a subsurface drainage system.

Boron. Boron is an essential nutrient for plant growth but is required in very minimal amounts. It is water soluble and is found in many water sources used for irrigation. Boron can become toxic to turfgrasses if the concentration in the irrigation water exceeds 1 to 2 parts per million. An additional problem is accumulation, since boron can form chemical complexes that are not readily leached from the soil.

Sodium. The presence of sodium in irrigation water is of great concern in turfgrass culture. The rate at which soil adsorbs sodium from water is known as the *sodium adsorption ratio* (SAR). This ratio is used for classifying the sodium hazard of water sources. Water with an SAR above 10 is likely to produce a sodium buildup in the soil unless gypsum is applied periodically. Injury may occur on sodium-sensitive plants owing to sodium accumulation within the plant tissue without the sodium having similar harmful effects on the physical properties of the soil. The effect of sodium in the deflocculation of clay soils is particularly critical on intensively trafficked turfgrass areas because of the decrease in aeration, water infiltration, and soil water percolation.

Irrigation waters have been divided into four classes in terms of the SAR. The classification is based primarily on the effect of sodium on soil physical conditions, i.e., on average conditions of soil, drainage, climate, sodium tolerance, and low salinity level.

S1—Low-sodium water (SAR of 10 or less). Can be used for irrigation on almost all soils with little danger that the exchangeable sodium will accumulate to harmful levels.

S2—Medium-sodium water (SAR of 10.1 to 18). Presents an appreciable sodium hazard in fine-textured soils possessing a high cation exchange capacity. The hazard is especially great under low leaching conditions unless gypsum is present in the soil. Can be used on coarse-textured or organic soils that have good permeability.

S3—High-sodium water (SAR of 18.1 to 26). Can produce harmful levels of exchangeable sodium in most soils. Such soils require special management, including provisions for good drainage, high leaching, and possibly even additions of organic matter. Soils high in gypsum may not develop harmful levels of exchangeable sodium from this irrigation water. Chemical amendments may be required to replace the exchangeable sodium developing in soils, with the exception that use of such amendments may not be feasible if high-sodium waters also have a very high salinity level.

S4—Very high-sodium water (SAR above 26.1). Generally unsatisfactory for irrigation purposes. The only exceptions would be at low and perhaps even medium salinity levels and where the solution of calcium from the soil or use of gypsum or other amendments makes the use of this water feasible.

Interpreting Salinity and Sodium Hazards. The classifications of individual salinity and sodium hazards in irrigation water just presented are quite simplified. Proper interpretation is much more complex. An integrated diagrammatic classification is shown in Figure 9-21. It should be used in conjunction with the two salinity and sodium water classification systems previously described. A number of variations from these guidelines need to be taken into account. Thus, water quality analyses should be interpreted by a qualified professional.

The complexity of interpretation is illustrated as follows. Irrigation water sometimes dissolves sufficient calcium from calcareous soils to decrease the sodium hazard appreciably. This should be taken into account in the use of C1-S3 and C1-S4 water classifications. For calcareous soils with high pH values or for noncalcareous soils, the medium status of waters in classes C1-S3, C1-S4, and C2-S4 may be improved by the addition of gypsum to the water. Similarly, it may be beneficial to add gypsum to soils on a periodic basis if C2-S2 and C2-S3 water classifications are used.

Preferably, water quality problems should be analyzed and solved on an individual basis after an assessment of all related factors. The concentration of individual constituents must be known before water quality can be evaluated. In the case of sodium as well as of several other salts, the indirect effects on the soil and the direct effects on grass growth must be considered. There is also the question of combined effects from several salts. For example, high concentrations of both sodium and bicarbonates are especially undesirable. Similarly, it is difficult to set precise limits on the maximum acceptable sodium level because its reaction is influenced by the quantity of calcium and magnesium in the soil.

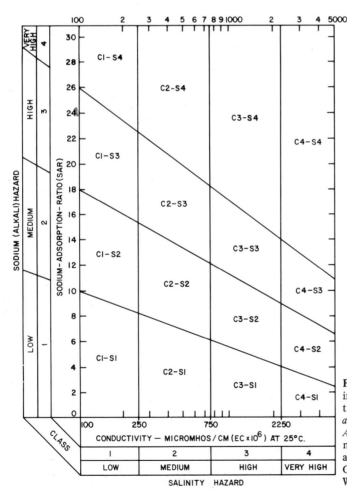

Figure 9-21. Diagram for the integrated classification of irrigation waters. (From *Diagnosis and Improvement of Saline and Alkali Soils*. 1954. U.S. Department of Agriculture, Agricultural Handbook No. 60. U.S. Government Printing Office, Washington, D.C.)

For these reasons, it is best that a soil and water quality chemist/specialist be consulted for proper interpretation of water and soil analysis reports.

INSTALLATION

A well-designed irrigation system composed of good-quality components will not function correctly unless properly installed. Irrigation systems are installed under two distinctly different situations. One involves new construction sites, while the second involves an established turf on an operating golf course. In each case some unique problems can be encountered.

Selecting a Contractor

Once the design engineer has completed the plans, detailed working drawings, specifications, and bid documents, a contract can be let to accomplish the work. Some irrigation installation companies specialize in large golf course projects. In the case of new golf course construction, the irrigation installation company may bid as a subcontractor under the overall general contractor previously selected by competitive bidding. The irrigation installation company would be the prime contractor for installation of a new irrigation system on an established golf course.

The design engineer is usually responsible for preparation of the bid documents. This is followed by invitations to bid and specific instructions to bidders. In some cases, the bid procedure may call for prequalification. The preselection of qualified bidders involves an assessment of their overall capabilities and the quality of work performed on previous projects. The basic steps in the bidding procedure and selection of a contractor are the same as those for a golf course construction contractor, which are discussed in detail in chapter 2.

In some instances, the golf course management may choose to install an irrigation system on an "in-house" basis. This usually is done when there are budget restrictions and when the golf course superintendent has sufficient knowledge and experience to successfully install a quality irrigation system. If this approach is utilized, it is generally advisable that an independent design engineer experienced in golf course irrigation systems be employed. The design engineer's responsibilities would be to develop a set of accurate design plans, the specifications, and a list of materials; to advise on associated technical needs; and to make periodic visits during the actual installation to insure that the project is being properly executed. In this way, an irrigation system can be installed on an existing golf course over an extended period as funds become available and with minimal disruption of play. Usually the superintendent will need to employ some supplemental labor to accomplish such a project with efficiency and in a reasonable length of time.

Contract. Preparation of the contract for installation of an irrigation system is usually the responsibility of the design engineer. The contract includes descriptive articles on the (a) contract documents, (b) installation work involved, (c) time of commencement and completion of the work, (d) sum payable for the work, (e) progress payments, and (f) final payment. It is very important that the contract specify the time of commencement and completion of the work for installation of an irrigation system on an established, operating golf course. The contract may also include specifications as to how much sod removal and open trenching will be allowed at any one time. It is not unusual for the specifications to call for disruption of no more than one golf hole at a time on an established course. Information concerning contract documents and specifications are discussed in considerable detail in chapter 2. The principles involved in the contract for irrigation system installation do not differ greatly.

Installation Procedure

A quality installation of a golf course irrigation system is dependent on accurate design plans and specifications. The plans should be scaled accurately; show significant topographic variations; delineate physical features such as roads, buildings, trees, and rock outcroppings; and accurately depict property line boundaries beyond which watering should not be planned. A detailed soil map will assist the installation contractor in anticipating problems that might be encountered during trenching, for example, problems related to rock outcroppings, high density soils, peat bogs, poorly drained depressions, swampy areas, or stony soil types.

The installation contractor can then proceed to procure the resources needed based on the specifications. This is critical, since shortages of certain irrigation components are not uncommon and four to eight months may be needed to obtain these in some locations. The contractor should also assess specific equipment and labor requirements and develop plans for their procurement so the project can be completed within the specified time period. On completion of these preparatory planning stages, the actual irrigation system installation can be initiated. Major phases in an irrigation system installation project are illustrated diagrammatically in Figure 9-22.

Installation Inspector. The installation of an irrigation system on an eighteen-hole golf course is very complex and has many possibilities for error. Employment of a full-time, independent irrigation installation inspector throughout the project life is advisable, especially for a major project. It is imperative that the individual selected be fully knowledgeable and experienced in the principles of hydraulics and design engineering, be able to read detailed technical plans and specifications, and be experienced in civil engineering. The inspector should study the plans and specifications thoroughly before the installation project is initiated. The irrigation inspector is responsible for certifying that all installation activities are performed in accordance with the design plans and specifications. The inspector may be employed by the golf course management or by the design engineer representing the client. The installation inspector should be careful to avoid an inflexible attitude with respect to trivial construction details and yet be firm in insuring that all design plans and specifications critical to effective performance and functional longevity of the system being installed are executed.

Installation Planning. System installation must be in accordance with the designer's plans and specifications. Preinstallation planning can be particularly important in insuring that an irrigation system is installed on a new golf course in time for optimum planting or is completed on an existing golf course in the shortest possible time to minimize disruption of play. Development of a construction flow plan is quite helpful in completing installation as efficiently as possible with minimal delays. Such a plan can be particularly important in procurement of materials. Plastic piping and large pumps have been in short supply at times, with delays of up to six months in filling orders. It is usually the responsibility of the installer to be certain that all codes are followed and that the necessary permits, application for water connection, and related preliminary arrangements are complied with before initiation of the installation project. Finally, the installer should locate any existing underground utility lines or similiar hazards that might complicate installation of the irrigation system.

If the installation involves conversion of an existing irrigation system from manual to automatic, the best approach is initiation of conversion at the site of the master controller and/or power supply. This enables the installer to make an operations check and pressure test of each section as the changeover is completed. Otherwise, testing and use of completed sections cannot be done because the power supply is to be installed at a later stage in the installation. In other words, once the manual system is converted, no water is available in the system without the proper power supply.

Pump System. Pumps must be mounted on a sturdy base, which in most cases is concrete with a rubber pad positioned between the concrete base and the pump mountings to function in absorbing vibrations during normal operation. The design specifications and installation of a pumping system should be the responsibility of an expert in the field. The more complex systems typically required for golf course irrigation operations include a series of pumps and motors, jockey pump, check valve, gate valve, pressure-reducing valve, automatic vent valve, bypass control valve, pressure gauges, pressure switches, drain valve, shutoff valve, pressure tank, strainers, and an elaborate electrical control system.

A recent development is the preassembled pumping station designed and built to the specific needs of a given golf course irrigation system (Fig. 9-23). The station involves not only a network of pumps and motors but also the jockey pump, valves, gauges, pressure switches, strainers, and electrical control system needed in a complex modern golf course pumping station. In many locations in the country no

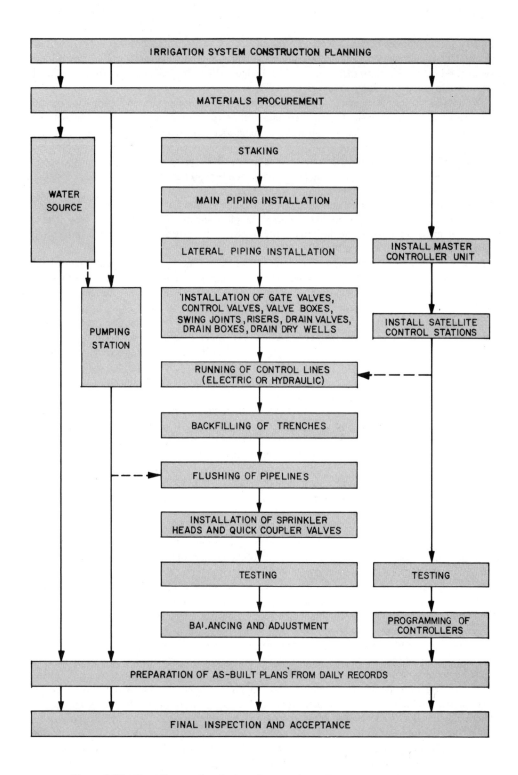

Figure 9-22. Flow diagram for the installation of a golf course irrigation system.

Figure 9-23. A preassembled pumping station. (Photo courtesy of Pumping Systems Incorporated, Dallas, Tex.)

qualified experts are available to successfully design and install a golf course pumping station. Thus, the prefabricated pumping station is a particularly attractive option, since on-site set up can be accomplished with minimum professional expertise. Installation involves setting the station in place on a standard concrete base, connecting it to the irrigation system water source and power supply, and ultimately pressure testing, adjusting, and activating it.

In addition to the concrete pump mounting, many pumping stations are protected by a pump house, which is a permanently constructed structure with a concrete floor plus concrete block walls (Fig. 9-24). The pump house serves to protect the pumping station from damage and weathering associated with climatic stresses, animals, and vandalism. The pump house should be well louvered to provide adequate ventilation for heat generated from the motors. Where a pump house is not employed, the specifications should call for pump motors to be waterproof.

There can be great variation in the water intake arrangement associated with a pumping station. It can be a simple suction pipe extending into the water source with the appropriate protection, a pump pit in the case of a vertical turbine pump, or a direct connection to a municipal water source with backflow preventer and a simple booster pump (Fig. 9-25). The size and shape of a pump pit will vary depending on the type of water supply, quantity of water to be pumped, and need for dissipating turbulence within the pit. The suction intake should be positioned in the midzone. If the intake is too near the bottom or surface of the water source, turbulence is created that can draw soil, debris, and air into the pumping system.

Staking. The first step in actual installation is the layout or staking of the system, including the locations of main lines, sprinkler heads, valves, and other key features. Staking must be done with exacting fashion so that sprinkler head spacings are uniform and the original design specifications are followed. Accurate staking is accomplished with measuring tapes and surveyors' instruments.

Staking the location of each sprinkler head enables the installer to make sure the design matches the area where the system is to be installed. Any errors in the original plan will become apparent at this time and can be corrected before trenching is initiated. Correction involves moving stakes or even adding extra sprinkler heads. Significant changes should be discussed and approved by the designer and client. The stakes also act as a guide for the actual trenching operation. It is advisable for the designer of the system to supervise the actual staking.

Trenching. Trench routing is determined by the design layout, including the zoning arrangement. The preferred trenching plan should involve the maximum number of long cuts and least number of cross-overs. Trench width is dictated by the pipe size and the space needed for workmen to accomplish

Figure 9-24. A permanently constructed pump house.

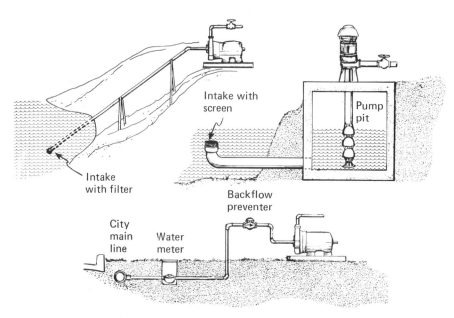

Figure 9-25. Three types of water intake arrangement: a simple suction pipe extending into the water source with the appropriate protection (*top left*), a pump pit for a vertical turbine pump (*center right*), and a direct connection to a municipal water source with a backflow preventer and booster pump (*bottom*).

the installation. The trench depth varies depending on the (a) height specified for the sprinkler riser assembly, (b) soil depth needed to provide protection against freezing, and (c) slope needed to provide proper drainage for winterizing pipelines. The width and depth of the trench should be no greater than absolutely necessary to minimize the amount of soil dug, facilitate soil compaction during backfilling, and minimize disturbances to any existing turf.

A wide range of trenching machines is available (Fig. 9-26). Properly dug trenches are on grade and on line, as shown in the plan and subsequent staking. The trench bottom should be smooth, free of rocks, and in a continuous line at the specified grade. A smooth trench bottom is needed to fully support the pipe. Wedging or blocking of pipe is not advisable. Where the bottom of a trench is variable due to the presence of rocks or a hard impermeable soil, approximately 2 to 3 inches (5 to 7.6 centimeters) of sand or stone-free soil should be added to the bottom of the trench before the pipe is installed.

When pipe is to be installed under an established turf, the trenching operation should be done with as little disruption as possible. The usual procedure is to cut, roll, lift, and place the sod near the planned trench for replacement after backfilling is completed. In some cases, a plastic sheet is laid parallel to the trench in such a way that excavated soil falls on the sheet. This greatly facilitates the backfilling procedure and subsequent cleanup. Occasionally the topsoil is segregated from the subsoil by making two passes with the trenching machine and throwing the soil to opposite sides. This procedure allows the topsoil to be replaced on top. A good installation contractor does not cut sod and trench too far in advance of the follow-up installation activities. By proper coordination of trenching and subsequent laying and backfilling, installation can be accomplished with minimum disruption in daily play.

Pipe Laying. Storage, handling, and eventual placement of pipe in the trench should be done with great care. Most manufacturers provide suggestions relative to how a particular pipe is to be handled and installed and the joints assembled. Careful lowering of pipe into place, proper handling of joints, and care in keeping soil out of lines are all characteristics of a quality, experienced irrigation installer. Failure to take precautions to avoid getting dirt into the irrigation lines may translate into months or even years of problems in debris removal from nozzles and remote control valves plus the likelihood of an inferior irrigation pattern in the interim.

The installation is normally started at the water source. The sequence involves installation of a main line, then the valves, lateral lines, and sprinkler-riser assembly. Cement, asbestos, and heavy-duty plastic pipe must be laid on a sand base free of rocks or similar hard objects. It is important that thrust blocks be placed at all ells and tees, as specified by the manufacturer and design engineer (Fig. 9-27). Precautions must be taken to allow for anticipated temperature expansion and contraction in the piping. Depending on the particular type of pipe, this may involve simple snaking of pipe from side to side in the trench or installation of expansion joints. The bell and ring connection used in asbestos-cement and certain polyvinyl-chloride piping compensates for expansion.

Figure 9-26. A trenching machine in operation.

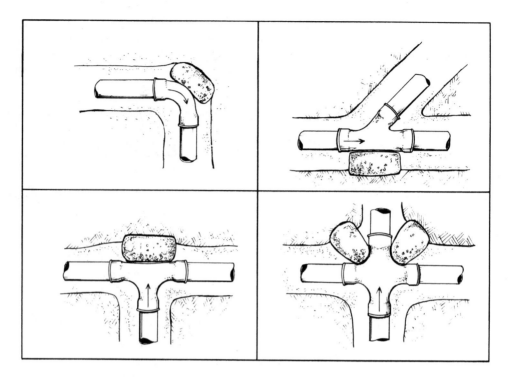

Figure 9-27. Diagram showing proper use of a thrust block.

Pipe Pulling. A recent innovation in pipe installation on established turf is the method termed pipe pulling. The procedure involves digging holes at the sites where sprinkler heads, tees, and control valves are to be placed. The pipe is then pulled underground through the previously dug holes by means of a vibrating mole-plow attachment (Fig. 9-28). The pipe is cut at the specified location in each hole and the appropriate fittings installed. This pipe-pulling technique is less expensive and presents fewer problems in disruption of the turf and associated play than does trenching. However, difficulties may be encountered in dense, fine-textured soils and in rocky soils where excessive abrasion or grooving of the pipe may occur. It is also difficult with this method to install pipe on a specified grade so that the pipe can be gravity drained to avoid freezing damage.

Installing Risers and Valves. It is generally advisable that the sprinkler riser or riser assembly be installed at the same time the pipe is installed to minimize the chance of soil entering the piping. A swing-joint arrangement is used, since it allows flexibility in future sprinkler head cap adjustments because of changing surface grade and it absorbs shocks when golf carts and heavy equipment pass over the sprinkler head. Sprinkler heads should not be attached to the risers until after all piping has been flushed clean of dirt and debris that may have entered the system during installation.

Gate valves, control valves, and drain valves are also installed in coordination with pipe laying. Each should be installed as outlined in the design engineer's specifications and in accordance with the manufacturer's recommendations. Most remote control valves are also designed for direct underground burial. However, the installation of valve boxes and drain boxes is advisable. In the case of larger installations with numerous valves, it is usually best that as large a number of valves as possible be grouped in a box to facilitate location and access for servicing.

Drain valves, either automatic or manual, are then installed as specified in the design plan. They should be installed at all low points in the system and should include a sump pit in the case of small short

Figure 9-28. A pipe-pulling machine in operation (*top*) and close-up of the pipe entry point (*bottom*).

lines (Fig. 9-29) or a large pit connected to a subsurface drainage system for large mains and longer pipe lines. Automatic drain valves should be installed exactly as specified by the manufacturer, including at the proper angle, and should not be positioned on the far end of a line due to problems with dirt accumulating on the inlet screen.

Installing Control Lines. Control lines should be run in the pipe trenches whenever possible. Either electric wire or hydraulic tubing is run by the most direct route from the control point to the appropriate valves in the trenches along with the piping. The control lines should be installed in accordance with the engineer's and manufacturer's specifications and carefully checked to see that all connections are secure. As with piping, it is advisable that an allowance for expansion and contraction be included at 100-foot (30-meter) intervals, usually in the form of loops. The control lines should be installed in such

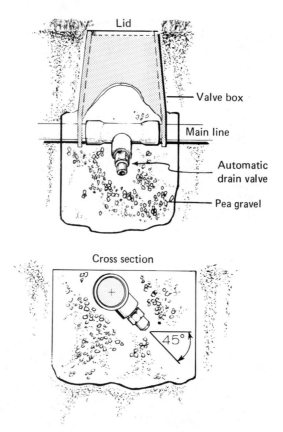

Figure 9-29. Diagram of a drain valve-sump pit arrangement.

a manner as not to crush or kink them and deep enough to avoid disruption from cultivation practices, such as coring and slicing. Electric control lines must have waterproof connections.

Controllers. There are two basic types of controllers: wall-mounted and pedestal. The wall-mounted type usually involves a master control panel located in the operations office of the maintenance building. This master controller is commonly a preconstructed package unit. Thus, installation involves attachment to the wall followed by hookup of the electrical power source, the control lines to all zone satellite controllers, and other possible accessories, such as a rain shut-off switch.

Associated with the master controller is a series of satellite controllers positioned at strategic locations around the golf course so that an operator can view all areas under control of each satellite. This allows the irrigation maintenance specialist to readily check the operational status of all components in the system on a regular basis. The satellite controller typically is mounted on a pedestal installed on a concrete base. A template or similar-type mount is embedded in the concrete at the time it is laid to provide a connection point for the pedestal cabinet. Also positioned in the concrete slab are two underground conduits extending directly down and then horizontally outward as 3-inch (7.8-centimeter) elbows (Fig. 9-30). The electrical wire or hydraulic lines can then be pulled through the conduit upward into each satellite controller.

Accessories associated with the satellite controller may include a heat source for protection against freezing, a master switch, a safety device in case of power failure, and a hookup for the electrical supply to the satellite controller. Any satellite or wall-mounted controller located outside should be weather-resistant to provide protection for the operational panel and clock. All controllers

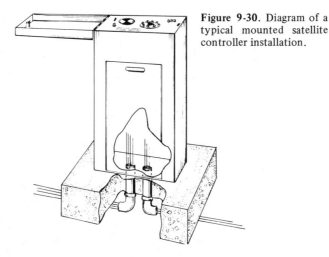

Figure 9-30. Diagram of a typical mounted satellite controller installation.

should be grounded to the earth to eliminate the potential hazard of an electrical shock. Installation of a lightning suppression device should be seriously considered and is essential in areas where lightning is common.

Partial Backfilling. Sand or stone-free fine-textured soil should be utilized in partial backfilling of the trench following installation of piping and associated irrigation equipment. The pipe should be covered to a depth of 3 to 4 inches (7.6 to 10 centimeters) so that pipe damage from rocks and other debris during backfilling and compaction operations is minimal. It is generally advisable that joints or fittings associated with the main line not be covered so they may be checked for possible leakage. Initial backfilling should be done in the cool part of the day, especially in warm climates, to minimize the effects of heat expansion.

Line Flushing. After the piping has been installed, connected to the pumping station/main water source, and covered with sufficient soil to prevent movement, the pumping station should be activated and sufficient water passed through all piping, fittings, and risers to insure that dirt, pipe chips, and other debris present in the lines have been flushed out.

Installing Sprinkler Heads. Immediately following line flushing, the sprinkler heads are installed to minimize the chance of extraneous material entering the piping. Often the sprinkler heads are attached while line flushing is in progress. The procedure involves connecting the sprinkler head closest to the valve first and then connecting heads progressively out along the line from the valve. This approach increases the pressure and flow on the outermost reaches of the line, thus facilitating better flushing of debris.

Following their connection, the sprinkler heads should be set to the desired level. In the case of an existing turf, the sprinkler head cap normally is set flush with the soil level. In the case of new construction, the sprinkler heads usually are installed slightly above the projected rough grade level. They are left to operate in this position until initial turf establishment has been achieved and then lowered to the more permanent finished grade after most of the soil settling has occurred. A triple swing joint in a riser connection facilitates this operation.

Pressure Testing. Design specifications may call for testing of the main lines at pressures exceeding the normal operating pressure of the system. This is the portion of the system that is usually under constant pressure. Partial backfilling is required before pressure testing to insure that the pipe sections remain anchored in place after pressure activation. The joints are generally left uncovered to detect possible leaks. Pressure testing may involve a simple visual inspection for leakage at exposed joints or a more comprehensive assessment in which the system is brought to a given pressure and then the pressure and water loss over a specified time are monitored.

Figure 9-31. Mechanical backfilling unit in operation.

Finish Backfilling. After successful line flushing and pressure testing, the remainder of the pipe joints are manually covered with stone-free sand or fine-textured soil. Then the remainder of the trench is backfilled, usually by mechanical means (Fig. 9-31). The subsoil should be backfilled first, then the topsoil. Most fine-textured soils require some type of mechanical firming, such as use of a powered vibrating tamper. If mechanical firming is done, an effort should be made to duplicate a degree of compaction comparable with that of the original material. Uniform settling of the backfilling material is enhanced by frequent watering during backfilling.

Backfilling should bring the soil back to the original surface level with a slightly higher rise in the center of the trench, which is a provision for anticipated future settling. Where the sod is to be transplanted back onto the site, final backfilling should be to a slightly lower subgrade to accommodate replacement of the sod at the original turfed surface level. If the trench is to be resodded, proper plant-bed preparation of the surface soil zone should be accomplished prior to transplanting.

Adjustment and Balancing. At this point, any required final adjustments and balancing of the total system should be accomplished to achieve the desired operating pressure and water distribution. This includes final adjustment in the sprinkler head cap to a surface height that conforms to the surrounding conditions. Final testing also includes setup and operation of the controller through an entire cycle to confirm that the system is fully operational.

As-Built Plan Preparations. As work progresses through the staking, trenching, and installation phases, some changes in the original design plan are inevitable. All such changes should be noted on a daily basis on a preliminary as-built plan. It is critical that this be done daily rather than at some later date. Specific changes that should be noted include the positioning of piping, gate valves, remote control valves, quick couplers, control tubing and wiring, domestic water lines, and drain valves. After successful testing and programming of the entire system, a final as-built plan must be prepared with complete accuracy. It is then submitted to the client, who should keep it as a permanent record and future reference for use in maintenance, winterizing, repairs, or additions to the system. It is important to note that the as-built plan usually differs from the original design engineer's plan.

MAINTENANCE

A new irrigation system, once installed and made fully operative, has an initial period of minimal maintenance. However, long-range plans must be made in terms of budget, labor, and an adequate repair inventory to maintain the system in its originally designed operational state. As with any complex mechanical device, an automatic irrigation system requires constant attention in terms of adjustment, maintenance, and repair if it is to function properly. Such components as the automatic controllers, control valves, rotary-head drive mechanisms, nozzles, hydraulic or electrical control lines, screens, fittings, and pumping system are prone to the effects of weathering, rodent damage, wear, vandalism, and damage from improper use.

Thus, a full-time worker is often required in the warm climatic regions to maintain the complex components of an automatic irrigation system. The individual must be properly trained and fully knowledgeable in upkeep and repair of the system to keep it functional.

A complete visual check of all sprinkler heads and an operational check of the associated controller systems should be conducted at a five- to seven-day interval. Some operators also make a brief daily check during the syringe cycle. Use of this maintenance check system establishes that the control system is working properly and, if not, gives an indication of what repairs or adjustments are needed. It also indicates to the operator the type of water distribution that is being achieved both in terms of the duration the sprinkler runs in relation to the program set at the controller and the pattern of water dispersement from the sprinkler.

Nozzles should be checked periodically for excessive wear and replaced as needed. It is also important that a check be made daily for sticking rotary sprinkler heads and leaky valves that cause low head drainage. Similarly, screens and filters must be checked and cleaned periodically, with the specific interval determined by the amount of debris and sand introduced from the water source. Appropriate adjustments or repairs are made whenever a component of the system is not functioning properly.

An irrigation system maintenance checklist can be used as a method of repair control (Fig. 9-32). Whenever a problem is identified, it is noted on the checklist and a card is given to the individual in charge of irrigation repairs. Appropriate adjustments or repairs are then made. Once the problem is corrected and the system made functional, the card is signed, dated, and placed in a permanent file. This card system facilitates communications on the specific repair needs and provides a permanent record from which operating efficiency and repair costs can be ascertained.

To insure that the irrigation system can be repaired quickly when breakdowns occur, it is important that an adequate inventory of spare parts needed for repairs be stocked. The inventory should include at least two spare controller timing mechanisms; a working supply of remote control valves, electric lines or hydraulic tubing, sprinkler heads, and associated parts; a range in sizes and types of piping utilized on the course for repair of breaks, plus the associated couplings for pipe repair; and a few selected sizes of gate valves. The appropriate types of specialized irrigation repair tools dictated by the particular system utilized are also needed.

Winterizing

In most of the northern cool regions of North America, the irrigation system must be drained to prevent pipe breakage during the winter, assuming the potential soil frost depth extends below the depth of pipe burial. The irrigation system should be drained prior to the first severe freeze. The preferred method is for irrigation lines to be blown out with an air compressor. The drain outlets are positioned over a gravel sump or dry well, which is preferably connected to a drain line system.

The actual procedure to follow in blowing water out of an irrigation and pumping system may vary from the following outline depending on the type of equipment involved. If any aspects are unclear, it is

---

IRRIGATION CONTROL CHECKLIST

DATE _____   ZONE _____   COURSE _____

Valve or Head No.	Set Time	Actual Time	Spray Pattern	Nozzle Pressure	Rotation	Comments
1						
2						
3						
4						
5						

Figure 9-32. Irrigation system maintenance checklist.

critical that the design engineer for the irrigation system and the manufacturer of the pumping system be asked to provide a detailed written procedure for draining and winterizing the systems.

Drainage of Irrigation System

1. A week before the scheduled draining of the system, the superintendent should study the irrigation drawings and prepare a sequence of steps planned for the orderly drainage of all main and lateral irrigation lines.
2. Turn off the water supply, open all drain outlets that flow directly into drain lines or similar outlets, insert quick coupler keys in the high and low points in each line to facilitate air replacement as water drains from the lines, and secure or arrange for the rental of an appropriate-sized air compressor.
3. Connect the appropriate-sized compressor into the main irrigation line near the water source. Irrigation lines 4 to 8 inches (10 to 20 centimeters) in diameter can be blown out most readily by means of two 125- to 250-cubic-feet-per-minute (3.54- to 7.08-cubic-meters-per-minute) air compressors, while systems with 3-inch (7.6-centimeter) diameter lines or less can be blown out relatively quickly with one 125-cubic-feet-per-minute air compressor. Allow the compressor to build up pressure before opening any drainage outlets.
4. Open each remote control valve, beginning at the water source on the main line and then the lateral line nearest the water source. Allow sprinklers to drain until only air comes out. Then close the valve. Continue this procedure to the end of the line and then repeat the same steps on each more distant lateral off the main line until all water has been removed from each lateral, riser, and sprinkler head.
5. Repeat step 4 to insure full water removal from all irrigation lines. Again, start from the water source and work toward the ends of each of the outlying laterals. Open each drain outlet slightly and blow out any remaining water, close for a short period, and then reopen to establish that all water has been removed.
6. Close the drain lines to prevent surface water from entering the irrigation lines through the drain valve during periods of winter thawing.

Drainage of Pumping System

1. Study the water flow route through the piping, gate valves, check valves, and related portions of the pumping system, being careful to identify all drain outlets.
2. Drain pump volutes by removing the bottom plug or opening the drain cock.
3. Drain or remove the suction drop pipe.
4. Drain pressure-reducing valves by blowing out or loosening the cover bolts.
5. Turn all pump motors off and cover motors to protect windings against possible rodent damage.
6. Drain pressure gauges, switches, tank sight glasses, tank air chargers, and similiar equipment that is subject to freezing.
7. Make sure all oil- or grease-lubricated bearings are well covered with lubricant.
8. Cover any exposed metal, such as the shaft, with protective lubricant to eliminate corrosion.
9. Finally, program automatic valves to operate once a day for five minutes to prevent the solenoid plunger from sticking and reduce moisture in the solenoid coil and automatic controller contacts.

OPERATION

The objective of any golf course irrigation system is to enable the superintendent to irrigate the course in a manner that provides as close to optimum playing conditions as is possible. It should be noted that optimum playing conditions and optimum turfgrass conditions are usually not the same. All too often, golf courses in the United States are overirrigated from the standpoint of optimum golfing conditions. This is due to the (a) pressures of club members for soft greens and lush turf, (b) improper operating practices of the golf course superintendent, and/or (c) limitations or improper design restrictions of the irrigation system itself.

The perfect golf course irrigation system has yet to be installed. Thus, irrigation practices remain one of the most challenging and difficult day-to-day decision-making responsibilities of the golf course superintendent. The techniques employed by the superintendent often determine the effectiveness of the irrigation system. Knowledgeable operation and total familiarity with the capabilities of the system are essential requirements for the qualified golf course superintendent.

Too frequently, irrigation practices fail because they have been established by habit or by calendar reference dates. Actually, good irrigation practices are dictated on a day-to-day basis by the specific turfgrass needs, soil characteristics, and projected weather conditions. Thus, the criteria affecting the decision-making process concerning irrigation involve a dynamic, ever-changing set of conditions which must be assessed by a golf course superintendent with intimate knowledge of the criteria.

A responsible superintendent will make a daily assessment of the soil moisture levels at key indicator sites throughout the golf course. Consideration must also be given to the temperature, atmospheric relative humidity, cloud cover, and wind conditions affecting the evapotranspiration rate, plus the anticipated rainfall for the next few days. Finally, an assessment must be made as to the capabilities and weaknesses of the irrigation system in relation to applying the needed amount of water within a specific period of time. Based on these evaluations, decisions are made regarding when to water and how much water to apply.

The situation is even more complicated because soil moisture content may vary at different locations on the golf course. Some sites may tend toward perpetual wetness, while others may be prone to rapid drying. Consequently, the irrigation program must be adjusted for the variable soil and drainage conditions within the golf course itself. Prolonged dry weather may dictate the use of manually set hose end sprinklers connected to quick coupling valves to supplement normal irrigation system applications on selected sites. Similarly, care must be taken to properly irrigate very wet sites and to avoid overwatering of adjacent slopes, which can result in surface runoff onto these low, wet areas.

Essentially, the golf course superintendent compensates for inadequacies in irrigation system design or for special problem sites on the golf course by supplementing the automatic or semiautomatic system with manual irrigation methods when needed. The need is not uncommon during extremely dry periods.

When to Irrigate

The ultimate decision as to when irrigation is needed requires visual assessment of the water status of both the turf and the soil. Visual turf assessment involves use of the footprinting technique and signs of actual wilt. Both indicate the current water status of a turf and whether water must be applied soon. In contrast, visual assessment of the soil moisture level gives a projection of potential water needs over the next few days and aids in planning upcoming irrigation practices. A soil probe is the best tool for this assessment, assuming the person is familiar with the appearance of soils under various moisture conditions (Fig. 9-33).

Soil moisture should be checked to an 8-inch (20-centimeter) depth at a number of key locations on the golf course. By experience, the golf course superintendent identifies these indicator sites where turfgrass moisture stress first occurs. Thus, a visual assessment of turf and soil water status is partially an art developed through experience.

A sensor known as a tensiometer is capable of measuring soil moisture. Manual tensiometers can be inserted into the soil to determine the soil water status. Other tensiometer models can be permanently connected to the irrigation system controller in such a way as to produce a truly automatic irrigation system. Unfortunately, these units have proven impractical as an extension of the automatic irrigation system under certain field conditions. The amount of soil area sampled is so limited, the golf course soils are so variable, and the rooting depth and cutting height of various turfgrasses are so different on golf courses that is is difficult to use a tensiometer system for comprehensive monitoring. Thus, irrigation decisions remain the responsibility of the golf course superintendent.

One aid in making irrigation decisions consists of a small evaporative pan arrangement that indicates the evaporative demand of the atmosphere on a daily basis. The amount of irrigation water applied is based on 85 percent of the pan evaporation rate. A number of types of evaporative surface devices can be devised and interconnected in such a way that the amount of water lost per day can be assessed, usually linearly in inches (Fig. 9-34). The pan should be read at the same time daily and the original water level reestablished. Computers may become available in the future that can monitor the individual evaporative rates, and calculate the irrigation requirement for the specific location.

The preferred time of day for irrigating most golf courses, from the agronomic standpoint, is the late portion of the nocturnal period and the early morning. However, limitations of some fairway irrigation systems may dictate irrigating for the full nocturnal period on two consecutive nights to fully cover an eighteen-hole course.

It is important that irrigations be scheduled so that excessive amounts of soil water are not present when intense traffic is anticipated. This will minimize the potential for soil compaction and insure optimum playing conditions.

A light, daily irrigation is frequently applied to putting greens just prior to dawn, especially if the root zone has a high infiltration rate. This serves the dual purpose of irrigation plus removal of dew, exudates, and frost that may have formed on the turfgrass surface. This approach offers more favorable playing conditions in early morning and also eliminates the need for such manual procedures as poling or hose dragging of greens.

During summer heat and drought stresses, watering of the greens and even the tees may be necessary at midday, particularly the cool-season turfgrasses. This very light, midday watering technique is termed *syringing*. It can be used to correct a turfgrass stress situation, such as wilt or heat stress, so the turf can survive until normal irrigation during the nocturnal period. When wilt potential is high, the superintendent or the assistant superintendent should inspect all greens and tees daily near midday and sometimes even twice per day during extreme heat and drought stress when the turfgrass root

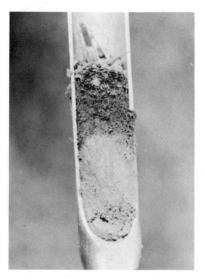

Figure 9-33. Use of a soil probe to determine the moisture status of a soil. Note the well-defined boundary between the light dry soil and the dark moist soil.

Figure 9-34. Small evaporative pan used on a golf course to monitor the daily evaporative demand.

system is quite short. Syringing must be done whenever wilt is imminent. Any delay could mean extensive loss of turf, particularly when the turf is composed of annual bluegrass or bentgrass.

Midday irrigation, other than syringing, has several disadvantages including (a) the potential for unsatisfactory water distribution patterns due to high winds that typically occur at midday, (b) a higher amount of water loss by direct evaporation to the atmosphere, and (c) inconvenience to golfers. Irrigation in late afternoon or early evening also has disadvantages in that the turf remains moist throughout the nocturnal period, thus increasing potential for pathogen invasion and subsequent disease development.

A specific frequency of irrigation cannot be recommended on an absolute basis. Frequency is dictated by existing environmental and soil conditions. It may range from daily on greens in midsummer to three to five times per week on tees during the summer to once every seven to fourteen days during the spring and fall on fairways.

Amount of Water to Apply

The golf course superintendent should attempt to apply an amount of water equivalent to that removed from the soil since the last irrigation to field capacity. The amount of water removed is determined by the quantity of water lost to the atmosphere through evapotranspiration plus that which moves downward through the soil as free gravitational water. The actual amount of water that can be applied also depends on the water retention characteristics of the soil. Fine-textured soils have a higher water retention capability than coarse-textured sandy soils.

Overirrigation must be avoided. If continued on a long-term basis, it causes serious decline in the soil oxygen level, root growth, and overall turfgrass quality and increases the potential for disease development and soil compaction. In addition, overirrigation is wasteful, since much water can be lost through surface runoff and gravitational percolation. Overwatering also encourages annual bluegrass encroachment. Turfgrass symptoms of overirrigation include a yellowish, chlorotic appearance and thinning of the stand.

Figure 9-35. Double-ring in-filtrameter used to monitor the infiltration rate of fairway soil.

An important dimension in irrigation is the rate of water application per unit of time. This rate should be adjusted to the maximum rate at which water enters the soil, termed the infiltration rate. The infiltration rate can range from as low as 0.05 inch (1.3 millimeters) per hour on very fine-textured silty clay soils to more than 4 inches (10 centimeters) per hour on mature sandy root zones. Failure to select the appropriate water application rate can result in objectionable water loss by surface runoff. On sites where the soil infiltration rate is extremely low, an irrigation system is needed that applies water in short, frequent intervals over the nocturnal irrigation period. The rate of water application is controlled primarily by the sprinkler head nozzle size, type of sprinkler head, and operating time.

The soil infiltration rate is best determined by a double-ring infiltrameter arrangement, as shown in Figure 9-35. The procedure usually involves prewetting followed by application of a specified amount of water and monitoring of the depth of water which enters the soil in one hour.

The soil infiltration rate can change through time, as a result of the (a) introduction of golf carts, (b) increased traffic on the golf course, (c) increased use of water containing sodium, which causes deflocculation of the clays, (d) accumulation of thatch or mat, and (e) deposition of clay and silt during flooding, by wind, or by poor-quality irrigation water and topdressing.

BIBLIOGRAPHY

A limited number of references relate to golf course turf irrigation:

Anonymous. 1966. *Rainfall-Evapotranspiration Data — United States and Canada.* The Toro Company, Minneapolis, Minn., 63 pp.
Anonymous. 1974. *Sprinkler Irrigation Manual.* Johns-Manville, Fresno, Calif., 27 pp.
Beard, J. B. 1973. *Turfgrass: Science and Culture.* Prentice-Hall, Inc., Englewood Cliffs, N.J., 658 pp.
Camenga, B. C. 1974. *Design Information for Large Turf Irrigation Systems.* The Toro Company, Riverside, Calif., 157 pp.
Camenga, B. C. *Residential and Commercial Turf Irrigation Systems Information.* The Toro Company, Riverside, Calif., 223 pp.
Gray, A. S. 1961. *Sprinkler Irrigation Hand Book.* 3rd ed. Rain Bird Sprinkler Manufacturing Corp., Glendora, Calif., 44 pp.
Pair, C. H., Hinz, W. W., Reid, C., and Frost, K. R. 1975. *Sprinkler Irrigation.* Sprinkler Irrigation Association, Silver Spring, Md., 615 pp.
United States Salinity Laboratory Staff. 1954. *Diagnosis and Improvement of Saline and Alkali Soils.* USDA Agricultural Handbook No. 60. U.S. Government Printing Office, Washington, D.C., 160 pp.
Watkins, J. A. 1977. *Turf Irrigation Manual.* Telsco Industries, Dallas, Tex., 353 pp.

Some good articles on golf course irrigation can be found in current periodicals. Articles published prior to 1972 are cited by Beard, J. B., Beard, H. J., and Martin, D. P. 1977. *Turfgrass Bibliography: 1672 to 1972.* Michigan State University Press, East Lansing, Mich., 730 pp.

Chapter 10
Pests and Stresses

PROBLEM DIAGNOSIS

A distinct change in the uniformity, color, and/or density of a turf suggests that a potential problem is developing. Early diagnosis and correction of a problem can avoid further deterioration to the point where serious weed invasion may occur. The problem may be due to environmental stress, adverse soil conditions, or a pest attack of significant dimensions. Successful control of a pest problem or correction of an environmental stress is dependent on correct diagnosis. Certain problems are easily diagnosed even by a neophyte, whereas other problems are more sophisticated and can be positively diagnosed only by someone with previous experience with the symptoms involved.

Initial recognition of an impending problem typically is based on grass symptoms. Early problem indicators include a decline in shoot growth, loss of green color, and decreased density. These symptoms may occur in specific sizes and shapes, such as rings or circular patches, or as general thinning in irregular patterns. Another common shoot symptom is increased proneness to wilting, which also can occur in particular sizes and shapes. Footprinting and purpling symptoms are signs of water stress caused by a developing problem with the root system.

The appearance of aboveground shoot symptoms suggests the need for a detailed search for more specific plant and/or soil symptoms. This is best done by cutting a turf plug and the associated underlying soil to a depth of at least 4 inches (10 centimeters). Individual plants in the turf plug can be examined for symptoms of injury. The investigation should include the leaf, stem, and root portions. The turf plug should also be checked for presence of an objectionable thatch layer. It is also important that the soil be inspected for the presence of a disagreeable smell or color, suggesting an anaerobic condition, and of soil layering or compaction problems. Finally, the turf plug should be examined for the presence of fungal growths, such as mycelium or fruiting bodies, as well as for shoot- and root-feeding insects.

Damaged turf plugs are best sampled along the edge of an affected area so that both normal and injured plants are included in the plug. A turf plug with only dead shoots and root systems offers far less potential for correct diagnosis of the problem.

Once the turfgrass plant and soil symptoms have been completely described, additional factors or key indicators can be used to make the best possible diagnosis of the problem. These include (a) time of the year when injury occurred, (b) environmental conditions at the site, such as a sunny versus shaded area, (c) soil conditions, such as very wet versus very dry and presence of a soil layering or compaction problem, (d) which grass species in the affected area were injured and which were not affected, and (e) pesticide application history.

Figure 10-1. Simple aids that can be used to help in the diagnosis of developing turf problems: (*left to right*) Stimpmeter and three golf balls, soil sampling probe, turf/soil profile probe, knife, measuring tape, hand lens, and camera.

Certain physical aids facilitate diagnosis. Included are a stimpmeter, soil sampler, sharp knife, and 10-power hand lens for magnification of minute characteristics (Fig 10-1). In addition, a binocular microscope for detailed examination of leaf, stem, and root tissues may be useful. Finally, a camera can be used to make a permanent visual record for future reference.

On-site diagnosis of a problem is preferable to attempting diagnosis only from a turf plug. If the golf course superintendent is unable to diagnose the problem, he or she may have to submit a sample to a diagnostic laboratory operated by the state cooperative extension service or to one of the private companies servicing the turfgrass industry. In this situation, one or two plugs should be sampled from the perimeter of the affected area to insure that some green tissue remains. These samples must be collected before the turf is treated with a pesticide. The plug should be from 4 to 8 inches (10 to 20 centimeters) in diameter and 3 to 4 inches (7.5 to 10 centimeters) deep. These plugs should be transported or shipped by the fastest means possible in an aerated, moist, protected container to insure arrival in a condition representative of the original field situation. A small plant sample or a single grass plant wrapped in an airtight container often arrives dead and moldy, which negates successful diagnosis of the problem. Accompanying the turf should be a complete description of the symptoms and site conditions, such as the turfgrass cultural program being utilized, soil test results, whether the site is located in a sunny or shady area, whether the soil is under abnormal droughty or wet conditions, and the climatic conditions at the time stress occurred. All such detailed information greatly aids rapid, accurate diagnosis.

Once diagnosis has been made, appropriate corrective measures can be initiated. Disappearance of the symptoms usually indicates that the diagnosis was correct, although a change in weather may produce the same effect. It is advisable that a record be kept of the problem occurrence, diagnosis, and corrective measures taken (Fig. 10-2).

The remainder of this chapter is devoted to pest and environmental problems and includes descriptions of specific symptoms, conditions under which they are most likely to occur, and the appropriate procedures to correct or minimize the problem. To facilitate referencing, symptoms and corrective measures are presented in outline form along with extensive illustrations.

PESTICIDE USAGE

Federal Environmental Pesticide Control Act

In an effort to place tighter controls on the use and handling of pesticides, the United States government introduced the Federal Environmental Pesticide Control Act (FEPCA) in 1972. This law

PROBLEM REPORT

Golf course _____ Location _____

Date _____

Location of problem _____

Date of problem occurrence _____

Weather/temperature for a week prior to problem _____

Soil type and moisture conditions _____

Species and cultivar injured _____

Description of symptoms _____

_____

_____

Diagnosis (identification of problem) _____

_____

_____

Corrective measures implemented _____

_____

_____

_____

Confirmation of diagnosis _____

_____

Cost of correction (chemicals and labor) _____

_____

Remarks _____

_____

_____

_____

_____

_____

_____

Figure 10-2. Representative report form used in diagnosing turfgrass problems.

provided sweeping changes in the Federal Insecticide, Fungicide, and Rodenticide Act (FIFRA) of 1947. The Environmental Protection Agency (EPA) was given the authority to administer the provisions of the FEPCA. Prior to 1972, the use of pesticides was not subject to federal regulation; use and application were controlled by each state's laws and regulations.

Among the important provisions of the FEPCA is the requirement that every pesticide be registered with the EPA and that all pesticides be classified either for general use or restricted use, or both. Products classified for general use can be marketed openly and used by the general public. Those classified for restricted use can be used legally only by certified applicators. A restricted-use pesticide is one which the EPA has determined may cause unreasonable adverse effects on the environment without regulatory restriction. Registration of pesticides which the EPA determines are unsafe for any use is suspended and the pesticide must be taken off the market.

The law provides for testing and certification of pesticide applicators by state agencies, following standards established by the EPA. A certified applicator is a person authorized by law to use or supervise the use of any restricted-use pesticide. A private applicator is a certified applicator who uses or supervises the use of restricted-use pesticides on his or her own or rented property for producing agricultural commodities. The title "commercial applicator" pertains to those certified applicators not included in the description of a private applicator and includes golf course personnel.

The old law, the FIFRA, applied primarily to the pesticide product and its labeling and had no provision for enforcement of proper use. FEPCA makes it unlawful to use a registered pesticide in a manner inconsistent with its labeling. In the original 1972 law, if a pesticide were labeled for one pest and one crop, its use for control of another pest on the same crop was considered a label violation. Under recent amendments, use is allowed for any pest on the labeled crop. In addition, recent amendments permit (a) fertilizer-pesticide mixes, unless specifically prohibited on the pesticide label, (b) use of any pesticide at less than the label-recommended rate, and (c) application of pesticides by means other than those outlined on the label, unless specifically prohibited.

In addition to the above, FEPCA and its amendments include provisions and standards for many different aspects of the manufacture, transport, sale, use, and disposal of pesticides. At the golf course level, many safety practices once suggested for use are now required by law. These include standards for such areas as record keeping, storage and disposal procedures, and filling and mixing methods. It is important for golf course personnel to check regularly with the local cooperative extension office, state university, or EPA officials for complete details on pesticide laws and how they affect golf course use.

Pesticide Selection

Once the cause of a pest problem is diagnosed and the assessment has been made that the pest is a serious threat to the turf, the appropriate pesticide must be selected. The general trend has been to select a pesticide specific for the particular pest problem(s) diagnosed, rather than a broad-spectrum preventive pesticide to be used throughout the growing season. In some cases, more than one pest problem may be associated with the injury symptoms, which dictates selection of a pesticide or combination of pesticides that will be effective on all problems affecting the turf.

A second consideration is selection of the appropriate form of the pesticide. Formulations of pesticides may include wettable powders (WP), dusts, emulsifiable concentrates (EC), flowables, granulars (G), baits, and gas fumigants. It should be remembered that the trade-off between effective control of a particular pest and injury to the desirable turfgrass species may vary among various formulations of a particular pesticide. Thus, selection of the formulation that is most effective for the particular pest problem and causes the least phytotoxicity to the turfgrass species is important.

The third dimension in use of a pesticide is selection of the proper rate of application. This should be based on the manufacturer's label recommendations. Increasing the rate above that recommended on the label will not enhance control in most cases and may even decrease the effectiveness of the pesticide as well as increase the potential for injury to the desirable turfgrass species.

Table 10-1. Signal Words
on Pesticide Labels That Indicate Approximate Human Toxicity

Signal Words/Symbol	Approximate Toxicity
Danger, Poison, skull and crossbones symbol	Highly toxic
Warning	Moderately toxic
Caution	Slightly toxic

Selection of the specific pesticide should also be based on the degree of handling safety relative to the level of expertise of the personnel applying it. The degree of toxicity is indicated on the label (Table 10-1). Selection of the least toxic pesticide from the human toxicology standpoint is advisable, assuming adequate control of the particular pest problem can be achieved.

The method of application of a particular pesticide formulation may be dictated by the type of equipment available, assuming equal effectiveness of different methods in pest control. It is imperative that the pesticide be applied in the manner described on the label to insure effective pest control and safety to humans and the environment. Furthermore, the rate of travel over an area with a particular type of applicator should be within the range prescribed on the label, as this is important in achieving the specified pesticide application rate.

Occasionally, the golf course superintendent wishes to combine several pesticides or a pesticide with another chemical, such as a fertilizer or wetting agent, to reduce the cost of application in relation to the upcoming turfgrass maintenance requirements. Some pesticides and/or other chemicals can be mixed compatibly. Mixing of others can result in chemical reactions that greatly alter the potential for effective pest control and may increase phytotoxicity. In some cases, a precipitate may occur that can clog the sprayer apparatus. Thus, it is important that, before any pesticides and/or chemicals are mixed, the label on the pesticide container is checked to insure that this approach is feasible.

Finally, proper pesticide selection and use involves following the manufacturer's directions on the label concerning the proper time and conditions under which the application should be made. It is not unusual for the label to specify the particular time of day, temperature range, and stage of turfgrass or weed growth when the pesticide should be applied. In addition, application of pesticides under minimal wind velocities is always advisable so that problems of drift can be avoided.

Once the pesticide is selected, it is imperative that the applicator *read and understand all the information on the pesticide label* before handling is attempted and that he or she seek knowledgeable help if any aspect of usage is unclear.

Pesticide Storage

Preferably, pesticides should be stored in a separate building, but a corner on the first floor of a larger building may be used. The storage site should be in an area where flooding is unlikely and should be downwind and downhill from sensitive areas such as houses, ponds, and play areas. Runoff or drainage from the site that could contaminate surface or groundwater should not be possible.

Pesticides should be stored in a cool, dry, airy room which is fireproof and can be tightly locked. Weatherproof warning signs should be hung on every door and window. Windows should be barred so that children and other people cannot get in. A drainage system should be built to collect any runoff water, which may otherwise contaminate surface or groundwater. Supplies of detergent or soap, hand cleanser, and water are a must in the storage area. Absorptive calcined clay, activated charcoal, vermiculite, or sawdust should be readily available at the storage site to soak up spills and leaks. Hydrated lime and bleach should be available to neutralize the pesticide in an emergency. A shovel, broom, dustpan, and fire extinguisher should also be on hand.

Hot areas should be avoided when storing pesticides. Liquids can expand in glass and metal containers and then splash out under pressure when the container is opened. Some formulations will catch on fire when they get too hot, and others may break down and lose their strength.

Herbicides should be stored apart from other pesticides, since they can vaporize and interact with nearby pesticides. When the contaminated pesticide is used, the herbicide vapors in it may injure or kill sensitive plants. All highly toxic pesticides should be stored together in a special area. A special disposal area should be established for surplus pesticides and containers being held for disposal.

Pesticide containers should be checked regularly for corrosion, leaks, and loose caps. If a container is damaged, the pesticide should be put in a sturdy, sealable container, which should then be relabeled. Sometimes the label from the damaged container can be firmly fastened to the new container. Unlabeled pesticides are worthless, should be treated as surplus pesticides, and should be held for disposal. Partly empty pesticide containers should be resealed and returned to storage. Pesticides should never be stored in anything used as a food or drink container. Pesticides stored in fruit jars, milk cartons, and so on are a common source of accidental poisoning. The same protective gear that was used during application should be worn while cleaning and putting away pesticides, containers, and equipment.

Safety in Filling and Mixing

Some pesticides, such as baits, dusts, dry granular materials, and aerosols, can be used just as purchased. However, many golf course applicators use concentrated pesticides that must be mixed with water or some other liquid.

Whenever possible, it is best that the pesticide not be added to the spray tank until just before the material is to be applied. An applicator is most likely to be harmed by a pesticide during the mixing phase, since that is when the concentrated form is handled. Therefore, all safety precautions listed on the label should be strictly adhered to during mixing. Bare hands should never be used when mixing highly toxic materials. Protective gear, including rubber gloves, goggles, clothing, and a respirator, should be worn during the filling and mixing operation (Fig. 10-3). If a concentrate is spilled or splashed on clothing, it should be immediately washed off and the clothes changed. If a concentrate is spilled on the floor or ground, it should be cleaned up immediately. Soap, water, and good washing facilities should be maintained at the mixing site.

The environment is easily harmed by careless mixing and filling procedures. Suction hoses should be equipped with good antisiphoning devices, such as check valves, so that the spray mixture from the tank will not escape down the hose into the original water source. If the tank is allowed to run over during filling, the overflow will often end up as toxic puddles on the ground. Spray equipment should never be left unattended while it is being filled.

Compatibility must be determined before two or more pesticides are put together in a tank mix. The pesticides must be compatible both chemically and physically. Chemical incompatibility may result in a loss of pesticidal activity, increased toxicity to the applicator, or injury to the treated turf. Mixing physically incompatible pesticides may cause lumps to form in the tank or liquid/solids to settle out of suspension. Some compatibilities are listed on the label and others can be checked on compatibility charts available from manufacturers. Spray adjuvants (e.g., wetting agents, emulsifiers, foaming agents, stickers) should only be used in accordance with label recommendations.

Safe Application of Pesticides

Safe application of pesticides begins with thorough mixing of the correct kinds and amounts of materials in a properly calibrated and operating sprayer. Thereafter, effective application depends on the weather. Pesticide application should be avoided on windy days. High winds increase drifting and result in loss or poor distribution on the target area. Drifting pesticides increase the possibility of injury to wildlife, other sensitive vegetation, and the applicator or bystanders. Water contamination could also be a problem. The applicator is legally responsible for any injury or money loss of crops due to pesticide drift onto nontarget areas.

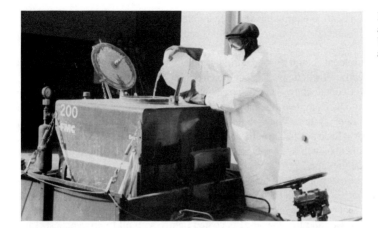

Figure 10-3. The appropriate protective clothing to be worn when mixing and applying pesticide sprays.

Figure 10-4. Kill of adjacent nontarget turf area caused by lateral washing of nonselective herbicide off a path.

Spray applications should not be made just before a heavy rain. Rain may not only reduce the effectiveness of the application but subsequent runoff can injure adjacent turf areas (Fig. 10-4).

Protective gear should be worn at all times when handling and applying pesticides. Rubber gloves, goggles, protective clothing, and a respirator should be standard equipment in most cases. The applicator should never eat, drink, or smoke while handling pesticides and should always wash thoroughly after each application. Employees should be carefully supervised to insure that they follow all safety precautions. They should always work in pairs when handling and applying pesticides.

At the end of each day the applicator(s) should shower, washing thoroughly with soap and water. Clothes that have been exposed to pesticides should be stored and washed separately. They should not be washed in streams or ponds and the person who is to wash them should be warned of possible dangers.

Equipment Cleaning

All of the pesticide in the tank should be used, if possible. If some spray material is left it can be sprayed on other label-approved areas at the recommended dosage. If it cannot be used up, it must be drained into appropriate containers and stored for proper disposal. When the tank is empty, the pressure should be released from the application equipment and the equipment returned to the proper cleaning area, a place where residue will not endanger people or animals and will not cause water pollution from runoff.

Protective clothing and equipment should be used during the cleaning operation. The pesticide label should be checked for any specific instructions. The equipment tank is drained or the hopper emptied, the pesticide being caught in a container for later disposal. Nozzles should be removed from spray equipment and cleaned separately. Complete flushing of the system is accomplished by starting the motor and operating the full sprayer system. Water should be added to the tank and the system flushed, the rinse water being caught for safe disposal. This procedure should be repeated until the water is clear. Tanks containing certain chemicals, such as 2, 4-D, may require special treatment with ammonia or other materials, as specified on the label.

After this initial cleaning, the exterior parts of the equipment should be flushed with water to remove excess pesticide and the interior should be flushed with a mixture of water and light oil. The oil coats interior surfaces and helps prevent rust. Sprayer nozzles should be thoroughly cleaned with kerosene or detergent, using a soft bristle brush, and the nozzle parts coated lightly with oil to prevent rust. Line strainers should be removed, cleaned, and replaced. Hoses should be disconnected, the pump drained. Equipment should be stored in a dry, protected area.

Disposal of Containers

Even after a pesticide container has been rinsed out properly, it still contains small amounts of pesticide. All containers should be triple rinsed, as this has been found to be a very effective cleaning and safety practice. Rinse water should be dumped in the spray tank if possible, never on the ground.

Empty containers should be separated into three categories for disposal: (a) those that burn, (b) those that will not burn, and (c) those containing mercury, lead, cadmium, arsenic, or inorganic pesticides. Burnable containers are usually composed of wood, cardboard, or paper. Small quantities of these may be burned if local laws allow burning. Large quantities of burnable containers should be held for proper disposal in accordance with local, state, and federal regulations.

Nonburnable containers are usually metal, glass, or plastic. Some types may be sent back to the manufacturer for reuse. Before the containers are shipped back they should be resealed carefully and the outside completely washed off. Metal drums that cannot be returned can be crushed with a backhoe, front-end loader, truck, or tractor and stored in a proper area for future disposal. Glass containers may be carefully broken and plastic containers cut apart and stored. An empty 55-gallon drum makes a good storage container for smaller empty containers. The drum can be stored in a special "disposal" section of the pesticide storage area.

Containers with mercury, lead, cadmium, arsenic, or inorganic pesticides must be handled differently. These containers may be wood, cardboard, paper, metal, plastic, or glass. Special methods, such as encapsulation, may be necessary for safe disposal. Encapsulation involves sealing the excess pesticide and container in a sturdy, waterproof container so that the contents cannot possibly get out. These containers should never be burned. Federal and state regulations should be checked for their proper disposal. Some may be crushed and placed in a 55-gallon drum separate from the drum containing regular nonburnable pesticide containers.

Methods of disposing of pesticides and containers include incineration and chemical degradation. Incineration involves burning in a special high-temperature pesticide incinerator designed to reduce pesticides and containers to harmless gases and solid ashes. This method cannot be used for pesticides or containers with mercury, lead, cadmium, arsenic, or inorganic pesticides. The local county extension agent, state college, or EPA office can provide information about the location of the nearest incinerators. Some pesticides can be chemically degraded into nontoxic materials. Methods are specific for each compound. The manufacturer or local EPA officials can provide information about specific techniques.

Record Keeping

Records must be kept with regard to pesticide applications. Besides meeting government requirements, proper record keeping can help establish proof of proper use in damage suits, is helpful in finding the cause of an error, and facilitates a comparison of results obtained from different pesticides. Record keeping also tends to reduce pesticide misuse and aids in purchasing only the required amounts of pesticides needed each year.

The more information recorded, the more useful it will be. A standard form should be filled out immediately after each pesticide application (see chapter 11). Required information includes:

1. Date of application and time of day
2. Certified applicator's name and registration number
3. Name of person actually applying the pesticide
4. Specific turf area or ornamental involved
5. Target pest
6. Equipment used
7. Pesticide used (common name, trade name, formulation, active ingredient, and lot number)
8. Total formulation added to tank or hopper
9. Amount of mixture used
10. Amount or numbers treated (acres, trees, etc.)
11. Additional comments (location, weather, severity of infestation, etc.)

WEEDS

Five major components of turfgrass quality are uniformity, density, smoothness, texture, and color. Plants that disrupt the uniformity of turfs in terms of either texture or density are considered undesirable in high-quality turfs and thus are referred to as weeds. A uniformly dense, smooth surface free of changes in leaf texture is a necessary attribute of quality putting greens. At the other end of the spectrum, a diverse array of textures, vertical shoot growth rates, and densities are more acceptable in the rough areas. Specific weeds associated with green, tee, and fairway turfs are summarized in chapters 3, 4, and 5, respectively. These chapters also discuss general concepts of weed control as they relate to each of these three types of turfgrass cultural systems on golf courses. The reader is referred to them for further information.

Weed Characteristics

Turfs thinned by environmental stresses, pest attacks, or human traffic are the most likely to be invaded by weeds. A weedy species can be described as one that is opportunistic in terms of having growth characteristics that permit it to invade a turf area rapidly should even the smallest of openings occur. These characteristics include rapid germination and seedling emergence, aggressive growth habit, and a rapid vertical shoot growth rate. Weeds may be disseminated by seed, vegetatively, or both, depending on the particular species involved. Many weed seeds have a strong dormancy factor, which permits them to persist in the soil for an extended period until conditions are favorable for germination and emergence. Most weed species are prolific seed producers, especially the annuals. Vegetative propagules may include nodes on rhizomes or stolons as well as bulbs and tubers. The dormancy factor in seeds and in certain types of vegetative propagules is a survival mechanism that facilitates the capability of weeds to survive extended droughts, very cold winters, flooding, and similar adversities. The dispersal of weed seeds and propagules occurs by wind; surface water movement; animals, especially birds; and the activities of humans by movement on contaminated shoes, maintenance equipment, soil, sod, and vegetative plant material.

Maximum effectiveness of herbicides in weed control is achieved by application when the weed is most susceptible to kill. Thus, knowledge of the life history of each problem weed is important. Plants are classed as annuals, biennials, or perennials, depending on the duration they live. *Annuals* grow from seed to a mature plant, flower, produce new seed, and die in one year or less. Both summer annuals and winter annuals occur in turfs. Also, the same species, such as annual bluegrass, can behave as a summer annual in the north and a winter annual in the south of North America. Typically, the annual weeds are more easily controlled with herbicides than are the perennials.

Biennials live for two years, the first year's growth being vegetative, typically a rosette of leaves, while a flower stalk and seed are formed the second year, after which the plant dies. The third category of weeds, *perennials,* live and, in some cases, produce seed year after year. Many perennial weedy species also have the capability to reproduce by vegetative plant parts, such as stolons, rhizomes, nutlets, and bulbs. Perennial weeds possessing this capability can only be controlled if the associated surface and underground plant parts are killed chemically or are physically removed by raking or pulling.

Most weedy species are more easily killed with use of less herbicide while in the seedling stage. Certain mature perennial species will proliferate an underground network of rhizomes or roots with nutlets that can only be killed with a systemic herbicide by translocation to these below-ground organs. A nonsystemic or contact herbicide kills only those aboveground tissues on which it is applied. This is another reason for controlling perennial weedy species in the seedling stage.

Environmental Effects

The climate in a particular region dictates the particular weedy species that will be the greatest problem on golf courses in the area. There are exceptions, such as annual bluegrass, crabgrass, and similar species which are ubiquitous across North America. Seasonal variations in temperature affect the time of year when a weed germinates from seed and when the weed can compete favorably within the turfgrass community. Each weed species has an optimum temperature range for seed germination and growth. For example, crabgrass and goosegrass are most active during periods of high temperature, whereas shepherdspurse grows in the cool temperatures of the fall and spring. Water is another significant factor affecting the competitive ability of weeds. It is the primary requirement in initiation of seed germination as well as in supporting subsequent growth. The combination of wet soils plus excess irrigation is highly favorable for a number of weed species, including annual bluegrass, crabgrass, chickweed, and nutsedge. Excessive irrigation of golf course turfs is one of the major factors encouraging annual bluegrass invasion. In contrast, quackgrass can compete very favorably in relatively dry soil conditions. Finally, light intensity has a significant effect on the weed population in shaded versus full-sun areas. Species such as crabgrass and goosegrass require light for seed germination and thus are usually not found under the shade canopies of trees.

Cultural Effects

The foundation of a good weed control program is a turfgrass cultural system that insures the best possible turfgrass density and competitive vigor. The soil management program should maintain a pH and nutritional level which favor a dense competitive turf, that is, a pH between 5.8 and 7.2 and phosphorus and potassium levels maintained in the adequate range based on soil tests. In addition, an adequate nitrogen fertilization level should be maintained. Thinning because of a low fertility level is especially favorable for weed seed germination and invasion. An excessively high nitrogen fertility level can also weaken the desirable turfgrass species, especially the root system, which increases their proneness to disease attacks. Such a situation can also lead to increased weed invasion.

Irrigation and mowing are basic cultural practices affecting weed invasion. Whenever possible, irrigation should be deep and as infrequent as possible in relation to the rooting depth of the desirable turfgrass species. Frequent, light irrigation tends to enhance weed seed germination but sometimes cannot be avoided when the turf is shallow rooted. The potential for weed invasion generally increases

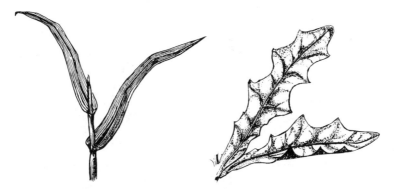

Figure 10-5. Comparison of the parallel veination in grassy weeds (*left*) with the branching network of veins in broadleaf weeds (*right*).

as the mowing height is lowered on tees and fairways, since increased light penetration to the soil surface facilitates weed seed germination and emergence. However, the needs of the game dictate relatively close cutting heights varying from very close on greens to slightly higher cuts on tees and fairways. Thus, the turfgrass manager must be especially careful in terms of allied cultural practices such as fertilization, irrigation, pH adjustment, vertical cutting, and turf cultivation to insure the maximum turf density possible to discourage weed invasion.

Finally, the timing of vertical cutting and turf cultivation can be important in affecting the potential for weed invasion. These practices result in openings in the turf which permit light penetration to the soil surface and thus enhance weed seed germination and seedling emergence. Thus, vertical cutting and turf cultivation should not be scheduled when conditions are favorable for seed germination of problem weeds.

Diagnosis

Weedy species are frequently grouped in terms of broadleaf weeds and grassy, or narrow-leaf, weeds. The grassy weeds are monocotyledons, while the broadleaf weeds are dicotyledons. These two groups are distinguished by the parallel veins extending longitudinally in the leaves of grassy weeds and the secondary branching or netted vein system in the broadleaf weed species (Fig. 10-5). Most broadleaf weeds also have a relatively wide leaf compared with the grasses. These two groupings are commonly used, since herbicides available for use in turfgrass weed control can be grouped similarly in relation to the target species on which they are most effective. Generally, removal of grassy weeds from desirable turfgrass species is more difficult than is the case for broadleaf weeds. Furthermore, even greater difficulty is encountered in selectively removing perennial weedy grasses from the desirable perennial turfgrasses, because of the similarities between the species.

The first step in weed control is identification of the specific turfgrass weed species causing a problem and of the desirable species in the turfgrass community which are to be retained. Detailed descriptions and illustrations of the forty-five weeds most commonly found on golf courses across North America are presented in Figure 10-6. Table 10-2 presents information about algae and moss problems. In addition, twenty-three desirable turfgrass species for golf courses are presented in Appendix A, including a discussion of identification procedures, a key for identification, and a detailed description of the important features used in identification. Bahiagrass, bentgrass, bermudagrass, kikuyugrass, and tall fescue are illustrated in the appendix, but these grasses may be considered weeds in a turfgrass community composed of one or more distinctly different desirable species. If difficulties are encountered in identification of weed species or desirable turfgrasses found on a particular site, the assistance of a knowledgeable specialist from the county cooperative extension service should be sought.

GRASSY WEEDS

ANNUAL BLUEGRASS
Poa annua L.

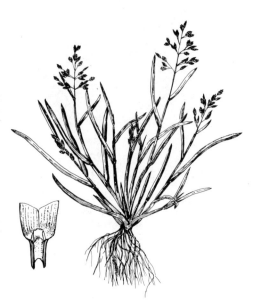

Annual or *perennial,* reproducing by seed and by spreading stoloniferous growth habit with rooting at lower nodes. *Roots* fibrous. *Culms* flattened, erect to spreading, vernation folded. *Sheaths* flattened, overlapping. *Ligule* 1- to 4-mm-long membrane, acute. *Leaf blades* soft to lax, 1 to 3 mm wide, smooth, bright light green, boat-shaped tip. *Panicle* pyramidal, open, 3 to 7 cm long, branches few and spreading. *Spikelets* crowded, three to six flowers about 4 mm long. *Occurrence* throughout North America; behaves as winter annual in the south, summer annual in the far north, and perennial in cool climatic regions; prefers wet, compacted soils and is adapted to very close cutting heights of putting greens; responds to intense irrigation and fertilization; can form a good-quality turf but lacks tolerance for environmental stresses.

BARNYARDGRASS

Echinochloa crusgalli (L.) Beauv.

Annual, reproducing by seed, bunch growth habit. *Roots* fibrous, rather shallow. *Culms* stout, erect to decumbent, often branching from base, vernation rolled. *Sheaths* smooth. *Ligule* absent. *Leaf blades* smooth, elongate, 5 to 15 mm wide, flattened, light green. *Panicle* erect or nodding, green or purple tinged, 10 to 20 cm long. *Racemes* numerous, 2 to 4 cm long, spreading, ascending, sometimes branched. *Spikelets* crowded, about 3 mm long excluding awns. *Occurrence* throughout United States, except extreme Southeast; prefers moist, fertile soils.

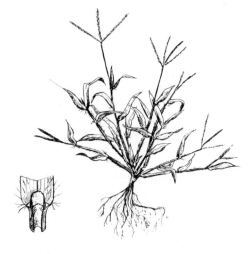

CRABGRASS, LARGE

Digitaria sanguinalis (L.) Scop.

Annual, reproducing by seed, decumbent stems branching and spreading, often purplish. *Culms* stout, smooth, up to 3 to 12 dm long when prostrate, rooting at nodes, flowering shoots ascending, vernation rolled. *Sheaths* densely covered with long hair, especially lower ones, rough to the touch, often more or less pilose. *Leaf blades* lax, 5 to 15 cm long, 4 to 10 mm wide, somewhat hairy. *Racemes* 5 to 15 cm long with 3 to 13 fingerlike segments in whorls at top of stem. *Spikelets* along one side of rachis, about 3 mm long. *Occurrence* throughout United States.

Figure 10-6. Forty-five grassy and broadleaf weeds most commonly found on golf courses across North America.

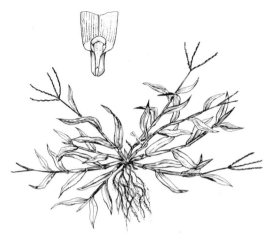

CRABGRASS, SMOOTH

Digitaria ischaemum (Schreb.) Schreb. ex Muhl

Annual, reproducing by seeds. *Culms* 0.2 to 4 dm tall, usually decumbent-spreading, venation rolled. *Leaf blades* 2 to 10 cm long, 3 to 6 mm wide, smooth, bluish to purplish. *Racemes* mostly two to six, commonly purple, 4 to 10 cm long, rachis with thin wings wider than midrib. *Spikelets* on one side of rachis, solitary or in twos, about 2 mm long. *Occurrence* throughout United States, except for arid Southwest and southern Florida.

DALLISGRASS

Paspalum dilatatum Poir.

Perennial, reproducing by seeds, bunch growth habit, short rhizomes. *Culms* tufted, stoutish, 4.5 to 17 dm tall, smooth except ligules and crowded spikelets, venation rolled. *Ligule* 1.5 to 3 mm-long membrane. *Leaf blades* elongated, 10 to 25 cm long, 4 to 12 mm wide, smooth. *Racemes* three to five, 5 to 19 cm long, loosely ascending, spreading. *Spikelets* egg shaped, tapering to a point, 2.8 to 4 mm long, 2 to 2.5 mm broad. *Occurrence* in warm climatic region of southern United States.

FOXTAIL, GREEN

Setaria viridis (L.) Beauv.

Annual, reproducing by seeds, tufted. *Culms* branching at base, sometimes spreading, 20 to 40 cm tall, venation rolled. *Ligule* band of hairs. *Leaf blades* flat, usually less than 15 cm long, 5 to 15 mm wide, smooth. *Panicle* erect or somewhat nodding, densely flowered, green or purple, cylindric but tapering at summit, usually 1.5 to 15 cm long, 1 to 2.3 cm wide. *Bristles* one to three below each spikelet. *Spikelets* 1.8 to 2.5 mm long, green, the green to purplish bristles upwardly rough to the touch, spreading-ascending. *Occurrence* throughout United States, especially the Midwest.

FOXTAIL, YELLOW

Setaria glauca (L.) Beauv.

Annual, reproducing by seeds, tufted. *Culms* flattened, erect to prostrate, mostly 5 to 12 dm tall, branching at base, vernation rolled. *Sheaths* keeled. *Ligule* band of hairs. *Leaf blades* as much as 25 cm long and 3 to 10 mm wide, flat, twisted in a loose spiral with hairs long and soft toward base above. *Panicle* dense, evenly cylindric, spikelike, yellow at maturity, mostly 1.5 to 12 cm long, 0.9 to 1.4 cm thick, axis densely hairy. *Bristles* 5 to 20 in a cluster, 3 to 8 mm long. *Spikelets* 3 mm long. *Occurrence* throughout United States.

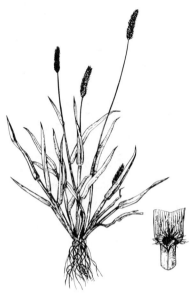

GOOSEGRASS

Eleusine indica (L.) Gaertn.

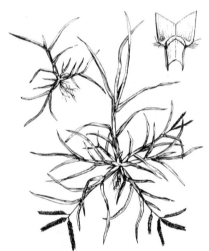

Annual, reproducing by seeds, coarse tufted. *Roots* fibrous. *Culms* 15 to 60 cm long, erect or decumbent at base, flattened, smooth, vernation folded. *Sheaths* flattened, keeled, smooth, margin sometimes pilose. *Ligule* short marginal hairs, 1 mm long or less. *Leaf blades* flat or folded, smooth but sometimes slightly rough, 3 to 8 mm wide, 5 to 25 cm long. *Spikes* 4 to 15 cm long, fingerlike with two to six fingerlike segments 2.5 to 7.5 cm long, crowded, whorled. *Spikelets* sessile on one side of rachis, 3 to 5 mm long, three to six florets along edges of rachilla, crowded. *Occurrence* throughout United States, except for northern plains and mountainous region; persists on compacted soils and closely mowed putting greens.

JOHNSONGRASS

Sorghum halepense (L.) Pers.

Perennial, reproducing by seeds and large, scaly rhizomes (up to 1 m long). *Roots* freely branching, fibrous. *Rhizomes* stout, creeping, with purple spots, usually with scales at nodes. *Stems* erect, stout, 5 to 15 dm tall, vernation rolled. *Sheaths* smooth. *Ligule* 2 to 3 mm membrane, hairs. *Leaf blades* alternate, simple, smooth, flat, 20 to 50 cm long, less than 2 cm wide. *Panicles* large, purplish, hairy, 15 to 50 cm long. *Spikelets* sessile, 4.5 to 5.5 mm long, egg shaped, with flat-lying straight hairs, the readily deciduous awn 1 to 1.5 cm long, bent abruptly, twisted below. *Occurrence* southern two-thirds of United States, especially the humid Southeast.

Figure 10-6. *Grassy weeds/continued*

KNOTGRASS

Paspalum distichum L.

Perennial, reproducing by seeds and by long, flat stolons to form a loose mat. *Culms* creeping, rooting at hairy nodes, with ascending culms 1 to 6 dm long, vernation rolled. *Sheaths* loose, flattened. *Ligule* 0.1 mm membrane, very blunt. *Leaf blades* short, flat, 2 to 8 cm long, 2 to 5 mm wide, usually crowded, sometimes sparsely hairy on margins, ciliate at base. *Racemes* two, strictly terminal, 1.5 to 7 cm long, ascending and often incurring; *spikelets* solitary, 2.5 to 4 mm long, 1.3 to 1.5 mm wide, egg shaped, abruptly acute, sparsely hairy, pale green. *Occurrence* throughout southern warm climatic region and western states; prefers wet soils.

NIMBLEWILL

Muhlenbergia schreberi J. F. Gmelin

Perennial, reproducing by seeds. *Roots* fibrous. *Culms* slender, smooth, diffuse, branching, spreading, decumbent at base, often rooting at lower nodes, but not forming definite creeping stolons, 1.5 to 6 dm long, freely forking into capillary ascending branches, vernation rolled. *Ligule* very short membrane. *Leaf blades* flat, thin, mostly less than 5 cm long, smooth, 2 to 4 mm wide, spreading or loosely ascending. *Panicles* terminal and axillary, threadlike to linear-cylindric, slender, loosely flowered, lax, nodding, 6 to 18 cm long. *Occurrence* humid eastern half of United States; prefers moist soils.

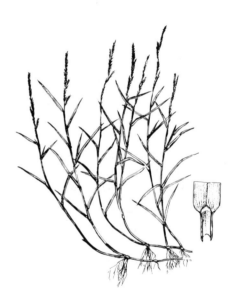

NUTSEDGE, YELLOW

Cyperus esculentus L.

Perennial, a sedge reproducing by seeds and weak threadlike stolons, terminated by hard tubers. *Tubers* 1 to 2 cm long. *Roots* fibrous. *Stems* erect, 2 to 9 dm tall, simple, triangular. *Sheaths* closed, mostly basal. *Leaf blades* three ranked, pale green, 4 to 9 mm wide, about as long as stem. *Umbel* terminal, simple to compound, the longest involucral leaf much exceeding the umbel. *Spikelets* 0.5 to 3 cm long, 1.5 to 3 mm broad, yellowish to golden brown, strongly flattened, mostly four ranked (occasionally two ranked) along wing-angled rachis, blunt, tip acute to round. *Occurrence* throughout United States, especially warm humid Southeast.

QUACKGRASS

Agropyron repens (L.) Beauv.

Perennial, reproducing by seeds and extensive, long, slender rhizomes. *Roots* arising only at nodes. *Culms* 3 to 12 dm tall, smooth, with three to six joints, hollow at tip, vernation rolled. *Sheaths* lower ones hairy, upper ones smooth or slightly pilose. *Ligules* 0.5 mm long membrane. *Auricles* distinct, long, clasping. *Leaf blades* soft, flat, with crowded fine ribs, rough or sparsely pilose above. *Spike* dense or lax, 0.5 to 2.5 dm long, two to nine short-awned florets in compressed spikelet (0.6 to 2.2 cm long). *Occurrence* throughout cool and transitional climatic regions of United States, especially the Great Lakes states.

RESCUEGRASS

Bromus willdenowii Kunth

Annual or *biennial,* reproducing by seeds, bunch growth habit. *Roots* fibrous. *Culms* erect to spreading, as much as 100 cm tall, sometimes decumbent at base, vernation rolled. *Sheaths* smooth or hairy, flattened. *Ligule* large, 2.5 mm long membrane. *Leaf blades* smooth to hairy, 2 to 12 mm wide. *Panicle* open, narrow to pyramidal, erect to nodding. *Spikelets* green, sometimes tinged purple, flattened, 2 to 3 cm long, 6 to 12 flowers. *Occurrence* throughout warm climatic region of southern United States.

SANDBUR, FIELD

Cenchrus pauciflorus Benth.

Annual, at times a short-lived perennial, reproducing by seeds. *Roots* fibrous, sometimes rooting at nodes of stems. *Culm* stout, decumbent or erect, sometimes with many spreading branches from the base. 5 to 80 cm tall, smooth, vernation folded. *Sheaths* laterally flattened, smooth. *Ligule* short, ciliate, membrane 2 to 6 mm wide. *Spike* short, composed of two to four sessile, smooth spikelets enclosed in sharp spiny burs (8 to 40 spines). *Burs* sharp, straw colored to mauve or purple. *Occurrence* southern warm climatic region, especially Texas.

Figure 10-6. *Grassy weeds/continued*

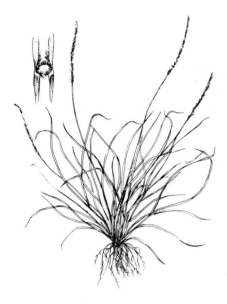

SMUTGRASS

Sporobolus poiretii (Roem. & Schult.) Hitchc.

Perennial, reproducing by seeds. *Culms* solitary or tufted, 3 to 10 dm tall, erect, smooth, wiry, with two or three leaves, vernation rolled. *Ligule* line of short hairs. *Leaf blades* flat to slightly rolled inward, rather firm, 10 to 30 cm long, 2 to 5 mm wide at base, slenderly tapering. *Panicle* linear-cylindric, stiff, one-fourth to one-half the entire length of plant, 10 to 40 cm long, branches close to central axis or ascending. *Spikelets* 1.5 to 2 mm long, shining, crowded on slender, erect branches. *Occurrence* warm transitional climatic regions of southern United States.

TORPEDOGRASS

Panicum repens L.

Perennial, spreads by extensive rhizome network. *Rhizomes* elongated, heavy, clothed at base with bladeless overlapping sheath. *Culms* tall, rigid, erect or ascending from nodes of rhizomes, vernation folded. *Sheaths* usually overlapping, loose, hairy margins. *Ligule* 1 mm long. *Leaf blades* flat or folded, 2 to 5 mm wide, somewhat hairy to smooth. *Panicle* open, 7 to 12 cm long, branches stiffly ascending. *Spikelets* 2.2 to 2.5 mm long, egg shaped, sharply pointed. *Occurrence* in coastal regions of southeastern United States, especially on sandy soils along Gulf Coast.

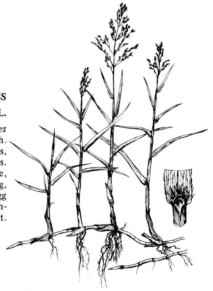

VELVETGRASS

Holcus lanatus L.

Perennial, reproducing by seeds. *Roots* fibrous. *Culms* erect to semierect, vernation rolled. *Sheaths* smooth, split. *Ligule* 0.5 to 2 mm long membrane. *Leaf blades* grayish, velvety-hairy. *Panicle* 8 to 15 cm long, contracted, pale purplish tinged. *Spikelets* 4 mm long. *Occurrence* cool climatic and transitional regions of northern United States and Canada; prefers moist fertile soils.

BROADLEAF WEEDS

CHICKWEED, COMMON

Stellaria media (L.) Cyrillo

Annual or *winter annual,* weakly tufted, reproducing by seeds and creeping stems, rooting at nodes. *Roots* fibrous, shallow. *Stems* much branched, often trailing, matted or loosely ascending, up to 8 dm long, minutely hairy in lines. *Leaves* opposite, simple, usually 1 to 3 cm long, oblong-ovate, pointed tip, smooth, upper leaves sessile, lower leaves petiolate, egg shaped, often hairy toward base or on petioles, 0.5 to 4 cm long. *Flowers* solitary or in few-flowered terminal, pedicels ascending, recurved, frequently hairy. *Sepals* lanceolate-oblong, 3.5 to 6 mm long, blunt to acute, usually with long shaft hairs. *Petals* five, white, small, shorter than sepals, two parted or absent. *Occurrence* throughout United States; prefers cool, moist, or shaded sites east of Mississippi River.

CHICKWEED, MOUSE-EAR

Cerastium vulgatum L.

Perennial, reproducing by seeds, occasionally spreading by creeping stems. *Roots* fibrous, branched, shallow. *Stems* sticky-hairy, slender, 1.5 to 5 dm long, partly spreading to erect, often rooting at lower nodes, forming mats. *Leaves* opposite, small, 1 to 2 cm long, 3 to 12 mm wide, one nerved, very hairy, attached directly at stem, oblong to lanceolate. *Inflorescence* open, mature pedicels 5 to 12 mm long. *Sepals* 4 to 6 mm long, oblong-lanceolate, hairy. *Petals* (sometimes absent) 4 to 6 mm long, notched at tips. *Occurrence* throughout United States, except for southernmost arid areas; prefers cool, moist, shaded sites.

CLOVER, WHITE

Trifolium repens L.

Perennial, or *winter annual* in warm climates, a legume reproducing primarily by seeds and spreading by stoloniferous stems. *Roots* moderately fibrous. *Stems* prostrate growing, rooting at nodes, forming mats, usually smooth. *Leaves* broadly elliptical to egg shaped, crescent-shaped watermark on upper surface, three sessile leaves borne on pedicels that develop from crown and nodes of stolons. *Flowers* white to pinkish, globular in shape, composed of 40 to 100 florets, seedheads borne on long stalks arising from basal nodes. *Occurrence* throughout cool and warm, humid climatic regions; prefers moist, imperfectly drained, nitrogen-deficient soils, responds to high potassium levels, can persist under close mowing of putting green.

Figure 10-6. *Broadleaf weeds/continued*

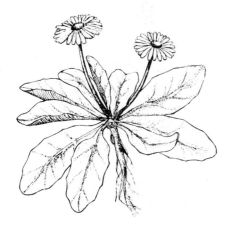

DAISY, ENGLISH

Bellis perennis **L.**

Perennial, reproducing by seeds. Low growing. *Roots* moderately fibrous. *Stems* very short, at soil surface. *Leaves* oval, toothed in a basal whorl. *Flowers* numerous, showy white or pinkish, borne on prominent, upright, short stalks. *Bracts* involucre, equal in about two rows. *Occurrence* primarily in western region of United States.

DANDELION

Taraxacum officinale **Weber**

Perennial, reproducing by seeds and from root crowns. *Taproot* thick, 6-dm deep, many-branched crowns, milky juice. *Stems* very short, wholly underground, producing a rosette of leaves at surface. *Leaves* 5 to 40 cm long, shape varies from lobeless or entire to divided into many shallow to deep-cut lobes with long soft points and intermediate small teeth, a larger lobe at tip, or edges merely toothed, narrowed at base into short hollow petiole, hairy. *Flower heads* 2 to 5 cm in diameter, solitary at end of naked hollow stalk 5 to 75 cm long. *Receptacles* flat or convex, naked. *Flowers* strap-shaped ray flowers, golden yellow, five notched at tip, 100 to 300 per head. *Bracts* green to brownish surrounding flower heads in two rows, outer row hanging down, one-third to one-half as long as inner, erect row. *Occurrence* throughout United States, especially in cool climatic region.

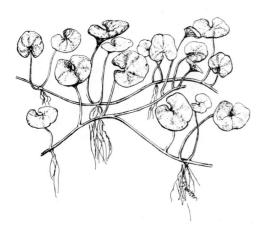

DICHONDRA

Dichondra **sp. Forst**

Perennial, reproducing by seeds. Low, creeping growth habit. *Roots* fibrous. *Stems* prostrate, growing in a dense mat, rooting at nodes. *Leaves* kidney shaped, entire, 6 to 40 mm wide, hairy, borne on elongated stems. *Flowers* inconspicuous, pale green, borne on peduncles. *Occurrence* warm, humid climatic region, especially along Gulf Coast and in irrigated turfs of southern California.

DOCK, CURLY

Rumex crispus L.

Perennial, reproducing by seeds. *Taproot* large, yellow, somewhat branched. *Stems* smooth, erect, single or in groups from root crown, simple to inflorescence, up to 1 m tall. *Leaves* simple, mostly basal, smooth, 15 to 30 cm long, lanceolate, larger leaves rounded to nearly heart shaped at base, wavy-curly margins, upper leaves alternate, base a short petiole with a papery sheath surrounding stem. *Inflorescence* large, many erect or ascending branches, few to many linear leaves intermingled. *Flowers* small, greenish, becoming reddish brown at maturity, in dense clusters of ascending racemes in branches at ends of stems, on slender pedicels of 5 to 10 mm long. *Occurrence* throughout United States in rough and fairways.

GROUND IVY

Glechoma hederacea L.

Perennial, reproducing by seeds and creeping stems. *Roots* shallow. *Stems* 3.8 to 7 dm long, creeping, rooting at nodes, numerous erect flowering branches, four angled, smooth. *Leaves* opposite, palmately veined, petioled, rounded, kidney shaped, round-toothed edges, bright green, smooth, 1 to 3 cm in diameter, with minty odor. *Flowers* small, in axillary clusters. *Calyx* tubular, with five equal teeth, hairy, persistent. *Corolla* bluish purple to purplish, two lipped, upper lip erect. *Occurrence* cool, humid and transitional climatic zone, primarily east of Mississippi River.

HEALALL

Prunella vulgaris L.

Perennial, reproducing by seeds and short runners that root at nodes, can form a dense mat. *Stems* erect, 0.5 to 6 dm tall, ascending or prostrate, mostly tufted, simple or branched, four angled, hairy, becoming nearly smooth with age. *Leaves* opposite, pinnately veined, moderately long petioles, margins entire or irregularly toothed, ovate-oblong, hairy or smooth, 2.5 to 10 cm long. *Flowers* sessile, in a close thick spike, three in axils of each rounded membranous bract. *Bracts* mostly bristly-ciliate. *Calyx* irregularly ten nerved, 7 to 10 mm long, green or purple, two lipped. *Corolla* blue or purple to white or pink, 1 to 2 cm long, two lipped. *Occurrence* throughout United States; responds to moist, irrigated, fertile soils and tolerates close mowing heights.

Figure 10-6. *Broadleaf weeds/continued*

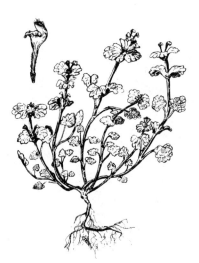

HENBIT

Lamium amplexicaule **L.**

Biennial or *winter annual,* reproducing by seeds and spreading by rooting stems. *Roots* fibrous. *Stems* decumbent, numerous ascending branches, frequently rooting at lower nodes, 10 to 40 cm tall, slender, smooth, four angled. *Leaves* opposite, circular, palmate venation, hairy, rounded teeth, lower leaves petioled, doubly crenate lobed, 1 to 2 cm long, upper leaves sessile and clasping stem. *Flowers* in whorls in axils of upper leaves. *Corolla* tubular but two lipped, about 1 to 1.5 cm long, pinkish to purple, surrounded at base by calyx (5 to 6.5 mm long), five sharp teeth, spotted. *Occurrence* throughout United States, especially east of Mississippi River; prefers fertile soils.

KNOTWEED, PROSTRATE

Polygonum aviculare **L.**

Annual, reproducing by seeds. *Taproot* thin. *Stems* 10 to 100 cm long, prostrate or loosely ascending to erect, main stem corrugated, much branched, forming mats. *Leaves* alternate, entire, sharp pointed to rounded at end, narrowed at base, blue-green, lanceolate to oblong, 5 to 30 mm long, 1 to 8 mm wide, petioles very short, united to short sheath, veinless. *Flowers* in axillary clusters, perfect, small. *Occurrence* throughout United States; well adapted to intense traffic and soil compaction.

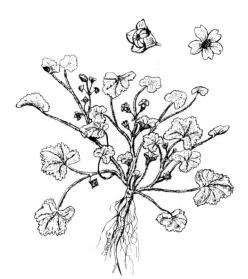

MALLOW, COMMON

Malva neglecta **Wallr.**

Annual or *biennial,* reproducing by seeds. *Taproot* short, straight. *Stems* 10 to 30 cm long, procumbent or branching at base, nearly erect, or spreading with tips generally turned up, hairy. *Leaves* alternate, round heart to kidney shaped, 2 to 6 cm wide, simple, on very long slender petioles, toothed with five to nine shallow rounded lobes or lobeless, hairy. *Flowers* small, with five whitish or pale lilac petals, borne singly or in clusters in axils of many leaves. *Petals* about 1 cm long, twice as long as calyx. *Occurrence* throughout United States; primarily in wet, humid regions east of Mississippi River.

MEDIC, BLACK

Medicago lupulina L.

Annual, biennial, or sometimes acting as a *perennial,* a legume reproducing by seeds. *Taproot* shallow. *Stems* slender, procumbent or prostrate, branched at base, 30 to 60 dm tall, sparsely hairy. *Leaves* alternate, petioled, three parted, center leaflet on a short stalk, leaflets 5 to 15 mm long, broadly obovate, sparingly hairy. *Peduncles* slender, hairy; *Flowers* 3 to 4 mm long, crowded in spikelike racemes (not over 12 mm long). *Calyx* five cleft, persistent. *Corollas* yellow, 1.5 to 2 mm long, longer than the hairy calyx. *Petals* five standard, two lateral wings and two lower wings fused into a keel. *Occurrence* throughout the United States, especially in eastern Midwest.

PEARLWORT, BIRDSEYE

Sagina procumbens L.

Annual or *perennial,* propagated primarily vegetatively, forms a very dense, patchy mat. *Roots* fibrous. *Stems* prostrate, spreading, smooth. *Leaves* linear-thread shaped. *Flowers* small, at apex of peduncles, four to five petals, undivided, shorter than the broadly blunt sepals. *Occurrence* cool humid regions of Northeast and eastern Midwest; prefers wet, poorly drained soils; adapted to close mowing of putting greens.

PLANTAIN, BROADLEAF

Plantago major L.

Perennial, sometimes an *annual,* reproducing by seeds. *Leaves* alternate in rosettes, basal, 0.5 to 3 dm long, blades thick, roughish, minute hairs, elliptic to broadly egg shaped, strongly ribbed, wavy or angular-toothed margin, petioles broad, usually green, hairy at base. *Spikes* dense, blunt, at ends of stems, 0.1 to 5 dm long. *Flowers* sessile, bracts smooth, broadly egg shaped with slender keel. *Sepals* smooth, elliptic, rounded keel, 1.5 to 2 mm long. *Occurrence* throughout United States; responds to moist fertile soils.

Figure 10-6. *Broadleaf weeds/continued*

PLANTAIN, BUCKHORN

Plantago lanceolata L.

Perennial, reproducing by seeds. *Taproot* strong with tough, slender rootlets. *Stems* erect, leafless, 10 to 30 cm tall, terminating with a flower spike. *Leaves* all basal in a rosette, blades lanceolate to oblong, ascending or spreading, 5 to 30 cm long, 0.6 to 5 cm wide, three to five prominent veins running lengthwise, tapering into petiole. *Scape* tough, grooved angled, elongating, 2 to 8 dm tall, stiff haired above. *Spikes* dense, at beginning of flowering slenderly ovoid-conic, tapering apex, at maturity cylindric and blunt, 1.5 to 10 cm long. *Flowers* numerous, 5 mm broad, inconspicuous, forward sepals united, 3 to 3.5 mm long, corolla lobes 2 to 3 mm long. *Bracts* thin, papery, broadly egg shaped, margin wavy. *Occurrence* throughout United States, especially east of Mississippi River in cool, humid region and transitional zone.

PURSLANE, COMMON

Portulaca oleracea L.

Annual, reproducing by seeds and stem fragments on moist soil. *Taproot* heavy. *Stems* succulent, smooth, fleshy, prostrate, usually purplish red, forming mats, freely branched, 10 to 56 cm long, smooth. *Leaves* alternate or nearly opposite, often in clusters at ends of branches, thickened, sessile, margins smooth, broad rounded tips, 0.4 to 2.8 cm long. *Flowers* yellow, sessile, solitary in leaf axils or several together in leaf clusters at ends of branches, 3 to 10 mm broad, including five pale yellow petals. *Calyx* lower portion fused with ovary, upper part with two free sepals, pointed at tip, 3 to 4 mm long. *Occurrence* throughout United States, especially east of Mississippi River; prefers fertile soils.

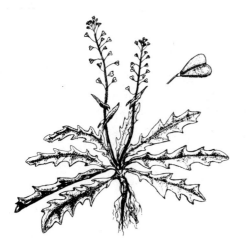

SHEPHERDSPURSE

Capsella bursa-pastoris (L.) Medic.

Annual or *winter annual,* reproducing by seeds. *Taproot* branched, thin. *Stems* erect, branched, 1 to 6 dm tall, covered with gray hairs. *Leaves* alternate, simple, variously toothed or lobed, in a rosette at base, coarsely lobed, clasping stem with pointed lobes, coarsely serrate, 5 to 10 cm long, stem leaves arrow shaped. *Flowers* small, white, four petaled, about 2 mm wide, borne in elongated racemes at ends of branches on slender pedicels. *Occurrence* throughout North America.

SORREL, RED

Rumex acetosella L.

Perennial, reproducing by seeds and creeping rhizomes. *Roots* and *rhizomes* extensive but shallow. *Stems* slender, erect, 1.5 to 4.5 dm tall, branched at top, several stems from one crown or from rhizomes. *Leaves* alternate, simple and entire, a rosette of basal leaves in early growth, stem leaves arrow shaped with two basal lobes somewhat divergent, thick, smooth, narrowly lanceolate, 2.5 to 7 cm long, acid to taste. *Inflorescence* of slender racemes near top of plant, erect in panicles. *Flowers* yellow to red, male and female flowers on different plants, nodding on short-jointed pedicels, outer sepals lanceolate. *Occurrence* throughout United States, especially in the transition zone east of Mississippi River; prefers wet, acidic soils of low fertility.

SPEEDWELL, COMMON

Veronica officinalis L.

Perennial, reproducing by seeds and creeping stems. *Stems* prostrate, rooting at base, stout, hairy, flowering branches erect or ascending. *Leaves* opposite, simple, oblong, toothed, hairy, 2.5 to 6 cm long, 1 to 3 cm broad, short petioled. *Peduncles* stout, ascending. *Flowers* in dense axillary racemes, pedicels shorter than calyx. *Calyx* lobes blunt, nearly equal in size. *Corolla* pale blue to lilac or lavender, or white, marked with darker lines, 5 to 6 mm in diameter, with blunt lobes. *Occurrence* cool, humid and transitional climatic region east of Mississippi River; prefers acidic soils.

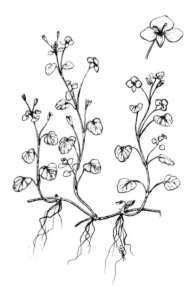

SPEEDWELL, CREEPING

Veronica filiformis Sm.

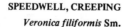

Perennial, reproducing by seeds and spreading by creeping stems. *Roots* shallow, fibrous. *Stems* prostrate, rooting at nodes. *Leaves* opposite, egg shaped to round, 5 to 10 mm in diameter, margins scalloped. *Flowers* pale blue to white on slender threadlike stalks. *Occurrence* cool, humid climatic region of northeastern United States; prefers moist, shaded sites.

Figure 10-6. *Broadleaf weeds/continued*

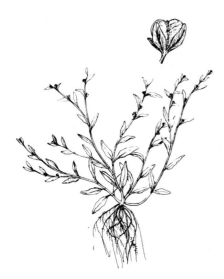

SPEEDWELL, PURSLANE

Veronica peregrina L.

Annual or *winter annual,* reproducing by seeds. *Roots* fibrous. *Stems* erect, simple, or branching from base, smooth, 1 to 4 dm tall, lower half with opposite leaves, upper half bearing flowers. *Leaves* simple, narrowly oblong, 1.5 to 3 cm long, often blunt, entire, sessile or narrowed to a petiolelike base, lower leaves opposite, upper leaves alternate. *Bract leaves* similar to stem leaves but progressively smaller. *Flowers* small, in axils or bracts, sessile or short stalked. *Sepals* subequal. *Corolla* white. *Occurrence* throughout humid climatic region of United States; prefers wet, fertile soils.

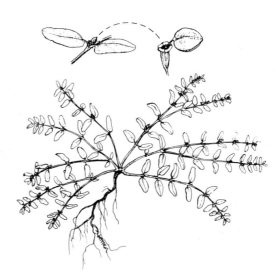

SPURGE, PROSTRATE

Euphorbia supina Raf. ex Boiss.

Annual, reproducing by seeds. *Stems* slender, prostrate or ascending, branching from near base, forming mats 1 to 9 dm in diameter, soft hairy, often reddish, with a milky juice. *Leaves* opposite, 4 to 17 mm long, egg shaped to oblong, toothed to nearly entire, smooth, often purple mottled. *Flowers* solitary in branch axils or in dense leafy lateral clusters. *Occurrence* humid areas of Midwest, eastern United States, and along Pacific coast.

SPURGE, SPOTTED

Euphorbia maculata L.

Annual, reproducing by seeds, germinating late in spring or early summer. *Taproot* shallow. *Stems* simple or much branched, erect or spreading, 0.8 to 1 m tall, with milky juice, crisp-hairy at young tips, soon becoming smooth and firm. *Leaves* oblong, falcate, 0.8 to 3.5 cm long, edges slightly toothed, borne on short petioles, with a conspicuous reddish spot or blotch. *Flowers* solitary or clustered, with minute petals in form of a cup, peduncle 0.5 to 5 mm long. *Occurrence* eastern two-thirds of United States, along Pacific coast, and in desert regions of Arizona.

WILD CARROT

Daucus carota **L.**

Biennial, reproducing by seeds. *Taproot* bearing a rosette of leaves the first season. *Stems* erect, branching, slender, hollow, ridged, bristly-hairy, 3 to 16 dm high, bearing scattered stem leaves. *Leaves* alternate or basal, oblong, pinnately nearly compound, ultimate segments lanceolate or oblong, often lobed, somewhat hairy, stem leaves sessile with a sheathing base, basal leaves long petioled. *Flowers* in flat-topped umbels, which become concave as fruits mature, 6 to 15 cm broad. *Occurrence* throughout United States.

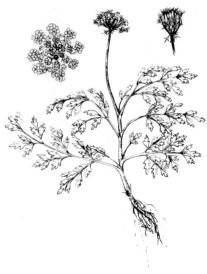

WILD GARLIC

Allium vineale **L.**

Perennial bulbous herb, outer layers of bulb formed from sheathing leaves of foliage leaves. *Stem* stiff, erect, leafy to near middle, 0.3 to 1.3 m tall. *Leaves* two ranked, with sheathing bases, leaf blades circular, hollow in cross section, striped, distinct odor, younger ones easily flattened, slenderly tapering. *Spathe* usually one, dry, thin, short, beaked, edges united above. *Umbel* projecting through base of deciduous spathe, nearly head shaped, 2 to 5 cm in diameter. *Occurrence* eastern and central United States, except northern border states, plus Pacific Northwest coastal areas.

YARROW, COMMON

Achillea millefolium **L.**

Perennial, very variable, reproducing by seeds and underground rootstocks, has offensive odor and bitter taste. *Stems* simple or somewhat forked above, 3 to 10 dm high, web-hairy to smooth. *Stem leaves* 8 to 20 cm, smooth to loosely hairy, dissected into fine segments. *Flowers* very compound, flattish top, 0.6 to 3 dm broad. *Involucre* slenderly cylindric, scales pale. *Ligules* usually whitish, passing to pink or deep rose purple, short-oblong, 1.5 to 2.5 mm long. *Receptacle* greatly prolonged in fruit. *Occurrence* throughout United States, except for Southwest, but especially in Northeast and central Midwest; prefers droughty, infertile soils; tolerates very close mowing.

Figure 10-6. *Broadleaf weeds/continued*

Table 10-2. Description, Symptoms, Environmental Factors, and Control of Algae and Moss

	Algae	*Moss*
Plant Description	Minute, single-celled, threadlike green plant; forms a thin, dense, green scum over soil surface; not a parasite; spores disseminate by wind and rain; blue-green is most common type.	Branched, threadlike, green plant; forms a tangled, thick, green mat over soil surface; not a parasite; spores disseminate by wind and rain.
Problem Symptoms	Dense, green scum forms a relatively impermeable surface layer; if the scum dries, a tough, black, impermeable, parchmentlike crust forms, which may crack and peel.	Can form very thick, distinct patches that disrupt the surface qualities of closely mowed turfs.
Environmental Factors Favoring Growth	Wet, humid, full sun conditions; compacted, waterlogged, fertile soils; thin, weak turf.	Wet, humid, shady conditions; acidic, infertile, poorly drained, waterlogged soils; excessive thatch; thin, weak turf.
Preventive Cultural Practices	Avoid excessive irrigation; insure adequate drainage through proper contouring and installation of drain lines, french drains, and dry wells, where needed; turf cultivation by coring or slicing especially advisable on fairways; root zone modification to a sandy mix on greens and tees; select best adapted turfgrass species and cultivars.	Avoid excessive irrigation; insure adequate drainage through proper contouring and installation of drain lines, french drains, and dry wells, where needed; turf cultivation by coring or slicing especially advisable on fairways; root zone modification to a sandy mix on greens and tees; adjust pH to between 6 and 7; insure adequate soil fertility and control excessive thatch/mat accumulation; select best adapted turfgrass species and cultivars.
Control	Apply copper sulfate at 2 to 3 ounces per 1,000 sq. ft. or mancozeb (Fore®); remove large areas of dead scum crust by spiking/raking; apply 2 to 3 lbs. of hydrated lime per 1,000 sq. ft.	Ferrous sulfate at 4 to 7 ounces* per 1,000 sq. ft. or ferrous ammonium sulfate at 10 ounces* per 1,000 sq. ft.; vertical power raking will assist in breaking up and partially removing the thick moss layer prior to chemical treatment; after death the remainder of the moss layer should be spiked/raked for removal of any remaining impervious layer.

*Caution: These rates will injure bentgrass on greens.

Weed Control

A high percentage of the potential weeds in turfs are controlled simply by execution of a well-planned, effective turfgrass cultural system. A thin, weak turf encourages the invasion and spread of weedy species. Thus, selection of well-adapted turfgrass species and cultivars combined with the proper mowing, fertilization, irrigation, turf cultivation, vertical cutting, insect control, and disease control practices will result in a dense, vigorous turf which has optimum capability to repel weed invasion.

Too intense a cultural program will enhance the potential for invasion of certain weedy species, such as annual bluegrass. Excessively close mowing, and especially scalping due to improper mowing frequency, must be avoided. Also, excessive irrigation or nitrogen nutritional levels result in a succulent turf that is less vigorous in terms of potential weed invasion and is more prone to disease attacks which result in bare areas ideal for weed invasion. Finally, the timing of vertical cutting and turf cultivation should be scheduled so that conditions are optimum for the desirable species to fill in the openings and least favorable for germination of weed seeds.

Sanitary Practices. Certain weedy species can be avoided primarily through proper sanitary practices. These include purchasing seed, sod, plugs, and vegetative plant material free from seed and vegetative propagules of weedy species. The same applies to purchase of soil and topdressing; this material also can be fumigated immediately after delivery, as most soils are contaminated with weed seed.

Finally, the golf course superintendent should be ever cognizant that seeds and vegetative propagules of weedy species can be readily transported from infested to noninfested areas on maintenance equipment such as mowers, vertical cutters, and turf cultivation units. Thorough cleaning, preferably with steam, before moving the equipment onto a noninfested area is an important sanitary practice.

Mechanical Control. Most of the more erect growing weeds will be controlled simply by frequent mowing, especially at heights of 1 inch (2.5 centimeters) or less. The proper mowing frequency contributes significantly in cutting off seedheads before viable seeds are produced to further contaminate an area. Fence rows, ditch banks, steep slopes, and similar minimal maintenance areas should be mowed at a frequency that prevents seed formation. These mechanical approaches are basically sanitary practices.

A second type of mechanical control involves physical removal of individual weeds by hand pulling or spudding, especially from greens and in some cases even tees. This approach is most effective on annual broadleaf weeds and is much less effective on perennial grassy species with deep underground rhizomes. Hand spudding should be accomplished before seedhead formation occurs and before deep rootstalks or rhizomes are formed for maximum effectiveness with perennial weedy species. Although somewhat laborious, hand weeding of scattered individual plants from greens is usually preferred, since it avoids potential herbicide phytotoxicity to the desirable species.

Preplant Control. Many future problems can be avoided by control of seeds and vegetative propagules of weeds existing in the soil prior to planting. Fallowing is a method of mechanical preplant weed control. It involves tillage of the soil at four- to six-week intervals. The objectives are to bring dormant weed seeds and vegetative plant propagules to the surface where conditions favor their growth and then to destroy all developing weeds. Adequate moisture must be available through either rainfall or irrigation to insure rapid seed germination or growth from vegetative propagules. The main disadvantages of fallowing are the extended length of time, as much as one year, needed to achieve mechanical weed control and the high potential for erosion. Also, the effectiveness in controlling certain weedy species is limited. For these reasons, chemical means of preplant weed control may be needed.

Fumigation. Soil fumigation is used for preplant chemical control of weeds, seeds, fungal pathogens, nematodes, insects, and rodents. Soil fumigation is more commonly practiced on intensively maintained sites, such as putting greens and tees, and on quarantine areas where complete eradication of a particular pest problem is desired. It is also used for killing potential pests in materials to be used in preparation of a soil root zone or topdressing mix. An effective soil fumigant should have as short a residual period as possible, preferably not more than three weeks. The common soil fumigants and their proper use are summarized in Table 10-3. A polyethylene cover is used to prevent upward atmospheric loss of the toxic vapors (Fig. 10-7).

Proper on-site soil preparation prior to fumigation includes deep tillage to a depth of at least 8 inches (20 centimeters) to facilitate movement of the fumigant to lower soil depths. Soil temperatures at a 2- to

Table 10-3. Characteristics of Fumigants Utilized on Golf Courses

Fumigant	Application Method*	Aeration Time (days)
Metam-sodium (Vapam®)	Apply as liquid drench, pack, and cover with water seal or polyethylene sheet	15 - 20
Methyl bromide and its combinations[†]	Release gas under polyethylene cover with all edges sealed in soil	2 - 3

*Both have minimum exposure time of 48 hours at soil temperatures above 60 °F (16 °C) before aeration can be initiated.

[†]Requires special handling due to high human toxicity.

All chemicals suggested for use should be applied in accordance with the directions on the manufacturer's label as registered under the Federal Insecticide, Fungicide, and Rodenticide Act. Mention of a trademark or proprietary product does not constitute a guaranty or warranty of the product by the author, the United States Golf Association, or the publisher and does not imply approval to the exclusion of other products that also may be suitable. The use of certain pesticides effective against turfgrass weeds, diseases, insects, small animals, and related pests may be restricted by some state, provincial, or federal agencies; thus, be sure to check the current status of the pesticide being considered for use.

Figure 10-7. Polyethylene cover being put into place, followed by fumigation with methyl bromide. (Photo courtesy of W. Daniel, Purdue University, West Lafayette, Ind.)

4-inch (5- to 10-centimeter) depth must be above 60 °F (16 °C) to further enhance downward movement of the fumigant. Finally, the soil should be moist to insure maximum biological activity of the problem pests to be controlled, since this increases their proneness to kill by the fumigant treatment. If adequate rainfall does not occur, the site should be irrigated for at least two weeks prior to the scheduled fumigation to insure proper moisture level. Individuals involved in the application of fumigants should always be cognizant that most fumigants are quite toxic to humans. They should only be applied by properly trained professionals utilizing the proper protective gear, including an appropriate gas mask or respirator, goggles, and protective clothing.

Herbicides

Even when biological, mechanical, and sanitary weed control practices are fully implemented, certain weedy species will still invade and persist in golf course turfs. The appropriate herbicide must then be selected to correct the problem. A range of herbicides are labeled for use on golf course turfs (Table 10-4).

Herbicides can be grouped according to whether they are applied preplant, preemergence, or postemergence. The preplant types (soil fumigants) were just discussed. *Preemergence herbicides* are those applied, usually to established turfs, before emergence of a specified weed or group of weeds. Since most preemergence herbicides are absorbed by root systems, it is important that they be washed off the leaves and into the soil by irrigation or rainfall to insure maximum absorption. This is important also because certain types of herbicides are subject to photochemical decomposition. In contrast, *postemergence herbicides* are applied to specific weeds after they emerge within a turfgrass community. Since postemergence herbicides are applied foliarly, it is important that the time between application and rain be sufficient to insure phytotoxicity. A rain immediately after application can wash much of the herbicide off the foliage. The effectiveness of postemergence herbicides also depends on adequate leaf area to insure absorption. The preemergence types usually have a considerably longer residual than the postemergence types. This is an advantage in controlling germinating weed seeds, but it also extends the duration of potential phytotoxicity to desirable species, which can be a problem if selectivity is marginal.

Whether or not the herbicide is actively translocated into the plant affects how it is utilized. *Contact, or nonsystemic, herbicides* kill only those parts of the plant on which they are applied. Death occurs very rapidly after application. Contact herbicides are utilized on annual weedy species or where nonselective total kill of vegetation is desired. In contrast, *systemic herbicides* are usually absorbed by the roots and translocated throughout the plant. Translocation is critical in achieving phytotoxicity in perennial weed species which possess underground rhizomes, nutlets, or rootstalks. For maximum effectiveness of systemic herbicides, the target weed must be physiologically active. Death of weeds treated with a systemic herbicide may take one to four weeks. Most systemic herbicides also exhibit selectivity in their phytotoxic characteristics.

Selectivity. The ability of a herbicide to control weeds within a turf community without killing or seriously injuring the desirable turfgrass species is termed selectivity. A *nonselective herbicide* is phytotoxic to all plants within the turfgrass community and thus is essentially a contact herbicide, as previously described. In contrast, a *selective herbicide* kills the target weed species without seriously injuring the desirable turfgrass species. The selectivity of most herbicides is relative. Most herbicides normally considered as possessing selective traits will kill desirable turfgrass species if applied at rates above that recommended on the label. Thus, selectivity is achieved through use of the proper rate, time, and application. Also, the selectivity of a herbicide varies depending on the particular turfgrass species and cultivar involved. The relative selectivities among the common turfgrass species used on golf courses are summarized in Table 10-5.

In terms of relative selectivity, the desirable turfgrass species may be injured without any obvious aboveground symptoms under certain conditions. For example, the root system is particularly vulnerable to injury, in comparison with the shoots. Under water-stress conditions, injury may be expressed in the form of increased proneness to visual wilt symptoms. Finally, the timing of preemergence

**Table 10-4. Trade Names
and Use Characteristics of Common Turfgrass Herbicides Used on Golf Courses**

Herbicide		Mode of Action*					
Common Name	Some Trade Names	Preemergence	Postemergence	Contact	Systemic	Nonselective Grass Killers	Selective Herbicides
Asulam	Asulox		X		X		X
Atrazine	AAtrex	X	X				X
Benefin	Balan	X					X
Bensulide	Betasan, Pre-San	X					X
Bentazon	Basagran		X		X		X
Bromoxynil	Brominal, Buctril, Nu-Lawn Weeder		X				X
2,4-D	Amine No. 4, Chipco Turf Herbicide D, Dacamine, DMA-4, Weedar 64, Weed-Rhap		X		X		X
Dalapon	Basfapon, Dowpon		X		X	X	
DCPA	Dacthal, DAC 893	X					X
Dicamba	Banex, Banvel, Banvel D, Mediben		X		X		X
DSMA	Arrhenal, Chipco Crab Kleen, Crab-E-Rad, Dal-E-Rad, Methar, Weed-Hoe		X		X		X
Endothall	Accelerate, Endothal, Endothal Turf Herbicide, Hydrothal 47		X		X		
Glyphosate	Roundup		X		X	X	
MCPA	Chiptox, Weedar MCPA		X		X		X
Mecoprop (MCPP)	Chipco Turf Herbicide MCPP, Compitox		X		X		X
Metribuzin	Sencor	X	X		X		X
MSMA	Daconate 6, Trans-Vert		X		X		X
Oxadiazon	Ronstar	X			X		X
Paraquat	Ortho Paraquat CL		X	X		X	
Pronamide	Kerb	X	X		X		X
Siduron	Tupersan	X			X		X
Simazine	Princep	X			X		X

*Based on usage at label rates.

All chemicals suggested for use should be applied in accordance with the directions on the manufacturer's label as registered under the Federal Insecticide, Fungicide, and Rodenticide Act. Mention of a trademark or proprietary product does not constitute a guaranty or warranty of the product by the author, the United States Golf Association, or the publisher and does not imply approval to the exclusion of other products that also may be suitable. The use of certain pesticides effective against turfgrass weeds, diseases, insects, small animals, and related pests may be restricted by some state, provincial, or federal agencies; thus, be sure to check the current status of the pesticide being considered for use.

herbicide applications relative to the scheduled date for winter overseeding of bermudagrass putting greens and tees is especially critical, since most of the commonly used winter overseeding grasses, such as perennial ryegrass, fine fescue, and bentgrass, lack the desired level of tolerance.

Soil Sterilants. Chemicals present in the soil that are toxic to plants for extended periods are termed *soil sterilants.* The duration a soil remains devoid of higher plant life depends on the particular chemical used, its rate of application, and the prevailing environmental conditions that affect leaching and

Table 10-5. Comparative Tolerance of Established Turfgrasses to the Common Herbicides

Herbicide	Annual Bluegrass	Bahiagrass	Bentgrass, Creeping	Bermudagrass	Bluegrass, Kentucky	Buffalograss	Centipedegrass	Fescue, Red	Fescue, Tall	Ryegrass, Perennial	St. Augustinegrass	Zoysiagrass
Asulam			T*							T		
Atrazine			m*				T			T	T*	
Benefin		T	m	T	T	T	T	T	T	T	T	T
Bensulide		T	T	T	T	T	T	T	T	T	T	T
Bentazon		T	T	T	T		T	T		T	T	T
Bromoxynil		T	T	T			T	T		T		
2,4-D	m	T	T‡	T	T	m	T	T	T	T		T
DCPA		T	m†	T†	T	T	T	m	T	T	T	T
Dicamba	T	T	m	T	T		T	T	T	T		T
DSMA, MSMA	m	m	m	T	T	T		T	m			m
Endothall			m	T	T				T	T	T	
Mecoprop (MCPP)	T	T	T	T	T		T	T	T	T		T
Oxadiazon		T		T	T		T		T	m		T
Pronamide		I		T		T	T					T
Siduron			T*,†	m	T			T	T	T		T.
Simazine			T*				T				T	T‡

NOTE: Blanks or no notation indicate severe injury. The user should be sure to confirm specific species and cultivar tolerance by checking the label on the product under consideration.

T Adequate tolerance with proper use according to label.
m Marginal tolerance; injury can occur.

*Variability among cultivars within a species may occur. The user should be sure to check label.

†Not labeled for closely mowed turfs such as greens.

‡Injury may occur under high-temperature stress.

decomposition. Soil sterilants have no specific role in the maintenance of golf course turfs. However, they are useful in preventing plant growth under fences, in parking lots, and in similar areas that are difficult to mow. The water solubility of the soil sterilant is an important factor to consider, owing to the potential for movement in surface water onto adjacent turf areas where damage may occur.

Broadleaf Weed Control. Most broadleaf weed problems are controlled by three main herbicides, 2,4-D, mecoprop, or dicamba, or a combination of these, as shown in Table 10-6. All are systemic, selective herbicides that usually are foliarly applied for postemergence control, often in combinations of two or three rather than singly. Dicamba can cause injury to ornamental shrubs and trees and should not be applied near the root systems of such species. Mecoprop and 2,4-D can injure flowers, ornamental shrubs, and trees through misapplication, as by wind-aided drift or volatile vapors.

Broadleaf herbicides should be applied when moisture and temperature favor active growth of the target weed. Where the broadleaf weed population is large, a second postemergence treatment may be needed at approximately a two-week interval to achieve acceptable control, especially with certain species that are difficult to control. Postemergence broadleaf weed control in cool-season grass turfs often is best accomplished in late summer or early fall. Control at this time facilitates rapid filling in of the resultant openings by the desirable grass species, since temperature and moisture conditions usually

Table 10-6. Five Common Herbicides and the Broadleaf Weeds They Control Selectively

2, 4-D *	Dicamba†	Mecoprop	2,4-D * + Mecoprop	2,4-D * + Mecoprop + Dicamba†
Aster	Carpetweed	Chickweed,	Chickweed,	Bedstraw
Bindweed‡	Chickweed,	common	common	Bindweed
Buttercup	common	Chickweed,	Chickweed,	Black medic
Canada thistle‡, §	Chickweed,	mouse-ear	mouse-ear	Burdock
Carpetweed	mouse-ear	Clover, red	Clover, white	Carpetweed
Chicory	Chicory	Clover, white	Dandelion	Chickweed
Dandelion§	Clover, bur	Dandelion	Dock, curly	Chicory
Dock‡	Clover, white	Dicondra	English daisy	Clover
Ground ivy‡	Dock, curly	Ground ivy	Ground ivy	Dandelion
Healall‡	English daisy	Knotweed	Knotweed	Dichondra
Kochia§	Hawkweed	Lambsquarters	Plantain,	Dock
Lambsquarters§	Henbit	Pigweed	broadleaf	Ground ivy
Mallow	Knotweed	Plantain	Plantain,	Healall
Morning glory	Lawn burweed		buckhorn	Henbit
Mustard§	Pepperweed		Red sorrel	Knotweed
Pennywort‡	Purslane		Speedwell	Lambsquarters
Pigweed§	Red sorrel		Spurweed	Lespedeza
Plantain§	Speedwell		Stitchwort	Mallow
Purslane	Spurge		Wild garlic	Morning glory
Ragweed§	Spurry		Wild onion	Peppergrass
Red sorrel‡	Spurweed		Yarrow	Pigweed
Shepherdspurse§				Plantain
Spurweed				Purslane
Wild carrot				Ragweed
Wild garlic‡				Red sorrel
Wild lettuce				Shepherdspurse
Wild onion‡				Speedwell
Yellow rocket§				Spurge
				Spurweed
				Wild carrot
				Wild garlic
				Wild lettuce
				Wild onion
				Wood sorrel
				Yarrow

NOTE: Effectiveness of herbicide combinations in controlling a specific weed will vary depending on the ratio of ingredients and labeled rate of application.

An individual weed may appear in more than one column.

*Not for use on turfs composed of carpetgrass and most cultivars of St. Augustinegrass.

†Not for use in the vicinity of trees or areas underlaid by roots of desirable trees and shrubs.

‡Difficult to control with 2, 4-D alone. Applications should be repeated at 7- to 10-day intervals.

§Also controlled by MCPA alone.

are more favorable for growth. Broadleaf weed control in warm-season species typically is accomplished in late spring or fall, depending on the region of the country, or during the winter when the warm-season turfgrasses are dormant. The latter approach is more common with use of such herbicides as paraquat, atrazine, or metribuzin.

Grassy Weed Control. Annual weedy grasses can be controlled either by preemergence or postemergence herbicide application (Tables 10-7 and 10-8). Selective, systemic preemergence herbicides must be applied in the spring prior to germination of the target weed species. Postemergence herbicides, such as the organic arsenicals, also can be used to control many annual weedy-grass species. Best control is achieved with such a herbicide if it is applied when the weedy-grass species is in an early growth stage. Multiple applications at ten- to fourteen-day intervals are usually required. Best control is achieved by allowing development of the largest amount of leaf surface possible to maximize absorption and translocation. Annual bluegrass control presents special problems, especially on bentgrass turfs. These problems are discussed in chapter 3.

Nonselective herbicides are occasionally used in turfgrass culture. For example, nonselective grass killers, such as dalapon and glyphosate, are systemic postemergence herbicides that are phytotoxic to grasses. Such herbicides are used in both spot treatment and treatment of large areas for control of both annual and perennial grass species which cannot be controlled selectively. Following a period for translocation and kill of both the aboveground and belowground plant parts, the dead foliage can be removed from the area, the root zone tilled, and the area reestablished by sodding, seeding, or sprigging.

Table 10-7. Perennial Grassy Weeds That Can Only Be Controlled Nonselectively

Weed (Common and Scientific Name)	Herbicide Treatment
Bentgrass* (*Agrostis* spp.) Bermudagrass* (*Cynodon* spp.) Kikuyugrass (*Pennisetum clandestinum*) Nimblewill (*Muhlenbergia schreberi*) Orchardgrass (*Dactylis glomerata*) Quackgrass (*Agropyron repens*) Tall fescue* (*Festuca arundinacea*) Torpedograss (*Panicum repens*) Velvetgrass (*Holcus lanatus*)	Apply nonselective systemic herbicide, such as glyphosate (Roundup℗) or dalapon (Dowpon℗), to actively growing foliage as spot treatment or general application or Use soil fumigant and then reestablish area by sodding, seeding, or sprigging

*Used as a desirable turfgrass but may also occur as weed in turf of other species.

Table 10-8. Grassy Weeds and Sedges and the Herbicides Used in Their Selective Control

Grassy Weed/Sedge (Common and Scientific Name)	Selective Herbicides*	
	Preemergence Application	Postemergence Application[†]
Annual bluegrass (*Poa annua*)	Benefin, bensulide, DCPA, oxadiazon, or pronamide	Endothall or pronamide
Bahiagrass (*Paspalum notatum*)		DSMA or MSMA
Barnyardgrass (*Echinochloa* spp.)	Benefin, bensulide, DCPA, oxadiazon, or siduron	DSMA or MSMA
Crabgrass: Large (*Digitaria sanguinalis*) Smooth (*Digitaria ischaemum*)	Benefin, bensulide, DCPA, oxadiazon, or siduron	Asulam[§], DSMA, or MSMA
Dallisgrass (*Paspalum dilatatum*)		DSMA or MSMA
Fall panicum (*Panicum dichotomiflorum*)	Bensulide or oxadiazon	
Foxtail: Green (*Setaria viridis*) Yellow (*Setaria glauca*)	Benefin, bensulide, DCPA, or siduron. Oxadiazon for use on green foxtail only	
Goosegrass (*Eleusine indica*)	Benefin[‡], bensulide[‡], DCPA[‡], or oxadiazon	Asulam or metribuzin[§]
Rescuegrass (*Bromus willdenowii*)		Endothall
Sandbur, Field (*Cenchrus pauciflorus*)	DCPA	DSMA or MSMA
Yellow nutsedge (*Cyperus esculentus*)		Bentazon, DSMA[‡], or MSMA[‡]

*The user should be sure to check label for species and cultivar tolerance and selectivity.

[†]DSMA or MSMA are applied postemergence in two treatments 10 to 14 days apart, preferably when weed is in a young stage.

[‡]Labeled, but control is marginal to ineffective in same locations.

[§]Label approved only in selected states.

INSECTS AND RELATED PESTS

There are over two million different kinds of insects, but relatively few pose a significant problem to turfgrasses. The severity of insect attacks on golf course turfs is not as highly correlated to the intensity of culture as is the case for disease-causing pathogens. The severity and frequency of insect attacks tend to be greater on warm-season than on cool-season turfgrasses. Specific insect problems common to warm-season and cool-season turfgrasses on greens, tees, and fairways are summarized in chapters 3, 4, and 5, respectively. In addition, general concepts of insect control as they relate to the three types of turfgrass cultural systems employed on golf courses are discussed in these chapters, and the reader is referred to them for further information.

Insect Description

Insects of the Insecta class (phylum Arthropoda) are very small members of the animal kingdom. They are characterized by three pairs of legs, a pair of antennae, a segmented body (head, thorax, and abdomen), and usually wings. There are other classes of arthropods which are nuisances in turfs. With the exception of the mites, however, they do not threaten direct damage to turfgrasses. The Arachnida class encompasses mites, spiders, scorpions, and ticks, species characterized by two main body segments, four pairs of jointed legs, wings, and the absence of antennae. Other nuisance pests include the centipedes of the Chilopoda class, which have a single pair of legs per body segment and more than five pairs of legs on a wormlike body. The millipedes of the Diplopoda class have two pairs of legs per body segment and more than five pairs of legs on a wormlike body. As the majority of turfgrass injury problems are caused by species in the Insecta class, the remainder of this discussion will be devoted primarily to these.

Insects can damage turfgrasses by direct feeding or by soil burrowing activity, which creates soil mounds or raised turfs that disrupt the surface quality of closely mowed turfs, especially putting greens. Mole crickets and certain species of ants, bees, and wasps are primarily objectionable in terms of soil mounding or tunneling that damages the turf either by smothering or by uplifting and severing the root system, which increases proneness to death by desiccation.

An understanding of the life cycle of each problem pest insect is important, since this is the basis for effective control with the least amount of pesticide. The two basic types of life cycle are simple and complete metamorphosis. Simple metamorphosis involves the development of a young nymph, from an egg, that possesses eye and wing structures similar to those of the adult. The nymph progresses through molting stages with associated increases in size until the adult develops. The number of molts can range from four to eight. Examples include the chinch bug and grasshopper. In complete metamorphosis the insect develops through distinctly different forms, starting with the egg and progressing to the wormlike larva, the pupa, and eventually the adult insect, usually possessing wings. Examples include the cutworm and fall armyworm.

Insects with a complete metamorphosis life cycle usually cause the majority of turfgrass injury during the larval stage, when they actively feed by chewing on the root and/or shoot system. In contrast, many of the insects associated with a simple metamorphosis cause turf damage by sucking vital juices from the turfgrass plant. Examples include the scale insects, leafhoppers, chinch bugs, and ground pearls.

An understanding of the insect life cycle is important to be able to apply appropriate control when the insect is most vulnerable. Many insects are best controlled in a relatively young nymphal stage, after a majority of the eggs have hatched but before significant turfgrass injury occurs. Knowledge concerning the time of year and specific environmental conditions when adults are most likely to lay eggs is critical. With this information, the time when the vulnerable stage occurs can be reliably predicted and thus serve as a basis for selecting the appropriate time for application of an insecticide. Some insects are best controlled in the larval stage prior to deposition of eggs.

Diagnosis

The pest insect or mite must be located and identified to insure selection of an insecticide that will effectively control the problem with the least possible broad-spectrum damage to nontarget insects. Regular inspections of golf course turf areas are important if serious injury from insect pests is to be avoided. Many pest insects feed nocturnally on shoots and remain hidden in the thatch or soil during the day. Others feed totally underground on the root system. Thus, it is quite possible for substantial damage to occur before the problem is recognized. Certain types of pest insect problems are unpredictable in their seasonal occurrence as well as from year to year in a given location.

Initial symptoms frequently include an increased proneness to wilt, owing to lack of roots for absorption of water or interference with upward translocation of water due to tunneling activity in the stems. Typical symptoms of insect damage include general yellowing, restricted shoot growth, defoliation of leaves and shoots, and lack of roots. Damage may become visible as irregular patches which gradually expand.

A detailed examination for problem insects should include cutting of a turf plug and thorough examination of the sod for root injury symptoms as well as injury to the aboveground shoots and lateral stems. This close examination should also reveal the actual insect. Use of a $10 \times$ magnifying glass is advisable, especially if the presence of mites, scale insects, or smaller stem-tunneling insects is suspected. Symptoms associated with each of the common insect pests on golf courses are summarized in Table 10-9. Figure 10-8 illustrates damage and the causative pests. Figure 10-9 shows the rastral patterns used to identify the white grub species.

A pyrethrum test often is helpful in pest insect diagnosis. It involves sprinkling of a mixture of 2 percent pyrethrum in 1 gallon of water over a 1-square-yard turf area encompassing both damaged and undamaged turfs. If present, many insects will emerge to the surface within ten minutes owing to the irritating effects of the pyrethrum. A common household detergent will serve the same purpose with less potential for foliar burn. White grubs and larvae of billbugs do not respond well to the pyrethrum test. Thus, careful digging around the turfgrass roots and the thatch is an appropriate procedure for diagnosing these pests.

Insect Control

A properly maintained, healthy turf is more likely to recover from insect injury. Such turfs have the capability of functioning at an adequate quality level even in the presence of scattered, low populations of pest insects. Only when major attacks of a particular pest insect occur and the damage threshold is exceeded are insecticide applications needed.

Preventive approaches to minimizing problems with destructive pest insects are generally preferred. Included are sanitary practices and use of resistant cultivars. Certain types of relatively immobile insects can be controlled through sanitary practices. Introduction of such insects as ground pearls can be avoided by not bringing contaminated sod, soil, or turfgrass equipment into noninfested areas. A second option is the use of resistant turfgrass cultivars. Unfortunately, available cultivars resistant to insect damage are rather limited in comparison with those resistant to turfgrass diseases.

Once a particular pest insect is known to be present in damaging numbers, the appropriate insecticide can be selected and applied. The modern approach is control of only the particular problem insect which threatens to cause serious turfgrass damage, rather than insecticide applications on a continuous basis throughout the season. The turf should be well irrigated one day prior to application of the insecticide. This maximizes control of shoot-sucking or -chewing insects, since the insecticide can remain for the longest possible period before the next irrigation is required or rainfall occurs. In the case of root-feeding pest insects, the insecticide should be thoroughly watered in immediately after application for maximum effectiveness. It is generally preferable that insecticide applications be avoided during temperature extremes above 90 °F (32 °C) or below 60 °F (16 °C).

Table 10-9. Turfgrass Injury Symptoms, Causal Insects, Host Species, and Methods of Control

Turfgrass Injury Symptoms	Causal Insect or Related Pest	Description of Pest	Life History and Habits	Major Turfgrasses Attacked	Methods of Control
Irregular, brown patches of dead grass					
Roots pruned to 1 inch or less below soil surface; sod easily lifted or rolled back; C-shaped white grubs found by lifting sod	**White grub** Asiatic garden beetle (*Maladera castanea*) Black turfgrass ataenius (*Ataenius spretulus*) European chafer (*Rhizotropus majalis*) Japanese beetle (*Popillia japonica*) June beetle (*Phyllophaga* spp.) Northern mask chafer (*Cyclocephala borealis*) Oriental beetle (*Anomala orientalis*) Southern mask chafer (*Cyclocephala immaculata*) Rastral patterns used to identify grub species in Figure 10-9	Grubs grayish white, brown head, 3 to 38 mm long, 6 legs, C-shaped resting position; adult a hard-shelled beetle, yellow brown to black, some bright blue green or yellow with metallic luster	Most adults emerge in summer, *Phyllophaga* during spring; larvae hatch from eggs and feed on roots 0 to 4 inches below surface; life cycle of a few months to 2 or 3 years or longer	Most turfgrasses	Bendiocarb, diazinon, trichlorfon,[1] chlorpyrifos,[1] ethoprop, isophenphos,[2] pirimiphos ethyl[2] fensulfothion[1][2]; from preirrigation suggested; after application, drench into soil root zone with water; *Bacillus japonica* for Japanese beetle only
Yellowish patches gradually progressing to brown; close examination reveals grass stems hollowed out or severed at base from feeding activity of larvae and adults, respectively	**Turfgrass weevil** (*Hyperodes* spp.)	Larva 1 to 4.5 mm long, straight, legless, creamy white with dark brown head; adult weevil 3.5 mm long with elongated snout; young adults orange to brown, turning mottled brown to dull gray or black	Eggs deposited in holes in outer leaf sheath; larvae hatch in 4 to 9 days; larvae actively feed in stem, adults on blades; one to two generations per year	Annual bluegrass	Chlorpyrifos, diazinon,[2] or isophenphos[2]

Turfgrass Injury Symptoms	Causal Insect or Related Pest	Description of Pest	Life History and Habits	Major Turfgrasses Attacked	Methods of Control
Small spots expanding to large, irregular areas; young larvae feed in stems; move below ground as they mature to feed on roots; larvae may be found by digging inside the perimeter of affected area	**Bilbug** Bluegrass (*Sphenophorus parvulus*) Hunting (*S. veratus vestitus*) Phoenix (*S. phoeniciensis*)	Larvae white, legless, 6 to 16 mm long with hard yellowish-brown to reddish-brown head; adults small (6.3 to 8 mm long), hard-shelled, gray to black to brown beetles with distinct long snout	Eggs laid in grass stems, hatch in 3 to 14 days; larvae feed for several weeks before forming pupae in the soil; adults form within a few days; one to multiple generations occur annually depending on location	Bahiagrass Bermudagrass Kentucky bluegrass Zoysiagrass	Carbaryl, chlorpyrifos, diazinon, isophenphos,[2] or propoxur[2]; drench with water after treatment; may need to reapply in 2 to 3 weeks
Small wilted patches, soon turn yellow, enlarge to 2 to 3 feet, then turn brown; typically occurs during hot, dry weather in sunny sites; chinch bugs found by close examination of grass shoots near soil surface and in thatch, flotation method can also be used for positive diagnosis	**Chinch bug** Common (*Blissus leucopterus leucopterus*) Hairy (*B. leucopterus hirtus*) Southern (*B. insularis*)[3]	Adults 4 to 5 mm long with black body, reddishyellow legs, and short or fully developed wings; each front wing primarily white with an irregular black patch at middle of outer margin; small nymphs bright red; large nymphs blackish; all stages feed by sucking plant juices	Eggs laid in lower sheaths of grasses over several weeks; nymphs emerge after 1 to 2 weeks and have 5 stages, followed by active adult feeding for 6 to 10 weeks; number of generations per year is one to two in north and two to seven in south	Bahiagrass Bentgrass Bermudagrass Bluegrass Centipedegrass Red fescue St. Augustinegrass Zoysiagrass (depending on *Blissus* species)	Bendiocarb, carbaryl, carbophenothion, chlorpyrifos, diazinon, ethion, isophenphos,[2] propoxur,[2] or propyl thiopyrophosphate; irrigate turf prior to treatment; afterwards water in; may need to reapply after 4 to 6 weeks for southern chinch bug

(Continued)

Table 10-9/Continued

Turfgrass Injury Symptoms	Causal Insect or Related Pest	Description of Pest	Life History and Habits	Major Turfgrasses Attacked	Methods of Control
Plants defoliated to the soil					
Irregular yellow to brown patches; signs of feeding activity on both leaves and stems; close examination reveals silk-lined burrows near turf surface where larvae remain in daytime	**Sod webworm** Bluegrass (*Crambus teterrellus*) Corn root (*C. caliginosellas*) Grass (*Herpetogramma licarsisalis*) Striped (*C. mutabilis*) Tropical (*H. phaeopteralis*)	Larvae slender, grayish, plain to black spotted caterpillar, about 2 cm long; adult is white to grayish to brown moth with snout-like projection from head, wing span of over 2.5 cm folded close to body when at rest	Adults rest in shrubbery and sheltered areas during day, at night they drop eggs on turf during flight or lay eggs on grass shoots; eggs hatch in 1 week; larvae feed nocturnally for 3 to 4 weeks and hide in tunnels lined with grass debris; pupa stage is 1 week; life cycle is 5 to 6 weeks with two to five generations annually	All turfgrasses	Bendiocarb, carbaryl, chlorpyrifos, diazinon, ethion, ethoprop, isofenphos,[2] methomyl, pirimiphos-ethyl,[2] propoxur, propyl thiopyrophosphate, toxaphene, or trichlorfon; apply in late afternoon or evening, with irrigation delayed as long as possible; *Bacillus thurieg* is effective against tropical sod webworm
Circular to irregular whitish patches, leaves skeletonized; close examination reveals numerous greenish larvae feeding along perimeter; occurs as sporadic problem; flotation method aids detection	**Armyworm** (*Pseudaletia unipuncta*)	Larvae dark green, smooth, hairless, 2.5 to 3.8 cm long; head greenish brown; one stripe along each side, plus broad stripe down back; adult brownish-gray moth with small white spot near center of each front wing	Eggs laid at night; larvae hatch and feed nocturnally on leaves and stems for 3 to 4 weeks, then burrow 2 to 3 inches into soil to form pupae; approximately three generations per year	All turfgrasses	Chlorpyrifos, diazinon, toxaphene, or trichlorfon; apply in late afternoon or evening, delay irrigation as long as possible; repeat applications may be needed in some regions

Turfgrass Injury Symptoms	Causal Insect or Related Pest	Description of Pest	Life History and Habits	Major Turfgrasses Attacked	Methods of Control
Circular to irregular whitish patches; large grass areas may be eaten to soil surface during severe outbreaks; numerous larvae evident during severe attack	**Fall army worm** (*Spodoptera frugiperda*)	Young larvae white with black heads, darken on maturity, 2.5 to 3.8 cm long, wide dark stripes on each side of light midstripe on back, next to each dark stripe is wavy stripe with some red, head with inverted white *Y*; adult ashgray moth with mottled fore wings having white or light-gray spots near tips, hind wings white with smokey-brown edge	Adults lay eggs on leaves at night and cover with light grayish fuzz; emerging larvae curl up inside leaf sheath, suspend from plants by threads, and move about soil surface; larvae feed 2 to 3 weeks, then burrow 2 to 3 inches into soil and pupate; adults emerge in 10 to 14 days; from one to ten generations per year depending on latitude	Most turfgrasses, especially bermudagrass	Chlorpyrifos, diazinon, toxaphene, or trichlorfon; apply in late afternoon or evening with irrigation delayed until the next day; repeat applications may be needed in some regions
Plants severed at soil surface by 1.5 to 2 inch-long brownish-black caterpillars; pyrethrin test aids diagnosis	**Cutworm** (*Noctuidae* family)	Larvae thick-bodied 3.8 to 5 cm-long caterpillars; greenish gray, brown, or black, often with spots or stripes; adults night-flying moths of somber color, wing span of 2.5 to 3.8 cm	Moths lay eggs on grass leaves at night; larvae feed at night on leaves and stems, in daytime hide in holes under debris or in thatch/mat; one generation per year for most species, two to four per year for some	All turfgrasses	Carbaryl, chlorpyrifos, diazinon, toxaphene, or trichlorfon; apply in late afternoon or evening

(Continued)

Table 10-9/Continued

Turfgrass Injury Symptoms	Causal Insect or Related Pest	Description of Pest	Life History and Habits	Major Turfgrasses Attacked	Methods of Control
Stunted, thin turf; individual plants may turn brown or die					
Close examination reveals whitish moldy-appearing material on stems and crown; most commonly occurs in shaded sites and turfs with excess thatch/mat	**Bermudagrass scale** (*Odonaspis ruthae*)	Adult female wingless, legless, covered by white, cone-shaped or oval, moderately convex secretion of 1 to 1.75 mm in diameter; resembles small oyster shell; male one-half size of female with one pair of wings	Newly hatched nymphs mobile, but within few hours settle down, insert mouth parts into stem to suck juices, lose antennae and legs, and begin sessile existence; stems within leaf axils are primary attack sites	Bermudagrass, St. Augustine-grass	Carbophenothion or diazinon; apply as spray and repeat in 3 to 4 weeks
Examination of turf reveals white cottony secretion on crowns, stems, and nodes	**Rhodesgrass mealybug** (*Antonina graminis*)	Adults 1.6 mm in diameter, globular, dark purplish brown with white cottony covering; females 3 mm in diameter, males one-third this size	Gives birth to living young; larvae wedge beneath leaf sheaths at nodes or in crown, insert mouthparts, and begin immobile existence; felted, waxy covering is secreted; life cycle is 50 to 60 days with up to five generations annually	Bermudagrass, St. Augustine-grass	Successful biological control implemented in Texas following release of wingless parasite *Neadusmetia sangwani* Rao.; carbophenothion or diazinon; apply as spray and repeat in 3 to 4 weeks

Turfgrass Injury Symptoms	Causal Insect or Related Pest	Description of Pest	Life History and Habits	Major Turfgrasses Attacked	Methods of Control
Infested turfs turn brown in summer and die in fall in irregular spots; examination of sod plug to 2-inch soil depth reveals globular, whitish shells attached to roots	Ground pearls (*Margarodes meridonalis*) (*Eumargarodes laingi*)	Immature stages occur in soil as small, pearl-like cysts; scale insect covered with hard, whitish, globular shell up to 3 mm in diameter	Nymphs hatch from eggs, crawl onto grass roots, and attach needlelike mouthparts; protective, pearl-like covering formed rapidly, under which nymph matures and leads sessile existence; 1-year life cycle	Bermudagrass Centipedegrass St. Augustinegrass	Fumigate with methyl bromide and reestablish; follow sanitary practices to prevent introduction[4]
Stunted, tufted shoots due to severely shortened stem internodes; shoots become yellowish, turn brown, and die, which leads to turf thinning	Bermudagrass mite (*Eriophyes cynodeniensis*)	Extremely small, white, 8-legged, oblong mites which can barely be seen with 10X hand lens; two distinct pairs of legs near head; no antennae or wings	Eggs hatch in 5 to 6 days; life cycle of 3 instars completed in 5 to 6 days; mites live beneath leaf sheath where they suck juices from stem; several generations occur per season	Bermudagrass	Carbophenothion or diazinon; repeat application at 2- to 3-week interval may be needed
Bleached or dry areas; white to brown dots on leaves; small 6 mm-long hopping insects spring up when turf is walked on	Leafhoppers Aster (*Macrosteles fascifrons*) Clover (*Aceratagallia sahguinolenta*) Lawn (*Recila hospes*) Painted (*Endria inimica*) Potato (*Empoasca fabae*)	Adults whitish green, yellow, or brownish gray, may be speckled or mottled; small, wedge shaped, very active insect 4 to 6 mm long, which flies or jumps short distances when disturbed; nymphs various colors but wingless	Eggs inserted into leaf tissue, hatch 5 to 14 days later; both adults and nymphs suck juices by puncturing leaves and stems	All turfgrasses	Carbaryl or diazinon; apply at 4- to 5-week intervals if damage becomes severe

(Continued)

411

Table 10-9/Continued

Turfgrass Injury Symptoms	Causal Insect or Related Pest	Description of Pest	Life History and Habits	Major Turfgrasses Attacked	Methods of Control
Stunted thin turf; individual plants may turn brown or die					
Turf unthrifty, slow growing; emerging leaves and stem apex damaged; individual plants turn brown and die; small black flies may be seen hovering over turf; examination of stems near soil surface reveals larvae tunneling	**Frit fly** (*Oscinella frits*)	Mature larvae 4 mm long, yellow, with black curved mouth-hooks; adults shiny black, about 4 mm long, with small yellow markings on legs	Larvae overwinter in stems; pupation occurs in spring, followed by emergence of adults; eggs laid on leaves; larvae hatch and feed by tunneling in stems near soil surface; most damage caused by larvae	All grasses, bentgrass and bluegrass being most susceptible	Diazinon; irrigate well before treatment and delay watering again as long as possible
Soil mounding or tunneling that smothers or lifts turf, which dries out and dies					
Burrows uproot turfgrass plants and soil during noctural feeding; objectionable on closely mowed turfs, especially putting greens; pyrethrin test aids detection	**Mole cricket** Puerto Rican, or Changa (*Scapteriscus vicinus*) Southern (*S. acletus*) Short-winged (*S. abbreviatus*) Northern (*Neocurtilla hexadactyla*)	Adult 6 mm wide, covered with fine hairs, with distinct broad, shovel-like fore tibia used in burrowing; southern mole cricket greenish gray with light markings on thorax; Puerto Rican mole cricket creamy to dark brown	Mating flights during early spring; females lay eggs few inches below soil surface; nymphs hatch and feed nocturnally on roots, especially in moist soils; adults emerge in late summer - early fall; one or two generations per year	Most turfgrasses, especially bahiagrass and bermudagrass	Bendiocarb, chlorpyrifos, diazinon, ethoprop, or propoxur; apply when night temperatures at least 60 °F (16 °C) and soil moist; irrigate before and after spray or granular application (but do not irrigate when using a bait)

Turfgrass Injury Symptoms	Causal Insect or Related Pest	Description of Pest	Life History and Habits	Major Turfgrasses Attacked	Methods of Control
Distinct soil mounds of varying size smother turf, may create obstructions to mowing, and are especially objectionable in disrupting surface smoothness of putting greens; certain species, such as fire ant, can impart painful stings	**Ants** (*Formicidae* family)	Adults range greatly in size depending on species and caste; may be shiny black to reddish yellow in color; possess distinct, large abdomen, 6 legs, and pair of antennae	Have distinct social organization including construction of elaborate nests, occupied by queen, adult workers, eggs, larvae, and pupae; mounding activity by adult worker ants	All turfgrasses	Carbaryl, chlorpyrifos, or diazinon; drench into soil root zone with water; may only need to spot-spray hills

[1] Controls only selected species of grubs.

[2] Label approved only in selected states.

[3] Feeds almost exclusively on St. Augustinegrass.

[4] No insecticide use label issued; sanitary practices must be followed to prevent introduction.

WHITE GRUB

A. Damage to turf in a rough.
B. Sod is pulled back to expose typical problem grub population. (Photo courtesy of James A. Reinert, University of Florida, Agricultural Research Center, Fort Lauderdale, Fla.)
C. Close-up of typical white grubs: European chafer (*left*) and Japanese beetle (*right*). (Photo courtesy of H. Tashiro, Department of Entomology, New York State Agricultural Experiment Station, Geneva, N.Y.)
D. Close-up of adult European chafer. (Photo courtesy of H. Tashiro.)

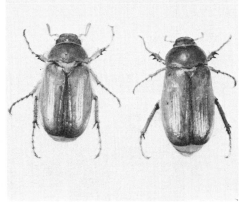

Figure 10-8. Symptoms of turf injury and the associated pest insect frequently found in golf course turfs.

A

B

TURFGRASS (HYPERODES) WEEVIL

A. Turfgrass weevil damage to annual
    bluegrass in putting green surrounds. (Photo
    courtesy of H. Tashiro.)

BLACK TURFGRASS
(ATQENIUS SPRETULUS)

B. Close up *(left to right)* of larva, pupa,
    callow adult, and mature adult. (Photo
    courtesy of H. Tashiro.)

BILLBUG

A. Billbug damage to turf in irrigated rough. (Photo courtesy of James A. Reinert, University of Florida.)
B. Bluegrass billbug larvae. (Photo courtesy of H. Tashiro.)
C. Bluegrass billbug adult. (Photo courtesy of H. Tashiro.)

Figure 10-8. *Turf injuries and associated pests/continued*

A

B

CHINCH BUG

A. Chinch bug damage to turf on collar of a green.
B. Chinch bug adult. (Photo courtesy of H. Tashiro.)

A

B

C

SOD WEBWORM

A. Sod webworm damage to a Kentucky bluegrass turf.
B. Sod webworm larva. (Photo courtesy of H. Tashiro.)
C. Sod webworm moth. (Photo courtesy of H. Tashiro.)

A

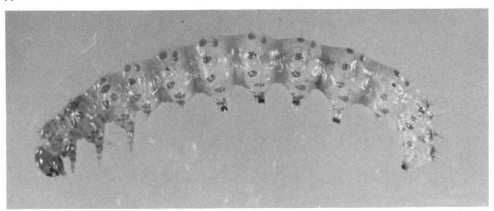

B

TROPICAL SOD WEBWORM

A. Tropical sod webworm damage to bermudagrass. (Photo courtesy of James A. Reinert, University of Florida.)

B. Tropical sod webworm larva. (Photo courtesy of James A. Reinert, University of Florida.)

C. Tropical sod webworm moth. (Photo courtesy of James A. Reinert, University of Florida.)

C

Figure 10-8. *Turf injuries and associated pests/continued*

A

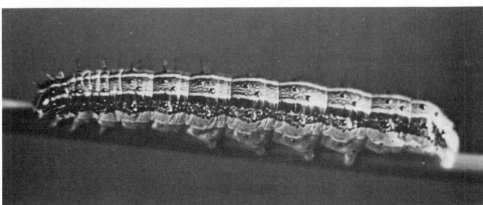

B

C

FALL ARMYWORM

A. Fall armyworm damage to a bentgrass turf.
B. Fall armyworm larva. (Photo courtesy of V. R. Coleman, University of Georgia, Athens, Ga.)
C. Fall armyworm moth. (Photo courtesy of James A. Reinert, University of Florida.)

A

B

CUTWORM

A. Damage caused by cutworms feeding on a putting green.

B. Black cutworm larvae. (Photo courtesy of James A. Reinert, University of Florida.)

C. Black cutworm moth. (Photo courtesy of R. Rings and G. Berkey, Ohio Agricultural Research and Development Center, Wooster, Ohio.)

C

Figure 10-8. *Turf injuries and associated pests/continued*

A

B

C

SCALE INSECTS

A. Bermudagrass scale. (Photo courtesy of James A. Reinert, University of Florida.)
B. Rhodesgrass mealybug. (Photo courtesy of James A. Reinert, University of Florida.)
C. Ground pearls: cluster (*left*) and close-up (*right*). (Photos courtesy of James A. Reinert, University of Florida.)

A

B

BERMUDAGRASS MITE

A. Bermudagrass fairway turf damaged by bermudagrass mite. (Photo courtesy of James A. Reinert, University of Florida.)

B. Close-up of stunted, tufted growth of a bermudagrass shoot apex caused by bermudagrass mite. (Photo courtesy of James A. Reinert, University of Florida.)

C. Magnified close-up of bermudagrass mites. (Photo courtesy of James A. Reinert, University of Florida.)

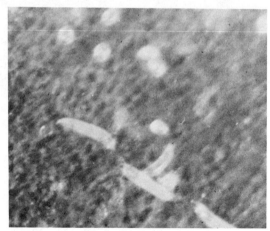

C

Figure 10-8. *Turf injuries and associated pests/continued*

A

MOLE CRICKET

A. Mole cricket damage to a bermudagrass tee. (Photo courtesy of James A. Reinert, University of Florida.)
B. Close-up of changa mole cricket. (Photo courtesy of James A. Reinert, University of Florida.)

B

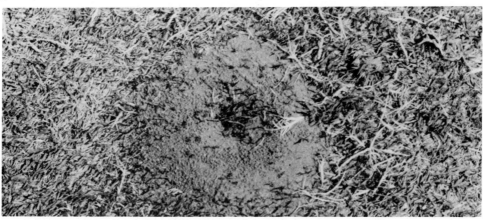

ANTS   Close-up of a typical ant mound in a closely mowed turf.

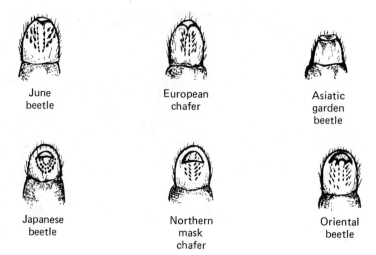

June
beetle

European
chafer

Asiatic
garden
beetle

Japanese
beetle

Northern
mask
chafer

Oriental
beetle

Figure 10-9. Characteristic rastral patterns used in identification of six common white grubs.

The options available in insecticides are much more limited than is the case for herbicides or fungicides. Most have a relatively short residual nature. This dictates frequent applications if an insect problem persists. The insecticides labeled for turf use are summarized in Table 10-10. Insecticides are applied in the form of baits, dusts, granules, sprays marketed as wettable powders, soluble powders, or emulsifiable concentrates. Sprays are applied in amounts needed to thoroughly wet the aboveground shoots, commonly 1 gallon of spray per thousand square feet (3.5 liters per are).

Most insecticides can cause injury to humans and animals if improperly used. The operator must thoroughly read and understand the directions on the label and practice all special precautions recommended. Appropriate protective devices, including respirators, goggles, and protective clothing, should be worn whenever recommended. Also, guidelines concerning handling and storage must be followed.

SMALL ANIMALS

Damage to turfgrass caused by small animals is a much less frequent occurrence than damage caused by disease and insects, but it can be very severe where it does occur. Typically, it takes the form of soil mounding, burrowing, and tearing away of the turf. Burrowing activity elevates the sod and severs the root system to the extent that grass may be weakened or even die as a result of desiccation. Many small animals cause damage in seeking food such as grubs, worms, or crickets. Some small animals live in or under the sod, while larger animals migrate to the turfgrass area while feeding and live in surrounding areas such as fence rows, ditches, and minimal maintenance woodland areas. Occurrence of damage by small animals may be seasonal as a result of climatic conditions, the life cycle of their insect food source, and the breeding-activity cycle of the animal involved. The activities of small animals are nonspecific in that all turfgrass species are subject to damage.

Damage symptoms caused by common small pest animals are summarized in Table 10-11 and illustrated in Figure 10-10.

Table 10-10. Common Insecticides Used on Golf Courses and the Insects and Mites They Are Labeled to Control

Common Name	Some Trade Names	White Grubs	Turfgrass Weevil	Sod Webworm	Rhodegrass Mealybug	Mole Cricket	Leafhoppers	Frit Fly	Fall Armyworm	Cutworm	Chinch Bug	Billbug	Bermudagrass Scale	Bermudagrass Mite	Armyworm	Ants
Bendiocarb	Turcam	x*		x		x				x						x
Carbaryl	Sevin	m*		x		b	x		m	x						
Carbophenothion	Trithion				x					x		x	x			
Chlorpyrifos	Dursban, Lorsban, Proturf Insecticide III	x*		x		xb	x		x	x		x	x			x
Diazinon	Diazinon, Spectracide, Proturf Insecticide I			x		x	x		x	x		x	x			x
Ethion	Ethion	x	x†	x		x	x		x	x						x
Ethoprop	Mocap, Proturf Nematicide/Insecticide	x*				x										
Fensulfothion	Dasanit, Terracur P	x*														
Isofenphos	Oftanol	x†	x†	x†							x†	x†				
Malathion	Cython, Karbofos, Malathion					b										
Methomyl	Lannate			x												
Pirimiphos-ethyl	Primicid	x†		x†						x†						
Propoxur	Blattanex, Baygon, Suncide			x		xb				x	x†	x†				
Propyl thiopyrophosphate	Aspon			x							x					
Toxaphene	Toxaphene								x	x					x	
Trichlorfon	Dylox, Proxol	x		x					x	x					x	

x Labeled for control.
m Labeled, but control is marginal to ineffective in some locations.
b Bait
*Controls only selected species of grubs.
†Label approved only in selected states.

All chemicals suggested for use should be applied in accordance with the directions on the manufacturer's label as registered under the Federal Insecticide, Fungicide, and Rodenticide Act. Mention of a trademark or proprietary product does not constitute a guaranty or warranty of the product by the author, the United States Golf Association, or the publisher and does not imply approval to the exclusion of other products that also may be suitable. The use of certain pesticides effective against turfgrass weeds, diseases, insects, small animals, and related pests may be restricted by some state, provincial, or federal agencies; thus, be sure to check the current status of the pesticide being considered for use.

Table 10-11. Injury Symptoms, Causal Animals, and Methods of Control

Injury Symptoms	Causal Pest	Description of Pest	Animal Activities and Habits	Protectants and Controls
Animal burrows and associated soil mounds				
3 to 5 inch-diameter, open burrows; bare ground around burrows from animals feeding on green vegetation	**Ground squirrel** (*Spermophilus* spp.) Several species, each in specific regions of western North America	Rodent ranging from 8 to 11 inches long with bushy tail of 5 to 8 inches in length; gray to brown mottled color striping; internal cheek pouches opening just inside lips for carrying food	Subterranean dweller digs extensive burrows which remain open year-around; tends to live in large colonies in open, grassy, or rocky areas; main food seeds, green vegetation, and insects; feeding activity primarily in daytime	Poison baits are common control, with best type determined by testing; can use anticoagulants where poison hazard to humans and other animals is high; fumigation effective on moist soils; trapping with modified station bait-box trap effective and safe, but slow for large numbers
Distinct round to fan-shaped, fresh earth mounds with burrows 4 to 12 inches below ground	**Pocket gopher** (*Geomys* and *Thomomys* spp.)	Rodent 6 to 8 inches in length; tail 3 to 4 inches long; blunt head with small eyes and ears; external fur-lined cheek pouches for carrying food; large incisor teeth not covered by lips; fore feet with long slender claws for digging	Solitary, digs extensive tunnels 4 to 12 inches below ground, which facilitates feeding on roots; occasionally feeding involves defoliation of surface vegetation within body length of burrow opening	Trapping by placing specially designed trap directly in excavated burrow, followed by careful covering of opening and daily checking; poison-grain baits placed in burrows effective in some situations; fumigation generally less effective
Numerous small ¼- to ½-inch soil mounds or castings; primarily a problem on putting greens where mounds disrupt surface smoothness needed for ball roll	**Earthworm** Burrowing activities beneficial in enhancing soil aeration, infiltration, percolation, and organic matter content	Large soil-dwelling annelid worms; genus *Lumbricus* is one of the more common in North America	Worms retreat downward in dry weather, whereas under waterlogged conditions they move to surface; they emerge at night to feed on dead plant debris; activity favored by moist soils with pH near neutral and high organic matter content	Earthworms generally encouraged in fairways and roughs due to their beneficial activities; however, on putting greens their castings on surface can become objectionable and thus dictate need for chemical control

Injury Symptoms	Causal Pest	Description of Pest	Animal Activities and Habits	Protectants and Controls
Raised tunnels and soil mounds Raised ridges of uplifted sod running randomly across surface with occasional cone-shaped, loose mounds of soil; starnosed mole produces extremely large soil mounds	**Mole** (*Scapanus* spp.)	Not a rodent; has soft, dense fur; is 7 to 9 inches long with short tail of 1 to 2 inches; distinguished by long pointed snout and no external eyes or ears; no cheek pouches; numerous small teeth that do not protrude; shovel-like forepaws have short, heavy claws	Very active soil-burrowing animal; prefers moist grassy areas; digging involves deep burrows and near-surface tunneling, which creates sod ridges above ground; burrowing associated with constant feeding on soil insects, larvae, and earthworms along with seeds and roots	Best control is trapping with special mole traps placed in runway; second approach is removal of food supply by use of soil insecticides; fumigation of limited success due to extensive burrowing; poison baits have been of limited effectiveness
Bare runways and holes in sod Extensive network of barren runways, nesting areas, and holes through turfgrass canopy; mice may be seen in daytime during summer activities; is common occurrence under winter snow cover; shoots are defoliated	**Vole** (*Microtus* spp.) **Mouse** (*Muridae* family)	Stout-bodied rodents; large head; brown color; 4 to 6 inches long with soft body fur; almost hairless, short tail of 1 to 2 inches	Dig 1 to 2 inch-diameter burrows straight down into ground and cut elaborate network of surface runways in turf vegetation between burrows; feed on seeds and on green vegetation by chewing off at soil surface; can cause extensive turf damage under winter snow cover	Poison baits sometimes helpful; protect against winter damage by removal of excess vegetation from adjacent fence rows, ditch banks, roadsides, and woodlands which function as feeding reservoir for population buildups

(Continued)

Table 10-11/Continued

Injury Symptoms	Causal Pest	Description of Pest	Animal Activities and Habits	Protectants and Controls
Turf torn and dug out				
Large irregular patches where turf has been dug out as result of search for grubs, insects, and worms	**Armadillo, badger, raccoon, and skunk**	Descriptions well known; digging activity in turf areas in search of food relatively infrequent but can cause extensive damage where it occurs	Digging primarily during night, as these animals have nocturnal feeding habits	Trapping with modified station bait-box trap suggested if nightly pattern occurs, or removal of food source by use of appropriate soil insecticide
Numerous small holes ½- to 1-inch deep and ¼- to ½-inch wide at surface; most commonly problem on putting greens	**Birds** Associated with large groups of birds, such as black birds and starlings; evidence of damage indicated by birds working on turf area	Descriptions well known	Digging due to birds feeding on insect larvae found in turf; this is biological indicator of impending insect attack on turf	Remove food source by application of insecticide, which will also prevent turf damage from feeding activity of larvae
Worn, depressed animal runways in turf				
6- to 12-inch-wide trails extending across turf; also irregular patches of dark green and/or dead, light tan turf	**Dogs, etc.** Large, four-legged animals that tend to follow a routine path	Descriptions well known	Distinct trails created by routine daily traffic of dogs and certain other large four-legged animals; dogs from adjacent residences may urinate on specific turf areas	Install fence, if continuing problem anticipated

A

B

C

PEST ANIMALS

A. Ground squirrel and open burrow. (Photos courtesy of R. Johnson and R. Timm, Department of Forestry, Fisheries, and Wildlife, University of Nebraska, Lincoln, Neb.)

B. Pocket gopher and earth mounds. (Photos courtesy of R. Johnson and R. Timm, University of Nebraska.)

C. Earthworm castings on a green.

Figure 10-10. Symptoms of turf damage caused by small burrowing or digging animals.

D

E

F

PEST ANIMALS

D. Mole tunnel across a green.
E. Runway developed by voles when turf was covered with snow.
F. Armadillo damage.

Figure 10-10. *Turf damage from small animals/continued*

G   H

PEST ANIMALS

G. Badger damage.
H. Skunk damage.

Figure 10-10. *Turf damage from small animals/continued*

NEMATODES

There has been a tendency in the past to blame difficult to diagnose turfgrass injury problems on the nematode. This is because (a) the nematode is not visible to the human eye, (b) its injury symptoms are general in nature and are caused by a broad array of other pest and environmental stresses as well, and (c) injury in many instances is associated with a disease complex involving one or more other pest or environmental stresses. Additionally, knowledge and research information concerning the types and significance of nematode problems on various turfgrass species are very limited. Most nematodes are beneficial in that they contribute to the decomposition of organic matter. Only a few are a problem in terms of damaging turfgrasses.

Characteristics. Nematodes are roundworms which are for the most part microscopic. Accurate identification of a particular nematode species must be done by a qualified nematologist using specialized equipment in a laboratory. Parasitic nematodes feed on grass by sucking the predigested cellular contents from the host. Depending on the species, feeding may be by insertion of a hollow spear or stylet into the plant from an external location or by insertion of the body inside the plant tissue. The nematode reproduces by eggs laid either in the soil or inside the host plant. Thus, the location of the nematode and its egg are important factors to consider when selecting the type of chemical control to be utilized on established turfs. Nematodes are capable of very limited movement in the soil, usually less than 1 foot (30 centimeters). Thus, their introduction into turfgrass areas is usually the result of human activities such as dissemination on turfgrass maintenance equipment; in irrigation and drainage water; and on soil, sod, and vegetative plant material.

Injury Symptoms. Nematodes feed on all parts of the turfgrass plant, depending on the nematode species, with the most frequently attacked portion being the root system. Thus, many injury symptoms associated with nematodes are those typically associated with a shortened root system. One of the first symptoms is an increased tendency to wilt. Subsequently, the shoots may become stunted in irregular patches and appear yellowish/chlorotic. Eventually, the symptoms progress to general thinning of the turf. These symptoms can also be attributed to numerous other environmental and pest stresses. Examination of the root system reveals shortened, brown roots which may have galls caused by root knot nematodes or stubbly swellings of the root tips from stubbly root nematodes (Fig. 10-11).

Figure 10-11. Bermuda-grass turf with a healthy root system (*left*) and a typical short, brown root system caused by parasitic nematodes (*right*). (Photo courtesy of C. Laughlin, Department of Plant Pathology and Weed Science, Mississippi State University, Miss.)

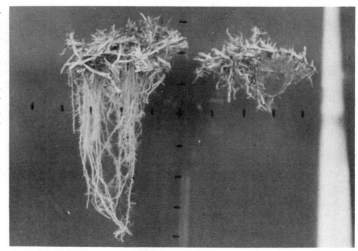

More typically, nematodes are associated with a disease complex in which significant turfgrass injury is the result of a combination of stresses, such as disease and environmental stress plus the presence of parasitic nematodes. Correction of the other environmental or pest stresses frequently alleviates the problem. Chemical nematode control is not needed under these conditions, since the turfgrass host can live and perform adequately in association with a relatively high nematode population, providing no additional significant stresses occur.

A decision to chemically treat for nematode control should not be based strictly on visual turfgrass injury symptoms. Rather, the presence of significant levels of parasitic nematodes should be confirmed by a detailed laboratory analysis. A set of turf-soil samples should be collected and submitted to a reputable diagnostic laboratory equipped to identify and quantitatively measure the number of parasitic nematodes present. Sample collection should consist of 1- to 2-inch (2.5- to 5-centimeter) diameter plugs taken to a depth of 6 to 8 inches (15 to 20 centimeters) from the problem area. The sample should include turf and roots as well as soil. Several cores from one problem area can be placed in a single plastic bag and sealed to prevent drying. A similar set of samples should be collected from an adjacent, normal-appearing turfgrass area of comparable soil type and environmental growing conditions. Each bag should be clearly labeled as to the site and turf condition where the collections were made. The samples should then be submitted to the diagnostic lab, care being taken to keep them cool and moist. Exposure to heat or dryness will result in severe loss of the nematode population. It is preferable if the samples are personally delivered to the diagnostic laboratory. Finally, it is important that a trained, qualified specialist make an interpretation of the nematode analysis, giving due consideration to the particular turfgrass symptoms and environmental conditions under which the problem developed.

Problem Correction. There are relatively few locations in North America where a serious parasitic nematode problem has been diagnosed and confirmed. Just because a significant level of parasitic nematodes has been confirmed at a particular problem site does not necessarily mean that the nematodes are the cause of the problem. The first approach should be adjustment of cultural practices and control of other potential disease and insect problems before serious consideration is given to chemical nematode control. This should be the general approach until there is unquestionable proof that a nematode problem exists in the area.

One of the best approaches for proving that a nematode problem exists is appropriate chemical treatment of a small adjacent area and study of the turfgrass response. Assuming all stresses have been corrected, a positive response is the final proof that a nematode problem exists.

The first approach when a nematode problem is confirmed is quarantine of the area, assuming it is relatively small. Nematodes move very little unless aided by human activity. The quarantine approach restricts spread of the problem until eradication can be achieved through fumigation. Good sanitary practices are the best preventive measures in a quarantine program. Contaminated equipment, sod, vegetative sprigs, and soil should not be moved from the infected area to healthy areas. The best fumigation procedures available should be employed as soon as possible to eradicate the nematodes in the infected area.

The use of nematicides is a common approach on golf course turfs with an extensive nematode infestation. The type of nematicide selected depends on whether treatment is to be done before turf establishment or whether the nematode problem has been found in an existing turf. Nematode eradication prior to turf establishment is much preferable.

Nematicides applied to established turfs are typically watered in immediately after application. The nematicide selected should be label approved for that particular use. The specific nematicides available for use on turfgrass areas vary depending on which labels have been approved from state to state. Safety procedures in the handling and application of nematicides should be carefully adhered to, since many are highly toxic in comparison with most pesticides available for turfgrass use.

DISEASES AND VIRUSES

Turfgrass diseases are a greater problem on golf courses than is the case for most types of turf use. This is due to close mowing, heavy fertilization, intense irrigation, and constant bruising from traffic and divoting. Disease problems are most severe on putting greens, especially those composed of bentgrass or annual bluegrass turfs in contrast to bermudagrass. Tees are also subject to high disease activity if the cultural system utilized involves a cutting height and nutritional level similar to those employed on greens. Fungicide programs are commonly used on these types of turf during periods when the potential for disease development is high. Roughs are at the other end of the spectrum, diseases being an infrequent problem and fungicides rarely being employed. Intermediate between greens-tees and roughs are fairway turfs, which are subject to some disease problems. The frequency and severity of disease increase as the cutting height is lowered or the fertilization and irrigation regimes are increased. Fairways composed of bentgrass and/or annual bluegrass are subject to more severe disease problems than are fairways composed of species such as Kentucky bluegrass, zoysiagrass, and bermudagrass. Finally, the severity of disease problems is typically greater on cool-season grasses than on warm-season grasses, especially in the more humid climatic regions of the country.

Specific diseases common to warm-season and cool-season turfgrasses on greens, tees, and fairways have been summarized in chapters 3, 4, and 5, respectively. In addition, general concepts of disease control as they relate to the three types of turfgrass cultural systems on golf courses have also been discussed in these chapters, and the reader is referred to them for further information.

Causal Pathogen

A disease on a turf is simply the visual result of a causal agent, termed a *pathogen*. Disease symptoms are the first readily recognized visual evidence of adversity, which may be caused by a biological stress. The potential causal pathogens of disease include fungi, viruses, nematodes, and bacteria. Most of the serious diseases of turfgrasses on golf courses result from the activity of fungi; only one significant disease is caused by a virus. Thus, most of the discussion in this section is devoted to diseases caused by fungi.

Disease development depends on (a) the availability of an active parasite, such as a fungus or virus, (b) an acceptable host possessing a growth rate that favors parasitic activities of the pathogen, and (c) a favorable microenvironment, particularly moisture and temperature.

Fungi are low forms of plant life that grow as threadlike structures termed *mycelia*. They produce spores and similar seedlike units which are readily spread by wind, water, traffic, turfgrass maintenance equipment, and infected plant material, such as grass clippings. *Spores* are essentially minute propagating units which, under favorable conditions, germinate and initiate mycelial growth that can infect a host plant. The fungus can survive stress periods and can overwinter in forms such as *sclerotia,* which are compact, hard resting bodies, or *conidia,* which are specialized asexual reproductive cells. All four structures, the mycelia, spores, sclerotia, and conidia, can function in the spread and/or survival of a fungus, depending on the particular fungus.

Fungi are incapable of manufacturing their own food and thus live as *saprophytes,* by feeding on dead plant material, or as *parasites,* by obtaining their food by infecting living plants. Many of the common turfgrass fungi have the capability to survive as saprophytes on dead organic matter in the turfgrass canopy and then, when environmental conditions are favorable, infect the protoplasm of live plants where they feed as parasites. This combined form is termed a *facultative parasite*. With the parasitic form, a distinct series of steps leads to the evolution of disease symptoms. These steps are (a) inoculation of the host plant, (b) penetration into the host plant, especially through mower wounds, (c) infection of cells in the host plant, and (d) an incubation period of a few days to several weeks during which the fungal pathogen spreads through the tissues but the actual disease symptoms are not yet visually apparent on the host turfgrass plant (Fig. 10-12).

Environmental Effects

Symptoms of each disease develop under specific temperature, moisture, humidity, and light regimes. Excessively wet conditions are particularly favorable for the development of most fungal-caused diseases. Wet, humid weather combined with poor soil drainage and excessively frequent irrigation are very favorable for development of most diseases caused by fungi. Similarly, frequent extended dews in early morning are particularly favorable for fungal growth and infection of the turfgrass plant. Temperature is the second important environmental factor that controls the time of year when a particular fungal-caused disease is most likely to occur. Thus, *Fusarium* patch, *Typhula* blight, LTB, SLTB, snow scald, and spring dead spot commonly occur during the winter, while brown patch and *Pythium* blight typically occur in the warm humid portions of the growing season. Shade effects are particularly striking in terms of disease activity. Low light intensity combined with high humidities and

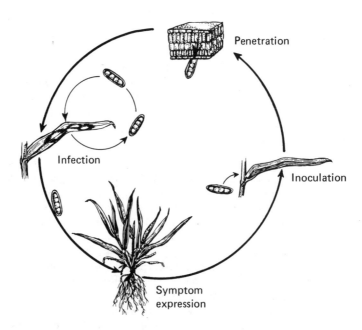

Figure 10-12. Diagrammatic representation of a fungal disease cycle.

moderate temperatures and the resultant delicate, succulent shoot tissues result in a condition that makes the host plant especially prone to fungal attack and disease development.

Cultural Effects

Maintenance of a potential host turf in a healthy, actively growing state makes it much less prone to fungal attack. Thus, good cultural practices are the first requisite in minimizing the damaging effects of turfgrass diseases. This approach starts with selection of turfgrass species and cultivars that are well adapted to the climatic conditions and cultural practices to be utilized on the particular site. In addition, it is important that the cultivars selected possess resistance to the more serious disease-causing pathogens in the locality, whenever such cultivars are available.

Many turfgrass diseases are caused by relatively weak pathogens working on a host plant that has been weakened by environmental stresses or improper cultural practices. Potential for disease development is greater when the mowing height is lower than the optimum for a species. Similarly, increased mowing frequency enhances potential for disease development, since the resultant wounds at leaf tips are ideal avenues for invasion by the fungal pathogen. Nevertheless, putting greens must be mowed frequently. From the nutritional standpoint, high potassium levels generally have been shown to reduce the severity of damage from most disease-causing fungi. With most fungi, a high nitrogen level produces a soft, succulent tissue that favors fungal disease development in the host plant. Exceptions are dollar spot, red thread, and rust, where the weakened condition of the host plant due to a low nitrogen level results in an increased severity of disease incidence.

Proper water management is an important dimension in a cultural program designed to minimize disease problems. The irrigation program should be designed to maintain the turf in as dry a condition as possible. Deep, infrequent irrigation is preferred whenever practical. From a timing standpoint, predawn or early morning irrigations are preferred. Early morning irrigation or syringing, particularly on greens and tees, functions in the removal of dew and leaf exudates, which are particularly favorable for fungal development. Turf cultivation by coring or slicing improves soil water infiltration and percolation and thus encourages surface drying. Finally, avoidance of an excessive thatch/mat accumulation is important in minimizing the amount of dead organic matter on which the saprophytic fungal pathogens can survive until environmental conditions are favorable for parasitic activity. Improper irrigation practices and compacted poorly drained soil are perhaps the most important factors in disease development on golf course turfs.

Disease Diagnosis

Accurate diagnosis of the cause of a problem is essential before corrective cultural practices and/or chemical control are/is initiated. Too frequently a putting green is sprayed repeatedly with various fungicides to correct expanding circular patches of injured turf, without success. As a last resort the area is examined in detail, only to find that insects are the actual cause of the problem rather than fungi.

A golf course superintendent should be familiar with the appearance of healthy, nondiseased turf on the particular green, tee, or fairway before diagnosis of a diseased turf is attempted. Disease identification is most easily accomplished on turfs where the causal pathogen is, or has recently been, active. Thus, a turf plug of 4 to 12 inches (10 to 30 centimeters) in diameter, which includes the soil, should be collected from the outer edge of the damaged area so that healthy turfgrass plants are included in the sample. A disease problem cannot be diagnosed accurately from a single leaf of the plant. Both the turfgrass shoots and roots should be carefully examined, preferably with the aid of a $10 \times$ hand lens. In addition, access to a binocular microscope allows the superintendent to examine affected plants in much greater detail. From this examination, plus (a) an assessment of the turfgrass species affected and those not affected, (b) the overall turf symptoms, and (c) the environmental conditions and cultural practices employed on the site where the disease occurred, the golf course superintendent can make the best possible diagnosis of the disease problem (see Table 10-12 and the color section on turfgrass diseases and nutrient deficiencies following page 452).

Table 10-12. Injury Symptoms, Causes, Host Species, and Control of the Common Turfgrass Diseases and Virus

Injury Symptoms	Disease and Causal Organism	Conditions Favoring Disease Development	Major Turfgrass Hosts*	Cultural Practices That Minimize Disease Occurrence†	Methods of Control
Large circular dead patches					
Up to 5 ft. in diameter; leaves appear olive green, then wilt, turn light brown, and die to form light-brown, circular patches; center of patch may recover creating a brown ring; spreads rapidly	**Brown patch** and **yellow patch** (*Rhizoctonia solani, R. cerealis,* and *R. oryzae*), also causes damping off of seedlings	Wet, humid, warm (75 to 90°F [23 to 32°C]) conditions; cold-weather forms exist; morning dews; excessive thatch/mat; high nitrogen fertility; poor soil drainage; excessive irrigation	Annual bluegrass Bentgrass Bermudagrass Fescue Ryegrass St. Augustinegrass Zoysiagrass	Improve soil drainage; remove dew in early morning; cultivate by coring or slicing; avoid excessive nitrogen fertilization and irrigation; reduce shading; improve air movement	Anilazine, benomyl, captan, chlorothalonil, cycloheximide+PCNB, cycloheximide+thiram, iprodione, mancozeb, maneb+zinc sulphate, PCNB, thiophanate-ethyl, thiophanate-ethyl+thiram, thiophanate-methyl, thiophanate-methyl+mancozeb, thiram, thiram+cadmium compounds, or triadimefon
1 to 3 ft. in diameter, sunken, with bleached, straw color; appears at spring greenup; roots and stolons may have black rot	**Spring dead spot** (pathogen unknown)	High late summer-early fall nitrogen fertility; dry soil conditions; excessive thatch/mat	Bermudagrass	Maintain moist soil and moderate nitrogen fertility level in fall; control thatch; use less susceptible cultivars	None; very slow recovery unless soil is disturbed by forking or use of spade or rotary tillers
Up to 2 ft. in diameter; light brown to straw colored; may form a ring as a result of turf recovery in center or invasion of off-type species	**Takeall patch** or **Ophiobolus patch** (*Gaeumannomyces graminis,* var. *avenae*—formerly *Ophiobolus graminis,* var. *avenae*)	Moist, cool (40 to 70°F [4 to 21°C]) weather; low nitrogen fertility; excessive thatch/mat; alkaline soil pH; common problem of the Pacific Northwest now appearing on east coast	Bentgrass	Reduce soil pH; avoid use of alkaline soil amendments and liming materials	Sulfur applied at 2 lbs./1,000 sq. ft.; use sulfur containing fertilizers such as ammonium sulfate; fumigate soil with methyl bromide

Injury Symptoms	Disease and Causal Organism	Conditions Favoring Disease Development	Major Turfgrass Hosts*	Cultural Practices That Minimize Disease Occurrence†	Methods of Control
Up to 2 ft. in diameter with whitish-gray leaves matted together; light gray mycelia may be visible; brownish or black sclerotia may be embedded in leaves and crowns	**Typhula blight** or gray snow mold (*Typhula incarnata* or *T. ishikariensis*)	Wet, humid, cold (30 to 40 °F [-1 to 4 °C]) weather; typically occurs under wet slush or thawing snow; high nitrogen fertility; more common in colder portion of cool humid region	Annual bluegrass Bentgrass Fine fescue Kentucky bluegrass Perennial ryegrass	Use moderate fall nitrogen fertilization to avoid excessive shoot growth; insure rapid drainage	Anilazine, cadmium compounds, chloroneb, iprodione, thiophanate-ethyl+thiram, thiram, thiram+PMA, or triadimefon. For golf greens only: mercury chlorides, PCNB, or PMA
Up to 2 ft. in diameter, irregular shape, straw colored; may have white to gray cottony mycelia at edges; brownish-black irregular sclerotia on leaves and stems	**LTB and SLTB snow molds** (*Coprinus* sp.—low-temperature basidiomycetes)	Winter snow cover; wet, thawing snow; high nitrogen fertility in fall; excessive thatch; common in Canadian prairie provinces	Chewings fescue Kentucky bluegrass Red fescue	Use moderate, late summer-fall nitrogen fertilization to avoid excessive shoot growth; control thatch accumulation	Mercury chlorides or thiram+cadmium compounds; PCNB labeled for use in Canada
Irregular patches up to 2 ft. in diameter, but usually less than 12 in.; initially wilting, progresses to tan or straw-colored dead areas; may appear as circle with green center (frog-eye)	**Fusarium blight** (*Fusarium roseum* and *F. tricinctum*)	Low soil moisture; medium high temperatures of 70 to 90 °F (21 to 32 °C); high light intensity; excessive thatch/mat; has nitrogen fertility	Kentucky bluegrass	Irrigate to prevent wilt; control thatch/mat; avoid excessive nitrogen fertilization; use resistant cultivars	Benomyl, iprodione, mancozeb, thiophanate-ethyl, thiophanate-methyl, or triadimefon; drench into root zone prior to disease occurrence; fungicides may be ineffective

(Continued)

Table 10-12/Continued

Injury Symptoms	Disease and Causal Organism	Conditions Favoring Disease Development	Major Turfgrass Hosts*	Cultural Practices That Minimize Disease Occurrence†	Methods of Control
Circular dead patches					
Up to 12 in. in diameter; leaves become water soaked, turn reddish brown and then bleach; pink mycelia may be visible in early morning; fall forms appear as 1 to 2 in.-diameter patches which enlarge	*Fusarium* patch or pink snow mold (*Gerlachia nivalis*, var. *nivalis*—formerly *Fusarium nivale*)	Wet, humid, cloudy, cold (32 to 50°F [0 to 10°C]) weather; also develops under snow if soil not frozen; high nitrogen fertility in fall; excessive thatch/mat accumulation; more common in cold humid region	Annual bluegrass Bentgrass Fine fescue Ryegrass	Use moderate fall nitrogen fertilization to avoid excessive shoot growth; control excessive thatch; remove dew in early morning; improve air movement	Benomyl, iprodione, mancozeb, PCNB, PMA, thiophanate-ethyl+thiram, thiophanate-methyl, thiophanate-methyl+mancozeb, thiram, thiram+PMA, or triadimefon; mercury chlorides are labeled for putting-green use only; sulfur applied at 2 lbs./1,000 sq. ft.; sulfur containing fertilizer is effective in Pacific Northwest
Up to 6 in. in diameter; water-soaked leaves and sparse gray mycelial patches which bleach almost white and coalesce; black sclerotia up to 7 mm in leaf axils and crowns	**Snow scald** or *Sclerotinia* snow mold (*Myriosclerotinea nivalis*—formerly *Sclerotinea borealis*)	Snow cover of long duration; develops on unfrozen, acid soils, especially high organic soils; primarily a problem in Canada	Most cool-season turfgrasses	Use moderate fall nitrogen fertilization to avoid excessive shoot growth, adequate phosphorus fertilization	Mercury chlorides and quintozene labeled for use in Canada; remove or spread snow drifts to encourage rapid melting
Small circular spots may coalesce into larger patches					
2 to 24 in. in diameter, but typically small, light tan patches with distinctive reddish cast; pink to reddish mycelia threads extend out ¾ inch from lesions on the leaf or pink gelatinous mycelia mass	**Red thread** and **pink patch** (*Laetisaria fuciformis* and others)	Wet, humid, moderate temperature (60 to 70°F [15 to 21°C]) conditions; heavy dews; low to deficient nitrogen fertility; more common in colder portion of cool humid region	Annual bluegrass Bentgrass Chewings fescue Kentucky bluegrass Red fescue Ryegrass	Increase nitrogen fertilization judiciously	Cadmium compounds, chlorothalonil, cyclohexi-mide+thiram, mancozeb, thiophanate-ethyl, thiophanate-methyl, thiophanate-methyl+mancozeb, or thiram+cadmium compounds

Injury Symptoms	Disease and Causal Organism	Conditions Favoring Disease Development	Major Turfgrass Hosts*	Cultural Practices That Minimize Disease Occurrence†	Methods of Control
1 to 6 in.-diameter patches of irregular shape or even streaks; leaves initially water soaked to greasy, then turn tan; white to gray, cottony mycelial growth may be evident in early morning on green leaves; can spread very rapidly	**Pythium blight** or cottony blight (*Pythium* spp.), also causes damping off of seedlings	Wet, humid, cloudy, rainy weather with high (80 to 90 °F [26 to 32 °C]) temperatures; primarily found on poorly drained soils with pH of 7.0; high nitrogen fertility; spread mechanically by mowers	All cool-season grasses Bermudagrass	Provide adequate drainage; avoid excessive irrigation and high nitrogen fertilization; improve air movement	Chloroneb, cycloheximide+PCNB, ethazole, mancozeb, metalaxyl, propamocarb, or zineb
1 to 2 in. in diameter; distinct straw- to tan-colored sunken spots; leaves turn yellow green, water soaked, and finally bleach to tan color; white to tan banding of leaf blades on perimeter of patch; sparse mycelial growth may be visible in early morning on necrotic leaves	**Dollar spot** (*Sclerotinia homoeocarpa*)	Moderately dry soil; humid with moderate temperatures of 70 to 80 °F [21 to 26 °C]; morning dews; low to deficient nitrogen fertility; excessive thatch/mat; close, frequent mowing	Annual bluegrass Bentgrass Bermudagrass Fine fescue Kentucky bluegrass Ryegrass	Increase nitrogen fertility judiciously; control excessive thatch/mat buildup; remove dew in early morning	Anilazine, benomyl, cadmium compounds, chlorothalonil, cycloheximide, cycloheximide+PCNB, cycloheximide+thiram, iprodione, mancozeb, maneb, maneb+zinc sulfate, PCNB, thiophanate-ethyl, thiophanate-ethyl + thiram, thiophanate-methyl, thiophanate-methyl+mancozeb, thiram, thiram+cadmium compounds, or triadimefon

(Continued)

Table 10-12/Continued

Injury Symptoms	Disease and Causal Organism	Conditions Favoring Disease Development	Major Turfgrass Hosts*	Cultural Practices That Minimize Disease Occurrence†	Methods of Control
Small circular spots					
1 to 3 in. in diameter; copper-colored patches; small reddish lesions may cover entire blade	**Copper spot** (*Gloeocercospora sorghi*)	Wet, acid soils, cool (68 to 75 °F [20 to 23 °C]) temperatures; most common in Northeast	Bentgrass	Provide good drainage	Anilazine, cadmium compounds, chlorothalonil, mancozeb, thiophanate-ethyl, thiophanate-ethyl+thiram, thiophanate-methyl, thiophanate-methyl+mancozeb, thiram+cadmium compounds, or triadimefon
Circular rings of darker green and or dead turf					
2 to more than 15 ft. in diameter; mushrooms may be present in ring, which tends to be hard and impermeable to water penetration; ring is from 4 to 12 in. wide; ring interior usually has green turf	**Fairy ring** (many species of Basidiomycetes, with *Marasmius oreades* being widespread)	Enhanced by decaying organic matter, especially buried wood and stumps; excessive thatch/mat accumulation; high nitrogen fertility; high soil moisture	All turfgrasses	Deep core and drench with water plus wetting agent, keep wet 2 weeks; symptoms of some species masked by nitrogen fertilization	Fumigate with metam-sodium or methyl bromide and reestablish turf; or remove infested sod and soil, replace with clean soil and reestablish
General thinning of turf					
Yellow appearance progressing to red, then brown; elongated pustules enlarge in rows parallel to veins, which rupture leaf epidermis; reddish-brown spores	**Rust** Leaf, Stem, and Crown (*Puccina* spp.)	Moist, humid, moderate (60 to 90 °F [15 to 32 °C]) weather; low to deficient nitrogen fertility; partially shaded environment; infrequent mowing	Kentucky bluegrass Ryegrass Tall fescue Zoysiagrass	Increase nitrogen fertilization judiciously	Anilazine, chlorothalonil, cycloheximide, cycloheximide+PCNB, cyclohexi-mide+thiram, mancozeb, maneb, maneb+zinc sulfate, oxycarboxin,‡ PCNB, thiophanate-methyl+mancozeb, triadimefon, or zineb

Injury Symptoms	Disease and Causal Organism	Conditions Favoring Disease Development	Major Turfgrass Hosts*	Cultural Practices That Minimize Disease Occurrence†	Methods of Control
Yellowish chlorosis, then turns brown; yellowish to brown leaf lesions; may form irregular patches up to 2 ft.; shoots readily pulled out and are black at base	**Anthracnose** (*Colletotrichum graminicola*)	Dry soil and high atmospheric humidity with heat stress of 80 to 85 °F [26 to 29 °C]; low to deficient nitrogen fertility; compacted soils	Annual bluegrass Fescue Kentucky bluegrass Ryegrass	Apply adequate nitrogen fertilization; correct soil compaction; cool turf by syringing	Thiophanate-methyl+ mancozeb
Yellowish chlorosis, then turns brown; numerous oblong, gray to ash-brown leaf lesions with purple margins	**Gray leaf spot** (*Piricularia grisea*)	Wet, humid, rainy weather with warm temperatures of 70 to 80 °F (21 to 26 °C); intense dews; high nitrogen fertility; common in spring following rains	St. Augustinegrass	Use low nitrogen fertilization; provide adequate drainage	Chlorothalonil, cyclohexi-mide+PCNB, cyclohexi-mide+thiram, or thiram
Curling of leaf tips, long, narrow, yellowish streaks on leaves that turn gray; epidermal cells may rupture to expose black spore masses	**Smuts** Stripe and Leaf (*Ustilago* and *Urocystis* spp.) Blister (*Entyloma* spp.)	Dry, moderately cool (55 to 65 °F [12 to 18 °C]) weather; high nitrogen fertility; excessive thatch/mat accumulation; typically occurs in late spring or early fall	Bentgrass Kentucky bluegrass	Reduce nitrogen fertilization in summer; control thatch/mat accumulation	Benomyl, PCNB, thiophanate-ethyl, or thiophanate-methyl; drench into root zone immediately; apply on dormant grass

441

(Continued)

Table 10-12/Continued

Injury Symptoms	Disease and Causal Organism	Conditions Favoring Disease Development	Major Turfgrass Hosts*	Cultural Practices That Minimize Disease Occurrence†	Methods of Control
General thinning of turf					
General yellowish chlorosis; initially pale-green to yellowish leaves, progresses to distinct stippling; shoots gradually thin over 3 to 5 years	**SAD** or St. Augustine Decline (Panicum Mosaic Virus-Strain SAD, or PMV-SAD)	Wet, hot weather; low nitrogen fertility; spread mechanically by mowing	St. Augustinegrass	Use high irrigation and fertilization levels to provide healthy, rapidly growing turf which delays thinning	No chemical control; use resistant cultivars
Elongated to circular lesions with gray to tan centers and purplish to brown margins; leaves turn tan to straw colored if crown rot develops	*Helminthosporium* diseases Brown blight, leaf blotch, leaf spot, melting out, net blotch, red leaf spot, zonate eye spot (*Drechslera, Bipolaris,* and *Exserohilum* spp.); also causes damping off of seedlings	Wet, humid conditions; cool temperatures of 55 to 70 °F (12 to 21 °C), except for bermudagrass; short days and low light intensity; high nitrogen fertility; close mowing; excessive irrigation	Bentgrass Bermudagrass Fine fescue Kentucky bluegrass Ryegrass Tall fescue	Improve drainage; use moderate nitrogen fertility levels; raise cutting height	Anilazine, captan, chlorothalonil, cycloheximide, cycloheximide+PCNB, cycloheximide+thiram, iprodione, mancozeb, maneb, maneb+zinc sulfate, PCNB, thiophanate-ethyl, thiophanate-ethyl+thiram, thiophanate-methyl+mancozeb, thiram+cadmium compounds, or zineb
Raised chlorotic tufts in turf					
Mottled turf caused by 0.5 to 3-in. yellowish, chlorotic tufts; white, downy growth develops as streaks parallel to veins on upper leaf surface	**Downy mildew** or yellow tuft (*Sclerophthora macrospora*)	Problem most evident on putting greens but occurs on higher mowed turfs; wet, humid, cool to warm (70 to 80 °F [21 to 26 °C]) weather; high nitrogen fertility; spreads by surface water movement	All turfgrasses	Use less susceptible cultivars; mask unevenness on greens by increasing mowing frequency; provide good drainage; use nitrogen judiciously	No fungicides labeled; can apply iron sulfate to mask symptoms

White or slimy substance on leaves

Injury Symptoms	Disease and Causal Organism	Conditions Favoring Disease Development	Major Turfgrass Hosts*	Cultural Practices That Minimize Disease Occurrence‡	Methods of Control
White to gray, dusty patches of fungal growth on leaves and stems; areas enlarge; chlorotic lesions may develop; entire leaf turns yellow	**Powdery mildew** (*Erysiphe graminis*)	Moist, humid, cool (55 to 70°F [12 to 21°C]) weather; high nitrogen fertility; severe in shaded environments with limited air circulation	Bermudagrass Fine fescue Kentucky bluegrass	Reduce shading problem; improve air circulation; use moderate nitrogen fertilization	Cycloheximide, cycloheximide+PCNB, cycloheximide+thiram, or triadimefon
Milky white to gray, almost translucent, slimy, irregular shaped mass of up to 12 in. covering turf; turns ash gray	**Slime mold** (*Physarum cinereum, Mucilago spongiosa*)	Wet, humid, cloudy weather with warm temperatures of 70 to 90°F (21 to 32°C)	All turfgrasses	Brush mold off grass; follow by washing with a strong spray of water	None needed

Seedling kill

Injury Symptoms	Disease and Causal Organism	Conditions Favoring Disease Development	Major Turfgrass Hosts*	Cultural Practices That Minimize Disease Occurrence‡	Methods of Control
Young grass seedlings die just after emergence, or seeds or seedlings may rot before emergence; initially, seedlings appear water soaked, then blacken, shrivel, and turn brown	**Damping off, root rot, seed rot** (*Pythium, Rhizoctonia, Fusarium,* and *Drechslera* spp.)	Wet, cool soils of 40 to 60°F (4 to 15°C); high nitrogen fertility; common in winter overseeding	All turfgrasses	Insure good drainage; avoid excessive irrigation; use high-quality seed at recommended planting rate, depth, and time	Captan or ethazole; also see control for specific pathogen listed elsewhere in this table

*The severity of the disease on a specific turfgrass species may vary in different climatic regions of the country. Be sure to contact the local state extension service regarding suggested disease control practices for that area.

†Use of resistant cultivars is always desirable, if available.

‡Label approved only in selected states.

Some turfgrass diseases can be diagnosed conclusively only by a qualified professional plant pathologist. When the diagnosis is inconclusive or tentative, it is advisable for the golf course superintendent to submit samples of the diseased turf to a reliable plant disease diagnostic lab, such as one of those operated by the state agricultural extension service. Laboratory diagnosis of diseases caused by fungi will require from two to fourteen days, depending on whether the fungal agent must be cultured. It is preferable for the turf sample to be delivered personally to the laboratory or else carefully shipped in a container that insures the grass will arrive without being further injured during shipment by heat, cold, drought, or light exclusion.

Fungicides

In some situations fungicides must be applied for disease control to prevent extensive damage to the turf, particularly on greens and tees (Fig. 10-13). Fungicides are pesticides that kill or inhibit the growth of fungi which can cause disease. A fungicide is usually most effective and can be applied at a lower rate if treatment is accomplished before the disease becomes severe; a virulent attack that is allowed to progress will require more frequent, higher rates of fungicide application to correct. This latter approach is termed *curative* disease control. A second approach is *preventive* disease control, in which the fungicide is applied prior to disease development to prevent infection by the pathogen. In the past, preventive disease control on golf courses has involved applications of broad-spectrum fungicides throughout the year. The modern trend is to a preventive program in which a fungicide is selectively used at the time of year when a particular disease is most likely to occur. In some cases, more than one fungus is involved in a particular disease syndrome, and the fungicide selected should have a range of effectiveness that encompasses these particular fungi. The common turfgrass fungicides and the diseases they control are summarized in Table 10-13.

Fungicides can be grouped into two types based on how they protect the host turfgrass plant against infection. *Nonsystemic fungicides* control disease by killing the spores, mycelia, and other fungal parts as they occur externally on the surface of the host plant. Because of their external placement, nonsystemic fungicides are effective for two to seven days, depending on how rapidly they are removed by the effects of mowing, irrigation, and rainfall. For this reason, the use of nonsystemic fungicides in a preventive program dictates application at fairly frequent intervals. In contrast, *systemic fungicides* are absorbed and translocated through the plant, where they control infections by killing the fungus within the host. This type of fungicide is a relatively recent development; examples include benomyl, iprodione, propamocarb, thiophanate-ethyl, thiophanate-methyl, and triadimefon. In addition, some fungicides, such as chloroneb, cycloheximide, and PCNB, have a limited degree of systemic activity.

Figure 10-13. Fungicide spray application by helicopter.

Table 10-13. Common Turfgrass Fungicides and the Diseases They Are Labeled to Control

| Fungicide | | Diseases Controlled | | | | | | | | | | | | | | |
Common Name	Some Trade Names	Brown Patch	Copper Spot	Dollar Spot	Fusarium Blight	Fusarium Patch	Gray Leaf Spot	Helminthosporium Diseases	LTB and SLTB Snow Molds	Powdery Mildew	Pythium Blight	Red Thread	Rusts	Smuts	Snow Scald	Typhula Blight
Anilazine	Dyrene; Proturf Fungicide III	m		x		x							x			
Benomyl*	Tersan 1991	x	x	x	x	x							x			m
Cadmium Compounds	Caddy, Cadminate		x	x								x		x		x
Captan	Captan 50, Orthocide	x						x								
Chloroneb	Proturf Fungicide II, Tersan SP										x					
Chlorothalonil	Daconil 2787, Proturf 101V Broad Spectrum Fungicide	x	x	x			x	x				x	x			x
Cycloheximide	Acti-dione TGF			x			x	x		x		x	x			
Cycloheximide + PCNB	Acti-dione RZ	x		x			x	x		x	m	x	x			
Cycloheximide + thiram	Acti-dione + thiram	x		x			x	x		x	x	x	x			
Ethazole	Koban 30, Terrazole										x					
Iprodione*	Chipco 26019	x		m	x	x†		x								
Mancozeb	Fore	x	x	m		x		x			m	m	x			x
Maneb	Dithane M-22	x		m				x					x			
Maneb + zinc sulfate	Tersan LSR	x		m				x					x			
Mercury Chlorides	Calo-Clor, Calo-Gran					x			x						x‡	x
Metalaxyl	Subdue										x					
Oxycarboxin	Plantvax												x†			
PCNB (quintozene)	Terraclor	x	x	x		x		x	x‡				x	x	x‡	x
Phenylmercuric acetate (PMA)	PMAS		x	x		x†										x
Propamocarb*	Banol Turf Fungicide										x†					
Thiophanate-ethyl*	Cleary 3336	x	x	x	x	x		x				x	x	x		x

(Continued)

Table 10-13/Continued

Common Name	Some Trade Names	Anthracnose	Brown Patch	Copper Spot	Dollar Spot	Fusarium Blight	Fusarium Patch	Gray Leaf Spot	Helminthosporium Diseases	LTB and SLTB Snow Molds	Powdery Mildew	Pythium Blight	Red Thread	Rusts	Smuts	Snow Scald	Typhula Blight
Thiophanate-ethyl + thiram	Bromosan		x	x	x		x		x								x
Thiophanate-methyl*	Fungo 50, Proturf Systemic Fungicide		x	x	x	x	x						x		x		
Thiophanate-methyl + mancozeb	Duosan, Proturf, Fungicide 7	x	x	x	x		x		x				x	x			
Thiram	Chipco Thiram 75, Spotrete, Tersan 75, Thiramad		m		m		m	m									m
Thiram + Cadmium compounds	Cad-Trete, Cleary's Granular Turf Fungicide, Kromad		x	x	x				x	x			x				
Thiram + PMA	Proturf Broad Spectrum Fungicide		x	x	x	x	x										
Triadimefon*	Bayleton			x	x		x		x		x			x			x
Zineb	Dithane Z-78								x			m		x			x

NOTE: Combinations of fungicide and fertilizer not included.

x Labeled for control.

m Labeled, but control is marginal to ineffective in some areas.

*Systemic-type fungicide (tolerance to this fungicide can develop); others are nonsystemic or contact types.

†Label approved only in selected states.

‡Labeled for use in Canada, but not the United States.

All chemicals suggested for use should be applied in accordance with the directions on the manufacturer's label as registered under the Federal Insecticide, Fungicide, and Rodenticide Act. Mention of a trademark or proprietary product does not constitute a guaranty or warranty of the product by the author, the United States Golf Association, or the publisher and does not imply approval to the exclusion of other products that also may be suitable. The use of certain pesticides effective against turfgrass weeds, diseases, insects, small animals, and related pests may be restricted by some state, provincial, or federal agencies; thus, be sure to check the current status of the pesticide being considered for use.

Because of their internal action, the systemic fungicides are effective for a much longer period of time than are the nonsystemic ones. Thus, the frequency of fungicide application may range from two to four weeks. Since the systemic fungicides are absorbed primarily by the turfgrass root system, they should be applied in fairly large volumes of water as a drench or else be watered in immediately after spray application.

Once the disease has been diagnosed properly and the appropriate fungicide selected, it is important that the fungicide be applied according to the manufacturer's directions. The golf course superintendent or an authorized certified representative must read the label thoroughly. Fungicides can be applied as a spray or in granular form. It is important that the sprayer or spreader be accurately calibrated for the rate of application specified and that it function properly to insure uniform application. Most nonsystemic fungicides that are sprayed on are applied at a rate of 3 to 5 gallons of water and fungicide mix per thousand square feet (10.5 to 17.5 liters per are), with the 5-gallon rate preferred. However, the proper procedure concerning spray application volumes is to follow the manufacturer's recommendations. Pesticide handling, storage, application, and clean-up procedures should follow the label specifications of the manufacturer. Procedures to follow in this regard have been covered previously in this chapter.

NUTRIENT DEFICIENCIES

Visual symptoms of a nutrient deficiency indicate that serious problems will occur if the condition is not corrected. Symptoms involving chlorosis, necrosis, reduced tillering, and lack of growth portend weed invasion and eventual severe loss of stand of certain desirable grass species. Thus, early recognition of a developing nutrient deficiency is important. In the case of potassium and phosphorus, regular soil testing is used as a guide to fertilization to insure that deficiencies never develop.

Symptoms of deficiencies of twelve nutrients are described in Table 10-14; six are illustrated in the color section on turfgrass diseases and nutrient deficiencies following page 452. Deficiencies of nitrogen and iron are most commonly observed, followed by deficiencies of sulfur and potassium. Deficiencies of the other eight nutrients are infrequently observed and typically occur in limited locations on specific soil types. It should be kept in mind that similar types of symptoms also can be associated with turfgrass pest and other stress problems. However, the latter usually are more localized and occur as irregular patches or in circular patterns.

Soil Test

The best approach to solving a majority of the nutrient deficiency problems is the preventive approach of soil testing. Soil tests take the guesswork out of fertilization, prevent the development of nutrient deficiencies, and insure the best possible efficiency and economy in utilization of applied nutrients in the form of fertilizers. The application of two essential nutrients, nitrogen and iron, is not based on soil test results.

A soil test is the best diagnostic tool available for assessing phosphorus and potassium needs. Soil tests also provide information on calcium, magnesium, and pH levels. On request, most laboratories will analyze micronutrient, salinity, and sodium levels. The results of these soil tests serve as a guide for proper application of most nutrients. Testing avoids the waste of excessive fertilizer applications and also insures that nutrients are applied in the proper proportions.

Soil tests should be made prior to establishment and then annually during the establishment phase and until soil nutrient levels stabilize. After the pH levels and nutrients have been brought into the desired range, a soil test is needed at one- to three-year intervals. Longer intervals are usually followed for fine-textured, unmodified soils, while more frequent intervals are employed for greens and tees constructed of a sandy root zone mix. The sandy mix has a low nutrient holding capacity and is prone to nutrient leaching, which causes rapid depletion of nutrients.

Table 10-14. Symptoms of Twelve Nutrient Deficiencies Most Commonly Observed on Turfgrasses

Nutrient	Shoot Symptoms*			Frequency of Occurrence	Conditions Increasing Probability of Occurrence
	Initial	Intermediate	Advanced		
Nitrogen	Stunting of shoot growth; older, lower leaves turn pale green; decreased tillering	Yellowish chlorosis develops across entire leaf blade and progresses toward base	Tips of lower, older leaves become tan, which progresses to base; decreased shoot density; eventual necrosis of leaves	High	Coarse, sandy soils; high leaching from intense rainfall or irrigation
Iron	Youngest, actively growing leaves exhibit interveinal yellowing	Chlorosis spreads to older, lower leaves	Plants become spindly; leaf blades turn nearly white or ivory	Medium-high	Alkaline soils; high soil phosphate, manganese, zinc, or arsenic levels; high organic-matter content in soil; waterlogging; excessive thatch
Potassium	Leaves soft and tend to droop; excessive tillering	Interveinal yellowing, especially older leaves; midvein remains green	Leaf margins become scorched; leaf tips roll and wither	Medium-low	Coarse, sandy soils; high leaching from intense rainfall or irrigation
Sulfur	Older, lower leaves become pale green	Interveinal areas of leaf blades become yellowish green; midvein may remain green	Faint scorching of leaf tips, which progresses toward base along each margin; eventually entire leaf withers	Medium-low	Coarse, sandy soils; minimal organic-matter content in soil; high leaching from intense rainfall or irrigation
Phosphorus	Leaves turn dark green; plants tend to be spindly; shoot growth reduced	Leaf blades turn dull blue green, with purplish coloration along entire margins and in main veins near base	Dull reddish color progresses from leaf tip to base, followed by necrosis; leaf tips wither	Low	Acid or extremely alkaline soils; cold temperatures
Magnesium	Older, lower leaves turn cherry red along margins, extending to midvein; shoot growth reduced as leaves turn pale green	Coloring tends to become blotchy; older leaves turn blotchy	Necrosis	Low	Coarse, sandy soils; high leaching from intense rainfall or irrigation; acid soils

Nutrient	Shoot Symptoms*			Frequency of Occurrence	Conditions Increasing Probability of Occurrence
	Initial	Intermediate	Advanced		
Calcium	Younger, upper leaves turn reddish brown along margin, gradually extending to midvein	Older leaves develop reddish-brown color in interveinal area	Coloration fades to rose red; leaf tips become withered	Rare	Coarse, sandy soils; high leaching from intense rainfall or irrigation; highly acid soils
Manganese	Interveinal yellowing of leaf blades with tips remaining green; shoot growth reduced	Small, distinct necrotic spots form; midvein remains green; leaf blades tend to droop	Entire leaf discolors, then withers and rolls	Rare	Alkaline soils; high leaching from intense rainfall or irrigation; high phosphorus and iron levels
Zinc	Shoot growth stunted	Youngest leaves thin and tend to shrivel	Leaves darken and become desiccated	Rare	Alkaline soils
Copper	Tips of youngest, actively growing leaves become bluish	Leaf tips become necrotic	Necrosis progresses toward leaf base	Rare	Highly alkaline soils; high organic matter content in soil; coarse, sandy soils; high leaching from intense rainfall or irrigation
Molybdenum	Older, lower leaves turn pale green	Interveinal areas of leaf appear mottled and yellowish	Necrosis and withering; stunting of plants	Rare	Acid soils
Boron	Discoloration of shoots; stunting of growing point	Leaves become stubby, producing rosette appearance	Sporadic streaks develop in interveinal area of leaf blades	Rare	Highly alkaline or acid soils; high leaching from intense rainfall or irrigation

*The progression of individual nutrient-deficiency symptoms on turfgrass shoots varies slightly depending on particular turfgrass species involved. For further details see Beard, J. B. 1973. *Turfgrass: Science and Culture.* Prentice-Hall, Inc., Englewood Cliffs, N.J.

Accurate soil testing is dependent on (a) collection of representative soil samples, (b) analysis by a reputable soil testing laboratory equipped to process and analyze turfgrass samples, and (c) proper interpretation of results in relation to specific turfgrass soil and cultural conditions on the golf course.

The soil samples should be collected and submitted to a reputable laboratory for testing well in advance of the scheduled fertilization date. The testing procedure usually takes a minimum of two to six weeks. The procedures involved in soil sampling are outlined as follows:

1. Secure appropriate, clean equipment and materials for collecting the soil samples. These include a soil sampling probe, a set of 1-pint soil testing boxes or bags provided by the testing laboratory, and a set of clean paper bags or plastic containers to be used for mixing the samples (Fig. 10-14).

2. Analyze and identify the specific areas from which composite soil samples are to be collected. Included are each green and tee, plus one or more samples collected from each fairway and rough. A study of the soil and of topography maps will aid in identifying the number of composite samples that should be taken from each fairway. If the entire fairway consists of a single soil texture with the same slope, fertilization history, and drainage characteristics, one composite sample is adequate. However, if the fairway possesses significant variations in these features, a separate composite sample is needed for each site condition. Separate soil test samples also may be taken periodically from the adjacent rough areas.

3. The collection of each soil sample involves compositing twelve to fifteen samples collected randomly from the area using the soil sampling probe. Sample the soil to a depth of 2 to 4 inches (5 to 10 centimeters), depending on the recommendations of the soil testing lab, the sampling depth being measured from the soil surface. Separate and discard the turf, if recommended by the testing laboratory, and place the cores in a clean paper bag or plastic container and mix thoroughly.

4. Place 1 pint (or more as specified by the lab) of the composited soil in the sample container and identify it properly as to the area from which the soil sample was taken.

5. Submit the samples to a reputable soil testing laboratory experienced in conducting turfgrass soil tests. The appropriate soil testing fee should accompany the samples. It is important to provide as much information as possible concerning the soil conditions and turfgrass cultural practices associated with each site from which a sample is collected. This includes (1) the particular turfgrass species and cultivar being grown, (2) site conditions, such as topography and drainage, and (3) turfgrass cultural system, such as the irrigation and clipping removal practices. Also indicate whether the turf has been established; the desired intensity of culture, extent of traffic; and specific use, such as green, tee, fairway, or rough. It is important to indicate whether any arsenic herbicides have been applied in the past, since the phosphorus soil test analysis is affected by the arsenic level in the soil. Thus, the lab needs to know the history of arsenic applications to insure proper phosphorus soil test analysis and interpretation. Finally, it is essential to include a return address.

6. On completion of the soil analyses, a report will be mailed from the testing laboratory. The report normally includes (a) a description of the soil texture, (b) the existing soil reaction (pH) and recommended liming or acidification rates, and (c) the existing soil phosphorus, potassium, calcium, and magnesium levels along with specific application rates required to bring these soil nutrients into the desired range for maintenance of the particular turfgrass species involved.

Sometimes a superintendent will submit the same samples to more than one soil testing laboratory. It should be kept in mind that the actual nutrient levels reported from different laboratories may not be the same, since the soil test analysis, specifically nutrient extraction procedures, may differ among laboratories. However, the general recommendations concerning the specific amounts of each nutrient to be applied should be comparable.

Figure 10-14. Representative materials used in collecting soil samples for testing.

The individual interpreting the soil test results should be knowledgeable concerning the specific soil types involved along with the proper turfgrass fertilization principles and practices for golf courses. Finally, a permanent record of the soil test results should be maintained, as discussed in chapter 11.

ENVIRONMENTAL STRESSES

During a year, golf course turfs are subject to numerous environmental stresses, which the superintendent attempts to modify, minimize, or even prevent through the specific turfgrass cultural practices selected. Loss of turf owing to environmental stresses is very complex and a fairly common occurrence. Since the causes are very complex, this dimension of golf turf culture usually is the least understood of any agronomic area. The truly professional golf course superintendent is knowledgeable in this significant aspect of turfgrass culture. The superintendent who relies solely on past experiences lacks the knowledge to prepare properly the various golf course turfs for the wide array of environmental stresses that may occur over the course of a year. A basic understanding of the turfgrass environment and associated stresses is acquired through formal education or through extensive independent reading and study.

Acquired knowledge about environmental stresses can be used in numerous ways. First, with an understanding of the species and cultivar tolerances to each type of stress, the superintendent can assess the stresses most likely to occur in a given location and can select the particular species and cultivar likely to perform best in this environment. The superintendent should also know which cultural practices can be employed to minimize environmental stresses. The basic approach may involve manipulation of the environment surrounding the turf and/or adjustment of the physiological condition of the turfgrass plant to improve its tolerance to anticipated stress.

Understanding the conditions that favor a particular environmental stress permits the superintendent to forewarn club officials and golfers when the stress may occur. It is appropriate for the superintendent also to delineate the steps that have been taken to minimize the chance for turf injury. This approach offers positive evidence that the superintendent is knowledgeable about the existing conditions and problems on the golf course. The golfers and club officials should keep in mind that in certain situations turf loss may occur despite such preventive steps, owing to the fact that no turfgrass cultivars are tolerant to all possible environmental stresses that may occur in a specific location.

Environmental stress problems are severe in the transitional zone between the warm and cool climatic regions. This is the zone where neither warm- nor cool-season grasses are well adapted to one or more of the environmental stresses which occur during the year.

The superintendent must be able to diagnose the particular cause, should a turf be injured by environmental stress. Specific criteria for diagnosis include (a) time of year, (b) associated environmental conditions, (c) soil condition, including topography and drainage, and (d) the particular turfgrass species and cultivars that were injured and those that survived. With this information, plus knowledge of the symptoms associated with each type of turfgrass stress damage, the best possible diagnosis can be made. On determining the cause of damage, the superintendent can assess the preventive cultural practices that were employed and evaluate whether any cultural techniques could be adjusted to reduce the potential for such injury in the future.

The environmental stresses discussed in this chapter are those that result in direct injury to the turf. However, it should be kept in mind that less severe environmental stresses may also cause severe injury if they weaken the turf and then complex with some other type of soil, traffic, or pest stress. The complex of factors causing the injury makes correct diagnosis a difficult problem.

Injury symptoms, causes, and prevention of the common types of winter and summer environmental stresses are covered here. For a detailed discussion of the turfgrass environment and associated environmental stresses, the reader is referred to *Turfgrass: Science and Culture*, by J. B. Beard, 1973, Prentice-Hall, Englewood Cliffs, N.J.

Winter Stresses

Winter injury encompasses all types of damage to turfs occurring during the winter. The commonly occurring types of winter injury will be discussed in this section, except for low-temperature diseases, such as *Fusarium* patch, spring dead spot, *Typhula* blight, and snow scald, which are covered in another section of this chapter. The specific cause of winter injury may be difficult to diagnose, since an interaction of several types of stress may be involved owing to the diverse range of environmental, soil, and cultural factors which affect winter survival. Winter desiccation, direct low-temperature kill, and traffic effects are the major types of winter injury, other than the low-temperature diseases previously mentioned. Turf injury under ice sheets from oxygen suffocation or toxic accumulations is an infrequent occurrence. More typically, turf damage associated with ice sheets occurs during their freezing or thawing. Similarly, heaving is a relatively infrequent occurrence and is associated primarily with seedling turfs planted too late in the growing season to form a sod.

Symptoms, causes, and prevention of the common types of winter injury are summarized in Table 10-15, and representative types of winter injury are shown in Figure 10-15. From the cultural standpoint, it should be remembered that any practice carried out in the fall that enhances the reserve carbohydrate level and general health of the turf will maximize the potential for winter survival. Proper control of turfgrass plant and soil water relations is the most critical factor in minimizing the effects of most types of winter injury.

Summer Stresses

Discussion in this section emphasizes primarily atmospheric or external stresses imposed directly on turfgrass plants. The major summer environmental stresses of concern on turfgrasses typically are associated with heat or water. Often they occur in combination and are difficult to distinguish. Damage caused by turfgrass pests such as diseases, viruses, insects, mites, and small animals is discussed in a separate section of this chapter, as are soil stresses.

A turf may enter a brown dormancy phase if not irrigated during periods of extreme water stress. It should be kept in mind that a dormant turf composed of creeping perennial turfgrasses is basically a healthy turf. Development of a brown dormant turf is a normal occurrence under severe water stress. It enables the turf to survive, the shoots regrowing from nodes on basal crowns and lateral stems once moisture again becomes available, assuming the drought period has not been excessively long.

Seventeen Common Turfgrass Diseases Found on Golf Courses

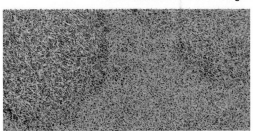

Brown patch, close-up of active development. (Photo courtesy of E. I. du Pont de Nemours & Company, Wilmington, Del.)

Brown patch turf symptoms, fungus no longer active. (Photo courtesy of E. I. du Pont de Nemours & Company, Wilmington, Del.)

Spring dead spot, turf symptoms. (Photo courtesy of Mallinckrodt, Inc., St. Louis, Mo.)

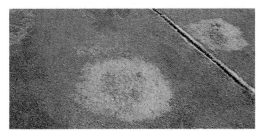

Takeall patch, turf symptoms. (Photo courtesy of Mallinckrodt, Inc., St. Louis, Mo.)

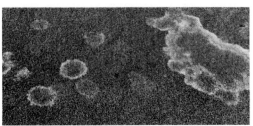

Typhula blight, turf symptoms. (Photo courtesy of J. M. Vargas, Jr., Michigan State University, East Lansing, Mich.)

Typhula blight, close-up of sclerotia. (Photo courtesy of J. M. Vargas, Jr., Michigan State University, East Lansing, Mich.)

Fusarium blight, turf symptoms. (Photo courtesy of E. I. du Pont de Nemours & Company, Wilmington, Del.)

Fusarium blight, close-up. (Photo courtesy of E. I. du Pont de Nemours & Company, Wilmington, Del.)

Fusarium patch, turf symptoms from fall activity. (Photo courtesy of J. M. Vargas, Jr., Michigan State University, East Lansing, Mich.)

Fusarium patch, close-up of leaf injury. (Photo courtesy of E. I. du Pont de Nemours & Company, Wilmington, Del.)

Red thread, turf symptoms. (Photo courtesy of E. I. du Pont de Nemours & Company, Wilmington, Del.)

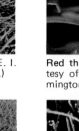

Red thread, close-up of active mycelia. (Photo courtesy of E. I. du Pont de Nemours & Company, Wilmington, Del.)

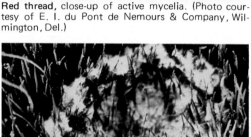

Pythium blight, turf symptoms. (Photo courtesy of E. I. du Pont de Nemours & Company, Wilmington, Del.)

Pythium blight, close-up of active mycelia. (Photo courtesy of Dr. D. J. Blasingame, Mississippi State University, Mississippi State.)

Dollar spot, turf symptoms on green. (Photo courtesy of E. I. du Pont de Nemours & Company, Wilmington, Del.)

Dollar spot, close-up of lesion. (Photo courtesy of E. I. du Pont de Nemours & Company, Wilmington, Del.)

Copper spot, turf symptoms. (Photo courtesy of Mallinckrodt, Inc., St. Louis, Mo.)

Copper spot, close-up of spore masses. (Photo courtesy of E. I. du Pont de Nemours & Company, Wilmington, Del.)

Fairy ring, turf symptoms. (Photo courtesy of Mallinckrodt, Inc., St. Louis, Mo.)

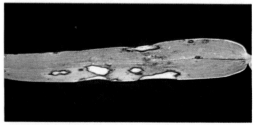

Gray leaf spot, lesions on leaf. (Photo courtesy of Mallinckrodt, Inc., St. Louis, Mo.)

Rust, turf symptoms. (Photo courtesy of Diamond Shamrock Corporation, Cleveland, Ohio.)

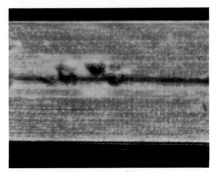

Rust, close-up of lesions. (Photo courtesy of J. M. Vargas, Jr., Michigan State University, East Lansing, Mich.)

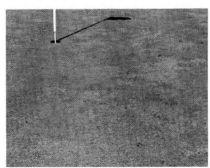

Anthracnose, turf symptoms on green. (Photo courtesy of J. M. Vargas, Jr., Michigan State University, East Lansing, Mich.)

Helminthosporium disease, close-up of lesion. (Photo courtesy of TUCO, Division of The Upjohn Company, Kalamazoo, Mich.)

Stripe smut, close-up. (Photo courtesy of Mallinckrodt, Inc., St. Louis, Mo.)

Yellow tuft, turf symptoms. (Photo courtesy of J. M. Vargas, Jr., Michigan State University, East Lansing, Mich.)

Powdery mildew, turf symptoms. (Photo courtesy of E. I. du Pont de Nemours & Company, Wilmington, Del.)

Powdery mildew, close-up. (Photo courtesy of E. I. du Pont de Nemours & Company, Wilmington, Del.)

Foliar symptoms of six essential nutrient deficiencies in three cool-season turfgrasses. (Photos courtesy of O. J. Noer Research Foundation, Milwaukee, Wis.)

Table 10-15. Common Winter Injuries to Turf and Their Symptoms, Causes, and Prevention

Injury	Symptoms	Causes	Practices That Minimize Injury		
			Cultural	Soil	Specific Protectants
Winter desiccation					
Atmospheric	Leaves turn distinctly white but remain erect; occurs most commonly on high locations exposed to drying winds; can range from small irregular patches to extensive kill of large areas	Drying atmospheric environment, including high winds and low humidity; soil water absorption reduced or may be inoperative because soil is frozen	Maintain moderate nitrogen level; eliminate any thatch problem	Do not core in late fall leaving holes open	Use winter protection cover: polyethylene (4-6 mil.) cover, saran shade cloth (94%), topdressing (0.4 yd^3/1,000 sq. ft.); windbreaks such as snow fence or brush; natural organic mulches such as straw
Soil	Leaves turn distinctly white and are semierect; tissues including crown are very dry and brittle; commonly occurs in more extensive pattern over turf than does atmospheric desiccation	Extended periods of soil drought due to drying atmospheric environment and lack of precipitation, snow, or irrigation	Maintain moderate nitrogen level; irrigate or haul water to critical greens and tees	Same as above	Same as above
Low Temperature					
Direct kill	Leaves initially appear water soaked, turn tan colored and progress to dark brown; leaves limp and tend to lay as mat over soil; distinct, putrid odor frequently evident; occurs most commonly in poorly drained areas such as soil depressions; frequently appears as large, irregular patches	Rapid decrease in temperature, particularly adjacent soil temperatures; most commonly occurs at soil temperatures below 20°F (−7°C) during late winter - early spring freezing and thawing periods	Maintain moderate nitrogen level and high potassium level; use high cutting heights; eliminate any thatch problem; avoid excessive irrigation	Provide rapid surface drainage by proper contours, open catch basins, and ditches; provide adequate subsurface drainage by drain lines, modify soil with coarse-textured materials, slit trenches, and dry wells; cultivate turf, especially by coring and slicing when compaction is a problem	Use winter protection cover; enhance snow accumulation with snow fence or brush; natural organic mulches such as straw; soil warming by electricity

(Continued)

Table 10-15/Continued

Injury	Symptoms	Causes	Practices That Minimize Injury		
			Cultural	Soil	Specific Protectants
Low temperature					
Chilling	Leaves of warm-season grasses turn tan to white when exposed to temperatures below 55 °F (13 °C)	Chloroplast/chlorophyll complex disrupted, thus photosynthesis ceases	Maintain moderately high nitrogen level; use chill-tolerant warm-season cultivars		Use gibberellin within 12 hours of exposure to chilling temperatures, assuming subsequent temperatures rise above 55 °F (13 °C)
Traffic					
On frozen turfgrass leaves	Erect, white to light-tan leaves appear in shape of footprints or wheel tracks where they were impressed onto turf	Pressure of traffic (shoes, animals, or wheels) on rigid, frozen leaves mechanically ruptures cells; problem most commonly occurs during early morning hours	Apply a light application of water in early morning (most effective when soil not frozen and air temperature is above freezing)		Withhold or divert traffic from turfgrass areas during periods when leaf and stem tissues are frozen
On wet, slush-covered turf	Leaves initially appear water soaked, turn whitish brown, and progress to dark brown; leaves limp and tend to lay as mat over soil; irregular shapes associated with previous patterns of concentrated traffic	Snow cover thaws to slushy condition, causing increased hydration of turfgrass crowns; traffic, including snowmobiles, forces wet slush into intimate contact with turfgrass crowns; kill occurs if this event is followed by a decrease in temperature to below 20 °F (−7 °C)		Provide rapid surface drainage by proper contours, open catch basins, and ditches; physical removal of slush may be needed	Withhold traffic on turfgrass areas during wet, slushy conditions, especially if drastic freeze anticipated

Injury	Symptoms	Causes	Practices That Minimize Injury		
			Cultural	Soil	Specific Protectants
Ice cover	Irregularly shaped, tan-colored patches corresponding to sites where ice cover persisted; infrequent occurrence, annual bluegrass being most prone to injury	Impermeable ice layer causes buildup of gases, such as CO_2 and cyanide, to toxic levels	Maintain moderate nitrogen levels and high potassium level	Provide rapid surface drainage by proper contours, open catch basins, and ditches; provide adequate subsurface drainage by drain lines, soil modification with coarse-textured materials, slit trenches, and dry wells; cultivate turf, especially by coring and slicing, when compaction is problem	Apply black material such as lampblack, charcoal, or dark-colored fertilizer, at temperatures above 32° F (0° C) to absorb radiant energy that thaws ice; mechanically remove upper ice cover if in place more than 50 days
Heaving	Young seedling, including crowns and roots, lifted out of soil; roots broken and plants turn tan colored	Repeated freezing and thawing of ice layers on surface of wet soils lifts seedlings out of soil, and they are killed by desiccation	Avoid late planting dates; encourage deep rooting	Same as above	Apply straw mulch to seedlings planted late; enhance snow accumulation by use of snow fence or brush; roll in heaved seedlings at time of first thaw

455

A

B

C

A. Winter desiccation of higher exposed areas on a green.
B. Low-temperature kill of turf on a fairway.
C. Low-temperature kill of annual bluegrass on a collar, apron, and surrounds, but Penncross creeping bentgrass on green is not affected.

Figure 10-15. Representative types of winter injury.

D

E

F

D. Shoot injury caused by golf-cart traffic when tissues were frozen.

E. Extensive ice cover on a fairway. (Photo courtesy of A. E. Anderson, West Newton, Mass.)

F. Snow fence in place to enhance the accumulation of protective snow cover.

Many problems associated with summer atmospheric stresses can be minimized by turfgrass cultural practices which insure maximum root development. This is particularly true of water stress and also of heat stress, since the ability of roots to absorb water from as great a portion of the soil profile as possible is essential in maintaining adequate transpirational cooling. Thus, the following review of cultural practices that are important in maximizing root growth is appropriate.

1. Maintenance of soil pH between 5.7 and 7.5.
2. Minimization of soil compaction through turf cultivation by coring and slicing or by root zone modification to a sandy mix in the case of greens and tees.
3. Prevention of waterlogged soil conditions by insuring surface drainage through proper contouring and by internal drainage through use of drain lines, slit trenches, catch basins, and root zone modification to a sandy mix in the case of greens and tees.
4. Minimization of potential problems from pesticides toxic to the root system. Of particular concern are herbicides, which should be used only as needed to control a serious pest problem.
5. Control of potentially serious insect, disease, and nematode pests that feed on the root system.
6. Maintenance of adequate soil potassium levels.
7. Avoidance of excessive nitrogen fertilization that forces shoot growth at the expense of root development.
8. Employment of soil management practices that minimize the development of saline or sodic soil problems.
9. Maintenance of as high a cutting height as possible within the confines of the particular use on greens, tees, or fairways.
10. Avoidance of excessive thatch accumulation that encourages root development in the thatch/mat layer only.

Adjustment of cultural practices to maximize root growth development results in a turf with much better potential to survive summer stresses. The importance of roots in relation to turfgrass culture is overlooked by some superintendents. Warm-season grasses generally possess more extensive root systems than do cool-season turfgrasses. In addition, because of the very close mowing height, turfgrasses growing on putting greens possess a much shorter root system than do turfgrasses on tees, and fairway turfgrasses produce an even deeper root system.

Symptoms, causes, and prevention of the common types of summer stress injury are summarized in Table 10-16, and representative types of summer injury are shown in Figure 10-16.

Other Environmental Stresses

Trees are a valuable asset in the golf course landscape and even enter the playing strategy of some golf holes. However, the modified microenvironment beneath trees may create difficulties in turfgrass culture. In addition, tree roots compete with turfgrasses for available nutrients and water. Because of these canopy microclimate and root effects, cultural practices in the shade of trees should be adjusted in comparison with practices on the same turfgrasses growing in adjacent areas exposed to the sun's full radiation. Turfs growing in shade typically are lower in shoot density; have a shorter root system; have more erect stems; exhibit a more rapid rate of stem and leaf elongation; and possess more succulent, delicate tissues that are prone to traffic stress. These turfgrass responses are due to the low light levels caused by canopy screening plus tree root competition for water and nutrients. The restricted wind movement; high relative humidity; and more succulent, delicate tissues result in increased proneness to turfgrass diseases. Thus, the primary problems in growing turfgrasses in a shady environment are (a) lack of light, (b) a microenvironment that results in increased potential for diseases, (c) turfgrasses that are more susceptible to diseases and wear stress, and (d) tree root competition. Symptoms of these problems and approaches that minimize shade effects on turfgrasses are summarized in Table 10-17.

Table 10-16. Common Summer Injuries to Turf and Their Symptoms, Causes, and Prevention

Injury	Symptoms	Causes	Practices That Minimize Injury		
			Cultural	Soil	Specific Protectants
Heat					
Indirect stress	Decreased root growth followed by slowing of shoot growth; reduced density; eventual cessation of growth along with darker green to blue-green color	Soil temperatures (above 75 °F [24 °C] for cool-season species and above 100 °F [38 °C] for warm-season species) that exceed optimum range for metabolic/growth processes	Maintain transpiration cooling through irrigation and enhancement of root growth; raise cutting height; maintain moderately low nitrogen level; control any thatch/mat problem	Provide rapid surface drainage by proper contouring and drainage ways, adequate subsurface drainage by drain lines, slit trenches, catch basins, and root zone modification to a sandy root zone in the case of greens and tees	Syringe 1 to 3 times a day during heat stress, especially on closely mowed bentgrass greens and tees; insure air movement across greens and tees
Direct kill	Shoots turn tan to white in large irregular patches; leaves tend to remain erect	Lethal heat levels cause precipitation of protoplasm in cells	Same as above	Same as above	Use heat-tolerant species and cultivars; syringe 1 to 3 times a day during heat stress, especially on closely mowed bentgrass greens and tees; insure air movement across greens and tees
Scald	Shoots turn tan to brown with scorched appearance in depressional areas; leaves tend to lay prostrate to soil	Shallow pools of standing water in soil depressions plus high sunlight cause rapid rise in water temperature to lethal levels	Raise cutting height; maintain moderately low nitrogen level; control any thatch or mat problems	Same as above	Remove shallow pools of standing water from greens immediately (a squeegee can be used) until soil drainage problem is corrected
Desiccation					
Atmospheric (wet wilt)	Irregular patches of turf wilt and die within short period at midday due to internal water stress; shoots erect with white to tan color	Shoots desiccate because rate of transpiration exceeds rate of water absorption by roots, even if soil moisture adequate—wet wilt	Enhance root growth; maintain moderately low nitrogen level and high potassium and iron levels; irrigate to maintain adequate soil moisture	Cultivate turf by coring or slicing to enhance water infiltration	Syringe 1 to 3 times a day as needed to prevent wilt, especially on closely mowed greens

(Continued)

Table 10-16/Continued

Injury	Symptoms	Causes	Practices That Minimize Injury		
			Cultural	Soil	Specific Protectants
Desiccation Soil drought	Shoots erect with white to tan color over large areas that have not been irrigated; extensive cracks form in clay soils	Lack of rainfall or irrigation over extended period, along with high summer evapotranspiration rates, causes death of shoots by desiccation	Enhance root growth; maintain moderately low nitrogen level, high potassium level; limit use of herbicides, especially preemergence	Cultivate turf by coring or slicing to enhance water infiltration	Use drought-resistant species and cultivars
Wear	Leaves and stems bruised, torn, and worn away in distinct patterns where intense traffic has occurred	Mechanical wearing away of turfgrass shoots from severe pressure and twisting action of foot and vehicular traffic	Raise cutting height; maintain moderately low nitrogen level, high potassium level; use moderate irrigation; provide moderate thatch/mat cushion	Improve soil resiliency through turf cultivation by coring or slicing	Rotate traffic patterns by planned movements of cups and tee markers; use design features that tend to distribute traffic over wide areas; use cart paths where traffic is highly concentrated
Flooding Submergence	Leaves prostrate with tan to brown color and signs of rapid decomposition in large irregular areas that have been under water for an extended period	Death associated with complex set of conditions created by anaerobic environment	Maintain moderate but adequate nutritional levels		Construct perimeter dikes to prevent flooding; elevate greens and tees; keep water moving and cool
Soil deposition*	Soil layer covering turf following flood	Flood waters carrying eroded soil slow to velocity where soil can settle out			Remove deposited soil from greens and tees so that turf is exposed, then wash turf; on fairways remove deposits of more than 1 in. (2.5 cm)

*Same effects result from high winds, especially in more arid regions.

A

B

C

A. Fairway with a drainage problem that can lead to many types of summer stress problems.
B. Scald injury to a fairway turf.
C. Submergence injury to a fairway turf.

Figure 10-16. Representative types of summer injury.

D. Heat stress injury to annual bluegrass on a fairway.
E. Water stress (wilt) injury to a bentgrass putting green.
F. Turf wear damage and soil compaction in a rough.

Figure 10-16. *Summer injuries/continued*

Problems with turfgrasses in certain urban areas have increased owing to high atmospheric pollutant levels in certain localities. The effects of atmospheric pollutants on turfgrasses can be very subtle in terms of general growth suppression and discoloration. Occasional acute exposures to high concentrations of atmospheric pollutants can cause necrosis of shoots. Ozone, peroxyacetyl nitrates (PAN), and sulfur dioxide are the most common types of atmospheric pollutants that cause damage to turfs. Occasionally other pollutants, such as fluorides, chlorine, and similar toxic gases, may be present adjacent to manufacturing areas. Basic understanding of injury symptoms, preventive cultural practices, and relative species/cultivar susceptibilities to various types of atmospheric pollutants is limited. What little information is available is summarized in Table 10-17.

Table 10-17. Turf Injuries from Shade and Atmospheric Pollutants and Their Symptoms, Causes, and Prevention

Injury	Symptoms	Causes	Practices That Minimize Injury		
			Cultural	Soil	Specific Protectants
Shade					
Tree canopy	Reduced shoot density; increased elongation and more erect growth of leaves and stems; shortened roots; increased disease; less wear tolerance	Lack of light; tree-root competition; modified microenvironment favors disease development; delicate, succulent shoots more prone to wear stress	Raise mowing height; avoid excessive nitrogen fertilization; use deep irrigation; apply fungicides as needed; select shade-tolerant turfgrasses	Insure rapid drainage of excess surface water	Increase light penetration through canopy by selective thinning of crown and pruning of lower limbs; enhance air movement by judicious removal of shrubs and trees in avenue of prevailing winds; rapid removal of fallen tree leaves
Tree roots	Lack of vigor and shoot growth; shortened roots; loss of green color; increased proneness to wilt	Tree roots permeate surface root zone of turfgrass and absorb much of water and available nutrients; one tree can affect entire adjacent green or tee	Increase fertilization rate and/or frequency; increase amount of irrigation water applied by extending duration of irrigation	Dig trench around perimeter of greens, tees, and fairways from 2 to 3 ft. (6 to 9 dm) deep to sever roots from adjacent trees, then refill; repeat every 4 to 6 years	Deep probe fertilization of trees; select deep-rooted trees
Atmospheric pollutants					
Ozone (O₃)	Tan spotting or transverse banding of leaf blades; bleaching and necrosis of blades follows	Destruction of chloroplasts	Select tolerant turfgrasses; maintain moderate growth rate		
Peroxyacetyl nitrates (PAN)	Tan spotting or transverse banding of leaf blades	Destruction of chloroplasts	Same as above		

(Continued)

Table 10-17/Continued

Injury	Symptoms	Causes	Practices That Minimize Injury		
			Cultural	Soil	Specific Protectants
Atmospheric pollutants					
Sulfur dioxide (SO_2)	Interveinal yellow chlorosis or bleaching of leaf; then necrosis of leaf tip as collapse of marginal and interveinal tissues results in dull, water-soaked appearance	Destruction of chlorophyll	Select tolerant turfgrasses; maintain moderate shoot-growth rate; avoid application of sulfur-containing fertilizers		
Fluoride	Leaf tips have gray-green, water-soaked appearance; lesions turn light tan to reddish brown and extend down blade as uniform front	High flouride levels emanating from nearby chemical manufacturing plant	Select tolerant turfgrasses		Request that the manufacturing facility reduce fluoride emissions level

Table 10-18. Common Soil Stresses and Their Symptoms, Causes, and Prevention

Stress	Symptoms	Causes	Practices That Minimize Injury		
			Cultural	*Soil*	*Specific Protectants*
Chemical					
Acid pH	Reduced shoot growth; short, brown, spindly roots; dark-green color; increased tendency to wilt; soil pH less than 5.2	Increase in soluble aluminum concentration to toxic level; reduced availability of certain nutrients	Avoid excessive irrigation which increases leaching; limit use of acidifying fertilizers	Apply liming materials as needed, based on soil tests	Conduct regular soil tests
Alkaline pH	Reduced shoot and root growth; soil pH 7.5 to 8.4	Reduced nutrient availability, especially iron	Avoid excessive irrigation with water high in calcium or magnesium; limit use of fertilizers containing calcium or magnesium	Apply acidifying materials as needed, based on soil tests; use acidifying fertilizers, such as ammonium sulfate, when feasible	Same as above
Saline soil	Reduced shoot and root growth; increased tendency to wilt; blue-green color; tip burn of leaves; shoot thinning; white deposit on soil surface; soil tests show conductivity greater than 4 mmhos/cm at 25 °C	High salt content in soil solution impairs water and nutrient absorption by roots	Irrigate deeply so that amount of water applied exceeds rate of water loss by evapotranspiration, thus insuring downward leaching of salts; select salt-tolerant turfgrasses	Maintain physical soil condition that facilitates soil water infiltration and resultant downward leaching of soils; cultivate by coring or slicing as needed to correct compaction problem; install drain lines, if needed	Conduct periodic soil tests for salinity level; if feasible, use water source with low level of total dissolved salts
Sodic soil	Reduced shoot and root growth; soil tests show exchangeable sodium percentage greater than 15 and/or pH of 8.5 or higher; soil impermeable to water	High sodium level causes deflocculation of clay and loss of soil structure, poor aeration, low water infiltration, and severe compaction; net result is unfavorable environment for growth	Apply turfgrass wetting agent as needed to partially alleviate problem; cultivate turf	Apply sulfur or gypsum to displace sodium on soil colloids; after a time for reaction, irrigate to leach sodium out of root zone; install drain lines, if needed	Conduct periodic soil tests for sodium level; use water source with low sodium adsorption ratio (SAR) if feasible

(Continued)

465

Table 10-18/Continued

Stress	Symptoms	Causes	Practices That Minimize Injury		
			Cultural	Soil	Specific Protectants
Chemical					
Petroleum spills	Specific type of petroleum spill evident by sight and smell; shiny, oily, water-soaked appearance; turf turns yellow to brown; leaf rolling	Direct phytotoxicity to turfgrass shoots; kill may also involve heat stress aspect	Use cultural practices that favor optimum growth	Remove and replace soil which has been contaminated as result of high-volume spill	Remove spill from turf by immediately sprinkling detergent over spill area, thoroughly wetting, and then completely removing suds with a vacuum
Pesticide residues	Unusually short root system or death of shoots whose cause cannot be attributed to any other stress; certain preemergence herbicides of particular concern	Direct toxicity to sensitive roots or uptake and translocation to shoots where phytotoxicity occurs	Irrigate to enhance downward leaching of water-soluble pesticides	Cultivate turf by coring or slicing to encourage downward leaching	Application of fine charcoal counteracts by absorption, effective only on certain pesticides
Physical					
Compaction	Restricted rooting; reduced shoot growth; soil lacking in resiliency; reduced soil aeration and water infiltration; difficulty in pushing cup cutter or soil probe into soil; algae on bare soil areas	High soil density impairs percolation of soil water and restricts aeration needed to support root growth; may also be physical impedance to root growth	Avoid excessive irrigation; maintain as high a cutting height as allowable, plus high density, which serve as a cushion against compaction stress	Insure adequate drainage of excess water; cultivate turf by coring or slicing; modify soil to sandy root zone in case of greens and tees	Select cup and tee marker placements that distribute traffic over wide area; golf course design features that minimize traffic concentration; use cart paths in areas of very intense traffic; limit golf play when soils are water saturated

| | | | Practices That Minimize Injury | | |
Stress	Symptoms	Causes	Cultural	Soil	Specific Protectants
Hydrophobic soils (localized dry spots)	Irregular patches of hard, dry soil very difficult to rewet; increased tendency for turfgrass wilt; very common on sandy soils	Soil repels water due to high contact angle of water with surface of soil or thatch	Maintain adequate soil moisture by irrigation; control developing thatch/mat problem; syringe if needed	Cultivate turf, preferably by coring or deep forking; response enhanced if accomplished just before wetting agent is applied	Apply an effective turf-grass wetting agent and water in immediately; most effective if applied before hydrophobic stress occurs on areas regularly subject to localized dry spots
Waterlogging	Restricted root growth; reduced shoot growth; yellowish chlorosis; continuously wet, soggy soil conditions	Excess water fills soil pores, causing depletion in soil oxygen level needed to maintain root growth; toxic organic acids and gases may be formed	Avoid excessive irrigation	Cultivate turf by coring or slicing	Provide surface drainage by proper contours and drainage ways and sub-surface drainage by drain lines, slit trenches, and catch basins; modify greens and tees to sandy root zone

Figure 10-17. Putting green damaged by hydraulic oil spill (*top*) and an extensive hydrophobic soil problem on a fairway (*bottom*).

SOIL STRESSES

The soil types existing on the site of golf course construction dictate, to a great extent, the types and severity of soil stresses that may occur. Soil stress problems related to compaction and excess water are prevented by construction of a sand root zone, especially on greens and tees where culture and traffic are most intense. The resultant sandy root zone has both a low water-holding capacity and a low nutrient retention, which may lead to other stresses (but ones that are more easily prevented). It should be recognized that soil-related problems impact on all dimensions of turfgrass growth and quality. Thus, turfgrasses adversely affected by one or more of the soil stresses characterized in Table 10-18 will be more prone to injury from the environmental stresses just discussed. Stress problems associated with soils can be grouped into chemical and physical problems. Nutrient deficiencies were discussed previously in this chapter and are not included in Table 10-18. Figure 10-17 shows symptoms of two types of soil stresses.

Chapter 11

Management

ORGANIZATION

The organizational structure of golf clubs, including the triumvirate and general manager concepts, was discussed in chapter 1. It is equally important that each golf course superintendent develop an organizational structure for the golf course maintenance department. An organizational chart can identify the many different elements in the organization and their relationship to each other. Each box in an organizational chart represents a particular job assignment and an area of responsibility. Lines with arrows connecting individual boxes identify the direction and path of responsibility, authority, accountability, and communication. The higher an element or box on the organizational chart, the broader the range of assigned responsibilities.

A typical golf course green department organizational plan is shown in Figure 11-1. No one organizational structure meets the needs of all golf course operations. Thus, this basic structure can be modified as needed, depending on the particular situation. Each element or subunit should have a clearly stated set of objectives which contribute to the overall objectives of the department. In addition, the objectives of each subunit should be coordinated in such a way that they support and contribute to the other subunits. There should be minimal overlap of objectives and responsibilities. Overlap is counterproductive and can lead to friction among employees.

The organizational structure should be reevaluated periodically and modified as needed, based on changes in the overall objectives of the golf club operation. Lack of a clear objective or lack of productivity in a subunit suggests that the particular subunit needs to be discontinued or that the objectives and lines of authority need revision to better fit operational needs.

Job Description

Employees work best if they know what is expected of them. Every position or subunit in the organizational chart should have a formal written description of its duties and responsibilities. Each prospective employee should be given a copy of the appropriate job description and of the organizational chart. A job description can be utilized in informing potential employees as to the specific duties, level of training, and expertise required to fulfill the objectives of the position. It is also used to measure the actual performance of an employee in relation to the position objectives.

The job description also can be utilized as an effective morale builder. If the employee fully understands the management objectives and position description, he or she is in the best position to perform adequately and to experience the enjoyment of successful accomplishment of the assigned responsibilities and approbation from his or her superior. The net result is high employee morale. The employee also has enhanced confidence in his or her ability to do the assigned task.

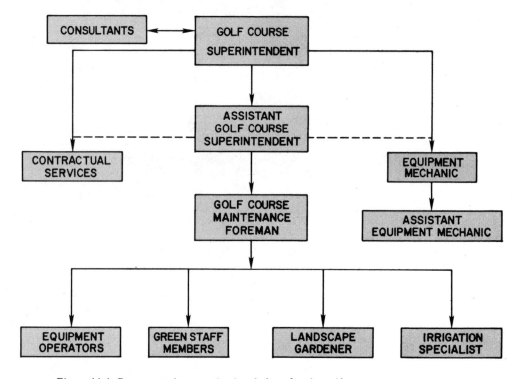

Figure 11-1. Representative organizational chart for the golf course green department.

The position description should state (a) to whom the person holding the position is responsible, (b) the specific duties and skills required, (c) the extent of authority, and (d) the subpositions for which the individual is responsible within the organizational structure. A set of typical job descriptions follows, based on the organizational chart shown in Figure 11-1. These are general outlines; detailed duties for each position vary depending on the specific needs and size of the staff at each golf course.

GOLF COURSE SUPERINTENDENT

Definition. A golf course superintendent is entrusted with the development and management of a golf course. The responsibilities are to supervise the construction and maintenance of the golf course (or courses), to supervise the servicing and repair of turfgrass maintenance and construction equipment, to keep appropriate records, and to prepare budgets and reports.

Typical Tasks. Plans, organizes, and directs the construction of putting greens, tees, fairways, roughs, and bunkers. Supervises the maintenance of putting greens, tees, fairways, roughs, bunkers, and related areas. Supervises the planting and cultural practices involved in growing various turf-grasses, trees, and ornamental plants. Supervises the efficient operation of an equipment service and repair shop. Procures supplies and materials within budgetary limitations. Keeps records of annual maintenance activities and costs. Prepares and presents the annual golf course maintenance budget. Participates in interviewing, hiring, and discharge of employees.

Prerequisites. A degree in agronomy/horticulture/plant/soil sciences desired, or equivalent knowledge. Experience in all phases of golf course management and turf culture. Certified and/or licensed in pesticide usage. Participating knowledge of the game of golf. Thorough knowledge of the construction, establishment, and maintenance practices employed on golf course putting greens, tees, fairways, roughs, and bunkers; planting and culture of turfgrasses used on golf courses; the planting, cultivating, and pruning of ornamental plants, shrubs, and trees; the characteristics and proper use of various fertilizers and soil conditioners; pest control methods and materials; drainage methods; and watering practices and irrigation systems, including wells, pumps, and automatic controls. Knowledge of construction and maintenance of the maintenance facility, shelters, fences, bridges, golf cart paths, service roads, parking lots, ponds, and streams.

Ability to train, motivate, and effectively direct, through the assistant golf course superintendent and foreman, the work of employees in a safe, efficient manner; procure, maintain an inventory of, and supervise the proper use of chemicals, pesticides, parts, materials, and supplies; prepare clear, concise reports; prepare annual budget estimates and execute the authorized expenditures; keep needed records relating to expenditures, payrolls, personnel, operations, equipment, chemicals, weather, and safety; and maintain effective employee and public relations.

ASSISTANT GOLF COURSE SUPERINTENDENT

Definition. Under the general supervision of the golf course superintendent, directs and participates in the construction and maintenance of a golf course; supervises the operation, maintenance, and repair of motorized and mechanical equipment; and performs related tasks as required.

Typical Tasks. Assists in planning, scheduling, and supervising the construction and maintenance of putting greens, tees, fairways, roughs, bunkers, and associated support facilities. Supervises repair and maintenance of all mechanical and motorized equipment used on the golf course. Instructs equipment operators in the safe, efficient operation and care of mowing and other equipment. Supervises and participates in the operation and maintenance of pumps, irrigation, and drainage systems.

Prerequisites. A degree in agronomy/horticulture/plant/soil sciences desired. Certified and/or licensed in pesticide usage. Participating knowledge of the game of golf. Working knowledge of the construction, establishment, and maintenance practices employed on golf course putting greens, tees, fairways, roughs, and bunkers; planting and culture of the turfgrasses used on golf courses; planting, cultivating, and pruning of ornamental plants, shrubs, and trees; proper use of fertilizers and soil conditioners; pest control methods and materials; drainage methods; watering practices and irrigation systems; and equipment operation, servicing, and repair. Ability to schedule and supervise work to achieve the most efficient utilization of employees and equipment.

GOLF COURSE MAINTENANCE FOREMAN

Definition. Under general supervision of the superintendent or assistant superintendent, assists in directing and participates in construction and maintenance of the golf course and performs related tasks as required.

Typical Tasks. Oversees the ongoing daily work activities of the green staff members in an efficient, safe manner. Periodically works with the golf course staff on the many facets of their work responsibilities.

Prerequisites. Ability to direct and take an active part in golf course construction and maintenance activities.

EQUIPMENT MECHANIC

Definition. Under direction, makes major and minor mechanical repairs on a variety of gasoline and diesel powered equipment; keeps all equipment in efficient, operable condition at all times; organizes and maintains a clean service area and maintenance building; and performs related tasks as required.

Typical Tasks. Inspects, adjusts, diagnoses, and repairs mechanical defects in the many types of golf course maintenance equipment. Does mower grinding/sharpening. Performs general overhaul of motors. Repairs transmissions, differentials, carburetors, distributors, fuel pumps, steering systems, starters, generators, universal joints, hydraulic systems, and high-pressure pumps and valves. Installs and adjusts brakes. Installs batteries, tires, wiring, and glass. Does machining or welding work in making fittings used in automotive equipment. Does occasional automotive painting or body and fender repair work. Maintains records of preventive maintenance, repairs made, orders, and time worked.

Prerequisites. Working knowledge of light and heavy construction and maintenance equipment and automotive apparatus. Skill in the use of a wide variety of equipment repair tools and in the making of various types of mechanical repairs. Knowledge of the theory, care, and operation of internal combustion engines and of mower grinding, sharpening, and adjustment. Ability to diagnose mechanical troubles and schedule appropriate preventive maintenance work.

ASSISTANT EQUIPMENT MECHANIC

Definition. Under supervision, assists equipment mechanic in the repair and maintenance of motorized equipment, independently does a variety of mechanical repair and maintenance work, services motorized equipment, and performs related tasks as required.

Typical Tasks. Assists equipment mechanic. Does work in overhauling and repairing automotive and other powered equipment. Cleans working areas after repair work is completed. Assists in electric and gas welding. Lubricates and services automotive equipment. Inspects equipment for operating deficiencies and makes routine adjustments where necessary. Fills automotive equipment with gas and oil. Inspects, changes, and repairs tires. Maintains operating records. May do body repair and painting work. Repairs and adjusts the engines and cutting mechanisms on a wide variety of heavy and light mowing equipment.

Prerequisites. Working knowledge of the general operation of gasoline and diesel engines. Knowledge of proper methods for servicing automotive equipment and of the sharpening, repair, and adjustment of power mowing equipment. Ability to understand and follow oral and written directions. Aptitude for mechanical problem diagnosis and repair work methods. Mechanical ability. Ability to use common mechanical tools.

EQUIPMENT OPERATOR

Definition. Under direction, operates motorized equipment and trucks used on the golf course and does related tasks as required.

Typical Tasks. Operates gang mowers or tractor-drawn mowers in mowing golf course areas. Operates mechanical loaders in moving soil, debris, and other materials. Drives a dump truck. Maintains, lubricates, and makes minor adjustments to equipment.

Prerequisites. Knowledge of safe, efficient mechanical operation of trucks and other motorized equipment. Mechanical aptitude. Ability to follow oral and written directions.

GREEN STAFF MEMBER

Definition. Under supervision, works on the diverse range of activities involved in golf course maintenance and construction, does semiskilled grounds construction and maintenance work, and performs related tasks as required.

Typical Tasks. Operates powered equipment in mowing golf course putting greens, aprons, and tees. Waters and fertilizes putting greens, tees, fairways, and roughs. Grades and prepares a soil plant bed, lays sod, plants vegetative material, and seeds putting greens, tees, fairways, and roughs. Changes cups and tee markers. Maintains ball washers and water hazards. Assists in spraying chemicals on greens and tees. Rakes and maintains bunkers. Assists in construction of new greens, tees, and fairways by grading, preparing soil, and planting. Operates dump trucks and other light equipment in hauling materials and removing debris. Trims trees and prunes shrubbery. Cultivates shrubs and flowers.

Prerequisites. Knowledge of the tools, methods, and materials used in golf course and grounds landscape construction and maintenance work. Ability to safely operate trucks and motorized equipment and to follow oral and written directions.

LANDSCAPE GARDENER

Definition. Under supervision, is responsible for the care and maintenance of the ornamental plants, shrubs, and trees on the clubhouse grounds and selected golf course sites; operates equipment associated with the maintenance of ornamental plants; and does related tasks as required.

Typical Tasks. Prepares soil plantbeds, establishes by seed or transplants, and maintains annual and perennial flowers in aesthetically pleasing arrangements. Plants and maintains ornamental shrubs and trees, tasks that include appropriate pruning, trimming, root feeding, and pest control. Operates mechanical and power equipment utilized in the maintenance of ornamental plants and trees.

Prerequisites. Knowledge of the characteristics and cultural requirements of ornamental plants, shrubs, and trees adapted to the region and of the proper use of fertilizers, soil conditioners, and pesticides utilized in the maintenance of ornamentals. Ability to safely operate trucks and motorized equipment.

IRRIGATION SPECIALIST

Definition. Under supervision of the superintendent or assistant superintendent, operates, services, and repairs the varied components of an irrigation system and performs related tasks as required.

Typical Tasks. Operates, maintains, and repairs a complex irrigation system, including leaks in distribution lines, valves, risers. Repairs control lines and sprinkler heads. Maintains and repairs the master and satellite controllers. Operates and maintains the well and pumping station. Periodically inspects the various components of the irrigation system to insure that they are operating properly.

Prerequisites. Working knowledge of basic electricity and hydraulics related to an irrigation system, including automatic valves and controllers, and of various types of pumps and pumping systems.

Management by Objective

Every job description in an organizational structure should have specific objectives. These objectives must be reasonable, realistic, attainable, and properly communicated to each individual within the organization. Management by objective is essentially a means of justifying each position in an organization so that maximum productivity is achieved. It focuses on the overall goals of the organization regardless of the managerial or employee level involved. The objectives established by the golf course superintendent must be in line with those policies established by the green committee, owner, or a delegated management representative. As a further extension of this concept, every position within the organization must have an objective or series of objectives that are coordinated with and contribute to those of the total golf course organization. Positions with objectives·and functions that do not support the overall objectives should be terminated or reevaluated and a new job description and objectives established that are in line with the overall objectives of the organization. The concept of management by objective applies not only within the golf course green department but also among the golf department, house department, and other groups associated with the overall organization.

Finally, for the individual to achieve the objectives of a supervisory position, he or she must be given authority to plan and execute those objectives. It follows that he or she must also be accountable for accomplishing the established objectives. Thus, responsibility and authority are delegated downward through the organizational structure to subordinates, while accountability is an upward reaction by subordinates in response to an assignment.

Chain of Command

To achieve the objective(s) of the position, the individual holding it must be given authority to plan and execute those objectives. The chain of command should be well conceived and thoroughly stated. To maximize effectiveness, the management objectives should be contained in a formal document, all or parts of which have been circulated to all policy-making bodies and subordinate supervisory personnel in the chain of command. It is critical that each employee have a clear understanding of the individual(s) to whom he or she is responsible in terms of meeting the objectives of the position and also of the specific individuals under his or her supervision, if any. The chain of command concept does allow an individual to have two or more supervisors. However, under the unity-of-command concept, an individual is accountable to only one individual for any one particular activity or area of responsibility. The golf course superintendent should constantly check to insure that the areas of responsibility for each position are well identified and that the associated lines of communication are operating smoothly without intervention from individuals acting in a supervisory role without authority delegated by the superintendent.

Delegation of Responsibility

Maximum productivity and job satisfaction are best achieved by delegating responsibility for decision making as far down the organizational structure as is possible. This technique insures the most efficient use of time for upper-level supervisors. The superintendent frees time from day-to-day work activities to the more important primary responsibility of short- and long-range planning. The delegation of authority also increases the value of middle-level supervisory personnel and allows individual workers to build job morale and enthusiasm through experiencing accomplishment of the responsibilities assigned.

Delegation of authority can only be implemented successfully if individuals in middle supervisory positions have been formally trained and given an opportunity to experience the wide range of activities and problems encountered in day-to-day golf course operations. Within this concept, it is important that the middle-level supervisory employees selected have the capability to make decisions. Also, each individual should be given only that level of responsibility which he or she can accomplish efficiently and successfully. In delegating responsibility, the second-line supervisor should be fully informed as to what is expected in terms of performance. The scope or extent of authority should be clearly communicated.

In delegating responsibility and authority, it is important that employees under a middle-level supervisor be informed of this action by the superintendent. Upward communication is also important in successful delegation of responsibility. The superintendent should be informed whenever an important objective has been accomplished. In addition, the superintendent should be informed in advance whenever potential trouble is expected and immediately informed whenever unexpected problems arise. Information concerning a problem should be accompanied by details of the actions taken to correct the problem. The superintendent can then review the situation and either approve the actions taken or suggest modifications based on a more extensive range of experience and knowledge.

Decision Making

The golf course superintendent is in a responsible management position and must make decisions that are not predetermined by consistent policies or procedures. This is particularly true under the diverse range of soil, environmental, budgetary, and personnel conditions commonly found. Decision

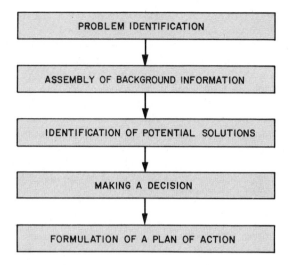

Figure 11-2. Sequence of logical steps used in the decision-making process.

making is essentially a problem-solving process. Success is based on taking sufficient time to thoroughly think through the problem and generate ideas for possible solutions. The decision-making process should follow a logical sequence (Fig. 11-2). Such a procedure avoids snap judgments which may or may not lead to the most efficient, successful answer to the problem. In other words, decision making should not be based solely on past experience, although this is an important component.

Problem Identification. The first step in a logical decision-making process is identification of the problem. Substantial time may be required to discuss the situation with the appropriate personnel, to make detailed observations, and finally to conduct an in-depth analysis of the basic problem. It is important that surface manifestations of a basic underlying problem or problems not be interpreted as the problem. For example, high cost in raking bunkers might appear to be related to either improper equipment or low-quality labor. However, an in-depth analysis might reveal the basic problem is low employee morale. Thus, proper diagnosis is important, since the solutions to the problems are quite different. In some cases there may be a combination of situations, each of which must be addressed separately to solve the overall problem. Thus, problem identification should be based on a comprehensive assessment of the situation with use of as wide a range of informational sources as possible.

Assembly of Background Information. The second step is collection of background information and data concerning the problem. The superintendent should be strongly motivated to seek the best possible solution based on available information without bias from preconceived concepts. It is important to establish that the information collected is valid and based on sound data, if possible. Established facts should be identified and opinions should be distinguished in terms of the backgrounds of the individuals offering them. It is important that information be obtained from primary sources rather than secondhand or thirdhand.

Identification of Potential Solutions. The third phase is listing of a series of possible options for solving the problem based on the best available information. A detailed study of the available information should result in a number of possible solutions. Adequate time should be allocated to arrive at the most logical options.

Making a Decision. The fourth phase is evaluation of the relative merits of each approach. It is essential that this phase be objective and logical. Objectivity can be accomplished by an assessment of the options in terms of (a) their potential for solving the problem completely or partially, (b) whether they are permanent or short-term, (c) their feasibility from a practical standpoint and from a cost-effective standpoint, and (d) their acceptability from the standpoint of the golfing clientele and the employees who must execute them. In some cases, simple experiments on a turf nursery will aid in assessing the feasibility of use of a particular pesticide, chemical, cultural technique, or type of equipment under the actual conditions on the golf course. After a thorough assessment of the options for solving the problem, the best possible decision can be made.

Formulation of a Plan of Action. Finally, the superintendent should develop a plan of action to employ in solving the problem. The situation should be monitored thereafter to insure that the solution or plan of action has in fact solved the problem. If the solution has not been effective or has only partially solved the problem, the situation must be reevaluated based on the results observed. The superintendent should assess whether the correct plan of action was devised or whether the problem was improperly diagnosed in the first place. The decision-making process may need to be repeated to insure a permanent, long-term solution to the problem.

Use of a Consultant. As an aid in the decision-making process or to assess the correctness of existing practices, a majority of the golf courses in the United States seek the aid of one or more outside consultants. The management of a golf course poses an extremely diverse range of problems and requires a wide range of expertise. Each golf course superintendent has stronger capabilities in certain aspects than in others. The use of consultants to insure sound decision making and efficient, economical use of funds is standard operating procedure. Consultants may be called on for help with agronomic dimensions of turfgrass culture, landscaping, golf course architecture, irrigation design, water quality, or engineering.

Turfgrass science consultants typically are the most commonly employed. The golf course budget is planned with a certain amount devoted to this need. The United States Golf Association Green Section employs a group of regional agronomists whose primary responsibility is consulting on golf course maintenance problems. Some states offer the services of a turfgrass extension specialist who is available to advise on turfgrass management problems on a nonfee basis. Qualified, reputable turfgrass consultants are also available among university turfgrass researchers and private consultants. Selection of a consultant should be based on careful study of the individual's proven technical expertise as well as history in problem solving at other golf courses.

Consultation typically involves a minimum of one-half and up to one full day for a visitation and detailed analysis. The golf course superintendent and management group should be prepared to make available all records of turfgrass cultural practices, including detailed information concerning fertilizer and pesticide usage, plus soil test and water quality analyses. After the detailed visitation and any needed follow-up analyses, the golf club should expect a formal written report including the consultant's observations and diagnoses of specific problems which golf club personnel have identified. The consultant is reimbursed for all travel expenses and receives a fee that is agreed on in advance.

Planning

The superintendent is charged with the responsibility of achieving certain goals for the golf course organization. Planning involves the development by the superintendent of a realistic work program which will insure the successful accomplishment of the management objectives set forth for the golf course. Essentially, it is a program statement of short-term and long-term activities and the best way to accomplish those activities with the resources available. A well-conceived and executed plan is an organizational tool that allows the golf course superintendent to achieve the most efficient utilization of both human and physical resources.

First, a policy statement of objectives is prepared and approved by the policy-making body of the golf club. This statement of objectives concerning golf course playing conditions and associated budgetary aspects should include both an annual policy statement and a long-term policy plan for the upcoming five or more years. The golf course superintendent is then responsible for developing an operations plan to successfully accomplish the established policy objectives within the guidelines of the approved budget. A major portion of the management responsibility is planning.

Proper planning and scheduling of golf course maintenance and construction activities reduces the number of unexpected emergency problems that may arise. A properly conceived plan provides a sound basis for determining the physical and human resources required to accomplish the objectives. The plan should contain a time dimension that insures accomplishment of objectives within the designated guidelines and that allows the superintendent to assess the ongoing progress of each project. Essentially, this plan serves as a measure of both individual and organizational performance.

In developing the annual, weekly, and daily plans of work it is important to insure that the goals established can be reasonably attained. A poor plan can lead to frustration on the part of both supervisors and employees. The superintendent should seek input from middle-level supervisors and, where appropriate, the greens staff members concerning possible improvements in the plan of work. These are the people actually responsible for the work; with their previous experience they may be able to make a very important contribution to the proposed plan of work. This opportunity to provide input generates pride in being a part of the decision-making process rather than just responding to arbitrary dictatorial work orders. In establishing the daily and weekly plans of work, the superintendent should be sure that these plans are consistent with the long-range goals included in the annual and five-year plans. Finally, the superintendent should be ever cognizant that the annual, weekly, and daily work plans are guidelines subject to change according to existing conditions. These plans should be dynamic, even though they are formal documents.

Long-Range Plan. Each golf course superintendent should maintain a formally written long-term plan of five years or more. It should be updated annually to insure continuity and should be within the policy goals established by the club officers, golf course owner, or policy-making authority. The long-range plan typically includes such aspects as architectural design, drainage, water source, irrigation system, and so on.

Annual Plan. An annual plan describes a program of work that can be used in the development of budget requests. It should be based on the objectives established for the particular year. It also serves as a base from which labor requirements and material/equipment purchases are established for the upcoming year. The annual plan of work insures the efficient utilization of labor and equipment by scheduling major work activities at intervals throughout the year. Major projects should be scheduled in relation to anticipated golfing activities.

The annual plan of work typically is divided on a monthly or seasonal basis oriented in relation to the major tournaments and golfing events scheduled for the course. The annual plan of activities usually includes a program of work related to the maintenance of putting greens, tees, fairways, roughs, and bunkers, plus any new construction outlined in the five-year plan for that particular year. Activities scheduled on a yearly-monthly plan of work typically include fertilization, pest control, turf cultivation, winter overseeding, bunker perimeter trimming, bunker sand replacement, tree planting, tree trimming, equipment repair, mower grinding and sharpening, employee training, and upkeep of the maintenance facility.

Weekly Plan. The superintendent should also establish a weekly plan of work in consultation with the assistant superintendent and golf course foreman. Special nonrecurring work projects should be scheduled in such a way that normal maintenance activities on putting greens, tees, fairways, roughs, and bunkers are not adversely interrupted. Minor adjustments in the normal scheduling of cultural practices on green, tee, and fairway turfs should also be reviewed in relation to seasonal weather and soil conditions plus the anticipated intensity of play and available work force. In addition, the weekly plan is influenced by the accomplishments of the previous week. For example, a particular project may have been delayed due to wet soil conditions caused by intense rains.

Daily Plan. A daily plan of work is established under the guidelines of the weekly plan. After the completion of a given day, the superintendent typically reviews the accomplishments for that day with the assistant golf course superintendent and/or golf course foreman. Based on this review, a detailed plan for the upcoming day is developed. It is important that the daily program of work be thoroughly understood by the individuals charged with the responsibility for supervising its execution. The daily work should be scheduled so that there is the least possible interference with normal play on the golf course. For example, turf cultivation and topdressing should be accomplished on days when the course is closed or when play is anticipated to be light. Decisions concerning the activities for a given day should be based on information provided by the local weather service concerning potential for rain, high wind, or similar adverse conditions which affect the specific cultural practices that can be accomplished. An alternate daily work plan should be developed in case the primary plan of work is interrupted by inclement weather, equipment breakdowns, or illness of employees. In particular, indoor work should be planned for extremely adverse weather conditions. Finally, the superintendent should insure that all employees are fully informed as to the work plan for the upcoming day and that they have a general overview of the plan for each week.

PERSONNEL

The recruitment, selection, training, motivation, and keeping of quality golf course maintenance personnel is an important dimension in achieving the objectives of a quality golf course. Compared with the agronomic science of turfgrass maintenance, more art and a significant amount of experience are utilized in effectively performing this dimension of the golf course superintendent's responsibilities. Certain precepts are basic in the selection, training, and retention of personnel. Nevertheless, the superintendent must be flexible and use good judgment to meet the needs of each employer-employee relationship in order to achieve maximum productivity. Proper communication with each employee as to the needs and objectives of the particular work assignment and a willingness to listen to the concerns and ideas of the employee are needed.

Superintendent Position

The selection of a properly trained, experienced golf course superintendent is the foundation on which an efficient, successfully executed golf course maintenance program is established. There is no substitute for experience in the training of a qualified golf course superintendent. Experience usually involves a combination of (a) work experience on the general golf course staff and (b) employment as an assistant golf course superintendent under the supervision of a mature, properly trained, well-qualified golf course superintendent.

In addition, a majority of the golf course superintendent positions on modern, quality golf courses require a formal course of college study. This is particularly true in view of the large budget which a superintendent is charged to expend in an efficient manner. Through trial-and-error techniques and experience gained over a number of years at one golf course, an individual may develop a very successful management system without understanding why certain cultural practices are used. This lack of knowledge will restrict the individual in his or her ability to move successfully from one golf course to another with a drastically different environment, soil, turfgrass species, and budget conditions. An individual who has received formal education in these aspects of golf course maintenance or has become educated through lifelong study of the field plus attendance at numerous state, regional, or national turf educational conferences is in a much better position to interpret varying conditions from one golf course to another and to diagnose the problems unique to each golf course. The net result will be the ability to assume the responsibilities at a new golf course with minimal errors. These potential difficulties emphasize the need for formal training for a position as a modern golf course superintendent.

Some club officials attempt to save money by ignoring the importance of both experience and formal training. In some cases, a superintendent position is filled by a long-term, hard-working employee who is thought to know the golf course and is willing to assume the responsibilities at a very modest salary or by a recent graduate of a two-year technical college or four-year bachelor of science program who lacks experience and is willing to take a chance at a modest salary. In most cases, both of these approaches are false economy. Typically, the formally trained, experienced golf course superintendent will more than repay his or her additional salary through sound basic decisions, proper problem diagnosis, and efficient labor utilization which translates into a more economical maintenance system relative to the golf course playing quality achieved.

The procedure followed at most golf clubs is to establish a search and selection committee, which is charged with the responsibility of obtaining the best-qualified golf course superintendent available. A majority of the committee members should possess some knowledge and/or actual experience in the operations and problems encountered in the management of golf course turfs. For this reason, the green committee typically is assigned to serve as the search and selection committee. It is imperative that the incumbent superintendent be informed of his or her discharge before a search is initiated for a new superintendent. The procedure to be followed in distributing announcements concerning the position as well as the formal process for screening the applicants should be agreed on by the committee in advance. The first responsibility of the search and selection committee is to update the job description outlined in the first section of this chapter. The job description should be modified as needed to fit the specific needs and conditions of the particular golf course.

Once the job description has been prepared and approved by the appropriate policy-making bodies, an announcement of the position opening is released and distributed. Four common contacts are the (1) Golf Course Superintendents Association of America-Employment Referral Service, (2) local and state chapters of the Golf Course Superintendents Association, (3) state universities and two-year technical schools actively involved in training golf course superintendents, and (4) consultants. The job announcement should be sent to city and state employment organizations to comply with the Equal Employment Opportunity law in terms of no race, sex, age, religion, or handicap biases. In all these cases, circulation of the position announcement is on a cost-free basis. Ads also can be posted in golf and turfgrass publications.

Applicants for the position should be required to prepare a personal resume summarizing educational background, experience, employment history, and addresses/phone numbers of three or more references. The search and selection committee may request a written recommendation from the individuals cited as references, may choose to make direct contact by telephone, or may use a combination of these approaches.

Once an extensive search has been completed and the resumes with recommendations accumulated, the applicants are narrowed to a group of two to five. Basically, the procedures involved in selecting a golf course superintendent are comparable to those discussed in detail for the golf course architect in chapter 2. The leading candidates are contacted and brought to the golf course for a formal interview. Members of the search and selection committee may actually visit the golf course where the final candidate is currently employed to gain a firsthand assessment of the situation and golf course condition.

The formal interview should involve an inspection of the golf course, including the maintenance facility, irrigation system, golf course maintenance equipment, and other areas of responsibility. Each candidate should have an opportunity to spend some time visiting with the managers of the house and golf departments. After viewing the actual golf course, physical facilities, and operations personnel, the candidate meets with the search and selection committee for a period of time. A relaxed, private atmosphere is suggested in which committee members have an opportunity to interview the candidate in depth and ask specific questions to obtain a better overall assessment of his or her qualifications for the position. During the same interview, the candidate should have an opportunity to ask committee members specific questions concerning operations and policies that will affect his or her capabilities to accomplish the objectives established for the golf course. After the search and selection committee completes the formal interview of the final candidates, a choice is made or the position is reopened for additional applicants.

Employment Contract. The position offer should be accompanied by a contract. Both the golf club and the superintendent should be protected by a memorandum of agreement or a contract concerning the superintendent's services. It should include the duties of the superintendent, extent of authority, specific responsibilities, immediate supervisor, salary, and list of benefits. In contrast to an oral contract, a formal written contract is valid and enforceable, which is particularly important at golf clubs where there is a constant change in club officials. The specific contract contents depend on the particular needs and conditions of the golf club. Two contracts varying in degree of detail are presented in Figure 11-3 to show what may be included. At the time this formality is completed, the other applicants for the position should be informed and given an expression of appreciation for their interest in applying for the position.

Staff Recruitment and Hiring

Successful training, motivation, and supervision of a dependable, productive golf course maintenance staff often depends on an active recruitment program for the best available personnel. Too often the hiring of golf course green staff and laborers is a rather passive affair involving a brief newspaper announcement or word-of-mouth. The first step in recruitment is preparation of a brief announcement of each position opening. The job announcement should be sent to the state and city employment organizations to comply with the Equal Employment Opportunity law in terms of no race, color, religion, sex, national origin, or handicap biases. An advertisement can also be placed in the help wanted columns of local newspapers.

Seasonal employees frequently can be secured with the aid of high-school counselors, college advisors of undergraduate turf majors, and/or instructors in two-year technical training programs in the turfgrass and ornamental horticulture areas. This approach increases the probability of securing employees interested in turfgrass management and thus becoming productive members of the staff.

The next step in the hiring process is interviewing of applicants. First, each applicant should be asked to fill out an application for employment form, such as the one shown in Figure 11-4. The golf course superintendent or an assigned representative interviews each applicant after reviewing the completed employment application. One objective of the interview should be to insure that the applicant fully understands the job responsibilities and any special job-related qualifications. It is helpful if the applicant is provided with a copy of the formal job description.

A properly conducted interview will permit the golf course superintendent to assess the background and employment history of the applicants so that each can be placed in a position which best meets his or her qualifications. The interview should include a detailed review of the individual's (a) work history, (b) types of experience gained during previous employment, (c) specifics of formal education, special schools, and training successfully completed, and (d) any other qualifications that contribute to proper placement. It is important that the interviewer avoid asking any questions that cannot be asked on an employment form. If any unfavorable references have been received, the individual should be given the chance to defend himself or herself. Any formal testing that is required as part of the hiring process should be conducted after the interview has been completed.

After accumulation of appropriate information, a check of references, and a thorough interview of all applicants, the final step is deciding which individual(s) will be hired. Criteria involved in the selection include qualifications in relation to the job description along with the level of interest, dependability, and potential to develop.

Once the position has been offered and the applicant has accepted, an employment voucher should be initiated. In some cases this is a short, formal document which the employee signs, as does the golf course superintendent. Finally, the employment agencies, newspapers, and other sources which had originally been provided the job description should be notified that the position has been filled.

SAMPLE EMPLOYMENT CONTRACT 1

THIS AGREEMENT MADE AND ENTERED INTO on this _____ day of

_____ , 19 _____ , by and between _____

_____ ,

hereinafter called the Employer, and _____

_____ ,

hereinafter called the Superintendent, WITNESSETH:

The parties hereto agree that the Superintendent shall be employed by the Employer upon the following terms and conditions:

1. *Duties.* The Employer shall employ the Superintendent, and the Superintendent shall serve the Employer as the Employer's golf course superintendent, to directly supervise the maintenance of said course in accordance with accepted standards and practices in the locality of the Employer. During the term of this Agreement, the Superintendent shall devote his/her best efforts and entire working time to advance the interests of the Employer and shall not directly or indirectly be engaged with any business that conducts a business in competition with the Employer. The Superintendent shall be responsible for hiring, with the Employer's consent and agreement as to salary, adequate assistants and staff properly to carry out his/her duties. The Superintendent shall at all times conduct himself/herself in a manner that will not discredit nor reflect adversely on the Employer, and shall perform his/her duties in accordance with the skill and care of an experienced golf course superintendent.

2. *Compensation.* The compensation to be paid to the Superintendent under this Agreement shall be at the rate of $ _____ a year, payable in accordance with the Employer's practice for full-time employees [or specify payments as weekly, twice a month, etc.] .

3. *Term.* The term of the employment of the Superintendent shall be for a period of _____ years commencing _____ , 19 _____ . This Agreement may be renewed or extended by the agreement of both parties; provided, however, that in the event that the Employer or the Superintendent does not desire to renew or extend this Agreement, such party shall so advise the other party at least 90 days prior to the expiration of this Agreement by giving written notice by certified mail. If by reason of illness, disability, or other incapacity the Superintendent is unable to perform his/her duties for a period of 90 consecutive calendar days, the Employer may terminate this Agreement upon 30 days' notice to the Superintendent. This Agreement shall terminate in the event of the death of the Superintendent, effective the date of such death. The Employer may terminate this Agreement for cause, effective the date the Employer so notifies the Superintendent in writing.

4. *Vacation.* The Superintendent shall be entitled to four (4) weeks of vacation with pay in each year of employment, such vacation to be timed in conjunction with the reasonable needs of the Employer.

5. *Reimbursement for Expenses.* The Superintendent shall be reimbursed in full for reasonable expenses incurred while attending educational meetings, both local and national, which have been previously approved by the Employer. The Employer also shall reimburse the Superintendent for all items of traveling, entertaining, and miscellaneous ex-

Figure 11-3. Two sample employment contracts for a golf course superintendent: Contract 1 is very detailed, and Contract 2 is simple and abbreviated. (Contract 1 adapted from material provided by the Golf Course Superintendents Association of America. Contract 2 adapted from material provided by the GCSAA as originated by Robert M. Williams, Bob O'Link Golf Club, Highland Park, Ill.)

penses reasonably incurred while away on business on behalf of the Employer, but payment shall be made only against a signed itemization listing of such expenditures. The Employer shall pay the Superintendent's dues to local and national turfgrass organizations approved by the Employer.

6. *Miscellaneous.* The Employer shall furnish at its expense a pickup truck for the Superintendent to carry out his/her duties. If the Superintendent is required to furnish his/her own transportation for Employer's business, he/she shall be compensated at the rate of _____ ¢ per mile. The Employer shall reimburse the Superintendent for moving expenses in an amount not to exceed $ _____ and shall provide the Superintendent with adequate housing and utilities for his/her family. The Employer shall provide Superintendent and the members of his/her immediate family with health and accident and disability insurance and shall provide the Superintendent with life insurance in an amount equal to his/her annual compensation. The Superintendent shall be entitled to participate in any pension plan provided by the Employer for which he/she is eligible. The Employer shall provide the Superintendent with meals at his/her discretion, and the Superintendent shall be extended the privileges of the golf course and the clubhouse, including guests, in good taste, subject to the rules of the Employer.

7. *Arbitration.* Any claim or controversy arising out of or relating to this Agreement or the breach thereof shall be settled by arbitration to be held at the Employer's location and to be conducted in accordance with the rules of the American Arbitration Association by a committee of three turfgrass experts, one to be appointed by the Superintendent, one to be appointed by the Employer, and one to be selected by the two arbitrators so chosen, and the judgment or award rendered by said committee acting as arbitrators may be entered in any court having jurisdiction thereof. The party which did not prevail in arbitration shall bear the expense of such proceeding. [Note that such a provision may encourage an employee to arbitrate a matter he/she would not think worth the greater expense of litigation.]

8. *Notice.* Any Notice to be given pursuant to the provisions of this Agreement shall be in writing and by registered mail and mailed to the parties at the following addresses:

(Employer)	(Address)
(Superintendent)	(Address)

9. *Assignment.* This Agreement shall inure to the benefit of and shall be binding upon the Employer, its successors and assigns.

IN WITNESS WHEREOF, the parties hereto have signed this Agreement the date and year first above written.

_____
(Employer)

By: _____
President

_____
(Superintendent)

Figure 11-3/Continued

LETTER OF UNDERSTANDING AND AGREEMENT BETWEEN _____

_____

(the Superintendent) and _____

Club (the Club). _____

is hereby engaged as golf course superintendent of the Club for a period of _____ years,

commencing _____ , 19 _____ . Renumeration will be at the rate of $_____

for the first year and $ _____ for the second year. The Club's and the Superintendent's

objective is to mutually bring about and maintain a top-quality golf course.

Chain of Command and Responsibilities

1. The Superintendent will be responsible only to the Green Committee and its chairman or
   to _____ .

2. All purchases for the maintenance of the golf course, including equipment and supplies,
   shall be the responsibility of the Superintendent after previous approval of a budget
   through regular channels of the Green Committee or _____ .

3. The Superintendent shall have the entire responsibility of hiring, firing, and directing all
   personnel for grounds and green maintenance; the salaries of such persons shall be subject
   to the approval of the Green Committee.

4. The Superintendent and the Green Committee will be responsible for the direction and
   policing of golf carts on the golf course.

Privileges

1. The Superintendent shall have the privileges of the course and the clubhouse, including
   guests, in good taste, in accordance with the rules of the Club.

2. Meals shall be available to the Superintendent at his/her discretion.

3. A month's vacation with pay in each year is allowed, timed in conjunction with the
   Green Committee.

4. The Club will pay for reasonable expenses incurred by the Superintendent for educational
   meetings, not to exceed $_____ in one year.

It is the combined thinking of the Superintendent and the Green Committee that the course
maintenance be brought to top condition and maintained as such.

_____
(President)

_____
(Superintendent)

Figure 11-3/*Continued*

Staff Training

All new employees should be given indoctrination sessions during which the overall objectives, structure, chain of command, and specific work responsibilities are reviewed. Special emphasis should be placed on safety guidelines and procedures. In addition, formal on-the-job training sessions will usually be required to insure that the employee can successfully execute the responsibilities of the position with maximum efficiency and safety. An employee who has been properly oriented to and trained in the responsibilities of a position will be better motivated to successfully perform the duties of that position.

Most golf course operations hire a number of seasonal employees. Thus, a common procedure is to hold meetings two to three days per week at which the initial indoctrination, safety regulations, and operating guidelines are reviewed and discussed with the group. These planning sessions can be supplemented with on-the-job training sessions covering the specific work activities of each individual.

It is preferable for the golf course superintendent to assume responsibility for instructing new employees. This permits the superintendent to become better acquainted with the new employee and to set the tone in terms of the level of job performance and attitude desired. By personally conducting the training session, the golf course superintendent also has better assurance that the individual's assigned tasks are accomplished in the desired manner. When time constraints do not permit the superintendent to conduct the session, the assistant superintendent or foreman can be called on. It is important that the individual delegated to conduct the training session has the ability to communicate effectively with and train new employees.

The specific information and activities the new employee is to be taught should be carefully determined and then summarized in a detailed written outline. Successful training of new employees depends on selection and presentation of information which the employee wants to know or perceives as of immediate importance to job performance. In other words, the knowledge or skill being taught should be useful in meeting a present responsibility.

Even though an employee may work in only a small portion of the general golf course operation, it is important for each staff member to understand the general concepts of the entire operation. A basic premise in any training program is that a well-informed staff member evolves into a well-trained individual who takes a greater interest in what he or she is doing. The more interest an employee has in the assigned work, the more likely that he or she will experience job satisfaction.

A number of golf courses have developed an ''operations manual'' covering overall procedural guidelines and containing a brief explanation of the operations involved in golf course maintenance, including courtesies to golfers and the fundamentals of golf etiquette. New employees should be encouraged to take the manual home for detailed study.

The best approach in any training session is to cover even the most basic fundamentals. Nothing should be assumed in the training process. For example, each employee should have a basic understanding of the game of golf and the rules of etiquette by which golf is played. The material should be presented in a simple, direct manner. To maximize the effectiveness of a training experience, the instructor should utilize a range of techniques including movies, slides, charts, group discussions, case histories, and actual on-site demonstrations.

On-the-job training is one of the best approaches to successful training of new golf course employees. New employees should have the opportunity to participate in the learning process. Retention of information or skills will be better if the trainee has repeated opportunities to practice or use what has been learned. Thus, training for specific activities is best scheduled just prior to periods when the activities will be performed on a regular basis.

New employees should be encouraged to ask questions and to offer alternate viewpoints. Such free give-and-take sessions permit them to participate in the learning process and to demonstrate their level of competence in a skill area based on previous experience. From that reference point the instructor can present new ideas and approaches in such a way as to reinforce or improve existing skill levels.

APPLICATION FOR EMPLOYMENT AT _____
                                    an equal opportunity employer

Notice to Applicant:

We appreciate your interest in our organization and assure you that we are sincerely interested in your qualifications. A clear understanding of your background and work history will aid us in placing you in a position that best meets your qualifications and our needs.

Date _____

Position desired: _____

Are you interested in: full-time _____ , part-time _____ , or seasonal _____

employment?

Are you willing to work: nights _____ , weekends _____ , holidays _____ ?

When are you available to start work? _____

Name: _____

Current address: _____ Current phone no.: _____

How long have you lived at current address: _____

Permanent address: _____ Permanent phone no.: _____

Who should be contacted in case of accident or emergency (give name and address)? _____

_____ Social Security no: _____

Are you either a United States citizen or a permanent resident alien? Circle: yes or no.

Do you have any physical or mental defects that would impair your ability to perform the job

for which you have applied? _____

_____

Are you willing to submit to a physical examination? _____

Have you worked for a golf course before? _____

If so, what was your position? _____

Show final grade completed: Grade School _____ High School _____ College _____

In detail, list special schools or training. _____

_____

_____

_____

(over)

Figure 11-4. A representative form that can be used as a formal document when individuals make application for employment. (Regulations with respect to equal employment opportunity vary from state to state. Thus, be sure to check the specific regulations in your state as they pertain to this Application for Employment form.)

PRESENT AND PAST EMPLOYMENT

(Last job first)

Show dates From To	Kind of Work Performed	Name and Address of Employer	Immediate Superior	Salary	Reason for leaving

REFERENCES (Personal, not employer)

Name	Address	Occupation	How long have you known?

May we contact those listed above? Yes _____   No _____

The answers to the foregoing are true to the best of my knowledge and belief.

_____
(Signature)

Applicant Do Not Write Below This Line

Personnel data requirements to be filled in by Department Head:

Beginning Date: _____   Salary: _____

Position: _____

Status: ( ) Full-time   ( ) Part-time   ( ) Seasonal
           Regular

Remarks: _____

_____

_____

_____

Figure 11-4/_Continued_

Another effective approach involves use of case histories. A specific problem is presented and the instructor encourages the new employees to develop possible approaches to solving it. With guidance from the instructor, the best practical solution to the problem can be brought out along with the specific principles on which the solution is based.

It is essential for the instructor to schedule follow-ups to the training exercises where the performance and progress of new employees in achieving the previously taught skills can be established. Individuals who are not progressing rapidly should be tutored privately on needed improvements and how they can be achieved. At the same time, they should be encouraged to continue their learning experience.

In some situations, a short internship for new employees is advisable following the training session. In this case, the intern accompanies a good, experienced employee during execution of specific activities. This allows the intern to observe the actual location, timing, and execution of various work responsibilities. The next phase involves a practice period during which the intern is responsible for the nursery and/or practice green for one to two weeks before being assigned to mow the regular greens on the golf course.

In addition to indoctrination and training of new employees, many golf course superintendents conduct an ongoing education program for all employees. This may involve a discussion session once a week or a more formal educational session one to two times a month. Typically, a specific subject is addressed, such as proper use of lubricants, identification of diseases, safety procedures in the operation of mechanized vehicles, or maintenance and repair of irrigation system components.

Finally, the golf course superintendent must pursue an active continuing education program to insure constant updating of information about techniques, chemicals, and equipment. This is achieved by regular attendance at state field days and turfgrass conferences as well as periodic participation at national conferences. Typically, the golf course sponsors the superintendent's participation at such educational events. Just one new idea, concept, or technique gained during a two- to three-day meeting usually will more than pay for the cost of attendance at the meeting. Furthermore, the superintendent should invite the assistant superintendent and foreman to attend some of the educational events. This not only will further their education but will improve morale and pride of these key supervisory personnel.

Staff Motivation and Morale

An important responsibility of the superintendent is to provide a mental and physical working environment that motivates employees to do their best. This environment also fosters employee morale or esprit de corps. Every person wants an enjoyable job and one which he or she can take pride in accomplishing.

Some supervisors motivate employees to perform better only through fear or a monetary reward system. However, evaluations reveal that receiving recognition for a job well done and job satisfaction are more important to most employees. The superintendent, assistant superintendent, and foreman should personally acknowledge, either verbally or in writing, an individual's accomplishment of a task efficiently and effectively (Fig. 11-5). Expressions of appreciation and compliments are highly valued by the worker and also generate pride and loyalty to all concerned. By the same token, it is important that criticism or discipline be constructive and that the employee be given a basic understanding of how to accomplish the task properly so that the error will not be repeated.

Another dimension in motivation and morale of employees is for them to be informed about the overall objectives and day-to-day activities planned for the golf course. This can be accomplished by a ten- to fifteen-minute meeting each morning before the workday is begun. It is important that information be provided in advance concerning special projects that will be assigned to the crew. This instills in each staff member a feeling of being knowledgeable about overall objectives and about how his or her particular work responsibilities fit within these objectives.

EMPLOYEE COMMENDATION

Date _____

Name _____ Dept. _____ Position _____

I feel that it is appropriate to give recognition in the form of this written commendation to the above named employee, and would like to have this document become part of his/her permanent employment record.

_____

Statement:

Supervisor _____

Date _____

Figure 11-5. Form letter used for employee commendation.

The superintendent must always remember that each employee may have personal problems and at times may need to talk with someone concerning these problems. Thus, the superintendent should provide an atmosphere that encourages confidence. The superintendent should take the time to listen carefully to what the individual is saying. Whenever it is sensed that an employee may need to discuss something, the superintendent should sympathetically express concern and offer to talk the problem over in an effort to help find a solution.

Job security is a high priority concern of most employees. Every effort should be made to plan work activities so that they can be distributed throughout the year. This will maximize the number of employees that can be retained year-round.

Each person must be treated with respect. Work assignments should be made as interesting and as challenging as possible. Rotating employees among various work assignments helps maintain interest and at the same time gives stability in accomplishing daily work activities should one employee become ill or be on vacation.

Finally, good working conditions should not be overlooked. Significant improvements have been made in this area in the past decade. Clean restrooms, a separate locker room and lounge area, and a shower all contribute to enjoyable working conditions and enhance employee attitudes, job satisfaction, and productivity.

The superintendent who pays attention to these factors demonstrates concern for employee welfare. The net result will be employee motivation to perform job responsibilities at a very high level with the overall goal of efficiently maintaining a high-quality golf course.

In working with employees, the attentive golf course superintendent can identify individuals that he/she may encourage to continue in the field and make it a profession. Many of today's golf course superintendents started as laborers, were elevated to positions of authority, and eventually attended college for formal training in the turf management profession (Fig. 11-6). It is the responsibility of the superintendent to identify these people, provide encouragement, and even help them progress through the appropriate training programs. Such recruitment efforts are needed to insure that knowledgeable, conscientious, hard-working turf managers are available for the future. These activities should also be part of staff training and morale building.

Figure 11-6. Formal college education in turfgrass science is an integral part of the modern golf course superintendent's training.

Communication

Clear, concise communication at a level which the recipient fully comprehends is the cornerstone for success of any golf course superintendent. Effective communication is needed at all levels of the chain of command: the assistant superintendent, foreman, and staff and also club officials, golfers, and other departmental managers, such as the golf pro and house manager. Failure to communicate with the latter groups has led to the downfall of many superintendents competent from the technical standpoint.

It is important for the superintendent to select carefully the terminology he or she uses, since comprehension of turfgrass terms most probably varies considerably among these groups. The effectiveness and efficiency with which the superintendent communicates with the golf course officials and golfers themselves are essential in gaining the respect and support of these groups, who are just as concerned with golf course playing conditions as the superintendent.

Courteous, friendly greetings to golfers encountered on the course is one level of communication which may involve not only the golf course superintendent but the assistant superintendent, foreman, and staff as well. The superintendent should also keep the golfing clientele informed as to the status of the golf course by such means as posting announcements on bulletin boards or preparing a superintendent's column for the monthly club newsletter. It is particularly important to post notices of scheduled events, such as turf cultivation, extensive vertical cutting, and winter overseeding of greens. Such approaches keep the membership well informed and thus minimize rumors that may be false, confusing, and counterproductive. The superintendent should also make an effort to communicate several times a week with the golf professional and house manager concerning course conditions, potential problems, and steps being taken where problems have arisen. Managers of these other departments frequently have more contact with golfers than does the superintendent and thus can be another avenue for disseminating information concerning progress and developments in golf course turfgrass maintenance as well as an avenue for feedback from the golfers.

Meetings should be scheduled regularly between the major department heads to update plans, establish objectives, discuss problems, explore solutions, and generally keep each other informed concerning the various facets of the golf club operation. This approach is essential, since the overall objectives in all departments of a golf course organization are the same. It is imperative that all operating departments work mutually to achieve the objectives. The superintendent should also make a personal effort to establish frequent informal communications among the department managers to insure the most harmonious management team possible.

Techniques. The superintendent occupies a management position in which 60 to 80 percent of the time is concerned with speaking, listening, writing, and reading, all forms of communication. There are various levels of communication, such as the informal face-to-face interchange and use of a telephone and the more formal written types including (a) letters, (b) reports and recommendations to the green committee and membership, (c) budget preparation and presentation, and (d) record keeping. Communication is also involved in interacting with others for the purpose of seeking ideas and opinions to have a better basis on which to make decisions.

The purpose of communication is to transmit or receive information. Its success is based on directing messages to the proper audience or individual. It is important that the receiver of the information has the attitude, interest, and willingness to understand what is being communicated. The selection of words and terminology used to communicate messages should be based on the ability of the recipient to understand them. In other words, the superintendent should be constantly alert in communicating with staff, since these individuals do not necessarily know everything that the superintendent knows. It is equally important to avoid excessive communications. Constantly bombarding a recipient with superfluous information can lead to an inability to communicate truly important issues or actions desired.

Oral work assignments should include (a) general information, (b) the mission to be accomplished, and (c) a detailed plan to follow. In providing instructions to subordinates or staff concerning daily or weekly work objectives, the superintendent should get feedback from them to insure that they understand what has been communicated. The approach should be to teach the staff how to do a task rather than just telling them what to do. It is also important that the superintendent properly train the middle supervisors to insure that they effectively communicate the objectives and assigned day-to-day work activities.

In most communication, certain objectives guide word selection. Sometimes this word selection is not as important as the manner in which the communication is delivered. In other words, facial expressions and body language are also involved in conveying certain meanings or attitudes. A routine communication presented in an uptight manner because of other problems faced by the superintendent may cause negative reception. Thus, it is essential that the superintendent be aware of mannerisms, tone of voice, and body language utilized to insure effective transmission of the desired message to the recipient.

Formal Reports. Written reports should be concise and orderly. The problem or issue should be clearly stated before a solution or alternative solutions are proposed. Issues or conditions affecting the ultimate solution should also be stated. Reading of formal reports is facilitated by employing wide margins, double spacing, and an organized format with the appropriate headings and subheadings. A brief summary can be presented at the beginning of lengthy reports to increase the impact.

Operations Manual

An operations manual containing guidelines for the diverse range of golf course operations and activities is an important component in a sound, efficient management system. The manual is a basic reference that can be used during the initial training period and as a readily available reference aid for all employees. Contents of the handbook may include (1) a summary outline of the organizational chart and chain-of-command procedures to be followed, (2) procedures to follow in daily turfgrass maintenance activities, such as greens mowing, operation of the irrigation system, raking of bunkers, changing of cups, moving of tee markers, (3) detailed safety procedures utilized in the shop, equipment operation, and handling of chemicals, and (4) procedures to be followed in the maintenance and care of equipment.

The operations manual is a very specific document which relates to the needs of a particular golf course. Thus, it is typically prepared by the golf course superintendent. The document should be as brief and concise as possible to encourage employees to read it. It is important that it be written in a manner and with word selection which permit employees to fully comprehend the message. An outline format is a very effective approach for some portions of the manual. The operations manual is a living document that should be constantly updated to meet current conditions and needs. Employees should be encouraged to take a copy home to read at their convenience.

Safety

The superintendent must always be cognizant that he or she is responsible for employee safety. A health and safety program should be initiated during the new employee indoctrination sessions and the superintendent should be constantly alert for violations of the established safety guidelines for the golf course. Repeated violations of these guidelines by an employee should be documented in writing. Failure to comply with the guidelines is cause for discharge. The golf course superintendent and supporting supervisory staff should be fully knowledgeable of all Occupational Safety and Health Act (OSHA) safety regulations and stay up to date on new or altered guidelines. In addition, periodic training and discussion sessions for existing employees can serve as a continual reinforcement of the need to follow safe procedures in all types of day-to-day golf course operations. Appropriate safety guidelines should be posted in a high visibility area as a constant reminder. Safety in day-to-day operations, whether it be in equipment operation or pesticide use, is habit forming. The need for speed in accomplishing a task is no justification for ignoring safe operating procedures and techniques. Details concerning safety procedures for equipment and chemicals are found in chapters 8 and 10.

Staff Reprimand and Discharge

Every effort should be made to insure that each employee fully understands his or her responsibilities and how each assigned task is to be accomplished. A well-organized and effectively communicated plan of work for the staff contributes significantly to minimizing disciplinary problems. In addition, the superintendent should set a good example for the entire work staff in terms of timeliness, honesty, attitude, and work characteristics.

Employees who fail to comply with the rules or to do assigned tasks must be disciplined. The reprimand should be accomplished in private and as soon as possible after the failure has been noticed. It is important that rules enforcement be impartial and consistent. The employee should have an opportunity to present his or her side of the story. The superintendent should listen with an open mind in as informal an environment as possible. After careful evaluation with emotional issues under control, the reprimand should be issued, if warranted. The proper approach is constructive criticism of performance, not of the individual. After the reprimand, the superintendent should insure that the employee understands what he or she has done wrong. A record should be kept of the disciplinary actions.

An employee whose record shows chronic violations may need to be discharged. The process of discharge should involve thorough documentation, including initial oral warnings, oral warnings with a notation in the employee's file, and finally a written warning signed by the supervisor and the employee involved (Fig. 11-7). Should the employee refuse to sign, a witness should be used. Once the decision has been made to terminate an employee, the person should be given the opportunity to resign. The resignation should be in writing to avoid unjustified unemployment compensation claims and to protect against possible EEO charges. Further, a resignation is desirable from the employee's standpoint in terms of self-respect and future employment opportunities. Should the employee refuse to resign, the only alternative is official issuance of a discharge after thorough documentation as to the details and seriousness or repetitiveness of the firing offense(s).

The superintendent should guard against on-the-spot firing. It is particularly important that all employees be treated equally in relation to firing offenses. Treatment should be based on a detailed examination of the circumstances. The superintendent should always be cognizant that discharge of an employee means a loss of the income invested in hiring and training that employee and of productive time before a properly trained new employee can be brought into the organization.

Efficient Personnel Management

Typically, 70 percent of a golf course operating budget is devoted to salaries and wages. Thus, maximizing the efficiency of employees without sacrificing quality is an important objective in achieving efficient utilization of funds. All facets of management discussed in this chapter contribute to maximizing efficiency in the use of manpower resources. Included are proper personnel training, effective communication, and delegation of authority. Attention to proper safety practices in all operations minimizes injuries and therefore lost time. By the same token, proper record keeping concerning labor requirements of various golf course maintenance operations permits the superintendent to establish costs for various activities. This information can then be used to assess where savings may be achieved without sacrifice of quality. On the other hand, the superintendent should avoid investing so much time in record keeping that the additional information generated does not contribute significantly to an ongoing efficient golf course management system. Minicomputers will probably be used increasingly to add efficiency in golf course management operations.

The superintendent should conduct job analyses periodically. Sufficient time must be taken to stand back and ask, ''Is there a better way to do this job without sacrificing quality?'' Perhaps purchase or lease of a particular piece of equipment would permit the job to be done more efficiently and also would eliminate less pleasant work tasks. Time and motion studies of the activities of the staff and equipment operations are valuable. One of the areas where efficiency frequently can be increased is in the routing of men and equipment from the maintenance facility over the golf course as they perform their daily responsibilities. The superintendent should study the size, shape, and physical characteristics of the

EMPLOYEE WARNING

Date _____

Name _____ Dept. _____ Position _____

Nature of Warning

Has employee been warned previously?   1st   2nd   3rd

Employee's Remarks

Date: _____ Employee's signature _____

Action Taken

Date: _____ Supervisor's signature _____

Figure 11-7. Form used to formally reprimand an employee.

property which affect the routing and efficiencies that can be achieved. Sometimes a decentralized system of several outlying equipment buildings may be more efficient than one centrally located service building. In some cases, the selection of a different means for transporting personnel should be considered. The use of motorized two-wheel vehicles is increasing for this reason. Through these management activities a well-trained, experienced golf course superintendent can achieve substantial savings in golf course operating costs. Such contributions alone more than justify a higher salary, without taking into consideration the technical expertise in agronomic practices that such a professional brings to the position.

RECORDS

A good record-keeping system plays an ever increasing role in the efficient, effective management of a golf course operation. It is important that the superintendent be able to assess on a regular basis current expenditures as compared with budget projections and the actual expenditures for the previous year. Only through good accounting procedures can this be accomplished. In organizing a record-keeping system, the superintendent should be sure that it is compatible with the system used by the golf club accountant.

The superintendent needs to establish cost centers in order to determine quickly how funds have been spent and the labor resources allocated. A daily log is needed to record the receipt of chemicals, parts, and other supplies as well as to keep an inventory of remaining stock. This information is summarized and posted to the appropriate cost center on a monthly basis.

Records are essential for the preparation of progress reports, the annual report, the next year's proposed budget, and the long-range plan. A record system also is necessary to evaluate efficiency and generate maintenance costs for greens, tees, fairways, roughs, bunkers, trees, and similar facilities. Such information provides justification for the next year's budget proposal. If adjustments in priorities due to budget restrictions become necessary, the superintendent can inform club officials as to the amount of money required for each activity. This, along with a statement of impact on overall golf course playing conditions, can be used to justify or to eliminate the activity. In other words, a good record-keeping system provides a sound basis to justify specific expenditures such as for equipment.

Most authorities recommend and some state laws dictate that certain employee records be kept. Weekly and monthly payroll summaries can be derived from daily time cards. OSHA requires that employment and safety records be maintained for each employee. Other federal and state laws direct that a log showing procurement and use of chemicals and pesticides must be kept. Included in this log are the type of chemical, the amount, and location where applied. Thus, an accurate and readily understood record-keeping system is very important in the operation of a complex, modern golf course.

Log of Daily Operations

A log of daily operations and observations should be maintained. Generally the record is hand entered into a permanently bound logbook. This daily log should be considered the minimum form of record keeping on golf courses. Typically, it lacks the detail afforded by a record-keeping system containing all or a major portion of the components and forms described in the remainder of this section. Thus, this log should be considered a basic component but not the sole form of record keeping needed in a highly efficient, successful golf course operation.

Daily Operations Record System

A time card and time clock usually are used to record the daily work period for each employee. In addition, the foundation of a comprehensive record system is the requirement that each employee fill out a daily log presenting a breakdown of hours spent on various tasks along with the particular equipment utilized. Many types of daily work record systems are in use on golf courses. A relatively simple system is presented in this section as an example.

EMPLOYEE DAILY LOG

_____ Golf Course   Date _____

Employee Name	Job Number	Equipment Number	Hours (nearest ¼)		Fuel (gal)	Remarks, Problems, or Repairs
			Labor	Equipment		
Daily Total						

Figure 11-8. Employee daily log used to record labor and equipment activities.

JOB CODE IDENTIFICATION LIST

Areas or Facility		Job Activity		Job Activity	
Unit Code	Description	Job Code	Description	Job Code	Description
01--	Greens	--01	Mowing	--22	Site preparation
02	Collars	02	Trimming (rotary)	23	Construction
03	Aprons	03	Edging	24	Drainage
04	Tees	04	Fertilization	25	Soil processing
05	Fairways	05	Irrigation	26	Fumigation
06	Surrounds	06	Topdressing	27	Seeding
07	Rough	07	Vertical cutting	28	Sprigging
08	Intermediate rough	08	Spiking	29	Sodding
09	Bunkers	09	Turf cultivation	30	Planting
10	Club grounds	10	Dew removal	31	Pruning
11	Trees/shrubs	11	Disease control	32	Snow removal
12	Pond/lake	12	Insect control	33	Cleaning
13	Stream/ditch	13	Animal control	34	Repair
14	Parking lots	14	Aquatic weed control	35	Servicing/adjustment
15	Shelters/drinking water	15	Weed control	36	Winterizing
		16	Sand raking	37	Purchasing
16	Fence	17	Cup changing	38	Crew training
17	Maintenance building	18	Tee marker placement	39	Conference/field day
		19	Ball washer/towels	40	Administrative
18	Cart paths/roads	20	Trash removal	41	Vandalism repair
19	Irrigation system	21	Root zone modification	42	Repair

Figure 11-9. Comprehensive job code identification list used in the daily operations record system.

Employee Daily Log. The employee daily log is the only form used in this system that needs to be explained to each employee (Fig. 11-8). Primary emphasis should be placed on job codes or cost centers, usually a single-column item. To identify the specific task, a job code is assigned, normally a four-digit number. The first two digits designate specific areas, such as greens, tees, fairways, as shown in the left column of Figure 11-9. The last two digits represent the particular activity or practice, as shown in the right two columns of Figure 11-9. For example, use of job code 0101 in the employee daily log denotes that the greens have been mowed.

Job Code Identification List. To facilitate use of this system, a job code identification list is posted in the work area where employees assemble for cleanup and termination of the day's activities. In addition, it may be printed on the back of the employee daily log form. The code designation ''00'' can be used on the daily log form so the employee may add in the remarks column specific activities not included in the job code identification list. The job code identification list shown in Figure 11-9 is very comprehensive. A less extensive list can be used.

Any imminent problems or malfunctions noted should be indicated in the remarks column. When the mechanic accomplishes the indicated repairs or adjustments, an ''OK'' note is made in the remarks column by the mechanic.

Monthly Summary. At the end of each month, the information from the employee daily log can be entered on a monthly labor and a monthly equipment utilization form (Fig. 11-10). Each form should be large enough to enter a full month on one page. This consolidation is done by the superintendent or, more typically, by the assistant superintendent. These monthly summaries provide the superintendent an opportunity to review the activities of the past month and possibly to identify areas where greater efficiencies can be accomplished in the upcoming months. The two monthly labor and equipment utilization summaries can be included in the monthly progress report to the green committee and club officials. This report usually contains a comparison of the amount budgeted for each category with the amount actually spent to date for that budget category.

Annual Summary. Annual summaries of labor utilization and equipment utilization can be compiled at the end of the growing season or fiscal year from the monthly forms previously described. These summaries serve as consolidated references and show the (a) total annual hours expended for labor activities and equipment operation, (b) hours devoted to labor and equipment operation on specific areas, such as greens, tees, and fairways, and (c) amount of time that each maintenance task required on each area. These annual summary forms are most indicative of the total golf course maintenance operation and are particularly valuable in budget preparation (Fig. 11-11).

Record System Utilization. Based on these records, a projection of expenditures for each month in the upcoming fiscal year can be prepared for the accountant and the club officials (Fig. 11-12). Expenses can be summarized in general categories and then broken down into specific activities. The maintenance of accurate annual records generated from the employee daily logs and the monthly utilization records are a valuable aid in justifying proposed budget expenditures to course officials. This record-keeping system provides base data which are valuable in determining labor costs for specific activities as well as for comparing performance efficiency of each employee.

Similar detailed information on costs can be obtained for each piece of equipment. These data allow the superintendent to (a) forecast engine overhaul requirements, (b) schedule specific maintenance servicing, and (c) project the date for replacement of each unit. Seasonal equipment needs also become apparent from this record-keeping system. Such information can be useful in budget preparation, since equipment maintenance and repairs can be scheduled when most convenient and employment of additional part-time laborers can be avoided. These data also permit evaluation of specific pieces of equipment not used frequently. The superintendent can determine if lack of use is due to downtime, an inferior product, improper operating practices, or a shift in basic maintenance requirements on the golf course. In some cases, an accurate record-keeping system may identify a piece of equipment which it would be more economical to rent due to infrequent use. In contrast, for those types of equipment that show very high use, purchase of a more efficient machine could prove more economical due to fewer man-hours required in completing the task.

Equipment Records

In addition to records concerning equipment utilization, three additional record forms are to be considered. One is an equipment inventory form that describes each unit purchased. It includes details concerning the original purchase arrangements and projected life expectancy (Fig. 11-13).

The second form contains the preventive maintenance and repair records for each piece of equipment (Fig. 11-14). This log is a record of all scheduled preventive maintenance inspections as well as nonscheduled repairs required for the specific unit. It provides an overall maintenance history including the types and frequency of repair as well as the costs involved in servicing the unit. This basic maintenance record for each piece of equipment may be kept in a file folder for that particular unit. The folder may also contain operating manuals, parts manuals, work orders, and inspection forms.

MONTHLY LABOR UTILIZATION SUMMARY

_____ Golf Course   Month _____

Job Description	Job Number	1	2	3	4	5	6	7	8	9	10	11	12	13	14	15	16	17	18	19	20	21	22	23	24	25	26	27	28	29	30	31	Total Hours

Figure 11-10. Monthly labor utilization summary form. A monthly equipment utilization summary form would be comparable.

ANNUAL LABOR UTILIZATION SUMMARY

_____ Golf Course   Year _____

Job Description	Job Number	Jan.	Feb.	Mar.	Apr.	May	June	July	Aug.	Sept.	Oct.	Nov.	Dec.	Total Hours

Figure 11-11. Annual labor utilization summary form. An annual equipment utilization summary form would be comparable.

PROJECTED MONTHLY BUDGET EXPENDITURES

_____ Golf Course   Year _____

Account Number	Category	Jan.	Feb.	Mar.	Apr.	May	June	July	Aug.	Sept.	Oct.	Nov.	Dec.	Total
	Personnel													
	Salaries													
	Wages													
	Benefits													
	Fertilizers													
	Water													
	Irrigation facilities													
	Chemicals													
	Drainage													
	Bunker sand and topdressing mix													
	Seed, sprigs, and sod													
	Petroleum supplies													
	Equipment parts and service													
	Landscaping													
	Golf course equipment													
	Fences, bridges, shelters, and drinking fountains													
	Maintenance building													
	Electricity/gas/fuel oil													
	Equipment depreciation													
	Contract services													
	Insurance													
	Miscellaneous													
	Contingency													
	Monthly Totals													

Grand Total _____

Figure 11-12. Form for projected monthly budget expenditures. The form for actual monthly expenditures by budget category would be comparable or can be combined in the same form.

EQUIPMENT INVENTORY

_____ Golf Course

Date Received	Unit Number	Description	Make and Model	Serial Number	Supplier	Cost	Expected Life (Years)	Date Sold or Junked

Figure 11-13. Golf course equipment inventory form.

EQUIPMENT PREVENTIVE MAINTENANCE AND REPAIR SERVICE RECORD

Unit Number ________ Unit Make ________ Engine Make ________

Description ________ Unit Model ________ Engine Model ________

Date Purchased ________ Unit Serial No. ________ Engine Serial No. ________

Date	*Problem Reported*	*Date and Hours/Miles Service Due*	*Date and Hours/Miles Service Performed*	*Date Repairs Completed*	*Man Hours Needed*	*Parts Used*	*Total Cost Parts and Labor*

Figure 11-14. Equipment preventive maintenance and repair record form.

A wall chart showing preventive maintenance schedules is usually placed in the service shop. This chart contains a list of all equipment units and the projected dates, hours, or miles when they should have preventive maintenance servicing. With such a chart, the superintendent and mechanic can plan the servicing work for times when the equipment is least likely to be in use. For units not equipped with an hour meter or speedometer, preventive maintenance scheduling can be established by calendar dates based on the historical average operating hours or use for each unit.

The third form involves a log of equipment parts procurement and utilization (Fig. 11-15). This form serves as an organized reference in inventorying the parts stock. It insures that replacement parts are requisitioned sufficiently early so that they are on hand when needed and thus costly downtime is avoided.

Fuel and Power Records

The substantial increase in energy costs has emphasized the need to maintain proper inventory and cost control records for fuel and lubricants (Fig. 11-16). The employee daily log can be a source of information regarding fuel consumption for each piece of equipment. A log of fuel use may also be maintained at the pumps. The mechanic is usually in charge of regularly checking the fuel inventory and requisitioning replacement supplies well in advance of the projected date when existing supplies will be exhausted. This watchful concern in ordering fuel and power stocks is particularly important in times of variable availability. Records of gasoline use are vital where one storage tank is used as the source for all golf course vehicles, including those of departments other than maintenance. They facilitate proper accounting procedures so charges can be made to the appropriate cost center or department. For example, gasoline for golf carts is charged to the golf department and for clubhouse vehicles to the house department. Records of gasoline use are also needed for recovery of fuel tax on gasoline used for agricultural (nonhighway) use.

Pesticide, Fertilizer, and Seed Records

Records concerning the acquisition and use of pesticides, chemicals, fertilizers, and seeds are important from several standpoints (Fig. 11-17). A current or running inventory of stocks is needed so that requisitions can be initiated as needed to avoid depletion of stocks. Proper use of this inventory also insures that older stocks are used before they deteriorate to an unacceptable extent or, in the case of seeds, before an excessive decline in germination occurs. A stock number should be assigned to a lot when received, entered on the record form, and clearly marked on the stock containers.

Detailed records should be kept by the superintendent concerning the purchase, storage, and use of pesticides (Fig. 11-18), fertilizers, and chemicals. A minimum set of utilization records is required by such governmental units as the Environmental Protection Agency. The record should include the stock number, trade and generic names, quantity of material applied, method of application, specific area to which applied, name of the individual supervising the application, date applied, and weather conditions at the time of application.

Water Records

Both the amount of water used and the trends in water quality must be monitored to insure efficiency. A log of the amount of water pumped or purchased should be kept on a monthly or, in some cases, a weekly basis. Certain states have a law specifying that water use records be kept. The rate of water use should be read from a water meter and recorded at the same time each week. This information facilitates an evaluation of irrigation practices in relation to year-to-year weather trends. In the future, such long-term records may be vital in justifying golf course water needs for irrigation to municipal or county water allocation authorities or control boards. This external control of water use may be applicable even when the water comes from a well within the golf course property.

EQUIPMENT PARTS, PROCUREMENT, AND USAGE LOG

_____ Golf Course

Date of Requisition	Part Description	Name of Supplier	Number of Units Ordered	Cost	Date Received	Date Used

Figure 11-15. Equipment parts, procurement, and usage form.

FUEL AND POWER RECORDS
(Amount Used and Cost)

—— Golf Course   Year ——

Month	Gasoline	Diesel Fuel	Motor Oil	Lubricants	Electricity	Gas, Coal, Fuel Oil

DAILY GASOLINE/DIESEL FUEL LOG

—— Golf Course   Year ——

Date	Gallons		Oil	Equipment Number and Name	Operator
	Gasoline	Diesel			

Figure 11-16. Monthly inventory record of fuel and power, including amount used and cost (*top*), and daily gasoline/diesel fuel log (*bottom*).

PESTICIDE PROCUREMENT AND INVENTORY RECORD

_____ Golf Course

Date Ordered	Trade and Generic Names	Mfg. Batch Number	Name of Supplier	Amount Ordered	Date Received	Stock Number	Date Used

Figure 11-17. Pesticide procurement and inventory record form. Similar forms can be employed for fertilizers and seeds.

PESTICIDE UTILIZATION RECORD

Golf course name _____ Location _____

Name of certified supervisor _____ Registration no. _____

Address _____

Application date _____ Time _____ A.M. _____ P.M.

Name of employee(s) applying pesticide _____

Pesticide(s) used and dosage(s):

Pesticide(s) (Common Name, Trade Name, and Formulation)	Stock No.	Concentration(s) and Active Ingredient	Dilution in Carrier	Gallons or Pounds of Diluted Material Applied per Acre or Specified Area

Total formulation added to tank or hopper _____ Amount of mixture applied _____

Wetting agent _____ Rate _____ Other material _____

Target pest(s) _____

Extent and type of plant injury _____

Plant species treated _____

Description and
measurement of area treated _____

Application equipment used _____

Speed of machine _____ MPH _____ RPM _____

Nozzle size _____ Pressure maintained _____ Spreader setting _____

Weather conditions during application _____

Air temperature _____ Wind velocity _____ Wind direction _____

Cloudy _____ No. of days since last rainfall _____ Amount of rain _____

Observations and notes _____

Figure 11-18. Detailed form for pesticide utilization records.

Regular analysis of water quality is essential if effluent water is used for irrigation (Fig. 11-19). Regulatory agencies in some states require monitoring, on a specified regular basis, of all effluent water used for turfgrass irrigation. The monitoring of effluent water quality provides information concerning potentially harmful chemicals as well as beneficial constituents. Knowledge about the amounts of plant nutrients in the water is critical when determining fertilizer programs. Without this knowledge, a balanced fertilizer program cannot be developed. Such knowledge is essential when the nutrient content of the effluent water is subject to substantial daily variation. Following of trends in water quality in other water sources is also important to detect shifts that could lead to future problems.

Soil Test Records

A summary set of records of soil tests is usually maintained (Fig. 11-20). This form allows soil test results to be consolidated so that they can be evaluated in terms of year-to-year trends and so that potential problems are easily identified. For comparisons to be valid, it is important for the soil tests to be conducted in the same manner. This includes depth of sampling, time of year sampled, and analysis by the same laboratory or by laboratories utilizing the same extraction and analytical procedures.

Weather Records

Keeping on-site weather records is not a common practice at most golf courses, but it should be in the future (Fig. 11-21). The responsibility for collecting and recording this information is frequently assigned to the assistant golf course superintendent. Weather records are of particular importance in isolated locations where there is no Weather Bureau reporting station. Information on seasonal weather trends can serve as a basis for scheduling future cultural practices as well as for the diagnosis of problems associated with stresses and pests that develop in response to certain weather conditions. Soil temperature monitored on a daily or weekly basis is a particularly effective indicator of the status of turfgrass shoot growth, root initiation and growth, recuperative ability, weed seed germination, time of preemergence herbicide applications, disease development, and timing of turf establishment, especially scheduling of winter overseeding. Course weather records can be supplemented by monthly weather record summaries, which are available from the U.S. Department of Commerce for a nominal fee.

Cultural Practice Records

Superintendents should maintain a log of specific cultural practices utilized on the major turfgrass areas, such as greens, tees, fairways, and roughs. This log includes:

1. Fertilization: date, rate, spreader setting, and type of fertilizer applied
2. Materials applied for adjustment of pH or for correction of a sodic condition: date, rate, and type of material applied
3. Vertical cutting: date, depth of blade setting, and number of passes
4. Turf cultivation: date, type, size of tines or blades, and number of passes
5. Pesticide application: date, material applied, rate, and method of application
6. Topdressing: date, amount applied, and specific soil mix utilized
7. Mowing practices: cutting height, frequency, mowing pattern, type of mower, and clipping disposition
8. Any other practices, such as major changes in irrigation practices or use of a wetting agent

Personnel Records

The Federal Wage and Hour Law stipulates a minimum wage and requires payment of one and one-half times the regular hourly rate for each hour over forty an employee works in a given seven-day work week. Under the Fair Labor Standards Act, certain records must be kept. The superintendent

RECORD OF EFFLUENT WATER QUALITY

_______________ **Golf Course**

Date	Nutrient Level			Salinity	Potential Problem Elements						
	Nitrogen	*Phosphorus*	*Potassium*		*Boron*	*Cadmium*	*Copper*	*Mercury*	*Nickel*	*Sodium*	*Zinc*

Figure 11-19. Form employed to monitor quality of water sources used for turfgrass irrigation.

SOIL TEST RECORD

Location _______________

Golf Hole	*pH*			*Phosphorus*			*Potassium*			*Calcium*			*Magnesium*			*Salinity*			*Sodium*		
	19__	19__	19__	19__	19__	19__	19__	19__	19__	19__	19__	19__	19__	19__	19__	19__	19__	19__	19__	19__	19__
1																					
2																					
3																					

Figure 11-20. A typical soil test record form.

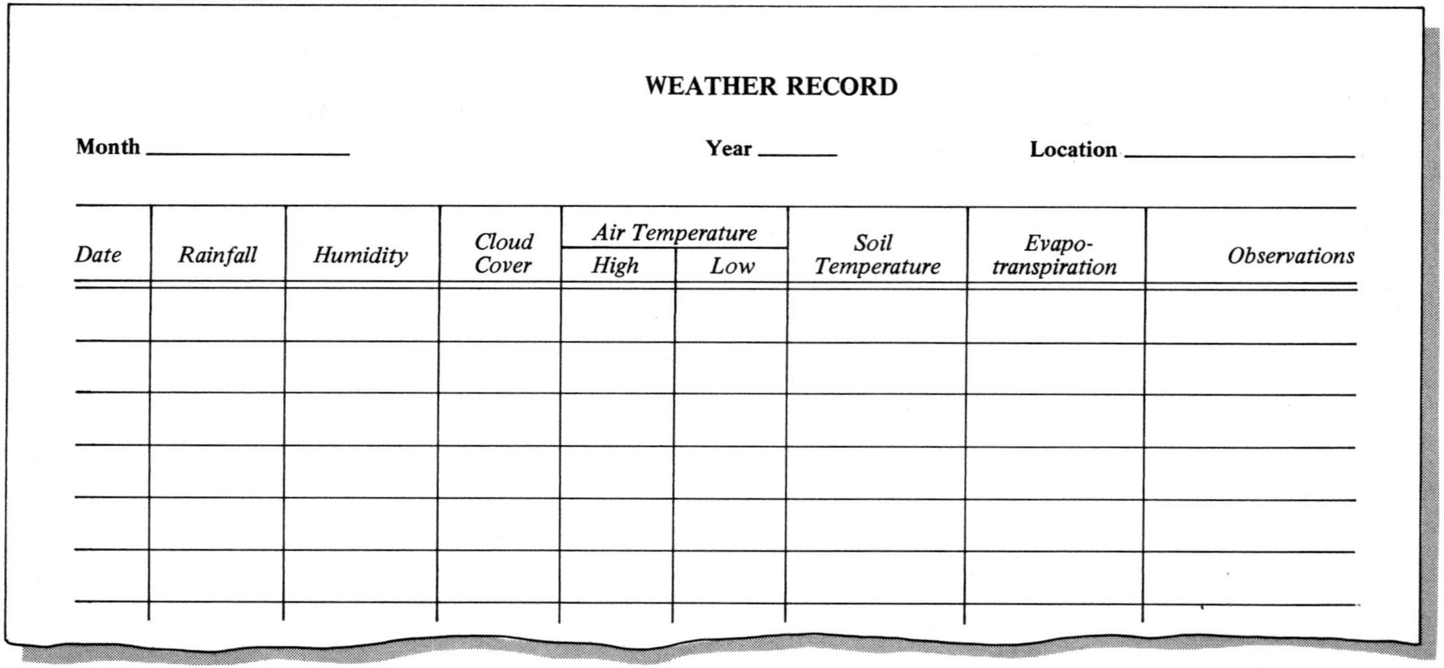

WEATHER RECORD

Month _____   Year _____   Location _____

Date	Rainfall	Humidity	Cloud Cover	Air Temperature		Soil Temperature	Evapo-transpiration	Observations
				High	Low			

Figure 11-21. A typical weather record form.

should check the labor laws annually to be sure that the proper employee records are being kept. The basic employment and earning records, such as daily time cards, must be preserved for at least two years.

Records concerning occupational accidents and illness are required by OSHA and the state Workers' Compensation Board. In some cases, a health evaluation form must be completed by a physician before the worker can begin official employment.

BUDGET

One of the more important basic responsibilities of a golf course superintendent is preparation of the course maintenance budget. Budget preparation is typically stipulated in both the superintendent's job description and contract with the golf club. The budget should reflect, in financial terms, all grounds maintenance requirements for the following year and should be presented in a form that is easily understood by the green committee and/or manager/owner. A detailed explanation and justification for each budget category request, along with accurate estimates, greatly enhance the probability of receiving adequate funding to maintain the golf course in accordance with the stated objectives and standards for the particular facility.

Assuming the budget has been properly prepared, it can be utilized throughout the year as a reference perspective in achieving the original objectives. It can also function as an aid in assuring that funds are spent in an orderly, programmed manner. Unusual or unexpected demands on funds to meet a maintenance crisis are more likely to occur if the budget procedure is haphazard. Thus, a properly prepared budget allows identification and control of (a) all expenses, (b) means and methods for cost reduction, and (c) human factors that can be manipulated to improve efficiency. A properly prepared budget is an essential tool in achieving cost controls and is critical to a smooth-running operation.

Two types of budgets should be developed: capital and operating. A capital budget is prepared covering expenditures for equipment and items with a life expectancy of more than one year. In contrast, the operating budget is prepared for expenditures associated solely with the upcoming year.

Budget Preparation

The golf course budget is developed systematically in a series of stages. The starting point in preparing an operating budget is a review of club and departmental objectives for the coming year. The superintendent should obtain a statement from the green committee or owner regarding maintenance objectives, policies, and planned improvements. This information provides the superintendent with a base from which to establish priorities in the maintenance plan for those budget items necessary to achieve the stated objectives. Long-range objectives should be reviewed at regular intervals by the appropriate club officials so the superintendent is properly informed as to the changing desires of the golf club members or owner.

Every major capital budget item should be clearly explained with emphasis on the positive aspects. Factors to consider include member/owner objectives and ultimate satisfaction, economic trends, general labor availability, number of employees required to meet the objectives, and the time schedule needed to accomplish long-range improvements. The establishment of target dates for completion of specific projects is an effective way to determine the practical timing of projects and their relationship to ongoing maintenance practices.

The next stage is for the superintendent to conduct a complete evaluation of present maintenance practices and techniques, with the goal of achieving possible efficiencies and/or improvements. Budget preparation is a time to evaluate the accomplishments of the past year as well as how golf course funds are to be utilized in the coming year. In other words, a properly prepared course maintenance budget shows the current golf course condition and the financial plan needed to support proposed future activities, both short- and long-term.

SAMPLE GOLF COURSE MAINTENANCE BUDGET

1. Capital Improvements

		Unit Cost	Total
A.	Rebuilding putting greens No. 7 and 10	_____	_____
B.	Planting 24 oak trees	_____	_____

2. Capital Expenses

   A. Equipment replacement

	Unit Cost	Total
2 Triplex greensmowers	_____	_____
1 Hydraulic, 7-gang rough mower	_____	_____
1 Powered mechanical topdresser	_____	_____

   B. File cabinet (4 dr.) replacement | _____ | _____ |

   Grand Total $ _____

3. Operating Expenses

Account Number	Category	Previous 3 years			Current Year		Proposed 19_
		19_ Actual	19_ Actual	19_ Actual	Proposed 19_	Projected 19_	
	Personnel Salaries Wages Benefits Fertilizers Water						
	Irrigation facilities Chemicals Drainage Bunker sand and topdressing mix Seed, sprigs, and sod						
	Petroleum supplies Equipment parts and service Landscaping Golf course equipment Fences, bridges, shelters, and drinking fountains						
	Maintenance buildings Electricity/gas/fuel oil Equipment depreciation Contract services Insurance Miscellaneous Contingency						
	Grand Total						

Figure 11-22. Representative golf course maintenance budget.

The secondary objectives are originated, planned, and executed by the golf course superintendent to accomplish the prime objectives. Past records of routine maintenance practices are of considerable value in planning this aspect of the budget. Specific needs are established to accomplish the prime objectives. Included are projected costs for labor, equipment, chemicals, supplies, and special projects. The best aids in determining these costs are past cost records, experience, and current distributor information. The superintendent should attempt to obtain realistic costs and should not hesitate to seek appropriate advice from experts.

The budget may include statements regarding (a) whether the current year's standards of operation and support equipment will be sufficient to meet next year's needs, (b) the specific improvements that the club members or owner desire, (c) the current financial status and outlook for next year, and (d) new federal or state laws which affect the cost of operations. Budget estimates that reflect an accurate appraisal of these factors are more likely to be approved.

A good record-keeping system is essential for preparation of a projected budget. It makes the task much easier, since there is a reference base of past costs. For example, labor costs can be derived from past records and adjusted in accordance with (a) projected inflation rates, (b) adjustments in the maintenance program, and (c) specific improvement projects proposed for the upcoming year to meet long-range objectives. Projected needs for equipment will become apparent from the records. The level of maintenance and repair costs for each piece of equipment provides information needed to decide whether the purchase of a replacement unit is in order. If a unit is to be replaced, good records permit realistic projections for maintenance and repair costs. Thus, accurate annual records are valuable in justifying the proposed budget expenditures to course officials.

Some summary guidelines for budget preparation include the following:

1. The budget should be prepared well in advance of the fiscal year.
2. The budget activity is a team effort. Involvement of the assistant superintendent, foreman, and mechanic can provide alternate viewpoints, serve to educate with regard to course maintenance objectives, and aid in building morale. However, final decisions as to specific budget proposals must rest with the superintendent.
3. Involvement of club officials and management personnel in planning the budget contributes to a successful presentation and ultimate approval of the budget.
4. The budget and maintenance program should be prepared jointly.
5. Accurate records, judicious purchases, proper purchasing procedures, and realistic cost controls are necessary in preparing and executing the budget.
6. Budgeting of one phase of the course maintenance program must be coordinated with and related to budgeting of other phases as well as to the total golf course budget.
7. Budget requests should be realistic; there should be no padding or across-the-board percentage increases or cuts.

Once the primary objectives have been established and approved for both ongoing course maintenance and long-range improvements and construction, they should be adhered to during the budget year. This assures that no unexpected catastrophic events will occur. In some situations, an alternate budget for support of unanticipated contingencies may be advisable. In these cases, a plan for higher-than-anticipated as well as less-than-anticipated income should serve as the base.

Budget Content

The method of organizing a budget varies with the type of facility, requirements of the management or owner, organization of the record system, and experience of the course superintendent. The budget proposal usually contains two distinct aspects (Fig. 11-22). One aspect includes the capital improvement expenditures. This phase of the budget includes costs for acquisition of equipment plus expenditures for course improvements whose life expectancy is longer than one year. Each capital expenditure should be accompanied by a detailed justification. The other aspect of the budget covers proposed operational expenditures for maintenance of the golf course during the upcoming year.

CATEGORIES INCLUDED IN A GOLF COURSE BUDGET

Capital Improvements. Expenditures listed improve the value of the property, such as (a) building construction — additions, pump-house, bridges, shelters, or cart paths, (b) course changes — green, tee, or bunker construction, and (c) tree plantings.

Capital Expenses. Equipment, including vehicles and trucks, constitutes the major portion of this category. Lockers, permanent tools, and office furniture are also included.

Operating Expenses
> *Personnel*
>> Salaries: Superintendent, assistant superintendent, foreman, equipment mechanic, assistant equipment mechanic, and irrigation specialist.
>> Wages: Permanent employees, seasonal employees, and extra workers.
>> Benefits: Includes vacation time, sick leave, social security, workers' compensation, unemployment, hospitalization insurance, life insurance, retirement, uniforms, meals, and superintendent expense allowance.

> *Fertilizer.* Specific types and quantities based on a preplanned program, with fertilizer on hand taken into account. An effort should be made to not store fertilizer over a year.

> *Water (if purchased).* Approximate cost established by averaging gallonage from past five years and adding any anticipated rate increase.

> *Irrigation Facilities.* Age of the system and the costs for past repair for piping, controllers, control lines, valves, and sprinkler heads are considered. Allowing a contingency sum for possible major pump repairs during the year is wise.

> *Chemicals.* Includes herbicides, fungicides, insecticides, nematicides, and fumigants. Present inventory should be included to keep chemicals revolving in storage.

> *Drainage.* Projected costs for repair of drain lines, french drains, ditches, stream banks, ponds, and surface contours.

> *Bunker Sand and Topdressing Mix.* Based on preplanned maintenance for year ahead.

> *Seed, Sprigs, and Sod.* Any planned construction or renovation projects as well as routine overseeding and sodding needs should be considered. Includes purchase of cool-season grass seed for winter overseeding of dormant bermudagrass in warm climates.

> *Petroleum Supplies.* Gasoline, diesel fuel, oil, and lubricant use records should be kept for accurate cost projections. Purchase of any additional new equipment should be taken into account, along with anticipated rate increases.

> *Equipment Parts and Service.* Costs projected for mechanical repairs from past cost records with consideration for new or different equipment. Equipment rentals and leasing would be covered in this category.

> *Landscaping.* Amount for annual flowers, bulbs, border edging, ornamental shrubs, tree pruning, and tree replacement program.

> *Golf Course Equipment.* Flags, flagsticks, out-of-bounds and hazard stakes, ropes, cups, tee markers, benches, ball washers, and towels. Past records of vandalism may give an estimate of how much to budget in this category.

> *Fences, Bridges, Shelters, and Drinking Fountains.* A designated amount should be allowed for maintenance and repair of these items.

> *Maintenance Building(s).* Amount for painting, repair, window replacement, plumbing, and heating facilities.

> *Electricity/Gas/Fuel Oil.* Costs projected from past cost records and anticipated rate increases.

> *Equipment Depreciation.* A detailed depreciation schedule to fund the purchase of new equipment.

Contract Services. Based on past records and projected plans, plus anticipated cost increase. May include turfgrass consultant, architect, engineer, surveyor, repair specialist, and tree maintenance contractor.

Insurance. Includes fire, property loss, and liability insurance.

Miscellaneous. May include office supplies and printing, telephone, vehicle licenses, pesticide applicators' licenses, association dues, educational conference/field day expenses, and summer lodging for student workers.

Contingency. An amount to cover unanticipated expenses for replacement of turf and trees caused by flooding, tornadoes, hurricanes, winterkill, extended droughts, scald, epidemic pest attacks, and vandalism.

Long-Range Planning

Every golf course should maintain a long-range plan for capital improvements. Five years is usually the practical maximum in long-range planning for a specific project, while three years is considered intermediate. The program should be updated each year, one year being added and the current year dropped. Without such planning, capital improvement projects tend to be hit or miss, which usually results in increased costs. Examples of long-range projects include the rebuilding of a green, tee, bunker, or total golf hole; extensive renovation of an irrigation system; installation of a fairway drainage system; a major tree planting program; other landscape projects; and construction of a new maintenance building. Examples of short-term capital improvement projects include installation of french drains to correct problems in depressional areas, extension of an irrigation line within a fairway, replacement of bunker sand, and extension of a cart path. Such short-term projects can be completed within a year. Priorities should be established for projected long-range projects.

Most long-range projects involve relatively large expenditures, which emphasizes the need to make long-range financial plans. The treasurer or club controller must be involved in the long-range planning process. Generally, costs for major improvement projects should be prorated over several years. Major equipment expenditures should be amortized for a number of years. The exact period should be determined by the accountant. This emphasizes to club officials that a given piece of equipment must be replaced within a specified period. Capitalization of equipment purchases within a single year may lead officials to defer replacement of needed equipment or cause them to not anticipate future large equipment expenditures. On the other hand, the funds generated by short-term depreciation schedules may have a favorable impact on the club's financial structure. For the same reason, leasing rather than purchasing equipment must be considered. In most cases, it is the responsibility of the superintendent to provide background information and justification statements for major capital expenditures. Appropriate information relating to the projected cost estimates should be sought. This may involve the employment of a golf course architect, landscape architect, or design engineer to develop the most feasible plan and specifications to accomplish the stated objectives. It is imperative that the proposed improvements be studied in detail and evaluated to insure that they fit within the overall master plan and objectives of the golf course.

Budget Presentation

Presentation of a budget to the green committee, owner, or governing authority is the responsibility of the superintendent. Much detailed planning is needed to successfully present and defend a proposed budget. One approach to presentation is to summarize the highlights of the budget and then to give appropriate supporting information. A short history may be appropriate for capital improvement projects. A copy of the proposed budget should be sent to each committee member prior to the budget meeting.

The presentation should be as short and concise as possible, yet must effectively communicate the budget proposal and justification. Simple language is better than trade jargon and scientific terms, since club officials are usually unfamiliar with these. Use of visual aids to communicate concepts and plans is always desirable. These aids may range from a marking pencil and scratch pad to drawings, charts, models, pictures, or a slide presentation. During the verbal assessment of certain capital improvements, both the advantages and disadvantages of the concept should be presented. Personal touches in the presentation and enthusiasm are effective. Also, it is helpful if the major features of the budget are discussed with key members of the club management team and green committee before the actual budget meeting. Finally, it is important that sufficient time be allocated following the budget presentation for discussion and questions.

Purchasing Procedures

An orderly, well-delineated purchasing procedure should be established. The objective is securing of the best possible quality materials at minimum cost. Requisitioning, buying, and receiving are the three main phases of procurement. The proper information must be included on the requisition to insure purchase of the correct item. All bids and contracts must be carefully prepared, and where required, presented in accordance with legal precepts. The purchasing and procurement policies are most effective when coordinated and integrated with the procedures utilized in the overall golf course operation. No single purchasing procedure can be recommended for use on all golf courses, owing to the great diversity of financial structures from course to course.

The superintendent must have a certain degree of latitude in the purchase of items officially approved in the budget. However, certain guidelines must be followed to avoid the development of serious financial problems. In general, it is suggested that (a) all invoices for materials and supplies be properly accepted by the superintendent or an authorized representative before payment is made, (b) approval from the appropriate club officials be obtained in advance of a capital expenditure in excess of the amount mutually agreed on, and (c) monthly budget summaries be prepared and distributed to the superintendent and appropriate club officials.

Considerable budgetary savings can be made if the procurement of equipment and supplies is properly programmed or scheduled and if equipment and supplies are acquired in the appropriate quantities. Improper purchasing policies are evidenced by overstocking of materials and equipment, buying the wrong item for a particular need, spoilage and deterioration of supplies, downtime due to delay in delivery of repair parts, and an excessive number of back orders. An inventory of existing supplies and equipment parts should be checked and a budget for the particular replacement needs established prior to any procurement action.

Adequate specifications, quality purchasing, reliable suppliers, early buying, and an understanding of the realistic needs for a golf course are all important in prudent buying. Buying locally is good public relations but is advisable only if the local dealer can offer good value, service, and price. It is best to deal with companies possessing a reputation for reliable service, quality products, and an understanding of golf course policies and problems. The particular dealer selected should have demonstrated a willingness and capability to give prompt delivery, adjustments and exchanges, and efficient equipment servicing and to stock repair parts in amounts needed to insure that they are readily available. Ordering well in advance avoids problems associated with last-minute purchases and permits time to compare and test items before a final decision is made. In addition, early ordering often permits a real savings by enabling the superintendent to take advantage of preseason price reductions.

Adjusting to a Tight Budget

Keys to controlling spiralling maintenance and operating costs within the framework of a reasonable budget are efficient labor operations and improved maintenance practices. A limited budget often calls for superior management. For this reason, a well-trained, experienced golf course superintendent will more than recover a somewhat higher salary through management efficiencies.

Certain categories of the golf course budget offer the most potential for economies. Since 65 to 70 percent of the budget is allocated to labor costs, economies in this area will have a substantial impact. Labor costs can be reduced by intelligent purchasing of high-capacity equipment and non-labor-intensive supplies, skillful management strategies, careful hiring practices, and efficient record keeping. The proper labor-saving equipment will quickly pay for itself through reduced labor expenditures. Examples include three-gang mowers, power sand rakes, and large powered rotary mowers. Two-way radio communication facilities allow more efficient utilization of staff and equipment, which in turn produces economies in maintenance.

Strategies related to maintenance practices and programs should be judiciously evaluated for possible budgetary savings. Costly hand trimming around poles, trees, and buildings often can be eliminated by use of an appropriate contact herbicide or growth regulator. Instead of poling manually to remove dew from fairway turf, a hose or chain section pulled behind two maintenance vehicles can be an effective labor-saving alternative. A syringe cycle on an automatic irrigation system also removes dew quickly and economically.

A well-planned and executed equipment maintenance program requires expenditures in the present but may produce future savings. Well-maintained machinery often lasts beyond the tax depreciation period. Also, proper storage of equipment, chemicals, fertilizer, and topdressing can prevent deterioration and thus save money.

Consideration should be given to the feasibility of rescheduling certain turfgrass maintenance practices. Many staff hours are lost annually by interruptions due to intense play. Thus, scheduling of projects at times when they can be completed without undue interruption is advisable.

Year-round staff members should be recognized and encouraged, since their experience, cooperation, and loyalty can facilitate budget economies. Club members or managers should be aware that providing funds or defraying expenses for these loyal employees to attend schools, conferences, seminars, and field days is a good investment. Similarly, projects should be planned well in advance so a year-round work program keeps permanent staff members busy throughout the year, not just during the golfing season. A number of work projects on a golf course can be planned as off-season winter tasks to provide year-round employment.

The superintendent's efforts to economize within a constrained budget should be communicated to the club members and manager. Priorities should be carefully honed and established in preparing and executing an alternate budget to deal with reduced funds. The aid of club members and officials should be enlisted when adhering to these priorities. A tight budget demands sound management strategies and more efficient utilization of machinery and manpower resources.

Budget Comparisons

Golf courses differ in their budget requirements and should not be compared dollar for dollar. There is no established standard for a golf course maintenance budget. Thus, great variability exists in how costs and expenditures are categorized. True costs may not be reflected in the totals and expenditures may not be charged to the correct category or cost center. For example, one course budget may group golf course maintenance expenses with expenditures for the swimming pool or tennis courts, whereas another golf course may utilize a more elaborate accounting system under which the expenditures are specifically categorized.

Variables among courses will affect the operating budget. For example, a hilly course will require a greater expenditure for fuel than a level course. Wooded areas necessitate increased labor expenditures for trimming, leaf removal and disposal, and tree root pruning. Courses with streams, ponds, or lakes will generally require added expenditures for maintenance. Soil types frequently vary among golf courses and will dictate different irrigation, turf cultivation, drainage, and fertilization practices. Courses also may be planted to different turfgrass species and cultivars, which can be reflected in maintenance cost. The crew size may vary depending on the particular types and sizes of maintenance

Figure 11-23. An architect's drawing table and storage cabinet. (Photo courtesy of D. O. Miller, Saucon Valley Country Club, Bethlehem, Pa.)

equipment purchased. Courses in distinctly different geographical regions will have grasses that vary considerably in their water and nutrient requirements. Climatic conditions and length of the growing season likewise impact on these and other cultural practices.

Golf course maintenance costs are affected by (a) number of rounds played annually, (b) number of days per week the course is open for play, (c) extent of winter play, (d) intensity of play and local rules with regard to interruption of play for work, (e) course design, (f) size of greens, tees, fairways, bunkers, and rough, (g) mowing frequency for greens, tees, and fairways, (h) amount of golf cart traffic and whether cart paths exist, (i) type of irrigation system and water source, (j) extent of irrigated turf, and (k) quality of labor force and unionization. While comparison of operating costs between golf courses in certain subcategories is possible, the likelihood of misinterpretation is great when overall budget totals are the only means of comparison.

PLANS AND DRAWINGS

A permanent, up-to-date record of all physical facilities and ''as-built'' plans must be maintained for a golf course. For example, failure to maintain an updated set of irrigation plans and drawings can lead to great waste in time and money when trying to locate drain and irrigation lines for repair or renovation projects. All changes, additions, or modifications to a particular item should be accurately recorded on the appropriate set of plans or blueprints.

In the case of an irrigation system, there is a distinct difference between the original plan drawn by a design engineer and the actual system installed. A design for the latter is termed an *as-built plan* and is of great significance in both regular maintenance and future adjustments to the system. A complete, current set of plans is needed so that when there is a change in supervisory personnel, such as a superintendent, equipment mechanic, or irrigation specialist, the incoming person will have the necessary information to execute his or her responsibilities with minimum delay. Much time can be wasted in attempting to contact previous personnel or trying to find out from hourly laborers the location of valves, piping, drain lines, and electrical lines.

It is advisable that three sets of plans be maintained, one set to be kept in the operations office of the maintenance facility, the second set in the clubhouse office, and the original with the architect. This duplication is a preventive step should the set normally placed in the maintenance building be lost to fire or vandalism. The frequently used plans may be placed on a wall rack, which facilitates ready reference. It is advisable that plans be individually protected in plastic covers. The addition of new or altered details on a plan is best accomplished with use of an architect's drawing board (Fig. 11-23) and a simple set of drawing tools. The types of plans most commonly maintained for a golf course operation include the following:

1. Golf course layout
2. Topographic map
3. Soils map
4. Drainage system layout
5. Irrigation system layout
6. Tree and shrub landscape plan and inventory
7. Golf cart paths and service roads
8. Sewer, electrical, gas, TV cable, and telephone layouts
9. Maintenance facility plans
10. Shelters, drinking fountains, and pump-house plans
11. Foot and vehicular bridge plans
12. Property variances and easements
13. Long-range architectural changes
14. Property survey
15. Aerial photos and surveys

Chapter 12

Other Aspects of Golf Course Operation

CHAMPIONSHIP/TOURNAMENT PREPARATION

Preparations for competitive events range from relatively simple ones for a club championship to the elaborate organizational structure required to host a major tournament or a national championship (Fig. 12-1). The golf course portion of tournament preparation usually falls under the responsibility of the regular green committee, which for championship preparation may be termed the grounds committee. Continuing effective communication among superintendent, grounds committee, and overall organization committee is important in successful preparation of a course for any major golf event. The goal of the grounds committee is to prepare a golf course that possesses uniform playing conditions in line with the particular level of tournament or championship play involved. Discussion in this section is oriented to the elaborate preparations required for championship play, such as the United States Golf Association (USGA) Open Championship. Appropriate aspects can be selected for use in smaller tournaments. The reader is referred to the USGA, Golf House, Far Hills, New Jersey 07931 for more detailed information.

Course Setup

The golf course is set up for competition by a tournament official who, in concert with representatives of the golf course, defines the (a) distance for each hole, (b) fairway mowing height and contours, including narrowing where necessary to provide an exacting test, (c) mowing heights for the intermediate and primary roughs, and (d) placement of tee markers and cups during each day of the competition. Any major changes requiring rebuilding of greens, tees, bunkers, or fairways should be completed at least one year in advance of a scheduled competition.

The difficulty of course setup depends on the nature of the competition. The USGA policy is that a course should provide a good test of golfing ability without being tricky. The USGA Open and Amateur championships are expected to play more difficult than the Junior and Senior competitions. For example, Stimpmeter green speeds for the Open and Amateur are expected to be in the range of 112 to 120 inches (2.8 to 3 meters), while for other championships a slightly lower speed is acceptable, depending on such circumstances as the location and time the championship is held.

The golf course must be prepared properly so that all competitors play the same course — there must be no confusion and no misunderstanding. Out-of-bounds, regular water hazards, lateral water hazards, obstructions, and ground-under-repair must all be marked with either stakes or painted lines. Out-of-bounds stakes are painted white and ground-under-repair is marked with white painted lines, while regular water hazards are marked yellow and lateral water hazards are marked red. An obstruction is

Figure 12-1. Golf course during a major championship.

usually marked with a sign. Any existing artificial distance or directional markers are usually removed before a major championship.

Putting Greens

The cultural system for putting greens should be organized so that all greens are as uniform in putting quality as possible. The practice putting green should be maintained to achieve the same degree of uniform putting quality as the regular greens. The mower bench setting is typically in the range of ⅛ to 3/16 inch (3.2 to 4.8 millimeters), depending on the type of mower and bedknife utilized. The mowing frequency should be daily for several months prior to scheduled play, with double mowing beginning four days prior to the first practice round and continuing through the event. Early morning double mowing is preferred over single mowing in the evening and single mowing the next morning.

The irrigation program should be carefully planned so that all greens peak at the time of the championship. The goal is firm greens that reward only well-executed shots. Irrigation water should be applied only as needed to maintain uniform, moderate turfgrass growth and color. Excessive irrigation leads to soft greens and increased capability to hold improperly executed shots. The greens should be firm but resilient, with a true, nonslippery putting surface. The greens should not be rolled or mowed to the extent that the ball can gain speed when putted down all but the severest of slopes.

Matted, fluffy turf on greens cannot be tolerated for championships. Excessive organic material can be eliminated by vertical cutting, brushing, and raking plus a judicious combination of cultivation and topdressing, if needed. Where a mat problem exists, light topdressing may be required as frequently as six to eight times in the fall and spring preceding a scheduled competition. All mat or puffiness problems should be eliminated at least one year in advance of a competition.

Green Speed

The Stimpmeter can be utilized to monitor the speed of each green and thus provide guidance to the superintendent in achieving uniformity of putting quality for all eighteen greens on the golf course during tournament competition. One approach is to measure each green daily after mowing. If any green does not meet the speed standard established, it can be mowed again before competition starts.

The putting green speed standard for championship play as monitored by the Stimpmeter has been established as 126 inches for fast, 114 inches for medium-fast, 102 inches for medium, 90 inches for medium-slow, and 78 inches for slow (Table 3-1 on page 100).

Cup Placement

Many factors must be taken into account when selecting the location of the hole for each day of a tournament. The placement must be fair, play well, and be free from surface imperfections. The USGA has the following guidelines concerning cup placement for tournament play.

1. The design of the hole as the architect intended it to be played should be studied. The length of the shot to a green and how it may be affected by the probable conditions for the day, such as wind and other weather elements, condition of the turf from which shots will be played, and holding quality of the green, must be known.

2. There must be enough putting green surface between the hole and the front and sides of a green to accommodate the required shot. For example, for a long iron or wood shot to a green, the hole should be located deeper in the green and further from its sides than may be the case for a short pitch shot. In any case, it is recommended that the hole be located at least five paces from any edge of a green. If a bunker is close to the edge or the ground slopes away from the edge, the distance may well be greater, especially if the shot is more than a pitch. Consideration should be given to allowing a fair opportunity for recovery after a reasonably good shot that just misses a green.

3. An area 2 to 3 feet (0.6 to 0.9 meter) in radius around the hole should be in good condition without any steep slopes or changes in the degree of slope. In other words, the holing-out area of a green should be as nearly level as possible and of uniform grade, but need not be exactly level. In no case should holes be located in tricky places or on sharp slopes where a ball can gather speed. A player above the hole should be able to putt with a reasonable degree of boldness, not purely defensively.

4. The condition of nearby turf must be considered, care being taken to avoid old plug holes that have not completely healed.

5. Holes should be cut as nearly on the vertical as possible, not perpendicular with the surface contour of a green.

6. There should be a balanced selection of hole locations for the entire course with respect to left, right, central, front, and back positions. For example, left positions put a premium on drawn or hooked shots. Balanced selection usually requires that the location of each cup be recorded when changed.

7. For a competition played over several days, the course should be kept in balance daily as to degree of difficulty. In stroke competition, the first hole of the first round is as important as the last hole of the last round. Thus, the course should not be set up appreciably more difficult for any round. The old concept of making the course progressively harder round after round is fallacious. One form of balanced daily treatment is selection of six quite difficult hole locations, six that are somewhat less difficult, and six of moderate difficulty.

8. An effort should be made to anticipate players' traffic patterns in early rounds to avoid locating many holes where exit and entrance routes could spoil potentially good hole locations for later rounds.

9. In match play, a hole location may be changed during a round, if necessary, provided the opponents in each match will play the same location. In stroke play, Rule 36-4a in the *Rules of Golf* requires that all competitors in a single round play with each hole cut in the same position. When thirty-six holes are played in one day, it is not customary for the hole locations to be changed between rounds, but no rule prohibits this. All competitors must be informed if hole locations are changed.

10. The greenkeeper who cuts the holes should make sure that the rules of golf are observed, especially the requirements that the hole liner not exceed 4.25 inches (10.8 centimeters) in outer diameter and that it be sunk at least 1 inch (2.5 centimeters) below the putting green surface.

11. During the practice days before a competition, it is advisable to locate holes in areas not likely to be used during play, preferably at the fronts and backs of greens, bearing in mind the areas that will be adversely affected by foot traffic patterns.

Collar and Putting Green Surrounds

A collar of about 30 inches (76 centimeters) in width is maintained around the putting green for championship/tournament play. The cutting height is slightly under fairway height, at 0.4 to 0.6 inch (⅜ to ⅝ inch or 9.5 to 16 millimeters). Immediately outside the collar is an intermediate rough mowed at approximately 2 inches (5 centimeters) high. This intermediate zone between the collar and the putting green surrounds may range in width from 2 to 6 feet (0.6 to 1.8 meters), depending on the nature of the shot and the contours surrounding the green. A wider width is used for a more difficult shot, whereas a narrower width is desired if the shot is relatively easy. The intermediate cutting height is maintained to the perimeter of bunkers adjacent to the green as well as between bunkers and to the crest of mounds closely surrounding the putting green. Extending beyond is the deeper rough, which may be maintained at a cutting height of 4 to 8 inches (10 to 20 centimeters), depending on the density and uniformity of the turf.

Tees

All tees are mowed at a height of 0.4 to 0.5 inch (⅜ to ½ inch or 9.5 to 13 millimeters) on a daily basis during championship play. Irrigation should be practiced only if needed to prevent wilt and to encourage an adequate recuperative rate. Proper watering produces a firm, dry turf, which is essential to the proper stance. It is usually advisable for tees on par-3 holes to be protected during practice rounds. On the other hand, competitors should be allowed use of the full length of all tees during their preparation for the tournament. The best compromise is to leave the par-3 tees open for their full length on the left one-third. The remaining two-thirds of the holes can be protected by means of wire netting laid across the surface (Fig. 12-2) or by roping off the area.

Figure 12-2. Protection of a tee on a par-3 hole during practice rounds before a major tournament.

Tee markers are moved daily during tournament competition. A single set of blue tee markers is used most commonly. A paint mark can be used to designate each day's placement to the greenkeeper. Only one uniform set of tee markers should remain on the course during major championships to avoid errors or confusion on the part of contestants. Any tee marker containing information that is not correct for the particular competition must be removed.

Fairways

Decisions regarding fairway widths should be made at least one year prior to a major competition. Wide fairways place a premium on distance, while narrow fairways demand accuracy. Most major tournaments require narrowing of the fairways, which necessitates a change in cutting height of what ultimately will be the intermediate or primary rough. On a fairway converted to a higher cut rough, the turf tends to become dense and heavy owing to the irrigation pattern and higher nitrogen fertility level previously used. The result is a much more difficult condition than is normally desired for intermediate and primary roughs. Thus, the shift to narrower fairways, from 30 to 35 yards (27 to 32 meters) wide in the landing areas, should be initiated one year prior to a major championship or tournament. Fertilization and irrigation of the newly added primary rough areas must be avoided so a more uniform, representative rough is formed throughout the golf course.

Certain cultural practices required to bring the fairway turf into desired tournament condition need to be completed well in advance. All fairway areas should possess a firm, tight turf. Alternation of hard and soft spots across the fairway must be corrected to achieve a uniformly firm playing surface. Such variations can be avoided through proper cultivation and irrigation practices. Similarly, fluffiness is undesirable in fairway turfs. Correction can be achieved through raking, brushing, or combing for a few weeks prior to the scheduled competition if the problem is minor or through more extensive renovation and vertical cutting early in the season prior to the scheduled competition if serious fluffiness or a thatch problem exists. No objectionable weeds should be present, especially patchy clumps such as clover. Any existing bare areas should be spiked, planted, and topdressed sufficiently early to achieve a uniform, dense fairway turf throughout. Depressions from settling of old irrigation or drainage trenches should be leveled by raising the sod and/or topdressing. This is especially important in the landing areas.

The fairway cutting height for tournament competition is usually between 0.5 and 0.75 inch (1.3 and 1.9 centimeters). Fairways must be closely mowed so that golfers can impart the spin necessary for control over every type of shot. The desired cutting height is initiated at the beginning of the season during which the event is to be held. This height is maintained throughout the season leading up to the competition, and one mowing every three to four weeks is a cross cut. The higher the cutting height, the greater the mowing frequency to achieve the desired tight, firm turf surface. Just prior to and during the event, the fairways should be mowed daily. During the competition, divots marks in the fairway on short par-4 holes and in the area of the third shot on par-5 holes should be filled with topdresssing to minimize problem lies in the primary landing areas.

Rough

The area of most concern is the intermediate and primary roughs. The intermediate rough typically consists of a 6-foot (1.8-meter)-wide mowing swath along both sides of each fairway. The height of this rough may range from 1.5 to 2 inches (4 to 5 centimeters). The latter is usually utilized in the USGA Open and Amateur championships. The purposes of a 2-inch (5-centimeter)-high intermediate rough are to prevent a ball that comes to rest just off the edge of the fairway from rolling into the deep rough and to avoid a severe difference in shot difficulty for a ball hit just a few inches off target as compared with a ball hit badly off line.

Outside the intermediate rough is the primary rough. This is typically mowed at between 3 and 6 inches (7.6 and 15 centimeters) in height, depending on the caliber of the championship and the turf density in the primary rough. Bermudagrass typically is mowed in the lower portion of the range, while cool-season grasses are mowed in the higher portion. No standard cutting height is given for the rough, as the character of the grass stand determines this to a great extent. Where the grass stand is thin and weak, a cutting height of 6 to 8 inches (15 to 20 centimeters) may be desirable. In contrast, a dense matted turf that has been irrigated may dictate a cutting height of 4 inches (10 centimeters) or less. The objective when selecting the cutting height for a primary rough is to prevent a player from making a full recovery shot. The primary rough should not be so deep as to make recovery impossible or to increase significantly the prospects for a lost ball. By the same token, the rough should not be so thin that a wood or a long iron shot can be played with ease.

The type of mower used on the primary rough will necessitate some variation in the specified cutting height. Reel mowers may be used at cutting heights less than 4 inches (10 centimeters), while rotary mowers are preferred at heights of 4 inches or higher. The suction action of rotary mowers lifts the leaves to a more vertical position so they are cut at a more uniform height. The rotary mower has additional advantages in removing unsightly seedheads and other extraneous growth that often develop when turfs are allowed to grow at high heights. The result is a more uniform-appearing turf, since the desired height can be maintained throughout the tournament by mowing with a rotary mower as needed rather than by merely ceasing to mow the roughs at some predetermined time prior to the tournament. The latter approach results in more shaggy, inconsistent growth in many places and a progressively more difficult rough as the tournament progresses, which is usually not advisable.

Major fertilization or liming applications scheduled for the rough should be accomplished two years in advance of the tournament. This allows sufficient time to enhance turf density without allowing excessively lush growth. Patches of unusually thin turf should be fertilized to thicken the sod and thus eliminate the possibility of a full-distance recovery shot. By the same token, excessively lush grass where a ball may be lost or hidden should also be corrected. Weed control, especially of patchy weeds such as clover, should be accomplished by herbicide treatment during the year preceding the scheduled competition. Any weeds that survive this treatment can be eliminated early in the year prior to the tournament.

Bunkers

The desired sand-particle size distribution, shape, and color for bunkers are as described in chapter 7. In particular, the reader is referred to Table 7-1 (page 265) for specifications related to sand-particle size ranges. If a large amount of sand is required in one or more bunkers, it should be in place at least six months in advance of the scheduled championship. If a small amount of sand (1 inch [2.5 centimeters] deep or less) is to be added for cosmetic purposes only, it should be in place at least one month in advance of the competition. If no rainfall occurs, it is important that the newly added sand be fully wetted by irrigation so that it settles properly. Players should not be able to putt out of bunkers. A grassy lip of 3 to 4 inches (7.6 to 10 centimeters) must be developed on the greenside perimeter face of bunkers to prevent this. Sand on the bunker face must be sufficiently shallow (2 inches [5 centimeters] deep) to prevent balls from imbedding.

Posttournament Cleanup

Deployment of a large number of litter bags and daily emptying will significantly reduce the litter problem. The preparation of route plans and operating instructions for vehicle drivers involved in the setup of auxiliary facilities required for a major championship will minimize the amount of turf wear and rutting problems during wet weather. Such preventive measures will reduce the amount of costly posttournament repair.

Some reestablishment of turf can be anticipated after any major tournament with a large gallery in attendance. Reestablishment involves turfgrass cultivation by coring or slicing, usually in multiple directions and up to four times. Subsequently, the area should be seeded (Fig. 12-3) and then watered

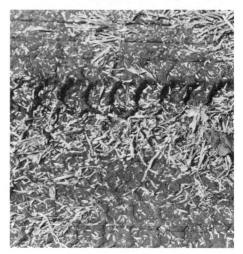

Figure 12-3. Turfgrass renovation seeding operation on a rough. Area thinned by intense gallery traffic (*top*), centrifugal seeder in operation (*bottom left*), and close-up of seed on bare spot (*bottom right*).

daily at midday until turf establishment is achieved. Satisfactory recovery should be anticipated within four to six weeks, assuming favorable growing conditions following the tournament. Another approach that has been successful in certain situations involves broadcasting seed before the event over areas where serious thinning is anticipated and allowing the gallery traffic to press the seed into the soil.

A significant amount of soil compaction can be anticipated wherever gallery traffic has been intense, even if severe turf wear and thinning have not occurred. These areas should also be cored or sliced in multiple directions immediately after the tournament.

Checklist for Championship Preparation

Greens

1. Mow daily for several weeks in advance.
2. Develop firm, true greens; do not overwater.
3. Begin to eliminate any matted, fluffy turf one year in advance.
4. Topdress as needed the preceding fall and spring.
5. Do not core during the spring and summer before the event unless absolutely necessary.
6. Hand-water during the event.

Tees

1. Maintain a firm dry turf; do not overwater.
2. Install tee signs one week in advance.
3. Protect a portion of par-3 tees during practice days.

Fairways

1. Establish the fairway outlines specified by tournament officials one year in advance.
2. Eliminate any hard or soft spots.
3. Avoid fluffiness; rake, brush, or comb, if necessary.
4. Eliminate weeds, especially clover.
5. Mow at championship height throughout the season.
6. Mow daily during competition.
7. Topdress divot marks daily.

Roughs

1. Eliminate any dense clover areas during preceding year.
2. Fertilize where necessary more than one year in advance.
3. Establish the cutting heights specified by tournament officials one year in advance.

Bunkers

1. Install any needed fresh surface sand (1 inch [2.5 centimeters] or less) no later than one month in advance; if 4 to 6 inches (10 to 15 centimeters) is to be added it must be accomplished at least six months in advance.
2. Establish 3- to 4-inch (7.6- to 10-centimeter) grassy lips on greenside bunkers.
3. Ascertain that sand in face is reasonably shallow and firm.

Other

1. Suggest yellow flags on solid white or cream-colored flagsticks.
2. Remove all artificial direction or distance markers and directional signs.
3. Erect any bridges needed for the gallery.
4. Provide red and yellow stakes or spray paint to define the boundaries of water hazards.
5. Define all out-of-bounds carefully; provide extra stakes.
6. Provide white paint in spray cans for marking any ground-under-repair.
7. Beginning ten days in advance, place holes in areas of greens not likely to be used during competition.
8. Paint soil strip above cup liners white daily during the competition, especially if it is to be televised.
9. Arrange for care of putting greens and bunkers during play.
10. Begin to install gallery ropes and stakes four days before practice rounds start.
11. Check gallery ropes and stakes daily during competition.
12. Install tents and any temporary comfort stations at least one week in advance.

13. Install any platforms required for photographers at least one week in advance.
14. Cooperate in installation of broadcasting equipment, including prearranging entrance routes and parking areas.
15. Provide tables, chairs, and public address system for the awards ceremony.
16. Control movement of trucks and other heavy vehicles; guard against ruts.
17. Supply whiting (spray paint) and marking devices to gallery committee.
18. Consider setting up a walkie-talkie system for key staff members to insure rapid communications.
19. Inventory equipment as soon as possible after completion of the event.

SHELTERS

The primary function of shelters is to provide protection during unfavorable weather conditions, particularly thunderstorms with associated lightning. Features added to shelters in recent years include restrooms, first-aid pack, refrigerated drinking water, lightning rods, communications equipment, and snack bar facilities. The actual combination of facilities selected beyond those required for protection from unfavorable weather depends on the specific needs, desires, and budget of the club. Oxygen should be available for emergencies at two or more locations.

Characteristics Desired

Characteristics and structural features to be considered when designing shelters for golf courses include (1) simple yet functional design, (2) safety from severe wind, lightning, rain, snow, and flooding, (3) durable, long-lasting construction materials, (4) minimal maintenance requirement, (5) visibility and accessibility to golfers, caddies, and maintenance staff, (6) minimal susceptibility to damage from vandals, (7) sufficient size and proper design to allow protection for golf carts as well as players, if desired and affordable by the club, and (8) compatibility with the golfing landscape. Well-conceived landscaping adds greatly to the attractiveness of the shelters (Fig. 12-4). Shelter construction costs depend on the (a) type of facility, (b) size, (c) construction materials utilized, and (d) cost of running electricity, water, and phone lines.

Figure 12-4. An attractive, well-landscaped shelter.

Site Selection

Each shelter should be clearly visible and accessible to golfers so it can be located readily when the need arises. All individuals on the golf course must seek safe shelter immediately when thunderstorms appear. Lightning is a serious threat to persons on a golf course. Thus, shelters should be located where the possibility of lightning strikes is minimal. Normally, a low area in a dense woods or group of trees is safest, but the low area must not be prone to flooding. Hilltops, elevated locations, open fields, lakes, wire fences, overhead lines, railroads, and similar structures that attract lightning should be avoided. Trees having a high moisture content, especially those with a single leader, such as hemlock, pine, poplar, spruce, tulip, oak, and maple, also are more likely to attract lightning, as are individual tall trees. Beech, birch, and horse chestnut have multiple trunks and are rarely struck by lightning. Information applicable to local conditions can be obtained by consulting local lightning protection companies and arborists.

The clubhouse, pro shop, halfway house, and maintenance facility can also serve as shelters during emergencies. Thus, the locations of these structures are of concern when selecting shelter sites across the golf course. The number of shelters per golf course can vary considerably depending on the arrangement of the golf holes. The normal range is from two to six per eighteen holes.

Architectural plans for any golf course should include the approximate location and orientation of shelters. Shelter construction is preferably accomplished while the golf course is being built and not after the architect and prime contractor leave. Construction is usually done by a subcontractor, although golf course superintendents with construction experience have successfully completed such projects.

Design and Construction

Shelters should be large enough to accommodate a minimum of two and preferably four foursomes (Fig. 12-5). Six square feet (0.56 square meter) per person is suggested. The main function of the shelter is golfer safety. More people can be accommodated in smaller shelters if they do not try to squeeze pull-type golf carts in as well. Most people walked when shelters were first used on golf courses, but this is not now the case. Where the golfing membership prefers to provide shelter for all equipment, elaborate shelters can be constructed with entrances that allow double-row parking and complete drive-through for golf carts. The shelter should be convenient and large enough to protect at least four foursomes and their equipment. At least 36 square feet (3.3 square meters) per golf cart is suggested.

From an economic standpoint, it is desirable that the same architectural design and construction materials be used in all shelters. Coordination of the structural theme with the clubhouse, pro shop, and maintenance building is also desirable from an aesthetic standpoint. The shape of the shelter may vary from rectangular to cylindrical. Shelters with corners more easily do damage to and are damaged by golf carts. In some cases, posts or similar barriers placed at the corners and entrances can be utilized to minimize this problem. Shelters can be designed so that protection from wind and unfavorable weather is provided on two sides no matter from which direction the wind originates.

Structural Types. Minimal maintenance is a major consideration in constructing shelters. Buildings vary from simple straw roofs and poles for support to secure shelters built with reinforced concrete floors, brick walls, steel beams, and 4- to 6-inch (10- to 15-centimeter) steel pipe in concrete to brace the overhang. Some have bare earthen floors, while others have a reinforced concrete, asphalt, brick, or wood floor. The roof may consist of shingles, tar paper, gravel and tar, reinforced prestressed concrete, plastic, plywood, or straw thatch. Although prestressed concrete is strong and relatively permanent, it is heavy and usually requires brick or masonry walls for support.

The types of construction materials selected depend on the projected function. Shelters that house restrooms and possibly even irrigation pumps should have walls constructed of brick, stone, or concrete, plus reinforced concrete floors at least 4 inches (10 centimeters) thick. The floors are usually

Figure 12-5. Types of shelters used on golf courses.

sloped outward or to a floor drain to facilitate cleaning by washing down with a hose. Rough brushed concrete requires no maintenance, is easy to clean, and is rough enough so golfers with spiked shoes are not prone to slipping. The inclusion of vents with screen covers provides needed ventilation.

Vandalism Protection. Potential vandalism problems must be kept in mind when designing shelters and rest stations, as these structures are prone to abuse. In some situations, one or more sides of the building can be left open so that the inner area is readily visible, thus discouraging misuse. This arrangement also enhances ventilation of the shelter.

In some areas, shelters need iron security bars, preferably of an ornamental type, placed over windows and vents to prevent entrance by vandals. Skylights can substitute for windows and are usually inaccessible. Light fixtures should be placed high enough that light bulbs cannot be reached easily and/or should have metal guards around them. Properly located skylights may eliminate the need for electricity in some types of shelters. Coin-operated machines on the outside of the shelter may need to have locked wrought-iron cages placed around them for night security. Finally, burglar alarms are being used more commonly in locations where vandalism is a continuing problem.

Lightning Protection for Shelters. Every shelter needs lightning protectors for the safety of golfers. The best protection is a standard lightning rod protection system. Details on installation of conductors, air terminals, and maintenance requirements can be found in the Lightning Protection Code, available from the National Fire Protection Association, 470 Atlantic Avenue, Boston, Massachusetts 02110, or from the American National Standards Institute, 1430 Broadway, New York, New York 10018.

An alternate method of lightning protection for shelters is known as a ''cone of protection'' and consists of grounded rods or masts and overhead conductors. It is described in Section 31 of the Lightning Protection Code. This system is feasible for small structures but can be more expensive than a standard lightning rod system.

Down conductors need to be shielded with nonconductive materials that are resistant to impact and climatic effects and which extend to a height at least 8 feet (2.4 meters) above the ground to prevent persons from coming into direct contact with the conductor. Shelters with earthen floors must be provided with a lightning protection system having approved grounding electrodes interconnected by an encircling buried, bare conductor suitable for such service or provided with radial conductors extending out at least 10 feet (3 meters) from the electrode and away from the building.

Maintenance

All shelters should be inspected for the presence of biting and stinging insects. These nuisance insect problems are kept under control by use of the appropriate insecticide(s). This may be a daily activity in some locations and at times of the year when insect populations are large.

Restrooms should be inspected and cleaned and needed supplies replenished daily when the golf course is open for play. Trash receptacles must be of adequate size and placed in prominent positions to encourage disposal of all trash and waste paper. Daily pickup of windblown or discarded paper waste is a necessity. Restrooms and snack bars may have to be locked nightly in locations where vandalism is a continuing problem.

Wooden structures require more repair and maintenance and are also more prone to vandalism than are brick, concrete, stone, or steel structures. Wood has to be painted or stained regularly, the specific frequency depending on local climatic conditions. Staining is usually preferable to painting. Concrete and brick veneer walls require minimum maintenance. Similarly, prestressed concrete, gravel, and asphalt shingle roofs have a low maintenance requirement.

First-aid kits should be inspected weekly for needed restocking. The minimum contents include a box of assorted bandaids, headache tablets, salt tablets, and a mild medicine or disinfectant for cuts, bruises, and insect bites/stings.

DRINKING WATER

Site Selection

The sites selected for drinking-water fountains should be visible to golfers and located where water needs will be greatest. The time required for a golfer to move from the No. 1 tee to the first drinking fountain is the initial consideration. Normally, fifty-five to sixty-five minutes are required to play through the fifth hole, approximately eleven to thirteen minutes per hole. The fifth hole is an appropriate site for a drinking fountain, since it is roughly the halfway point on the front nine, with the golfers returning to the clubhouse after four more holes. In approximately forty-four to fifty-two more minutes, golfers can obtain a drink at the clubhouse before proceeding to the No. 10 tee. The time interval and fountain placement for the back nine are similar to those for the front nine. It is also advantageous to position each drinking fountain where players from two or more holes can use it and where players will be least likely to be struck by errant golf balls.

Types

Four main types of drinking-water fountains are used on golf courses in North America (Fig. 12-6). Electric refrigerated fountains have become the most popular type in recent years, particularly in the warmer portions of the country. Most require a 110- to 120-volt power source for operation, although models are available that operate off low voltage irrigation control wires. Heaters may be needed to prevent freezing of the water during spring and fall in cooler climates. Gas-refrigerated water fountains are occasionally used but are less desirable than the electric types.

A second common drinking fountain is one that operates off pressurized water lines. These fountains do not require electrical power and thus the water is not refrigerated. In some cases, the water is cooled by running it through a copper coil system packed in ice. A 40-gallon (151-liter) tank placed 6 feet (1.8 meters) underground can also be used to keep the water near 55 °F (13 °C) in the cool climatic zone.

The third type of fountain is a portable keg. These portable units may need tending several times during the day. Ice can be added to cool the water. The main advantage of the portable keg is minimal installation cost, but the operating cost is rather high in terms of personnel to transport and maintain cold drinking water as needed by golfers.

Finally, there are the spring-fed and shallow well hand-pump types of drinking facilities. Courses having flowing springs with quality water possess an ideal, low-cost drinking water source.

Water Source

Water used for drinking fountains must be approved for human consumption by the appropriate local health authorities. Either the county or city health unit will assess the water quality and approve its use for drinking purposes. Municipal water is the most common source of drinking water on golf courses. A well is sometimes drilled if municipal water is not available. This can be a costly source, especially if a deep well must be drilled. Use of lake water is not advisable unless it has been passed through a filter and purification plant that meets local health standards for drinking water. Also, water for drinking purposes should not be obtained directly off the water distribution lines used for golf course irrigation because of the potential for back siphon contamination. The one exception is where locally approved antisiphon and/or vacuum breaker units are installed and the water quality is acceptable.

Installation

Refrigerated electric or gas water fountains require the installation of power lines as well as water lines. Installation cost of a drinking fountain can become extremely high if these lines must be run a great distance. Electric fountains must be protected from lightning by special resistors which protect against electrical surges created in the power line connecting the fountains.

Spring-fed hand pump

Portable jugs

Fountain with pressurized water line

Electric refrigerated fountain

Figure 12-6. Four main types of drinking-water fountains used on golf courses.

The water spout or basin of the fountain should be positioned approximately 40 inches (1 meter) above ground level. Provision for the removal of excess water from the drinking fountain vicinity is important to avoid wet, muddy conditions. All excess water collected in the water fountain basin should be drained through appropriate pipes to a drain field of a septic tank or similar specially constructed drainage bed located at least 20 feet (6 meters) away from the drinking fountain. In addition, the surface surrounding the water fountain should be contoured to insure rapid removal of excess water.

Maintenance

All water fountains must be inspected daily and any water leaks or drainage problems repaired immediately. The fountains should be cleaned regularly to maintain a high sanitary standard. Electrical line connections to the fountain are inspected each month to avoid worn, exposed wires that could result in electrical shocks. Metal fountains can be improved aesthetically by applying an imitation wood grain, brick contact covering, or wood veneering.

GOLF CART PATHS

The thought of asphalt surface paths forming a series of roads running the length and breadth of a golf course seemed ridiculous only a few years ago. Golf was envisioned as a sport that provided physical exercise and enjoyment from walking. Golf carts were only for players who were physically handicapped or of such advanced age that they could only enjoy golf by riding from tee to green.

Today, most golf courses have permanent paths or roads to accommodate powered golf carts (Fig. 12-7). The major change occurred during the 1960's. At this writing, the golf cart and its influence on the game, course design, and turfgrass culture are a reality. For example, the *Rules of Golf* now include a ruling allowing relief from roads constructed of man-made materials.

Why Golf Carts?

Changes in golf course design and golf philosophy have accentuated the use of golf carts. Changes in what players expect from the game and how it is played in North America have been prompted by many pressures. Among them are:

1. Medical considerations. Many golfers have to use a golf cart to play the game. The golf cart has extended the years a person can enjoy the game.
2. Decline of the caddie. Caddies were once an institution on golf courses and caddying provided juvenile employment. Now caddies are few in number.
3. Revenue. Many golf courses, whether private, semiprivate, or daily fee, have found a lucrative revenue source in golf carts. Also, having cart paths through wet areas can keep a course open for play when walking would be unpleasant and/or damaging to the course.
4. Convenience and comfort. Golf carts provide the convenience expected by today's leisure-oriented society.
5. Terrain. Hilly or long golf courses are less physically demanding to play with the use of golf carts.
6. Golf course design. The architect can allow more distance between a green and the next tee. This permits greater flexibility when designing a golf course on a particular piece of land.

Golf Cart Problems

The problems associated with golf carts vary depending on (a) the intensity of their use, (b) whether the course design accommodates golf carts, and (c) the specific soil texture, drainage, and turfgrass characteristics of the course. Disadvantages of regular golf cart usage include:

1. Distraction. Golf carts in motion during play can disturb a golfer's concentration. Also, gasoline-powered carts can be noisy and smokey.
2. Danger. Improperly operated golf carts can become involved in accidents that cause material damage, personal injury, liability, and sometimes even death.

Figure 12-7. Extensive path system for golf carts on a golf course.

3. Loss of golf course beauty. The signs, ropes, and/or paint sometimes needed for traffic control and/or permanent cart paths are an intrusion into the pastoral beauty classically associated with a golf course.
4. Less exercise. Walking a golf course is a mild exercise. The use of golf carts reduces this physical benefit.
5. Alteration of the game. Personal contact among golfers is lessened. Carts paths, bare soil from severe wear, and ruts caused by golf cart traffic can result in erratic ball bounces and unplayable lies. Also, the cart itself can cause golf rule problems, as can the associated paths.
6. Golf course damage. Above-ground damage to turf is readily evident and proportional to golf cart traffic intensity. Disruptions in surface smoothness that affect ball lie may also occur if golf carts are operated on excessively wet soil. Even more significant, long-term damage results from the hidden, below-ground effects of soil compaction.

Cultural practices can sometimes be adjusted sufficiently to minimize turfgrass wear and soil compaction problems where golf carts are used at light to moderate intensities and/or where course design minimizes concentration of golf cart traffic. This is accomplished by (a) selection of wear-tolerant turfgrasses, (b) regular turf cultivation by coring and slicing, (c) adjustments in fertility and irrigation practices to increase turfgrass wear tolerance yet maintain adequate recuperative potential, and (d) manipulation of golf cart traffic patterns to achieve a more uniform distribution over the golf course.

There is a point when the intensity of golf cart traffic in relation to golf course conditions results in a degree of soil compaction and turfgrass wear that can only be alleviated by the installation of cart paths. This situation has become common on many golf courses in North America.

When to Install Cart Paths

Scarred, bare areas may result from intense golf cart traffic regardless of the cultural practices employed (Fig. 12-8). Soil erosion becomes an increasing problem on these bare areas, with the eroded soil being deposited on adjacent turfed areas. In addition, some golfers and golf carts traveling in the vicinity tend to move along the turfed fringe rather than over the muddy soil. The result is an ever-enlarging area of bare soil.

The most common solution to this problem is installation of cart paths that confine the intense traffic and allow the surrounding area to be revegetated. If the choice is between cart paths and aesthetically displeasing bare areas, cart paths should be installed. This does not mean that cart paths are advocated. Rather, when all else fails, cart paths are the only realistic solution to bare, eroded areas.

Cart Path Placement

The extensiveness of a cart path system varies from limited paths around tees and greens of selected holes to a system that traverses the entire length of the golf course. The system chosen depends on the (a) basic golf course design relative to the traffic intensity, (b) intensity of play, (c) funds available for cart path installation and maintenance, (d) availability of caddies, and (e) philosophy of club members toward golf carts.

The cart path system should be placed correctly. Otherwise, new traffic problems can be introduced that are just as undesirable as the original problem. One approach is for the cart path system to be installed when the golf course is constructed. In this case, the system is included as part of the design plans drawn by the golf course architect. The second approach is installation of a cart path system after the golf course has become operational and definite golf cart wear areas have developed. A placement and design system is then used that will minimize the chance of new wear areas developing. The second approach is commonly used. The primary advantage is more assurance that golfers will use the paths than if the architect tries to project in advance where golf cart traffic concentrations will occur. A disadvantage is that golfers may develop bad habits regarding where they drive golf carts, and these will be difficult to correct at a later date.

A third approach where funds are limited is development of a cart path master plan for the entire course. Segments are then installed as funds become available over a period of years. Cart path

Figure 12-8. Barren, muddy area caused by unavoidable concentration of golf cart traffic.

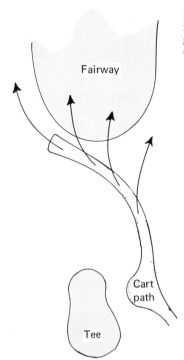

Figure 12-9. A cart path exit of flared design, which reduces turf-grass wear by distributing golf cart exit points over a wider area.

Fairway

Cart path

Tee

segments are first installed in areas where turf wear is most severe. With this piecemeal procedure a comprehensive cart path system is eventually completed.

Every effort should be made to insure that the cart path system fulfills the originally intended functions, since it is a very expensive golf course accessory. A decision as to cart path placement should involve the studious, logical reasoning of where traffic concentrations will realistically occur over a given golf course layout. Major considerations include the (a) site topography, (b) location and type of nonturf vegetation, and (c) playing strategy for each hole. Cart paths should be placed where they are least visible and least likely to come into play.

Cart paths are most commonly used in routing traffic from a green to the next tee. A mistake frequently made with relatively short paths is to extend the path from the tee straight outward toward the fairway, where it ends abruptly. Traffic concentrated immediately off the end of the path produces a bare, scarred area which must be constantly resodded or the cart path periodically lengthened. This situation can be avoided by (1) having the path swing in an arc at its terminus, which encourages golf carts to exit at random locations along the arc depending on where the golfer's ball has been hit, (2) using a flared cart path terminus along with portable barriers which guide traffic off at selected points along the path (Fig. 12-9), or (3) using a combination of the previous two.

Other traffic control techniques can also be employed in cart path installation, for example, the installation of a low curb between the path and adjacent tee bank. In the case of a narrow collar between a green and bunker, traffic can be directed away by positioning the cart path outside a protective mound or bunker extension. Cart path placement from tee to green of each hole is a compromise. The best approach has been to locate the cart path in the rough within 20 to 30 feet (6 to 9 meters) of the fairway perimeter. The path should not be placed on the immediate edge of the fairway or between the fairway and a bunker. Sometimes one path can serve two holes in the case of parallel fairways.

Cart Path Design

Narrow cart paths have often been designed in an effort to make them less obvious, to lessen their effect on play, and to reduce costs. Design of too narrow a path results in wearing of the edges, which eventually break down and become muddy/dusty bare areas. Most modern cart paths have a width of 6 to 9 feet (1.8 to 2.7 meters). The 8- to 9-foot width is preferred for three main reasons: it is easier for golf carts to stay on a path of this width, this width allows operation of golf course maintenance equipment on the same path, and mechanical asphalt-laying machines are available in 8-foot (2.4-meter) widths. Excavation and installation costs may be less for an 8-foot path than for a narrower one, which must be hand installed. Widths of more than 8 feet should be planned for sharp turns and intense two-way traffic areas, such as around the clubhouse, golf shop, first tee, and tenth tee. It is also advisable that parking areas be provided in locations where more than two golf carts may congregate at a time.

Cart path design should insure safety for riders, especially on hilly terrain. Potential problems can be minimized by avoiding (a) sharp turns, (b) steep slopes on paths oriented toward water or steep drop-offs, (c) excessively steep uphill slopes, which are difficult to climb, and (d) downhill inclines that lead to dangerous cart velocities. Guard rails, walls, or curbs should be installed on paths adjacent to bodies of water or steep drop-offs. Turns should be wide, sweeping, and adequately banked for safe passage, especially on downhill paths.

The surface contour of cart paths will vary with the situation. The main concern is allowing surface water to flow freely over or off the cart path. A crown-shaped surface with the center 3 to 4 percent higher than the edges is typical on level terrain to provide surface drainage. In contrast, the cart path surface is sloped to one side or the other on hilly terrain. In a few cases, it is shaped as a swale, which acts as a channel for the removal of excess surface water. Another option is installation of curbing to guide the water to an appropriate drainage outlet.

Cart Path Materials

A wide range of cart path surfacing materials are available. Criteria to be considered in the selection of a material include (a) cost, (b) availability, (c) wear tolerance, (d) course topography, (e) effects on play, (f) aesthetics, and (g) long-term maintenance requirements.

Material costs vary greatly, with the hard-permanent surfaces ranking high compared with the soft, loose, organic types. Availability is of most concern with organic types, since a local supply exists only in certain portions of the country and hauling expenses can negate any cost advantage. The surface material selected must be tolerant of intense traffic from golf carts and spiked shoes. Course topography frequently dictates which material(s) can be used. Loose, light-weight surfacing materials are prone to wash onto adjacent turfs in hilly terrain where high-velocity water movement occurs. The influence of the surface material on play is a consideration where the path is in close proximity to the playing area. A soft, resilient material minimizes erratic ball bounces.

Finally, long-term maintenance costs of the surface should be evaluated. Although a loose-type material might have a low initial cost, considerable expense may result over the long term in the hand raking and shoveling required at three- to five-week intervals to collect and redistribute material washed from the path. Thus, nonwashing, permanent-type cart path materials are definitely preferred on inclines where high-velocity water movement is likely.

The availability of materials and topography are the most significant factors affecting the decision as to which surfacing material to use.

Subbase. A wide range of materials function acceptably for cart path surfaces if properly installed, including soft, loose materials, if used on level terrain. A qualification for proper installation usually includes a 4-inch (10-centimeter)-deep subbase of crushed rock or stone under the path. This subbase provides needed drainage and stability to the surface material. Use of a crushed stone subbase is especially important where an organic surfacing material is used.

Hard-Permanent Surfacing. Included in this category are asphalt, concrete, stone, and crushed rock by-products. These materials are stable and relatively permanent once installed.

Asphalt is the most widely used surfacing material for cart paths on golf courses. It is relatively quick and easy to install, especially if a paving machine is used. Characteristics include relatively good stability and permanence, but also high initial installation cost.

Concrete is stable, permanent, and maintenance-free. It is utilized under the same conditions as asphalt. Which material is selected frequently depends on availability and comparative costs. Reinforced concrete has performed better than asphalt on clay soil sites prone to frequent shrinking and swelling.

Quarry screenings, gravel, stone, or crushed rock by-product materials tend to be somewhat cheaper than asphalt or concrete. Thus, a common procedure when finances are limited is initial installation of the crushed stone-type materials. Continuous cart operation tends to settle and stabilize this material so that it can serve as the subbase for an asphalt or concrete covering at some future date. In the interim, this material offers an economic alternative and is not as prone to washing as are loose, organic materials. It is important that an aggregate size range, which readily compacts to a stabilized bed, be obtained. If not, there is a tendency for loose stones to be thrown out into the turf, where they can be hit by a mower. This may result in costly damage to the cutting edge and is also a potential human safety problem, should stones be thrown out from a rotary mower.

Organic Surfacing. Included in the organic materials group are wood chips, tan bark, pine needles, licorice root, nut hulls, rubber chips, and sawdust. These materials perform quite well on level areas not prone to erosion. The organics are relatively low in cost compared with the permanent types, assuming a local supply is available. They are also softer and thus better absorb the impact of a ball striking the surface. For this reason, organic materials frequently are used on cart paths in areas which repeatedly come into play. Most organics require periodic reapplication to replace losses from erosion, weathering, and decomposition. It is important that relatively undecomposed organic materials be avoided because they decompose very rapidly, resulting in an undesirable soft and odorous mess.

New Developments. A recent innovation not yet fully tested under golf course conditions are honeycomb or matrix structures. They are composed of wear-resistant material ranging from concrete to plastic and are structurally designed to carry the weight of repeated golf cart, vehicle, and foot traffic. A material with regularly spaced openings or cells in various geometric configurations, if properly installed over a well-drained subbase and coarse-textured root zone, allows adequate water infiltration downward into the soil and the growth of turfgrasses in the spaces (Fig. 12-10). This interspersed vegetation provides cooling of the surface and also blends into the adjacent turfed landscape. The full potential for this type of cart path is yet to be determined.

Cart Path Construction

Detailed specifications concerning cart path construction should be drawn up and a contract signed with the contractor making the successful bid. The following discussion encompasses some important considerations in cart path construction. Construction details vary depending on the type of surface selected.

The first step in construction is staking out the cart path in accordance with the architect's plan. Next, any existing sod is cut out. The better turf is retained for resodding the edges of the path after construction has been completed. The soil should then be removed to a sufficient depth so that the ultimate cart path surface is level with the surrounding topography. Excessively high cart paths create problems in operating mowing equipment, while surfaces lower than the surrounding area are prone to water accumulation. The depth of soil removal is usually from 5 to 7 inches (12 to 17 centimeters).

Next, the 3- to 4-inch (7.6- to 10-centimeter)-deep stone subbase is put down. An angular crushed stone of 0.5 to 1 inch (1.3 to 2.5 centimeters) in size provides the proper subsurface drainage and stability. Special care should be taken during filling to prevent a cave-in of the sides. This is a severe

Figure 12-10. A concrete matrix being installed (*top*), which will support cart traffic while turfgrass grows in the open cells (*bottom*). (Photos courtesy of Don Parsons, Knollwood Men's Club, Granada Hills, Calif.)

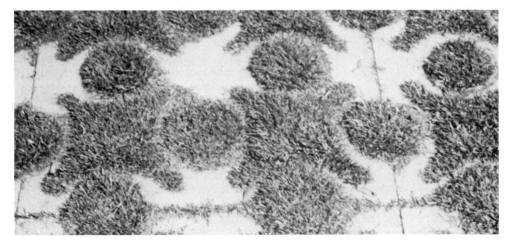

problem on more sandy soils. The best procedure to prevent side-wall caving problems is to install edge barriers, such as pliable plywood, during construction. The edging barrier provides cleaner lines and a neater appearance. It also reduces costly hand shoveling required to reestablish the sides after soil cave-ins have occurred. After the crushed stone has been put down, it should be firmly compacted with use of a heavy roller. An alternative to a stone subbase that has been effective in some locations is a 4-inch (10-centimeter)-deep asphalt layer, without a base, laid on undisturbed, well-drained soil or on existing rocky subbase materials.

The final step in cart path construction is installation of the surfacing material. A 3- to 4-inch (7.6- to 10-centimeter) layer is commonly recommended, especially for the asphalt and organic materials. Installation specifications for the surfacing material selected should follow those typically used for highway construction. The surface material is compressed immediately after application. For asphalt, this is achieved with a surface roller which applies between 200 and 400 pounds of pressure per square inch (1,380 to 2,760 kPa). The surface roller is operated at a relatively slow speed, not exceeding 150 feet (45 meters) per minute.

After cart path construction is completed, the adjacent soil should be recontoured to bring the surface grade in line with the cart path surface so that mowing can be accomplished easily with multiple gang units. Abrupt high spots lead to scalping and objectionable bare areas. The turfed edge is best reestablished by sodding, using the sod collected during the initial stripping of the cart path site. There is also the option of seeding, but sodding is preferred because the area can be opened sooner for golf cart use.

Sometimes painting of permanent traffic control lines is advisable in areas where several golf carts will be operated at a time, for example, parking areas and locations of intense golf cart traffic such as around the golf shop, practice putting green, and first tee.

Who Does the Construction? The decision as to who will install the cart path depends on the (a) cost, (b) size of the project, (c) time of year when the work must and can be accomplished, and (d) relative capabilities of the maintenance staff versus a local contractor to accomplish the project at minimal cost. Reliable contractors with the capability of installing cart paths are usually available. In some cases, the golf course superintendent and the green staff may have comparable capabilities. The arrangement selected depends on the resources and expertise available.

A major cart path installation encompassing an entire eighteen-hole golf course is most commonly assigned to an outside contractor. The contract may specify that all work is to be done by the contractor or that a portion of it is to be done by the golf course maintenance staff. The latter situation typically involves clean-up and resodding or seeding of bare areas adjacent to the cart path.

Limited cart path construction around selected greens and tees may be accomplished by the golf course maintenance staff. In this case, the needed rental equipment must be available and the work must be accomplished during a time of the year when critical turfgrass maintenance activities are less demanding. It is also important that additional monies be allocated, so this add-on project can be accomplished without sacrifice of normal maintenance operations.

Encouraging Cart Path Use

A golf operation that has chosen to invest considerable money in a cart path system must take steps to insure its use. The most important step in encouraging cart path use is proper placement, as discussed earlier. However, on most courses, cart paths must be routed in some places in patterns that are less convenient or different from traffic patterns followed in the past. Additional traffic aids must be employed in these situations to encourage cart path use. Such aids may include signs, chains, ropes, lines, landscape plantings, or mounds. These aids must be properly positioned to direct cart traffic onto the paths. Once a new traffic pattern is established, it is hoped that golfers will adopt it so that the aids can be removed eventually.

Sometimes more drastic measures may be necessary to direct traffic onto the appropriate cart paths, such as installation of new bunkers, grassy mounds, trees, and/or shrub plantings. Measures may also be needed to insure that golf carts remain on the path at key locations. This can be achieved through appropriate placement of curbings, ropes, and railings (Fig. 12-11).

Rules and restrictions for golf cart use in relation to the cart paths may have to be established. For this approach to be effective, a serious membership education program should be presented regarding the rules of proper golf cart use. Some club rules require that golf cart operators stay on the path or lose their cart privileges for a period of time.

Golf cart use is restricted to the paths on some golf courses having a complete path system, with no deviations from this rule being allowed. Where a path system exists only on certain portions of a course, golf cart use may be restricted to the paths on those holes having them and be allowed at random over the turf on the other holes, except for normal restrictions around tees and greens.

Less strict regulations limit golf carts to paths only during wet soil conditions in an effort to minimize soil compaction problems. Similarly, cart paths may be installed from tee to green only on holes that have continually wet soils, with golf cart traffic restricted to the paths on these holes to minimize soil rutting and compaction.

Figure 12-11. The use of curbing (*top*) and railings (*bottom*) along cart paths to guide golf cart traffic.

In summary, there are no absolute guidelines concerning golf cart use on a cart path system. The rules and regulations a course adopts will depend on the (a) extent of the cart path system, (b) topography, (c) soil drainage conditions, and (d) wishes of the golfing clientele.

BRIDGES

Flowing rivers, deep ditches, and arroyos are fairly common features in the golf course landscape and may dictate installation of bridges to facilitate movement of golfers, golf carts, and associated maintenance equipment. The Swilcan Burn bridge is a well-known historical feature of the eighteenth hole at the St. Andrews course in Scotland. The siting of bridges should be part of the golf course architect's original master plan. Bridge placement on a given golf hole is determined by the anticipated route of golfer traffic, the desire not to interfere with play, the need to avoid excessive concentration of traffic, and aesthetic value. Golf cart paths frequently are associated with the entrance and exit to a bridge, except for those designed strictly for pedestrian traffic.

Characteristics and structural features to be considered when designing bridges for golf courses include (1) adequate width and structural strength for the anticipated traffic, (2) proper safety features, including side handrails, (3) adequate height so that water flow is not impeded at full flood stage, (4) building of end abutments into the banks to avoid redirection of flow that causes erosion problems, (5) use of durable, long-lasting construction materials, (6) minimum maintenance requirement, and (7) simple yet functional design compatible with the surrounding golf course landscape. Both the width and structural weight-load capacity selected will depend on whether the bridge is to be used only as a walkway, for both pedestrian and golf cart traffic, or as a multipurpose structure for all types of golf course vehicles, including those used for turfgrass maintenance. In some cases, the bridge must be wide enough to accommodate the large seven- to nine-gang hydraulic mowers, tractors, and trucks utilized on the course. The design specifications for load capacity should be based on sound engineering principles. In the case of walking bridges with wooden flooring, placement of a rubberized mat or asphaltic material over the surface will provide walking comfort and prevent wood deterioration from the action of golf shoe spikes.

It is desirable for the same architectural design and construction materials to be used for all bridges. Furthermore, it is aesthetically desirable for the bridge design to be coordinated with the theme of other buildings and structures on the course. Bridges should be designed and constructed of materials that are the least prone to damage from vandalism. Structural materials may range from wood to structural steel to concrete and attractive stone (Fig. 12-12).

SECURITY FENCES

The increase in vandalism and burglaries on golf courses is causing much concern about how to prevent these destructive acts. The cost of vandalism at some clubs is substantial. Records indicate that thefts of flagsticks, ball washers, tee markers, and benches alone can represent a replacement cost of from $2,500 to $4,000 per year. Restrooms, rain shelters, or halfway houses may need repair or replacement. The ever-rising cost for repairs may justify installation of a security fence around the perimeter of the club's property as well as expenditures for security patrols and alarm systems in key buildings throughout the property. Vandalism on golf courses also involves turf damage, especially on greens, from deliberate operation of motor vehicles over the area.

Golf courses that have constructed security fences around the perimeter have found the investment worthwhile. Their harshness can be moderated through proper landscaping and/or painting them dark brown (Fig. 12-13). A security fence, however, is only a deterrent. It will not prevent the determined vandal or burglar from encroaching, but it will stop most casual walk-on traffic, which may also be a significant problem. A security fence can also relieve the club of some liability if lawsuits should develop. A number of guidelines must be considered in the installation of a security fence.

1. Check the building code for the area. Is there a limit or minimum fence height? How close can the fence be placed to the property line or intersections where motorists' vision may be obstructed as a result of a fence? Is there an easement from a pipeline, highway, or railway?
2. If possible, consider a tension-type fence as opposed to a support railing on top of the fence. A tension-type fence is more difficult to climb.
3. Use H-shaped posts to support the fence. These posts are extremely strong and have long life spans, since they do not have inside surfaces that will corrode.
4. Consider setting the fence post in concrete. Tri-set bases may be needed in very soft, low-lying areas.
5. Plan a fence of 6 to 9 feet (1.8 to 2.7 meters) in height.
6. Use barbed wire on top of the fence, if codes permit.
7. Survey the property to be sure the fence is placed on golf course property.
8. Have the maintenance staff prepare the right-of-way area for the fence line. A substantial cost can be saved for the golf course by having the maintenance staff clear the fence line.
9. Arrange for an outside contractor professionally equipped to install the fence.

Figure 12-12. Three types of bridge construction for pedestrian and golf cart traffic: wooden (*top*), precast concrete (*center*), and steel (*bottom*).

Figure 12-13. A perimeter security fence.

PONDS AND LAKES

Ponds and lakes may function in diverse roles on a golf course, such as (a) in the playing strategy of a golf hole, (b) as the primary water source for irrigation, or (c) as a reservoir for water being pumped from a well or municipal supply in situations where the water delivery rate does not meet the water demand rate of the irrigation system. During the early planning of a dam construction project, it is important to determine whether the prospective site falls under the jurisdiction of a governmental authority such as in a state dam act or the federal Wetlands Law. If such laws apply, appropriate steps must be taken to insure compliance, including securing of any required permits.

Site Selection

The first step in planning a golf course pond or modest-sized lake is site selection. The preferred site is a small valley or disc-shaped depressional area which has a natural capability to hold water once the appropriate earthen dam structure is constructed. On essentially flat terrain, the site must be excavated. The soil taken out can be utilized as subbase material for greens, tees, bunkers, and extended grassy mounds, which add topographic variability to the course.

After the prospective sites have been identified, the extent of the water source must be characterized. Where the impoundment site is developed primarily through excavation with minimal surface runoff water entering the pond, the availability of an adequate artificial water source must be established. Such a water source typically involves a well and pump arrangement, or it may involve pumping or diverting water from a nearby stream. If the latter, the quantity of water available from the stream through the season must exceed the anticipated rate of water loss from the pond by evaporation and downward seepage through the soil.

Where the potential site is a natural valley, the size of the watershed draining through the site must be determined. This is best done by walking the outer perimeter of the watershed and drawing it on an aerial photograph. The acreage of the watershed can then be estimated by appropriate measurements made directly from an aerial photograph. The runoff characteristics of the watershed can be evaluated at the same time. This assessment includes the slope of the terrain, soil infiltration rate, and vegetative cover. The resulting runoff coefficient can be combined with the watershed data to establish the peak amount of runoff water passing through the site based on a 20-, 50-, or 100-year storm intensity. In many parts of the country, the main problem is an excessively large watershed for the proposed site rather than one of inadequate size. Very large watersheds necessitate installation of costly outlet structures on the dam site. For this reason, the site selected should be such that surface drainage is limited to the immediate surrounding area. Also, ponds constructed on sites draining a relatively large watershed have the added problem of silting. This problem is most severe if a significant portion of the watershed is outside the actual golf course property and the soil is not properly stabilized with a grass cover.

Another vital dimension in site selection is assessment of the soil profile by means of test borings. A clay subsoil is desired for the pond site. Topsoil underlaid with rock, gravel, or sand lenses may dictate an alternate pond site. Ponds can be constructed on some types of coarse-textured soils but involve increased costs for a bottom seal or liner to impede the anticipated downward water seepage. The lake should be oriented relative to the direction of the prevailing winds, whenever feasible. Orientation of the lengthwise dimension of a pond perpendicular to the direction of strong prevailing winds minimizes wave action that can cause deterioration in the shoreline. A qualified specialist from the Soil Conservation Service can offer assistance in site selection, including watershed assessment and soil profile characterization.

Design

The actual design of the dam as well as of the associated emergency spillway and mechanical spillway must be done by a qualified engineer. Proper design of the dam is critical in avoiding a costly washout. Most golf course ponds have an earthen dam and a grassed emergency spillway, plus a mechanical spillway in certain situations (Fig. 12-14). The actual sizes of the dam, emergency vegetative spillway, and mechanical spillway, if required, will be dictated by the size of impoundment and the anticipated maximum runoff volume from the watershed. The watershed assessment procedure is discussed in the next section of this chapter, on waterways and ditches. If the pond is to be designed for fishing, a minimum depth of 10 feet (3 meters) should be planned to insure sufficiently cool water temperatures in the summer, to avoid extensive ice formation in the winter, and to minimize excessive encroachment of water weeds which are favored by shallow water depths.

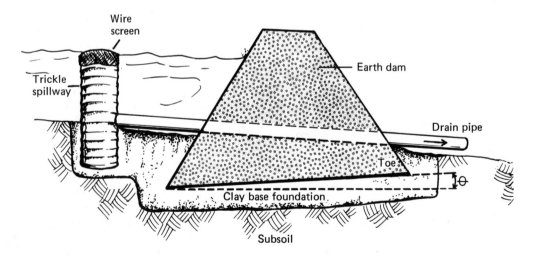

Figure 12-14. A cross-sectional perspective showing a dam, core base foundation, and mechanical (trickle) spillway.

The dam itself can fail due to (a) overturning, (b) settlement at the toe, termed crushing, or (c) sliding horizontally on its base. Overturning of a dam is caused primarily by failure to design and construct the proper cross section for the dam, including the height and width. Crushing, or settlement at the toe, occurs because the toe pressure of the dam is more than the bearing capacity of the underlying soil. Thus, it is essential that soil profile borings and load tests be conducted at the dam site for proper evaluation of the soil bearing capacity. Horizontal sliding typically is due to improper subbase preparation prior to dam construction. The preferred foundation base is a clay soil. Thus, the topsoil is usually removed down to the clay subsoil, if present, or a deep clay base foundation is constructed. Such deep excavation not only provides a slide-resistant factor but also prevents underwashing of the footing. In addition, the foundation bed can be designed with the lower end oriented toward the impoundment so that any tendency to slide will be met with increased resistance owing to the uphill action required. Finally, excavation of a rough bottom on the foundation base will provide increased friction and therefore greater resistance to horizontal slide.

In addition to the earthen dam itself, it is essential that a vegetatively stabilized emergency spillway of adequate size be constructed. The emergency spillway provides a means for release of excess water during intense rains that could otherwise result in a dam washout or whose release could only be avoided by construction of an excessively large, expensive dam including a mechanical spillway. The height of the emergency spillway above the mechanical spillway relative to the freeboard (the height from the base of the vegetative emergency spillway to the top of the dam) must be accurately established with use of sound engineering principles.

The size and form of the lake or pond may be functional in nature but should also be aesthetically pleasing. The shape, size, and placement of the pond should be carefully studied so that the pond blends with and compliments the surrounding landscape including trees, shrubs, stone, and grass. The pond may also be designed to feature moving water and biological life, such as birds and fish. Rather than a single pond, the design may involve a series of pools through a small valley with water flowing from one pool to the next lower pool. In more elaborate designs, a continuous flow of water from one pond to another down through a series of connecting streams is maintained by use of a recycling pump arrangement. An attractive feature in such a system is a waterfall, which also functions in aerating the water and minimizing stagnation. Potential problems may develop where a large amount of surface water enters the upper end of the pond during the rainy season, owing to a high content of silt and contaminants. In this case, a design may be found that lets this excess surface water flow around the pond. The siltation problem can be partially alleviated by construction of a catch or silt-settling basin just above the pond inlet. The basin can be dredged out periodically to remove the settled silt and soil-absorbed nutrients.

Construction

The first step is surveying and staking of the perimeter of the water impoundment area and the dam site. The site is then cleared of tree and shrub vegetation. Topsoil must also be removed, especially on small pond construction sites where clay subsoil is needed for the earthen dam. The dam subbase or foundation is prepared to the specified depth, width, and length by excavation. Filling of the earthen dam is initiated at this point. Soil of a specified texture is excavated and hauled to the dam site, where it is moved into place. It is critical during all phases of dam construction that the soil be properly compacted by earth-moving machinery. The earthen dam is built up to the width, height, and length specified by the design engineer. Coordinated with the dam construction is the installation of any drop or mechanical spillway specified in the contract.

The pond floor above the earthen dam requires no further preparation if it is composed of a fine-textured soil, such as clay. However, steps must be taken to prevent water loss by downward seepage on sites where the pond floor is sandy or gravelly. The particular approach used in sealing a pond will be determined by the soil conditions on the site, the degree of seepage control required, the use to be made of the pond, and any potential limitations in terms of the total area, depth, and side

Figure 12-15. Bentonite being placed on the floor of a pond (*top*) and a view after incorporation into the surface soil layer (*bottom*).

slopes of the lake. Three types of linings should be considered when attempting to prevent a soil seepage problem: (a) soil linings, (b) flexible membrane linings, and (c) rigid linings.

The soil-lining approach involves hauling a relatively impermeable clay soil from a local deposit to the site and layering it across the floor of the pond. A fine-textured, dense soil possessing a very high clay content is preferred for this purpose. Successful use of this technique depends on a local supply of clay soil and the distance the material must be hauled to the pond site. The depth of clay required to line a pond site effectively depends on the quality of the clay soil utilized. Finally, successful use of the technique depends on proper compaction of the clayey soil layer.

Bentonite is another form of soil lining and is purchased commercially for this purpose. It is distributed over the pond floor at the specified rate and incorporated into the surface soil layer (Fig. 12-15), with subsequent addition of water to initiate the sealing process. Successful use of bentonite is dependent on the soil type on the pond floor, the rate of bentonite application, and the particular type of bentonite used. This method of soil lining is not very successful where the pond floor is composed of permeable gravelly soils or where the water has a high calcium content.

Four major types of flexible membrane linings are available for use on ponds and lakes: polyethylene, polyvinyl chloride, butyl rubber, and asphalt. This type of lining is preferred for sealing pond floors composed of coarse-textured sand and gravel. The asphalt and butyl rubber membranes are used much less frequently than the two others because of much higher cost and difficulties in installation.

The polyvinyl chloride (PVC) lining is more resistant to puncture during installation and is less costly to install than is polyethylene (PE), but the PE lining has much better longevity once in place. The PE lining is preferred due to better long-term performance, if properly installed. Placement of a crushed stone or gravel layer over the lining is suggested. This functions in (a) protection against puncture, (b) holding the lining in position, and (c) reducing the potential rooting areas of certain aquatic weeds.

The rigid linings are various types of concrete and asphalt. Their use has decreased following development of the PE and PVC linings. They are very high in cost and are also subject to cracking and deterioration from weathering, which eventually result in increased seepage.

The slope of the floor around the pool edges should be relatively steep so that growth of water weeds is minimized. A side slope of 10 to 1 is suggested for at least 1 to 2 feet (0.3 to 0.6 meter) below the water surface to minimize wave destruction of the shoreline. The remainder of the pond floor should have a 4 to 1 or 5 to 1 slope.

The edge of the shore may be a retaining wall of logs or may consist of concrete riprap, coarse gravel, crushed stone, gabion diking, or large rocks. This type of construction allows the turfed area to extend to the shoreline and facilitates ready maintenance and trimming of the grassed edge. A shoreline with a retaining wall constructed of logs, large rocks, or similar material permits a greater pond depth to the edge and thus prevents waterlogging of the adjacent turf area. This facilitates mowing throughout the season. In addition, the construction of a retaining wall or the use of crushed rock or concrete-stone riprapping around the shoreline aids in controlling bank erosion by wave action.

The shoreline can be constructed to serve as a natural buffer zone to organic materials, grass clippings, silt, and inorganic nutrients that might otherwise enter the pond and adversely affect water quality. Materials such as stone, crushed rock, and concrete rock act as a natural filter. Either crushed stone or concrete-stone riprapping should be used where substantial fluctuations in the water level are anticipated. This form of shoreline construction prevents bank erosion during high water levels and development of extensive mud flats during the low water levels.

The final step in pond construction involves stabilization of the earthen dam and shoreline area surrounding the impoundment. This must be done quickly and successfully throughout the area to avoid the erosive action of water. Grass establishment is achieved by procedures similar to those described in the rough construction section of chapter 6. The permanent grasses selected for planting are basically the same as those utilized on roughs; they should be adapted to semiwet conditions and of a deep-rooted, sod-forming type. In addition, an increment of perennial ryegrass or cereal rye may be needed to insure quick stabilization during the establishment phase of the permanent sod grasses. This is particularly important when dam construction is completed at a time of the year unfavorable for grass establishment and/or when the potential for soil erosion from intense rains is high. Use of a mulch, such as straw, for soil stabilization and a favorable microclimate during grass establishment are particularly critical in soil stabilization of the pond area, as is the use of the appropriate seedbed fertilization procedure. In some situations, selective or strip sodding may be needed to insure soil stabilization.

Maintenance

The grassed area on the dam and surrounding the pond should be fertilized as needed to maintain a grass stand sufficient to stabilize the area against soil erosion. Irrigation is sometimes also required to fully achieve this objective.

The two primary problems with the pond or lake proper are algae and aquatic weeds. Algae problems are reduced by good water circulation and/or by periodic water replacement if the pond is used as a storage reservoir for irrigation. Algae problems are especially severe during warm summer months when the water temperature rises. Lakes with a depth of 10 feet (3 meters) or more have a more limited

Figure 12-16. A fountain-pump system being used for oxygenation of pond water.

algae problem. Mechanical aeration of the water can contribute significantly to control of algae, especially in shallow ponds. The use of a fountain-pump arrangement is typical (Fig. 12-16). Cooled water is drawn from the lower pond depths and pressurized so that it can be sprayed into the air, where it is oxygenated and in turn falls to the water surface where a mixing action results. The net effects are oxygenation of the water and minimizing of the stratification of warm water near the surface so that conditions are less favorable for algae growth.

A range of water weeds may occur depending on the region of the country. Cattails and water brush grow predominantly around the edges of the pond or lake. These can be controlled by mowing; by manual removal, if done frequently at first appearance; or by deepening of the pond. A severe algae problem and certain water weeds can be controlled by chemical means. The main considerations in selecting the appropriate chemical are (a) whether the fish population is to be preserved in the pond, (b) the specific aquatic weed species, and (c) whether the water is to be used for irrigation of turf and ornamental areas. Conference with local authorities concerning aquatic weed control recommendations is advisable, since local conditions and regulations can vary.

WATERWAYS, DITCHES, AND STREAMS

Surface drainage ways can play an important role in the design and playing strategy of individual golf holes. Even more important, they are essential on many golf courses to insure rapid, effective removal of excess surface water. To minimize erosion problems, it is important that the routing, design specifications, and construction of waterways, ditches, and streams be based on sound engineering principles. A district Soil Conservation Service specialist or a qualified drainage engineer should be consulted, even for relatively small projects.

Design

The routing of a waterway, ditch, or stream should be planned with gentle bends and with a grade that does not allow water velocity to exceed the maximum allowable to avoid scouring and eroding of the channel (Fig. 12-17). The maximum allowable velocity for grassed waterways is 4 feet (1.2 meters) per second, while in ditch channels covered with riprap material such as stone it is usually 8 feet (2.4 meters) per second. Maximum safe water flow velocities can be achieved with ditch bottoms having a grade not exceeding 2 percent. This varies somewhat depending on the type of soil in the ditch bottom and whether it is stabilized with a grass cover or some sort of riprap or concrete arrangement. Where the routing and grade of a ditch channel result in water velocities exceeding the desired maximum, installation of drop spillways or check dams is generally advisable at appropriate intervals. These dams can be constructed of concrete, stone, logs, or similar materials.

The primary criteria affecting the design specifications of surface drainage channels are the maximum allowable flow velocity and the erosion probability. The former affects both cross-sectional shape and size, while the latter affects the grade. Peak rates of storm water runoff are estimated based on (a) the watershed size, (b) the projected rainfall intensity (in inches per hour) for the specific area based on a 20-, 50-, or 100-year storm record, and (c) a runoff coefficient which is expressed as a ratio of runoff to rainfall. The watershed is best estimated by actually walking the area and mapping it on an aerial photograph and then estimating the acreage as mapped. A 50-year storm frequency is commonly used as a base for stream and ditch runoff specifications. Finally, the runoff coefficient can vary considerably depending on the type of surface represented in the watershed. Coefficients range from 0.2 for wooded land to 0.35 for parks, golf courses, and lawns to 0.45 for suburban residential areas to 0.6 for dense urban residential areas to 0.75 for barren land to 0.95 for roofs, concrete, and asphalt. The area of the cross-sectional profile is established based on the runoff volume calculated for a given location.

The next step is selection of the cross section of the waterway, ditch, or stream. The three most common shapes of these are (a) a grassed waterway or swale with a parabolic cross section, used where water flow occurs only during rainstorms, (b) a ditch possessing a flat base and sloping sides, and (c) a stream with straight vertical sides permanently stabilized with a nonerosive material.

Figure 12-17. A serious erosion problem along a stream bank.

Figure 12-18. A properly designed, constructed, and maintained drainage ditch.

Figure 12-19. An attractive stone wall being used in stream bank stabilization.

Waterway. This type of surface drainage way is designed for short-term water flow immediately after rainstorms. The relatively broad, flat parabolic design distributes the water over a large surface area. Waterways are typically covered with a grass surface and maintained like a primary or secondary rough. The depth of such waterways is normally 10 to 24 inches (25 to 60 centimeters).

Ditch. Drainage ditches are designed to accommodate large water volumes and continuous flow situations (Fig. 12-18). The minimum depth is usually 4 feet (1.2 meters). An even greater depth is preferred where subsurface drain lines empty into the ditch. The ditch bottom should be flat with a minimum width of 4 feet. The slope of the sides should preferably be 2 to 1 or, if mowed, not less than 3.5 to 1.

Stream. Permanent stream bank stabilization is frequently practiced on golf courses to minimize potential erosion problems. Characteristics desired in vertical walls of streams include good stability, minimum long-term degradation, provisions for lateral seepage of water from the adjacent area into the stream, and reasonable cost (Fig. 12-19). Walls constructed of concrete or a combination of mortar and natural stone, concrete blocks, or bricks are frequently unsatisfactory because they do not allow seepage water accumulating behind the walls to drain into the stream. As a result, hydrostatic pressures build up to the point where the wall becomes cracked and deteriorates. Wooden walls, such as those made from railroad ties (Fig. 12-20), are satisfactory if properly anchored but have a relatively short life span in comparison to the cost involved. Stream bank stabilization can also be achieved by a combination of steel H beams driven into the base of the creek followed by installation of precast concrete slabs positioned between the beams. This arrangement has good long-term stability and permits lateral seepage of water.

A newer method of stream bank stabilization which has proven to be cost effective is the use of gabions. A gabion wall is composed of a series of rectangular baskets made of heavily galvanized steel wire mesh of triple-twist weave with openings of 3.5 to 4.5 inches (9 to 11.4 centimeters) (Fig. 12-21). The gabions may be subdivided into cells of comparable size by interior wire mesh partitions. When put into place along the edge of a stream bank, the gabion cells are filled with stones of 4 to 8 inches (10 to 20 centimeters) in diameter. The lid is then closed and the top edge laced to the upper edge of the gabion. Such gabion walls are free-standing and thus have the advantage of not requiring an expensive anchoring procedure during construction. Gabions facilitate natural seepage of ground water, which avoids buildup of hydrostatic pressures. Also, they can be subjected to natural settling processes without deteriorating. Finally, the installation can be accomplished by a golf course staff without exceptional expertise or equipment. The top of the gabion can be covered with several inches of soil and a turf sodded over the area to provide a distinct grassy surface which extends to the very edge of the stream. Such an arrangement blends nicely into the golf course landscape and reduces both mowing and trimming costs.

Maintenance

Proper maintenance of ditches and stream banks is important not only from the aesthetic and playability standpoints but also in facilitating rapid removal of excess surface water. Grass, weeds,

Figure 12-20. Stream bank stabilization by means of a wooden wall of railroad ties.

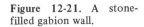

Figure 12-21. A stone-filled gabion wall.

leaves, soil, stone, wood, metal, and similar debris should not be allowed to accumulate to the extent that the drainage channel cannot function properly. All ditches and streams should be inspected regularly during the rainy season and any objectionable debris removed and soil slides corrected.

Soil slides that may block the normal flow of water should be removed and the slopes repaired and stabilized immediately. If a power grader, drag line, or backhoe is used in this operation, it is very important not to undercut the toe of the slope. Such undercutting leaves a vertical wall at the base of the slope which is a probable site for future soil sloughing and erosion. Accumulations of soil above the desired subgrade should be corrected by the same procedure to avoid adverse water velocities which increase erosion potential.

A chemical growth regulator can be used to suppress excessive growth of grassy vegetation within the boundaries of a ditch. The growth regulator selected should have minimal effects on the root system to avoid potential soil erosion problems. Objectionable weeds should be cut out as they develop (if minor) or they can be chemically controlled. Care must be exercised to use only those chemicals permitted and prescribed by EPA regulations. Special precautions are required if the water may be used downstream for crop irrigation, animal drinking, or human consumption. Some situations may negate the use of herbicides for vegetation control. All weeds and tall grass should be cut and cleaned from ditches to facilitate rapid removal of excess water.

LANDSCAPING

Where golf originated on the linksland of Scotland there were no trees. This totally open style of golf course landscaping continues to be an excellent one for locations where it is natural to the environment, but in most areas where the game is played today trees are normal features of the surroundings. A course where trees are scarce or nonexistent looks oddly barren, and golfers on a treeless course are deprived of the considerable benefits that trees and ornamental plantings provide. Properly selected and positioned trees perform four distinct—but often interrelated—functions: architectural, aesthetic, engineering, and economic.

These are some of the more important architectural uses for trees:

1. To add to the challenge (shot values) of golf holes by guarding doglegs and entrances to greens, by forming chutes through which shots must be played, and by forcing players to choose between alternative routes of play or shot types.
2. To indicate and control the line of play by drawing lines of sight (but seldom unnaturally straight ones) that influence golfer alignment.
3. To provide targets, especially when landing areas or greens are out of sight.
4. To better define targets, such as greens, that without trees would have only the sky as a backdrop.
5. To prevent very errant shots from leaving the course property or coming to rest in impossible positions.
6. To improve visibility of balls in flight by setting them off against a tall green backdrop or by shielding golfers' eyes from the low-lying afternoon sun when they play closing holes that head west.
7. To provide reference points to help locate balls that have strayed from the ideal line of play.
8. To assist golfers in gauging distance by providing depth perception and proportion cues and by use as yardage markers.

Aesthetically, the overriding objective is to make the golf course look natural in its surroundings and to develop and sustain within the golfer a harmonious feeling during each step of his or her round. Additionally, the landscape should be interesting and should contribute a certain delight to the golfer's senses and enjoyment of the course in all seasons. Tree and ornamental plantings help to achieve these aesthetic objectives in the following ways:

1. By breaking up the monotony of green turf and taking away the barren look.
2. By screening out the disruptive sights — and, to some extent, the sounds and smells — of a busy, highly structured "artificial" world, thus providing a sense of seclusion and a relaxing atmosphere.
3. By connecting different course features through drawing lines of sight.
4. By tying the course to the surrounding space through shaping that space, framing it, providing emphasis for pleasing focal points, and giving a sense of proper proportion.
5. By decorating the landscape to a tastefully restrained degree with plantings that provide variety, contrast, and seasonal interest.

There are several important engineering uses for trees:

1. To influence the normal flow of traffic and, where necessary, positively control it.
2. To give a greater measure of safety from errant shots to golfers and to adjacent properties.
3. To modify environmental forces with windbreaks and shady places carefully located to provide relief from the sun for buildings and golfers without an adverse impact on fine turf areas.
4. To enhance such resource conservation objectives as erosion control and preservation of wildlife habitats.

The direct economic functions that can be served by trees are largely unexploited by golf facilities at present. But some almost inadvertent uses are being made of trees and tree products for firewood, fruits and nuts, construction lumber, wood for furniture (especially black cherry and black walnut), maple syrup, wood chips for mulches, leaves for composting, and the development of larger, more valuable trees in nursery areas for eventual use as shade trees, ornamental specimens, and even Christmas trees.

In addition to the functions that must be served, many plant characteristics should be considered before a particular tree, shrub, ground cover, or flower is selected. The major criteria are discussed here in some detail, and emphasis is on tree selection. All ornamental plants have certain limitations as well as virtues. Selection of a plant species is based on a balance of outstanding features and an assessment of potential problems compared with those of alternative plants.

When placing a plant or allowing one to remain, the definition of a weed as a ''plant out of place'' should be kept in mind. Locations causing unfair interference with golf play are to be avoided. Also, maintenance of fine turfs can be impeded by shade effects, litter, and root encroachment.

Trees

The following characteristics should be considered when selecting trees for golf course use:

1. Rooting habit. Trees with large masses of feeder roots near the surface are seldom desirable for planting near greens, tees, and other areas where root competition will adversely affect the turf. Large roots that project above the soil surface may cause mowing problems and can disrupt asphalt or concrete roadways and cart paths. The location of drain lines, sewer lines, and similar underground facilities must also be taken into consideration, since roots can render them inoperative. Many trees are noted for their surface rooting, but the most troublesome include willow (*Salix* spp.), fig (*Ficus* spp.), elm (*Ulmus* spp.), beech (*Fagus* spp.), poplar (*Populus* spp.), cottonwood (*Populus* spp.), and eucalyptus (*Eucalyptus* spp.).

2. Foliage type. Trees are classified by foliage type as either deciduous (losing their leaves each year) or evergreen (retaining their leaves for more than a year). The problem with deciduous trees is that the autumn leaf fall produces litter that often must be removed immediately to avoid damage to the turf and interference with play. Trees such as maple (*Acer* ssp.), oak (*Quercus* spp.), tulip tree (*Liriodendron tulipifera*), and sycamore (*Platanus* spp.) can present substantial litter problems. Deciduous trees planted as screens along roadways or buildings function well only when they have leaves.

3. Fruiting. Fruit produced by trees can be detrimental to golf course maintenance operations. Trees with undesirable fruits include sweet gum (*Liquidambar* spp.), olive (*Olea* spp.), catalpa (*Catalpa* spp.), Osage orange (*Maclura* spp.), horse chestnut (*Aesculus* spp.), pine (*Pinus* spp.), and spruce (*Picea* spp.). Not only is fallen fruit unsightly, but if allowed to remain on the ground, it also clogs and dulls mowers. A local nurseryman should be consulted for the availability of variants that do not produce objectionable fruit.

4. Crown shape. Most mature trees display a characteristic crown shape ranging from the well-defined egg shape of a little-leaved linden (*Tilia cordata*) to the very irregular shape of a honey locust (*Gleditsia triacanthos*). Selection of a tree for its crown shape can be very important and is affected by the purpose for which a tree is used. For example, narrow upright trees may be used to create a screen. If a tree species is selected on the basis of its shape, proper spacing is necessary to allow the desired form to develop. Spacing too close to other trees or buildings can adversely affect the final shape of a tree that should be broad and spreading. Also, variants that differ in crown shape are available in many species. For example, there are variants of Norway maple (*Acer platanoides*) in crown shapes ranging from broad spreading to narrow columnar.

5. Density of foliage and shade potential. The crown density (shade potential) of tree species as it affects the maintenance of the turf beneath the canopy can be very important. The shade from most trees will affect turfgrass growth, but certain species have more negative effects than others. Trees with dense crowns close to the ground produce more shade than those with crowns that are more open and well off the ground (Fig. 12-22). Crown density is an especially important characteristic for trees that will be located near greens, tees, and similar areas where a high-quality turf is desired. Trees that should not be planted too close to intensely maintained turfgrass areas include Norway maple, beech, oak, and linden.

6. Susceptibility to insects and diseases. Pest-infested trees are unsightly. Also, maintaining the health of insect- and disease-susceptible tree species can require a continual and substantial investment of funds and effort. No tree is completely immune to insects and diseases, but species that are highly susceptible to many pests or to a very serious disease should be avoided.

These include American elm (*Ulmus americana*), coconut palm (*Cocos nucifera*), willow, the Lombardy and other poplars, and sycamore (*Platanus occidentalis*). Local horticulturalists should be consulted for other species that may be undesirable in the local area and for selections resistant to the more serious pest problems.

7. Susceptibility to ice and storm damage. This characteristic is of most importance in northern areas where snow and ice storms are more frequent and severe. Tree species with weak crotches, brittle wood, shallow roots, and high susceptibility to insects and diseases are most likely to be damaged by snow, ice, and wind. Although severe storms can completely ruin such trees, even mild storms can leave branch, twig, and leaf litter that must be cleaned up at considerable expense and inconvenience. Commonly planted trees that are very susceptible to storm damage include acacia (*Acacia* spp.), silver maple (*Acer saccharinum*), gray birch (*Betula populifolia*), Siberian elm (*Ulmus pumila*), poplar, and willow.

8. Height. The ultimate height of a mature tree can be of importance in many circumstances. Tall trees are advantageous if planted for shade, as a visual screen, or as a strategic hazard in the fairway or rough; they are a hindrance if planted under overhead obstructions, if they block a scenic view, or if they interfere with play off a tee. Around the clubhouse, trees should be selected that at maturity will be in scale with the buildings. For example, foundation plantings of large trees and shrubs are in harmony with large buildings but dominate smaller structures.

9. Longevity. The expected life span differs dramatically among various tree species. Some, such as certain oaks, can live hundreds of years, while others can be depended on for only twenty years or less. Trees of greater longevity should be selected if a tree or group of trees is planned as a permanent feature of the landscape. Lombardy poplars (*Populus nigra italica*), for example, are fast growing but are not dependable for long periods. This type of tree should be planted mainly to fill immediate needs while other species become established, though some of them may be valuable for planting in difficult sites where better species will not thrive. The western catalpa (*Catalpa speciosa*) is one that might be so used. In any case, every golf course should plan for the eventual loss of aging trees by interplanting young ones as replacements.

Figure 12-22. Comparison of a tree with a dense crown that sweeps close to the ground (*left*) to a species with a more open, high crown that permits turfgrass growth and ease of turf maintenance with large equipment (*right*).

10. Outstanding characteristics. In addition to attractive flowers or fruit, other interesting features make a tree species worthy of consideration for planting on a golf course. Among these are leaf shape or texture, fall color, bark texture or color, branching habit, and even fragrance. Almost all trees possess one or more of these outstanding characteristics. Popular favorites should not be relied on to the exclusion of lesser known but equally effective species.

Tree Planting for Putting Greens. Trees planted near greens should have features that will not interfere with turfgrass growth. These include deep rooting, minimum shading, absence of litter, strong branching, and good pest resistance. While few trees will fulfill all of these requirements, tree species with as many desirable features as possible should be chosen. For example, a tree may be deep rooting, strong, long lived, and litter free, yet cast deep shadows. This tree would be acceptable if positioned so that the shadows are not cast on the putting surface, at least not until late afternoon. Also, modern equipment can deal effectively with litter, though it is still a nuisance, and periodic root pruning will reduce the severity of tree-root competition. These practices, however, do require an extra and avoidable expenditure of resources.

Trees may be of any height, but high-branching species are usually preferred for areas likely to be in play. The outer foliage line of a tree at maturity should not be closer than 35 feet (10 meters) to the edge of a putting green. Tall, dense trees rarely should be located on the south side of putting greens in the northern hemisphere. If they must be so located, they should be spaced far enough apart so that direct sunlight reaches all parts of the green for most of the day.

Tree Planting for Tees. Tree species used in the vicinity of tees may possess different characteristics from those located around greens. For example, the trees can have lower branches and produce larger volumes of leaves than those near greens. However, adequate air circulation, sunlight, and branch height above a tee should be provided. Deep-rooting tree species are preferred to avoid root competition. Trees can be positioned closer to the tee in back than in front as long as there is adequate clearance for golf shots hit from all portions of the tee. Trees characterized by low overhanging branches should not be used near the front of long tees to avoid regular pruning. Sunlight must reach all parts of a tee during most of the day to insure a vigorous, dense turf with adequate recuperative potential. Properly placed trees and tall shrubs can provide welcome shade for golfers. The best location for benches is in a shaded area beside the tee with a full view of the upcoming fairway.

Tree Planting for Fairways. Trees have a definite strategic role in fairway design, but must not be overused. To be in proper scale with the surroundings and to effectively fulfill the strategic intent, trees positioned on and near fairways generally must be large, well-formed specimens (Fig. 12-23). This size requirement all but eliminates the planting of new trees in fairways and should be taken seriously when selecting plants for sites adjacent to fairways. For example, the use of small trees or shrubs on the edges of fairways as 150-yard markers can completely upset an otherwise balanced landscape. Such plantings should employ larger specimens that are neutral in appearance and in form and should be set well back from the fairway edges. The positioning is important to avoid creating unintended golfer obstacles from which it is not permissible to grant relief without penalty under the *Rules of Golf*.

Trees located near fairways should have a sufficiently open canopy and deep-feeding root system to allow the fairway turf adequate amounts of sunlight and nutrients. Litter potential should be reasonably low, although leaves and twigs are not quite so objectionable on fairways as on greens. High-branching trees will minimize interference with a player's swing and with mowing operations. Long-lived trees relatively free of insect and disease problems should be chosen, particularly for strategically important locations. Trees with seasonal characteristics such as good fall color, attractive bark, or fine summer foliage can be used to good effect. It is important to consider the positioning of trees in relation to irrigation sprinklers to avoid dry areas caused by the disruption of the normal sprinkler pattern by tree trunks or branches (Fig. 12-24).

Tree Planting for Roughs. Tree and shrub species for roughs can be of nearly any type. Much depends on the location of the golf facility, existing plant materials, and the desires of the golfers. Plant

Figure 12-23. Strategically positioned trees that affect play on a dogleg hole.

Figure 12-24. "Tree-shadow" pattern of dry turf caused by a tree that obstructs the spray from a major full-circle sprinkler head.

materials in the rough may be valued for their color, shape, bark, texture, specimen nature, massing use, or qualities as obstacles or barriers. They should allow medium to high amounts of light to penetrate to the turf and be at least moderately free of insect, disease, litter, and rooting problems. Species selection certainly is more critical for areas near fairways than for areas further out of play. Thorny species, for example, should be avoided in high traffic areas.

Overall Considerations. It is important that a variety of different tree species be chosen for placement around a golf course. Not only does this approach result in greater interest and enjoyment of the different colors, textures, fragrances, and shapes, but it minimizes the impact of severe damage to a specific tree species caused by a serious insect or disease outbreak. This lesson was learned when Dutch elm disease struck the American elm and left many golf courses void of trees.

Also to be considered are the many cultivated forms within a species. These intraspecies selections can vary in shape, height, flowering and fruiting characteristics, leaf color, leaf texture and shape, disease and insect resistance, and vigor. For example, variants of Norway maple range in color from normal green to the maroon of the Crimson King. The common honey locust has thorns and pods that make it a nuisance in most locations, but varieties such as Shademaster have no thorns or pods and are more suitable. Similarly, flowering dogwood (*Cornus florida*) normally displays white flowers, but the variant, Rubra, has reddish-pink flowers.

The use of specimen plants has become popular on many golf courses. Specimen trees are those selected specifically to show off one or more of their outstanding characteristics, such as beautiful flowers, seasonal foliage color, a special form, or unique texture. Specimen trees are often planted alone to further emphasize their qualities. The use of too many individual specimen plants tends to defeat the purpose and results in a jumble of oddities instead of a unified composition with interesting, attractive highlights. Occasional single specimens or small specimen clumps are certainly desirable if they fit naturally into the flow of the overall landscape from one area of the course to another. They also might be used to break up an otherwise artificial-looking, straight-line appearance along the perimeters of a fairway.

One means of creating a pleasing scene is to develop a background of evergreen trees and to plant a smaller, showier group of flowering trees, such as dogwood (*Cornus* spp.), flowering cherry (*Prunus* spp.), or crabapple (*Malus* spp.), in front of the evergreens. This is quite striking when the trees are in flower and is very popular if it can be seen from the clubhouse.

The number of plants and spacing are other important considerations when grouping trees. Groupings should contain an uneven number of plants spaced unequal distances apart. Each group should be individualistic but should have a center of interest. When using the same tree species, set two or three plants close together near the center to make that part seem larger and denser. Scatter the others more widely and irregularly. Always allow at least the minimum amount of space necessary for maintenance equipment to pass easily between trees (Fig. 12-25).

Figure 12-25. Spacing of trees should facilitate mowing of the surrounding turf with large, low-cost mowers. (Photo courtesy of The Toro Company, Minneapolis, Minn.)

Table 12-1 lists a number of trees for possible use on golf courses and the qualities to be considered in the selection of a species. The maximum hardiness zones for these trees and shrubs are shown on the map of the United States in Figure 12-26.

Shrubs, Ground Covers, and Flowers

Shrubs, ground covers, and flowers are commonly used to add heightened interest and beauty in nonplay areas, such as around the main entrance, clubhouse, pro shop, halfway house, shelters, pool, tennis courts, and along the route from a green to the next tee.

Shrubs. Shrubs are woody plants that normally have multiple stems and are less than 20 feet (6 meters) in height. Hundreds of excellent species of shrubs and their variants can be used on golf courses. Characteristics to be considered when selecting shrubs for planting are height, shape, density, hardiness, rooting habit, insect and disease susceptibility, fruiting habit, and foliage type. Important aspects of flowering include the time and duration of blooming and the flower color. By careful selection of a variety of plants from the many available flowering shrubs, it is possible to have at least one of them in flower throughout the growing season.

Though they are generally used around the clubhouse and similar facilities, shrubs can be planted successfully near tees and ponds and other places where they can add interest and create a special atmosphere. In most situations shrubs cannot be recommended for use in the vicinity of greens and fairways. Shrubs also can be of value in providing protection from errant shots, in directing traffic, in helping to prevent balls from going out-of-bounds, in screening unsightly areas, and in abating noise from nearby roadways.

Ground Covers. The use of ground covers usually is limited to out-of-play areas, around clubhouse facilities, and confined or difficult-to-maintain areas, such as steep slopes. One advantage to using a

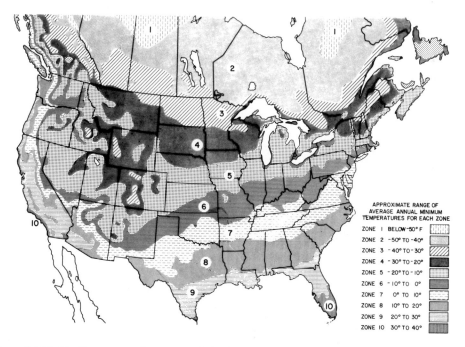

Figure 12-26. Hardiness zones for trees and shrubs in the United States. (From *Plant Hardiness Zone Map*, Agricultural Research Service, U.S. Department of Agriculture Publication No. 814.)

Table 12-1. Characteristics of Trees That Can Be Used on Golf Courses if Adapted to Local Conditions

Trees Scientific Name (Common Name)	Mature Height (Ft.)	Maximum Hardiness Zone (Fig. 12-26)	Primary Characteristics	Potential Problems
Abies concolor (Concolor or white fir)	75	3	Narrowly pyramidal evergreen/blue-green foliage	Cankers (*Cytospora* and others)
Abies homolepis (Nikko fir)	75	5	Narrowly pyramidal evergreen	Foliar burn/cankers
Acacia spp. (Acacia)	to 60	9	Gray-green evergreen foliage/yellow spring flowers/tolerant of poor, dry soils	Weak wood/short-lived/litter/shallow roots
Acer campestre (Hedge maple)	30	5	Shearable (for formal hedge)/tolerant of dry sites	Verticullium wilt. (Maples all highly susceptible where soil is infested)
Acer ginnala (Amur maple)	25	2	Red fall color/multistemmed if not trained	
Acer negundo (Box elder)	50	2	Fast growth/tolerant of poor, dry soils	Weak wood/litter/shade/weedy
Acer palmatum (Japanese maple)	20	5	Interesting shape and foliage/red fall color	
Acer platanoides (Norway maple)	60	3	Tolerant of poor sites	Dense shade/surface and girdling roots
Acer rubrum (Red or swamp maple)	60	3	Tolerant of moist soils/gray bark/red to yellow fall color/fast growth	Weak wood/shallow roots
Acer saccharinum (Silver maple)	60	3	Tolerant of wet soils/yellow fall color/fast growth	Weak wood/surface roots
Acer saccharum (Sugar maple)	60	3	Red to yellow fall color	Fails in poor or compacted soils
Aesculus carnea (Red horse chestnut)	50	3	Red spring flowers	Leaf blotch/surface roots/litter (fruitless varieties available)
Aesculus hippocastanum (Horse chestnut)	75	4	White spring flowers/tolerant of seashore conditions	Leaf blotch/surface roots/weak wood/litter (fruitless varieties available/weak roots/shade
Albizia julibrissin (Silk tree)	30	6	Pink summer flowers/tolerant of dry, alkaline soils	Webworm/mimosa wilt (resistant varieties available)
Alnus incana (Speckled alder)	40	2	Whitish-gray bark/tolerant of wet soils/fast growth/multistemmed if untrained	Foliar insects/short-lived/invasive roots
Amelanchier spp. (Shadbush, serviceberry)	to 40	4	White spring flowers/red to yellow fall color/tolerant of shade and of seashore conditions	Cedar rust
Araucaria excelsa (Norfolk Island pine)	100	10	Picturesque branching/evergreen/tolerant of seashore conditions	

Trees Scientific Name (Common Name)	Mature Height (Ft.)	Maximum Hardiness Zone (Fig. 12-26)	Primary Characteristics	Potential Problems
Arecastrum romanzoffianum (Queen palm)	40	10	Resistant to lethal yellows	Fails in poor, especially alkaline, soils (manganese deficiency)
Bauhinia blakeana (Hong Kong orchid tree)	20	10	Evergreen foliage/fragrant rose to red winter flowers/tolerant of poor, dry soils	Litter (large fleshy flower petals)
Betula nigra (River birch)	60	4	Tolerant of wet soils/yellow fall color	Short-lived
Betula papyrifera (Paper, canoe, or white birch)	60	2	Fast growth/white bark/yellow fall color	Fails in exposed sites
Betula pendula (European white birch)	50	2	White bark/yellow fall color	Birch borer/leaf miner/short-lived
Betula populifolia (Gray birch)	40	4	White bark/yellow fall color/multi-stemmed/tolerant of dry and wet sites and of seashore conditions	Birch borer/leaf miner/stem bending/short-lived
Brachychiton populneum (Bottle tree)	50	9	Swollen trunk/tolerant of poor, dry soils	
Bursera simaruba (Gumbo-limbo)	60	9	Interesting branching habit and bark	
Buxus sempervirens arborescens (Tree box)	25	6	Glossy evergreen/slow growth/multi-stemmed if untrained/shearable	Cankers/foliar burn/insects
Callistemon citrinus (Lemon bottle brush)	25	9	Red flowers/evergreen foliage/multi-stemmed if untrained	
Calocedrus decurrens (Incense cedar)	80	5	Tall, thin evergreen/fast growth/shearable	Intolerant of windy sites
Camellia japonica (Common camellia)	40	7	Red to white flowers/glossy evergreen	Intolerant of windy sites
Caragana arborescens (Siberian pea tree)	20	2	Yellow spring flowers/tolerant of poor, dry soils/clippable for an informal hedge	
Carpinus betulus (European hornbeam)*	50	5	Clippable/slow growth/tolerant of difficult sites	
Carpinus caroliniana (American hornbeam or ironwood)*	30	2	Tolerant of wet soil/red-orange fall color/clippable	Hard to transplant
Carya spp. (Hickory)	70	4	Most are tolerant of dry soils/yellow fall color	Litter (nuts)/hard to transplant
Castanea mollissima (Chinese chestnut)	40	4	White spring flowers/resistant to chestnut blight/yellow fall color	Litter (nuts, if two varieties planted together)
Casuarina equisetifolia (Australian pine)	50	9	Clippable evergreen/fast growth/tolerant of most soils and of seaside conditions	Litter/weak wood/surface roots

(Continued)

563

Table 12-1/Continued

Trees Scientific Name (Common Name)	Mature Height (Ft.)	Maximum Hardiness Zone (Fig. 12-26)	Primary Characteristics	Potential Problems
Catalpa speciosa (Western catalpa)	70	4	White spring flowers/fast growth/tolerant of most soils	Litter (pods)/weak wood/short-lived
Cedrus atlantica (Atlas cedar)*	100	6	Pyramidal evergreen	
Cedrus deodara (Deodar cedar)	120	7	Pendulous evergreen branches	Hard to transplant
Celtis spp. (Hackberry)	70	4	Tolerant of dry, difficult sites/fast growth	Shallow feeder roots/some susceptible to disfiguring witches'-broom
Cercidiphyllum japonicum (Katsura tree)*	60	4	Fast growth/red-yellow fall color/columnar when trained to a single stem	Shallow feeder roots
Cercis canadensis (Eastern redbud)	35	5	Rose spring flowers/shade tolerant	Weak wood/cankers
Chamaecyparis spp. (False cypress)	75+	5	Most are narrowly pyramidal/evergreen/central leaders clippable	Juniper blight (some resistant varieties available)
Chionanthus virginicus (Fringe tree)	25	4	White spring flowers/yellow fall color/usually multistemmed	
Cladrastis lutea (Yellowwood)*	50	3	Fragrant white spring flowers/yellow fall color/tolerant of most soils, including alkaline	Weak wood/shade/shallow roots
Cocos nucifera (Coconut)	80	10	Very long palm leaves/trunk usually leaning	Very susceptible to lethal yellows (disease-resistant varieties available)
Cornus florida (Flowering dogwood)	35	5	White spring flowers/red fall color/shade tolerant	Dogwood borer/crown canker
Cornus kousa (Kousa dogwood)	25	5	White spring flowers/red fall color	
Cornus mas (Cornelian cherry)	20	4	Yellow spring flowers/multistemmed if untrained	
Corylus colurna (Turkish hazelnut)*	40	4	Corky bark/tolerant of dry soils	Litter (nuts)
Crataegus crus-gallii (Cockspur hawthorn)	35	4	Red berries/tolerant of dry soils and seashore conditions/rust resistant	Apple scab/fire blight/thorns
Crataegus phaenopyrum (Washington thorn)	30	4	White spring flowers/red berries/red fall color/tolerant of dry soils/rust resistant	Apple scab/fire blight/thorns
Cryptomeria japonica (Cryptomeria, Japanese cedar)	50	6	Evergreen foliage/clippable/slow growth/tolerant of seashore conditions	Wind burn (dead foliage persistent)
Delonix regia (Royal poinciana)	40	10	Red summer flowers/fast growth	Litter (pods)/surface roots

Trees Scientific Name (Common Name)	Mature Height (Ft.)	Maximum Hardiness Zone (Fig. 12-26)	Primary Characteristics	Potential Problems
Diospyros virginiana (persimmon)	50	5	Good foliage/tolerant of most soils	Weak wood/hard to transplant
Elaeagnus angustifolia (Russian olive)	25	2	Fast growth/gray-green foliage/tolerant of wind, drought, and seashore conditions	
Eucalyptus citriodora (Lemon-scented gum)	70	9	Fragrant foliage/interesting bark/fast growth/tolerant of poor, dry soils and seashore conditions	Weak wood
Eucalyptus polyanthemos (Silver dollar gum)	70	9	Attractive foliage/fast growth/tolerant of poor, dry soils and seashore conditions	Not tolerant of wet soils
Fagus grandifolia (American beech)	75	3	Gray bark/slow growth/bronze fall color/clippable	Surface roots/dense shade/hard to transplant/beech bark insect-disease complex
Fagus sylvatica (European beech)	75	5	Gray bark/slow growth/bronze fall color	Surface roots/shade/beech bark insect-disease complex
Ficus retusa nitida (Indian laurel)	50	10	Glossy evergreen/shearable/tolerant of poor, dry soils/usually multistemmed	Aerial and surface roots/dense shade
Fraxinus spp. (Ash)	to 100	3	Fast growth/light shade	Weak wood/anthracnose/ash decline/litter (seedless varieties available)
Fraxinus uhdei (Evergreen ash)*	65	9	Compound leaves/fast growth	
Ginkgo biloba (Maidenhair tree)*	80	4	Yellow fall color/slow growth/tolerant of a wide range of sites, including alkaline soils	Fruit odor and litter (female plants)
Gleditsia triacanthos (Honey locust)*	60	4	Fast growth/casts light shade/tolerant of most soils, drought, and seashore conditions	Thorns/litter—pods (thornless and fruitless varieties available)
Gymnocladus dioica (Kentucky coffee tree)*	70	4	Fine, compound leaves/slow growth	Litter (pods on female trees)/weak wood
Halesia carolina (Carolina silver bell)*	40	5	White spring flowers/slow growth/multi-stemmed if untrained	Short-lived
Ilex aquifolium (English holly)	70	6	Glossy evergreen leaves/red berries (need female and male plants)/tolerant of shade and moist soils/shearable	Foliar burn
Ilex opaca (American holly)	50	5	Red berries (need female and male plants)/dull evergreen leaves/tolerant of shade, moist soils, and seashore conditions/shearable	Leaf miner

(*Continued*)

Table 12-1/Continued

Trees Scientific Name (Common Name)	Mature Height (Ft.)	Maximum Hardiness Zone (Fig. 12-26)	Primary Characteristics	Potential Problems
Jacaranda mimosaefolia (Jacaranda)	50	9	Fast growth/attractive foliage and bark/evergreen/often multistemmed if untrained	Weak wood
Juglans spp. (Walnut)	to 70	4	Fast growth/deep roots	Litter (nuts)/bacterial blight/hard to transplant
Juniperus chinensis (Chinese juniper)	35	4	Evergreen foliage/fast growth/tolerant of most soils/clippable	Juniper blight/several insects/cedar rust (blight- and rust-resistant varieties available)
Juniperus virginiana (Red cedar)	40	20	Evergreen foliage/fast growth/tolerant of poor, dry soils and seaside conditions/clippable	Juniper blight/several insects/cedar rust (blight- and rust-resistant varieties available)
Koelreuteria paniculata (Golden-rain tree)	30	5	Slow growth/yellow summer flowers/drought tolerant	Weak wood/canker/intolerant of acid soils
Laburnum watereri (Golden-chain tree)	30	6	Yellow spring flowers/often multistemmed if untrained	Short-lived
Larix spp. (Larch)*	to 60	to 1	Tolerant of wet soils/deciduous conifer/fast growth	Several insects
Liquidambar styraciflua (Sweet gum)*	60+	5	Red fall color/tolerant of wet soils	Litter (prickly seed balls)/hard to transplant
Liriodendron tulipifera (Tulip tree)	70+	4	Fast growth/yellow fall color/tolerant of moist soils	Weak wood/hard to transplant
Maclura pomifera (Osage orange)	50	4	Central leaders clippable/tolerant of dry, poor soils	Litter (fruit on female trees)/thorns
Magnolia acuminata (Cucumber tree)*	70	4	Fast growth	Scale/hard to transplant (all magnolias)
Magnolia grandiflora (Southern magnolia)	80	7	White, fragrant summer flowers/tolerant of seashore conditions	
Magnolia soulangiana (Saucer magnolia)	25	5	Several colors of spring flowers	
Magnolia stellata (Star magnolia)	20	5	White spring flowers/bronze fall color	
Magnolia virginiana (Sweet bay)	40	5	Tolerant of wet soil/fragrant flowers/good foliage	
Malus spp. (Crab apple)	to 40	to 2	Attractive fruit and flowers	Apple scab/cedar-apple rust/fire blight/powdery mildew/leaf spot/insects (disease-resistant varieties available)

Trees Scientific Name (Common Name)	Mature Height (Ft.)	Maximum Hardiness Zone (Fig. 12-26)	Primary Characteristics	Potential Problems
Maytenus boaria (Mayten tree)	35	9	Evergreen with pendulous branching habit/tolerant of seashore conditions/multi-stemmed if untrained	
Melaleuca leucadendron (Cajeput tree)	40	10	White summer flowers/fast-growing evergreen/tolerant of wet and dry soils and seashore conditions	Litter (exfoliating bark)/surface roots
Metasequoia glyptostroboides (Dawn redwood)	90	5	Deciduous conifer/fast growth/central leaders clippable	
Nyssa sylvatica (Sour gum, black tupelo)*	60	4	Red fall color/tolerant of wet soils and seashore conditions	Hard to transplant
Olea europaea (Common olive)	25	9	Gray-green evergreen/best in dry, poor soils/tolerant of seashore conditions/clippable	Litter (fruit)
Ostrya virginiana (Hop hornbeam)*	40	4	Yellow fall color/slow growth/tolerant of dry sites	Hard to transplant
Oxydendrum arboreum (Sourwood, sorrel tree)*	40	5	White summer flowers/red fall color/slow growth	
Parrotia persica (Persian parrotia)*	40	6	Red to yellow fall color	
Paulownia tomentosa (Empress tree)	40	7	Blue spring flowers/fast growth	Litter (pods)/dense shade
Phellodendron amurense (Amur cork tree)*	50	3	Light shade/furrowed bark/fast growth/tolerant of most soils	Litter—fruits on female plants (fruitless varieties available)
Phoenix canariensis (Canary Island date palm)	60	9	Attractive, long, arching leaves	
Picea spp. (Spruce)	to 75	2	Dense, pyramidal evergreens/tolerant of most soils and windy sites	Litter (cones)/Cytospora canker/several insects
Pinus banksiana (Jack pine)	50	2	Tolerant of dry, sandy soil	
Pinus cembra (Swiss stone pine)	60	2	Five-needle pine/almost columnar/slow growth	
Pinus densiflora (Japanese red pine)	60	4	Two-needle pine/picturesque branching/orange-red bark	Several insect pests, some quite damaging and difficult to control, have been affecting various pines on golf courses in some areas/cones may be a litter problem for most pines
Pinus flexilis (Limber pine)	55	2	Five-needle pine/slow growth	

(Continued)

567

Table 12-1/*Continued*

Trees *Scientific Name (Common Name)*	Mature Height *(Ft.)*	Maximum Hardiness Zone *(Fig. 12-26)*	Primary *Characteristics*	Potential *Problems*
Pinus nigra (Austrian pine)	70	4	Two-needle pine/tolerant of most soils/fast growth	*Diplodia* tip blight (on other two- and three-needle pines as well)
Pinus ponderosa (Western yellow pine)	90	5	Two-needle pine/yellow-green foliage/fast growth	
Pinus resinosa (Red pine)	70	2	Two-needle pine/fast growth	Intolerant of wet soils
Pinus rigida (Pitch pine)	60	4	Three-needle pine/tolerant of dry, rocky soil	
Pinus strobus (Eastern white pine)	100	3	Five-needle pine/fast growth	Some plants sensitive to air pollutants
Pinus sylvestris (Scots pine)	60	2	Two-needle pine/tolerant of moist or dry soils and seashore conditions/red bark on older parts	
Pinus thunbergii (Japanese black pine)	70	4	Two-needle pine/fast growth/picturesque form/very tolerant of seashore conditions	
Pinus wallichiana (Himalayan pine)	75	5	Blue-green foliage/fast growth	
Pistacia chinensis (Chinese pistache)	50	9	Slow growth/orange and red fall color/drought tolerant	
Platanus acerifolia (London plane tree)	80	5	Exfoliating bark/fast growth/tolerant of air pollution, alkaline soil, and seashore conditions/resistant to twig blight	Litter (fruit)/surface roots
Platanus occidentalis (Sycamore)	100	4	Exfoliating bark/fast growth/tolerant of alkaline soil	Litter (fruit)/anthracnose/surface roots
Populus spp. (Poplar, aspen, cottonwood)	to 100	3	Tolerant of difficult sites/yellow fall color/fast growth	Suckers/invasive surface roots/weak wood/litter (seeds, twigs)/short-lived/cankers
Prunus spp. (Ornamental cherry, plum, peach)	to 50	to 4	Showy flowers/some also with attractive fruit, good fall color and interesting bark	Litter (fruit)/several diseases and insects (many disease-resistant varieties available)/weak wood/short-lived
Prunus serotina (Black cherry)	70	3	Tolerant of difficult sites and seashore conditions/fruit liked by birds	Tent caterpillars
Pseudotsuga menziesii (Douglas fir)	100	4	Good evergreen foliage/tolerant of dry soil/fast growth/central leaders clippable	

568

Trees Scientific Name (Common Name)	Mature Height (Ft.)	Maximum Hardiness Zone (Fig. 12-26)	Primary Characteristics	Potential Problems
Pyrus calleryana (Callery pear)	30	5	White spring flowers/red fall color	Weak wood/fire blight/leaf spot/apple scab
Pyrus communis (Common pear)	60	4	White spring flowers/red fall color	Litter (fruit)/fire blight/leaf spot/apple scab
Quercus spp. (Oak)				In some areas, oaks may be troubled by gypsy moth defoliation. Oak wilt is a serious disease in some areas. Many oaks may present litter problems (acorns and leaves) and cast dense shade on turf areas.
Quercus alba (White oak)	75	4	Purplish fall color/slow growth/round-lobed leaves (less of a litter problem)/tolerant of seashore conditions	Anthracnose/hard to transplant
Quercus bicolor (Swamp white oak)	60	3	Tolerant of wet soils/yellow-red fall color/round-lobed leaves	Hard to transplant
Quercus borealis (Red oak)	70	3	Tolerant of dry soil/fast growth/red fall color/transplants well	
Quercus coccinea (Scarlet oak)	70	4	Red fall color/fast growth/tolerant of dry soil/less shade density	Hard to transplant
Quercus imbricaria (Shingle oak)	70	5	Shearable/slow growth/yellow-red fall color/leaves less of a litter problem	
Quercus palustris (Pin oak)	75	4	Fast growth/red fall color/transplants well	Fails in alkaline or poorly drained soils
Quercus phellos (Willow oak)	50	5	Fast growth/tolerant of moist soil/leaves less of a litter problem/transplants well	
Quercus robur (English oak)	75	5	Fast growth/round-lobed leaves	
Quercus velutina (Black oak)	100	4	Red fall color/tolerant of dry soil	Hard to transplant
Quercus virginiana (Live oak)	60	7	Evergreen/fast growth/tolerant of seashore conditions	
Robinia pseudoacacia (Black locust)	70	3	Light shade/tolerant of poor, dry soils and seashore conditions/fast growth/fragrant white late-spring flowers/furrowed bark	Shallow, invasive roots/weedy (suckers)/litter (pods and twigs)/borers

(Continued)

569

Table 12-1/Continued

Trees Scientific Name (Common Name)	Mature Height (Ft.)	Maximum Hardiness Zone (Fig. 12-26)	Primary Characteristics	Potential Problems
Roystonea regia (Royal palm)	70	10	Long feathery leaves/fragrant flowers/tolerant of seashore conditions	
Salix spp. (Willow)	to 60	2	Fast growth/tolerant of wet soils	Litter (twigs)/shallow, invasive roots/weak wood/cankers/several insects
Salix caprea (French pussy willow)	30	4	Early flowers/tolerant of moist soils	Short-lived/weedy (suckers)
Sassafras albidum (Common sassafras)*	40	5	Orange to red fall color/tolerant of poor, gravelly soils	Weedy (suckers)
Sciadopitys verticillata (Umbrella pine)*	50	5	Dense evergreen foliage/slow growth	Foliar burn
Sequoia sempervirens (Coast redwood)	100+	7	Narrow evergreen/attractive bark/fast growth/central leaders clippable	
Sophora japonica (Japananese pagoda tree)	60	4	Yellowish summer flowers/tolerant of poor, dry soils	
Sorbus aucuparia (European mountain ash)	40	3	White spring flowers/red berries/red fall color/fast growth	Fire blight/cankers/sun scald of trunk/borers/scale/foliar insects (especially Japanese beetle)
Stewartia pseudocamellia (Japanese stewartia)*	60	5	White summer flowers/purplish fall color/exfoliating bark/slow growth	
Styrax japonica (Japanese snowball)*	30	5	White spring flowers/slow growth	
Swietenia mahogani (Mahogany)	65	10	Leathery evergreen leaves	
Syringa amurensis japonica (Japanese tree lilac)	30	4	White summer flowers/cherrylike bark	Borers/scale
Taxodium distichum (Bald cypress)*	130	4	Tolerant of very wet soils/deciduous conifer/almost columnar	
Taxus cuspidata capitata (Upright Japanese yew)	50	4	Shearable/slow growth/tolerant of seashore conditions	Intolerant of wet soils
Thuja occidentalis (American arborvitae)	60	2	Columnar evergreen/tolerant of wet soils and seashore conditions/shearable/slow growth/shade-tolerant evergreen	Several insects
Thuja plicata (Giant arborvitae)	100+	5	Good evergreen foliage/shearable/slow growth	Several insects
Tilia americana (American linden)	70	2	Tolerant of poor sites/fast growth/fragrant summer flowers	Anthracnose/foliar insects (especially Japanese beetle)/dense shade

Trees Scientific Name (Common Name)	Mature Height (Ft.)	Maximum Hardiness Zone (Fig. 12-26)	Primary Characteristics	Potential Problems
Tilia cordata (Little-leaved linden)	70	3	Slow growth/formal shape/tolerant of most soils and seashore conditions/ fragrant summer flowers	Foliar insects (especially Japanese beetle)/dense shade
Tilia tomentosa (Silver linden)	70	4	Fast growth/formal shape/tolerant of most soils/silvery foliage underneath/ fragrant summer flowers	Dense shade/foliar insects (especially Japanese beetle)
Tristania conferta (Brisbane box)	60	10	Attractive evergreen foliage/exfoliating bark	Litter
Tsuga canadensis (Canada hemlock)	75	3	Dense evergreen/shearable/shade tolerant/ often multistemmed if untrained	Intolerant of dry, windy, or alkaline sites/mites/scale/canker
Ulmus americana (American elm)[†]				
Ulmus hollandica (Cultivars Christine Buisman and Groeneveld)	60	4	Resistant to Dutch elm disease (DED) and phloem necrosis (PN)	Litter (seeds and twigs)/foliar insects/ shallow roots
Ulmus parvifolia (Chinese elm)	40	5	Fast growth/interesting exfoliating bark/ reddish fall color/resistant to DED and PN/ tolerant of seashore conditions	Litter (seeds and twigs)/foliar insects/ shallow roots
Ulmus pumila (Siberian elm)	60	4	Fast growth/tolerant of dry, poor soils and seashore conditions/shearable/re- sistant to DED and PN	Litter (seeds and twigs)/invasive surface roots/weak wood (stronger- wooded varieties available)/foliar insects
Washingtonia robusta (Mexican fan palm)	90	10	Fan-shaped leaves/curved trunk/tolerant of seashore conditions	Surface roots
Zelkova serrata (Keaki tree)	80	5	Fast growth/tolerant of drought and alkaline soil/resistant to DED	Surface roots

*Remarkably free of disease problems

[†]Existing trees may warrant special care programs, but the species cannot be recommended for planting because of its extreme susceptibility to Dutch elm disease (DED) and phloem necrosis (PN). None of the disease-resistant elms currently available bear the classic umbrella shape of the American elm. This includes elms of Asiatic origin (Chinese and Siberian elms), of European origin (Scots elm and cultivars of *Ulmus hollandica*), and hybrid clones (Sapporo Autumn Gold and the Urban Elm) developed in the United States.

ground cover is reduced maintenance costs. Thus, the plant material selected should have qualities that fulfill this objective. Included are good density to reduce weed encroachment and freedom from serious pest problems so that maintenance requirements will be minimal. Shade tolerance is necessary if a ground cover is to be planted under trees. Most ground covers are not wear tolerant and therefore cannot be planted where traffic is anticipated. Table 12-2 lists a number of common ground covers and the important qualities to be considered in their selection and use.

Flowers. As with shrubs, the available varieties of herbaceous flowering plants for use on golf courses are very extensive, and they too are best planted in nonplay areas. Large masses of annuals or carefully planned perennial borders can add color and fragrance throughout the golfing season. It is advisable, especially for a perennial border, that a complete plan be drawn on paper before any planting is done. Important characteristics to be considered are plant height, flower color, time of bloom, foliage color and texture, fragrance, hardiness, special maintenance requirements, shade tolerance, and susceptibility to diseases and insects.

Annual, perennial, and bulbous-type flowers are especially useful around clubhouse facilities. Used with restraint, they can be effective around tees for beautification or traffic control, near ponds, along streams, and in naturalized settings. Many golf clubs prepare hanging baskets of flowers or foliage plants and display them in dining areas, on patios, around pools and tennis courts, and at halfway houses and shelters.

Sources of Additional Information

This section has discussed the functions of trees in golf course landscaping and the important factors to consider in selecting and placing trees and ornamental plant materials in various sites around a course. The accompanying table of characteristics of tree species has been designed to provide the most important information about a selected list of trees that often are planted or allowed to remain in this special kind of landscape. A table dealing with ground-cover plants and a map of the United States showing winter hardiness zones for trees and shrubs also have been included.

Those responsible for the development and maintenance of golf courses will want to know more than could be covered herein about tree forms and species, flower and shrub species, disease and insect problems important in certain areas, and the planting and care of trees and other landscape plants. County agricultural extension personnel can be contacted for further information specific to local conditions.

Reputable nurseries and greenhouses can be very helpful, especially concerning available species variants and their characteristics. Nursery and seed catalogues usually contain many pictures of plants and may offer some cultural advice. Also, USGA Green Section agronomists may be consulted. In addition, the following references should be of special interest and assistance.

Finally, because of the tremendous impact of landscaping on a golf course and the complexity of the subject, a qualified landscape architect with a knowledge of the game of golf should be consulted to develop a long-range program of planting and maintenance.

Brooklyn Botanic Garden. 1959. *The Hundred Finest Trees and Shrubs for Temperate Climates.* Brooklyn Botanic Garden, Brooklyn, N.Y. 90 pp.

Carpenter, P. L., Walker, T. D., and Lanphear, F. O. 1975. *Plants in the Landscape.* W. H. Freeman & Co., San Francisco, Calif. 481 pp.

Crockett, J. U. 1972. *Evergreens. The Time-Life Encyclopedia of Gardening.* Time-Life Books, New York. 159 pp.

Crockett, J. U. 1972. *Trees. The Time-Life Encyclopedia of Gardening.* Time-Life Books, New York. 160 pp.

Harrar, E. S., and Harrar, J. G. 1962. *Guide to Southern Trees.* Dover Publications, Inc., New York. 709 pp.

Johnson, W. T., and Lyon, H. 1976. *Insects That Feed on Trees and Shrubs, An Illustrated Practical Guide.* Cornell University Press, Ithaca, N.Y. 464 pp.

Nelson, W. R. Jr. 1979. *Planting Design: A Manual of Theory and Practice.* Stipes Publishing Co., Champaign, Ill. 186 pp.

Pirone, P. P. 1978. *Tree Maintenance.* 5th Ed. Oxford University Press, New York. 574 pp.

Preston, R. J. 1968. *Rocky Mountain Trees.* Dover Publications, Inc., New York. 285 pp.

Table 12-2. Ground Covers and Their Characteristics

Ground Covers Scientific Name (Common Name)	Maximum Hardiness Zone (Fig. 12-26)	Height (In.)	Flower or Other Characteristics	Site Considerations
Ajuga reptans (Bugleweed)	4	6	Blue	Shade or sun
Anthemis nobilis (Chamomile)	3	10	Daisy-type flowers	Tolerates drought/bunker lips
Calluna vulgaris (Heather)	4	24	Pink	Tolerates salt, wind, and drought
Comptonia peregrina (Sweet fern)	2	24	Fragrant/fine-textured foliage	Banks/full sun
Convallaria majalis (Lily of the valley)	2	8	White	Moist shade
Coronilla varia (Crown vetch)	3	24	Pink	Banks/tolerates moderate drought
Cotoneaster spp.	3 to 5	6 to 24	Red (berries)	Rocky areas/moist soils
Cytisus spp. (Brooms)	5 to 6	6 to 36	Yellow	Tolerates salt, drought, and wind
Erica carnea (Heath)	5	24	Pink	Full sun/tolerates salt and wind
Euonymus fortunei (Wintercreeper)	5	6	Good foliage	Banks, rocky areas
Festuca ovina glauca (Blue fescue)	3	10	Good foliage	Tolerates salt, wind, and drought
Hedera helix (English ivy)	5	8	Evergreen	Sun or shade
Hemerocallis fulva (Tawny daylily)	3	24	Orange flowers/reedlike leaf	Sun/tolerates wind and salt
Juniperus horizontalis (Creeping juniper)	2	6 to 12	Evergreen	Full sun/tolerates wind, salt, and drought
Liriope spicata (Creeping lily-turf)	4	12	Reedlike leaf/purple flowers	Sun or shade/tolerates drought
Lotus corniculatus (Bird's-foot trefoil)	3	2	Yellow	Sunny/dry banks
Pachysandra terminalis (Japanese pachysandra)	4	8	Evergreen	Light to dense shade
Parthenocissus quinquefolia (Virginia creeper)	3	12	Red fall color	Will climb
Phlox subulata (Moss pink)	2	6	Pink flowers/scalelike leaves	Full sun
Rosa wichuraiana (Memorial rosa)	5	12	White/fragrant	Sunny banks
Taxus baccata repandens (Spreading English yew)	5	24	Evergreen	Sun to deep shade
Vinca minor (Periwinkle)	4	6	Blue flowers/evergreen	Sun to deep shade

Sunset Books, 1979. *New Western Garden Book*. Lane Publishing Co., Menlo Park, Calif. 512 pp.
Tattar, T. 1978. *Diseases of Shade Trees*. Academic Press, Inc., New York. 361 pp.
Wigginton, B. E. 1963. *Trees and Shrubs for the Southeast*. University of Georgia Press, Athens, Ga. 304 pp.
Wyman, D. 1965. *Trees for American Gardens*. The Macmillan Co., New York. 502 pp.
Wyman, D. 1969. *Shrubs and Vines for American Gardens*. The Macmillan Co., New York. 613 pp.
Wyman, D. 1976. *Ground Cover Plants*. The Macmillan Co., New York. 192 pp.
Zion, R. 1968. *Trees for Architecture and the Landscape*. Van Nostrand Reinhold Co., New York. 284 pp.

PARKING LOTS

The parking lot is one of the first components of the golf facility the players see on arriving. It can lead to a first impression that is quite good or very unfavorable. The parking lot is also one of the last facilities the players see on leaving. It is to be hoped that they are left with a favorable overall impression and attitude. The contrast in impression created by a muddy or dusty parking lot having faded lines and crumbling pavement versus one with smooth, clean paving and well-defined parking stripes accented by properly maintained ornamental plantings can be imagined (Fig. 12-27). The parking lot should initiate and enhance the overall pastoral setting and aesthetics of the golf course. Unfortunately, the parking lot can become one of the most neglected components of a golf course facility. Proper design, construction, landscaping, and maintenance of parking lots can make a significant contribution in providing the golfer with a favorable overall impression and attitude.

Design

A local planning and zoning commission may exist whose ordinances require that a construction permit be obtained and certain design restrictions be met relating to proper drainage, construction guidelines, and entrances onto highways and roadways. Matching the parking lot design to the projected volume of traffic is vital in developing an efficient, functional facility. The design should be uncomplicated and possess a distinct flow pattern. In the case of irregular-shape lots, the services of a competent traffic design engineer or architect may be needed to develop the most effective design. There are three basic types of parking layouts:

90-degree right-angle layout. Provides a maximum number of cars per acre. Excluding approaches, accommodates a maximum of 170 cars per acre, with 149 cars preferred for more generous spacing. Permits entrance or exit in either direction. Only one entrance required.

60-degree diagonal layout. Provides easier access than the right-angle layout and takes less distance along the curb per car than does the 45-degree layout. Excluding approaches, accommodates a maximum of 158 cars per acre, with 140 cars preferred for more generous spacing. Two entrances or a turn-around required.

45-degree diagonal layout. Allows easy entrance into the parking space. Has the advantage that the aisle can be narrower, thus permitting use of a lot too narrow for right-angle parking. Excluding approaches, accommodates a maximum of 145 cars per acre, with 124 cars preferred for more generous spacing. Two entrances or a turn-around required.

Detailed specifications for various combinations of the three basic types of parking layouts are shown in Table 12-3. The particular layout selected should accommodate the optimum number of cars for the size and shape of area available. It is desirable that generous amounts of space be provided between cars for ease of entrance and exit, especially where golf equipment is involved.

A two-way drive entrance with a 20-foot (6-meter) width is suggested for all three basic types of layouts. The number of entrances and exits in the parking lot should be held to a minimum in relation to the anticipated volume of traffic to reduce congestion with street and sidewalk traffic. The inclusion of curbing facilitates maintenance of the parking lot. Sidewalks should be located on the side of the lot nearest the building.

Table 12-3. Parking Layout Standards

Type of Parking Arrangement	Standard Widths (Ft.)		Feet of Curb	Number of Cars/ Feet on Curb
	Minimum	Optimum		
Two-way 90 degree, both sides	54	68	9	11/99
Two-way 90 degree, one side	40	48	9	11/99
One-way 60 degree, both sides	55	65	10.5	9/94.5
One-way 60 degree, one side	36	45	10.5	9/94.5
Two-way 60 degree, both sides	55	65	10.5	9/94.5
Two-way 60 degree, one side	40	45	10.5	9/94.5
One-way 45 degree, one side	28	36	12.5	8/100
One-way 45 degree, both sides	45	54	12.5	8/100
Two-way 45 degree, both sides	50	60	12.5	8/100
Two-way 45 degree, one side	34	45	12.5	8/100
One-way parallel, one side	16	22	25	4/100
One-way parallel, both sides	24	32	25	4/100
Two-way parallel, one side	26	40	25	4/100
Two-way parallel, both sides	32	25	25	4/100

NOTE: From *Grounds Maintenance* 4(3): 17 - 22, 1969.

Driveways within the parking lot may vary in width. An optimum width of 12 feet (3.7 meters) is suggested for one-way drives, with the minimum being 9 feet (2.7 meters). In the case of two-way drives, the suggested optimum is 24 feet (7.3 meters), the minimum being 18 feet (5.5 meters). Unless space or budget is extremely limited, it is recommended that the wide driveway spacing be utilized. Should access to the service area of the clubhouse be through the parking lot, it is very important that turn-around space be adequate for large delivery trucks and that appropriate weight-load capacity for paving be provided along the projected route of travel.

The specific design selected will depend on the region of the country where the facility is located. For example, regularly spaced islands planted with ornamentals and trees can enhance aesthetics and add cooling shade to a parking area. However, in the more northerly climates, such islands can cause difficulty in plowing snow during the winter. Thus, the ease of snow removal must be weighed against the benefits of shade trees growing in the islands. Curbing should be used around all landscaped islands.

Construction

As in the case of golf courses, it is important that parking facilities be properly constructed so as to avoid the expense of resurfacing or rebuilding in a few years. The intensity of wear and weight loads anticipated on the parking lot must be projected and appropriate construction specifications selected to accommodate this level of use. It is essential that a good set of construction specifications be written which will serve as the basis for contractors' bids. Finally, the ongoing construction activities must be inspected regularly to insure that specifications are being met by the contractor.

Parking lot construction typically utilizes a concrete, asphalt, or asphalt-cement paving surface. Construction specifications call for the preparation of a subbase, the installation of a base, and finally the finished surface. The subbase should be rough leveled, graded to insure proper drainage as specified in the grading plan, and thoroughly compacted, with water being applied as required to achieve maximum compaction. Next, gravel or crushed rock of the specified size is applied. This usually involves the application of two 3-inch (7.6-centimeter) courses with thorough compacting between each course. Finally, the finish course of concrete or asphalt is applied according to the specifications, i.e., the specific type of material, thickness, and compaction pressure. The material must be uniformly

Figure 12-27. A properly maintained and aesthetically landscaped parking lot (*top*) and entrance way (*bottom*).

mixed and installed to the appropriate surface grade to insure drainage. Catch basins and subsurface drain outlets of adequate capacity must be provided.

Landscaping

One of the benefits of playing golf is the opportunity to be surrounded by an outdoor environment of trees, ornamentals, and green grass. This benefit should be extended to the parking area. The placement of large trees and/or flower beds on islands spaced throughout the parking lot as well as around the perimeter enhances the aesthetic surroundings as well as provides cool, shaded areas for parked cars. The latter can be particularly important in the warmer southern regions of North America. The placement of large trees should provide maximum shade potential in relation to the path of the rising and setting sun. The shade tree species selected for the parking perimeters and islands must have minimum problems with periodic drippings or deposits that can mar the surface of cars. Also to be avoided are shade tree species possessing large, shallow roots that can cause uplifting and possible breakup of asphalt or concrete parking lot surfaces.

In the construction of islands and perimeter areas, it is important that a good quality root zone soil mix be provided along with adequate subsurface drain lines, where needed. In addition, installation of an irrigation system will minimize long-term maintenance costs. Irrigation is quite important in the culture of trees and shrubs located in island areas, since the heat generated from adjacent surfaces increases the potential for water stress. Manual valves and hose outlets should also be included.

Adequate lighting for the parking lot is desirable. Lighting aids individuals using clubhouse facilities at night and at the same time serves a security function. Automatic time or photoelectric switches for controlling the lighting duration are advantageous.

Maintenance

The parking area should be kept clean of objectionable debris at all times. The frequency of sweeping will depend on the location and rate of debris accumulation. It usually varies seasonally and may range from daily to once a week. Large paper and plastic debris can be picked up manually, while more extensive accumulations of smaller particulate debris can be removed with powered vacuum or sweeper devices equipped with collection bags or bins (Fig. 12-28). In addition, immediate snow removal is important at golf facilities where the clubhouse is utilized for winter recreational and social activities.

Figure 12-28. Powered vacuum being used for debris clean-up on an asphalt parking lot.

Less frequently utilized practices include maintenance of clear, well-defined parking stripes, directional arrows, and no-parking zones. Repainting is done at least once annually, either by a contractor or by the green staff. In the case of asphalt parking areas, the surface will have to be resealed periodically with a liquid asphalt material. Renovation may also be required at intervals. This involves the cleaning and filling of cracks by means of an emulsified asphalt seal and/or spot patching involving the digging out of broken pavement to sound paving, shaping sides to a distinct vertical edge, applying a tack coat, filling with a surface coarse grade of asphalt patch material, firming, leveling, and applying a surface seal. Regular preventive maintenance involving the application of a surface seal and periodic renovation of cracks and minor spots avoids costly rebuilding of an entire parking lot.

Finally, the entrance should be made attractive through the use of landscaping, flowers, and a sign designating the name of the club. Entrances can be very simple or quite elaborate, depending on the objectives and image the golf facility wishes to project.

Appendix A
Species Characterization and Identification

VEGETATIVE IDENTIFICATION OF TURFGRASSES

The species composition of a turfgrass community is not necessarily what was planted on the golf course five, ten, or twenty years ago. The species dictates the cultural practices and pest control measures selected. Thus, the golf course superintendent must be able to identify by means of vegetative characteristics the turfgrass species commonly found on golf courses.

Each turfgrass plant is composed of a root system and a shoot system; the shoot system is composed of the stems and leaves (Fig. A-1). The leaves originate from solid, swollen joints on the stem called *nodes*. The stem portion connecting two adjacent nodes is termed an *internode*. Under the appropriate day length and temperature conditions certain species initiate flowering in which the stem elongates into a *culm* with an *inflorescence* borne at the tip.

Primary shoot growth results in turf density. These shoots originate mostly from *tillers* by intervaginal stem growth from the plant crown, with nominal internode elongation. In contrast, secondary lateral shoots are formed by extravaginal shoot growth involving outward lateral elongation of stems, which significantly enhances sod strength, recuperative potential, and lateral spread of turfs. Secondary lateral shoots that occur above ground are termed *stolons,* whereas those that occur below ground with roots initiated from the nodes are termed *rhizomes.* Some species possess both rhizomes and stolons. These two types of secondary lateral stem development result in a *creeping growth habit* with strong sod formation. In contrast, species possessing only primary shoot growth in the form of tillers have a noncreeping or *bunch growth habit*. Thus, the presence or absence of lateral stem development is a key feature in identification of turfgrass species.

The primary characteristic used in vegetative identification is the disposition of the youngest unexpanded leaf in the bud shoot, termed *vernation*. Vernation is either folded or rolled and is best observed by cutting a cross section of the stem just below the unexpanded leaf blade. The grass leaf is also an important structure in vegetative identification. The leaf consists of a lower *sheath* which surrounds the stem above the node from which it originates. Beyond the sheath is the expanded leaf *blade*. Three features associated with the junction between the leaf blade and leaf sheath are used in identification. The *ligule* is an erect tissue or appendage projecting from the inside of the grass leaf at this junction. The *collar* is a thickened zone on the outside or back of the leaf at the junction. The third structure, the *auricle,* is an earlike appendage projecting from either side of the collar at the junction of the leaf blade and leaf sheath.

The shape, size, color, hairiness, roughness, and characteristics of the margin of these key structures associated with the leaf are important in vegetative identification. The major types of vernation, auricle, sheath, ligule, collar, and leaf blade characteristics are summarized in Figure A-2.

The first step in identification is to confirm that the species is actually a grass rather than a sedge or a rush. Grasses have their leaves arranged in ranks of two, and a ligule usually is present. In contrast, sedges and rushes have leaves arranged in ranks of three, and the ligule is poorly developed or absent. Also, sedges possess a distinct triangular-shaped stem.

Vegetative identification of turfgrass genera is fairly simple, but species identification is more difficult and requires some experience. Cultivar identification within a species is extremely difficult even for the experienced turfgrass researcher.

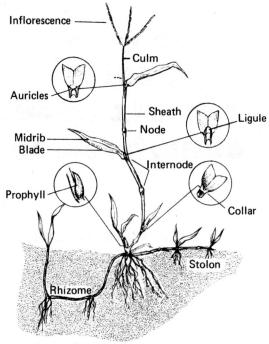

Figure A-1. The major grass structures used in vegetative identification.

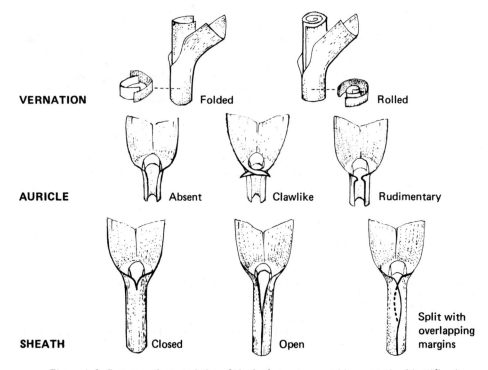

Figure A-2. Common characteristics of the leaf structure used in vegetative identification.

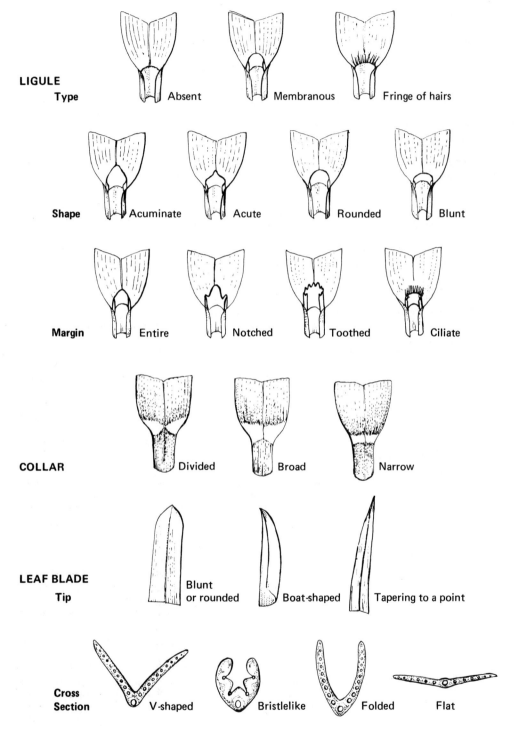

LIGULE

Type — Absent — Membranous — Fringe of hairs

Shape — Acuminate — Acute — Rounded — Blunt

Margin — Entire — Notched — Toothed — Ciliate

COLLAR — Divided — Broad — Narrow

LEAF BLADE

Tip — Blunt or rounded — Boat-shaped — Tapering to a point

Cross Section — V-shaped — Bristlelike — Folded — Flat

Figure A-2/*Continued*

Successful identification of turfgrasses depends on a detailed examination of several representative plants from the turfgrass community. The composition of the turfgrass species depends on topographic site, light exposure, and traffic intensity. These factors should be kept in mind when sampling plants to be used in identification. Specimens from moist habitats usually have larger, greener, and less hairy or rough surfaces than plants of the same species grown in a dry environment. Fresh, actively growing plants should be selected, since some of the characters used in vegetative identification are difficult to distinguish when portions of the plant are partially dried or damaged.

Once a set of representative plants has been selected from the turfgrass community, each distinguishing structure should be carefully examined. This includes both the shoot and the root system, starting from the apex and moving to the base of the plant. The size, shape, color, and types of structures present should be noted. Identification under field conditions can usually be accomplished with the aid of a sharp knife and an inexpensive hand lens of $10 \times$ magnification.

To correctly identify a species of turfgrass, the first step is to determine whether the leaf vernation is folded or rolled, (A) or (AA) in the following key. Next, the presence or absence of auricles, (B) or (BB) in the key, is determined. This is continued until the species name becomes clear.

Any vegetative key has certain limitations. For such a key to work, the number of species must be limited. However, despite limitations, this vegetative key is one of the best approaches to the identification of turfgrass species. The major turfgrasses plus some of the common grassy weeds that occur in golf course turfs are included in the key.

Vegetative Identification Key for the Common Turfgrasses

A.   Leaf vernation folded
>   **B.**   Auricles present, small, clawlike; ligule a very short, very blunt membrane; blades dull above, glossy below, veins prominent on upper side; basal sheaths smooth, glossy, reddish; plants tufted
>>   PERENNIAL RYEGRASS (*Lolium perenne*)

>   **BB.** Auricles absent
>>   **C.**   Creeping stolons present
>>>   **D.**   Blades petioled; sheaths greatly compressed
>>>>   **E.**   Ligule a fringe of very short hairs; sheaths with few hairs at margins and summit of keel; collar smooth; blades smooth, wavy, acute tip; culms branching
>>>>>   ST. AUGUSTINEGRASS (*Stenotaphrum secundatum*)

>>>>   **EE.** Ligule a ciliate membrane; collar hairy; blade margins ciliate; stolons thick, short-noded
>>>>>   CENTIPEDEGRASS (*Eremochloa ophiuroides*)

>>>   **DD.** Blades not petioled; sheaths compressed
>>>>   **E.**   Ligule a fringe of hairs
>>>>>   **F.**   Collar continuous, broad, hairy; leaves and sheaths very hairy; blades 4-5 mm wide, long acuminate tip, V-shaped; rhizomes and stolens present
>>>>>>   KIKUYUGRASS (*Pennisetum clandestinum*)

>>>>>   **FF.** Collar continuous, narrow, smooth, sparingly ciliate; sheaths and blades smooth or sparingly hairy
>>>>>>   **G.**   Blades 1.5-3 mm wide, flat, acuminate tip; scaly rhizomes and flat stolons present
>>>>>>>   BERMUDAGRASS (*Cynodon dactylon*)

>>>>>>   **GG.** Blades 4-8 mm wide, acute tip; rhizomes absent; nodes hairy, especially on stolons; stolons elongate with short internodes
>>>>>>>   CARPETGRASS (*Axonopus affinis*)

>>>>   **EE.** Ligule a very short, blunt membrane
>>>>>   **F.**   Blades 1 mm wide or less; margin of ligule irregular; stolons and rhizomes long, slender
>>>>>>   AFRICAN BERMUDAGRASS (*Cynodon transvaalensis*)

>>>>>   **FF.** Blades 4-8 mm wide; margin of ligule entire; stolons and rhizomes short, thick
>>>>>>   BAHIAGRASS (*Paspalum notatum*)
>>>>>>   Vernation variable, may also fall
>>>>>>   in group with leaves rolled

CC. Stolons absent
  D. Blades narrow, involute, bristlelike; prominent veins on upper surface
    E. Rhizomes present, forming dense sod; culms red, glossy at base; ligule medium short; extravaginal growth; blades smooth
    RED FESCUE (*Festuca rubra* var. *rubra*)
    EE. Rhizomes absent, forming spreading tufts
      F. Leaves bluish-green, 0.5-1.0 mm wide; culms erect, green or pink-tinged at base; ligule very short; intravaginal growth; sheath split
      SHEEP FESCUE (*Festuca ovina*)
      FF. Leaves bright green, 1-2 mm wide; culms red at base; sheath closed nearly to top
      CHEWINGS FESCUE (*Festuca rubra* var. *commutata*)
  DD. Blades V-shaped to flat; veins inconspicuous
    E. Blades with boat-shaped tip, transparent lines on either side of midrib
      F. Rhizomes usually absent, forming tufts
        G. Sheaths smooth, whitish at base; ligule long, acute tip; blades usually light green, parallel sided, wavy transversely; may spread by rooting at nodes
        ANNUAL BLUEGRASS (*Poa annua*)
        GG. Sheaths rough; ligule an acute, long membrane; blades light yellow-green, rough, acuminate tip, glossy below; thin stolons present
        ROUGH BLUEGRASS (*Poa trivialis*)
      FF. Rhizomes present, forming dense sod
        G. Blades acuminate, bluish-green; sheaths strongly compressed, keeled; rhizomes sparsely branched
        CANADA BLUEGRASS (*Poa compressa*)
        GG. Blades parallel sided; sheaths not strongly compressed or keeled
          H. Ligule short, very blunt membrane; sheaths smooth, somewhat keeled; rhizomes multibranched
          KENTUCKY BLUEGRASS (*Poa pratensis*)
    EE. Blades without boat-shaped tip, without transparent lines on either side of midvein
      F. Blades parallel sided with acute tip; prostrate growth habit; culms flattened; annual
      GOOSEGRASS (*Eleusine indica*)
      FF. Blades acuminate; upright growth habit; perennial
        G. Ligule a very blunt membrane; blades 4-10 mm wide, light green
        ORCHARDGRASS (*Dactylis glomerata*)
        GG. Ligule a fringe of hairs, fused at base; blades 2-4 mm wide, gray-green, flat to involute; sheaths overlapping
        SEASHORE SALTGRASS (*Distichlis spicata*)

AA. Leaf vernation rolled
  B. Auricles present
    C. Sheaths reddish at base; blades glossy below
      D. Margins of blades smooth; auricle long, clawlike; ligule short, blunt membrane; plants tufted
      ITALIAN RYEGRASS (*Lolium multiflorum*)
      DD. Margins of blades rough; auricle short; ligule a short, very blunt membrane; plants usually tufted
        E. Auricles generally without hairs or cilia on margins; blades flat, rough above
        MEADOW FESCUE (*Festuca pratensis*)
        EE. Auricles very small, generally with a few ciliate hairs; plants tufted
        TALL FESCUE (*Festuca arundinacea*)
    CC. Sheaths not reddish at base; blades not glossy below
      D. Rhizomes present, yellowish
        E. Blades flat, sparsely pilose above
        QUACKGRASS (*Agropyron repens*)

    EE. Blades flat, glaucous, blue-green, margins sharply toothed or barbed
            WESTERN WHEATGRASS (*Agropyron smithii*)

  DD. Rhizomes absent
   E. Auricles long, clawlike; collar divided
           CRESTED WHEATGRASS (*Agropyron cristatum*)

BB. Auricles absent
 C. Sheaths round
  D. Collar hairy, at least at base or on margins
   E. Sheaths not hairy
    F. Strongly stoloniferous
     G. Blades 2-4 mm wide; collar broad, continuous; strongly stoloniferous; ligule a fringe of hairs; leaf margin smooth
        JAPANESE LAWNGRASS (*Zoysia japonica*)

     GG. Blades 2-3 mm wide; collar only sparingly hairy; (otherwise same as *Z. japonica*)
        MANILAGRASS (*Zoysia matrella*)

    FF. Rhizomes short, stout, scaly; blades 1-2 mm wide; collar broad with hairy margins
        BLUE GRAMA (*Bouteloua gracilis*)

   EE. Sheaths and blades hairy
    F. Rhizomes present
        SIDEOATS GRAMA (*Bouteloua curtipendula*)

    FF. Rhizomes not present
        DOWNY BROMEGRASS (*Bromus tectorum*)

  DD. Collar not hairy
   E. Rhizomes and/or stolons present; perennial
    F. Ligule a fringe of hairs; collar broad, continuous
     G. Rhizomes present; blades smooth
        KOREAN VELVETGRASS (*Zoysia tenuifolia*)

     GG. Rhizomes absent; stolons well developed; blades sparsely pilose, 1-3 mm wide, curly, gray-green
        BUFFALOGRASS (*Buchloe dactyloides*)

    FF. Ligule membranous; collar narrow
     G. Sheaths closed to near top; ligule blunt, smooth on back; blades nearly smooth; rhizomes present
        SMOOTH BROME (*Bromus inermis*)

     GG. Sheaths split with overlapping margins; ligule acute, minutely hairy on back; blades flat with prominent veins on upper surface, acuminate tip
      H. Stolons absent or weak, forming tufts
       I. Blades 3-4 mm wide; ligule long; short rhizomes present
         REDTOP (*Agrostis alba*)

       II. Blades 1-3 mm wide; ligule medium short
        COLONIAL BENTGRASS (*Agrostis tenuis*)

      HH. Stolons well developed, not forming tufts
       I. Blades short, narrow, 1 mm wide; ligule short
        VELVET BENTGRASS (*Agrostis canina*)

       II. Blades 2-3 mm wide; ligule medium in length; stolons quite long
        CREEPING BENTGRASS (*Agrostis palustris*)

      HHH. Rhizomes hard, scaly, stout, deep, extensive
       I. Ligule 1-3 mm long
        AMERICAN BEACHGRASS (*Ammophila breviligulata*)

    EE. Rhizomes absent, plants tufted; annual or perennial
        F. Sheaths white with pink veins, smooth; annual

CHESS (*Bromus secalinus*)

        FF. Sheaths without pink veins, open
            G. Base of culms bulbous; ligule long, notched near front on each side; perennial

TIMOTHY (*Phleum pratense*)

            GG. Base of culms not bulbous; annual; decumbent-spreading, sometimes rooting at lower nodes
                H. Sheaths hairy, pilose; purplish; blades usually hairy below

LARGE CRABGRASS (*Digitaria sanguinalis*)

                HH. Sheaths smooth, bluish or purplish; blades smooth below

SMOOTH CRABGRASS (*Digitaria ischaemum*)

CC. Sheaths flattened
  D. Sheaths smooth
    E. Rhizomes present, scaly; tall, coarse perennial

JOHNSONGRASS (*Sorghum halepense*)

    EE. Rhizomes absent; annual
        F. Ligule absent

BARNYARDGRASS (*Echinochloa crusgalli*)

        FF. Ligule present, a fringe of hairs; sheath keeled

YELLOW FOXTAIL (*Setaria glauca*)

DD. Sheaths hairy
  E. Ligule membranous
    F. Sheaths white with pink veins
        G. Ligule margin even; back of ligule hairy; blades smooth to sparsely pilose

RESCUEGRASS (*Bromus willdenowii*)

        GG. Ligule margin notched, not hairy on back; plants grayish, velvety hairs

VELVETGRASS (*Holcus lanatus*)

    FF. Sheaths light green, often tinged with red
        G. Stolons present; blades hairy
            H. Ligule a long, blunt membrane; stolons long with hairy nodes

KNOTGRASS (*Paspalum distichum*)

            HH. Ligule a short, very blunt membrane; short, thick rhizomes and stolons present

BAHIAGRASS (*Paspalum notatum*)

        GG. Stolons absent, tufted; blades smooth; ligule a long, notched membrane

DALLISGRASS (*Paspalum dilatatum*)

  EE. Ligule a fringe of hairs; rhizomes absent
    F. Sheaths hairy; blades flat

GREEN FOXTAIL (*Setaria viridis*)

    FF. Sheaths smooth; blades flat

STINKGRASS (*Eragrostis cilianensis*)

ILLUSTRATED GUIDE OF THE COMMON TURFGRASS SPECIES AND THEIR IDENTIFYING CHARACTERISTICS

BAHIAGRASS

Paspalum notatum **Flugge.**

Vernation rolled or folded; *sheaths* flattened, sometimes hairy, keeled, overlapping; *ligule* membranous, 1 mm long, very blunt, entire; *collar* broad; *auricles* absent; *leaf blades* flat to folded, 4-8 mm wide, crowded at base, margins ciliate toward base; *stems* erect to ascending with short, stout, flattened rhizomes and stolons; *inflorescence* two to three suberect racemes; spikelets solitary.

BENTGRASS, COLONIAL

Agrostis tenuis **Sibth.**

Vernation rolled; *sheaths* round, smooth, split with overlapping hyaline margins; *ligule* membranous, 0.4-1.2 mm long, very blunt; *collar* conspicuous, narrow to medium broad, may be divided, smooth, light green; *auricles* absent; *leaf blades* flat, 1-3 mm wide, moderately rough above and on margins, prominent veins above, acuminate tip; *stems* erect, slender, tufted, stolons or rhizomes absent to weak and short; *inflorescence* open, loose, delicate, oblong to egg-shaped panicle, branches slender and clustered.

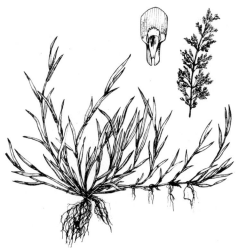

BENTGRASS, CREEPING

Agrostis palustris Huds.

Vernation rolled; *sheaths* round, smooth, split with overlapping hyaline margins; *ligule* membranous, 1-2 mm long, acute to oblong, may be notched; *collar* narrow to medium broad; *auricles* absent; *leaf blades* flat, 2-3 mm wide, smooth to minutely rough above, below, and on margins, prominent veins above, acuminate tip; *stems* erect or ascending from a spreading decumbent base, long, slender stolons rooting at nodes; *inflorescence* narrow, dense, contracted, pale purple panicle, branches clustered.

BENTGRASS, VELVET

Agrostis canina L.

Vernation rolled; *sheaths* round, smooth, split with overlapping hyaline margins; *ligule* membranous, 0.4-0.8 mm long, acute to oblong; *collar* medium broad; *auricles* absent; *leaf blades* less than 1 mm wide, flat, soft, smooth, veins prominent above, margins rough and hyaline, acuminate tip; *stems* erect, often tufted, decumbent at base with creeping, scaly stolons; *inflorescence* reddish, pyramidal-oblong, copiously flowered panicle, branches open at anthesis, sometimes contracting later.

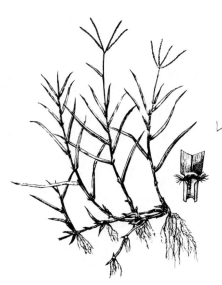

BERMUDAGRASS

Cynodon L. spp.

Vernation folded; *sheaths* flattened, loose, sparsely hairy, tufted hairs at throat, split with overlapping hyaline margins; *ligule* a fringe of white hairs, 1-3 mm long; *collar* continuous, narrow to medium broad, smooth, sparingly ciliate; *auricles* absent; *leaf blades* mostly flat, 1.5-3 mm wide, stiff, sparsely hairy above, usually smooth below, margins rough, tapering from base to acute tip; *stems* flattened, erect or ascending from a prostrate base, extensively creeping, strong, flat stolons and/or scaly, stout rhizomes that branch profusely and root at nodes; *inflorescence* four or five fingerlike spikes; spikelets sessile, closely appressed in two rows on a narrow, somewhat triangular rachis.

BLUE GRAMA

Bouteloua gracilis (H.B.K.) Lag. ex Steud.

Vernation rolled; *sheaths* round, smooth, split hyaline margins; *ligule* a fringe of hairs, 0.1-0.5 mm long, very blunt; *collar* medium broad, continuous, hairy margins; *auricles* absent; *leaf blades* flat or loosely involute, 1-2 mm wide, soft, hairy, rough above, acuminate tip, margins toothed; *stems* round, erect with stout, short, scaly rhizomes; *inflorescence* usually two spikes, sometimes one to three, on an erect culm, spike 2-5 cm long, spreading at maturity, rachis does not project beyond the spikelets.

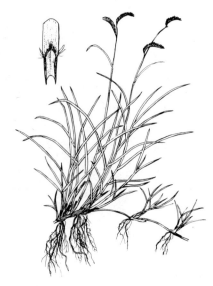

BLUEGRASS, KENTUCKY

Poa pratensis L.

Vernation folded; *sheaths* slightly flattened, smooth, somewhat keeled, split with overlapping hyaline margins; *ligule* membranous, 0.2-1 mm long, very blunt; *collar* medium broad, divided, smooth, yellowish-green; *auricles* absent; *leaf blades* V-shaped to flat, 2-4 mm wide, soft, usually smooth, keeled below, parallel sided, abruptly boat-shaped tip, transparent lines on each side of midrib, finely rough margins; *stems* slightly flattened, erect, relatively slender with long, slender, multi-branched rhizomes; *inflorescence* erect, open, pyramidal panicle with slender, spreading lower branches usually occurring in whorls of five.

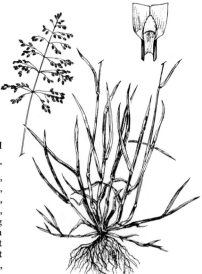

BLUEGRASS, ROUGH

Poa trivialis L.

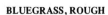

Vernation folded; *sheaths* flattened, retrorsely rough, keeled below, frequently purplish, split part way; *ligule* membranous, 4-6 mm long, acute, entire or sometimes ciliate; *collar* conspicuous, broad, smooth, divided; *auricles* absent; *leaf blades* flat or V-shaped, 1-4 mm wide, yellowish-green, soft, glossy, keeled below, strongly rough, tapering from base to narrowly boat-shaped tip, transparent lines on each side of midrib, margins rough; *stems* flattened, erect to somewhat decumbent at base with creeping, thin, leafy stolons rooting at nodes; *inflorescence* erect, oblong, open panicle with slender, spreading branches occurring in whorls of about five.

Illustrated Turfgrass Guide/*Continued*

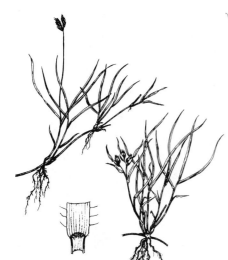

BUFFALOGRASS

Buchloe dactyloides (Nutt.) Engelm.

Vernation rolled; *sheaths* round, open, smooth; *ligule* a fringe of hairs, 0.5-1.0 mm long; *collar* broad, continuous, smooth; *auricles* absent; *leaf blades* flat, 1-3 mm wide, wavy, sparsely pilose, gray-green, margins rough; *stems* erect, round with well-developed stolons; *inflorescence* involves male and female flowers usually on separate plants; pistillate spikelets in clusters of four or five occur in sessile heads, partly hidden among leaves; staminate inflorescences have two or three short spikes on slender, erect culms, elevated above the leaves.

CARPETGRASS

Axonopus affinis Beauv.

Vernation folded; *sheaths* flattened, smooth; *ligule* short, fringe of hairs fused at base, about 1 mm long; *collar* continuous, narrow, smooth to sparingly hairy; *auricles* absent; *leaf blades* 4-8 mm wide, smooth or sparsely ciliate at base, margins ciliate toward tip; *stems* flattened, stout with elongated, branching stolons having short internodes, nodes densely hairy and leafy; *inflorescence* two to five racemes, usually three, on a long, slender, cylindrical seed stalk; spikelets sparsely pilose.

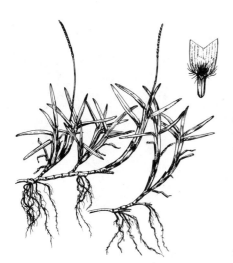

CENTIPEDEGRASS

Eremochloa Ophiuroides (Munro.) Hack.

Vernation folded; *sheaths* very flattened, fused-keel, conspicuously hyaline, smooth, grayish tufted hairs at throat, margins overlapping; *ligule* short membrane with short cilia longer than the purplish membrane, total about 0.5 mm; *collar* continuous, broad, constricted by fused keel, hairy, ciliate, tufted at lower edge; *auricles* absent; *leaf blades* flattened, 3-5 mm wide, blunt, keeled, ciliate with margins papillose toward base, smooth underside; *stems* erect to ascending, flattened with thick, leafy, short-noded, opposite-branched stolons; *inflorescence* spikelike racemes, smooth, subcylindric, terminal, axillary on slender peduncles.

FESCUE, CHEWINGS

Festuca rubra var. *commutata* Gaud.

Vernation folded; *sheaths* distinctly flattened, smooth or very short hairs, soon splitting, lower sheaths red at base; *ligule* membranous, 0.2-0.4 mm long; *collar* broad; *auricles* absent; *leaf blades* folded or involute, 1-2 mm wide, bristlelike, smooth, stiff to rigid, bluntly keeled, acuminate tip, smooth margins, *stems* oval, distinctly erect, mostly intravaginal growth; *inflorescence* erect, linear to arrow-shaped, narrow, contracted panicle.

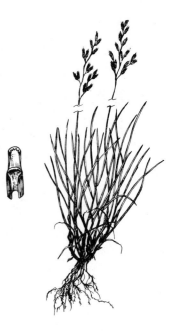

FESCUE, MEADOW

Festuca pratensis L.

Vernation rolled; *sheaths* round, smooth, split with overlapping hyaline margins, reddish at base; *ligule* membranous, 0.2-0.6 mm wide, very blunt, whitish-green; *collar* continuous, broad, smooth, pale yellow to yellow-green, thickened, frequently wavy; *auricles* small, blunt; *leaf blades* flat, 3-8 mm wide, smooth to rough and dull above, smooth and glossy below, veins prominent above, acuminate tip, rough margins; *stems* erect, tufted, occasional short, stout rhizomes; *inflorescence* erect or nodding, slender, somewhat contracted panicle.

 FESCUE, RED

Festuca rubra var. *rubra* L.

Vernation folded; *sheaths* oval to round, smooth to finely hairy, veins prominent, lower sheaths reddish, glossy, thin, disintegrating with age, open part-way; *ligule* membranous, 0.2-0.5 mm long, very blunt; *collar* narrow, indistinct, smooth; *auricles* absent or merely enlarged margins; *leaf blades* folded or involute, 0.5-1.5 mm wide, usually bristlelike, deeply ridged above, blunt keel, smooth, acute tip, margins smooth; *stems* oval to round, erect to ascending from a decumbent base, extravaginal growth, slender creeping rhizomes; *inflorescence* narrow, arrow-shaped, contracted panicle, branches rough, usually in pairs, unequal, reddish when ripe.

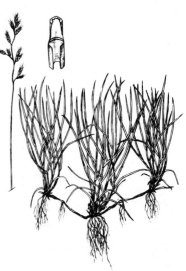

Illustrated Turfgrass Guide/*Continued*

FESCUE, SHEEP

Festuca ovina L.

Vernation folded; *sheaths* round, smooth, short, hairy, dull, split with overlapping margins; *ligule* membranous, 0.5 mm long, sometimes absent, very blunt; *collar* narrow, indistinct, smooth; *auricles* absent or merely enlarged at margins; *leaf blades* strongly folded or involute, 0.5-1 mm wide, firm, bristlelike, deeply ridged above, smooth below, grayish to bluish-green, acute tip, margins smooth; *stems* erect to ascending, tufted, rounded, stiff, intravaginal growth; *inflorescence* narrow, contracted panicle, sometimes almost spikelike, branches ascending.

FESCUE, TALL

Festuca arundinacea Schreb.

Vernation rolled; *sheaths* round, smooth, or occasionally rough, split with overlapping hyaline margins, reddish at base; *ligule* membranous, 0.2-0.8 mm wide, very blunt; *collar* conspicuous, broad, divided, usually hairy on margins, yellow-green; *auricles* small, narrow, celia present; *leaf blades* flat, stiff, 5-10 mm wide, rough above at least near tip, dull with veins prominent above, glossy keeled and smooth below at least at base, midrib prominent, acuminate tip, margins rough and hyaline; *stems* round, erect, stout, tufted; *inflorescence* erect or nodding, arrow to egg-shaped, somewhat contracted panicle, axis and branches rough; spikelets four to five flowered.

JAPANESE LAWNGRASS

Zoysia japonica Steud.

Vernation rolled; *sheaths* round to somewhat flattened, smooth with tufted hairs at throat, split with overlapping hyaline margins; *ligule* a fringe of hairs, 0.2 mm long; *collar* broad, continuous, hairy at least on margins; *auricles* absent; *leaf blades* flat, 2-4 mm wide, stiff, sparsely hairy above near base, smooth below, margins smooth; *stems* round, erect to ascending from a decumbent base, strongly stoloniferous and somewhat rhizomatous; *inflorescence* short, terminal, spikelike raceme; spikelets laterally flattened against slender rachis.

KIKUYUGRASS

Pennisetum clandestinum Hochst ex. Chiov.

Vernation folded; *sheaths* distinctly flattened, very hairy; *ligule* a fringe of hairs; *collar* continuous, hairy, broad; *auricles* absent; *leaf blades* 4-5 mm wide, elongated, hairy, ciliate margins, acuminate tip; *stems* leafy, very thick rhizomes and stolons; *inflorescence* two to four spikelets almost entirely enclosed in upper sheath of short culms, only stamens visible.

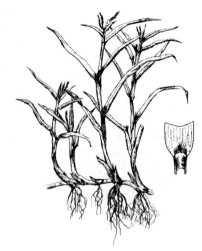

MANILAGRASS

Zoysia matrella (L.) Merr.

Vernation rolled; *sheaths* round or somewhat flattened, smooth, tufted hairs at throat, split with overlapping margins; *ligule* a fringe of hairs, 0.2 mm long; *collar* broad, continuous, hairy at least at base, margins hairy; *auricles* absent; *leaf blades* 2-3 mm wide, stiff, hairy above, especially near base, smooth below, acute tip, margins smooth; *stems* round, erect to ascending from a decumbent base, strongly stoloniferous and somewhat rhizomatous, rooting at nodes; *inflorescence* short, terminal spikelike raceme; spikelets laterally flattened against slender rachis.

RYEGRASS, ITALIAN

Lolium multiflorum Lam.

Vernation rolled; *sheaths* round, smooth, lower sheaths yellowish-green to reddish at base, split with tightly overlapping hyaline margins; *ligule* membranous, 1-2 mm long, blunt, entire; *collar* broad, may be divided; *auricles* prominent, narrow, clawlike; *leaf blades* flat, 3-7 mm wide, smooth, dull above, glossy below, veins prominent, acuminate tip, margins smooth and hyaline; *stems* round, erect to somewhat spreading, tufted; *inflorescence* erect, long narrow flat spike; awned spikelets positioned edgewise to rachis, alternating in two rows.

Illustrated Turfgrass Guide/*Continued*

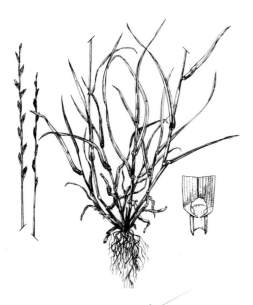

RYEGRASS, PERENNIAL

Lolium perenne L.

Vernation folded; *sheaths* somewhat flattened, smooth, loose, lower sheaths reddish at base, split with overlapping margins; *ligule* membranous, 0.5-1.5 mm long, very blunt; *collar* conspicuous, narrow to medium broad, divided, smooth; *auricles* small to moderate size, clawlike, soft; *leaf blades* flat, 2-5 mm wide, smooth, glossy below, dull with prominent veins above, keeled, acute tip, margins usually rough; *stems* flattened, erect to somewhat decumbent at base, tufted; *inflorescence* erect, long, narrow, flat spike; awnless spikelets positioned edgewise to rachis.

ST. AUGUSTINEGRASS

Stenotaphrum secundatum (Walt.) Kuntze

Vernation folded; *sheaths* flattened, keeled, loose, slightly ciliate toward tip and along margins; *ligule* inconspicuous fringe of hairs 0.3 mm long; *collar* continuous, extending through a petioled area, broad, smooth; *auricles* absent; *leaf blades* usually flat, petioled, 4-10 mm wide, smooth, wavy, bluntly acute tip; *stems* flattened, branching with extremely long, stout, creeping stolons having swollen nodes, short internodes, leaves clustered at each node; *inflorescence* short flowering culm bearing terminal and auxillary racemes.

WHEATGRASS, CRESTED

Agropyron cristatum (L.) Gaertn.

Vernation rolled; *sheaths* nearly round, smooth, veins separate, open; *ligule* membranous, 0.5-1.5 mm long, blunt, short ciliate margin; *collar* medium narrow, distinct, divided; *auricles* clawlike; *leaf blades* nearly flat, 2-5 mm wide, hairy, veins prominent above, midrib prominent below, smooth above, acuminate tip, margins weakly rough; *stems* round, erect to somewhat decumbent at base; *inflorescence* a spike; spikelets widely spreading.

Table A-1. Cool-Season Turfgrass Species Characterization

Species	Description				Environmental Adaptation				Soil Adaptation				Establishment				Cultural Requirements					Diseases
	Leaf Texture	Growth Habit	Polystand Compatibility	Wear Tolerance	Heat Hardiness	Cold Hardiness	Drought Resistance	Shade Adaptation	pH	Fertility	Moisture	Salinity	Establishment Method	Establishment Rate	Sod Formation Potential	Recuperative Potential	Cultural Intensity	Cutting Height (in.)	Nitrogen Requirement†	Irrigation Need	Dethatching Need	
Bentgrass:																						
Colonial	M	B	M	P	M	G	F	M	5.5–6.7	M	F	M	S	P	M	M	M	0.4–1.0	0.5–1.0	H		Dollar spot, brown patch, Helminthosporium diseases, Fusarium patch, Takeall patch, Pythium blight, red thread, Typhula blight
Creeping	M	St	P	P	M	E	P	G	5.5–6.5	H	G		S/V	P	G	H	H	0.2–0.8	0.5–1.4	H		
Velvet	Fi	St	P	P	M	G	P	E	5.0–6.0	M	F		S/V	P	G	H	H	0.2–0.5	0.5–1.0	H		
Bluegrass:																						
Annual	M	B-St	M	P	P	P	P	G	5.5–6.5	H	W	P	S	G	P	H	H	0.2–1.0	0.5–1.0	M		Same as bentgrasses
Kentucky	M	R	G	M	P	M	M	P	6.0–7.0	M	M	P	S/V	M	E	G	M	0.6–2.0*	0.4–1.0	M	M	Helminthosporium diseases, rust, stripe smut, Fusarium blight, powdery mildew
Rough	M	St	M	P	P	E	P	G	6.0–7.0	W	P	P	S	E	M	M	M	0.5–1.5*	0.5–1.0	H	L	
Fescue:																						
Chewings	Fi	B	G	M	F	G	G	E	5.5–6.5	L	L	P	S	M	M	L	L	0.7–2.5*	0.2–0.5	M		Helminthosporium diseases, red thread
Meadow	M	B	M	F	F	M	G	G	5.0–8.0	M	W	M	S	M	M	M	M	1.3–2.5	0.4–1.0	L		
Red	Fi	R	G	M	F	G	G	E	5.5–6.5	L	L	P	S	G	M	L	L	0.7–2.5*	0.2–0.5	M		
Sheep/hard	Fi	B	M	F	F	G	E	E	5.5–6.5	L	L	P	S	P	P	L	L	0.7–2.5	0.1–0.3	L		
Tall	C	B	G	G	G	M	G	M	4.7–8.5	M	M	M	S	E	P	M	M	1.7–2.5	0.4–1.0	L		Helminthosporium diseases, brown patch, Fusarium patch, Typhula blight
Ryegrass:																						
Italian	C	B	P	M	P	F	F	M	6.0–7.0	M	M	M	S	E	P	M	M	1.5–2.0	0.4–1.0	M		Pythium blight, rust, Fusarium patch, brown patch, Typhula blight, red thread
Perennial	M	B	M	G	F	F	E	F	6.0–7.0	M	M	M	S	E	P	M	M	0.5–1.5*	0.4–1.0	M		
Wheatgrass:																						
Crested	M	B	M	M	F	G	E	F	6.0–8.0	L	L	G	S	G	P	L	L	1.5–2.5	0.2–0.7	N		

SOURCE: Adapted from Beard, J. B. 1975. *How to Have a Beautiful Lawn*. Beard Books, College Station, Tex. For a more detailed discussion, see also Beard, J. B. 1973. *Turfgrass: Science and Culture*. Prentice-Hall, Englewood Cliffs, N.J.

Key

B	bunch	E	excellent	Fi	fine	H	high
C	coarse	F	fair	G	good	L	low
						M	medium
						N	none

P	poor	S	seeded	S/V	seeded or vegetative
R	rhizome	St	stolons	W	wet

*Certain cultivars can be mowed at 0.25 in. when used in winter overseeding greens.

†Pounds of nitrogen per 1,000 sq. ft. per growing month.

Table A-2. Warm-Season Turfgrass Species Characterization

Species	Description						Environmental Adaptation			Soil Adaptation			Establishment				Cultural Requirements					Major Pest Problems	
	Leaf Texture	Growth Habit	Polystand Compatibility	Wear Tolerance	Heat Hardiness	Cold Hardiness	Drought Adaptation	Shade Adaptation	pH	Fertility	Moisture	Salinity	Establishment Method	Establishment Rate	Sod Formation	Recuperative Potential	Cultural Intensity	Cutting Height (in.)	Nitrogen Requirement*	Irrigation Need	Dethatching Need	Diseases	Insects
Bahiagrass	C	B	M	G	E	E	E	M	6.5 - 7.5	L	L	P	S	M	M	P	L	1.5 - 2.5	0.1 - 0.4	L	L	Dollar spot, brown patch	Mole cricket
Bermudagrass: Common	M	R-St	M	G	E	E	P	P	5.5 - 7.5	H	L	G	S	G	M	G	M	0.5 - 1.5	0.5 - 1.0	M	L	Spring dead spot, dollar spot, brown patch, Fusarium patch, Pythium blight	Bermudagrass mite, armyworm, sod webworm, mole cricket
Improved	Fi	R-St	P	E	E	E	P	P	5.5 - 7.5	H	L	G	V	E	E	E	H	0.2 - 1.0	0.8 - 1.3	L	H		
Buffalograss	Fi	St	P	M	E	F	E	P	6.0 - 7.5	L	L	M	S/V	M	G	L	G	0.7 - 1.2	0.1 - 0.4	L	L		
Carpetgrass	C	St	P	P	E	P	G	G	4.5 - 5.5	L	W	P	S/V	M	F	L	M	1.0 - 2.0	0.2 - 0.4	M	L	Brown patch	
Centipedegrass	C	St	P	P	E	P	G	G	4.5 - 5.5	L	M	P	S/V	G	P	L	M	1.0 - 2.0	0.1 - 0.3	M	M	Brown patch, dollar spot	Ground pearls
Grama, blue	Fi	R	M	F	G	F	F	F	6.5 - 8.5	L	L	F	S	G	F	F	L	2.0 - 2.5	0.1 - 0.3	L	N		
Kikuyugrass	M	R-St	P	G	E	G	M	G	5.5 - 7.5	H	M	G	S/V	G	G	E	G	0.3 - 1.5	0.5 - 1.0	M	H	Helminthosporium diseases	
St. Augustinegrass	C	St	P	M	E	F	E	E	6.5 - 7.5	H	H	G	V	G	G	M	E	1.5 - 2.5	0.5 - 1.0	H	H	Brown patch, gray leaf spot, dollar spot, SAD, downy mildew	Chinch bug
Zoysiagrass: Japanese lawngrass	M	R-St	P	E	E	E	G	G	5.0 - 7.8	M	L	G	V	P	E	M	E	0.3 - 1.0	0.5 - 0.8	L	H	Rust, brown patch, dollar spot	Hunting billbug, sod webworm, armyworm
Manilagrass	F	R-St	P	E	E	E	G	G	5.0 - 7.8	M	L	G	V	P	E	M	E	0.3 - 1.0	0.5 - 0.8	L	H		

SOURCE: Adapted from Beard, J. B. 1975. *How to Have a Beautiful Lawn.* Beard Books, College Station, Tex. For a more detailed discussion, see also Beard, J. B. 1973. *Turfgrass: Science and Culture.* Prentice-Hall, Englewood Cliffs, N.J.

Key

B bunch	E excellent	Fi fine	H high
C coarse	F fair	G good	L low
M medium	P poor	S seeded	S/V seeded or vegetative
N none	R rhizome	St stolons	W wet

*Pounds of nitrogen per 1,000 sq. ft. per growing month.

TURFGRASS SEED IDENTIFICATION

Knowledge of the basic structural components of a grass seed are needed for successful seed identification. A seed is essentially a ripened floret. Its structures include the caryopsis, lemma, palea, and rachilla. The caryopsis is the fruit of the grass, which is enclosed in two chaffy bracts. The lower outer bract is the *lemma*, and the upper inner bract is the *palea* (Fig. A-3). The bristlelike extension of nerves from the tip of the lemma is the *awn*. In some cases, the awn originates from the middle to basal portion of the lemma, as in the bentgrasses. A swollen projection at the base of the lemma of some seeds is the *callus*. The final structure is the *rachilla*, which is a small stalklike segment that frequently remains attached to the base of a seed. These six structures vary in size, shape, texture, color, veination, thickness, hardness, and/or amount of hairs present, which in turn can be used in seed identification.

A number of representative seeds should be sampled for examination and eventual identification. Grass seeds vary significantly in size, depending on species, which causes stratification as the containers are handled. Thus, it is important for the seed lot to be well mixed and the sample drawn from random locations within the container rather than from the immediate surface.

Seed size is a major distinguishing characteristic of grass seeds and is the initial variable utilized in seed identification, as shown in the accompanying key. However, size can also vary somewhat depending on the environmental conditions under which seeds are grown.

All seeds are processed through a combine plus a series of mechanical seed cleaning and processing machines. As a result, certain structures used in identification can be damaged. The awns are especially prone to being broken off. Thus, it is important that a number of seeds be inspected during the identification process. Most of the common turfgrass seeds can be readily identified, with a few exceptions. Identification is difficult within genera such as the *Agrostis, Poa,* and fine-leafed species of *Festuca* and frequently requires the expertise of a trained seed analyst.

Seed Identification Key for the Common Turfgrasses

I. Very small seeds, 2.5 mm or less long (excluding awn); lemma and palea may or may not remain with caryopsis

    A. Awns usually present

        B. Palea minute; caryopsis soft; awns long, twisted, bent abruptly, arising from middle of lemma or lower; lemma finely granular, thin, transparent, 1.5-2.0 mm long, less than 0.5 mm wide; basal hairs short, stubby

                                VELVET BENTGRASS (*Agrostis canina*)

        BB. Palea thin, from one-half to three-fourths the length of lemma; caryopsis hard; awns numerous, twisted, arising from near base to about middle of lemma; lemma five-nerved, 1.7-2 mm long, 0.5 mm wide; basal hairs short, numerous

                                COLONIAL BENTGRASS (*Agrostis tenuis*)

    AA. Awns usually absent

        B. Seeds arrow- to egg-shaped; narrow, pointed tip

            C. Lemma keeled on the back above the callus, predominately five-nerved, 1.7-2 mm long, 0.5 mm wide; palea loose, broad, abruptly narrowed to a shoulderlike tip; basal hairs mostly short, stubby

                                CREEPING BENTGRASS (*Agrostis palustris*)

            CC. Lemma rounded or slightly flattened on back, tip three- to four-nerved, 2-2.5 mm long, 0.5 mm wide; palea tip very blunt or with broad, shallow notch

                                REDTOP (*Agrostis alba*)

        BB. Seeds boat-shaped to oblong

            C. Lemma with palea, hairy distinct keel, laterally compressed, firm, three-nerved, 1.5-2 mm long, lateral nerves close to margins, awnless; palea narrow, two-nerved, as long as the lemma; acute tip

                                BERMUDAGRASS (*Cynodon dactylon*)

            CC. Lemma without palea, faint keel, hard, margins slightly inrolled, smooth, 2-2.5 mm long; obtuse tip

                                CARPETGRASS (*Axonopus affinis*)

        BBB. Seeds broadly elliptic-oblong

            C. Lemma very broad, very blunt, membranous, five- to seven-nerved, 1.5-2.5 mm long, 0.8 mm wide; palea nearly as long as lemma, silvery white; grain plump, not grooved; awns absent

                                TIMOTHY (*Phleum pratense*)

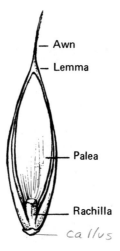

Figure A-3. Structures of the seed commonly used to identify grass seeds.

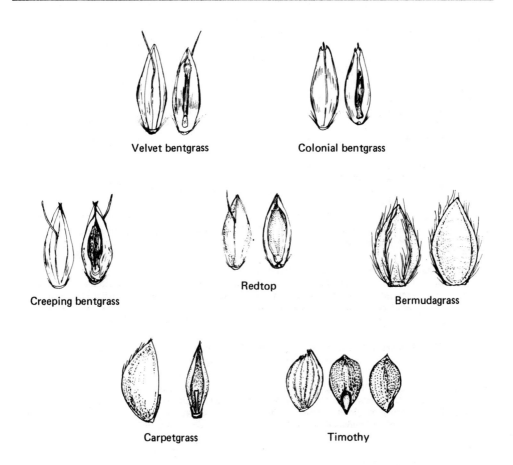

II. Small seeds, 2.5 to 4 mm long (exclusive of awn)
    A.   Single floret with glumes absent; lemma five-nerved, keeled along a heavy midnerve, 2.5-3 mm long; awns absent; pointed tip
        B.   Lemma usually hairy on the nerves with lower half long, silky; rachilla smooth, round
            C.   Hairs on keel of palea long, dense; no basal web; rachilla prominent, smooth
                                                  ANNUAL BLUEGRASS (*Poa annua*)
            CC. Hairs on keel of palea short, coarse, wide-spaced, do not extend to tip; basal web long, copious
                                          KENTUCKY BLUEGRASS (*Poa pratensis*)
        BB. Lemma usually not hairy, smooth or very finely granular; basal web short, scant; hairs on keel of palea short, fine, close-spaced, extending to tip
            C.   Tip folded; intermediate nerves distinct at base
                                          ROUGH BLUEGRASS (*Poa trivialis*)
            CC. Tip flares out; intermediate nerves obscure or lacking on lower half; rachilla round, smooth, prominent
                                        CANADA BLUEGRASS (*Poa compressa*)
    AA. One-flowered spikelet with first glume absent
        B.   Plano convex; papery glumes not persisting; fertile lemma strongly convex on back, oval, smooth, glossy, three-nerved, often slightly wrinkled transversely; 3-3.5 mm long, 2.75-3 mm wide
                                          BAHIAGRASS (*Paspalum notatum*)
        BB. Laterally compressed; glumes hard, stiff, smooth, short awned, completely enfolding a thin lemma and palea; palea thin, sometimes lacking; caryopsis may be hulled or unhulled with enfolding, hardened second glume present
            C.   Seeds narrowly lance-shaped, 3-3.5 mm long, 1 mm wide; bright yellowish straw color
                                        MANILAGRASS (*Zoysia matrella*)
            CC. Seeds broadly egg-shaped, short-pointed tip, 3.5-4 mm long, 1.5 mm wide; dull brownish with purplish tinge
                                    JAPANESE LAWNGRASS (*Zoysia japonica*)
  AAA. Spikelet with first glume winged at tip
        B.   Dorsally compressed; lemma very broad, very blunt, 2.5-3.5 mm long; awns absent
                            CENTIPEDEGRASS (*Eremochloa ophiuroides*)

III. Medium-sized seeds, 4 to 6 mm long (exclusive of awn)
    A.   Awns present, usually less than 1.5 mm long
        B.   Lemma 4 mm long, 0.5 mm wide, smooth or sparingly hairy at the callus and along the sharply keeled back
                                      BLUE GRAMA (*Bouteloua gracilis*)
        BB. Lemma 4-5 mm long, 1-1.5 mm wide, usually with short hairs at top and margin; awns mostly one-fifth the length of lemma
                                      SHEEP FESCUE (*Festuca ovina*)
    AA. Awns present, fine, more than 1.5 mm long
        B.   Lemma rounded on back, narrowly elliptic or oblong, 4-6 mm long, 1-1.5 mm wide, rough in upper portion; lemma smooth or sparingly rough; awns one-fifth to one-half the length of lemma; rachilla round with enlarged, flat tip
                                RED FESCUE (*Festuca rubra* var. *rubra*)
                       or CHEWINGS FESCUE (*Festuca rubra* var. *commutata*)
        BB. Lemma keeled, lance-shaped, 5-6 mm long, 1 mm wide; hairs on keel of palea short, stout, wide-spaced; awns one-third to one-half the length of lemma
                            CRESTED WHEATGRASS (*Agropyron cristatum*)
  AAA. Awns absent; pistillate spikelets occur in hard, whitish burrlike clusters of two to four surrounded by thick, hard, overlapping second glumes, each of which terminates in three rigid, acuminate lobes
        B.   Lemma of pistillate spikelet (hulled seed) membranous, 2.5-3 mm long, ovate, firm, dorsally compressed, broad below, three-nerved, usually glabrous; palea broad, obtuse, about as long as the body of lemma
                                BUFFALOGRASS (*Buchloe dactyloides*)

Annual bluegrass

Kentucky bluegrass

Rough bluegrass

Canada bluegrass

Bahiagrass

Manilagrass

Japanese lawngrass

Centipedegrass

Blue grama

Sheep fescue

Red fescue

Chewings fescue

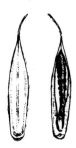

Crested wheatgrass

Buffalograss

IV. Large seeds, 6 to 9 mm long (exclusive of awn)
  A. Awns usually present
    B. Lemma long-pointed, elliptic or narrowly arrow-shaped, coarsely granular, rough on nerves, especially toward tip, rounded on back, acuminate tip; palea coarsely granular; awns 1-4 mm long; rachilla cylindrical, slender, tip expanded into a disc; callus wide (vertically), thick, heavy

TALL FESCUE (*Festuca arundinacea*)

    BB. Lemma narrowly oblong, 6.5-7 mm long, coarsely granular, wrinkled, somewhat flat at tip; palea smooth, lustrous toward tip; rachilla flat, wide, sides slightly bulged out at tip, tip not expanded into a disc; callus narrow (vertically) with a fine, clearcut rim; caryopsis may be curved backward

ITALIAN RYEGRASS (*Lolium multiflorum*)

  AA. Awns absent
    B. Lemma short-pointed, elliptic or narrowly arrow-shaped, 6-7 mm long, smooth, rounded tip; palea smooth, lustrous toward tip; rachilla cylindrical, slender, tip expanded into a disc; callus wide (vertically), thick, heavy

MEADOW FESCUE (*Festuca pratensis*)

    BB. Lemma narrowly oblong, 6-6.5 mm long, coarsely granular, somewhat flat, rounded at tip; palea smooth, lustrous toward tip; rachilla flat, wide with sides slightly bulged out at tip, tip not expanded into a disc; callus narrow (vertically) with a fine, clearcut rim

PERENNIAL RYEGRASS (*Lolium perenne*)

Tall fescue

Italian ryegrass

Meadow fescue

Perennial ryegrass

Appendix B

Seeding and Planting Guidelines

Table B-1. Turfgrass Seeding Guidelines for Golf Courses

Turfgrass Common Name	Approximate* Number of Seeds per Pound	Minimum Seed Purity (%)†	Minimum Seed Germination (%)†	Tee, Fairway, and Rough Seeding Rate‡		Optimum Seed Germination Temperatures§	
				Pounds per Acre	Kilograms per Hectare	°F	°C
Bahiagrass	272,400	70 - 75	70 - 75	160 - 320	180 - 360	86 - 95	30 - 35
Bentgrass:							
Colonial	8,720,000	95 - 98	85 - 90	20 - 45	22 - 50	59 - 86	15 - 30
Creeping	6,135,810	95 - 98	85 - 90	20 - 45	22 - 50	59 - 86	15 - 30
Velvet	11,800,000	90 - 95	85 - 90	15 - 30	17 - 34	68 - 86	20 - 30
Bermudagrass (hulled)	2,072,510	90 - 98	80 - 85	40 - 65	45 - 73	68 - 95	20 - 35
Bluegrass:							
Kentucky	1,391,510	90 - 95	75 - 80	45 - 65	50 - 73	59 - 86	15 - 30
Rough	2,092,940	90 - 95	80 - 85	45 - 65	50 - 73	⋯	⋯
Buffalograss	38,900	85 - 90	60 - 70	45 - 80	50 - 90	68 - 95	20 - 35
Carpetgrass	1,123,000	90 - 95	85 - 90	65 - 90	73 - 100	68 - 95	20 - 35
Centipedegrass	874,759	45 - 50	65 - 70	20 - 35	22 - 40	68 - 95	20 - 35
Fescue:							
Chewings	408,600	95 - 97	80 - 85	150 - 200	170 - 200	68 - 77	20 - 25
Meadow	227,000	95 - 97	85 - 90	300 - 390	300 - 390	68 - 86	20 - 30
Red	408,600	95 - 97	80 - 85	150 - 200	170 - 200	59 - 77	15 - 25
Sheep and hard	530,000	90 - 95	80 - 85	120 - 170	135 - 190	59 - 77	15 - 25
Tall	206,570	95 - 98	85 - 90	300 - 390	300 - 390	68 - 86	20 - 30
Grama, blue	900,000	40 - 50	70 - 75	65 - 110	73 - 123	58 - 86	15 - 30
Lovegrass	1,500,000	95 - 98	80 - 85	10 - 20	11 - 22	58 - 95	15 - 35
Ryegrass:							
Italian	190,680	95 - 98	90 - 95	300 - 390	300 - 390	68 - 86	20 - 30
Perennial	240,620	95 - 98	90 - 95	300 - 390	300 - 390	68 - 86	20 - 30
Wheatgrass, crested	320,000	85 - 90	80 - 85	130 - 220	145 - 245	59 - 86	15 - 30
Zoysiagrass	1,006,652	95 - 97	45 - 50	90 - 135	100 - 150	68 - 95	20 - 35

*Can vary up to ±10% depending on the cultivar.

†The underlined number is the preferred minimum percentage.

‡Where seed mixtures are utilized, the appropriate adjusted intermediate seeding rate should be used, based on the relative percentages of the various turfgrass species constituting the seed mixture. The lower seeding rate listed for each turfgrass species can be used in the rough if the budget is restricted and rapid turf establishment with minimum weeds is not of high priority. Use 30% to 50% of the listed rates when overseeding thin turfs.

§The optimum temperatures for seed germination as established by the Association of Official Seed Analysts. The first temperature represents a 16-hour period and the second an 8-hour period.

Table B-2. Vegetative Planting Guidelines for Golf Courses

Turfgrass Common Name	Greens		Tees		Fairways and Primary Roughs	
	Planting Method	Rate*	Planting Method	Rate*	Planting Method	Rate
Bentgrass	Stolonizing	8 to 12 bushels/ 1,000 sq. ft.	Stolonizing	5 to 8 bushels/ 1,000 sq. ft.	. . . . .	. . . . .
Bermudagrass	Stolonizing	12 to 16 bushels/ 1,000 sq. ft.	Stolonizing	6 to 10 bushels/ 1,000 sq. ft.	Sprigging	Row spacing of 10 to 18 in. with 3- to 6-in. sprig spacing in row
Buffalograss	. . . . .	. . . . .	. . . . .	. . . . .	Plugging	4-in. plugs on 12- to 24-in. centers
Centipedegrass	. . . . .	. . . . .	. . . . .	. . . . .	Plugging	4-in. plugs on 12- to 20-in. centers
Kikuyugrass†	. . . . .	. . . . .	Stolonizing	10 to 12 bushels/ 1,000 sq. ft.	Sprigging	Row spacing of 10 to 18 in. with 3- to 6-in. sprig spacing in row
St. Augustinegrass	. . . . .	. . . . .	. . . . .	. . . . .	Plugging	4-in. plugs on 12- to 24-in. centers
Zoysiagrass	. . . . .	. . . . .	Plugging or sodding	4-in. plugs on 10- to 18-in. centers	Plugging, sprigging (as per bermudagrass), or strip sodding	4-in. plugs on 10- to 18-in. centers or 4- to 12-in. strips in 12- to 18-in. rows

*One bushel of stolons is produced from one square yard of dense sod.
†Use only in areas already infested.

Appendix C
Fertilizer Characteristics

Table C-1. Comparative Salt Indices of Common Fertilizers

Fertilizer Carrier	Nutrient Content	Salt Index Per Equal Weights of Material*	Salt Index Per 20 lbs. of Plant Nutrients
Nitrogen:			
Ammonium nitrate	35.0% N	104.7	2.99
Ammonium sulfate	21.2% N	69.0	3.25
Calcium nitrate	15.5% N	65.0	4.19
Sodium nitrate	16.5% N	100.0	6.06
Urea	46.6% N	75.4	1.62
Natural organic	05.0% N	3.5	0.70
Phosphate:			
Normal superphosphate	20.0% P_2O_5	7.8	0.39
Concentrated superphosphate	48.0% P_2O_5	10.1	0.21
Monoammonium phosphate	12.2% N + 61.7% P_2O_5	29.9	0.41
Diammonium phosphate	21.2% N + 53.8% P_2O_5	34.2	0.46
Potash:			
Potassium chloride	60.0% K_2O	116.3	1.94
Potassium nitrate	13.8% N + 46.6% K_2O	73.6	1.22
Potassium sulfate	54.0% K_2O	46.1	0.85
Sulfate of potash-magnesia	21.9% K_2O	43.2	1.97
Miscellaneous:			
Dolomite	20.0% MgO	0.8	0.04
Magnesium oxide	100.0% MgO	1.7	0.00
Gypsum	32.6% CaO	8.1	0.25
Calcium carbonate	56.0% CaO	4.7	0.08

NOTE: A low salt index indicates less foliar burn potential.

*Based on sodium nitrate = 100.

Table C-2. Nitrogen Carriers and Their Characteristics

Nitrogen Carriers	Percentage N	Temperature Release Dependence*	Initial Response†	Residual Effect‡	Water Solubility*	Foliar Burn Potential*	Acidifying Potential*	Other Characteristics
Synthetic inorganic:								
Ammonium nitrate	31-35	L	F	N	H	H	M	Fire and explosion hazard; will absorb moisture rapidly unless coated
Ammonium sulfate	21	L	F	N	H	H	H	Strong acidifying properties; 24% sulfur
Calcium nitrate	15	L	F	N	H	H	L	Used infrequently; 19% calcium; absorbs moisture rapidly unless in airtight containers
Natural organic:								
Sewage sludge, activated	4-7	M-H	M-S	M	L	L	L	Contributes micronutrients, especially iron; substantial phosphorus content; nitrogen release depends on microbial activity
Sewage sludge, digested	1-3	M-H	S	M	L	L	L	Low nutrient content; may contain weed seeds and be difficult to distribute; nitrogen release depends on microbial activity
Tankage	7-10	M-H	M-S	M	L	L	M-L	Steam-treated refuse; used infrequently; nitrogen release depends on microbial activity
Synthetic organic:								
IBDU (isobutylidene diurea)	31	M	M-S	E	M-L	L	L	Nitrogen release affected by pH and water solubility; acidity enhances release; solubility determined by particle size
Urea	45	L	F	N	H	H	M-L	Gaseous ammonia loss potential
UF (Ureaformaldehyde)	38	H	M-S	E	M-L	L	L	Nitrogen release depends on microbial activity; nitrogen release above 55 °F, highest above 90 °F; usually 30% of total nitrogen is water soluble
Coated:								
Plastic resin-coated urea	10-20	H	M	E	L	L	L	Nitrogen release increases as higher temperatures increase degradation of coating
Sulfur-coated urea	32	M	M	E	L	L	H	Nitrogen release rate increases as increases in soil moisture and temperature enhance degradation of sulfur coating

NOTE: For a more detailed discussion see Beard, J.B. 1973. *Turfgrass: Science and Culture.* Prentice-Hall, Englewood Cliffs, N.J.

*H, high; M, medium; L, low.

†F, fast; M, medium; S, slc

‡E, extended; M, medium; N, nominal.

Table C-3. Phosphorus, Potassium, and Iron Carriers and Their Characteristics

Element	Carriers	Chemical Formula	Percentage Base Nutrient	Percentage Base Oxide	Percentage Other Nutrients	Characteristics
Phosphorus (P)	Concentrated superphosphate	$Ca(H_2PO_4)_2 \cdot H_2O$	18 - 20 P + 1S	42 - 46 P_2O_5	12 - 14 Ca	Similar to superphosphate but less calcium sulfate
	Diammonium phosphate (DAP)	$(NH_4)_2H_2PO_4$	20 - 23 P	46 - 53 P_2O_5	10 - 21 N	Ammonia loss on alkaline soils can be severe
	Monoammonium phosphate (MAP)	$NH_4H_2PO_4$	21 - 23 P	48 - 53 P_2O_5	10 - 12 N	Preferred to DAP when applied to alkaline soils
	Normal superphosphate	30% $Ca(H_2PO_4)_2 \cdot H_2O$ + 50% $CaSO_4$	8 - 9 P	18 - 20 P_2O_5	18 - 21 Ca and 12 S	
Potassium (K)	Potassium chloride	KCl	50 - 52 K	60 - 62 K_2O	42 Cl	Known as muriate of potash; high foliar burn potential
	Potassium nitrate	KNO_3	37 K	44 K_2O	14 N	Low salt concentration; low chloride; fire hazard
	Potassium sulfate	K_2SO_4	41 - 44 K	50 - 53 K_2O	18 S	Acidifying effect
	Sulfate of potash-magnesia	$K_2SO_4 \cdot 2MgSO_4$	18 - 22 K	22 - 26 K_2O	11 Mg and 15 S	Excellent magnesium source
Iron (Fe)	Chelated iron	FeDTPA, FeHEDTA, and FeEDTA	6 - 7 Fe	......	......	Long residual response due to being held in solution
	Ferrous ammonium sulfate	$(NH_4)_2(FeSO_4)_2 \cdot 6H_2O$	14 Fe	......	7 N and 15 S	Water soluble; usually foliarly applied
	Ferrous sulfate	$FeSO_4 \cdot 7H_2O$	19 - 21 Fe	......	18 S	Water soluble; usually foliarly applied

Appendix D
Conversion Tables

ENGLISH UNITS OF MEASURE

Length

1 yd	= 3 ft	= 36 in.
1 rd	= 5.5 yd	= 16.5 ft
1 mi	= 1,760 yd	= 5,280 ft

Area

1 ft^2 $\quad$ = 144 in.^{2}
1 yd^2 $\quad$ = 9 ft^2
1 acre $\quad$ = 4,840 yd^2 $\quad$ = 43,560 ft^2
1 mi^2 $\quad$ = 1 sect $\quad$ = 640 acres

Mass

1 lb $\quad$ = 16 oz
1 ton $\quad$ = 2,000 lb

Rate

1 lb/1,000 ft^2 $\quad$ = 43.6 lb/acre
100 lb/acre $\quad$ = 2.3 lb/1,000 ft^2
1 mph $\quad$ = 88 ft/min
1 ft^3/s $\quad$ = 448.83 gpm
$\quad\quad\quad$ = 23.8 acre-in./day
1 gal/min $\quad$ = 0.053 acre-in./day
1 gal/1,000 ft^2 $\quad$ = 43.6 gal/acre
1 acre-in. $\quad$ = 3,630 ft^3
$\quad\quad\quad$ = 27,154 gal
1 acre-ft $\quad$ = 43,560 ft^3
$\quad\quad\quad$ = 325,851 gal

Volume

1 cup $\quad$ = 16 tbsp $\quad$ = 48 tsp
1 pt $\quad$ = 2 cups $\quad$ = 16 fl oz
1 qt $\quad$ = 2 pt $\quad$ = 4 cups
1 gal $\quad$ = 4 qt $\quad$ = 8 pt
1 gal $\quad$ = 231 in.^{3} $\quad$ = 128 fl oz
1 bu $\quad$ = 4 pk $\quad$ = 1.244 ft^3
1 brl $\quad$ = 32.5 gal
1 ft^3 $\quad$ = 1,728 in.^{3} $\quad$ = 7.48 gal

METRIC UNITS OF MEASURE

Length

1 km = 1000 m
1 m = 10 dm
1 dm = 10 cm
1 cm = 10 mm

Area

1 km² = 10 ha
1 ha = 100 a
1 a = 100 m²

Volume

1 l = 100 cl
1 cl = 10 ml

Mass

1 MT = 1000 kg
1 kg = 1000 g
1 g = 1000 mg

Force

1 N = 1 kg·m/s²

Pressure

1 Pa = 1 N/m²
1 kPa = 1000 Pa

ENGLISH TO METRIC

METRIC TO ENGLISH

Mass

1 oz = 28.35 g	1 g = 0.053 oz
1 lb = 453.6 g	1 kg = 2.205 lb
1 ton = 0.907 MT	1 MT = 1.102 ton

Length

1 in. = 2.54 cm	1 cm = 0.394 in.
1 ft = 30.48 cm	1 cm = 0.033 ft
= 0.304 m	1 m = 39.37 in.
1 yd = 0.914 m	= 3.28 ft
1 mi = 1.609 km	1 km = 0.621 mi
= 1,609.3 m	= 1,093.6 yd

Area

1 in.² = 6.45 cm²	1 cm² = 0.155 in.²
1 ft² = 0.0929 m²	1 m² = 10.76 ft²
= 929 cm²	= 1.196 yd²
1 yd² = 0.836 m²	1 a = 1,076 ft²
1,000 ft² = 0.929 a	= 119.6 yd²
1 acre = 0.405 ha	1 ha = 2.47 acre
1 mi² = 2.59 km²	

Volume

1 in.³ = 16.39 cm³	1 cm³ = 0.061 in.³
1 fl oz = 29.57 ml	1 ml = 0.034 fl oz
1 ft³ = 0.028 m³	1 m³ = 35.31 ft³
1 pt = 0.473 l	1 l = 2.12 pt
1 qt = 0.945 l	= 1.06 qt
1 gal = 3.785 l	= 0.264 gal

ENGLISH TO METRIC

METRIC TO ENGLISH

Pressure

1 psi	= 6.9 kPa
1 atm	= 101.325 kPa
1 ft H_2O	= 2.988 kPa

1 kPa	= 0.145 psi
	= 0.0099 atm
	= 0.335 ft H_2O

Rate

1 lb/acre	= 1.12 kg/ha
1 lb/1,000 ft^2	= 0.488 kg/a
1 oz/gal	= 7.8 ml/l
1 pt/20 gal	= 1.65 ml/l
1 mph	= 1.61 km/hr
	= 44.7 cm/s

1 kg/ha	= 0.89 lb/acre
1 kg/a	= 2.05 lb/1,000 ft^2
1 g/cm^2	= 2.048 lbs/ft^2
1 g/cm^3	= 62.4 lbs/ft^3
1 kg/cm^2	= 14.223 lb/in.^{2}
1 km/hr	= 0.621 mph
	= .913 ft/s

FORMULAE

Circle

Ratio of circumference
to diameter = π = 3.1416
Area = πr^2
Circumference = $2\pi r$ = πD

Rectangle or Parallelogram

Area = bh

Right Triangle

Area = ½bh

Triangle

Area: sides a, b, c
s = ½(a + b + c)
Area = $[s(s-a)(s-b)(s-c)]^{1/2}$

Temperature

Fahrenheit (°F) = (⁹⁄₅°C) + 32
Celsius (°C)   = ⁵⁄₉ (°F − 32)
Kelvin (°K)   = 273.15 + °C

Cube

Volume = b^3

Sphere

Volume = ⁴⁄₃(πr^2)

Cylinder

Volume = $\pi r^2 h$

Cone

Volume = ⅓($\pi r^2 h$)

Nutrient Weight Conversion

Phosphorus (P) = 0.44(P_2O_5)
Potassium (K) = 0.83(K_2O)

Spray Mixtures

To determine the percentage of active ingredient in a spray mixture:

$$\frac{(\text{Lbs pesticide used}) \times (\% \text{ active ingredient})}{(\text{Gals of spray mixture}) \times (8.3)}$$

To determine the pounds of wettable powder needed to mix a spray containing a given percentage of active ingredient:

$$\frac{(\text{Gals of spray wanted}) \times (\% \text{ active ingredient}) \times (8.3)}{(\% \text{ active ingredient in pesticide used})}$$

To determine the gallons of emulsifiable concentrate needed to mix a spray containing a given percentage of active ingredient:

$$\frac{(\text{Gals of spray wanted}) \times (\% \text{ active ingredient wanted}) \times (8.3)}{(\text{Lbs active ingredient per gallon of concentrate}) \times (100)}$$

ABBREVIATIONS

English

atm	atmosphere
brl	barrel
bu	bushel
ft	foot
ft²	square foot
ft³	cubic foot
fl oz	fluid ounce
gal	gallon
gpm	gallons per minute
in.	inch
in.²	square inch
in.³	cubic inch
lb	pound
mi	mile
mi²	square mile
mph	miles per hour
oz	ounce
pk	peck
psi	pounds per square inch
pt	pint
qt	quart
rd	rod
sect	section
tbsp	tablespoon
tsp	teaspoon
yd	yard
yd²	square yard
yd³	cubic foot

Metric

a	are
cl	centiliter
cm	centimeter
cm²	square centimeter
cm³	cubic centimeter
dm	decimeter
g	gram
ha	hectare
kg	kilogram
km	kilometer
kPa	kilopascal
l	liter
m	meter
m²	square meter
m³	cubic meter
mg	milligram
ml	milliliter
mm	millimeter
MT	metric ton
N	Newton
Pa	Pascal

Time

hr	hour
min	minute
s	second

Glossary

Abaxial — Located on the side away from the axis.

Achene — A dry indehiscent one-seeded fruit formed from a single carpel.

Acid equivalent — The amount of active ingredient expressed in terms of the parent acid.

Active ingredient (ai) — The actual toxic material(s) present in a formulation.

Acuminate — Tapering gradually at the end, or apex.

Acute — Sharp pointed.

Adaxial — Located on the side toward the axis.

Alternate — Placed singly on opposite sides of the stem or axis at different heights.

Amendment, physical — Any substance, such as sand, calcined clay, peat, or sawdust, added to the soil to alter its physical properties.

Annual — A plant starting from seed and completing its life cycle in the same growing season.

Anther — The pollen-bearing part of the stamen.

Anthesis — The opening of the flower bud.

Apron — The fairway area in closest proximity to and in front of the putting green which adjoins the putting green collar; sometimes referred to as the approach. This area is normally mowed at fairway height, but sometimes is mowed with smaller equipment to preserve or improve on the quality of turf thereon.

Artificial turf — A synthetic surface simulating turf.

Auricle — Hornlike or clawlike appendage projecting from the base of the leaf blade or from the sheath apex; occurs in pairs to each side.

Awn — A bristlelike structure, usually extending from (attached to) the glumes or lemma of grasses.

Ball mark — Depression or tear in the surface of a turf, usually a green, made by impact of a ball.

Ball roll — The distance the ball moves (a) after striking the ground on termination of its air flight or (b) as a result of a putting stroke.

Bedknife — Stationary bottom blade of a reel mower against which the reel blades turn to produce a shearing cut.

Bench setting — Height the cutting plane (bedknife or rotating blade tip) of a mower is set above a hard, level surface.

Biennial — A plant starting from seed and requiring two years to complete its life cycle.

Biological control — Controlling a pest by its natural or introduced enemies.

Blade — Expanded portion of a leaf; the flat portion of a grass leaf above the sheath.

Blend, seed — A combination of two or more cultivars of a single species.

Bract — A leaflike or scalelike structure at the base of the flower of certain plants; a modified inflorescence leaf.

Broadcast application — Distribution of a chemical over an entire area.

Broadcast sprigging — Vegetative turf establishment by broadcasting stolons, rhizomes, or tillers and covering with soil.

Brushing — The practice of moving a brush against the surface of a turf to lift nonvertical stolons and/or leaves before mowing to produce a uniform surface of erect leaves.

Bunch-type growth — Plant development by intravaginal tillering at or near the soil surface, without production of rhizomes or stolons.

Bunker — A hazard consisting of an area of bare ground, often a depression, which is usually covered with sand. Grass-covered ground bordering or within a bunker is not part of the hazard.

Bur — A rough or prickly covering around seeds, fruits, or spikelets, as the bur of sandbur.

Calcined clay — Clay minerals, such as montmorillonite and attapulgite, that have been fired at high temperatures to obtain absorbent, stable, granular particles; generally used as amendments in soil modification.

Carpel — A portion of the ovary or female portion of the flower.

Cart path — A roadway constructed of asphalt, fine gravel, quarry dust, wood products, or other suitable materials for the purpose of facilitating movement of golf carts about the course with a minimum of injury to turfgrass areas.

Caryopsis — Dry, indehiscent fruit in which the single ovule wall is adhered to the pericarp: as seed in grasses.

Castings — Soil and plant remains excreted and deposited by earthworms in or on the turf surface or in their burrows.

Catcher — A detachable enclosure on a mower used to collect clippings.

Centrifugal spreader — An applicator from which dry, particulate material is broadcast outward as it drops onto a spinning disc or blade beneath a hopper.

Chemical trimming — Using herbicides or chemical growth regulators to limit turfgrass growth around trees, borders, walks, etc.

Ciliate — Fringed with hairs along the margin.

Cleavage plane, sod — A zone of potential separation at the interface between the underlying soil and an upper soil layer adhering to transplanted sod. Such separation is most commonly a problem when soils of different textures are placed one over another.

Clipping removal — Collecting leaves cut by mowing and removing them from the turf.

Clippings — Leaves and, in some cases, stems cut off by mowing.

Clonal planting — Vegetative establishment using plants of a single genotype placed at a spacing of 1 meter or more.

Cold water-insoluble nitrogen (WIN) — A form of fertilizer nitrogen not soluble in cold water (25 °C).

Cold water-soluble nitrogen (WSN) — A form of fertilizer nitrogen soluble in cold water (25 °C).

Coleoptile — A sheathlike structure covering the shoot of grass seedlings.

Coleorhiza — The sheath of a monocotyledonous embryo surrounding the radicle.

Collar — A part of the leaf; narrow band on the abaxial side, marking the place where the blade and sheath join.

Collar, turf — A narrow area of turf adjoining the putting surface which is mowed at a height intermediate between those of the fairway and the putting surface. This cut is normally $\frac{5}{16}$ to $\frac{1}{2}$ inch (8 to 13 millimeters). The collar width normally desired is approximately 36 inches (90 centimeters), but varies depending on the total green area.

Colorant—A dye, pigment, or paintlike material applied to turf to create a favorable green color when the grass is discolored, damaged, or dormant.

Combing—Using a comb, with fixed teeth or flexible tines, fastened in front of a reel mower to lift stolons and horizontal shoots so they may be cut by the mower.

Compaction, soil—The pressing together of soil particles into a more dense soil mass.

Compound shoot—Primary shoot plus one or more lateral shoots.

Cool-season turfgrass—Turfgrass species best adapted to growth during cool, moist periods of the year; commonly having temperature optimums of 15 to 24 °C (60 to 75 °F).

Coring—A method of turf cultivation in which soil cores are removed by hollow tines or spoons.

Corm—The enlarged lower internodes of some grasses.

Cotyledon—Seed leaves of the embryo which act as storage organs.

Creeping growth habit—Extravaginal stem growth at or near the soil surface which results in lateral spreading by rhizomes and/or stolons.

Crown—That portion of the grass plant which includes the stem apex, the unelongated internodes, and the lower nodes from which adventitious roots are initiated.

Culm—A jointed, usually hollow stem, not including the leaves; the jointed stem of grasses.

Cultipacker seeder—A mechanical seeder designed to place turfgrass seeds in a prepared seedbed at a shallow depth followed by firming of the soil around the seed. It usually consists of a tractor-drawn unit having a seed box positioned between ridged rollers, the front roller being offset from the rear.

Cultivar—A plant of a single species that differs from another in specific characters such as disease resistance, leaf width, and insect resistance.

Cultivation, turf—Working of the soil without destruction of the turf; e.g., coring, slicing, grooving, forking, spiking, and shattering.

Cup—Defined as hole. The "hole" shall be 4.25 inches (10.8 centimeters) in diameter and sunk at least 4 inches (10 centimeters) deep. If a lining is used, it should be sunk at least 1 inch (2.5 centimeters) below the putting green surface.

Cup cutter—A hollow, cylindrical tool with a sharpened lower edge used to cut a hole for a cup in a green or to replace small spots of damaged turf.

Cutting height—Of a mower, the distance between the plane of travel (base of wheel, roller, or skid) and the parallel plane of cut.

Decumbent—Lying flat; prostrate with apex growing upward.

Density, shoot—See **shoot density.**

Dethatch—Remove an excessive thatch accumulation either (a) mechanically, as by vertical cutting, or (b) biologically, as by topdressing with soil.

Dicot—A plant having two seed leaves or cotyledons; generally refers to broadleaf plants.

Dioecious—One-sexed, having either male or female flowers only; the staminate (male) and pistillate (female) flowers borne on different plants.

Disseminate—Scatter or spread seeds from the parent plant.

Divot—A piece of turf severed from the soil by a golf club or by ball impact on a soft green.

Dogleg hole—Hole that bends left or right in the area of the drive zone. Normally the strategy requires that a drive be placed to a specific area from which the ball can more easily be advanced toward the green from the bend in the fairway.

Dormancy—Resting stage through which a plant or ripe seeds usually pass and during which nearly all outward manifestations of life come to an almost complete standstill.

Dormant seeding—Planting from seed during late fall or early winter after temperatures become too low for seed germination.

Dormant sodding—Transplanting sod during late fall, winter, or early spring when temperatures are too low for shoot and root growth.

Dormant turf—Turfs that have temporarily ceased shoot growth as a result of extended drought, heat, or cold stress.

Dry spot—See **localized dry spot.**

Effective cutting height—The actual height of the cutting plane above the soil surface at which the turf is mowed.

Embryo—That portion of a seed that develops into a young plant.

Emergence—The time when the first leaf of a plant appears above the soil surface.

Endosperm—That portion of a seed that contains reserve food.

Entire—Without divisions, lobes, teeth, or hairs.

Eradication—Elimination of a living organism from a specified area.

Establishment, turf—Root and shoot growth following seed germination or vegetative planting needed to form a mature stable turf.

Extravaginal—Young vegetative stems that grow outside the basal leaf sheath by penetrating through the sheath.

Face, bunker—The slope or incline of a bunker constructed in the direction of the putting green, intended to create an added obstacle for a player to negotiate during play.

Fairway—There is no precise definition in the *Rules of Golf* for "fairway." It is deemed to be an area between the tee and putting green included in the term "through the green." In terms of maintenance, a fairway is that area of the course which is mowed at a height between 0.5 and 1.2 inches (1.3 to 3 centimeters), depending on grass species and cultural intensity.

Fascicled—A tuft of hairs or leaves crowded together.

Fertigation—Fertilizer application through an irrigation system.

Fertilizer burn—See **foliar burn.**

Fibrous roots—Long, slender roots of about equal size.

Filament—A slender stalk.

Flaccid—Limp; flabby.

Flail mower—A mower that cuts turf by impact of blades rotating in a vertical cutting plane relative to the turf surface. See also **impact mowing.**

Floret—The lemma and palea with the included flower (stamens and pistil); florets may be perfect, staminate, pistillate, or sterile.

Foliar burn—Injury to shoot tissue caused by dehydration owing to contact with high concentrations of chemicals; e.g., certain fertilizers and pesticides.

Footprinting, frost—Discolored areas of dead leaf tissue in the shape of foot impressions that develop after live, frosted turfgrass leaves are walked on.

Footprinting, wilt—Temporary foot impressions left in a turf when flaccid leaves of grass plants suffer incipient wilt and have insufficient turgor to spring back after being treaded on.

Forking—A method of turf cultivation in which a spading fork or similar solid-tine device is used to make holes in the soil.

Formulation—The form in which active ingredients and carriers are mixed, packaged, and sold.

French drain—See **slit trench drain.**

Frequency of clip—Distance of forward travel between successive cuts of mower blades.

Funiculus—The stalk of a nonsessile ovule.

Glabrous—No hairs or pubescence.

Glume—One of the pair of outer bracts at the base of a spikelet.

Golf cart—Can be either a motorized vehicle propelled by gas or electricity (batteries) which transports two golfers and their golf bags during play or a wheeled implement on which a golf bag is placed and guided about the course by the player during a round of golf (some of these are battery operated but most are manually guided by hand about the course and thus are called pull-carts).

Grading—Establishing surface soil elevations and contours prior to planting.

Grain, turf—The undesirable, procumbently oriented growth of grass leaves, shoots, and stolons on greens; a rolling ball tends to be deflected from a true course in the direction of orientation.

Grassy hollows and mounds—Grass-covered, distinctly shaped depressions and "chocolate drop" mounds in the primary rough or projecting into the fairway, which often function in the playing strategy of golf holes, serve as barriers, or merely add an aesthetic dimension.

Gravity spreader—An applicator from which dry, particulate material falls downward through controlled openings.

Greenkeeping—A term used in the past when referring to golf course maintenance. The term in use today is "golf course culture and management."

Grooving—A method of turf cultivation in which vertical rotating blades cut continuous slits through the turf and into the soil, with soil, thatch, and green plant material being displaced.

Hazard—Any bunker or water hazard. Bare patches, scrapes, roads, tracks, and paths *are not hazards*.

Herbaceous—Refers to plants with nonwoody stems that normally die back to the ground in the winter.

Herbicide—Any compound used to kill or inhibit the growth of a plant.

Hilum—The place of attachment of a seed to its stalk.

Hispid—With rough, bristly hairs.

Hot water-insoluble nitrogen (HWIN)—A form of fertilizer nitrogen not soluble in hot water (100 °C); used to determine the activity index of ureaforms. See **nitrogen activity index.**

Hyaline—Clear, translucent.

Hybrid—The progeny resulting from a cross of individuals that differ in one or more heritable characters.

Hydroplanting—Planting vegetative propagules (e.g., stolons) in a water mixture by pumping through a nozzle which sprays the mixture onto the plantbed. The water-propagule mixture may also contain fertilizer and a mulch.

Hydroseeding—Planting seed in a water mixture by pumping through a nozzle which sprays the mixture onto a seedbed. The water mixture may also contain fertilizer and a mulch.

Hypocotyl—That portion of the axis of an embryo or seedling situated between the cotyledons and the radicle.

Impact mowing—Mowing in which the inertia of the grass blade resists the impact of rapidly moving blades and is cut; characteristic of rotary and flail mowers and contrasts with the shearing cut of reel and sickle-bar mowers.

Inflorescence—The flowering part of a plant.

Intercalary meristem—A meristemic area located between two partially differentiated tissues.

Intermediate rough zone—A narrow 6- to 9-foot-wide strip of irrigated turf running parallel to each side of the fairway which is mowed at a height between those of the fairway and the primary rough.

Internode—Region of a stem or rachis between two successive nodes.

Interseeding—Seeding between sod plugs, sod strips, rows of sprigs, or stolons.

Intervaginal—Vegetative stems that grow upward within the enveloping basal leaf sheath.

Involute—Rolled inward from the edges.

Irrigation, automatic—A water application system in which valves are automatically activated, either hydraulically or electrically, at times preset on a controller. The system may or may not be integrated with an automatic sensing unit.

Irrigation, manual—Water application using hand-set and hand-valved equipment.

Irrigation, semiautomatic—A water application system in which valves respond directly to a manually operated remote-control switch.

Irrigation, subsurface—Application of water below the soil surface by injection or by manipulation of the water table.

Keel—A projecting ridge of a surface; the midrib of a glume.

Knitting—See **sod knitting.**

Lamina—The blade or expanded part of a leaf.

Lanceolate—Flattened, two to three times as long as broad; widest in the middle; and tapering to a pointed apex.

Lapping, mower (backlapping)—Backward turning of the reel against the bedknife while a fluid-dispersed grinding compound is applied.

Lateral shoot—Shoots originating from vegetative buds in the axils of leaves or from the nodes of stems, rhizomes, or stolons.

Lawn—Ground covered with closely mowed vegetation, usually grass.

Lawngrass—See **turfgrass.**

Layering, soil—Stratification within a soil profile, which may affect the conductivity and retention of water, soil aeration, and rooting; can be due to construction design, topdressing with different textured amendments, inadequate on-site mixing of soil amendments, or blowing and washing of sand or soil.

Leaf—One of the lateral outgrowths of a stem; produced in definite succession from the stem apex.

Leaflet—One of the divisions of a compound leaf.

Leaf mulcher—A machine that lifts leaves from a turf and shreds them small enough to fall down within the turfgrass canopy.

Lemma—The bract within a spikelet enclosing the germ side of a floret. A bract above the pair of glumes.

Ligule—A thin, often scarious projection from the summit of the leaf sheath in grasses; may be a membrane, a fringe of hairs, or absent.

Lip, bunker—An abutment of sod raised 3 to 4 inches (7.6 to 10 centimeters) above the sand level in the bunker and facing the putting green that prevents a player from putting out of the bunker.

Liquid fertilization—A method of nutrient application as a solution of dissolved fertilizer.

Localized dry spot—A dry spot of turf and soil surrounded by more moist conditions, which resists rewetting by normal irrigation or rainfall; often associated with thatch, hydrophobic soil, fungal activity, shallow soil over buried material, compacted soil, or elevated sites in the terrain.

Lodicules—The organs at the base of the ovary in a grass flower that swell and force open the lemma and palea at anthesis.

Low-temperature discoloration—The loss of chlorophyll and associated green color that occurs in turfgrasses under low-temperature stress.

Maintenance building—A permanent structure that functions as the operations headquarters for the golf course maintenance personnel as well as a protective area for equipment and storage of pesticides, chemicals, fertilizer, tools, and equipment.

Maintenance facility—A centrally located area on the golf course that encompasses the maintenance building, washing apron, parking lot, soil-topdressing area, petroleum storage area, and external work areas.

Maintenance, turf—See **turfgrass culture.**

Mat—Thatch intermixed with mineral matter that develops between the zone of green vegetation and the original soil surface; commonly associated with greens that have been topdressed.

Matting—Dragging a steel mat over the turf surface to work in topdressing and smooth the surface; also used to break up and work in soil lifted out by coring and grooving.

Membranous—Thin, often papery, rather soft.

Mesocotyl—The central region of the grass embryo between the coleoptile and the scutellar node.

Midrib—The main vein in the center of the leaf.

Mixture, seed—A combination of seeds of two or more species.

Monocot—A plant having one seed leaf or cotyledon.

Monoecious — Having the flowers differentiated as to sex; the staminate (male) and pistillate (female) flowers being in separate inflorescence but borne on the same plant.

Monostand — A turfgrass community composed of one cultivar.

Mowing frequency — The number of mowings per unit of time, or the interval in days between one mowing and the next.

Mowing height — See **cutting height.**

Mulch blower — A machine using forced air to distribute particles of mulch over newly seeded turf.

Nitrogen activity index (AI) — The percentage of cold water-insoluble nitrogen that is soluble in hot water, used with ureaformaldehyde compounds and mixtures containing such compounds.
$$AI = (\% \ WIN - \% \ HWIN \times 100)/\% \ WIN.$$

Node — A joint or enlarged area where leaves, roots, or branches of stems arise.

Nursegrass — See **temporary grass.**

Nursery, turfgrass — An area where turfgrasses are propagated for vegetative increase to provide a source of stolons, sprigs, or sod for vegetative planting.

Obtuse — Blunt or rounded at the end.

Off-site mixing — Mixing the soil and amendments for soil modification at a location other than the planting site.

Opposite — Arranged in pairs on opposite sides of a stem.

Oral toxicity — The degree of toxicity of a compound when it is ingested.

Out-of-bounds marker — A stake or fence that determines the out-of-bounds line.

Ovary — The organ in which the ovules are born; usually a basal cavity in the pistil.

Ovate — Egg-shaped.

Overseeding — Seeding into an existing turf. See also **winter overseeding.**

Ovule — Structure that, when fertilized, develops into a seed.

Palea — The inner bract of a floret; the bract enclosing the crease side of a kernel or the bract opposite the lemma.

Palmate — Diverging like the fingers of a hand.

Panicle — A type of inflorescence having the spikelets attached to the main axis (rachis) by branches and pedicels; spikelets are *not* sessile or individually pedicled on main axis.

Papillose — Having very small nipple-shaped projections.

Parts per million (ppm) — The number of parts by weight or volume of a given compound in one million parts of the final mixture.

Pedicel — A short stalk.

Peduncle — The stem that supports an inflorescence or a solitary flower.

Pegged sod — Use of pegs to hold sod in place on slopes and waterways until transplant sod rooting occurs.

Perennial plant — A plant that may or may not start from seed, may or may not produce seed, and requires more than two years to complete its life cycle.

Perfect, flower — Flower having both carpels and stamens.

Permanent yardage marker — A device permanently positioned in each tee at a known distance from the center of the putting green that serves as a reference point for golfers in determining the length of a hole from the point where the tee markers are placed.

Pesticide — Any chemical (or mixture) used to control unwanted plant or animal life to protect desirable organisms.

Phytotoxicity — The effect of a chemical that causes death or injury to plants.

Pilose — Hairy, usually soft.

Pistil — The female or seed-producing organ of a flower; consisting typically of ovary, style, and stigma.

Plantbed — A soil area prepared for vegetative propagation or seed germination and establishment of turf.

Plugging — Vegetative propagation of turfgrasses by plugs or small pieces of sod. A method of establishing vegetatively propagated turfgrasses as well as of repairing damaged areas.

Plumule — The apical bud of a plant embryo from which the mature plant's stem and leaves eventually develop.

Poling — Using a long bamboo switch or fiberglass pole to remove dew and exudations from turf by switching the pole in an arc while in contact with the turf surface; also used to break up clumps of clippings and earthworm casts.

Polystand — A turfgrass community composed of two or more cultivars and/or species.

Postemergence herbicide — A chemical applied to the foliage of weeds after emergence from the soil.

Practice green — A putting green area in close proximity to the clubhouse for the purpose of allowing golfers to practice away from the regular putting greens. This green should be representative of the regular greens (and not planted with experimental grasses) so that golfers can develop a touch for play on the regular greens.

Practice range — An area on the golf course property, usually within walking distance of the clubhouse, where players can practice with all clubs.

Preemergence herbicide — A chemical applied prior to the emergence of the weed from the soil.

Pregermination — Preconditioning of seed prior to planting by placing it in a moist, oxygenated environment at optimum temperature to favor more rapid germination after seeding.

Press rolling — Pushing of sprigs or stolons into the soil followed by firming of the soil around the vegetative propagules by means of a mechanical planter.

Primary rough — That portion of the rough immediately surrounding a fairway where errant balls are most likely to be found; it may be maintained at an intensity of culture between those of the fairway and the most distant secondary rough.

Primary shoot — The simple shoot stage in the development of a seedling.

Prophyll — The sheathlike structure covering the axillary bud in grasses; first leaf of a branch off the main axis.

Pseudothatch — The upper surface layer above a thatch which consists of relatively undecomposed leaf remnants and clippings.

PSI — Pounds per square inch.

Pubescent — With hairs.

Puffiness — Spongelike condition of turf that may result in an irregular surface.

Putting green — The area of the hole being played that is specially prepared for putting or otherwise defined as such by the committee. A ball is deemed to be on the putting green when any part of it touches the putting green. Putting greens are mowed between $\frac{5}{32}$ and $\frac{5}{16}$ inch (4 to 8 millimeters), depending on the quality desired.

Putting green surrounds — The immediate turfed area adjacent to and outside the collar, but not including the apron, that is usually maintained similarly to the primary rough.

Raceme — Type of inflorescence having the spikelets attached to the rachis by pedicels.

Rachilla — The main axis of a grass spikelet; the stem of a floret.

Rachis — The axis of the central stem of an inflorescence.

Rebuilding — The practices that result in complete change of a turf area.

Recuperative potential — The ability of turfgrasses to recover from injury.

Reel mower — A mower that cuts turf by means of a rotating reel of helical blades which pass across a stationary blade (bedknife) fixed to the mower frame; this action gives a shearing type of cut.

Reestablishment, turf — A procedure involving (a) complete turf removal, (b) soil tillage, and (c) seeding or vegetative establishment of new turf; does not encompass rebuilding.

Release rate, fertilizer — The rate of nutrient release following fertilizer application. Water-soluble fertilizers are termed fast release, while insoluble or coated soluble fertilizers are referred to as slow release.

Renovation, turf — Improvement usually involving weed control and replanting into existing live and/or dead vegetation; does not encompass reestablishment.

Reseeding, turf — To seed again, usually soon after an initial seeding has failed to achieve satisfactory establishment.

Residual response, fertilizer — Delayed or continued turfgrass response to slow-release fertilizers; lasting longer than the usual initial response from water-soluble fertilizers.

Resiliency — The capability of a turf to spring back when balls, shoes, or other objects strike the surface; thus, providing a cushioning effect.

Retrorse — Pointing backward and downward.

Rhizome — A jointed, underground stem that can produce roots and shoots at each node; may originate from the main stem or from tillers.

Rippling — A wave or washboard pattern on the surface of mowed grass, usually resulting from mower maladjustment, too fast a rate of mower travel, or too low a frequency of clip for the cutting height.

Roller, water ballast — A hollow, cylindrical body, the weight of which can be varied by the amount of water added; used for leveling, smoothing, and firming soil.

Root hair — Very delicate, whitish, outward prolongation of an epidermal root cell; occurs a short distance back of the root cap in great numbers; important in the absorption of water and nutrients.

Rotary mower — A powered mower that cuts turf by high-speed impact of a blade or blades rotating in a horizontal cutting plane.

Rough — Not specifically defined in the *Rules of Golf*. It is included in "through the green" as follows: "Through the green" is the whole area of the course except: (a) teeing and putting green of the hole being played and (b) all hazards on the course. In terms of maintenance, a rough is the area of the course surrounding the green, the tee, and the fairway of each hole that is mowed at a height between 1.5 and 4 inches (3.8 and 10 centimeters) depending on the grass species.

Row sprigging — Planting of sprigs in rows or furrows.

Scabrous — Rough to the touch.

Scald, turf — Shoots standing in relatively shallow water collapse and turn brown if sun heats water to lethal temperatures.

Scalping — The removal of an excessive quantity of green shoots at any one mowing which results in a stubbly, brown appearance from exposed stems, stolons, and dead leaves.

Scarifying, turf — See **vertical cutting.**

Scarious — Thin, dry, membranous, not green.

Scorching — See **scald.**

Scum — A layer of algae on the soil surface of thin turf; drying can produce a somewhat impervious layer that impairs subsequent shoot emergence.

Secondary rough — That portion of a rough outside the primary rough and most distant from the fairway that is mowed less frequently and higher than the primary rough and may have a woodland character.

Seed — The entire structure developed from the ovule after fertilization; a mature ovule.

Seed mat — A fabricated mat with seed (and possibly fertilizer/pesticide) applied to one side; the mat serves as the vehicle to (a) apply seed (and fertilizer), (b) control erosion, and (c) provide a favorable microenvironment for seed germination and establishment.

Semiarid turfgrass — Turfgrass species adapted to grow and persist in semiarid regions without irrigation, such as buffalograss, gramagrass, and wheatgrass.

Seminal root — A root arising from the base of the hypocotyl.

Sepal — Segment of the calyx.

Service road—A permanent paved or aggregate stabilized roadway capable of accommodating the weight and use frequency of service vehicles and maintenance equipment during normal golf course operations.

Sessile—Without a stem or stalk; a sessile leaf is without a petiole or leafstalk but is attached directly on the axis or stem of the plant.

Settling, soil—A lowering of the soil surface previously loosened by tillage or by excavation and refilling; occurs naturally in time and can be accelerated mechanically by tamping, rolling, cultipacking, or watering.

Shattering—A method of turf cultivation involving fragmentation of a soil mass usually by a vibrating mechanical mole device.

Shaving, turf—The cutting and removal of all verdure, thatch, and excess mat by means of a sod cutter followed by turfgrass regrowth from underground lateral stems. Used on bowling greens, especially bermudagrass.

Sheath—Basal tubular portion of a leaf surrounding the stem.

Shelter—A structure that serves as a retreat for players stranded on the golf course at a point distant from the clubhouse when sudden lightning and rainstorms occur.

Shoot density—The number of shoots per unit area.

Short-lived perennial—Turfgrasses normally expected to live only two to four years.

Sickle-bar mower—A mower that cuts grass by means of horizontal, rapidly oscillating blades which shear the gathered grass against a stationary blade.

Slicing—A method of turf cultivation in which vertically rotating, flat blades slice intermittently through the turf and the soil.

Slit trench drain—A narrow trench (usually 5 to 10 centimeters wide) backfilled to the surface with a material, such as sand, gravel, or crushed rock, to facilitate surface or subsurface drainage.

Slow-release fertilizer—Designates a fertilizer with a rate of dissolution less than that of completely water-soluble fertilizers; may involve compounds which dissolve slowly, materials that must be decomposed by microbial activity, or soluble compounds coated with substances highly impermeable to water. ''Slow release'' used interchangeably with ''delayed release,'' ''controlled release,'' ''controlled availability,'' ''slow acting,'' and ''metered release.''

Sod—Plugs, sprigs, or strips of turfgrass with adhering soil used in vegetative planting.

Sod cutter—A tool to sever turf from the ground; the length and thickness of the sod cut are adjustable.

Sod harvesting—Mechanical cutting of sod (for sale and/or transfer to a planting site) with a minimum of soil to facilitate ease of handling and rooting.

Sod heating—Heat accumulation in tightly stacked sod; may reach lethal temperatures.

Sod knitting—Sod rooting to the extent that newly transplanted sod is held firmly in place.

Sod production—The culture of turf to a quality and maturity that allow harvesting and transplanting.

Sod rooting—The growth of new roots into the underlying soil from nodes in the sod.

Sod strength—The relative ability of sod to resist tearing during harvesting, handling, and transplanting; in research, the mechanical force (newtons) required to tear apart a sod when subjected to a uniformly applied force.

Sod transplanting—Transfer to and planting of sod on a new area.

Sodding—Planting turf by laying sod.

Sodding, dormant—See **dormant sodding.**

Soil fumigant—A compound that kills most organisms in the soil by vapor action, usually permitting replanting soon after, e.g., metam-sodium or methyl bromide.

Soil heating—See **soil warming.**

Soil mix—A prepared root zone material used as a growth medium for turfgrass.

Soil modification—Alteration of soil characteristics by addition of physical amendments; commonly used to improve physical conditions of turf soils.

Soil probe — A soil sampling tool having a hollow cylinder with a cutting edge at the lower end.

Soil screen — A screen used to remove clods, coarse fragments, and trash from soil; may be stationary, oscillating, or in the case of cylindrical screens, rotating.

Soil shredder — A machine that crushes or pulverizes clods, large soil aggregates, and amendments to facilitate uniform soil mixing and topdressing.

Soil sterilant — A compound that, when applied to the soil, prevents the establishment of vegetation for a relatively long period.

Soil warming — The artificial heating of turf from below the surface, usually by electrical means, to prevent soil freezing and to maintain a green turf during winter.

Soiling — See **topdressing.**

Solid sodding — See **sodding.**

Spatulate — Widened at the top like a spatula.

Species — A group of individuals similar in structure and physiology, and capable of interbreeding to produce fertile offspring which are like the parents.

Spicate — Spikelike.

Spike — An inflorescence with an elongating axis, the rachis, bearing sessile spikelets.

Spikelet — The basic unit of a grass inflorescence consisting of the two glumes and one or more florets.

Spiking — A method of turf cultivation in which solid tines or flat pointed blades penetrate the turf and soil surface.

Spongy turf — See **puffiness.**

Spoon, coring — A method of turf cultivation involving curved, hollow, spoonlike tines that remove small soil cores and leave openings in the sod.

Spot seeding — The seeding of small, usually barren or sparsely covered areas within established turf.

Spot treatment — Chemical application limited to a small area of infestation.

Sprig — A stolon, rhizome, tiller, or combination used to establish turf.

Sprigging — Vegetative planting by placing of sprigs in furrows or small holes.

Spring greenup — The initial seasonal appearance of green shoots as spring temperature and moisture conditions become favorable; thus, breaking winter dormancy.

Spudding — The removal of individual weedy plants with a small spadelike tool which severs the root deep in the soil so the weed can be lifted from the turf.

Stamen — The part of a flower (male) that bears the pollen; its parts are the filament and anther.

Stand — The number of established individual shoots per unit area. See also **shoot density.**

Stigma — The part of a pistil that receives the pollen.

Stimpmeter — A portable device designed to measure the speed and uniformity of putting greens.

Stolon — A jointed, above-ground, creeping stem that can produce roots and shoots at each node and may originate extravaginally from the main stem of tillers.

Stolon nursery — An area used for producing stolons for propagation.

Stolonizing — Vegetative planting by broadcasting of stolons over a prepared soil and covering by topdressing or press rolling.

Strip sodding — Laying of sod strips at intervals, usually across a slope; turf establishment depends on spreading of the grass to form a complete cover; sometimes the area between the strips is interseeded.

Style — The prolongation of an ovary bearing the stigma.

Subgrade — The soil elevation constructed at a sufficient depth below the final grade to allow for the desired thickness of topsoil, root zone mix, or other material.

Summer dormancy — The cessation of growth and subsequent death of leaves of perennial plants due to heat and/or moisture stress.

Surfactant — Materials used in chemical formulations to impart emulsifiability, spreading, wetting, dispersibility, or other surface-modifying properties.

Synergism — Cooperative action of two agents, e.g., two chemicals, that produces greater effect than the sum of the two taken separately.

Syringing — Spraying turf with small amounts of water to (a) dissipate accumulated energy and cool the leaves by evaporating free surface water, (b) prevent or correct a leaf water deficit, particularly wilt, or (c) remove dew, frost, and exudate from a turf surface.

Tee — The area of the hole being played that is specially prepared for hitting the first shot of each hole. It contains the teeing ground, which is delineated by two tee markers.

Tee box — Old-time wooden structure placed on tee for use in ball washing, in sand storage to be used as a tee, and as a trash receptacle.

Tee marker — A portable device used to define the teeing ground from which play begins on each hole. Separate tee markers are recommended for use by the United States Golf Association to indicate the championship course (blue markers), the regular course (white markers), and the ladies course (red markers).

Teeing ground — The starting place for the hole being played; a rectangular area two club-lengths in depth, the front and the sides of which are defined by the outside limits of two tee markers. A ball is outside the teeing ground when all of it lies outside the stipulated area.

Temporary grass — Grass species not expected to persist in a turf; used as a temporary cover.

Texture — In turf, the composite leaf width, taper, and arrangement.

Thatch — An intermingled organic layer of dead and living shoots, stems, and roots that develops between the zone of green vegetation and the soil surface.

Thatch control — Prevention of excessive thatch accumulation by cultural manipulation and/or reduction of excess thatch by mechanical or biological means.

Tiller — The shoot of a grass plant originating intravaginally in the axis of a leaf in the unelongated portion of a stem.

Tip burn — Leaf tip necrosis resulting from lethal internal water stress caused by wind desiccation, salt, or pesticide accumulation.

Topdressing — A prepared soil mix added to a turf surface and usually physically worked in by matting, raking, and/or irrigating to smooth a surface.

Topsoil planting — A modification of stolonizing that involves covering the area with soil containing viable rhizomes and/or stolons for the purpose of establishing a turf cover.

Transitional climatic zone — The suboptimal zone between the cool and warm climates where both warm- and cool-season grasses can be grown.

Trimming — Cutting edges and corners of turf to form clearly defined, well-groomed lines.

Truncate — Cut off square, very blunt.

Turf — A covering of mowed vegetation, usually a turfgrass, growing intimately with an upper soil stratum of intermingled roots and stems.

Turfgrass — A species or cultivar of grass, usually of spreading habit, which is maintained as a mowed turf.

Turfgrass color — The composite visual color of a turfgrass community perceived by the human eye.

Turfgrass community — An aggregation of individual turfgrass plants that have mutual relationships with the environment as well as among the individual plants.

Turfgrass culture — The composite cultural practices involved in growing turfgrasses for purposes such as lawns, greens, sports facilities, and roadsides.

Turfgrass management — Development of turf standards and goals which are achieved by planning and directing labor, capital, and equipment with the objective of manipulating cultural practices to achieve those standards and goals.

Turfgrass quality — The degree to which a turf conforms to an agreed standard of uniformity, density, texture, growth habit, smoothness, and color, as judged by subjective visual assessment.

Turfgrass uniformity — The degree to which a turfgrass community is free from variations in color, density, and texture across the surface, as judged by visual assessment.

Umbel — A raceme in which the axis has not elongated; flower stalks arise at the same point.

Undulate — With a wavy surface or edge.

Variety — A division of a species.

Vegetative propagation — Asexual propagation using pieces of vegetation, i.e., sprigs or sod pieces.

Vein — One of the fibrovascular bundles forming part of the framework of a leaf.

Verdure — The layer of green living plant tissue remaining above the soil following mowing.

Vernation — Arrangement of the youngest leaf in the bud shoot; rolled or folded.

Vertical cutting — Involves a mechanical device having vertically rotating blades that cut into the face of a turf for the purpose of controlling thatch or grain.

Vertical mower — A powered mower that cuts turf by high-speed impact of blades revolving in a vertical plane; the blades can be of varied shapes and fixed or free swinging (flail).

Warm-season turfgrass — Turfgrass species best adapted to growth during the warmer part of the year; usually dormant during cold weather or injured by it; commonly having temperature optimum of 27 to 35 °C (80 to 95 °F); e.g., bahiagrass, bermudagrass, St. Augustinegrass, and zoysiagrass.

Washboard effect — See **rippling.**

Watering in — Watering turf immediately after the application of agricultural chemicals to dissolve and/or wash materials from the plant surface into the soil.

Wear — The collective direct injurious effects of traffic on a turf; is distinct from the indirect effects of traffic caused by soil compaction.

Wet wilt — Wilting of turf in the presence of free soil water when evapotranspiration exceeds water uptake by the roots.

Whipping pole — A bamboo stalk or similar pole used in poling turf.

Whorl — A cluster of several branches around the axis of an inflorescence; also a circular cluster of leaves around a stem.

Wind burn, turf — Death and browning, most commonly occurring on the uppermost leaves of grasses, caused by atmospheric desiccation.

Winter desiccation — The death of leaves or plants by drying during winter dormancy.

Winter discoloration — See **low-temperature discoloration.**

Winter fertilization — A late fall to winter application of fertilizer to turfgrasses at rates that maintain green color without causing adverse physiological effects; used in regions characterized by moderate winters for the species involved.

Winter overseeding — Seeding cool-season turfgrasses onto warm-season turfgrasses at or near their start of winter dormancy; used in mild climates to provide green, growing turf during the winter period when the warm-season species are brown and dormant.

Winter protection cover — A barrier placed over a turf to prevent winter desiccation, insulate against low-temperature stress, and stimulate early spring greenup.

Winterkill — Any injury to turfgrass plants that occurs during the winter period.

150-yard marker — A device or landscape landmark that some clubs use on each hole, except par-3's, to indicate that from the point where it rests to the center of the green is 150 yards (137 meters).

Information Sources

A range of national trade and technical periodicals published in North America disseminate information with major emphasis on golf course management or have portions devoted to subjects which apply to golf courses. In addition, there are numerous state and regional publications allied with local associations which are published by the various state and regional organizations. The national turfgrass publications are as follows:

Golf Course Management. Published ten times a year by the Golf Course Superintendents Association of America, 1617 St. Andrews Drive, Lawrence, Kansas, USA 66044.

Greenmaster. Published eight times a year by the Canadian Golf Superintendents Association, 698 Weston Road, Suite 32, Toronto, Ontario, Canada M6N 3R3.

Green Section Record. Published six times a year by the United States Golf Association, Golf House, Far Hills, New Jersey, USA 07931.

Grounds Maintenance. Published thirteen times a year by Intertec Publishing Corp., 9221 Quivira Road, Overland Park, Kansas, USA 66215.

Park Maintenance. Published twelve times a year by Madisen Publishing Division, P.O. Box 1936, Appleton, Wisconsin, USA 54913.

Southern Golf. Published five times a year by Brantwood Publications, Inc., P.O. Drawer 77, Elm Grove, Wisconsin, USA 53122.

Weeds, Trees, and Turf. Published twelve times a year by the Harvest Publishing Co., 9800 Detroit Avenue, Cleveland, Ohio, USA 44102.

Turf professionals who wish to review the older literature while studying a problem, preparing a talk, or writing an article are referred to *Turfgrass Bibliography: 1672 to 1972,* which should be available in most libraries. It is a compilation of over 16,000 references of the turfgrass literature by James B. Beard, Harriet J. Beard, and David P. Martin, published by the Michigan State University Press in 1977. In the development of this bibliography, two major centers for collection of turfgrass literature were established with the aid of the Noer Research Foundation. They are in the libraries at Michigan State University and Texas A&M University. Reprints of specific articles can be obtained from either of these libraries by writing directly to the director of the library or using the interlibrary loan system.

Index

Boldface numbers indicate pages on which index entries are discussed in greatest detail.